# Wine
## ALL-IN-ONE
## FOR
# DUMMIES®

by Ed McCarthy, Mary Ewing-Mulligan,
Maryann Egan, Tony Aspler, and Barbara Leslie

WILEY

Wiley Publishing, Inc.

# About the Authors

**Ed McCarthy** and **Mary Ewing-Mulligan** have written several *For Dummies* books on wine, including the bestselling *Wine For Dummies* and two of their favorites, *French Wine For Dummies* and *Italian Wine For Dummies.* They recently added *California Wine For Dummies* to their repertoire as well. They've taught hundreds of wine classes, visited nearly every wine region in the world, run five marathons, and raised 12 cats. Along the way, they've amassed more than half a century of wine experience between them.

Ed, a New Yorker, graduated from the City University of New York with a master's degree in psychology. He taught high school English in another life, while working part time in wine shops to satisfy his passion for wine and to subsidize his growing wine cellar. In 1999, Ed went solo as author of *Champagne For Dummies,* a topic on which he's especially expert. He's contributing editor to *Beverage Media,* a trade publication.

Mary is president of International Wine Center, a New York City school for wine professionals and serious wine lovers. As U.S. director of the Wine & Spirit Education Trust (WSET), the world's leading wine-education organization, she works to make the courses she offers in New York available in more parts of the United States. She's also a freelance wine writer. Mary's most impressive credential is that she was the first female Master of Wine (MW) in the United States and currently is one of only 26 MWs in the United States. (with 277 MWs worldwide). Both Ed and Mary are also columnists for the online wine magazine WineReviewOnline.com and are Certified Wine Educators.

**Maryann Egan** is the wine writer for *donna hay magazine,* a leading food magazine in Australia. She's also the author of *Australian and New Zealand Wine For Dummies.* Maryann holds a degree in Oenology (more commonly known as wine science) and has worked at several wineries, including the Yarra Valley's Wantirna Estate and Domaine Chandon's Yarra Valley operation.

**Tony Aspler** is the most widely read wine writer in Canada. He's recognized as the leading authority on Canadian wines and is the creator of the annual Air Ontario Wine Awards competition. Formerly the wine columnist for the *Toronto Star,* Tony coauthored *Canadian Wine For Dummies* and is the author of many other books on wine and food.

**Barbara Leslie** is the former publisher of *Winetidings,* Canada's oldest continually published wine magazine. Over the course of a 15-year career with the magazine, she did just about everything from tasting wine to writing and editing to typesetting and layout. Barbara is coauthor of *Canadian Wine For Dummies.*

## Publisher's Acknowledgments

We're proud of this book; please send us your comments at http://dummies.custhelp.com. For other comments, please contact our Customer Care Department within the U.S. at 877-762-2974, outside the U.S. at 317-572-3993, or fax 317-572-4002.

Some of the people who helped bring this book to market include the following:

*Acquisitions, Editorial, and Media Development*

**Compilation Editor:** Traci Cumbay

**Project Editor:** Kristin DeMint

**Acquisitions Editor:** Stacy Kennedy

**Copy Editor:** Jennifer Tebbe

**Assistant Editor:** Erin Calligan Mooney

**Editorial Program Coordinator:** Joe Niesen

**Technical Editor:** Tyler Colman

**Editorial Manager:** Michelle Hacker

**Editorial Assistants:** Jennette ElNaggar, David Lutton

**Art Coordinator:** Alicia B. South

**Cover Photo:** iStock

**Cartoons:** Rich Tennant (www.the5thwave.com)

*Composition Services*

**Project Coordinator:** Katherine Crocker

**Layout and Graphics:** Reuben W. Davis, Melissa K. Jester, Christine Williams

**Proofreader:** Leeann Harney

**Indexer:** BIM Indexing & Proofreading Services

*Special Help*
Victoria M. Adang, Amanda M. Gillum

---

*Publishing and Editorial for Consumer Dummies*

**Diane Graves Steele,** Vice President and Publisher, Consumer Dummies

**Kristin Ferguson-Wagstaffe,** Product Development Director, Consumer Dummies

**Ensley Eikenburg,** Associate Publisher, Travel

**Kelly Regan,** Editorial Director, Travel

*Publishing for Technology Dummies*

**Andy Cummings,** Vice President and Publisher, Dummies Technology/General User

*Composition Services*

**Debbie Stailey,** Director of Composition Services

# Contents at a Glance

# Table of Contents

# Introduction

*W*ine is easy to love: It tastes great, offers a fascinating range of flavors, and brings people together — at the dinner table and elsewhere. Everyone can enjoy wine, regardless of experience or budget.

Yet despite the pleasure it brings, wine can also be a source of anxiety. After all, you have to know strange names of grape varieties and foreign wine regions *and* be able to figure out whether to buy a $20 wine or an $8 wine that seem to be pretty much the same thing. You even need a special tool to open the bottle after you get it home!

All this complication surrounding wine will never go away, because wine is a very rich and complex field. But you don't have to let the complication stand in your way. With the right attitude and a little understanding of what wine is, you can begin to buy and enjoy wine. (And if you decide that wine is fascinating, you can find out more and turn it into a wonderful hobby!) *Wine All-in-One For Dummies* exists to help you feel more comfortable around wine by providing you with some basic wine knowledge.

Ironically, what will *really* make you feel comfortable about wine is accepting the fact that you'll never know it all — and that you've got plenty of company. You see, after you really get a handle on wine, you discover that *no one* knows everything there is to know about wine. There's just too much information, and it's always changing. And when you know that, you can just relax and enjoy the stuff!

## About This Book

Here, within one bright yellow-and-black cover, is a wealth of wine information. But don't let the book's impressive heft intimidate you; everything on these pages is lighthearted and straightforward — easy to digest, even. (Excellent, perhaps, with a crisp Sauvignon Blanc.)

Use this guide as a reference, opening it whenever you want to answer a question, revisit advice, or find recommendations for matching wine with a meal. The page you flip to is up to you; this isn't a typical, read-from-cover-to-cover kind of book. It's designed to be at the ready whenever you feel the urge to find out more about all things wine.

Please note that a book can't provide the most up-to-date pricing (especially when its readers may be shopping anywhere from San Francisco to Tanzania), so you might find that the prices here vary from those you find in your local wine shop. Use the prices provided as a rough estimate; if a wine is included at about $20, you might find it for $15 or $25, but you probably won't see it for sale for $100. Call your local wine merchant to find out exactly what a bottle is going for. The excellent Web site `www.wine-searcher.com` also can help nail down prices in any currency.

# Conventions Used in This Book

Following are a few helpful conventions used throughout *Wine All-in-One For Dummies:*

- *Italics* are used to provide emphasis, highlight new words or terms being defined, indicate certain foreign or scientific words, and point out specific words or phrases on a wine label. They also indicate the stressed syllable in a pronunciation (if no syllable is italicized, all syllables carry equal weight).

- `Monofont` is used for Web addresses.

- Sidebars, which are shaded boxes of text, consist of information that's interesting but not necessarily critical to your understanding of wine.

# Foolish Assumptions

Before we put this book together, we had to make some assumptions about who you, its reader, might be. We assume that you

- Know very little about wine but have a strong desire to find out more.

- Know something about wine, perhaps more than most people, but want to understand the subject better, from the ground up.

- Are already very knowledgeable about wine but realize that you can always discover more.

- Don't have a lot of ego invested in wine — or maybe you do and you're buying this book "for your sister-in-law."

- Are someone who prefers straight talk about wine over a lot of mumbo jumbo and jargon.

# How This Book Is Organized

*Wine All-in-One For Dummies* is a wine user's manual and a reference book, all in one. It includes very basic information about wine for readers who know nothing (or next to nothing) about wine, but it also features tips, suggestions, and more sophisticated information for seasoned wine drinkers who want to take their hobby to a more-advanced level. Here's a quick guide to what you can find where.

## Book I: Understanding Wine

This book is the grapevine, so to speak, of *Wine All-in-One For Dummies*. It's raw material to the other chapters' finished, delectable bottles. Here you find out about how grapes become wine, and you get all the practical information you need to confidently buy, serve, taste, and store wines that strike your fancy. You also get some guidance on pairing wine with food, a feat that can be delicious or disastrous depending on the combination you use.

## Book II: France: A Wine Superstar

French wines are a vast and confusing field — especially for people who don't speak French, who are accustomed to seeing wines named after grape varieties (which most French wines aren't), and who live an ocean away from the regions where French wines grow. Book II breaks down these barriers for you, taking you region by region through France's wine production.

## Book III: Italy: Small but Mighty

Italy is one of, if not *the,* most exciting wine countries on earth. The quality of Italy's wines has never been higher, and its range of wines has never been broader. Nor have more types of Italian wines ever been available outside of Italy. Although Italy's wines are more desirable and more available than ever, they're no more comprehensible. In fact, the proliferation of new wines and new wine zones has made Italian wine an even more confusing topic than it has always been. This book straightens all that out for you.

## Book IV: California and Elsewhere in North America

You probably drink California wine already; wines from California are the top-selling wines in the United States. Could you find other wines from California — other grape varieties, other tastes — that you might enjoy even more than what you already know? Probably. And Book IV takes you through the greats of California, as well as wonderful wines from other areas of North America.

## Book V: Australia and New Zealand: Powerhouses of the Southern Hemisphere

Australia and New Zealand have really started coming into their own, wine-wise; in fact, Australia now produces more wine than all but five other countries. Each year, the wines get better, and those at the lower end of the price spectrum continue to surprise critics; at the higher end, the wines just get more complex, subtle, and alluring. Turn to this book to glimpse the exciting wine regions of Australia and New Zealand, touring the dominant wine-production areas and getting recommendations for bargains, splurges, and more.

## Book VI: And More Wine Regions!

Book VI presents a mix of Old World wine countries (such as Spain and Germany) and New World stunners (such as Chile and South Africa). Turn here to explore the beauty of classics such as Portuguese Port and German Riesling and the excitement of electrifying flavors such as Argentine Malbec and South African Pinotage.

# Icons Used in This Book

Throughout *Wine All-in-One For Dummies,* icons guide your eye to certain tidbits within the text. Here's a rundown of the kind of information each icon highlights:

Some issues in wine are so fundamental that they bear repeating. We mark the repetitions with this symbol.

Wine snobs practice all sorts of affectations designed to make other wine drinkers feel inferior. But you won't be intimidated by their snobbery if you see it for what it is. (And you can discover how to impersonate a wine snob!)

This odd little guy is a bit like the 2-year-old who constantly insists on knowing "Why, Mommy, why?" But he knows that you may not have the same level of curiosity that he has. Where you see him, feel free to skip over the technical information that follows. Wine will still taste just as delicious.

Advice and information that will make you a wiser wine drinker or buyer is marked by this bull's-eye so you won't miss it.

There's very little you can do in the course of moderate wine consumption that can land you in jail — but you could spoil an expensive bottle and sink into a deep depression over your loss. This symbol warns you about common pitfalls.

Unfortunately, some of the finest, most intriguing, most delicious wines are made in very small quantities. Usually, those wines cost more than wines made in large quantities — but that's not the only problem. The real frustration is that those wines have very limited distribution, and you can't always get your hands on a bottle, even if you're willing to pay the price. Such wines appear next to this icon; here's hoping that your search proves fruitful!

# Where to Go from Here

Itching to find an earthy Zinfandel for dinner tonight? Book IV is here to help. Boning up on the great wine regions of France? Dig into Book II. If you're hoping for help in choosing the most efficient corkscrew, Book I has what you need.

Start wherever you like. *Wine All-in-One For Dummies* is designed so you can jump to whichever section most interests you at whatever moment you pick it up. Of course, overachievers or the intensely curious are welcome to keep turning pages from here to the back cover.

Cheers!

# Book I
# Understanding Wine

The 5th Wave                          By Rich Tennant

"All right, let's try this one more time. It's not that difficult — you just wiggle the cork with your thumbs until it slips gently from the bottle."

# In This Book . . .

This book gets you up and sipping even if you've never tasted wine in your life. In these chapters, you glimpse the behind-the-scenes action of winemaking, including why soil and climate are critical, and you get the information that prepares you to dive right into your first bottle (or case). You also get the goods on what wine labels really tell you, how to make sense of a restaurant wine list, and the best ways to make your wine-shop experience count. And, naturally, you find out about what to do with your wine after you buy it: how to store and serve it, and how to pair it with foods that make it sing.

Here are the contents of Book I at a glance:

# Chapter 1

# From Vine to Bottle: The Hows and Wines

. . . . . . . . . . . . . . . . . . . . . . . . . . . . . . . . . . . . . . . . . . . . . . . . . . . . . .

## In This Chapter

▶ Identifying the colors of the wine rainbow

▶ Distinguishing among table, dessert, and sparkling wines

▶ Examining the process (and variations) by which grapes become wine

▶ Visiting wineries for a behind-the-scenes look

. . . . . . . . . . . . . . . . . . . . . . . . . . . . . . . . . . . . . . . . . . . . . . . . . . . . . .

*P*lenty of people enjoy drinking wine but don't know much about it. Of course, knowing a lot of trivia about wine definitely isn't a prerequisite to enjoying it. But familiarity with certain aspects of wine can make choosing wines a lot easier, enhance your enjoyment of wine, and increase your comfort level with it. You can find out as much or as little as you like. Regardless, the journey begins in this chapter, where you discover the very basics of how wines are categorized, get an overview of the wine-making process, see how even the subtlest of variations in the grapes and/or the process affect the wine and its name, and find out a few tips for visiting wineries (should you ever feel tempted to do so).

## Surveying the Landscape: Wine Categories

Your inner child will be happy to know that when it comes to wine, liking some colors more than others is a-okay. You can't get away with saying "I don't like green food!" much beyond your sixth birthday, but you can express a general preference for white, red, or pink wine for all of your adult years. Cheers to that!

In addition to being sorted by color, wines are sorted into three categories: table, dessert, and sparkling. They further vary by alcohol content and carbonation. The following sections help you navigate among these basic descriptors, which you definitely need to know if you plan to drink in any sort of sophisticated environment.

## Sorting wine by color

Whoever coined the term *white wine* must have been colorblind. All you have to do is look at it to see that it's not white, it's yellow. But everyone's used to the expression by now, so *white wine* it is.

*White* wine is wine without any red color (or pink color, which is in the red family), which means that *White Zinfandel,* a popular pink wine, isn't white wine. But yellow wines, golden wines, and wines that are as pale as water are all white wines.

Red wines, on the other hand, really are red. Regardless of whether they're purple red, ruby red, or garnet, they're members of the red family.

The most obvious difference between red wine and white wine is color. The red color occurs when the colorless juice of red grapes stays in contact with the dark grape skins during fermentation and absorbs the skins' color. Along with color, the grape skins give the wine *tannin,* a substance that's an important part of the way a red wine tastes. (See Chapter 5 in Book I for more about tannin.) The presence of tannin in red wines is actually the most important taste difference between red wines and white wines.

Your choice of a white wine, red wine, or rosé wine will vary with the season, the occasion, and the type of food that you're eating (not to mention your personal taste!). Choosing a color is usually the starting point for selecting a specific wine in a wine shop or restaurant. Most stores and most restaurant wine lists arrange wines by color before making other distinctions, such as grape varieties, wine regions, or taste categories.

Although certain foods can straddle the line between white wine and red wine compatibility — grilled salmon, for example, can be delicious with a rich white wine or a fruity red — your preference for red, white, or pink wine will often be your first consideration in pairing wine with food.

Whatever your preference, the following sections clue you in to the intricacies of whites versus reds versus rosés.

## (Not exactly) white wine

Wine becomes white wine in one of two ways:

- First, white wine can be made from white grapes — which, by the way, aren't white. (Did you see that one coming?) *White* grapes are greenish, greenish yellow, golden yellow, or sometimes even pinkish yellow. Basically, white grapes include all the grape types that aren't dark red or dark bluish. If you make a wine from white grapes, it's a white wine.

- The second way a wine can become white is a little more complicated. The process involves using red grapes — but only the *juice* of red grapes, not the grape skins. The juice of most red grapes has no red pigmentation, only the skins do. So a wine made with only the juice of red grapes can be a white wine. In practice, though, very few white wines come from red grapes. (Champagne is one exception; Chapter 6 of Book II addresses the use of red grapes to make Champagne.)

- In case you're wondering, the skins are removed from the grapes by either *pressing* large quantities of grapes so the juice flows out and the skins stay behind — sort of like squeezing the pulp out of grapes, the way kids do in the cafeteria — or by *crushing* the grapes in a machine that has rollers to break the skins so the juice can drain away.

White wines fall into four general taste categories, not counting sparkling wine or the really sweet white wine that you can drink with dessert (both of which are described later in this chapter). If the words used to describe these taste categories sound weird, take heart — they're all explained in Chapter 5 of Book I. Here are the four broad categories of white wine:

- **Fresh and unoaked:** Some whites are crisp and light, with no sweetness and no oaky character. Most Italian white wines, such as Soave and Pinot Grigio, and some French whites, such as Sancerre and some Chablis wines, fall into this category.

- **Earthy:** Other whites are dry, fuller-bodied, unoaked, or lightly oaked, with a lot of earthy character. Some French wines, such as Mâcon or whites from the Côtes du Rhône region, have this taste profile.

- **Aromatic:** Characterized by intense aromas and flavors that come from their particular grape variety, these whites are either *off-dry* (that is, they aren't bone dry) or dry. Examples include a lot of German wines, as well as wines from flavorful grape varieties (think Riesling or Viognier).

- **Rich and oaky:** These whites are dry or fairly dry and full-bodied, with pronounced oaky character. Most Chardonnays and many French wines — such as many of those from the Burgundy region of France — fall into this group.

You can drink white wine anytime you like — which for most people means as a drink without food or with lighter foods. (Chapter 6 of Book I covers the dynamics of pairing wines with food.) A lot of people like to drink white wines when the weather is hot, because they're more refreshing than red wines, and they're usually drunk chilled (the wines, not the people).

Serving white wines cool, but not ice-cold, is ideal. Sometimes restaurants serve white wines too cold, and you actually have to wait a while for the wine to warm up before you drink it. If you like your wine cold, fine; but try drinking your favorite white wine a little less cold sometime, and you'll probably discover it has more flavor that way. You can find specific serving temperatures for various types of wine in Chapter 4 of Book I.

White wines are often considered *apéritif* wines, meaning wines consumed before dinner, in place of cocktails, or at parties. (If you ask the officials who busy themselves defining such things, an apéritif wine is a wine that has flavors added to it, as vermouth does. But unless you're in the business of writing wine labels for a living, don't worry about that.)

### Red, red wine

*Red* wines are made from grapes that are red or bluish in color. So guess what wine people call these grapes? Black grapes! (Of course, right?)

Red wines vary quite a lot in style. This fact is partly because winemakers have so many ways of adjusting their red-winemaking to achieve the kind of wine they want. For example, if winemakers leave the juice in contact with the skins for a long time, the wine becomes more *tannic* (firmer in the mouth, like strong tea; tannic wines can make your lips pucker). If winemakers drain the juice off the skins sooner, the wine is softer and less tannic.

Here are four red wine styles:

- **Soft and fruity:** Some reds are relatively light-bodied, with a lot of fruitiness and little tannin (like Beaujolais Nouveau wine from France, some Valpolicellas from Italy, and many under-$10 U.S. wines).

- **Mild-mannered:** These reds are medium-bodied with subtle, unfruity flavors (like less-expensive wines from Bordeaux, in France, and some inexpensive Italian reds).

- **Spicy:** Other reds are flavorful, fruity wines with spicy accents and some tannin (such as some Malbecs from France or Argentina, as well as Dolcettos from Italy).

- **Powerful:** Some reds are full-bodied and tannic (such as the most-expensive California Cabernets; Barolo, from Italy; the most-expensive Australian reds; and lots of other expensive reds).

Thanks to the wide range of red wine styles, you can find red wines to go with just about every type of food and every occasion when you want to drink wine (except the times when you want to drink a wine with bubbles, because most bubbly wines are white or pink). That's rather fortunate because red wine tends to be consumed more often as part of a meal than as a drink on its own.

One sure way to spoil the fun in drinking most red wines is to drink them too cold. Those tannins can taste really bitter when the wine is cold — just as in a cold glass of very strong tea. On the other hand, many restaurants serve red wines too warm. (Where do they store them? Next to the boiler?) If the bottle feels cool to your hand, that's a good temperature. For more about serving wine at the right temperature, see Chapter 4 of Book I.

### A rose is a rose, but a rosé is "white"

*Rosé* wines are pink wines. They're made from red grapes, but they don't end up red because the grape juice stays in contact with the red skins for a very short time — only a few hours, compared to days or weeks for red wines. Because this *skin contact* (the period when the juice and the skins intermingle) is brief, rosé wines absorb very little tannin from the skins. Therefore, you can chill rosé wines and drink them as you would white wines.

Of course, not all rosé wines are called rosés; that would be too simple. Many rosé wines today are called *blush* wines — a term invented by wine marketers to avoid the word *rosé* because back in the '80s, pink wines weren't very popular. Lest someone figures out that *blush* is a synonym for *rosé,* the labels call these wines *white.* But even a 5-year-old can see that White Zinfandel is really pink.

The blush wines that call themselves *white* are fairly sweet. Wines labeled *rosé* can be sweetish too, but some wonderful rosés from Europe (and a few from America) are *dry* (not sweet). Some hard-core wine lovers hardly ever drink rosé wine, but many wine drinkers are discovering what a pleasure a good rosé can be, especially in warm weather.

---

# Red wine sensitivities

Some people complain that they can't drink red wines without getting a headache or feeling ill. Usually, they blame the sulfites in the wine. What they probably don't know is that red wines contain far less sulfur than white wines. That's because the tannin in red wines acts as a preservative, making sulfur dioxide less necessary. Red wines do contain histamine-like compounds and other substances derived from the grape skins, which could be the culprits. Whatever the source of the discomfort, it probably isn't sulfites.

# Categorizing by alcohol content and more

In the following sections, you find out about the differences between three categories of wines: table wines, dessert wines, and sparkling wines.

### Table wine

Here's a real-world definition of *table wines:* They're the normal, nonbubbly wines that most people drink most of the time.

Officially, though, table wine — or *light wine,* as the Europeans like to say — is fermented grape juice whose alcohol content falls within a certain range. Furthermore, table wine isn't bubbly. (Some table wines have a very slight carbonation but not enough to disqualify them as table wines.) According to U.S. standards of identification, table wines may have an alcohol content no higher than 14 percent; in Europe, light wine must contain from 8.5 percent to 14 percent alcohol by volume (with a few exceptions). So unless a wine has more than 14 percent alcohol or has bubbles, it's a table wine or a light wine in the eyes of the law.

### Dessert wine

Because winemakers add alcohol to dessert wines during or after fermentation, many of these wines have more than 14 percent alcohol. That's an unusual way of making wine, but some parts of the world, like the Sherry region in Spain and the Port region in Portugal, have made quite a specialty of it.

*Dessert wine* is the legal U.S. terminology for these wines, probably because they're usually sweet and often enjoyed after dinner. That term is misleading, however, because dessert wines aren't always sweet, nor are they always consumed after dinner. (For example, Dry Sherry is categorized as a dessert wine, but it's dry and great *before* dinner.)

In Europe, this category of wines is called *liqueur wines,* which carries the same connotation of sweetness. You may also hear them called *fortified,* which suggests that the wine has been strengthened with additional alcohol.

### Sparkling wine

*Sparkling wines* are wines that contain carbon dioxide bubbles. Carbon dioxide gas is a natural byproduct of fermentation, and winemakers sometimes decide to trap it in the wine. Just about every country that makes wine also makes sparkling wine.

# The origin of the percent-alcohol benchmark

The regulations-makers didn't get the number 14 by drawing it from a hat. Historically, most wines contained less than 14 percent alcohol — either because there wasn't enough sugar in the juice to attain a higher alcohol level, or because the yeasts died off when the alcohol reached 14 percent, halting the fermentation. That number, therefore, became the legal borderline between wines that have no alcohol added to them (table wines) and wines that may have alcohol added to them (see the "Dessert wine" section in this chapter).

Today, however, the issue isn't as clear-cut as it was when the laws were written. Many grapes are now grown in warm climates where they become so ripe — and have so much natural sugar — that their juice attains more than 14 percent alcohol when it's fermented. The use of gonzo yeast strains that continue working even when the alcohol exceeds 14 percent is another factor. Many red Zinfandels, Cabernets, and Chardonnays from California now have 14.5 or even 15.5 percent alcohol. Wine drinkers still consider them table wines, but legally they don't qualify as such. (Technically, they're dessert wines and taxed at a higher rate.) Which is just to say that laws and reality don't always keep pace.

In the United States, Canada, and Europe, *sparkling wine* is the official name for the category of wines with bubbles. (Isn't it nice when everyone agrees?) *Champagne* (with a capital *C*) is a specific type of sparkling wine (made from certain grape varieties and produced in a certain way) that comes from a region in France called Champagne. It's the undisputed Grand Champion of Bubblies and perhaps the most famous wine overall. (For more specifics about Champagne, see Chapter 6 in Book II.)

Unfortunately for the people of Champagne, France, their wine is so famous that the name *champagne* has been borrowed again and again by producers elsewhere, until the word has become synonymous with practically the whole category of sparkling wines. For example, until a recent agreement between the United States and the European Union, U.S. winemakers could legally call any sparkling wine *champagne* — even with a capital *C*, if they wanted — as long as the carbonation wasn't added artificially. Even now, the American wineries that were already using that name may continue to do so. (Although they do have to add a qualifying geographic term such as *American* or *Californian* before the word *Champagne*.)

For the French, limiting the use of the name *champagne* to the wines of the Champagne region is a *cause célèbre*. European Union regulations not only prevent any other member country from calling its sparkling wines *champagne* but also prohibit the use of terms that even *suggest* the word *champagne*, such as fine print on the label saying that a wine was made by using the so-called "champagne method." What's more, bottles of sparkling wine from countries outside the European Union that use the word *champagne* on the label are banned from sale in Europe. The French are that serious.

# How Wine Happens

Although wine is, essentially, nothing but liquid, fermented fruit, the art of producing it actually involves two separate steps: the growing of the grapes, called *viticulture,* and the making of the wine, called *vinification.* (In some wine courses, students nickname the dual process *viti-vini.*)

Sometimes one company grows the grapes *and* makes the wine, as is the case with *estate-bottled* wines. And sometimes the two steps are completely separate. For example, some large wineries buy grapes from private grape growers. These growers don't make wine; they just grow grapes and sell them to whatever wine company offers them the highest price per ton. In the case of the very least expensive wines, the winery named on the label may have purchased not even grapes but wine (from bulk wine producers) and then blended the wines and bottled the final product as its own.

## Glimpsing the organic wine frontier

The new standards of organic agriculture established by the U.S. Department of Agriculture in 2002 contain two categories for wine:

- **Wine made from organically grown grapes:** These are wines whose grapes come from certified organic vineyards.

- **Organic wine:** These wines come from organically grown grapes and are also produced organically, that is, without the addition of chemical additives (such as sulfur dioxide) during winemaking.

These categories apply to imported wines sold in the United States, as well as to domestic wines. Many more brands, by far, fall into the first category than the second, because most winemakers do use sulfur dioxide when making their wines.

But not all wines from organically grown grapes are labeled as such. Some winemakers who are deeply committed to organic farming prefer to promote and sell their wines based on the wines' quality, not the incidental feature of their organic farming. For them, organic farming is a means to an end — better grapes, and therefore better wine — rather than a marketing tool. Also, the fact that a national definition of *organic* didn't exist in the past disinclined some wineries from using the word.

Now that formal categories exist, many more producers who farm organically will perhaps begin using the *O*-word on their labels. But the number of wines in the more rigid organic-wine category will probably remain small due to the sulfur dioxide restriction.

Regardless of who owns the responsibility for the two steps, both viticulture and vinification feature variables that affect various aspects of a wine, from color to taste and so on. Obviously, one of the biggest factors in making one wine different from the next is the nature of the raw material: the grape juice. Think back to the last wine you drank. What color was it? If it was white, odds are that's because it came from white grapes; if it was pink or red, that's because the wine came from red grapes. Did the wine smell herbal or earthy or fruity? Whichever, those aromas came mainly from the grapes. Was it firm and tannic or soft and voluptuous? Thank the grapes, with a nod to Mother Nature and the winemaker. Grapes are the main ingredient in wine, and everything the winemaker does, he does to the particular grape juice he has.

Each grape variety reacts in its own way to the farming and winemaking techniques that it faces. How the grapes grow — the amount of sunshine and moisture they get, for example, and how ripe they are when they're harvested — can emphasize certain of their characteristics rather than others. So can winemaking processes such as oak aging.

The *taste* of a wine involves not only the wine's flavors but also its aroma, body, texture, length, and so on. Naturally, the taste of a wine is also a subjective experience. Different wines appeal to different wine drinkers at different times.

- ✔ Some wines are intended to taste good to casual wine drinkers, whereas others are intended for experienced wine lovers.
- ✔ Some wines are intended to taste good right away, whereas others are intended to taste good down the road, after the wine has aged.

The following sections walk you through the many variations that affect the taste of the wines you drink.

## *Discovering differences among grape varieties*

Grapes are the starting point of every wine and therefore are largely responsible for the style and personality of each wine. The grapes that make a particular wine dictate the genetic structure of that wine and how it'll respond to everything the winemaker does to it.

Different varieties of grapes (Chardonnay, Cabernet Sauvignon, or Merlot, for example) make different wines. *Grape variety* refers to the fruit of a specific type of grapevine: the fruit of the Cabernet Sauvignon vine, for example, or of the Chardonnay vine. The specific grape variety (or varieties) that makes any given wine is largely responsible for the sensory characteristics the wine offers — from its appearance and aromas to its flavors and alcohol–tannin–acid profile.

All sorts of attributes distinguish each grape variety from the next. These attributes fall into two categories: personality traits and performance factors. *Personality traits* are the characteristics of the fruit itself — its flavors, for example. *Performance factors* refer to how the grapevine grows, how its fruit ripens, and how quickly it can get from 0 to 60 miles per hour.

### Personality traits

Skin color is the most fundamental distinction among grape varieties. Every grape variety is considered either white or red (or "black"), according to the color of its skins when the grapes are ripe. (A few red-skinned varieties are further distinguished by having red pulp rather than white pulp.) Additionally, red grape skins contribute tannin to wine, whereas white grape skins don't.

Individual grape varieties also differ from one another in these other ways:

- **Aromatic compounds:** Some grapes (such as Muscat) contribute floral aromas and flavors to their wine, for example; other grapes contribute herbaceous notes (as Sauvignon Blanc does) or fruity character. Some grapes have very neutral aromas and flavors and, therefore, make fairly neutral wines.

- **Acidity levels:** Some grapes are naturally disposed to higher acid levels than others, which influences the wine made from those grapes.

- **Thickness of skin and size of individual grapes (called *berries*):** Black grapes with thick skins naturally have more tannin than grapes with thin skins; ditto for small-berried varieties compared to large-berried varieties, because their skin-to-juice ratio is higher. More tannin in the grapes translates into a firmer, more tannic red wine.

## Splitting hairs: Grape species

The term *variety* actually has a specific meaning in scientific circles. A variety is a subdivision of a species. Most of the world's wines are made from grape varieties that belong to the species *vinifera,* which is itself a subdivision of the genus *Vitis.* This species originated in Europe and western Asia; other distinct species of *Vitis* are native to North America.

Grapes of other species can also make wine; for example, the Concord grape, which makes Concord wine as well as grape juice and jelly, belongs to the native American species *Vitis labrusca.* But the grapes of this species have a very different flavor from *vinifera* grapes — *foxy* is the word used to describe that taste (not kidding). The number of non-*vinifera* wines is small because their flavor is less popular in wine.

The composite personality traits of any grape variety are fairly evident in wines made from that grape. A Cabernet Sauvignon wine is almost always more tannic and slightly lower in alcohol than a comparable Merlot wine, for example, because that's the nature of those two grapes.

### Performance factors

The performance factors that distinguish grape varieties are vitally important to the grape grower because those factors determine how easy or challenging it will be for him to cultivate a specific variety in his vineyard — if he can even grow it at all. The issues include

- ✔ **How much time a variety typically needs to ripen its grapes:** In regions with short growing seasons, early ripening varieties do best.

- ✔ **How dense and compact the grape bunches are:** In warm, damp climates, grape varieties with dense bunches can have mildew problems.

- ✔ **How much vegetation a particular variety tends to grow:** In fertile soils, a vine that's predisposed to growing a lot of leaves and shoots can have so much vegetation that the grapes don't get enough sunlight to ripen.

The reasons some grape varieties perform brilliantly in certain places (and make excellent wine as a result) are so complex that grape growers haven't figured them all out yet. The amount of heat and cold, the amount of wind and rain (or lack of it), and the slant of the sun's rays on a hillside of vines are among the factors affecting a vine's performance.

## Viticulture 101: Understanding what affects grape growth and development

Grapes don't grow in a void. Where they grow — the soil and climate of each wine region, as well as the traditions and goals of the people who grow the grapes and make the wine — affects the nature of both the ripe grapes and the taste of the wine made from those grapes. That's why so much of the information about wine revolves around the countries and the regions where wine is made.

Growing grapes for wine is a fairly intricate process that *viticulturalists* (the folks who grow grapes; not surprisingly, *viticulture* refers to the process of growing grapes) are constantly refining to suit their particular soil, climate, and grape varieties. Many of the technical terms spill over into discussions about wine or crop up on wine labels.

Here are the expressions you're likely to encounter as you pore further over the many intricacies of wine:

- ✔ **Microclimate:** Every wine region has climatic conditions (the amount and timing of sun, rain, wind, humidity, and so on) that are considered the norm for that area. But individual locations within a region — the south-facing side of a particular hill, for example — can have a climatic reality that's different from neighboring vineyards. The unique climatic reality of a specific location is usually called its *microclimate.*

- ✔ **Canopy:** Left untended, grapevines grow along the ground, up trees, wherever they please really. Commercial viticulture involves attaching the shoots of vines to wires or trellises in a systematic pattern. The purpose of *training* the vine, as this activity is called, is to position the grape bunches so they get enough sun to ripen well and so the fruit is easy for the harvesters to reach.

    An *open canopy* is a trellising method that maximizes the sunlight exposure of the grapes. *Canopy management,* the practice of maneuvering the leaves and fruit into the best position for a given vineyard, is a popular phrase.

- ✔ **Ripeness:** Harvesting grapes when they're perfectly ripe is one of the crucial points in wine production, but one producer's "perfect ripeness" is another's "almost there" and yet another's "too late."

- ✔ **Low yields:** Generally speaking, the more grapes a grapevine grows (in other words, the higher its *yield* of grapes), the less concentrated the flavors of those grapes will be, and the lower in quality (and less expensive) their wine will be. Just about any wine producer anywhere can claim that his yields are low, because it's too complicated to prove otherwise. The proof is usually in the wine's flavor concentration: If the wine tastes thin or watery, be suspicious of the "low yield" claim.

## Examining vinification: The making of wine

The recipe for turning fruit into wine goes something like this:

1. **Pick a large quantity of ripe grapes from grapevines.**

    You can actually substitute raspberries or any other fruit, but 99.9 percent of all the wine in the world is made from grapes, because they make the best wines.

2. **Put the grapes into a clean container that doesn't leak.**

3. **Crush the grapes somehow to release their juice.**

    Once upon a time, feet performed this step.

4. **Wait.**

# Matching a noble grape variety to its ideal growing place

Bees have their queens, gorillas have their silverbacks, and humans have their royal families. The grape kingdom has its nobles, too — at least as interpreted by the human beings who drink the wine made from those grapes.

*Noble* grape varieties (as wine people call them) have the potential to make great — not just good — wine. Every noble grape variety can claim at least one wine region where it's the undisputed king. The wines made from noble grapes on their home turf can be so great that they inspire winemakers in far-flung regions to grow the same grape in their own vineyards. The noble grape might prove itself noble there, too — but frequently it doesn't. Adaptability isn't a prerequisite of nobility.

Classic examples of noble grape varieties at their best are

- The Chardonnay grape and the Pinot Noir grape in Burgundy, France
- The Cabernet Sauvignon grape in Bordeaux, France
- The Syrah grape in France's Northern Rhône Valley
- The Chenin Blanc grape in France's Loire Valley
- The Nebbiolo grape in Piedmont, Italy
- The Sangiovese grape in Tuscany, Italy
- The Riesling grape in the Mosel and Rheingau regions of Germany

Basic wine production is astoundingly simple, but today's winemakers have a bag of tricks as big as a sumo wrestler's appetite. That's one reason why no two wines ever taste exactly the same. Techniques vary according to the grapes the winemakers have and the type of wine they're making. (If you have trouble making decisions, don't ever become a winemaker. Every decision made during *vinification,* the process of making wine, affects the taste of the wine in one way or another.)

The following sections provide some insight into the basic winemaking process and the ways in which winemakers can (and do!) vary their approach to vinification.

### *The natural process: Fermentation and maturation*

After the grapes are harvested and crushed, *yeasts* (tiny one-celled organisms that exist naturally in the vineyard and, therefore, on the grapes) come into contact with the sugar in the grapes' juice and gradually convert that sugar into alcohol. Yeasts also produce carbon dioxide, which evaporates into the air. When the yeasts are done working, your grape juice is wine. The juice's sugar is gone, and alcohol is present instead. (The riper and sweeter the grapes, the more alcohol the wine made from them will have.)

Known as *fermentation,* this totally natural process doesn't require man's participation at all, except to put the grapes into a container and release the juice from them. Fermentation occurs in fresh apple cider left too long in your refrigerator, without any help from you. Even milk, which contains a different sort of sugar than grapes do, develops a small amount of alcohol if you leave it on the kitchen table all day long.

Fermentation can last three days or three months. After fermentation, the wine goes through a period called *maturation* (or *finishing*), when it settles down, loses its rough edges, goes to prep school, and gets ready to meet the world.

### The art: Variations in technique

A winemaker's technique is based on three factors: the price level, the taste profile he's seeking, and the type of wine drinker the winery is targeting. To create those variations, winemakers exercise their creativity during both the fermentation and the maturation periods.

How the wine tastes is the ultimate validation of any method used to produce a wine. The procedures themselves are meaningless if they don't create a wine that's appealing to the wine drinkers for whom that wine is intended.

Every one of the following factors can make a big difference in the taste of a particular wine:

✔ **What the juice is fermented in (oak barrel or stainless steel tank):** Oak barrels often lend oaky flavor and aroma to the wine, which many people find appealing; they can also affect both the texture of the wine and its color. Stainless steel, by contrast, is neutral and prevents oxygen exchange, which can help retain freshness in the fruit aromas and flavors.

You don't have to venture very far into wine before you find someone explaining to you that a particular wine was barrel-fermented or barrel-aged. Here's what the terminology means:

- The term *barrel-fermented* means that the grape juice was fermented in barrels (almost always oak).

- The term *barrel-aged* usually means that the wine was fermented elsewhere — usually in stainless steel tanks — and was then put into barrels, where it matured. If a wine is barrel-fermented, it's almost always barrel-aged as well.

Think all this talk of barrels is just mumbo jumbo? Well, if you're a fan of white wines, you just might care whether a white wine is barrel-fermented versus barrel-aged. Barrel-fermented wines actually end up tasting *less* oaky than simply barrel-aged wines, even though they may have spent more time in oak. That's because juice interacts differently with the oak than wine does.

- ✔ **The size of the barrel or tank used for fermentation:** Fermentation often occurs in a neutral vessel, such as a stainless steel tank. If oak barrels or tanks are used, the larger (and older) the vessel, the less the oak influence. Fermentation can even happen in the bottle, as is often the case for sparkling wine.

- ✔ **The type of oak barrel used for maturation (and fermentation, if applicable):** Not all oak is the same. Oak barrels vary in the origin of their oak, the amount of *toast* (a charring of the inside of the barrels) each barrel has, and how often the barrels have been used (their oaky character diminishes with use). Small barrels, commonly 225 liters and known as *barriques,* have a greater ratio of wood to wine. Thus, wines made in them generally have more discernable oak influence.

  Oak barrels are expensive — about $800 per barrel if they're made from French oak. (Most people consider French oak to be the finest.) If a winemaker is producing a huge quantity of a wine that will sell for $5.99, for example, he probably won't put the wine into new oak barrels because the cost of the barrels can add as much as $5 to the price of every bottle.

- ✔ **The temperature of the wine during fermentation:** Reds usually ferment faster and at a higher temperature; whites ferment more slowly and at a lower temperature.

- ✔ **How long the wine is allowed to mature:** Wine can mature for a couple weeks or a couple years, or anything in between. Generally, wines that emphasize freshness, such as a rosé, have a short maturation. More age-worthy wines are kept in the winery longer, either in the barrel or the bottle, before being released.

Depending on the type of wine being made, the whole process can take three months to five years — or even longer if the bank isn't breathing down the winery's neck.

# Visiting Wineries for a Firsthand Look

One of the best — and most fun-filled — ways to discover more about wine is to actually visit wine regions and, if possible, speak to the winemakers and producers about their wines. You get to immerse yourself in the region you visit by experiencing the climate firsthand, seeing the soil and the hills, touching the grapes, and so on. You can walk through the vineyards, visit nearby towns or villages, eat the local food, and drink the wine of the region.

You discover that there's something special about the people who devote their lives to making wine. Maybe it's their creativity or their commitment to bringing pleasure to the world through their labor. Whatever the reason, they're exceptional folk.

Don't let your limited (or nonexistent) ability to speak the local language prevent you from visiting wine regions. These days, English is the nearly universal language of the wine world. Even if the person you're visiting doesn't speak English, he invariably has someone available (his wife, his son, or his dog) who does. Besides, wine itself is a universal language. A smile and a handshake go a long way toward communicating!

Whenever you plan to visit a winery — especially one that's less geared toward tourism, which is the case in most of the wine world — you usually need to call or write ahead for an appointment. During your visit, you can simply sample the wines, talk to the winemaker or proprietor when he's available, take an informal tour of the winery, and buy some wine if you so choose (an especially nice idea if the wine isn't available back home).

The major exceptions to the appointment-first rule are a few of the large wineries in California that offer scheduled tours or self-guided visits. Many wineries in the United States also have tasting rooms that are open every day during the busy tourism months and on weekends during the winter. In these tasting rooms, you can sample wines (sometimes for a small fee), buy wine, and purchase souvenirs such as T-shirts or sweat shirts with the logo of the winery imprinted on them.

# Chapter 2

# Getting Familiar with Wine Tastes and Names

**In This Chapter**

▶ Looking at the characteristics of popular white and red grape varieties

▶ Figuring out how wines get their names

Gaze across manicured rows of grapevines in Napa Valley or ponder craggy terraces of rugged hillside vines in Portugal, and you're likely to be inspired by the synthesis of the elements that makes grapes, well, grapes. They're a juicy link between land and wine, and they also happen to give us one of the easiest ways of classifying wine and making sense of the hundreds of different types of wine that exist. In the sections to come, you glimpse grapes' range and find out how wines get their names. (Hint: Usually from the land itself or the grapes that go into them.)

## Savoring the Nuances in Taste among Grape Varieties

Snowflakes and fingerprints aren't the only examples of Mother Nature's infinite variety. Within the genus *Vitis* and the species *vinifera* are as many as 10,000 varieties of wine grapes. If wine from every one of these varieties were commercially available and you drank the wine of a different variety every single day, you'd need more than 27 years to experience them all!

Not that you'd want to. Within those 10,000 varieties are grapes that have the ability to make extraordinary wine, grapes that tend to make very ordinary wine, and grapes that only a parent could love. Most varieties are obscure grapes whose wines rarely enter into international commerce.

The following sections delve into the white and red grape varieties you're most likely to encounter. Why? Because they're the most important *vinifera* varieties in the wine world.

## A primer on white grape varieties

This section includes descriptions of the 12 most important white *vinifera* varieties today and the types of wine that are made from each grape. These wines can be varietal wines or place-name wines that don't mention the grape variety anywhere on the label (a common practice for European wines). These grapes can also be blending partners for other grapes in wines made from multiple grape varieties.

### Chardonnay

Chardonnay (shar-dohn-nay) is a regal grape for its role in producing the greatest dry white wines in the world — white Burgundies — and for being one of the main grapes of Champagne. Today it also ends up in a huge amount of table wine (see Chapter 1 in Book I for more on this particular wine category).

The Chardonnay grape grows in practically every wine-producing country of the world for two reasons: It's relatively adaptable to a wide range of climates, and the name Chardonnay on a wine label is (these days) a surefire sales tool.

Most Chardonnay wine receives some oak treatment either during or after fermentation. (For the best Chardonnays, oak treatment means expensive barrels of French oak; for lower-priced Chardonnays, oak treatment can mean soaking oak chips in the wine or even adding liquid essence of oak. See Chapter 1 in Book I for the scoop on how wine is made.) Except for northeastern Italy and France's Chablis and Mâconnais districts, where oak usually isn't used for Chardonnay, oaky Chardonnay wine is the norm, and unoaked Chardonnay is the exception.

Oaked Chardonnay is so common that some wine drinkers confuse the flavor of oak with the flavor of Chardonnay. If your glass of Chardonnay smells or tastes toasty, smoky, spicy, vanilla-like, or butterscotch-like, that's the oak you're perceiving, not the Chardonnay.

Chardonnay itself has fruity aromas and flavors that range from apple in cooler wine regions to tropical fruits, especially pineapple, in warmer regions. Chardonnay can also display subtle earthy aromas, such as mushroom or minerals. Chardonnay wine has medium to high acidity and is generally full-bodied (flip to Chapter 5 in Book I to find out more about these important characteristics of wine). Classically, Chardonnay wines are dry. But most inexpensive Chardonnays these days are actually a bit sweet.

Chardonnay is a grape that can stand on its own in a wine, and the top Chardonnay-based wines (except for Champagne and similar bubblies) are 100 percent Chardonnay. But less-expensive wines that are labeled *Chardonnay* — those selling for less than $10 a bottle in the United States, for example — are likely to have some other, far less distinguished grape blended in to help reduce the cost of making the wine. Anyway, who can even tell, behind all that oak?

### Riesling

The great Riesling (*reese*-ling) wines of Germany have put the Riesling grape on the charts as an undisputedly *noble* variety (a grape variety that excels when grown in a particular region). Riesling shows its real class in only a few places outside of Germany, however. The Alsace region of France, Austria, and the Clare Valley region of Australia are among these few.

Although Chardonnay has long been a favorite and is still the most popular white wine in America, Riesling has been winning away fans from Chardonnay. Maybe that's because Riesling is the antithesis of Chardonnay. Whereas Chardonnay is usually gussied up with oak, Riesling almost never is; whereas Chardonnay can be full-bodied and rich, Riesling is more often light-bodied, crisp, and refreshing. Riesling's fresh, vivid personality can make many Chardonnays taste clumsy in comparison.

The common perception of Riesling wines is that they're sweet, and many of them are — but plenty of them aren't. Alsace Rieslings are normally dry; many German Rieslings are fairly dry; and a few American Rieslings are dry. (Riesling can be vinified either way, according to the style of wine a producer wants to make.) Look for the word *trocken* (meaning dry) on German Riesling labels and the word *dry* on American labels if you prefer the dry style of Riesling.

High acidity, low to medium alcohol levels, and aromas/flavors that range from fruity to flowery to minerally are trademarks of Riesling.

Riesling wines are sometimes labeled as *White Riesling* or *Johannisberg Riesling* — both synonyms for the noble Riesling grape. With wines from Eastern European countries, though, read the fine print: Olazrizling, Laskirizling, and Welschriesling are from another grape altogether.

### Sauvignon Blanc

Sauvignon Blanc (saw-vee-nyon blahnk) is a white variety with a very distinctive character. It's high in acidity with pronounced aromas and flavors. Besides its herbaceous character (which people sometimes refer to as *grassy*), Sauvignon Blanc wines display mineral aromas and flavors, vegetal character, or — in certain climates — fruity character, such as ripe melon, figs, or passion fruit.

The wines are light- to medium-bodied and usually dry. Most of them are unoaked, but some are oaky.

France has two classic wine regions for the Sauvignon Blanc grape: Bordeaux and the Loire Valley, where the two best-known Sauvignon wines are called Sancerre or Pouilly-Fumé. In Bordeaux, Sauvignon Blanc is sometimes blended with Sémillon (see Table 2-1); some of the wines that are blended about fifty-fifty from the two grapes and fermented in oak are among the great white wines of the world.

Sauvignon Blanc is also important in northeastern Italy, South Africa, and parts of California, where the wines are sometimes labeled as *Fumé Blanc.* New Zealand's Sauvignon Blanc wines in particular are renowned for their fresh, flavorful style.

### Pinot Gris/Pinot Grigio

Pinot Gris (pee-noh gree) is one of several grape varieties called *Pinot:* There's Pinot Blanc (white Pinot), Pinot Noir (black Pinot), Pinot Meunier (who knows how that one translates), and Pinot Gris (gray Pinot), which is called *Pinot Grigio* (pee-noh *gree*-joe) in Italian. Pinot Gris is believed to have mutated from the black Pinot Noir grape. Although Pinot Gris is considered a white grape, its skin color is unusually dark for a white variety.

Wines made from Pinot Gris can be deeper in color than most white wines (although most of Italy's Pinot Grigio wines are quite pale). Pinot Gris wines are medium- to full-bodied, usually not oaky, and have rather low acidity and fairly neutral aromas (flip to Chapter 5 in Book I for details on these key characteristics of wine). Sometimes the flavor and aroma can suggest the skins of fruit, such as peach skins or orange rinds.

Pinot Gris is an important grape throughout northeastern Italy; it also grows in Germany, where it's called Ruländer. The only region in France where Pinot Gris is important is Alsace, where it really struts its stuff. Oregon has had good success with Pinot Gris, and more and more winemakers in California are now taking a shot at it. Because Pinot Grigio is one of the best-selling inexpensive white wines in the United States, countries such as Chile and Australia now grow this grape for mass-market wines and often call the wine Pinot Grigio.

### Other white grapes

Table 2-1 describes some other grapes whose names you see on wine labels, or whose wine you might wind up drinking in place-name wines without realizing it.

### Table 2-1    Other White Grapes and Their Characteristics

| *Grape Variety* | *Characteristics* |
| --- | --- |
| Albariño (ahl-ba-*ree*-nyo) | An aromatic grape from the northwestern corner of Spain — the region called Rias Baixas — and Portugal's northerly Vinho Verde region, where it's called *Alvarinho*. It makes medium-bodied, crisp, appley-tasting, usually unoaked white wines whose high glycerin gives them silky texture. |
| Chenin Blanc (shen-in blahnk) | A noble grape in the Loire Valley of France, for Vouvray and other wines. The best Chenin Blanc wines have high acidity and a fascinating oily texture (they feel rather thick in your mouth). Some good dry Chenin Blanc comes from California, but so does a ton of ordinary off-dry wine. In South Africa, Chenin Blanc is often called *Steen*. |
| Gewürztraminer (geh-*vairtz*-trah-mee-ner) | A wonderfully exotic grape that makes fairly deep-colored, full-bodied, soft white wines with aromas and flavors of roses and lychee fruit. France's Alsace region is the classic domain of this variety; the wines have pronounced floral and fruity aromas and flavors but are actually dry. A commercial style of U.S. Gewürztraminer is light, sweetish, and fairly bland, but a few wineries in California, Oregon, and New York do make good, dry Gewürztraminer. |
| Grüner Veltliner (*grew*-ner *velt*-lee-ner) | A native Austrian variety that boasts complex aromas and flavors (vegetal, spicy, mineral), rich texture, and usually substantial weight. |
| Muscat (moos-caht) | An aromatic grape that makes Italy's sparkling Asti (which, incidentally, tastes *exactly* like ripe Muscat grapes). It has extremely pretty floral aromas. In Alsace and Austria, Muscat makes a dry wine, and in lots of places (southern France, southern Italy, and Australia among them) it makes a delicious, sweet dessert wine through the addition of alcohol. |
| Pinot Blanc (pee-noh blahnk) | Fairly neutral in aroma and flavors, yet can make wines with a good deal of character. High acidity and low sugar levels translate into dry, crisp, medium-bodied wines. Alsace, Austria, northern Italy, and Germany are the main production zones. |

*(continued)*

**Table 2-1** *(continued)*

| Grape Variety | Characteristics |
|---|---|
| Sémillon (seh-mee-yohn) | Sauvignon Blanc's classic blending partner and a good grape in its own right. Sémillon wine is low in acid relative to Sauvignon Blanc and has attractive but subtle aromas — lanolin sometimes, although it can be slightly herbaceous when young. A major grape in Australia and southwestern France, including Bordeaux (where it's the key player in the dessert wine Sauternes). |
| Viognier (vee-oh-nyay) | A grape from France's Rhône Valley that's becoming popular in California, the south of France, and elsewhere. It has a floral aroma and is delicately apricot-like and medium- to full-bodied, with low acidity. |

## A primer on red grape varieties

Following are descriptions of 13 important red *vinifera* grape varieties. Expect to encounter these grapes in both varietal and place-name wines.

### Cabernet Sauvignon

Cabernet Sauvignon (cab-er-nay saw-vee-nyon) is a noble grape variety that grows well in just about any climate that isn't very cool. It became famous through the age-worthy red wines of the Médoc district of Bordeaux (which usually also contain Merlot and Cabernet Franc, in varying proportions). But today California is an equally important region for Cabernet Sauvignon — not to mention Washington, southern France, Italy, Australia, South Africa, Chile, and Argentina.

The Cabernet Sauvignon grape makes wines that are medium- to full-bodied and high in *tannin* (a substance that's an important part of the way a red wine tastes; check out Chapter 5 in Book I for details). The textbook descriptor for Cabernet Sauvignon's aroma and flavor is *blackcurrants* or *cassis;* the grape can also contribute vegetal tones to a wine when or where the grapes are less than ideally ripe.

Cabernet Sauvignon wines come in all price and quality levels. The least-expensive versions are usually fairly soft and very fruity, with medium body. The best wines are rich and firm with great depth and classic Cabernet flavor. Serious Cabernet Sauvignons can age for 15 years or more.

Because Cabernet Sauvignon is fairly tannic (and because of the blending precedent in Bordeaux), winemakers often blend it with other grapes; usually Merlot, which is less tannic than Cabernet Sauvignon and therefore an ideal partner. Australian winemakers have an unusual practice of blending Cabernet Sauvignon with Syrah.

Cabernet Sauvignon often goes by just its first name, Cabernet (although it isn't the only Cabernet), or even by its nickname, *Cab*.

### Merlot

Deep color, full body, high alcohol, and low tannin are the characteristics of wines made from the Merlot (mer-loh) grape. The aromas and flavors can be plummy or sometimes chocolatey, or they can suggest tea leaves.

Some wine drinkers find Merlot easier to like than Cabernet Sauvignon because it's less tannic. (But some winemakers feel that Merlot isn't satisfactory in its own right, and thus often blend it with Cabernet Sauvignon, Cabernet Franc, or both.) Merlot makes both inexpensive, simple wines and, when grown in the right conditions, very serious wines.

Merlot is actually the most-planted grape variety in Bordeaux, where it excels in the Right Bank districts of Pomerol and St. Emilion. Merlot is also important in Washington, California, the Long Island district of New York, northeastern Italy, and Chile.

### Pinot Noir

The late Andre Tchelitscheff, the legendary winemaker of some of California's finest Cabernets, once said that if he could do it all over again, he'd make Pinot Noir (pee-noh nwahr) rather than Cab. He's probably not alone. Cabernet is the sensible wine to make — a good, steady, reliable wine that doesn't give the winemaker too much trouble and can achieve excellent quality — and Pinot Noir is finicky, troublesome, enigmatic, and challenging. But a great Pinot Noir can be one of the greatest wines ever.

The prototype for Pinot Noir wine is red Burgundy, from France, where tiny vineyard plots yield rare treasures of wine made entirely from Pinot Noir. Oregon, California, New Zealand, and parts of Australia and Chile also produce good Pinot Noir. But Pinot Noir's production is rather limited, because this variety is very particular about climate and soil.

Pinot Noir wine is lighter in color than Cabernet or Merlot. It has relatively high alcohol, medium-to-high acidity, and medium-to-low tannin (although oak barrels can contribute additional tannin to the wine). Its flavors and aromas can be very fruity — often like a mélange of red berries — or earthy and woodsy, depending on how it's grown and/or *vinified* (made into wine). Pinot Noir is rarely blended with other grapes.

### Syrah/Shiraz

The northern part of France's Rhône Valley is the classic home for great wines from the Syrah (see-rah) grape. Rhône wines such as Hermitage and Côte-Rôtie are the inspiration for Syrah's dissemination to Australia, California, Washington, Italy, and Spain.

Syrah produces deeply colored wines with full body, firm tannin, and aromas/flavors that can suggest berries, smoked meat, black pepper, tar, or even burnt rubber (believe it or not). In Australia, Syrah (called *Shiraz,* which is pronounced shee-rahz) comes in several styles — some of them charming, medium-bodied, vibrantly fruity wines that are quite the opposite of the Northern Rhône's powerful Syrahs.

Syrah doesn't require any other grape to complement its flavors. However, it's often blended with Cabernet in Australia, and in the Southern Rhône, it's often part of a blended wine with Grenache and other varieties.

### Zinfandel

White Zinfandel (*zihn*-fuhn-dehl) is such a popular wine — and so much better known than the red style of Zinfandel — that its fans might argue that Zinfandel is a white grape. But it's really red.

Zinfandel is one of the oldest grapes in California; it therefore enjoys a certain stature there. Its aura is enhanced by its mysterious history: Although Zinfandel is clearly a *vinifera* grape, authorities were uncertain of its origins for decades. Never fear though. They've finally proven that Zinfandel's origin is an obscure Croatian grape.

Zin — as lovers of red Zinfandel call it — makes rich, dark wines that are high in alcohol and medium to high in tannin. They can have a blackberry or raspberry aroma and flavor, a spicy or tarry character, or even a jammy flavor (for more on flavors to watch for, see Chapter 5 in Book I). Some Zins are lighter than others and meant to be enjoyed young, whereas some are serious wines with a tannin structure that's built for aging.

### Nebbiolo

Outside of scattered sites in northwestern Italy — mainly the Piedmont region — Nebbiolo (nehb-be-*oh*-loh) just doesn't make remarkable wine. But the extraordinary quality of Barolo and Barbaresco, two Piedmont wines, prove what greatness it can achieve under the right conditions.

The Nebbiolo grape is high in both tannin and acid, which can make a wine tough. Fortunately, it also gives enough alcohol to soften the package. Its color can be deep when the wine is young but can develop orangey tinges within a few years. Its complex aroma is fruity (strawberry, cherry), earthy and woodsy (tar, truffles), herbal (mint, eucalyptus, anise), and floral (roses).

Lighter versions of Nebbiolo are meant to be drunk young — wines labeled *Nebbiolo d'Alba, Roero,* or *Nebbiolo delle Langhe,* for example — whereas Barolo and Barbaresco are wines that really deserve a *minimum* of eight years' aging before drinking.

### Sangiovese

Sangiovese (san-joe-*vay*-say) is an Italian grape that has proven itself in the Tuscany region of Italy, especially in the Brunello di Montalcino and Chianti districts. Sangiovese makes wines that are medium to high in acidity and firm in tannin; the wines can be light-bodied to full-bodied, depending on exactly where the grapes grow and how the wine is made. The aromas and flavors of the wines are fruity — especially cherry, often tart cherry — with floral nuances of violets and sometimes a slightly nutty character.

### Tempranillo

Tempranillo (tem-prah-*nee*-yoh) is Spain's candidate for greatness. It gives wines deep color, low acidity, and only moderate alcohol. Modern renditions of Tempranillo from the Ribera del Duero region and elsewhere in Spain prove what color and fruitiness this grape has. In more traditional wines, such as those of the Rioja region, much of the grape's color and flavor is lost due to long wood aging and blending with varieties that lack color, such as Grenache.

### Other red grapes

Table 2-2 describes additional red grape varieties and their wines, which you can encounter either as varietal wines or as wines named for their place of production.

| Table 2-2 | Other Red Grapes and Their Characteristics |
|---|---|
| *Grape Variety* | *Characteristics* |
| Aglianico (ahl-*yahn*-ee-co) | From southern Italy, where it makes Taurasi and other age-worthy, powerful red wines that are high in tannin. |
| Barbera (bar-*bae*-rah) | An Italian variety that, oddly for a red grape, has little tannin but very high acidity. When fully ripe, it can give big, fruity wines with refreshing crispness. Many producers age the wine in new oak to increase the tannin level of their wine. |

*(continued)*

**Table 2-2** *(continued)*

| Grape Variety | Characteristics |
| --- | --- |
| Cabernet Franc (cab-er-nay frahn) | A parent of Cabernet Sauvignon that's often blended with it to make Bordeaux-style wines. Cabernet Franc ripens earlier and has a more expressive, fruitier flavor (especially berries), as well as less tannin. A specialty of the Loire Valley in France, where it makes wines with place-names such as Chinon and Bourgeuil. |
| Gamay (ga-may) | Excels in the Beaujolais district of France. It makes grapey wines that can be low in tannin — although the grape itself is fairly tannic. Neither the grape called *Gamay Beaujolais* in California nor the grape called *Napa Gamay* is true Gamay. |
| Grenache (gren-ahsh) | A Spanish grape by origin, called *Garnacha* there. (Most wine drinkers associate Grenache with France's Southern Rhône Valley more than with Spain, however.) Sometimes Grenache makes pale, high-alcohol wines that are dilute in flavor. In the right circumstances, it can make deeply colored wines with velvety texture and fruity aromas and flavors that are suggestive of raspberries. |

# How Wines Get Their Names

Most of the wines that you find in your wine shop or on restaurant wine lists are named in one of two basic ways: either for their grape variety or for the place where the grapes grew. Sometimes, though, they're named after the winery that made them, or they get a seemingly random name that tells you nothing about the wine itself. And to complicate matters, occasionally the wines named after a certain place aren't really made from the grapes of that place — ah, the fun of discriminating between true and false advertising!

The following sections help you understand the meaning of each type of name and where those types of wines are from.

## Naming by grape

Generally speaking, American wines are named after the grape (like Chardonnay, Cabernet Sauvignon, Sauvignon Blanc, and so on). These wines are called *varietals,* and they're named after either the principal or the sole grape variety that makes up the wine. Some varietal wines are made entirely from the grape variety for which the wine is named, but that isn't a requirement. Each country (and in the United States, some individual states) has laws that dictate the minimum percentage of the named grape that a wine must contain if that wine wants to call itself by a grape name.

Most of the time, the labels of varietal wines don't tell you whether other grapes are present in the wine, what those grapes are, or the percentage of the wine that they account for. All you know is that the wine contains at least the minimum legal percentage of the named variety.

U.S. federal regulations fix the minimum legal percentage of the named grape at 75 percent (which means your favorite California Cabernet Sauvignon could have as much as 25 percent of some *other* grape in it). In Oregon, the minimum is 90 percent (except for Cabernet, which can be 75 percent). Looking overseas, the minimum legal percentage in Australia and the countries that form the European Union (EU) is 85 percent in some wine categories and 100 percent in others.

Interestingly, if a wine sold in the United States is named for two or more grape varieties — for instance, a Sémillon-Chardonnay — the label must state the percentages of each, and these percentages must total 100 percent. Now that's an honest varietal wine!

## Naming by place

Unlike American wines, most European wines are named for the region where their grapes grow rather than for the grape variety itself. Many of these European wines come from precisely the same grape varieties as American wines (such as Chardonnay, Cabernet Sauvignon, Sauvignon Blanc, and so on), but they don't say so on the label. Instead, the labels say Burgundy, Bordeaux, Sancerre, and so on to indicate the *place* where those grapes grow.

Is this naming convention some nefarious plot to make wine incomprehensible to English-only wine lovers who've never visited Europe and flunked geography in school?

Au contraire! The European system of naming wines is actually intended to provide more information about each wine — and more understanding of what's in the bottle — than varietal naming does. The thinking goes like this: The name of the place connotes which grapes were used to make the wine of that place (because the grapes are dictated by regulations), and the place influences the character of those grapes in its own unique way. Therefore, the most accurate name that a wine can have is the name of the place where its grapes grew. The only catch is that to harvest this more detailed information about the wine, you have to know something about the different regions from which the wines come. (For more on this European naming convention, see the nearby sidebar, "The terroir game.")

Wine labels from non-European countries also tell you where a wine comes from — usually by featuring the name of a place somewhere on the label. On an American wine label (or an Australian, Chilean, or South African label, for that matter), however, the place of origin isn't the fundamental name of the wine (as it is for most European wines); the grape usually is. As a result, the place-name on these bottles isn't in a large, easily identifiable font as it is on bottles of wine that are actually *named* after the place.

Place-names in non-European countries mean far less than they do in Europe. For example, the name Sonoma Valley *legally* means only that at least 85 percent of the grapes came from an area defined by law as the Sonoma Valley wine zone. The name Sonoma Valley doesn't define the type of wine, nor does it imply specific grape varieties, the way a European place-name does.

Some non-European wine origins are ridiculously broad. Just think how European winemakers must react to all those wine labels that announce a wine's place of origin simply as *California:* "Great. This label says that this wine comes from a specific area that's 30 percent larger than the entire country of Italy! Some specific area!" (Italy has more than 300 specific wine zones; see Book III for the lowdown.)

## The terroir game

*Terroir* (pronounced ter-wahr) is the guiding principle behind the European concept that wines should be named after the place they come from. *Terroir* is a French word that has no direct translation in English, so wine people just use the French word (for expediency, not snobbery).

You won't ever find a fixed definition of *terroir;* the word itself is based on the French word *terre,* which means soil. Consequently, some people define *terroir* as, simply, dirt (as in "Our American dirt is every bit as good as

their French dirt"). But *terroir* is really much more complex (and complicated) than just dirt. *Terroir* is the combination of absolute natural factors — such as topsoil, subsoil, climate (sun, rain, wind, and so on), the slope of the hill, and altitude — that a particular vineyard site has. Chances are no two vineyards in the entire world have precisely the same combination of these factors. So you may want to consider *terroir* to be the unique combination of natural factors that a particular vineyard site has.

When the place on the label is merely *California,* that information tells you next to nothing about where the grapes grew. California's a big place, and those grapes could come from just about anywhere. Same thing for all those Australian wines labeled *South Eastern Australia* — an area only slightly smaller than France and Spain combined.

# Naming in other, less common ways

Now and then, you may come across a wine that's named for neither its grape variety nor its region of origin. Such wines usually fall into three categories: branded wines, wines with proprietary names, or generic wines. Check out the following sections for an explanation of each category.

### Laying claim with a name: Brand-name wines

A *brand name* is traditionally the name of the company or person that makes the wine (called the *producer*), but for less-expensive wines, the brand name is likely to be an invented name. Most wines have brand names, including those wines that are named after their grape variety — like Cakebread (brand name) Sauvignon Blanc (grape) — and those that are named after their region of origin — like Masi (brand name) Valpolicella (place). These brand names are usually the name of the company that made the wine, called a *winery.* Because most wineries make several different wines, the brand name itself isn't specific enough to be the actual name of the wine. Robert Mondavi Cabernet Sauvignon, for example, is a wine made by Robert Mondavi Winery and named after the Cabernet Sauvignon grape. Fontodi Chianti Classico is a wine made by the Fontodi winery and named after the place called Chianti Classico.

But sometimes a wine has *only* a brand name. For example, the label says *Salamandre* and *red French wine* but provides little other identification.

Wines that have *only* a brand name on them, with no indication of grape or place — other than the country of production — are generally the most inexpensive, ordinary wines you can get. If they're from a European Union country, they won't even be *vintage dated* (that is, there won't be any indication of what year the grapes were harvested) because EU law doesn't entitle such wines to carry a vintage date.

### With no real rhyme or reason: Proprietary names

You can find some pretty creative names on wine bottles these days: Tapestry, Conundrum, Insignia, Isosceles, Mythology, Trilogy. Is this stuff to drink, to drive, or to dab behind your ears?

# Decoding common European place-names

| Wine Name(s) | Country | Grape Varieties |
|---|---|---|
| Beaujolais (boh-jhoe-lay) | France | Gamay |
| Bordeaux (red) (bor-doh) | France | Cabernet Sauvignon, Merlot, Cabernet Franc, and others* |
| Bordeaux (white) | France | Sauvignon Blanc, Sémillon, Muscadelle* |
| Burgundy (red) | France | Pinot Noir |
| Burgundy (white) | France | Chardonnay |
| Chablis (shah-blee) | France | Chardonnay |
| Champagne (sham-pahn-yah) | France | Chardonnay, Pinot Noir, Pinot Meunier* |
| Châteauneuf-du-Pape* (shah-toe-nuf-doo-pahp) | France | Grenache, Mourvèdre, Syrah, and others* |
| Chianti (key-*ahn*-tee) | Italy | Sangiovese, Canaiolo, and others* |
| Côtes du Rhône* (coat dew rone) | France | Grenache, Mourvèdre, Carignan, and others* |
| Port (Porto) | Portugal | Touriga Nacional, Tinta Barroca, Touriga Franca, Tinta Roriz, Tinto Cão, and others* |
| Pouilly-Fuissé (pwee-fwee-say), Mâcon (mah-cawn), St.-Véran (san-veh-rahn) | France | Chardonnay |
| Rioja (red) (ree-*oh*-hah) | Spain | Tempranillo, Grenache, and others* |
| Sancerre/Pouilly-Fumé (sahn-sehr)/(pwee-foo-may) | France | Sauvignon Blanc |
| Sauternes (saw-tairn) | France | Sémillon, Sauvignon Blanc* |
| Sherry | Spain | Palomino |
| Soave (so-*ah*-vae) | Italy | Garganega and others* |
| Valpolicella (vahl-poh-lee-t'*chell*-ah) | Italy | Corvina, Molinara, Rondinella* |

*Indicates that a blend of grapes is used to make these wines.*

Names like these are *proprietary names* (often trademarked) that producers create for special wines. In the case of American wines, the bottles with proprietary names usually contain wines made from a *blend* of grapes; therefore, no one grape name can be used as the name of the wine. In the case of European wines, the grapes used to make the wine probably weren't the approved grapes for that region; therefore, the regional name can't appear on the label.

**Book I**

**Under-standing Wine**

Although a brand name can apply to several different wines, a proprietary name usually applies to one specific wine. You can find Zinfandel, Cabernet Sauvignon, Chardonnay, and numerous other wines under the Fetzer brand from California, for example, and you can find Beaujolais, Pouilly-Fuissé, Mâcon-Villages, and numerous other wines under the Louis Jadot brand from France. But the proprietary name Luce applies to a single wine.

Wines with proprietary names usually are made in small quantities, are quite expensive ($40 to $75 or more per bottle), and are high in quality.

### False advertising with misleading place-names: Generic wines

Burgundy, Chianti, Chablis, Champagne, Rhine wine, Sherry, Port, and Sauternes are all names that rightfully should apply only to wines made in those specific places. However, these names have been used inappropriately for so long that they've lost their original meaning in the eyes of the government (exactly what Xerox, Kleenex, and Band-Aid are afraid of becoming).

After two decades of negotiation with the European Union, the U.S. government has finally agreed that these names can no longer be used for American wines. However, any wine that bore such a name prior to March 2006 may continue to carry that name. In time, generic names will become far less common on wine labels.

# Chapter 3

# Buying Wine

· · · · · · · · · · · · · · · · · · · · · · · · · · · · · · · · · · · · · · · · · · · · · · ·

## In This Chapter

▶ Knowing where you can go to buy your vino

▶ Selecting a good wine merchant

▶ Pulling useful details from labels to direct your wine shopping

▶ Finding the help you need to get the wine you want

· · · · · · · · · · · · · · · · · · · · · · · · · · · · · · · · · · · · · · · · · · · · · · ·

Common sense suggests that buying a few bottles of wine should be less stressful than, say, applying for a bank loan or interviewing for a new job. What's the big deal? It's only fermented grape juice.

Then again, maybe you've encountered a wine shop that wouldn't take back one of the two bottles of inexpensive wine that you bought the week before, even when you explained how awful the first bottle had been. Or maybe you're still reeling from the time you pretended you knew what you were doing and bought a full case — 12 bottles — of a French wine based on the brand's general reputation, not realizing that the particular vintage you purchased was a miserable aberration from the brand's usual quality. Or maybe you've just spent too many hours staring at shelves lined with bottles whose labels might as well have been written in Greek.

No matter the situation, the single most effective way to guarantee that you have good wine-buying experiences time and time again is to come to terms with your knowledge — or lack thereof — of the subject. Too much information about wine is constantly changing — new vintages each year, hundreds of new wineries, new brands, and so on — for *anyone* to presume that she knows it all, or for anyone to feel insecure about what she doesn't know.

After you've accepted the inevitable uncertainties you'll face when choosing a bottle of wine, arm yourself with the general knowledge presented in this chapter so you can effectively gauge whether your local wine retailer is in fact a quality vendor, understand the mumbo jumbo on wine labels, and ask the right questions of the retailer. Well, what are you waiting for? After all, there are so many wines out there and only so little time. . . .

# Surveying Your Options of Wine Retailers, Large and Small

Buying wine in a store to drink later at home is great for a number of reasons, not the least of which is that stores usually have a much bigger selection of wines than restaurants do — and they charge you less for 'em. You can examine the bottles carefully and compare the labels. And you can drink the wine at home from the glass (and temperature!) of your choosing.

On the other hand, you must provide your own wine glasses and open the bottle yourself (flip to Chapter 4 in Book I for how to do it). And that big selection of wines in the store can be downright daunting.

Depending on where you live, you can buy wine at all sorts of stores: supermarkets, wine superstores, general liquor stores, discount warehouses, or small specialty wine shops. As you find out in the following sections, each type of store has its own advantages and disadvantages in terms of selection, price, or service.

Wine is a regulated beverage in most countries, and governments often get involved in deciding where and how wine may be sold. Some states within the United States, such as Pennsylvania and New Hampshire, and some provinces in Canada, such as Ontario and Quebec, have raised government control of alcoholic beverage sales to a fine art, deciding not only *where* you can buy wine but also *which wines* are available for you to buy. If you love wine and live in one of those areas, take comfort in the fact that a) you have a vote; b) freedom of choice lies just across the border; and c) if the Iron Curtain can topple, there's hope for change in your local government, too.

## Supermarkets, superstores, and so on

Supermarkets and their large-scale brethren, discount superstores, make wine accessible to everyone. When wine is sold in supermarkets or discount stores, the mystique surrounding the product evaporates: Who can waste time feeling insecure about a wine purchase when much more critical issues are at hand, such as how much time is left before the kids turn into monsters and which is the shortest line at the checkout? And the prices, especially in large stores, are usually quite reasonable.

Some people in the wine business disapprove of the straightforward attitude toward wine in supermarkets and discount stores; they think wine is sacred and should always be treated like an elite beverage. At least you won't run into *them* as you browse the wine aisles in your supermarket.

Discount stores are good places to find *private label* wines — wines that are created especially for the chain and carry a brand name that's owned by the store. These wines are usually decent (but not great), and if you like 'em, they can be excellent values. Some of the "club" chains may also offer — in smaller quantities — higher-end wines than supermarkets do.

The downside of buying wine in these stores is that your selection is often limited to wines produced by large wineries that generate enough volume to sell to supermarket chains. And you'll seldom get any advice on which wines to buy. Basically, you're on your own. Well, except for the ever-present shelf-talkers.

To guide you on your wine-buying journey, many stores offer plenty of *shelf-talkers* (small signs on the shelves that describe individual wines). Take these shelf-talkers with a very large grain of salt. They're often provided by the company selling the wine, which is more interested in convincing you to grab a bottle than in offering information to help you understand the wine. Most likely, you'll find flowery phrases; hyperbolic adjectives; impressive scores; and safe, common-denominator stuff like "delicious with fish." (*Any* fish, cooked in *any* way?) When you see a shelf-talker, you can bet that the info on it will be biased and of limited value.

The bottom line is that supermarkets and discount superstores can be great places to buy everyday wine for casual enjoyment. But if what you really want is to find out about wine as you buy it, or if you want an unusually interesting variety of wines to satisfy your insatiable curiosity, you'll probably find yourself shopping elsewhere.

## Wine specialty shops

Wine specialty shops are small- to medium-sized stores that sell wine and liquor and, sometimes, wine books, corkscrews (see Chapter 4 in Book I for more on those), wine glasses, and maybe a few specialty foods. The foods sold in wine shops tend to be gourmet items rather than run-of-the-mill snack foods.

If you decide to pursue wine as a serious hobby, shops like these are the places where you'll probably end up buying your wine because they offer many advantages that larger operations simply can't. For one thing, wine specialty shops almost always have wine-knowledgeable staffers on the premises. Also, you can usually find an interesting, varied selection of wines at all price levels.

Wine shops often organize their wines by country of origin and — in the case of classic wine countries, such as France, by region (Bordeaux, Burgundy, Rhône, and so on). Red wines and white wines are often in separate sections within these country areas. There may be a special section for Champagnes and other sparkling wines and another section for dessert wines. Some stores are now organizing their wine sections by style, such as "Aromatic Whites," "Powerful Reds," and so forth. A few organize the wines according to grape varieties.

Some wine shops have a special area (or even a superspecial, temperature-controlled room) for the finer or more expensive wines. In some stores, it's a locked vaultlike room; in others, it's the whole back area of the store.

Over in a corner somewhere, often right by the door to accommodate quick purchases, you can usually find a *cold box,* a refrigerated cabinet with glass doors where bottles of best-selling white and sparkling wines sit. Unless you really *must* have an ice-cold bottle of wine immediately (the two of you have just decided to elope, the marriage minister is a mile down the road, and the wedding toast is only ten minutes away), avoid the cold box. The wines inside it are usually too cold and, therefore, may not be in good condition. You never know how long the bottle you select has been sitting there under frigid conditions, numbed lifeless.

Near the front of the store, you may also see boxes or bins of special sale wines. Sometimes *sale* wines are those the merchant is trying to unload because she has had them for too long, or they're wines that she got a special deal on (because the distributor is trying to unload them). When in doubt, try one bottle first before committing to a larger quantity.

Sale displays are usually topped with *case cards* — large cardboard signs that stand above the open boxes of wine — or similar descriptive material. Like shelf-talkers (described in the preceding section), case cards are typically unreliable for gleaning useful info; but because case cards are a lot bigger, there's more of a chance that some helpful tidbit may appear on them.

# Choosing a Fabulous Wine Merchant

Sizing up a wine merchant is as simple as sizing up any other specialty retailer. The main criteria are fair prices, a wide selection, staff expertise, and service. Also, the shop must store its wines in the proper conditions.

When you're a novice wine buyer, your best strategy is to shop around *with an eye to service and reliable advice more than to price.* After you've found a merchant who has suggested several wines that you've liked, stick with her, even if she doesn't have the best prices in town. Paying a dollar or so more for wines recommended by a reliable merchant (wines that you'll likely enjoy) makes better sense than buying wines in a cut-rate or discount store and saving a buck, especially if that store has no special wine adviser or if the advice you receive is suspect.

When you have more knowledge of wine, you'll have enough confidence to shop at stores with the best prices. But even then, price must take a backseat to the storage conditions of the wine (see the section "Judging wine storage conditions" later in this chapter).

## Evaluating selection and expertise

You won't necessarily know on your first visit whether a particular store's selection is adequate for you. If you notice many wines from many different countries at various prices, give the store's selection the benefit of the doubt. If you outgrow the selection as you discover more about wine, you can seek out a new merchant at that point.

Don't be too ready to give a merchant the benefit of the doubt when it comes to expertise, however. Some retailers are not only extremely knowledgeable about the specific wines they sell but also extremely knowledgeable about wine in general. On the flip side, some retailers know less than their customers. Just as you expect a butcher to know her cuts of meat, you should expect a wine merchant to know wine. Be free with your questions (such as, "Can you tell me something about this wine?" or "How are these two wines different?") and judge how willing and able the merchant is to answer them.

Expect a wine merchant to have *personal* knowledge and experience of the wines she sells. These days, a lot of retailers use the ratings of a few critics as a crutch in selling wines. They plaster their shelves with the critics' scores (usually a number like 90 on a scale of 100) and advertise their wines by these numbers. Selling by the numbers is one quick way of communicating an approximate sense of the wine's quality. (**Remember:** A good score doesn't guarantee you'll like the wine!) But the retailer's knowledge and experience of the wines simply must go beyond the critics' scores. If it doesn't, she's not doing her job properly.

## Considering customer service

Most knowledgeable wine merchants pride themselves on their ability to guide you through the maze of wine selections and help you find a wine that you'll enjoy. Trust a merchant's advice at least once or twice and see whether her choices are good ones for you. If she's not flexible enough — or knowledgeable enough — to suggest wine that suits your needs, obviously you need another merchant. Finding that out early on will have cost you only the price of a bottle or two of wine . . . which is much less costly than choosing the wrong doctor or lawyer!

Speaking of service, any reputable wine merchant will accept a bottle back from you if she has made a poor recommendation or if the wine seems damaged. After all, she wants to keep you as a customer. But with this privilege comes responsibility: Be reasonable. Ask ahead of time about the store's defective and unopened wine policy. You should return an *open* bottle only if you think the wine is defective — in which case the bottle should be mostly full! Hold on to the store's receipt and don't wait several months before returning an unopened bottle of wine. By that time, the store may have a hard time reselling the wine. After a week or two, consider the wine yours whether you like it or not.

## Judging wine storage conditions

Here's a fact about wine that's worth knowing early on: Wine is a perishable product. It doesn't go moldy like cheese, and it can't host e-coli bacteria, as meat can. It normally poses no health hazard beyond those associated with alcohol and certain individuals' sensitivities, even when it's past its prime. In fact, some wines — usually the more-expensive ones — can get better and better as they get older. But if wine isn't stored properly, its taste can suffer. (For advice on storing wine in your own home, check out Chapter 8 in Book I.)

When sizing up a wine shop, especially if you plan to buy a lot of wine or expensive wine, check out the store's wine storage conditions. What you don't want to see is an area that's warm — for example, wines stored near the boiler so they cook all winter, or wines stored on the top floor of the building where the sun can smile on them all summer.

The very best shops have climate-controlled storerooms for wine — although, frankly, these shops are in the minority. If a shop has a good storage facility, the proprietor will be happy to show it off to you because she'll be proud of all the expense and effort she put into it.

In better wine shops, expect to see most of the bottles (except for the inexpensive, large, juglike bottles) *lying in a horizontal position,* so their corks remain moist, ensuring a firm closure. A dry cork can crack or shrink and let air into the bottle, which spoils the wine. A short time upright doesn't affect wine much, so stores with a high turnover can get away with storing their fast-selling wines that way, but slower-selling, expensive bottles, especially those intended for long maturation in your cellar, fare better in the long run lying down.

In addition to room temperature and bottle orientation, you know you've found a retailer who hasn't stored wine properly if you encounter any of the following situations at the store:

- The dust on the wine bottles is more than ⅛-inch thick.
- Many of the white wines are dark gold or light-brown in color.

✔ The most recent vintage in the store is 1997.

✔ The colors on all the wine labels have faded from bright sunlight.

Unfortunately, the problem of wine spoilage doesn't begin at the retail outlet. Quite frequently, the *wholesaler* or *distributor* — the company from which the retailer purchases wine — doesn't have proper storage conditions either. And there have certainly been instances when wine has been damaged by weather extremes even before it got to the distributor — for example, while sitting on the docks in the dead of winter or summer, or while traveling through the Panama Canal. A good retailer either checks out the quality of the wine before she buys it or sends it back if she discovers the problem after she has already bought the wine.

If you don't know how a wine has been stored — and most of the time you won't — take these actions to minimize the risk of getting a bad bottle:

✔ First, patronize retailers who seem to care about their wine and who provide their customers with good service.

✔ Second, be attentive to seasonal weather patterns when buying wine or having it shipped to you. Be cautious about buying wine at the end of, or during, a very hot summer, unless the store has a good climate-control system. And never have wine shipped to you (other than quick deliveries from your local shop) at the height of summer or winter.

✔ Buy the best-selling, most popular wines — assuming you don't mind being a slave to taste trends. Wines that move through the distribution chain very quickly have less opportunity to be damaged along the way.

# Shopping for the Perfect Bottle: Decoding Labels

When many people first start buying wine, their repertoire is about as broad as a 2-year-old child's vocabulary. They buy the same brands again and again, because they know what to expect from them, and they like them well enough — both good reasons to buy a particular wine. But they also let themselves get stuck in a rut because they're afraid to take a chance on anything new.

If wine is really going to be fun, you may want to be a little more adventurous. To experience the wonderful array of wines in the world, experimenting is a must. New wines can be interesting and exciting. Now and then you might get a lemon, but at least you'll have discovered not to buy that wine again! If you know what information to look for on a label — specifically, what's important and what isn't — and how to interpret that information, you can make educated choices about which wines to try.

# First things first: Distinguishing between front and back

Many wine bottles have two labels. The front label names the wine and grabs your eye as you walk down the aisle, and the back label gives you a little more information, ranging from really helpful suggestions like *this wine tastes delicious with food* to oh-so-useful data such as *this wine has a total acidity of 6.02 and a pH of 3.34.*

Now, if you're really on your toes, you may be thinking: How can you tell the difference between front and back on a round bottle?

You judge front and back by label content. The U.S. government (and other governments) requires certain information to appear on the front label of all wine bottles — basic stuff, such as the alcohol content, the type of wine (usually *red table wine* or *white table wine*), and the country of origin — but it doesn't define *front label.* So sometimes producers put all that info on the smaller of two labels and call that one the front label. Then the producers place a larger, colorful, dramatically eye-catching label — with little more than the name of the wine on it — on the *back* of the bottle. Guess which way the back label ends up facing when the bottle is placed on the shelf? Here's a hint: You may need to turn the bottle around to find the info you're looking for.

# The mandatory content

Every bottle of wine has to feature the name of said wine somewhere on its label. That's a no-brainer. The confusing part is that the names aren't as straightforward as you may think (or hope!). As explained in Chapter 2 of Book I, the name of a wine can be any of the following:

- ✔ The name of the *grape* from which the wine was made
- ✔ The name of the *place,* or *places,* where the grapes grew (the wine region, and sometimes the name of the specific vineyard property)
- ✔ The name of the brand (that is, the winery, or *producer*)
- ✔ A special, fanciful name for that particular wine (called a *proprietary* name)

The name of the wine plus the name of the producer is the shorthand name most folks use when talking about a particular wine.

You may recognize some wine names as grape names and other names as place-names right off the bat. If you don't, don't panic. That's the kind of info you can look up.

Labels also have other bits of mandatory info on them, but the requirements vary somewhat by country. The sections that follow walk you through the terminology you're likely to encounter.

### For all wines sold in the United States

The federal government mandates that certain items of information appear on the labels of wines sold in the United States. Such items are generally referred to as *the mandatory* and include

- ✔ A brand name.

- ✔ Indication of class or type (table wine, dessert wine, or sparkling wine; you can read more about these types in Chapter 1 of Book I).

- ✔ The amount of alcohol by volume. Alcohol content can be expressed in degrees, such as 12.5 degrees, or as a percentage, such as 12.5 percent. If a wine carries the words *Table Wine* on its label in the United States, it doesn't have to state the alcohol percentage; however, the law requires it to have less than 14 percent alcohol by volume.

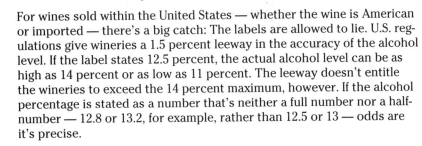

  For wines sold within the United States — whether the wine is American or imported — there's a big catch: The labels are allowed to lie. U.S. regulations give wineries a 1.5 percent leeway in the accuracy of the alcohol level. If the label states 12.5 percent, the actual alcohol level can be as high as 14 percent or as low as 11 percent. The leeway doesn't entitle the wineries to exceed the 14 percent maximum, however. If the alcohol percentage is stated as a number that's neither a full number nor a half-number — 12.8 or 13.2, for example, rather than 12.5 or 13 — odds are it's precise.

- ✔ Name and location of the bottler.

- ✔ Net contents, expressed in milliliters. The standard wine bottle is 750 milliliters, which is 25.6 ounces.

- ✔ The phrase *Contains Sulfites* (with very, very few exceptions).

- ✔ The standard government warning. (If you really want to know what it says, just pick up any bottle of wine and check out the back label.)

Wines made outside the United States but sold within it must also carry the phrase *imported by* on their labels, along with the name and business location of the importer.

### For all wines sold in Canada

Canadian regulations are similar to those for wines sold in the United States. They require wine labels to indicate the *common name* of the product (that is, *wine*), the net contents, the percentage of alcohol by volume, the name and address of the producer, the wine's country of origin, and the container size. Many of these items must be indicated in both English and French.

### *For wines produced or sold in the European Union*

Some of the mandatory information on American and Canadian wine labels is also required by the European Union (EU) authorities for wines produced or sold in the EU.

For wines produced in its member countries, the EU regulations also require additional label items. The most important of these additional items is an indication of a wine's so-called quality level — which really just lets you know the wine's status in the EU's hierarchy of place-names. In short, every wine made in an EU member country *must* carry one of the following items on the label:

- ✔ A registered place-name, often an appellation of origin, along with an official phrase that confirms the name is in fact a registered place-name

- ✔ A phrase indicating that the wine is a table wine, a status lower than that of a wine with a registered place-name

  Europeans have a distinctly different use of the term *table wine* from Americans. For U.S. wines, the table wine category encompasses all non-sparkling wines that contain up to 14 percent alcohol by volume.

If an EU wine has an official place-name, it falls into a European category called QWPSR (Quality Wine Produced in a Specific Region). The following phrases on European labels confirm that a wine is a QWPSR wine and that its name is therefore a registered place-name:

- ✔ **France:** *Appellation Contrôlée* (AC) or *Appellation d'Origine Contrôlée* (AOC), translated as "regulated name" or "regulated place-name." Also, on labels of wines from places of slightly lower status, the initials AO VDQS, standing for *Appellation d'Origine — Vins Délimités de Qualité Supérieure;* translated as "place-name, demarcated wine of superior quality." (See Chapter 1 in Book II for more on French place-names.)

- ✔ **Italy:** *Denominazione di Origine Controllata* (DOC), translated as "regulated place-name;" or for certain wines of an even higher status, *Denominazione di Origine Controllata e Garantita* (DOCG), translated as "regulated and guaranteed place-name." (Flip to Chapter 1 in Book III for the scoop on the Italian wine-classification system.)

- ✔ **Spain:** *Denominación de Origen* (DO), translated as "place-name;" and *Denominación de Origen Calificada* (DOC), translated as "qualified-origin place-name" for regions with the highest status (of which there are only two, Rioja and Priorat).

- ✔ **Portugal:** *Denominação de Origem* (DO), translated as "place-name."

- ✔ **Germany:** *Qualitätswein bestimmter Anbaugebiete* (QbA), translated as "quality wine from a specific region;" or *Qualitätswein mit Prädikat* (QmP), translated as "quality wine with special attributes," for the best wines.

If a European wine doesn't have a place-name — that is, it's a table wine — the label must include two phrases, which vary according to country. One term applies to table wines with a geographic indication (Italy actually has two phrases in this category), and another denotes table wines with no geographic indication smaller than the country of production. By country, these phrases are

- ✔ **France:** *Vin de pays* (country wine) followed by the name of an approved area; *vin de table* (see Chapter 1 in Book II)

- ✔ **Italy:** *Indicazione Geografica Tipica* (translated as "typical geographic indication" and abbreviated as IGT) and the name of an approved area, or *vino da tavola* (table wine) followed by the name of a geographic area; *vino da tavola* (see Chapter 1 in Book III)

- ✔ **Spain:** *Vino de la tierra* (country wine) followed by the name of an approved area; *vino de mesa*

- ✔ **Portugal:** *Vinho Regional* (regional wine) and the name of an approved area; *vinho de mesa*

- ✔ **Germany:** *Landwein* (country wine) and the name of an approved area; *Deutscher tafelwein*

Table 3-1 lists the European wine designations for easy reference.

| Table 3-1 | European Wine Designations at a Glance | | |
|---|---|---|---|
| *Country* | *QWPSR Designation(s)* | *Table Wine Designation with Geographic Indication* | *Table Wine Designation without Geographic Indication* |
| France | AOC AO VDQS | *Vin de pays* | *Vin de table* |
| Italy | DOCG DOC | IGT; *vino da tavola* (and geographic name) | *Vino da tavola* |
| Spain | DOC DO | *Vino de la tierra* | *Vino de mesa* |
| Portugal | DO | *Vinho Regional* | *Vinho de mesa* |
| Germany | QmP QbA | *Landwein* | *Deutscher tafel-wein* |

The phrase for a registered place-name in the United States is *American Viticultural Area* (AVA). But this phrase doesn't appear on wine labels. Nor does any such phrase appear on the labels of Australian or South American wines.

# Some optional label lingo

Aside from the mandatory information required by government authorities, all sorts of other optional lingo can appear on wine labels. These words can be meaningless phrases intended to make you think you're getting a special quality wine or words that provide useful details about what's in the bottle. Sometimes the same word can fall into either category, depending on the label. This ambiguity occurs because some words that are strictly regulated in some producing countries aren't regulated at all in others. The next few sections break down the terminology you may occasionally see in your wine wanderings.

### Vintage

The word *vintage* followed by a year, or the year listed alone without the word *vintage,* is the most common optional item on a wine label. Sometimes the vintage appears on the front label, and sometimes it has its own small label above the front label.

The *vintage year* is nothing more than the year in which the grapes for a particular wine grew; the wine must have 75 to 100 percent of the grapes of this year, depending on the country of origin. (*Nonvintage* wines are blends of wines whose grapes were harvested in different years.) An aura tends to surround vintage-dated wine, which causes many people to believe that any wine with a vintage date is by definition better than a wine without a vintage date. *In fact, no correlation exists between the presence of a vintage date and the wine's quality.*

Generally speaking, *what* vintage a wine is — that is, whether the grapes grew in a year with perfect weather or whether the grapes were meteorologically challenged — is an issue you need to consider a) only when you buy top-quality wines and b) mainly when those wines come from parts of the world that experience significant variations in weather from year to year, such as many European wine regions.

### Reserve

*Reserve* is one of the great meaningless words on American wine labels. The term is used to convince you that the wine inside the bottle is special. This trick usually works because the word has specific meaning and carries a certain amount of prestige on labels of wines from many other countries.

- ✔ In Italy and Spain, the word *reserve* (or its foreign language equivalent, which looks something like *reserve*) indicates a wine that has received extra aging at the winery before release. Implicit in the extra aging is the idea that the wine was better than normal and, therefore, worthy of the extra aging. Spain even has *degrees* of reserve, such as Gran Reserva.

✔ In France, the use of *reserve* isn't regulated. However, its use is generally consistent with the notion that the wine is better in quality than a given producer's norm.

In the United States, the word *reserve* has historically been used in the same sense — as in Beaulieu Vineyards Georges de Latour Private Reserve, the best Cabernet that Beaulieu Vineyards makes. But the word isn't regulated and so is bandied about so much that it no longer has meaning. For example, some California wines labeled *Proprietor's Reserve* sell for $6 a bottle. Those wines are not only the *least* expensive wines in a particular producer's lineup but also some of the least-expensive wines, period. Other wines are labeled Special Reserve, Vintage Reserve, Vintner's Reserve, or Reserve Selection — all utterly meaningless phrases.

### Estate-bottled

*Estate* is a genteel word for a wine farm, a combined grape-growing and wine-making operation. The words *estate-bottled* on a wine label indicate that the company that bottled the wine also grew the grapes and made the wine. In other words, the phrase suggests accountability from the vineyard to the winemaking through to the bottling. In many countries, the winery doesn't necessarily have to own the vineyards, but it has to control the vineyards and perform the vineyard operations.

Estate-bottling is an important concept to those who believe that you can't make good wine unless you know personally that the grapes are as good as they can possibly be. But great wines don't *have* to be estate-bottled, though. Ravenswood Winery — to name just one example — makes some terrific wines from the grapes of small vineyards owned and operated by private landowners. And some large California landowners, such as the Sangiacomo family, are quite serious about their vineyards but don't make wine them-selves; instead, they sell their grapes to various wineries. None of those wines would be considered estate-bottled.

Sometimes French wine labels carry the words *domaine-bottled* or *château-bottled* (or the phrase *mis en bouteille au château/au domaine*). The concept is the same as estate-bottled, with *domaine* and *château* being equivalent to the American term *estate*.

### Vineyard name

Some wines in the medium-to-expensive price category — costing about $25 or more — may carry on the label the name of the specific vineyard where the grapes for that wine grew. Sometimes one winery makes two or three different wines that are distinguishable only by the vineyard name on the label. Each wine is unique because the *terroir* of each vineyard is unique (see Chapter 2 of Book I for the scoop on *terroir*). These single vineyards may or may not be identified by the word *vineyard* next to the name of the vineyard.

Italian wines, which are really into the single-vineyard game, can have *vigneto* or *vigna* on their labels next to the name of the single vineyard. Or not. Using the word is optional.

### Other optional words on the label

Following are some other optional phrases and words you just might run into:

- ✔ **Old vines:** One additional expression on some French labels is *Vieilles Vignes* (vee-yay veen), which translates as "old vines," and appears as such on some Californian and Australian labels. Because old vines produce a very small quantity of fruit compared to younger vines, the quality of their grapes and of the resulting wine is considered to be very good. The problem is, the phrase is unregulated. Anyone can claim that his vines are old.

- ✔ **Superior:** The word *superior* can appear in French *(Supérieure)* or Italian *(Superiore)* as part of an AOC or DOC place-name (refer to the section "For wines produced or sold in the European Union," earlier in this chapter, for a refresher on these acronyms). It means the wine attained a higher alcohol level than a nonsuperior version of the same wine would have. Frankly, this distinction just isn't worth losing sleep over.

- ✔ **Classico:** The word *Classico* appears on the labels of some Italian DOC and DOCG wines when the grapes come from the heartland of the named place.

# Getting Help from the Wine Merchant

The following scene — or something very much like it — occurs in every wine shop every day (and ten times every Saturday):

> **Customer:** I remember that the wine had a yellow label. I had it in this little restaurant last week.
>
> **Wine Merchant:** Do you know what country it's from?
>
> **Customer:** I think it's Italian, but I'm not sure.
>
> **Wine Merchant:** Do you recall the grape variety?
>
> **Customer:** No, but I think it has a deer or a moose on the label. Maybe if I walk around, I can spot it.

Needless to say, most of the time that customer never finds the wine he or she is looking for.

When you come across a wine you like in a restaurant or at a friend's house, write down as much specific information about the wine from the label as you can. Don't trust your memory. If your wine merchant can see the name, she can give you that wine or — if she doesn't have that exact wine — she may be able to give you something very similar to it.

Being able to tell your wine retailer whatever you can about the types of wine that you've liked previously or that you want to try is to your advantage. Describe what you like in clear, simple terms and include any or all of the following information:

- ✔ **Desired wine characteristics:** For example, for white wine, you might use such words as "crisp, dry," or "fruity, ripe, oaky, buttery, full-bodied." For red wines, you might say "big, rich, tannic," or "medium-bodied, soft." Turn to Chapter 5 in Book I to discover other helpful descriptors.

- ✔ **Price range you're willing to pay:** Because the price of a bottle of wine can range from about $4 to literally hundreds of dollars, deciding approximately how much you want to spend and sharing that price range with your wine merchant is a good idea. Fix two ranges in your mind: one for everyday purposes and one for special occasions. These prices will probably change over time; the $6 to $10 range you start with for everyday wines often rises to $12 to $20 as you discover better wines. A good retailer with an adequate selection should be able to make several wine suggestions in your preferred price category.

  If a wine costs more than $10, be sure to ask the merchant what kind of storage the wine has experienced. Take any hemming and hawing on the part of the wine merchant to mean "poor." Also, ask how long the wine has been in the store — this factor is especially important if the store doesn't have a climate-control system. (See the section "Judging wine storage conditions," earlier in the chapter, for advice on how to respond to the answer you get.)

  A good wine merchant is more interested in the repeat business she'll get by making you happy than in trading you up to a bottle of wine that's beyond your limits. If what you want to spend is $10 a bottle, just say so and stand firm, without embarrassment. Plenty of decent, enjoyable wines are available at that price.

- ✔ **Food you're serving with the wine:** A good wine merchant is invaluable in helping you match your wine with food. Tell your wine merchant what kind of food you plan to have with the wine so she can narrow down your choices even more. After all, the wine you drink with your flounder probably isn't the one you want with spicy chili! The more info about the recipe or main flavors you can provide, the better your chance of getting a good match. (For guidance on pairing wine and food before you enter a wine shop, flip to Chapter 6 in Book I.)

  Even if you've already chosen a bottle, you may want to get the merchant's input by asking whether the wine you've selected will go well with the food you're planning to serve.

Provided you trust the wine merchant, and you don't think she's dumping some overstocked, closeout wine on you, you may also want to ask, "What are some particularly good buys this month?" If applicable, inquire why the wine is selling at such a low price. The merchant might know that the wine is either too old or otherwise defective; unless she comes up with a believable explanation for the unbelievable price, assume one of these scenarios is the case.

# Chapter 4

# Getting the Cork Out (And All That Comes After): Serving Wine

*T*here's more to serving a bottle of wine than just removing the cork and pouring (although pulling out that cork can be quite a challenge — fortunately, it's usually pretty easy to do after you get the hang of it). You also have to consider niggling details such as whether the wine needs to breathe before being served, what temperature it should be served at, which type of glass to use, and what to do if you don't finish the whole bottle. If your heart is racing at the thought of it all, rest easy! This chapter shows you how to handle a bottle of wine, from start to finish.

## Opening the Bottle

Before you can even think about removing the cork from a wine bottle, you need to deal with whatever's covering it. That's because most wine bottles have a colorful covering over the top of 'em known as a *capsule*. Wineries place capsules on top of corks for two reasons: to keep the corks clean and to create a fetching look for their bottles.

These days, many wineries use colored foil or plastic capsules rather than the traditional lead capsules. In keeping with the sheerness trend in fashion, other wineries use a transparent cellophane covering that lets the cork show through; sometimes this sheer look graces special *flange-top bottles*, a fancy type of wine bottle with a protruding, flat lip at the top. (Some flange-top bottles sport colorful plastic plugs on top of the cork rather than cellophane.) The flange-top seems to be going out of style, and that's fortunate, because many corkscrews just don't fit over its wide top!

The following sections walk you through the basic process of opening a wine bottle like a pro.

## Clearing the way to the cork

Sometimes wine lovers just can't bring themselves to remove the whole capsule out of respect for the bottle of wine they're about to drink. (In fact, traditional wine etiquette dictates that you not remove the entire capsule.) However, you might want to remove the entire capsule so that no wine can come into contact with the covering when you pour. (Better not to take chances with influencing the flavor of the wine.)

Many of the folks who like to leave the capsule partially intact use a gizmo called a foil cutter that sells for about $6 or $7 in wine shops, kitchen stores, or specialty catalogs. However, if you want to leave the capsule on, you're better off using your corkscrew's knife to cut the foil under the second lip of the bottle, approximately three-fourths of an inch from the top. The special foil cutter doesn't cut the capsule low enough to prevent wine from dripping over the edge of the foil into your glass.

When you encounter a plastic plug atop the cork rather than a capsule, just flick it off with the tip of a knife.

After removing the capsule or plug, wipe the top of the bottle clean with a damp cloth. Sometimes the visible end of the cork is dark with mold that developed under the capsule, and in that case, wipe all the more diligently. (If you encounter mold atop the cork, don't be concerned. That mold is actually a good sign: It means the wine has been stored in humid conditions. See Chapter 8 in Book I for info on humidity and other aspects of wine storage.)

## Removing the cork from a typical bottle of vino

Have you ever broken a cork while trying to extract it from the bottle, or taken an unusually long time to remove a stubborn cork while your guests smiled at you uneasily? Both scenarios have happened to just about everyone who has ever pulled a cork out of a wine bottle. It's enough to give anyone a case of corkophobia! If you use the right type of corkscrew, removing the cork is truly a cinch.

You can buy some really fancy corkscrews, some that attach to a counter or a bar, that are guaranteed to cost you $100-plus. Yes, most of them work very well, after you get the hang of them, but frankly, you don't need to spend that much on a corkscrew. Better to spend it on the wine!

### Knowing what to avoid: The corkscrew that mangles

The one corkscrew to avoid happens to be the most common type of corkscrew around: the Wing Type Corkscrew, a bright, silver-colored, metal device that looks like a cross between a pair of pliers and a drill. It mangles the cork, almost guaranteeing that brown flakes will be floating in your glass of wine.

When you insert this corkscrew into a cork, two "wings" open out from the sides. The major shortcoming of this device is its very short worm, or *auger* (the curly prong that bores into the cork), which is too short for many corks and overly aggressive on all of them.

Instead of finding out the hard way that this corkscrew just doesn't cut it (or, literally, cuts it too much!), invest a few dollars in a decent corkscrew right off the bat. The time and hassle you'll save will be more than worth the investment.

### Introducing the corkscrew you can't do without: The Screwpull

The one indispensable corkscrew for every household is the Screwpull. It's about 6 inches long and consists of an arched piece of plastic (which looks like a clothespin on steroids) straddling an inordinately long, 5-inch worm that's coated with Teflon (see Figure 4-1). The Screwpull comes in many colors and costs about $20 in wine shops, kitchen stores, and specialty catalogs. It's very simple to use, doesn't require a lot of muscle, and is the corkscrew of choice for most of the corks you might encounter.

## The shame and allure of the screwcap

When is a cork not a cork? When it's plastic or a screwcap! Formerly, only cheap, lower-quality wines had screwcap closures. But in recent years, more and more wine producers have switched from corks to screwcaps. Screwcaps are perfectly sound closures, technically speaking. And they prevent *cork taint*, a chemical flaw affecting a small percentage of corks, and consequently the wine in those bottles. A *corky wine* — that is, one affected with cork taint — is damaged either slightly or flagrantly. In the worst-case scenarios, corky wines give off an offensive odor similar to moldy or damp cardboard. Plastic corks solve this problem, but screwcaps solve it better by being more user friendly.

To use this corkscrew, simply place the plastic over the bottle top (after having removed the capsule, of course) until a lip on the plastic is resting on the top of the bottle. Insert the worm through the plastic until it touches the cork. Hold on to the plastic firmly while turning the lever atop the worm clockwise. The worm descends into the cork. Keep turning the lever in the same clockwise direction, and the cork magically emerges from the bottle. To remove the cork from the Screwpull, simply turn the lever counterclockwise while holding on to the cork.

**Figure 4-1:**
The
Screwpull
Corkscrew.

© Akira Chiwaki

Like many things in life, the Screwpull has a drawback: Because it's made of plastic, it can break. But if you opt for the stainless steel version, which costs about $30, your Screwpull should last indefinitely.

### Presenting yourself as a pro with the Waiter's Corkscrew

The Waiter's Corkscrew is probably the most commonly used corkscrew in restaurants worldwide. A straight or gently curved base holds three devices that fold into it, like a Swiss Army knife: a lever, a worm, and a small knife (see Figure 4-2). The latter is especially handy for removing the capsule from the bottle.

**Figure 4-2:**
The
Waiter's
Corkscrew.

© Akira Chiwaki

Using the Waiter's Corkscrew requires some practice. First, wrap your fist around the bottle's neck. The trick then is to guide the worm down through the center of the cork by turning the corkscrew. Turn slowly at first, until you're sure that the worm is actually descending into the middle of the cork and isn't off-center. After the worm is fully descended into the cork, place the lever on the lip of the bottle and push against the lever while pulling the cork up. Give a firm tug at the very end, or wiggle the bottom of the cork out with your hand.

*TIP*

If your cork ever breaks and part of it gets stuck in the neck of the bottle, the Waiter's Corkscrew is indispensable for removing the remaining piece. Insert the worm at a 45-degree angle; the rest of the steps are the same as if you were removing a cork that's flush with the top of the bottle. In most cases, you can successfully remove the broken cork.

The Waiter's Corkscrew sells for as little as $7, but designer versions can cost more than ten times that much.

### Hugging the cork: The Ah-So Corkscrew

The Ah-So Corkscrew — known as such because (according to wine legend, anyway) when people finally figure out how it works, they say, "Ah, so that's how it works!" — is a simple device made up of two thin, flat metal prongs, with one slightly longer than the other (see Figure 4-3). To use it, slide the prongs down into the tight space between the cork and the bottle (making sure to insert the longer prong first) using a back-and-forth seesaw motion until the top of the Ah-So is resting on the top of the cork. Then twist the cork while gently pulling it up.

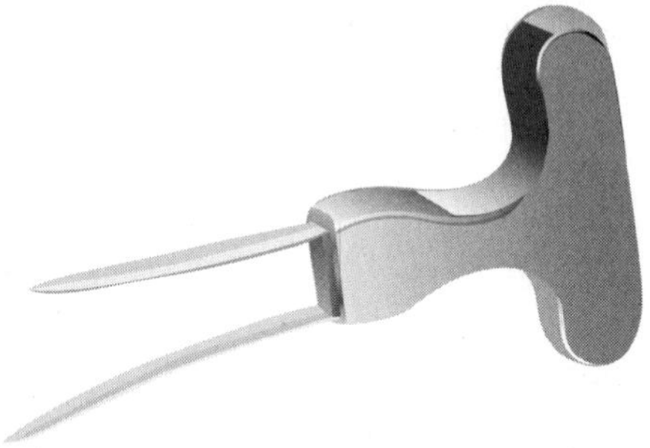

**Figure 4-3:**
The Ah-So
Corkscrew.

© Akira Chiwaki

Although more difficult to operate than the Screwpull (described earlier in this chapter), the Ah-So really comes into its own with very tight-fitting corks that no other corkscrews, including the Screwpull, seem to be able to budge. The Ah-So can also be effective with old, crumbly corks that don't give other corkscrews much to grip. (If you're into reusing items, another advantage of the Ah-So is that it delivers an intact cork that can be reused to close bottles of homemade vinegar or make cutesy bulletin boards.)

The Ah-So is useless with loose corks that move around in the bottle's neck when you try to remove them. It just pushes those corks down into the wine. At that point, you need another tool called a cork retriever (see the nearby sidebar "When cork gets in your wine" for details on this tool).

The Ah-So Corkscrew sells for around $6 to $9. It seems to be especially popular in California for some mysterious reason.

## Releasing the bubbly: Leave the corkscrew behind!

Opening a bottle of sparkling wine is usually an exciting occasion. After all, who doesn't enjoy the ceremony of a cold glass of bubbly? But you need to use a completely different technique than you'd use to open a regular wine bottle. The cork even looks different. Sparkling wine corks have a mushroom-shaped head that protrudes from the bottle and is enclosed by a wire cage that holds the cork in place against the pressure trapped inside the bottle.

The best way to remove the cork from a bottle of sparkling wine is with a gentle sigh rather than a loud pop. Here's how to do it:

1. **Hold the bottle at a 45-degree angle, resting the base of it on your hip.**

   Try wrapping a towel around the bottle if it's wet to avoid having it slip out of your hands.

2. **Twist the bottle while holding on to the cork so you can control the cork as it emerges.**

3. **When you feel the cork starting to come out of the bottle, push down against it with some pressure.**

   Press on the cork as if you don't want to let it out of the bottle.

4. **Hold the cork firmly as the pressure inside the bottle eases it out.**

   The cork comes out slowly, with a hiss or a sigh rather than a pop.

If you prefer hearing the cork pop, position yourself away from other people and fragile objects and simply yank out the cork. But be prepared to lose some of that precious wine, which will froth out of the bottle.

# When cork gets in your wine

Every now and then, even if you've invested in the right corkscrew and used it properly, you can still have pieces of cork floating in your wine. They can be tiny dry flakes that crumbled into the bottle, actual chunks of cork, or even the entire cork.

Before you start berating yourself for being a klutz, you should know that "floating cork" happens to everyone at one time or another, no matter how experienced they are. Cork doesn't harm the wine. And besides, there's a wonderful instrument called a cork retriever (no, it's not a small dog from the south of Ireland!) available in specialty stores and catalogs, although it's considerably more difficult to find than a corkscrew.

The *cork retriever,* designed for removing cork that had the nerve to fall into your wine, consists of three 10-inch pieces of stiff metal wire with hooks on the ends. This device is remarkably effective for removing floating pieces of cork from the bottle. Alternatively, you can just pick out the offending pieces of cork with a spoon after you pour the wine into your glass. (That's one occasion when it's rude to serve your guest first, because the first glass has more cork pieces in it.) Or you can pour the wine through a paper coffee filter (preferably the natural brown-paper filter, or a filter rinsed with hot water to remove the chemicals) into a decanter or pitcher to catch the remaining pieces of cork.

Every once in a while, you'll come across a really tight sparkling wine cork that doesn't want to budge. Try running the top of the bottle under warm water for a few moments or wrapping a towel around the cork to create friction. Either action should allow you to remove the cork successfully.

Never, ever use a corkscrew on a bottle of sparkling wine. The pressure of the trapped carbonation, when suddenly released, can send the cork *and* corkscrew flying right into your eye. If you absolutely require a gadget to remove a sparkling wine cork, you can purchase Champagne Pliers, a Champagne Star, or a Champagne Key. These devices are placed around the part of the cork that's outside the bottle. You can also try using regular pliers, although lugging in the toolbox will surely change the mood of the occasion.

If your bottle of bubbly has just traveled, let it rest for a while, preferably a day. Controlling the cork is difficult when the carbonation has been stirred.

If you're in the midst of a sparkling wine emergency and need to open the bottle anyway, a quick way to calm down the carbonation is to submerge the bottle in an ice bucket for about 30 minutes. Fill the bucket with one-half ice cubes and one-half ice-cold water.

# To Aerate or Not to Aerate (Or, Does Wine Really Breathe?)

Most wine is alive in the sense that it changes chemically as it slowly grows older. Wine absorbs oxygen and, like your own cells, it oxidizes. When grapes turn into wine in the first place, they give off carbon dioxide, just like people. So you could say that wine breathes, in a sense. But that's not what the server means when he asks, "Shall I pull the cork and let the wine breathe?"

The term *breathing* refers to the process of *aerating* the wine, meaning exposing it to air. Sometimes the aroma and flavor of a very young wine will improve with aeration. Many red wines and a few white wines — as well as some dessert wines — can benefit from aeration. (***Note:*** You can drink most white wines upon pouring, unless they're too cold. For more on proper wine temperatures, see the later section "Getting Temperature Right.")

Just pulling the cork out of the bottle and letting the bottle sit is a truly ineffective way to aerate your wine. The little space at the neck of the bottle is way too small to allow the wine to breathe much.

If you really want to aerate your wine, do one or both of the following:

✔ Pour the wine into a *decanter* (a fancy word for a glass container that's big enough to hold the contents of an entire bottle of wine). Practically speaking, it doesn't matter what your decanter looks like or how much it costs. In fact, the very inexpensive, wide-mouthed carafes are fine.

✔ Pour the wine into large glasses at least ten minutes before you plan to drink it.

## Considering the need for aeration

Perhaps you're wondering which wines benefit from aeration and which ones can go without it. Consider this section your guide.

One of the most famous fortified wines is Vintage Port (properly called Porto; see Chapter 2 in Book VI). Vintage Port needs breathing lessons — badly! Young Vintage Ports are so brutally tannic that they demand many hours of aeration (eight isn't too many). Even older Ports improve with four hours or more of aeration. Older Vintage Ports require decanting for another reason: They're chock-full of sediment. (Often, large flakes of sediment fill the bottom 10 percent of the bottle.) Keep Vintage Ports standing for several days before you open them.

Young, tannic red wines (see Chapter 5 of Book I for more on tannin) — such as Cabernet Sauvignons, Bordeaux, many wines from the Northern Rhône Valley, and many Italian wines — actually taste better with aeration because their tannins soften and the wine becomes less harsh.

Some very good, dry white wines — such as full-bodied white Burgundies and white Bordeaux wines, as well as the best Alsace whites — also get better with aeration. For example, if you open a young Corton-Charlemagne (a great white Burgundy) and it doesn't seem to be showing much aroma or flavor, chances are it needs some aeration. *Decant* the wine (pour it out slowly into a separate container without disturbing the sediment inside the bottle; see the following section for the decanting process) and taste it again in 30 minutes. In most cases, the wine improves dramatically.

**REMEMBER**

Contrary to what you might expect, the majority of red wines don't require decanting, aerating, or any special preparation other than pulling out the cork and having a glass handy, as you can see from the following list:

- ✔ Light- and medium-bodied, less tannic red wines, such as Pinot Noirs, Burgundies, Beaujolais, and Côtes du Rhônes; lighter red Zinfandels; and less imposing Italian reds, such as Dolcettos, Barberas, and lighter Chiantis. These wines don't have much tannin and, therefore, don't require much aeration.

- ✔ Inexpensive (less than $12) red wines. Same reason as the preceding.

- ✔ Tawny ports — in fact, any other Ports except Vintage Ports. These wines should be free from sediment (which stayed behind in the barrels where the wine aged) and ready to drink when you pour 'em.

## Removing sediment before aerating (if applicable)

Many red wines typically develop *sediment* (tannin and other matter in the wine that solidifies over time) after about eight years of aging. When dealing with an older wine, you want to remove this sediment because it can taste a bit bitter. Also, the dark particles floating in your wine, usually at the bottom of your glass, don't look very appetizing.

To remove sediment, keep the wine bottle in question upright for a day or two before you plan to open it so the sediment settles at the bottom of the bottle. Then carefully decant the wine: Slowly pour the wine out of the bottle into a decanter while watching the wine inside the bottle as it approaches the neck. Stop pouring when you see cloudy wine from the bottom of the bottle making its way to the neck. If you stop pouring at the right moment, all the cloudy wine remains behind in the bottle.

To actually see the wine inside the bottle as you pour, you need to have a bright light shining through the bottle's neck. Candles are commonly used for this purpose; they're certainly romantic, but a flashlight standing on its end works even better. (It's brighter, and it doesn't flicker.) Or simply hold the bottle up to a bright light and pour slowly.

## Aerating wine for the right amount of time

The younger and more tannic a wine is, the longer it needs to breathe. As a general rule, most tannic, young reds soften up with one hour of aeration. The glaring exception to the one-hour rule is found in many young Barolos or Barbarescos (red wines from Piedmont, Italy; see Chapter 2 in Book III); these wines are frequently so tannic that they can really make your mouth pucker. They often benefit from three or four hours of aeration.

If a wine needs aeration after decanting (that is, it still tastes a bit harsh), let it breathe in the open decanter. If the wine has a dark color, chances are it's still quite youthful and needs to breathe more. Conversely, if the wine has a brick red or pale garnet color, it probably has matured and may not require much aeration.

The older the wine, the more delicate it can be. Don't give old, fragile-looking wines excessive aeration. (Look at the color of the wine through the bottle before you decant; if it looks pale, the wine could be pretty far along its maturity curve.) The flavors of really old wines start fading rapidly after 10 or 15 minutes of being exposed to air.

# Getting Temperature Right

Serving wine at the ideal temperature is a vital factor in your enjoyment of wine. Taste the same wine at different temperatures and you'll find a surprisingly deep distinction.

Most red wines are best at cool room temperature, 62 degrees to 65 degrees Fahrenheit (16 degrees to 18 degrees Celsius). Once upon a time, in drafty old English and Scottish castles, that was simply room temperature. (Actually, it was probably warm, high-noon room temperature!) Today when you hear room temperature, you think of a room that's about 70 degrees Fahrenheit (21 degrees Celsius), don't you? Red wine served at this temperature can taste flat, flabby, lifeless, and often too hot — you get a burning sensation from the alcohol.

Ten or 15 minutes in the fridge does wonders for reviving red wines that have been suffering from heat exhaustion. But don't let the wine get too cold. Red wines served too cold taste overly tannic and acidic, making them decidedly unpleasant. Light, fruity red wines, such as the simplest Beaujolais wines, are most delightful when served slightly chilled at about 58 degrees to 60 degrees Fahrenheit (14 degrees to 15.5 degrees Celsius).

Are you wondering how to know when your bottle is 58 degrees to 60 degrees Fahrenheit? You can buy a nifty digital thermometer that wraps around the outside of the bottle and gives you a color-coded reading. Or you can buy something that looks like a real thermometer that you place into the opened bottle (in the bottle's mouth, you might say). Of course, you probably won't ever use them. Just feel the bottle with your hand and take a guess. Practice makes perfect.

Just as many red wines are served too warm, most white wines are definitely served too cold. The higher the quality of a white wine, the less cold it should be so you can properly appreciate its flavor.

To avoid the problem of warm bubbly, keep an ice bucket handy. Or put the bottle back in the refrigerator between pourings.

Table 4-1 indicates the recommended serving temperatures for various types of wines.

| Table 4-1 | Serving Temperatures for Wine | |
|---|---|---|
| *Type of Wine* | *Temperature °F* | *Temperature °C* |
| Most Champagnes and sparkling wines | 45° | 7° |
| Older or expensive, complex Champagnes | 52°–54° | 11°–12° |
| Inexpensive sweet wines | 50°–55° | 10°–12.8° |
| Rosés and blush wines | 50°–55° | 10°–12.8° |
| Simpler, inexpensive, quaffing-type white wines | 50°–55° | 10°–12.8° |
| Dry Sherry, such as fino or manzanilla | 55°–56° | 12°–13° |
| Fine, dry white wines | 58°–62° | 14°–16.5° |
| Finer dessert wines, such as a good Sauternes | 58°–62° | 14°–16.5° |
| Light, fruity red wines | 58°–60° | 14°–14.5° |

*(continued)*

**Table 4-1** *(continued)*

| Type of Wine | Temperature °F | Temperature °C |
|---|---|---|
| Most red wines | 62°–65° | 16°–18° |
| Sherry (other than dry fino or manzanilla) | 62°–65° | 16°–18° |
| Port | 62°–65° | 16°–18° |

# Believe It or Not, Glasses Do Matter

If you're just drinking wine as refreshment with your meal and you aren't thinking about the wine much as it goes down, the glass you use probably doesn't matter too much. A jelly glass? Why not? Plastic glasses? Great on picnics, not to mention in airplanes (where the wine's quality usually doesn't demand great glasses anyway).

But if you have a good wine, a special occasion, friends who want to talk about the wine with you, or the boss over for dinner, *stemware* (glasses with stems) is called for. And it's not just a question of etiquette and status: Good wine tastes better out of good glasses. Really.

Think of wine glasses as being like stereo speakers. Any old speaker brings the music to your ears, just like any old glass brings the wine to your lips. But (assuming you care to notice it) can't you appreciate the sound so much more, aesthetically and emotionally, from good speakers? The same principle holds true with wine and wine glasses. You can appreciate wine's aroma and flavor complexities so much more out of a fine wine glass.

Believe it or not, the taste of a wine changes when you drink it out of different types of glasses. Three aspects of a glass are important: size, shape, and thickness. All three elements and their effect on your wine experience are described in the next few sections.

Regardless of their size, shape, or thickness, good wine glasses always have one characteristic in common: They're clear. Those pretty pink or green glasses may look nice in your china cabinet, but they interfere with your ability to distinguish the true colors of the wine.

## Size

For dry red and white wine, small glasses are all wrong — besides that, they're a pain in the neck. You just can't swirl the wine around in those little glasses without spilling it, which makes appreciating the aroma of the wine almost impossible. And furthermore, who wants to bother continually refilling them? Small glasses work adequately only for Sherry or dessert wines, which have strong aromas to begin with and are generally consumed in smaller quantities than table wines. In most cases, larger is usually better.

To properly match glass size to wine, follow these guidelines:

- Glasses for red wines should hold a minimum of 12 ounces; many of the best glasses have capacities ranging from 16 to 24 ounces, or more.
- Glasses for white wines should hold 10 to 12 ounces, at minimum.
- Glasses for sparkling wines should hold 8 to 12 ounces.

Avoid filling your glass to the brim so you can have some margin of safety for swirling and smelling your wine. One-third capacity is the best fill-level for serious red wines. White wine glasses can be filled halfway, and sparkling wine glasses can be three-quarters full.

## Shape

Some wine glasses have very round bowls, whereas others have more elongated, somewhat narrower bowls. The next two sections highlight which shape is most appropriate for which wines.

Have a little fun with your stemware! When having dinner at home, try your wine in glasses of different shapes, just to see which glass works best for that particular wine.

### Tulips, flutes, and trumpets: Sparkling-wine glasses

You thought that a tulip was a flower and a flute was a musical instrument? Well, they also happen to be types of glasses designed for use with sparkling wine. The tulip (see Figure 4-4) is the ideally shaped glass for Champagne and other sparkling wines. It's tall, elongated, and narrower at the rim than in the middle of the bowl. This shape helps hold the bubbles in the wine longer, not allowing them to escape freely (the way the wide-mouthed, sherbet-cup-like, so-called Champagne glasses do).

The flute (see Figure 4-4) is another good sparkling wine glass; but it's less ideal than the tulip because it doesn't narrow at the mouth. The trumpet (see Figure 4-4) actually widens at the mouth, making it less suitable for sparkling wine but very elegant looking. Another drawback of the trumpet glass is that, depending on the design, the wine can actually fill the whole stem, which means the wine warms up from the heat of your hand as you hold the stem. Better to avoid the trumpet glass.

**Figure 4-4:**
Glasses for
sparkling
wine
(from left):
tulip, flute,
trumpet.

### *Oval or apple? Glasses for nonsparkling wines*

An oval-shaped bowl that's narrow at its mouth (see Figure 4-5) is ideal for many red wines, such as Bordeaux, Cabernet Sauvignons, Merlots, Chiantis, and Zinfandels. On the other hand, some red wines, such as Burgundies, Pinot Noirs, and Barolos, are best appreciated in wider-bowled, apple-shaped glasses (see Figure 4-5). Which shape and size works best for which wine has to do with issues such as how the glass's shape controls the flow of wine onto your tongue. (One glassmaker, Riedel Crystal, has designed a specific glass for every imaginable type of wine!)

**Figure 4-5:**
The
Bordeaux
glass (left)
and the
Burgundy
glass.

# How many glasses do I need, anyway?

Pinot Noir glasses. Riesling glasses. Burgundy glasses. Champagne glasses. What's a wine lover to do? Buy a different type of glass for each kind of wine? Actually, two different glasses for both red and white wines, plus one glass for sparkling wines, such as Champagne, should take care of most of your wine drinking needs.

One tall, oval-shaped glass, the so-called Bordeaux glass, is the glass of choice for all red and white wines except for Pinot Noirs, Barolos, and Chardonnays. You can use the wider-bowled, apple-shaped glass for all Pinot Noirs (including red Burgundy), Nebbiolo-based wines (such as Barolo and Barbaresco), and all Chardonnays (including white Burgundy and Chablis). The wider-bowled glass expresses the aromas of these wines better. For all sparkling wines, including Champagne, choose a tall tulip-shaped glass — definitely not the narrow flute, which does nothing for the wine's aromas.

You can buy fine, inexpensive wine glasses at any good home furnishing chain stores, such as Pottery Barn.

If you want something finer, try Riedel or Spiegelau Crystal. Riedel is an Austrian glass manufacturer that specializes in making the right wine glass for each kind of wine. Spiegelau, a German company now owned by Riedel, operates similarly, but its glasses are less expensive than Riedel's. Additionally, New York City–based Ravenscroft Crystal now offers quality crystal wine glasses at moderate prices. You can buy these glasses in many department stores, specialty shops, or glass companies.

The more you care to pay attention to the flavor of the wine, the more you truly appreciate and enjoy wine from a good wine glass. It's as simple as that!

## Glass thickness

Stemware made of very thin, fine crystal costs a lot more than normal glasses. That's one reason why many people don't use it and precisely why some people do. The better reason for using fine crystal is that the wine tastes better out of it. Whether the elegant crystal simply heightens the aesthetic experience of wine drinking or whether a more scientific reason exists has yet to be determined.

## Washing your wine glasses

Detergents often leave a filmy residue in glasses, which can affect the aroma and flavor of your wine. Clean your good crystal glasses by hand, using washing soda or baking soda. (Washing soda is the better of the two; it doesn't cake up like baking soda.) Neither product leaves any soapy, filmy residue in your glass. You can find washing soda in the soap/detergent section of supermarkets.

# After the Party's Over: Storing Leftover Wine

A *sparkling-wine stopper,* a device that fits over an opened bottle, is really effective in keeping any remaining Champagne or sparkling wine fresh (often for several days) in the refrigerator. But what do you do when you have red or white wine left in the bottle?

If the cork still fits, you can simply put it back into the bottle and place the bottle in the refrigerator. (Even red wines stay fresher there; just take the bottle out to warm up about an hour before serving it.) But four other methods are also reliable in keeping your remaining wine from oxidizing. These techniques are all the more effective if you put the bottle in the fridge after using them:

- ✔ If you have about half a bottle of wine left, pour the wine into a clean, empty, half-sized wine bottle and recork the smaller bottle.

- ✔ Use a handy, inexpensive, miniature pump called a Vacu Vin (available in most wine stores). This pump removes oxygen from the bottle, and the rubber stoppers that come with it prevent additional oxygen from entering the bottle. It's supposed to keep your wine fresh for up to a week, but it doesn't always work that well.

- ✔ Buy small cans of inert gas (available in some wine stores). Just squirt a few shots of the gas into the bottle through a skinny straw, which comes with the can, and put the cork back in the bottle. The gas displaces the oxygen in the bottle, thus protecting the wine from oxidizing. Simple and effective. Private Preserve is a good and highly recommended brand.

- ✔ A new device, called WineSavor, is a flexible plastic disk that you roll up and insert down the bottle's neck. Once inside the bottle, the disk opens up and floats on top of the wine, blocking the wine from oxygen.

To avoid all this bother, just drink the wine! Or, if you're not too fussy, just place the leftover wine in the refrigerator and drink it in the next day or two — before it goes into a coma.

# Chapter 5

# For Slurps and Gurgles: Tasting and Describing Wine

. . . . . . . . . . . . . . . . . . . . . . . . . . . . . . . . . . . . . . . . . . . .

## In This Chapter

▶ Using your eyes, nose, and tongue to properly taste wines

▶ Understanding the effect of acidity, tannin, and alcohol

▶ Unveiling the six mysterious concepts of wine quality

▶ Recording your tasting commentary for future reference

. . . . . . . . . . . . . . . . . . . . . . . . . . . . . . . . . . . . . . . . . . . .

**M**aybe you're a cynic; maybe right about now you're saying, "Hey, I already know how to taste. I do it every day, three to five times a day. All that wine-tasting humbug is just another way of making wine complicated."

And you know, in a way, you're right. Anyone who can taste coffee or a hamburger can taste wine. All you need are a nose, taste buds, and a brain. You also have all that it takes to speak Mandarin. Having the ability to do something is different from knowing how to do it and applying that know-how in everyday life, however.

This chapter takes you through a special process of tasting wine to help you enhance your everyday wine-drinking experience. You find out how to get your eyes and nose involved, distinguish a quality wine from a lesser one, and record your tasting observations for posterity.

## Knowing What to Do Before You Sip

You drink beverages every day, tasting them as they pass through your mouth. In the case of wine, however, drinking and tasting aren't synonymous. Wine is much more complex than other beverages. For example, most wines have a lot of different (and subtle) flavors, all at the same time, and they give you multiple sensations when they're in your mouth, such as softness and sharpness together.

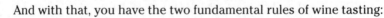

If you just drink wine, gulping it down the way you do soda, you miss a lot of what you paid for. But if you *taste* wine, you can discover its nuances. In fact, the more slowly and attentively you taste wine, the more interesting it tastes.

And with that, you have the two fundamental rules of wine tasting:

1. Slow down.
2. Pay attention.

The process of tasting a wine — that is, of systematically experiencing all the wine's attributes — has three steps. And believe it or not, the first two steps don't actually involve your mouth at all! First, you look at the wine; then you smell it.

## *Starting with the eyes*

Wines can vary a lot in appearance, even within their color category. Some whites are water pale, for example, while others are lemon yellow. The color isn't an indication of quality, but it can be a clue to the wine's style: Deeper colored wines are often (but not always) richer in flavor and generally "bigger" wines.

To observe a wine's appearance, tilt a (half-full) glass away from you and look at the color of the wine against a white background, such as the tablecloth or a piece of paper (a colored background distorts the color of the wine). Notice how dark or how pale the wine is, what color it is, and whether the color fades from the center of the wine out toward the edge, where it touches the glass. Also notice whether the wine is cloudy, clear, or brilliant. (Most wines are clear. Some unfiltered wines can be less than brilliant but shouldn't be cloudy.) Eventually, you'll begin to notice patterns, such as deeper color in younger red wines.

If you have time to kill, at this point you can also swirl the wine around in your glass (see the following section, "Savoring the scent") and observe the way the wine runs back down the inside of the glass. Some wines form *legs* or *tears* that flow slowly down. Once upon a time, these legs were interpreted as the sure sign of a rich, high-quality wine. Actually, a wine's legs are a complicated phenomenon having to do with the surface tension of the wine and the evaporation rate of the wine's alcohol. If you're a physicist, this is a good time to show off your expertise and enlighten your fellow tasters — but otherwise, don't bother drawing conclusions from the legs.

# Savoring the scent

The swirling and sniffing stage of tasting is the really fun part. You can let your imagination run wild, and no one will ever dare to contradict you. If you say that a wine smells like wild strawberries to you, how can anyone prove that it doesn't?

Before you roll your eyes or get overwhelmed, please know that: a) you don't *have* to apply this procedure to every single wine you drink; b) you won't look foolish doing it, at least in the eyes of other wine lovers; and c) it's a great trick at parties to avoid talking with someone you don't like.

### Perfecting the art of sniffing

To get the most out of your sniffing, swirl the wine in the glass first. But don't even *think* about swirling your wine if your glass is more than half full — unless of course you enjoy wearing your wine more than drinking it.

Keep your glass on the table and rotate it three or four times so the wine swirls around inside the glass and mixes with the air. Then quickly bring the glass to your nose. Stick your nose into the airspace of the glass (where the aromas are captured) and smell the wine.

Try different sniffing techniques until you have yours nailed down. For instance, some people like to take short, quick sniffs, whereas others like to inhale a deep whiff of the wine's smell. Keeping your mouth open a bit while you inhale can help you perceive aromas. (Some people even hold one nostril closed and smell with the other, but we think that's a bit kinky.)

When it comes to smelling wine, many people are concerned that they aren't able to detect as many aromas as they think they should. Smelling wine is really just a matter of practice and attention, as well as being in the right sur- roundings. Follow these tips to become a good wine sniffer:

- Don't wear a strong scent; it'll compete with the smell of the wine.

- Don't knock yourself out smelling a wine when strong food aromas are present. The tomatoes you smell in the wine could really be the tomato in someone's pasta sauce.

- Become a perpetual smeller. If you start to pay more attention to smells in your normal activities, you'll get better at smelling wine. Smell every ingredient when you cook, everything you eat, the fresh fruits and vegetables you buy at the supermarket, even the smells of your environment — like leather, wet earth, fresh road tar, grass, flowers, your wet dog, shoe polish, and your medicine cabinet. Stuff your mental database with smells so you'll have aroma memories at your disposal when you need to draw on them.

### Naming the many scents you smell

As you swirl, the aromas in the wine vaporize, so you can smell them. Wine has so many *aromatic compounds* (the atoms that bring the scent) that whatever you find in the smell of a wine probably isn't merely a figment of your imagination.

The point behind this ritual of swirling and sniffing is that what you smell should be pleasurable to you, maybe even fascinating, and that you should have fun in the process. As you sniff, free-associate. Is the aroma fruity, woodsy, fresh, cooked, intense, light? Your nose tires quickly, but it recovers quickly, too. Wait a moment and try again. Listen to your friends' comments and try to find the same aromas they smell.

Hang around wine geeks for a while, and you'll start to hear words such as *petrol, manure, sweaty saddle, burnt match,* and *asparagus* used to describe the aromas of some wines. "Yuck!" you say? Of course you do! Fortunately, the wines that exhibit such smells aren't the wines you'll be drinking for the most part — unless you really catch the wine bug right away. Whenever you do catch the wine bug, you may discover that those aromas, in the right wine, can really be a kick. Even if you don't come to enjoy those smells, you'll appreciate them as typical characteristics of certain regions or grapes.

Then there are the bad smells that nobody tries to defend. They don't pop up often, but they *are* out there, because wine is a natural, agricultural product with a will of its own. Often when a wine is seriously flawed, that shows immediately in the nose of the wine. Wine judges have a term for such wines. They call them DNPIM — Do Not Put In Mouth. Not that you'll get ill, but why subject your taste buds to the same abuse that your nose just took? Sometimes a bad cork is to blame, and sometimes some other sort of problem in the winemaking or even the storage of the wine is the culprit. Just rack it up to experience and open a different bottle.

# Bringing the Tongue into the Act

After you've looked at a wine and smelled it (see the previous sections in this chapter), you're finally allowed to taste it. Welcome to the time when grown men and women sit around and make strange faces, gurgling the wine and sloshing it around in their mouths with looks of intense concentration in their eyes. You can make an enemy for life if you distract a wine taster just at the moment when she's focusing all of his energy on the last few drops of a special wine.

Here's how the procedure goes. Take a medium-sized sip of wine. Hold it in your mouth, purse your lips, and draw in some air across your tongue, over the wine. (Be utterly careful not to choke or dribble, or else everyone will strongly suspect that you're not a wine expert.) Then swish the wine around in your mouth as if you're chewing it. Then swallow it. The whole process should take several seconds, depending on how much you concentrate on the wine. Wondering what to concentrate on? The next sections clue you in to just that.

## Feeling the basic taste sensations

Taste buds on the tongue can register various sensations, known as the basic tastes, which include sweetness, sourness, saltiness, bitterness, and *umami* (a savory characteristic). Of these tastes, sweetness, sourness, and bitterness are those most commonly found in wine. By moving the wine around in your mouth, you give it a chance to hit all of your taste buds so you don't miss anything in the wine (even if sourness and bitterness sound like things you wouldn't mind missing).

As you swish the wine around in your mouth, you also buy time. Your brain needs a few seconds to figure out what the tongue is tasting and make some sense of it. Any sweetness in the wine registers in your brain first because many of the taste buds on the front of your tongue — where the wine hits first — capture the sensation of sweetness. *Acidity* — which, by the way, is what normal people call sourness — and bitterness register subsequently. (While your brain is working out the relative impressions of sweetness, acidity, and bitterness, you can be thinking about how the wine feels in your mouth: heavy, light, smooth, rough, and so on.)

To find the right wine words for those taste sensations moving sequentially across your palate, check out the following sections.

### Sweetness (sweet versus dry)

As soon as you put wine into your mouth, you can usually notice either sweetness or the lack of it. In Winespeak, *dry* is the opposite of sweet. Classify the wine you're tasting as any of the following:

- *Dry*
- *Off-dry* (in other words, somewhat sweet)
- *Sweet*

Beginning wine tasters sometimes describe dry wines as sweet because they confuse fruitiness with sweetness. A wine is *fruity* when it has distinct aromas and fruit flavors. You smell the fruitiness with your nose; sweetness, on the other hand, is a tangible impression on your tongue. When in doubt, try holding your nose when you taste the wine; if the wine really is sweet, you'll be able to taste the sweetness despite the fact that you can't smell the fruitiness.

### Acidity (the backbone for whites)

All wine contains acid (mainly *tartaric acid,* which exists in grapes), but some wines are more acidic than others. Acidity is more of a taste factor in white wines than in reds. For white wines, acidity is the backbone of the wine's taste (it gives the wine firmness in your mouth). White wines with a high amount of acidity feel *crisp,* and those without enough acidity feel *flabby.*

Softness and firmness are actually *textural impressions* a wine gives you as you taste it. Just as your mouth feels temperature in a liquid, it also feels texture. Some wines literally feel soft and smooth as they move through your mouth; others feel hard, rough, or coarse. In white wines, acid is usually responsible for impressions of hardness or firmness (or crispness); in red wines, tannin is usually responsible. Low levels of either substance can make a wine feel pleasantly soft — or too soft, depending on the wine and your taste preferences.

You generally perceive acidity in the middle of your mouth — what wine-tasters call the *mid-palate.* You can also sense the consequences of acidity (or the lack of it) in the overall style of the wine — whether it's a tart little number or a soft and generous sort, for example. Classify the wine you're tasting as

- *Crisp*
- *Soft*
- *"Couch potato"*

Unfermented sugar contributes to an impression of softness, as can alcohol. But very high alcohol — which is fairly common in wines these days — can give a wine an edge of hardness.

### Tannin (the backbone for reds)

*Tannin* is a substance that exists naturally in the skins, seeds (or *pips*), and stems of grapes. Because red wines are fermented with their grape skins and pips, and because red grape varieties are generally higher in tannin than white varieties, tannin levels are far higher in red wines than in white wines. Oak barrels can also contribute tannin to wines, both reds and whites. Have you ever taken a sip of a red wine and rapidly experienced a drying-out feeling in your mouth, as if something had blotted up all of your saliva? That's tannin.

To generalize a bit, tannin is to a red wine what acidity is to a white: a backbone. Tannins alone can taste bitter, but some tannins in wine are less bitter than others. Also, other elements of the wine, such as sweetness, can mask the perception of bitterness (see the section titled "Balance" later in this chapter). You sense tannin — as bitterness, or as firmness or richness of texture — mainly in the rear of your mouth. If the amount of tannin in a wine is high, you also sense it on the inside of your cheeks and on your gums.

Depending on the amount and nature of its tannin, you can describe a red wine as

- *Astringent*
- *Firm*
- *Soft*

Red wines have acid as well as tannin, and distinguishing between the two as you taste a wine can be a real challenge. When you're not sure whether what you're perceiving is mainly tannin or acid, pay attention to how your mouth feels *after* you've swallowed the wine. Acid makes you salivate (saliva is alkaline, and it flows to neutralize the acid); tannin leaves your mouth dry.

### Body (fullness and weight)

A wine's *body* is an impression you get from the whole of the wine — not a basic taste that registers on your tongue. It's the impression of the weight and size of the wine in your mouth, which is usually attributable principally to a wine's alcohol. We say "impression" because, obviously, one ounce of any wine will occupy exactly the same space in your mouth and weigh the same as one ounce of any other wine. But some wines *seem* fuller, bigger, or heavier in the mouth than others.

Think about the wine's fullness and weight as you taste it. Imagine that your tongue is a tiny scale and judge how much the wine is weighing it down. Then classify the wine as any of the following:

- *Light-bodied*
- *Medium-bodied*
- *Full-bodied*

## Working nose and mouth: The flavor dimension

Until you let your nose in on the action, all you can taste in a wine are the sensations of sweetness, acidity, and bitterness and a general impression of weight and texture. Where have all the wild strawberries gone? They're still there in the wine, right next to the chocolate and plums.

To be perfectly correct about it, these flavors are actually *aromas* that you taste not through tongue contact, but by inhaling them up an interior nasal passage in the back of your mouth called the *retronasal passage.* When you draw in air across the wine in your mouth, you're vaporizing the aromas just as you did when you swirled the wine in your glass. See? There really is a method to this madness!

Wines have flavors (or *mouth aromas*), but wines don't come in a specific flavor. Although you may enjoy the suggestion of chocolate in a red wine that you're tasting, you wouldn't want to go to a wine store and ask for a chocolaty wine, unless you don't mind the idea of people trying not to laugh aloud at you.

Instead, refer to *families of flavors* in wine. In general, you have your

- ✔ **Fruity wines:** The wines make you think of all sorts of fruit when you smell them or taste them.
- ✔ **Earthy wines:** These remind you of minerals and rocks, walks in the forest, turning the earth in your garden, dry leaves, and so on.
- ✔ **Spicy wines:** These wines turn your mind to cinnamon, cloves, black pepper, or Indian spices, for example.
- ✔ **Herbal wines:** These make you think of mint, grass, hay, rosemary, and the like.

If you really love a wine and want to try another one that's similar but different (and it'll always be different, guaranteed), one method is to decide what families of flavors in the wine you like and mention that to the person selling you your next bottle.

Another aspect of flavor that's important to consider is a wine's *flavor intensity,* which is how much flavor the wine has, regardless of what those flavors are. Some wines are as flavorful as a Big Mac, whereas others have flavors as subtle as fillet of sole. Flavor intensity is a major factor to consider when pairing wine with food (as you can read in Chapter 6 in Book I), and it also helps determine how much you like a particular wine.

# *Answering the Quality Question: What's a Good Wine?*

After you go through all the rigmarole of properly tasting a wine, it's time to reach a conclusion: Do you like what you tasted? The possible answers are "yes," "no," an indifferent shrug of the shoulders, or "I'm not sure, let me take another taste" (this last one means you have serious wine-nerd potential).

Did you notice, by any chance, that nowhere among the terms to describe wines are the words *great, very good,* or *good?* Instead of worrying about crisp wines, earthy wines, and medium-bodied wines, wouldn't it just be easier to walk into a wine shop and say, "Give me a very good wine for dinner tonight"? Isn't *quality* the ultimate issue — or at least, quality within your price range, also known as *value?*

Wine producers constantly brag about the quality ratings that their wines receive from critics, because a high rating — which implies high quality — translates into increased sales for a wine. But quality wines come in all colors, degrees of sweetness and dryness, and flavor profiles. Just because a wine is high quality doesn't mean you'll actually enjoy it, any more than two-thumbs-up means you'll love a particular movie. Personal taste is simply more relevant than quality when it comes to choosing a wine.

Nevertheless, degrees of quality do exist among wines. But a wine's quality isn't absolute: How great a wine is or isn't depends on who's doing the judging. Read on for a better understanding of the characteristics that define a quality wine and advice on how to create your own numbering system.

## Evaluating the major characteristics

A good wine is, above all, a wine that you like enough to drink. After all, the whole purpose of a wine is to give pleasure to those who drink it. After that, how good a wine is depends on how it measures up to a set of (more or less) agreed-upon standards of performance established by experienced, trained experts. These standards involve mysterious concepts such as *balance, length, depth, complexity, finish,* and *trueness to type* (which is really *typicity* in Winespeak and *typicité* in Snobwinespeak). None of these concepts is objectively measurable, by the way.

### Balance

*Balance* is the relationship of the four components of wine (sweetness; acidity; tannin; and, oh yeah, alcohol) to one another. A wine is balanced when nothing sticks out as you taste it, such as harsh tannin or too much sweetness. Most wines are balanced to most people. But if you have any pet peeves about food — say, if you really hate anything tart or if you never eat sweets — you may perceive some wines to be unbalanced. If you perceive them to be unbalanced, then they're unbalanced for you. (Professional tasters know their own idiosyncrasies and adjust for them when they judge wine.)

Tannin and acidity are *hardening elements* in a wine (they make a wine taste firmer in the mouth), whereas alcohol and sugar (if any) are *softening elements.* The balance of a wine is the interrelationship of the hard and soft aspects of a wine, as well as a key indicator of quality.

### Length

*Length* is a word used to describe a wine that gives an impression of going all the way on the palate — meaning you can taste it across the full length of your tongue — rather than stopping short halfway through your tasting of it. Many wines today are very upfront on the palate — they make a big impression as soon as you taste them — but they don't go the distance in your mouth. In other words, these wines are *short*. Generally, high alcohol or excess tannin is to blame. Length is a sure sign of high quality.

### Depth

*Depth* is yet another subjective, immeasurable attribute of a high-quality wine. A wine is considered to have *depth* when it seems to have a dimension of verticality — that is, it doesn't taste flat and one-dimensional in your mouth. A "flat" wine can never be great.

### Complexity

There's nothing wrong with a simple, straightforward wine, especially if you enjoy it. But a wine that keeps revealing different characteristics of itself, always showing you a new flavor or impression — a wine that has *complexity* — is usually considered better quality. Some experts use the term *complexity* specifically to indicate that a wine has a multiplicity of aromas and flavors, whereas others use it in a more holistic (but less precise) sense to refer to the total impression a wine gives you.

### Finish

The impression a wine leaves in the back of your mouth and in your throat after you swallow it is its *finish* or *aftertaste*. In a good wine, you can still perceive the wine's flavors — such as fruitiness or spiciness — at that point. Some wines may finish *hot*, because of high alcohol, or *bitter*, because of tannin — both shortcomings. Or a wine may have nothing much at all to say for itself after you swallow.

### Typicity

In order to judge a wine's *typicity*, or whether it's true to its type, you have to know how that type is supposed to taste, which means you must know the textbook characteristics of wines made from the major grape varieties and wines of the world's classic wine regions. (For example, the Cabernet Sauvignon grape typically has an aroma and flavor of blackcurrants, and the French white wine called Pouilly-Fumé typically has a slight gunflint aroma.) Flip to Chapter 2 in Book I for those exciting details.

# The charm of an aged wine

Aged wines are a thing apart from young wines — and some wines don't really reach their full expression until they've aged. Try drinking a highly acclaimed young red Bordeaux, say a 1996 Château Lafite-Rothschild. You taste a mouthful of tannin, and although the wine has concentration, you probably wonder what all the fuss is about. Try it in 10 to 15 years; the assertive tannins have softened; a wonderful bouquet of cedar, tobacco, and blackcurrants emerges from the glass; and a natural sweetness of flavor has developed.

As a fine wine matures in the bottle, a series of chemical and physical changes occur. These changes are poorly understood, but their effects are evident in the style of a mature red wine.

✔ The wine becomes paler in color.

✔ Its aroma evolves from the fruity aromas (and often oakiness) it had when young to a complex leathery and earthy bouquet.

✔ Its tannic, harsh texture diminishes, and the wine becomes silky.

Mature wines seem to be easier to digest, and they go to your head less quickly. (Perhaps that's because we tend to drink them slowly, with reverence.) Besides visceral pleasure, they offer a special emotional satisfaction. Tasting an aged wine can be like traveling back in time, sharing a connection with people who have gone before in the great chain of humanity.

## *Decoding the critics' numerical systems and developing your own*

When a wine critic writes a tasting note, he usually accompanies it with a point score, which is a judgment of the wine's quality on a scale of 20 or 100. You see these numbers plastered all over the shelves in your wine shop and in wine advertisements.

Because words are such a difficult medium for describing wine, the popularity of number ratings has spread like wildfire. Many wine lovers don't bother to read the descriptions in a critic's wine reviews. Instead, they just run out to buy the wines with the highest scores. (Hey, they're the best wines, right?) Wines that receive high scores from the best-known critics sell out almost overnight as the result of the demand generated by their scores.

Numbers do provide convenient shorthand for communicating a critic's opinion of a wine's quality. But number ratings are also problematic for a number of reasons:

✔ The sheer precision of the scores suggests that they're objective, when in fact they represent either the subjective opinion of an individual critic or the combined subjective opinions of a panel of critics.

✔ Different critics can apply the same scale differently. For example, some may assign 95 points only to wines that are truly great compared to all wines of all types, whereas others could assign the same score to a wine that is great in its own class.

✔ The score likely reflects an evaluation of a wine in different circumstances than you'll taste it. Most critics rate wines by tasting them without food, for example, whereas most wine drinkers drink wine with food. Also, the wineglass the critic uses can be different from what you use; even this seemingly minor detail can affect the way the wine presents itself. (See Chapter 4 in Book I to find out how wineglasses can affect a wine's taste.)

✔ Number scores tell you absolutely nothing about how a wine tastes.

You may hate a wine that's rated highly. (Not only that, but you may end up feeling like a hopeless fool who can't recognize quality when it's staring him in the face.) Save your money and your pride by deciding what kinds of wine you like and then trying to figure out from the words whether a particular wine is your style, *regardless of the number rating.*

Despite the pitfalls of number ratings, you may be inclined to score wines yourself when you taste. Numbers can be very meaningful to the person assigning them. To start, decide which scale you want to use. A scale with 100 as the highest score is more intuitive than a scale ending in 20. (Most 100-point scales are actually only 50-point scales, with 50 points, not 0, representing the poorest conceivable quality.)

After deciding on your scale, create several groupings of points, and write down the quality level that each group represents. It can be something like this:

✔ 95–100: Absolutely outstanding; one of the finest wines ever

✔ 90–94: Exceptional quality; excellent wine

✔ 85–89: Very good quality

✔ 80–84: Above-average quality; good

✔ 75–79: Average commercial quality (a "C" student)

✔ 70–74: Below-average quality

✔ Below 70: Poor quality

Until you get the hang of using this system, you may just want to give each wine a range rather than a precise score, such as 80–84 (good) or 85–89 (very good). As you gain experience in tasting wine and rating wine quality, you'll become more opinionated and your scores will naturally become more precise.

# *Keeping Track of Tastings*

Some people have a special ability to remember tastes; others need to take notes to remember what they tasted, let alone what they thought of it. If you have the slightest difficulty remembering the names of wines, jot down the names of the ones you try and like so you can enjoy them, or similar wines, again. The following sections help you get started documenting your observations about the wines you taste.

Writing down comments about wines that you taste is also a good idea. Even if you're one of those lucky few who can remember everything you taste, writing your tasting notes now and then can be a good way to help discipline your tasting methods.

## *Taking notes when you taste*

A good starting point for note-taking is to write the letters

- ✔ *C* (for color and appearance in general)
- ✔ *N* (for nose)
- ✔ *T* (for taste, or mouth impressions)

Put one below the other, under the name of each wine on your tasting sheet, leaving space to record your impressions. When you taste, take each wine as it comes: If a wine is very aromatic, write lots of descriptors next to *N*, but if the aroma is understated, just write *subtle* or even *not much.*

Also, be sure to approach the wine sequentially as you taste it, noting its attack and evolution, and holding the wine long enough to describe its balance and texture too. Taste the wine again to determine what else it may be saying. Sometimes at that point you arrive at a summary description of the wine, like *a huge wine packed with fruitiness that's ready to drink now,* or *a lean, austere wine that will taste better with food than alone.* Your tasting notes may be a combination of fragmented observation — *high acid, very crisp* — and summary description.

At first, your own notes will be brief. Just a few words, like *soft, fruity* or *tannic, hard* are fine to remind you later what the wine was like. And as an evaluation of overall quality, there's absolutely nothing wrong with *yum!*

# Finding your own descriptive style

Some people think there's a right way and a wrong way to describe wine. Many *enologists* (people who've earned a degree in the science of winemaking), for example, usually favor a scientific approach to describing wine. This approach relies on descriptors that are objective, quantifiable, and reproducible — such as the level of acidity in a wine (which is measurable) or specific aroma and flavor descriptors (reproducible in laboratory tests). They dislike fanciful or unspecific terms, such as *rich, generous,* or *smooth.*

Other people who aren't scientists believe that strictly scientific descriptions usually fail to communicate the spirit of a wine. Even if you're all for noting the relative acidity, tannin, and alcohol levels of a wine, don't stop there! Describe the overall personality of a wine. Who cares if the language you use is more personal than universal?

If a wine inspires you to fanciful description, by all means go with it; only a cold-blooded scientist would resist. The experience of that wine will become memorable through the personal words you use to name it. (But try to avoid letting yourself be moved to poetry over every wine. The vast majority of wines are prosaic, and their descriptions should be too.)

When you do lapse into metaphor over a wine, don't necessarily expect others to understand what you mean, or even to approve. Literal types will be all over you, demanding to know what a rainbow tastes like and how a wine can possibly resemble a cat.

In the end, the experience of wine is so personal that the best anyone can do is to *try* to describe the experience to others. Your descriptions will be meaningful to people who share your approach and your language, especially if they're tasting the wine along with you. But someone else picking up your notes will find them incomprehensible. Likewise, you'll find some wine descriptions you read incomprehensible. Such is the nature of the exercise.

# Chapter 6

# Pairing Food and Wine

*E*very now and then, you encounter a wine that stops you dead in your tracks. It's so sensational that you lose all interest in anything but that wine. You drink it with intent appreciation, trying to memorize the taste. You wouldn't dream of diluting its perfection with a mouthful of food.

But 999 times out of 1,000, wine is better with food. Wine is meant to go with food. And good food is meant to go with wine.

But how best to marry the two? There are thousands of wines in the world, and every one is different. There are also thousands of basic foods in the world, each different — not to mention the infinite combinations of foods in prepared dishes. In reality, food-with-wine is about as simple an issue as boy-meets-girl. Not convinced? This chapter reassures you by explaining just how wine and food mix, sharing the two principles you need to know to pair like a pro, and providing some classic pairing combinations.

## How Wine and Food Work Together

Every dish is dynamic, made up of several ingredients and flavors that interact to create a (more or less) delicious whole. Every wine is dynamic in exactly the same way. When food and wine combine in your mouth, the dynamics of each change; the result is completely individual to each food-and-wine combination. (And, of course, each person's individual palate judges the success of each combination. Small wonder no rules exist!)

When wine meets food, several things can happen:

- ✔ **The food can exaggerate a characteristic of the wine.** For example, if you eat walnuts (which are tannic) with a tannic red wine, such as a Bordeaux (see Chapter 2 in Book II), the wine tastes so dry and astringent that most people would consider it undrinkable.

- ✔ **The food can diminish a characteristic of the wine.** Protein diminishes the impression of tannin, for example, and an overly tannic red wine — unpleasant on its own — could be delightful with rare steak or roast beef.

- ✔ **The flavor intensity of the food can obliterate the wine's flavor or vice versa.** If you've ever drunk a big, rich red wine with a delicate filet of sole, you've experienced this possibility firsthand.

- ✔ **The wine can contribute new flavors to the dish.** For example, a red Zinfandel that's gushing with berry fruit can bring its berry flavors to the dish, as if another ingredient had been added.

- ✔ **The combination of wine and food can create an unwelcome third-party flavor that wasn't in either the wine or the food originally.** You might get a metallic flavor when you eat plain white-meat turkey with red Bordeaux.

- ✔ **The food and wine can interact perfectly, creating a sensational taste experience that's greater than the food or the wine alone.** This scenario is what ideally happens every time you eat and drink, but it's as rare as a show-stopping dish.

Fortunately, what happens between food and wine isn't haphazard. Certain elements of food react in predictable ways with certain elements of wine, giving you a fighting chance at making successful matches. The major components of wine (alcohol, sweetness, acid, and tannin) relate to the basic tastes of food (sweetness, sourness, bitterness, and saltiness) the same way that the principle of balance in wine operates: Some of the elements exaggerate each other, and some of them compensate for each other.

Each wine and each dish has more than one component, and the simple relationships can be complicated by other elements in the wine or the food. Whether a wine is considered tannic, sweet, acidic, or high in alcohol depends on its dominant component. (Flip to Chapter 5 in Book I for more about these taste elements.)

The following sections outline some ways that food and wine interact, based on the components of the wine.

## The fifth wheel

Common wisdom was that humans can perceive four basic tastes: sweet, sour, salty, and bitter. But people who study food have concluded that a fifth taste exists, and there may be many more than that. The fifth taste is called *umami* (pronounced oo-*mah*-me), and it's associated with a savory character in foods. Shellfish, oily fish, meats, and cheeses are some foods high in umami taste.

Umami-rich foods can increase the sensation of bitterness in wines served with them. To counteract this effect, try adding something salty (such as salt itself) or sour (such as vinegar) to your dish. Although this suggestion defies the adage that vinegar and wine don't get along, the results are the proof of the pudding.

## Tannic wines

Tannic wines include most wines based on the Cabernet Sauvignon grape (including red Bordeaux, described in Chapter 2 of Book II), northern Rhône reds (see Chapter 5 in Book II), Barolo and Barbaresco (see Chapter 2 in Book III), and any wine — white or red — that has become tannic from aging in new oak barrels. These wines can

- ✔ Diminish the perception of sweetness in a food
- ✔ Taste softer and less tannic when served with protein-rich, fatty foods, such as steak or cheese
- ✔ Taste less bitter when paired with salty foods
- ✔ Taste astringent, or mouth-drying, when drunk with spicy-hot foods

## Sweet wines

Wines that often have some sweetness include most inexpensive California white wines, White Zinfandel, many Rieslings (unless they're labeled *dry* or *trocken*), and medium-dry Vouvray. Sweet wines also include dessert wines such as Port, sweetened Sherries, and late-harvest wines. These wines can

- ✔ Taste less sweet, but fruitier, when matched with salty foods
- ✔ Make salty foods more appealing
- ✔ Go well with sweet foods

## Acidic wines

Acidic wines include most Italian white wines (see Book III); Sancerre, Pouilly-Fumé, and Chablis (see Book II); traditionally made red wines from Rioja; most dry Rieslings; and fully dry wines that are based on Sauvignon Blanc. These wines can

- ✔ Taste less acidic when served with salty foods
- ✔ Taste less acidic when served with slightly sweet foods
- ✔ Make foods taste slightly saltier
- ✔ Counterbalance oily or fatty heaviness in food

## High-alcohol wines

High-alcohol wines include many California wines, both white and red; southern Rhône whites and reds (see Chapter 5 in Book II); Barolo and Barbaresco (see Chapter 2 in Book III); fortified wines such as Port and Sherry; and most wines produced from grapes grown in warm climates. These wines can

- ✔ Overwhelm lightly flavored or delicate dishes
- ✔ Go well with slightly sweet foods

# Pairing for Complement or Contrast

Two principles can help you match wine with food: the complementary principle and the contrast principle. The *complementary principle* involves choosing a wine that's similar in some way to the dish you plan to serve, whereas the *contrast principle* (not surprisingly) involves combining foods with wines that are dissimilar to them in some way.

The characteristics of a wine that can either resemble or contrast with the characteristics of a dish are

- ✔ **The wine's flavors:** Earthy, herbal, fruity, vegetal, and so on
- ✔ **The intensity of flavor in the wine:** Weakly flavorful, moderately flavorful, or very flavorful
- ✔ **The wine's texture:** Crisp and firm, or soft and supple
- ✔ **The weight of the wine:** Light-bodied, medium-bodied, or full-bodied

You probably use the complementary principle often without realizing it: You choose a light-bodied wine to go with a light dish, a medium-bodied wine to go with a fuller dish, and a full-bodied wine to go with a heavy dish. Some other examples of the complementary principle in action are

- **Dishes with flavors that resemble those in the wine:** Think about the flavors in a dish the same way you think about the flavors in wine — as families of flavors. If a dish has mushrooms, it has an earthy flavor; if it has citrus or other fruit elements, it has a fruity flavor (and so on). Then consider which wines would offer their own earthy flavor, fruity flavor, herbal flavor, spicy flavor, or whatever. The earthy flavors of white Burgundy complement risotto with mushrooms, for example, and an herbal Sancerre complements chicken breast with fresh herbs.

- **Foods with texture that's similar to that of the wine:** A California Chardonnay with a creamy, rich texture could match the rich, soft texture of lobster, for example.

- **Foods and wines whose intensity of flavor match:** A very flavorful Asian stir-fry or Tex-Mex dish would be at home with a very flavorful, as opposed to subtle, wine.

The contrast principle seeks to find flavors or texture in a wine that aren't in a dish but that would enhance it. A dish of fish or chicken in a rich cream and butter sauce, for example, may be matched with a dry Vouvray, a white wine whose crispness (thanks to its uplifting, high acidity) would counterbalance the heaviness of the dish. A dish with earthy flavors such as portobello mushrooms and fresh fava beans (or potatoes and black truffles) may contrast nicely with the pure fruit flavor of an Alsace Riesling.

You also apply the contrast principle every time you decide to serve simple food, like unadorned lamb chops or hard cheese and bread, with a gloriously complex aged wine.

In order to apply either principle, of course, you must have a good idea of what the food is going to taste like and what various wines taste like. That second part can be a real stumbling block for people who don't devote every ounce of their free energy to learning about wine. The solution is to ask your wine merchant. A retailer may not have the world's greatest knack in pairing wine with food (then again, he might), but at least he should know what his wines taste like.

# Some Tried-and-True Pairings

No matter how much you value imagination and creativity, don't waste your time reinventing the wheel. In wine-and-food terms, it pays to know the classic pairings because they work, and they're a sure thing.

Here are some famous and reliable combinations:

- ✔ Oysters and traditional, unoaked Chablis
- ✔ Lamb and red Bordeaux (Chianti also goes well with lamb)
- ✔ Walnuts and Stilton cheese with Port
- ✔ Salmon with Pinot Noir
- ✔ Gorgonzola cheese with Amarone
- ✔ Grilled fish with Vinho Verde
- ✔ Foie gras with Sauternes or late-harvest Gewürztraminer
- ✔ Braised beef with Barolo
- ✔ Soup with dry amontillado Sherry
- ✔ Grilled chicken with Beaujolais
- ✔ Toasted almonds or green olives with fino or manzanilla Sherry
- ✔ Goat cheese with Sancerre or Pouilly-Fumé
- ✔ Dark chocolate with California Cabernet Sauvignon

Sooner or later you're bound to experience a food-and-wine disaster — when the two taste miserable together. As long as the wine is good and the food is good, eat one first and drink the other afterward — or vice versa. No harm done!

# Chapter 7

# Ordering Wine When You're Dining Out

*W*hen you buy a bottle of wine in a restaurant, you get to taste it right then and there. Hello, instant gratification! If you've chosen well, you have a delicious wine that pairs beautifully with the food you've selected. You also get to bask in the compliments of your family and friends throughout the meal and go home feeling good about yourself. If you haven't chosen well . . . well, we all know *that* feeling! Fortunately, practice *does* make perfect, at least most of the time.

*Un*fortunately, restaurant wine lists can be infuriating. Most of them don't tell you enough about the wines. Sometimes there's nothing worth drinking, at least in your price range; other times you have so many choices that you're immobilized. All too frequently, the lists simply aren't accurate, which means you can spend ten good minutes of your life deciding which wine to order, only to discover that it's "not available tonight" (and probably hasn't been for months).

When you eat out, you may not feel like wading through the restaurant's wine list at all, knowing that it can be an ego-deflating experience. But don't give up without a fight. With a little guidance and a few tips, you can navigate the choppy waters of the restaurant wine list with ease.

# How Restaurants Sell Wine

Believe it or not, restaurateurs really do want you to buy their wine. They usually make a sizable profit on every sale; their servers earn bigger tips and become happier employees; and you enjoy your meal more, going home a more satisfied customer.

But traditionally (and, we trust, unwittingly), many restaurants have done more to hinder wine sales than encourage them. Fortunately, the old ways are changing . . . slowly.

Wines available for sale in a restaurant these days generally fall into four categories:

- House wines
- Premium wines
- Standard-list wines
- Special or reserve-list wines

The following sections take a look at each of these categories.

## The story behind house wine

The wine list at your average restaurant looks so imposing that you finally give up laboring over it. You hand it back to the server and say (either a bit sheepishly, because you're acknowledging that you can't handle the list, or with defiant bravado, signifying that you're not going to waste your time on this nonsense), "I'll just have a glass of white wine." Smart move or big mistake?

You'll probably know the answer to this question as soon as the house wine hits your lips. It might be just what you wanted — and you avoided the effort of plowing through that list. But in most cases? Big mistake.

Usually, a restaurant's *house wines* are inferior stuff that the restaurant owner is making an enormous profit on. (Cost-per-ounce is typically a restaurant owner's main criterion in choosing a house wine.) These wines usually include one white and one red, and sometimes also a sparkling wine. They're the wines you get when you simply ask for a glass of white or a glass of red.

House wines can be purchased by the glass or in a *carafe* (a wide-mouthed, handle-less pitcher). They can range in price from $4 to $10 a glass (with an average of $6 to $8). Often, the entire bottle costs the proprietor the price of one glass or less! No wonder the "obliging" server fills your glass to the brim.

If you do choose a house wine, you usually save money if you buy it by the carafe, if it's offered that way. Then again, you may not want an entire carafe of the house wine!

Under most circumstances, avoid the house wine. Only a small percentage of better restaurants — and wine-conscious restaurants, often located in enlightened places such as Napa or Sonoma — offer a house wine worth drinking. And it's practically never a good value. For the same reasons, avoid asking for "a glass of Chardonnay" or "a glass of Merlot."

If circumstances are such that a glass of wine makes the most sense (if you're the only one in your group who's having wine with dinner, for example), chances are you'll need to order the house wine, unless you're at a restaurant that offers premium selections by the glass as well (see the next section).

If the house wine is your only option, ask the server what it is. Don't be satisfied with the response, "It's Chardonnay." Ask for specifics: Chardonnay from where? What brand? Ask to see the bottle. Either your worst fears will be confirmed (you've never heard of the wine, or it has a reputation for being inferior), or you'll be pleasantly surprised (you *have* heard of the wine, and it has a good reputation). At least you'll know what you're drinking, for future reference.

## Premium pours

The word *premium* is used very loosely by the wine industry. You may think it refers to a rather high-quality wine, but when annual industry sales statistics are compiled for the United States, *premium* indicates any wine that sells for more than $7 a bottle in stores!

As used in the phrase *premium wines by the glass,* however, *premium* usually does connote better quality. Premium wines are reds and whites that a restaurant sells at a higher price than its basic house wines, usually in the range of $9 to $14 per glass. ***Note:*** Not every restaurant offers premium wines by the glass.

A restaurant may offer just one premium white and one premium red, or it may offer several choices. These premium wines aren't anonymous beverages, like the house red and white. Instead, they're identified for you somehow — on the wine list, on a separate card, verbally, by a display of bottles, or even on a chalkboard (if you're in a rather informal restaurant, that is). After all, why would you ever pay a premium for them if you didn't know what they were?

Ordering premium wines by the glass is a fine idea — especially if you want to have only a glass or two, or if you and your guests want to experiment by trying several wines — but be sure to do your math. You actually end up paying more for a premium wine if you order a bottle's worth of individual glasses than you would if you ordered a whole bottle to begin with.

If two or three of you are ordering the same wine by the glass — and especially if you might want refills — ask how many ounces are poured into each glass (usually 5 to 8 ounces) and compare the price with that of a 25.4-ounce (750-milliliter) bottle of the same wine. Sometimes you can have the whole bottle for the cost of only three glasses.

## The (anything but) standard wine list

The term *standard wine list* distinguishes a restaurant's basic wine list from its special, or *reserve,* wine list. Unfortunately, there's nothing standard about wine lists at all. They come in all sizes, shapes, and degrees of detail, accuracy, and user-friendliness (the latter usually ranging from moderate to nil).

If you're still hung up on the emotional-vulnerability potential of buying wine, don't even pick up a wine list. (Instead, turn to Chapter 3 of Book I and reread the pep talk about wine buying there.) When you're ready, read the "Conquering the Wine List" section later in this chapter to get a wine you'll like — with minimum angst involved.

## Special, or reserve, wine lists

Some restaurants offer a special, or *reserve,* wine list of rare wines available by the bottle to supplement their standard wine list. These special lists appeal to two types of customers: serious wine connoisseurs and "high rollers." If you're not in either category, don't even bother asking whether the restaurant has such a list (and not all restaurants have one). Then again, if you're not paying for the meal or if you seriously want to impress a client or a date, you may want to look at it! Try to get help with the list from some knowledgeable person on the restaurant staff, though: Any mistake you make can be a costly one.

# Conquering the Wine List

Your first step in the dark encounter between you and the wine list is to size up the opposition. Really good restaurants recognize that choosing a bottle of wine can take some time. In many restaurants, however, the servers don't give you enough time, so as soon as your server comes to the table, ask to see the wine list.

Besides communicating to the server that you feel comfortable with wine (whether that's true or not), asking for the list quickly gives you more time to study it. Oh, and an indirect benefit of this procedure is that the purposeful look in your eyes as you peruse the list will convince your guests that you know what you're doing. (Sometimes, however, the list is very small, with hardly any wines on it. Looking purposeful for very long is tough when you're studying a list like that.)

If your server asks, somewhat impatiently, "Have you selected your wine yet?" simply tell him (firmly) that you need more time. Don't be bullied into making a hasty choice.

For help deciphering what you find on the wine list, translating that into what you really want, and asking for help choosing a wine, check out the following sections.

## Paying attention to your first impression: A primer on presentation

Once upon a time, the best wine lists consisted of hand-lettered pages inside heavy leather covers embossed with the words *Carte des Vins* in gold. Today, the best wine lists are more likely to be laser-printed pages or cards that more than make up in functionality what they sacrifice in romance.

The more permanent and immutable a wine list seems, the less accurate its listings are likely to be — and the less specific. Such lists suggest that no one's really looking after wine on a day-to-day basis in that restaurant. Chances are many of the wines listed will be out of stock.

Sometimes, the list of wines is actually included on the restaurant's menu, especially if the menu is a computer-printed page or two that changes from week to week or month to month. Restaurants featuring immediate, up-to-date wine listings like this can be a good bet for wine.

A few restaurants have dared to go where no wine list has gone before: into the digital realm. Their wine lists — at least a few copies of them — are on portable computer screens, or e-books, that enable you not only to see the list of available wines and their prices but also to read background information by tapping a wine's name; you can even request a list of wines that are suitable for the food you're ordering. Of course, these lists have their downside: They're so much fun that you risk offending your friends by playing with the list for too long!

Many restaurants that are serious about wine publish their wine lists on the Internet. Before a special meal, you can go to the restaurant's Web site and make a short list of possible wines for your meal, a step that's guaranteed to boost your comfort level.

## Knowing what information you'll likely encounter

The more serious a restaurant is about its wine selection, the more information it gives you about each wine. Of course, there's no way of predicting exactly what you'll find on the list, other than prices, but most wine lists include the following additional information:

- ✔ **An item number for each wine:** *Item numbers,* which are sometimes called *bin numbers,* refer to the specific location of each wine in the restaurant's cellar or wine storage room. They make it easier for the server to locate and pull the wine quickly for you. They're also a crutch to help the server bring you the right wine in case he doesn't have a clue about wine, not to mention a crutch for *you* in ordering the wine in case you have no idea how to pronounce what you've decided to drink. (An added bonus of the item number? You can always pretend you're using it for the server's benefit.)

- ✔ **The name of each wine:** These names may be grape names or place-names (as explained in Chapter 2 in Book I), but they'd better also include the name of each producer (Château this or that, or such-and-such Winery). If they don't, you have no way of knowing exactly which wine any listing is meant to represent.

- ✔ **A vintage indication for each wine:** The *vintage* refers to the year the grapes were harvested. If the wine is a blend of wines from different years, it may say *NV,* for *nonvintage.* Sometimes, you'll see *VV,* which means the wine is a vintage-dated wine, but you're not allowed to know *which* vintage it is unless you ask. The restaurateur just doesn't want to bother changing the year on the list when the wine's vintage changes.

- ✔ **A brief description of the wines:** Don't expect to see descriptions if the list features dozens of wines.

- ✔ **Food pairing suggestions:** This information is helpful at times, but you may not always like — or agree with — the restaurateur's wine suggestion.

# Surveying the list with an eye toward organization

Start your review of the wine list by noting how it's organized. Read the headings on the wine list the way you'd read the chapter titles in a book that you were considering buying. Figure out how the wines are categorized and how they're arranged within each category. Notice how much or how little information is given about each wine.

The following sections offer some organization-specific information to help you understand how a particular wine list is set up.

### The grouping of the wines

Generally speaking, you may discover the wines arranged in the following categories:

- Champagne and sparkling wines
- (Dry) white wines
- (Dry) red wines
- Dessert wines

After-dinner drinks, such as Cognac, Armagnac, single-malt Scotches, grappas, or liqueurs, usually don't appear on the list. If they do, they have their own section near the back of the list.

Some restaurants further subdivide the wines on their lists according to country, especially in the white and red wine categories: French red wines, Italian red wines, American reds, and so on. These country sections may then be subdivided by wine region. France, for example, may have listings of Bordeaux, Burgundy, and possibly Rhône all under "French red wines." "American reds" may be divided into California wines, Oregon wines, and Washington wines.

Or you may find that the categories under white wines and red wines are the names of grape varieties — for example, a Chardonnay section, a Sauvignon Blanc section, and a miscellaneous "other dry whites" section, all under the general heading of white wines. If the restaurant features a particular country's cuisine, the wines of that country, say Italian, may be listed first (and given certain prominence), followed by a cursory listing of wines from other areas.

## Wine list power struggles

Usually, your table will receive just one wine list. An outmoded convention dictates that only the host (the masculine is intentional) needs to see the list. (It's part of the same outmoded thinking that dictates that females should receive menus with no prices on them.) Ask for additional lists if your party includes more than one decision-maker.

Invariably, the wine list is handed to the oldest or most important-looking male at the table. If you're a female entertaining business clients, this situation can be insulting and infuriating. Speak up and ask for a copy of the wine list for yourself. If it's important enough to you, slip away from the table and inform the server that you're the table's host.

### The sequence of the wines within each group

Often you'll find that within each category, the wines appear in ascending order of price with the least expensive wine listed first. Many a restaurateur is betting that you won't order that first wine out of fear of looking cheap. They figure you'll go for the second, third, or fourth wine down the price column, or even deeper if you're feeling insecure and need the reassurance that your choice is a good one. (Meanwhile, that least-expensive wine may be perfectly fine.)

Two recent trends in wine-conscious restaurants make ordering wine easier and decidedly more fun:

- **Progressive wine lists:** In a *progressive* wine list, the wines appear in a progressive sequence under each category heading. For example, under "Chardonnays," the wines are arranged by weight and richness, progressing from the lightest wines to the most intense, regardless of price.

- **Lists that use wine styles as their basic form of organization:** In these lists, the category headings are neither varietal nor regional. Instead, they describe the taste of the wines in each category, such as "Fresh, crisp, unoaked whites," or "Full-bodied, serious reds."

## Ordering the bottle you want

Plan to order your wine at the same time that you order your food — if not sooner. Otherwise, you may be sipping water with your first course.

In Table 7-1, you find a few types of wine that are on most restaurant wine lists and that are consistently reliable choices with food.

| Table 7-1 | Reliable Restaurant Wine Choices | |
|---|---|---|
| **Food Choice** | **Desired Wine Characteristics** | **Recommended Wine** |
| Delicately flavored fish or seafood | A crisp, dry white that isn't very flavorful | Soave, Pinot Grigio, or Sancerre |
| Mussels and other shellfish | A dry white with assertive flavor | Sauvignon Blanc from South Africa or New Zealand |
| Simple poultry, risotto, and dishes that are medium in weight | A medium-bodied, characterful, dry white | Mâcon-Villages, St.-Véran, or Pouilly-Fuissé |
| Lobster or rich chicken entrées | A full-bodied, rich white | California or Australian Chardonnay |
| Meaty fish, veal, or pork entrées | A full-bodied white with a honeyed, nutty character | Meursault |
| Asian-inspired dishes | A medium-dry white | Chenin Blanc, Vouvray, or German Riesling |
| White-meat poultry and fish that isn't too delicately flavored | A food-friendly red with a fairly low tannin level | Red Burgundy |
| Roast chicken | An easy-drinking, inexpensive red | Beaujolais (especially from a reputable producer, such as Louis Jadot, Joseph Drouhin, or Georges Duboeuf) |
| Spicy food | A versatile, flavorful, relatively inexpensive red | California red Zinfandel |
| Light- and medium-intensity foods | A lighter red that's delicious and young | Oregon or California Pinot Noir |
| Simple steak cuts | A basic French version of Pinot Noir | Bourgogne Rouge |
| Pizza | A dry, spicy, grapey, and relatively inexpensive red | Barbera or Dolcetto |
| Almost anything | A very dry, medium-bodied red | Chianti Classico |

## Asking for help selecting a wine

If, after sizing up the restaurant's wine list, you decide that you aren't familiar with most of the wines on it, don't be afraid to ask for help with your selection. If the restaurant is a fancy one, ask whether you can speak to the *sommelier* (pronounced soh-mell-yay) — technically, a specially trained, high-level wine specialist who's responsible for putting the wine list together and for making sure that the wines offered on the list complement the restaurant's cuisine. (Usually only the most wine-conscious establishments employ a sommelier.) If the restaurant isn't particularly fancy, ask to speak with the wine specialist. Often someone on the staff, frequently the proprietor, knows the wine list well.

Whoever on the restaurant staff knows the wine well is your best bet to help you select a wine. She will usually know what wines go best with the food you're ordering and will also be extremely appreciative of your interest in the list. Try consulting the sommelier, a wine specialist, or the restaurant's proprietor for suggestions.

Here are some face-saving methods for getting help choosing a wine when you're dining out:

- ✔ If you aren't sure how to pronounce the wine's name, point to it on the list, or use the wine's item or bin number (if there is one).

- ✔ Point out two or three wines on the list to the sommelier or server and say, "I'm considering these wines. Which one do you recommend?" This approach is also a subtle way of communicating your price range.

- ✔ Ask to *see* one or two bottles; your familiarity with the labels, seeing the name of an importer whose other wines you've enjoyed, or some other aspect of the label may help you make up your mind.

- ✔ Ask whether any half-bottles (375 milliliters) or 500-milliliter bottles are available. Sometimes they're not listed, but smaller bottles give you wider ordering possibilities. For example, you might drink one half-bottle of white wine and a half or full (750 milliliters) bottle of red wine.

- ✔ Mention the food you plan to order and ask for suggestions of wines that would complement the meal.

# Handling the Wine Presentation Ritual

In many restaurants, when you order a bottle, the wine presentation occurs with such solemnity and ceremony that you'd think you were involved in high church or temple services. The hushed tones of the server, the ritualized performance — the very seriousness of it all can make you want to laugh (but that seems wrong, kind of like laughing in church). At the very least, you may be tempted to tell your server, "Lighten up! It's just a bottle of fermented fruit juice!"

Actually, though, there's some logic behind the Wine Presentation Ritual. Step by step, the Ritual (and the logic) goes like this:

1. **The server or sommelier presents the bottle to you (assuming that you're the person who ordered the wine) for inspection.**

   The point of this procedure is to make sure that the bottle *is* in fact the bottle you ordered. Check the label carefully; about 15 to 20 percent of the time, it's either the wrong bottle or not the vintage shown on the list. Feel the bottle with your hand to determine whether its temperature seems to be correct; head to Chapter 4 in Book I if you're not sure what the correct temperature of a wine is. (This is also a good time to pretend you recognize something about the label, as if the wine is an old friend, even if you've never seen it before.) If you're satisfied with the bottle, nod your approval to the server.

2. **The server removes the cork and places it in front of you.**

   The purpose of this step is for you to determine, by smelling and visually inspecting the cork, whether the cork is in good condition, and whether the cork seems to be the legitimate cork for that bottle of wine. Once in your life, you may discover a vintage year or winery name on your cork. But most of the time, the presentation of the cork is inconsequential.

   In rare instances, a wine may be so corky (see Chapter 4 in Book I) that the cork itself will have an unpleasant odor. On even rarer occasions, the cork might be totally wet and shriveled or very dry and crumbly; either situation suggests that air has gotten into the wine and spoiled it.

   If the cork manages to raise your suspicions, you should still wait to smell or taste the wine itself before deciding whether to reject the bottle. But if you want to be a wise-guy, put the cork into your mouth, chew it, and then pronounce to the wide-eyed server that it's just fine!

3. **If your wine needs decanting, the server decants it.**

   For more info on decanting, flip to Chapter 4 in Book I.

4. **The server pours a small amount of wine into your glass and waits.**

   At this point, you're *not* supposed to say, "Is that all you're giving me?!" You're expected to take a sniff of the wine, perhaps a little sip, and then either nod your approval to the server or murmur, "It's fine." Actually, this is an important step of the Ritual because if something is wrong with the wine, *now*'s the time to return it — not after you've finished half the bottle! For a review of wine-tasting technique, turn to Chapter 5 in Book I before you head out to the restaurant.

If you're not really sure whether the condition of the wine is acceptable, ask for someone else's opinion at your table and then make a group decision. Otherwise, you risk feeling foolish by either returning the bottle later after it has been declared defective by one of your guests, or by drinking the stuff when it becomes clear to you later that something's wrong with it. Either way, you suffer. So take as long as you need to on this step.

If you decide that the bottle is out of condition, describe to the server what you find wrong with the wine, using the best language you can. (*Musty* or *dank* are easily understood descriptors.) Be sympathetic to the fact that you're causing more work for him, but don't be overly apologetic. (Why should you be? You didn't make the wine!) Let him smell or taste the wine himself if he wants to, but don't let him make you feel guilty.

Depending on whether the sommelier or wine specialist agrees that it's a bad bottle or thinks you just don't understand the wine, he may bring you another bottle of the same, or he may bring you the wine list so you can select a different wine. Either way, the Ritual begins again from the top.

5. **If you accept the wine, the server pours the wine into your guests' glasses and then finally into yours.**

   Now you're allowed to relax.

---

## Twice the price

A few profit-minded restaurateurs train their servers to maximize wine sales in every way possible — even at the customers' expense. For example, some servers are trained to refill wine glasses liberally so that the bottle is emptied before the main course arrives (which can happen all the more easily when the glasses are large). Upon emptying the bottle, the server asks, "Shall I bring another bottle of the same wine?" Depending on how much wine is in everyone's glass and how much wine your guests tend to drink, you may not *need* another bottle, but your tendency will be to say yes to avoid looking stingy.

An even trickier practice is to refill the glasses starting with the host, so that the bottle runs dry before each of the guests has had a refill. How can you refuse a second bottle at the expense of your guests' enjoyment?! You'll have to order that second bottle — and you should let the manager know how you feel about it when you leave. (But remember, these nefarious restaurant practices are the exception rather than the rule.)

# Chapter 8

# The Urge to Own: Collecting Wine

## In This Chapter

▶ Setting up your wine-collecting game plan

▶ Knowing where to find the wines you desire

▶ Storing your wine the right way, regardless of the space you have available

▶ Documenting what's in your collection

*M*ost people consume wines very quickly after buying them. If that's your custom, you have plenty of company. But many people who enjoy wine operate a bit differently. Oh, sure, they buy wine because they intend to drink it; they're just not exactly sure *when* they'll drink it. And until they do drink it, they get pleasure out of knowing that the bottles are waiting for them. If you count yourself in this second group, you're probably a wine collector at heart. The chase, to you, is every bit as thrilling as the consummation.

Suppose you *are* a wine collector at heart. You read about a wine that sounds terrific. Your curiosity is piqued; you want to try it. But your local wine shop doesn't have it. Neither does the best store in the next town. Or maybe you decide to balance your wine collection by buying some mature wines. But the few older wines you can find in wine shops aren't really what you want.

How do other wine lovers manage to get their hands on special bottles of wine when you can't? This chapter clues you in to their methods as well as how to balance your inventory, choose good wines to stockpile, create suitable storage conditions, and keep track of the wines you have on hand.

## Creating a Wine-Collecting Strategy

If you're a closet wine collector, developing a wine-buying strategy can prevent a haphazard collection of uninteresting or worthless bottles from happening to you. (And even if you never intend to have a wine collection, putting at least a little thought into your wine purchases is always worthwhile.) A strategy ensures that your inventory is balanced so you don't find yourself drinking the same type of wine over and over and over again; it also helps you purchase wines you actually like. The next two sections guide you on both strategy-setting fronts.

## Planning for a balanced inventory

The first step in formulating a wine-buying strategy is to consider

- ✔ How much wine you drink
- ✔ How much wine you want to own (and can store properly)
- ✔ How much money you're prepared to spend on wine
- ✔ What types of wine you enjoy drinking

Unless you strike a balance on these issues, you can end up broke, bored, frustrated, or in the vinegar business!

A balanced inventory is varied in the following ways:

- ✔ **By name:** A well-planned wine inventory features a range of wines. It can be heavy in one or two types of wine that you particularly enjoy, but it has other types of wine too. If you like California Cabernet Sauvignons, for example, you may decide to make them your specialty. But consider that you may grow weary of them if you have nothing else to drink night after night. By purchasing other wines as well, you can have the fun of exploring different types of wine.

- ✔ **By category:** Table wines, of course, are the bulk of most wine collections. But having a few apéritif wines (such as Champagne or dry Sherry) and dessert wines (such as Port or sweet white wines) on hand is a good idea so you're prepared when occasions arise.

- ✔ **By price:** Another hallmark of a balanced collection is a healthy selection of inexpensive wines ($8 to $18 a bottle) that you can enjoy on casual occasions and important wines that demand a special occasion. Purchasing only expensive wines is unrealistic. You need wines that you can open at any time with anyone.

## Selecting good wines for collecting

Unless your intention is to fill your cellar with wines that bring you the greatest return on investment when you later sell them — in other words, unless you aren't interested in actually drinking the wines you own — you should like a wine before buying it. (We're not talking about all those bottles you buy while you're playing the field and experimenting with new wines — just those that you're thinking of making a commitment to by buying in quantity.) Liking a wine before you buy it sounds like the plainest common sense, but you'd be surprised at how many people buy a wine merely because somebody gave it a high rating!

The following sections run through some great everyday wines, as well as some top collectible, age-worthy wines. You certainly aren't limited to the wines listed here, but use the ideas as a guide when you're just starting out.

**Book I**

**Under-
standing
Wine**

### Everyday wines to have on hand

What you stock as everyday wines depends on your personal taste. Great candidates for everyday white wines include

- ✔ Simple white Burgundies, such as Mâcon-Villages or St.-Véran
- ✔ Sauvignon Blancs from New Zealand, France (Sancerre and Pouilly-Fumé), and California
- ✔ Pinot Gris/Pinot Grigio from Oregon, Alsace, and Italy
- ✔ Italian Pinot Bianco
- ✔ Flavorful Italian whites such as Vermentino, Verdicchio, or Falanghina
- ✔ Grüner Veltliner from Austria
- ✔ Riesling from Germany, Austria, or Alsace
- ✔ Moschofilero from Greece
- ✔ Albariños from Spain

For everyday red wines, try Italian reds such as Barbera, Dolcetto, Montepulciano d'Abruzzo, Valpolicella, and simple (under $20) Chianti. These red wines are enjoyable young; versatile enough to go well with the simple, flavorful foods many people eat every day; and sturdy enough to age for a couple of years if you don't get around to them (that is, they won't deteriorate quickly).

Other recommended everyday red wines include Beaujolais, Côtes du Rhône, and lighter-bodied (under $15) Bordeaux.

### Reputable age-worthy wines

In planning your wine collection, include some age-worthy wines that you buy in their youth when their prices are lowest. Many of the better red wines, such as Bordeaux, Barolo, and Hermitage, often aren't at their best for at least ten years after the vintage — and some of them are difficult to find after they're ready to drink. Aging is also the rule for some fine white Burgundies (such as Corton-Charlemagne); better white Bordeaux; Sauternes; German Rieslings and late-harvest wines; and Vintage Port, which usually requires about 20 years of aging before it matures!

Top choices for age-worthy white wines include

- Above all, grand cru and premier cru white Burgundies — such as Corton-Charlemagne, Bâtard- and Chevalier-Montrachets, Meursault, and Chablis Grand Crus
- Better (over $30) white Bordeaux
- Great German and Austrian Rieslings
- Alsace Rieslings or Gewürztraminers

Among the many long-lived red wines, some likely candidates for *cellaring* (the term for letting wines mature) are

- Fine Bordeaux
- Grand cru and premier cru Burgundies
- Big Italian reds, such as Barolo, Barbaresco, Chianti Classico Riserva, Brunello di Montalcino, Taurasi, and Super-Tuscan blends
- From Spain: Rioja, Ribeira del Duero, and Priorato wines
- From California: Better Cabernet Sauvignons (and Cabernet blends)
- From the Rhône: Hermitage, Côte Rôtie, and Cornas
- Portugal's Barca Velha and other good Douro table wines
- Australia's Grange (Penfolds), the Henschke Shiraz wines, such as Hill of Grace, and other superpremium Shirazes

Other age-worthy wines include

- Finer Champagnes (usually Vintage Champagnes and prestige cuvées)
- The finest dessert wines, such as late-harvest German Rieslings, French Sauternes, sweet Vouvrays from the Loire Valley, Vintage Port, and Madeira

# Getting the Wines You Want

Wine lovers who've really caught the collecting bug face a dreadful Catch-22: The more desirable a wine is, the harder it is to get. And the harder it is to get, the more desirable it is.

Several forces conspire to frustrate buyers who want to get their hands on special bottles. First, some of the best wines are made in ridiculously small quantities. Quantity and quality aren't necessarily incompatible in winemaking, but at the very highest echelons of quality, there usually isn't much quantity to go around.

Today, many small-production wines sell *on allocation,* which means that distributors restrict the quantity that any one store can purchase, sometimes limiting stores to as few as six bottles of a particular wine. Most stores, in turn, limit customers to one or two bottles. Certain wines are allocated in such a way that they're available primarily at restaurants.

The issue of allocations leads to the second factor preventing equal opportunity in wine buying: Wine buying is a competitive sport. If you're there first, you get the wine, and the next guy doesn't. Buying highly rated wines is especially competitive. When a wine receives a very high score from critics, a feeding frenzy results among wine lovers, leaving little (if anything) for Johnnies-come-lately.

A final factor limiting availability of some wines is that wineries usually sell each wine just once, when the wine is young. In the case of many fine wines, such as top Bordeaux wines, the wine isn't at its best yet. But most wine merchants can't afford to store the wine for selling years later. This means that aged wines are usually hard to get.

When the wine plays hard to get, you have to play hardball, which means you have to look beyond your normal supply sources. Your allies in this game are wine auction houses, wine shops in other cities, and, in the case of domestic wines, the wineries themselves.

## *Buying wines at auctions*

The clear advantage of buying wine through auction houses is the availability of older and rarer wines. In fact, auction houses are the principal source of mature wines — their specialty. (In general, you can obtain younger wines at better prices elsewhere.) At auctions, you can buy wines that are practically impossible to obtain any other way. Many of these wines have been off the market for years, sometimes decades!

The main disadvantage of buying wine at auction is that you don't always know the storage history (or *provenance*) of the wine you're considering buying. The wine may have been stored in somebody's warm apartment for years. And if the wine does come from a reputable wine collector's temperature-controlled cellar, and thus has impeccable credentials, it'll sell for a very high price.

Also, almost all auction houses charge a *buyer's premium,* a tacked-on charge that's 15 to 20 percent of your bid. In general, prices of wine at auctions range from fair (rarely, you even find bargains) to exorbitant.

If you're personally present at an auction, be careful not to catch auction fever. The desire to win can motivate you to pay more for a wine than it's worth. Carefully thought-out, judicious bidding is in order. To plan your attack, you can obtain a catalog for the auction ahead of time, usually for a small fee. The catalog lists wines for sale by lots (usually groupings of 3, 6, or 12 bottles) with a suggested minimum bid per lot.

## Buying wine via catalog or Internet

A real plus to buying wine online or perusing wine shop catalogs and order-ing from your armchair is, of course, the convenience (not to mention the time savings). Most major wine retail stores have good Web sites and issue a wine catalog two or more times a year to customers on their mailing lists; just give 'em a call to obtain a free catalog.

Other advantages of buying wine long-distance include the availability of scarce wines — sometimes the *only* way to buy certain wines is by catalog, because sought-after wines made in small quantities aren't available in every market — and (sometimes) lower prices than you might pay in your home market.

If a wine you want is available locally, but you don't live in a market where pricing is competitive, you may decide that you can save money by ordering the wine from a retailer in another city — even after the added shipping costs.

One minor disadvantage of buying wine by catalog or online is that an adult usually must be available to receive the wine. Also, because wine is perishable, you have to make certain that it's not delivered to you during hot (above 75 degrees Fahrenheit) or cold (below 28 degrees Fahrenheit) weather. Spring and autumn are usually the best times for wine deliveries.

Because wine contains alcohol, it doesn't move as freely through com-mercial channels as other products do. Each state must decide whether to permit wineries and stores outside its borders to ship wine to its residents, and under which conditions. By requiring consumers to buy wine only from local, licensed retail stores or wineries, a state government can be sure it's getting all the tax revenue it's entitled to on every wine transaction within its jurisdiction.

Most wine shops and wineries are sympathetic to out-of-state customers, but out-of-state deliveries are risky for their businesses, depending on the regu-lations in their state and the destination state. The risk is all theirs too: The store or winery can lose its license, whereas all the buyer loses is any wine that's confiscated by the authorities.

If you want to buy wine from an out-of-state winery or merchant, discuss the issue with the people there. If shipping to you isn't legal, the shop owner can sometimes find a solution, such as holding the wine for you to pick up in person or shipping it to a friend or relative in a legal state. However, different rules apply when you purchase wine from an out-of-state winery that you're visiting. Wine drinkers may legally ship home wines that they purchase during visits to out-of-state wineries, so buy all the wine you want — just be sure to factor the shipping costs into your final total.

**Book I**

**Under-standing Wine**

### Some U.S. wine stores worth knowing

Listing *all* the leading wine stores that sell wine by catalog, newsletter, or the Internet would be impossible. But the purveyors listed in Table 8-1 are some of the best. Most of them either specialize in catalog sales or in certain kinds of fine wine that can be difficult to obtain elsewhere. The major Web sites for purchasing wine online are those of these bricks-and-mortar wine shops. Table 8-1 lists the stores and their main wine specialties, as well as their contact information and locations.

| Table 8-1 | Top U.S. Wine Shops and Their Specialties | | | |
|---|---|---|---|---|
| *Wine Store* | *Location* | *Phone Number* | *Web Site* | *Wine Specialty* |
| Acker Merrall & Condit | New York, NY | 212-787-1700 | `www.acker wines.com` | Burgundy, California Cabernets |
| Astor Wines & Spirits | New York, NY | 212-674-7500 | `www.astor wines.com` | French, California, Spanish |
| BLM Wine + Spirits | Allston, MA | 617-734-7700 | `www.blm wine.com` | Italian, Burgundy, Rhône |
| Burgundy Wine Company | New York, NY | 212-691-9092 | `www. burgundy wine company. com` | Burgundy, fine California Chardonnay and Pinot Noir, Rhône |
| Calvert Woodley | Washington, D.C. | 202-966-4400 | `www.calvert woodley. com` | California, Bordeaux, other French |
| Chambers Street Wines | New York, NY | 212-227-1434 | `www. chambers street wines.com` | Loire, biodynamic/ organic wine |

*(continued)*

### Table 8-1 *(continued)*

| Wine Store | Location | Phone Number | Web Site | Wine Specialty |
|---|---|---|---|---|
| The Chicago Wine Company | Wood Dale, IL | 630-594-2972 | www.tcwc.com | Bordeaux, Burgundy, California |
| Corti Brothers | Sacramento, CA | 916-736-3803 | www.cortibros.biz | Italian, California, dessert wines |
| D&M Wines & Liquors | San Francisco, CA | 415-346-1325 | www.dandm.com | Champagne |
| Garnet Wines & Liquors | New York, NY | 212-772-3211 | www.garnetwine.com | Bordeaux, Champagne (great prices) |
| Hart Davis Hart Wine Co. | Chicago, IL | 312-482-9996 | www.hdhwine.com | Bordeaux, Burgundy |
| Kermit Lynch Wine Merchant | Berkeley, CA | 510-524-1524 | www.kermitlynch.com | French country wines, Burgundy, Rhône |
| Le Dû's Wines | New York, NY | 212-924-6999 | www.leduwines.com | French, Italian, small estates |
| MacArthur Beverages | Washington, D.C. | 202-338-1433 | www.bassins.com | California, Burgundy, Bordeaux, Italian, Rhône, Alsace, Australian, German, Vintage Port |
| McCarthy & Schiering | Seattle, WA | 206-524-9500, 206-282-8500 | www.mccarthyandschiering.com | Washington, Oregon |
| Mills Fine Wine & Spirits | Annapolis, MD | 410-263-2888 | www.millswine.com | Bordeaux, other French, Italian |
| Morrell & Co. | New York, NY | 212-688-9370 | www.morrell.com | California, Italian, French |

| Wine Store | Location | Phone Number | Web Site | Wine Specialty |
|---|---|---|---|---|
| North Berkeley Imports | Berkeley, CA | 800-266-6585 | www. north berkeley imports. com | French, Italian |
| PJ's Wine Warehouse | New York, NY | 212-567-5500 | www. pjwine.com | Italian, Spanish |
| Pop's Wines & Spirits | Island Park, NY | 516-431-0025 | www.pops wine.com | California, Italian, Bordeaux, Long Island |
| The Rare Wine Company | Sonoma, CA | 800-999-4342 | www.rare wineco.com | Italian, French, Port, Madeira |
| Rosenthal Wine Merchant | New York, NY | 212-249-6650 | www.mad rose.com | Burgundy, Rhône, Loire, Italian |
| Royal Wine Merchants | New York, NY | 212-689-4855 | www.royal wine merchants. com | French (especially rare Bordeaux), Italian, Burgundy, hard-to-find wines |
| Sam's Wines & Spirits | Chicago, IL | 877-342-3611 | www.sams wine.com | French, Italian, California |
| Sherry-Lehmann Wine and Spirits | New York, NY | 212-838-7500 | www. sherry-lehmann. com | Bordeaux, Burgundy, California, Italian |
| Twenty-Twenty Wine Merchants | West Los Angeles, CA | 310-447-2020 | www.2020 wines.com | Bordeaux (especially rare, old), California, Burgundy |
| Vino | New York, NY | 212-725-6516 | www.vino site.com | Italian |

*(continued)*

**Table 8-1 (continued)**

| Wine Store | Location | Phone Number | Web Site | Wine Specialty |
|---|---|---|---|---|
| Wally's | Los Angeles, CA | 310-475-0606 | `www.wallywine.com` | Italian, California, French, Champagne |
| The Wine Club | San Francisco, CA | 415-512-9086 | `www.thewineclub.com` | Bordeaux, California |
| Zachys Wine and Liquor, Inc. | Scarsdale, NY | 800-723-0241 | `www.zachys.com` | Bordeaux, Burgundy |

### Some wine Web sites to point the way

Here are a few Internet sites worth checking out when you want to purchase wine online — all are great resources to point you to specific merchants:

- `www.wineaccess.com`: Wine Access calls itself a "wine shopping community." In fact, it's a mall of sorts, where you can purchase wine from numerous participating wine shops across the United States or from participating wineries. The site also features news about trends and ways to sign up for newsletters.

- `www.klwines.com`: Californian retailer K&L Wines' critically acclaimed Web site is easy to navigate and features a comprehensive inventory, knowledgeable commentary, and a blog.

- `www.wine-searcher.com`: Wine Searcher searches for wines that you name and lists stores and prices for them, including merchants outside the United States.

- `www.wineweb.com`: The Wine Web gives you the ability to buy wine through participating retailers or wineries.

# Creating a Home for Your Wines

If you've decided to collect wine — or if you discover that a wine collection is happening to you — please take heed: Poorly stored wines make disappointment after disappointment inevitable.

The following are key features of a good wine storage area:

- The temperature stays cool, ideally in the 53 degrees to 59 degrees Fahrenheit range.

- The temperature is fairly constant (wide swings in temperature aren't good for the wine).

- The area is damp or humid, with a minimum of 70 percent humidity and a maximum of 95 percent (mold sets in above 95 percent).

- The area is free from vibrations, which can travel through the wine; heavy traffic; and motors cycling on and off, such as in refrigerators or washers/dryers.

- The area is free from light, especially direct sunlight (the ultraviolet rays of the sun are especially harmful to wine).

- The storage area is free from chemical odors, such as paints, paint remover, and so on.

If you plan to keep wines indefinitely, you really need a wine storage facility with controlled temperature and humidity. Controlled conditions are especially important if you live where the temperature exceeds 70 degrees Fahrenheit for any length of time. Without proper storage, you may be tempted to drink those fine wines long before they reach their best drinking period, or worse yet, the wines may die an untimely death in your closet, garage, or warm cellar.

The good news is that if you have enough space in your home to section off a part of it to use for storage and can integrate climate and humidity control in that space, you can have your very own wine cellar. If space is limited, you're not out of luck — you can simply purchase a portable wine cave and call it a day!

If you plan to build a wine cellar or buy a wine cave, allow for expansion in your wine collection. Like most waistlines, wine cellars inevitably grow larger with the passing years.

## A wine cellar, most likely a do-it-yourself project

If the place where you intend to store your wine is very cool (below 60 degrees Fahrenheit) and very damp (75 percent humidity or higher) year-round — like in your recently inherited Scottish castle, for example — you can be the lucky owner of a *passive wine cellar*. (It's called passive because you don't have to do anything to it, such as cool it or humidify it.) Usually, only deep cellars completely below ground level with thick stones or comparable insulation can be completely passive in temperate climates. Passive cellars are certainly the ideal way to store wines, and you can save a lot of money on their upkeep.

However, most collectors are neither lucky enough to have a passive wine cellar nor fortunate enough to be able to create one without extraordinary expense and trouble (bulldozers, wrecking crews, and so on). But second best — an artificially cooled and/or humidified room — is far better than nothing.

The following sections provide a little do-it-yourself guidance for building your own makeshift wine cellar.

### Establishing the right conditions

When creating a makeshift wine cellar, make sure you include the following components:

- ✔ **Humidity control:** Buy a *hygrometer* (an instrument that measures humidity) for your wine storage area. A hygrometer gives the percentage of humidity and a digital reading of the temperature. (Hygrometers are available through wine accessory catalogs, such as *The Wine Enthusiast,* www.wineenthusiast.com.)

  During cold weather periods, humidity can drop very low in wine storage rooms — often below 50 percent. A large humidifier can help raise the humidity. If you don't want to invest in a humidifier, try placing several large buckets of water in the room. They may not be as effective as a large humidifier, but they'll help.

- ✔ **Climate control:** Professional cooling units are available, and you can find them advertised in wine accessory catalogs and wine magazines. These climate-control devices humidify and cool the air in a room. These units come in various capacities to suit rooms of different dimensions. Many require professional installation and typically cost from $600 to $2,400, depending on their capacity.

- ✔ **Insulation:** Your choice of insulation is of utmost importance. The ideal insulation is a 3-inch-thick, thermoplastic resin called polyurethane. It's odorless, doesn't absorb moisture, and makes a fine seal. Even when a cooling unit isn't running, temperatures will change extremely slowly in most wine rooms with this kind of insulation.

  Fiberglass insulation is bad news because it absorbs the moisture created by your cooling unit.

### Organizing for easy retrieval

Racking systems vary from elaborate redwood racks to simple metal or plastic types. The choice of material and configuration really hinges on how much you want to spend and your own personal taste.

Large, diamond-shaped wooden (or synthetic composition) racks are popular because they efficiently store up to eight bottles per section and make maximum use of space. Such racks also permit the easy removal of individual bottles.

A rack configuration that gives each wine its own cubbyhole is more expensive; if you're checking out such racks, consider whether any of your oversized bottles (such as bulbous sparkling wine bottles) may be too large to fit the racks. (And consider whether your half-bottles may be too small!)

Some collectors prefer to store their wine in the wines' original wooden crates. (Many classic wines, such as Bordeaux and Vintage Port, come in these crates; you can also usually pick up empty wooden crates in wine stores.) The crates are beneficial for storing wine because the wine remains in a dark environment inside the case, and the temperature changes very slowly thanks to the mass of wine bottles packed together in the closed case. The downside? Retrieving a bottle from the bottom row of the case can be rather inconvenient.

Cardboard boxes aren't suitable for wine storage. The chemicals used to make the cardboard can eventually affect the wine. Also, over time, the cardboard boxes become damaged from the moisture in the air, assuming that you're maintaining the proper level of humidity in your cellar.

## A portable wine cave, if space is limited

If you live in a house that has either a cellar or a separate area for your wine, consider yourself fortunate. But what if you live in cramped quarters and have no space to spare? In such a case, you have three choices:

- ✔ Leave your wine in a friend's or relative's house (provided he has adequate storage facilities — and you trust him not to drink your wine!).
- ✔ Rent storage space in a refrigerated public warehouse.
- ✔ Buy a *wine cave* — also known as a *wine vault* — a self-contained, refrigerated unit that you plug into an electrical outlet.

The first two options are barely acceptable because they don't give you immediate access to your wine. Making a trip every time you want to get your hands on your own wine is downright inconvenient. And both of these options rob you of the pleasure of having your wines readily available in your home where you can look at them, fondle the bottles, or show them off to your friends.

That makes the best storage solution a wine cave. Many wine caves resemble attractive pieces of furniture, either vertical or horizontal credenzas. Some have glass doors, and all of them can be locked. Wine caves range in size and capacity from a tiny unit that holds at most 24 bottles to really large units that hold up to 2,800 bottles, with many sizes in between. Prices range from $300 to about $8,000. You can find wine caves advertised extensively in wine accessory catalogs and in the back pages of wine magazines.

If purchasing a wine cave isn't financially feasible at the moment, don't turn to your refrigerator as a cool storage option. In fact, good wine or Champagne should be left in the refrigerator for no more than a week. Not only is the refrigerator motor harmful, but the excessively cold temperature (as low as 35 degrees Fahrenheit) tends to numb and flatten the wine's flavors.

# Keeping Track of Your Inventory

When you're not only a wine drinker but also a wine collector, you become aware that you need to keep track of all your wine so that

- ✔ You can find a bottle quickly when you're looking for it.

- ✔ You know what you own. (Many a bottle has gone over the hill because the owner forgot she had it!)

- ✔ You can show off your wine collection to your friends (something akin to showing your baby's pictures).

You can keep track of your wine in many different ways. A wine inventory on paper should include a list of the specific wines in your collection, the number of each, and the location. If you're especially thorough, you may want to also record the

- ✔ Vintage

- ✔ Producer

- ✔ Wine name

- ✔ Appellation

- ✔ Region

- ✔ Country

- ✔ Type (red, white, rosé, sparkling, apéritif, or dessert)

- ✔ Quantity owned

- ✔ Price paid (per bottle)

- ✔ Value (the latest estimated worth, per bottle)

- ✔ Size of bottle (to indicate 1.5-liter magnums, half bottles, and so on)

You don't need anything fancy for your inventory. A plain old notebook or a standard spreadsheet is a perfectly serviceable option that costs nothing (or next to nothing). But of course you can buy special software and log books for the project.

# Book II
# France: A Wine Superstar

"I want a Champagne that says 'Congratulations on your promotion even though we both know you don't deserve it.'"

# In This Book . . .

**W**hy did France become the most famous place in the world for wine? For one thing, the French have been doing it for a long time — making wine, that is. Even before the Romans conquered Gaul and planted vineyards, the Greeks arrived with their vines.

Equally important is the magical combination of climate and soil that yields grapes that make breathtaking wines. And what grapes! France is the home of almost all the renowned varieties in the world: Cabernet Sauvignon, Chardonnay, Merlot, Pinot Noir, Syrah, and Sauvignon Blanc, just to name a few.

The chapters in this book take you through the magnificent winemaking regions of this standard-setting nation, which (not coincidentally!) has the highest per capita wine consumption of any major country.

Here are the contents of Book II at a glance:

# Chapter 1

# French Wine Today

**S**ome people are just born with certain talents. Some countries are just born with certain gifts. In the case of France, the ability to grow wine grapes and make good wine is hard-wired into the land and the people who live there. That's why France is not only the greatest wine-producing country on Earth but also the greatest wine culture.

France has been the leader of the winemaking world for centuries. It's number one in wine consumption and, in many years, wine production. In the quality department, the most critically acclaimed, most treasured red wines, white wines, sparkling wines, *and* sweet wines all come from France. The country's renown is such that winemakers from all over the world find inspiration and motivation in French wines. This chapter helps you better understand the allure of French wines by exploring France's natural talents, the concept of *terroir,* the wide range of French wines, and the intricacies of French wine laws and labels.

## Natural Talents: Climate and Soil

France's thousands of years of winemaking experience count for a lot. But the fact is, France had a couple other things going for her since Day One: climates extremely suitable for growing high-quality wine grapes and the right types of soils in the right climates.

France is large by European standards — in fact, it's the largest country in western Europe — but compared to countries such as the United States or Australia, it isn't really such a big place. (All of France could fit easily into Texas, for example, with plenty of room to spare.) And yet, France has a strong diversity of soil types and climates. Each of France's major wine regions has different growing conditions for its grapes. (Figure 1-1 depicts France's wine regions.)

**Figure 1-1:**
France's
wine
regions.

The following sections help you better understand the role that France's diversified climates and soils — as well as her people's years of experience — play in making the country such a key player in the world's wine scene.

## Climate ups and downs

Because French wines are so acclaimed, wine people tend to credit France with having an ideal location for grape-growing and winemaking. The 45th parallel, which runs through the regions of Bordeaux and the Rhône Valley, has taken on mythical connotations as the It position for fine wine production.

In reality, though, a lot of seriously good wine comes from places that occupy a much more southerly position than France does — such as all of Spain and Portugal, California, and most of Italy (not to mention, in the Southern Hemisphere, Chile, Argentina, Australia, New Zealand, and South Africa!). Furthermore, plenty of France's wine regions are even more northerly than Bordeaux; Champagne and Alsace, for example, are situated about as north as wine grapes can viably grow. From a global perspective, France would seem to be out of the mainstream of wine production, latitude-wise.

But latitude doesn't tell the whole story. France has ideal climates for growing wine grapes thanks to where the country happens to be situated relative to the rest of Europe — and thanks to the lay of the land within France's borders.

- Water surrounds France on three sides: the Atlantic Ocean on the west, the English Channel on the north, and the Mediterrean Sea along part of the country's southern border. These bodies of water influence the climate of the land nearby. In particular, winds passing over the Atlantic's Gulf Stream carry moisture and warm air to western France, providing a climate that's more suitable for grape-growing than France's northerly position might suggest.

- The Massif Central, a high plateau in south-central France, blocks the Atlantic's maritime influence about halfway across the country. It also creates a particular climate in eastern France (cold winters and hot but relatively short summers) that's distinctly different from the damp, temperate climate in the west. Farther east, France is landlocked and mountainous, with the mighty Alps Mountains separating France from Italy and Switzerland.

- The Mediterranean Sea creates yet another climate pattern in southern France: warm, dry, long summers and mild, rainy winters.

According to the way experts categorize climates, in fact, France boasts all three of the major climates for grape-growing and wine production:

- ✔ The maritime climate (in the Bordeaux region and elsewhere in western France)

- ✔ The continental climate (in the regions of Alsace and Burgundy)

- ✔ The Mediterranean climate (in the southern Rhône Valley region and in southern France)

These different climates each favor the cultivation of different grape varieties and the production of different types of wine.

## The dirt on France's old dirt

The variation in soil types within France has to do with the geological origins of the European continent: the melting of polar ice caps, the drying of seas, the decomposition of rocks, and so forth. At least two books are devoted entirely to the subsoils and soils of France's wine regions — that's how complex the soils are.

Different wine regions of France have markedly different soils:

- ✔ Gravel in the western part of Bordeaux

- ✔ Chalky soil in Champagne, in the northeast

- ✔ Granite in Beaujolais, in the southeast

- ✔ Large stones in the Châteauneuf-du-Pape district of the southern Rhône Valley

Even within individual wine regions, the soil varies quite a lot. The difference between western Bordeaux and eastern Bordeaux is one classic example: Different soils in each area favor different grape varieties. Within the region of Alsace, the soils change literally from one hillside to the next; within Burgundy, soils change between vineyards separated from each other by the width of a cow path.

None of this is to say that French dirt is any better than any other country's dirt, though. What's important about France's soils is that they're the right soils in the right climates for the right grape varieties. Where the climate is rainy (as in Bordeaux), for example, the soil provides good drainage. Where there's an impressionable grape variety, such as Pinot Noir, the soil varies from patch to patch (as in Burgundy) to create compellingly individual wines.

## *Time's role in France's wine*

France's climate and soil are natural endowments, but choosing the right grape variety for each climate and soil is a human challenge. Enter those thousands of years of experience that the French have in growing grapes and making wines. Through centuries of trial and error, they've managed to discover which grape varieties do best where.

For most of France's history, wine grapes grew all over the country; transportation being difficult, each community had to produce its own wine in order to have any. That all changed in the 19th century, when the double whammy of vineyard devastation (via fungal diseases and the phylloxera bug) and better transportation (railroads) put many areas out of the grape-growing business. The French wine regions that exist today are the survivors — the regions whose climate, soil, and grape varieties make wines worth making.

# *French Wine-Think: Understanding Terroir*

Many French winemakers attribute every nuance in a wine to the particular place where the grapes grow — to the rain that falls or refrains from falling; the sun that shines down on the vineyard; the wind that warms or cools the air; and the soil that holds the rain or drains it, reflects the sun's heat back onto the grapes, or contains just the right minerals.

The French have a single word for the whole package of natural, interactive forces that affect the grapevine and its fruit: *terroir* (pronounced ter-wahr). *Terroir* encompasses

- ✔ The soil and subsoil of a vineyard, including its mineral content, fertility, and drainage
- ✔ How the vineyard is situated, on a slope, for example, or near a river
- ✔ The climate of the wine region, including sun, heat, wind, rain, and humidity
- ✔ The grape variety or varieties that grow in the vineyard

Every wine comes from a unique *terroir* and — in the French way of looking at wine — is what it is because of its *terroir*.

Of course, every French wine also has a winemaker who turns the fruit of the vineyard into wine. And there's no arguing with the fact that what the winemaker does — such as fermenting the grape juice at a certain temperature or aging a wine in a particular type of oak barrel — can affect the quality and style of the wine. For the most part, however, French winemakers perceive their responsibility as bringing out in the wine what the *terroir* put into the grapes. (And because of the long history of each region, the winemakers have a pretty good idea of what that is.)

The title that most French winemakers use — *vigneron* — suggests what they consider their role to be. The word means "winegrower," not "winemaker." Their wines grow from their vineyards, as opposed to being "made" in their wineries.

The concept of *terroir* is so fundamental to French wine that it even dictates how the wines are named: The overwhelming majority of French wines carry the name of the place where the grapes grow, because the place (rather than just the grape variety) is what makes the wines the way they are. Depending on the wine, the place might be any of the following (see the later section "Understanding a French Wine Label" for more on names and regions):

- ✔ A large wine region
- ✔ A district within a region
- ✔ A single vineyard

# The Variety of French Wine

When it comes to wine, quantity doesn't necessarily equate with quality. In fact, the opposite is often true: The smaller the quantity produced, the more concentrated and higher quality a wine will be. Luckily for the reputation of French wines, the huge quantity produced each year includes hundreds of different types of wine.

Variety, in fact, is the rule for French wines, which sell anywhere from less than $8 a bottle to several thousand dollars a bottle and are

- ✔ White, red, and pink
- ✔ Still (nonbubbly) wines and bubbly wines
- ✔ Dry wines, semidry wines, and sweet wines
- ✔ Simple wines for enjoying while they're young and serious wines that aren't at their best until they age for a few decades
- ✔ Handcrafted artisan wines made by small family wineries and mass-production wines made by large corporations

As you can see, French wines span the whole spectrum of what's possible in a wine. The following sections cover the characteristics of French wine in greater detail, from the grape varieties used to the wine styles made.

## The colors of France

France produces more red wine than white or *rosé* (pink) wine. Precise figures are hard to come by, because statistics tend to lump red wines with rosé wines (considering they're both made from red grape varieties). But we do know this: In 2005, 35 percent of the wine produced in France was white. Most of the remaining 65 percent was, most likely, overwhelmingly red (as opposed to rosé).

Rosé wines are made throughout France, and some of them are quite special, but they represent just a tiny part of the country's production.

## Dry, sweet, and bubbly

French wines are predominantly dry, nonsparkling wines. Sparkling wines represent less than 10 percent of France's production. Champagne itself — the major sparkling wine of France (and the world) — accounted for about 5.5 percent of French wine production in 2005. Many other regions also make sparkling wine, but in significantly smaller quantity than Champagne. (See Chapter 6 in Book II for the scoop on Champagne.)

Almost every region of France makes some type of sweet dessert wine, but no one region specializes in it. The quantity varies greatly from year to year, because sweet wine production often depends on specific weather patterns that don't visit a region predictably each year.

Quantity aside, France makes outstanding sweet wines. Sauternes, which is probably the world's most revered type of sweet wine in the eyes of serious wine collectors, carries the banner — but not without protest from the legendary sweet wines of the Loire Valley, such as Coteaux du Layon. Sweet wines from southern France, southwestern France, and the region of Alsace are also noteworthy.

## Collectable to highly affordable

French wine authorities apparently never heard the expression, "You can't be all things to all people." Or maybe, by the time that way of thinking evolved, the nature of French wines was already a *fait accompli.* However it happened, France has managed to satisfy wine drinkers across all price and ageability spectrums: from Château Lafite-Rothschild to Beaujolais Nouveau.

**Book II**

**France:
A Wine
Superstar**

France's finest wines enjoy the highest reputation of any wines anywhere, period. The best wines of the Champagne, Bordeaux, Burgundy, and Rhône regions dominate the cellars of the world's most celebrated wine collectors, as well as the auctions where rare wines are bought and sold. Bottles of mature wines from these regions can cost thousands of dollars each, depending on the wine and the vintage — that's how desirable these wines are.

But France makes plenty of midrange and inexpensive wines, too. In just about any good wine shop in the United States, you can find wines from southern France that sell for as little as $6 a bottle — good, everyday wines for casual enjoyment. Between the least expensive and the most precious French offerings are the majority of French wines — high-quality wines that cost from about $15 to $35 and are suitable either for drinking young or for aging a few years.

## *Regional characters*

In 1961, when he was president of France, Charles de Gaulle remarked, "How can you be expected to govern a country that has 246 kinds of cheese?"

The reason France has so many cheeses (now estimated at more than 700 types) is the same as the reason why it has so many wines: regional particularities. Wineries in different parts of France cultivate different grape varieties and make their wines in different ways. Even when two regions grow the same grape variety, their wines usually turn out to be distinctly different because of *terroir* differences (see the earlier "French Wine-Think: Understanding Terroir" section for more on *terroir*) or different winemaking traditions. The Sauvignon Blanc grape variety provides a good example of how the same grape makes different wines.

- In the Loire Valley, Sauvignon Blanc makes crisp, unoaked wines with concentrated, minerally flavors.

- In the Bordeaux region, winemakers frequently blend Sauvignon Blanc wine with Sémillon, making a fleshier, longer-lasting wine with more subtle flavors; often they use oak barrels, which give the wine a smoky or toasty character.

- In the south of France, Sauvignon Blanc wines have riper fruit flavors than those from either the Loire or Bordeaux.

Wine critics who sample thousands of wines each year complain about the "cookie cutter" wine phenomenon — that so many wines taste pretty much the same. Not so in France. Regional individuality is inbred among the French. That might make governing the country a challenge, but it makes drinking the country's wines an adventure.

# The grapes of France

Practically all the most famous grape varieties in the world are French varieties, meaning they either originated in France or became famous through their expression in French wines. (Chapter 1 in Book I explains grape varieties and how they differ.)

Which varieties are they? Name a variety, and chances are, it's French. Chardonnay? Yep. Merlot? Yes. Sauvignon Blanc? Right again. Cabernet Sauvignon, Pinot Noir, or Syrah? *Oui* to all three. (In fact, only two of France's top grape varieties aren't technically French. Riesling is a German variety, and Grenache originated in Spain, where it's called Garnacha.)

Over the centuries, different grape varieties have acclimated to certain regions of France. In some regions, winemakers make blended wines, from several grape varieties; in other regions, the wines derive from a single variety. Table 1-1 names the major white grape varieties of France and indicates in which of France's wine regions each grape is important. Table 1-2 does the same for France's major red grapes.

| Table 1-1 | France's Major White Grape Varieties | |
|---|---|---|
| *Grape Variety* | *Pronunciation* | *Region(s) Where Important* |
| Chardonnay | shar-dohn-nay | Burgundy; Champagne; Languedoc |
| Chenin Blanc | shen-in blahnk | Loire Valley |
| Sauvignon Blanc | saw-vee-nyon blahnk | Bordeaux; Loire Valley; southwestern France; Languedoc |
| Gewürztraminer | geh-*vairtz*-trah-mee-ner | Alsace |
| Pinot Gris | pee-noh gree | Alsace |
| Pinot Blanc | pee-noh blahnk | Alsace |
| Marsanne | mar-sahn | Rhône Valley |
| Muscadet | moos-cah-day | Loire Valley |
| Riesling | *reese*-ling | Alsace |
| Roussanne | roos-sahn | Rhône Valley |
| Sémillon | seh-mee-yohn | Bordeaux; southwestern France |
| Viognier | vee-oh-nyay | Rhône Valley; Languedoc |

| Table 1-2 | France's Major Red Grape Varieties | |
|---|---|---|
| *Grape Variety* | *Pronunciation* | *Region(s) Where Important* |
| Cabernet Sauvignon | cab-er-nay saw-vee-nyon | Bordeaux; southwestern France; Languedoc |
| Cabernet Franc | cab-er-nay frahn | Loire Valley; Bordeaux; southwestern France |
| Carignan | cah-ree-nyahn | Rhône Valley; southern France |
| Cinsault | san-soh | Rhône Valley; southern France |
| Gamay | ga-may | Beaujolais |
| Grenache | gren-ahsh | Rhône Valley; southern France |
| Merlot | mer-loh | Bordeaux; southwestern France; Languedoc |
| Malbec | mahl-bec | Southwestern France; Bordeaux |
| Mourvèdre | more-ved'r | Rhône Valley; southern France |
| Pinot Noir | pee-noh nwahr | Burgundy; Champagne |
| Syrah | see-rah | Rhône Valley; southern France |

Wine lovers often use a certain shorthand when talking about French grapes. Here's that shorthand decoded:

- **"Bordeaux varieties" (generally used in reference to red varieties):** Cabernet Sauvignon, Merlot, and Cabernet Franc, principally; Malbec and Petit Verdot are two minor red varieties of Bordeaux

- **"Red Rhône varieties":** Syrah, Grenache, Cinsault, and Mourvèdre

- **"White Rhône varieties":** Marsanne, Roussanne, Grenache Blanc, and Viognier

- **"Southern French varieties" (generally used in reference to reds):** Grenache, Cinsault, Mourvèdre, and Carignan

The wines of Bordeaux, southern France, and the Rhône Valley (the larger Southern Rhône, at least) are blends, made from several grape varieties in varying proportions. When winemakers from other parts of the world use these varieties together, they sometimes describe their wines as being "Bordeaux blends" or "Rhône blends," a more convenient lingo than naming all the varieties used.

# France's Wine Laws: The Opposite of Laissez-Faire

The first step toward understanding French wine names and labels is to realize that, in France, the government controls how wines may be named, and every wine name is a reflection of French wine law. In theory, you could discover all sorts of information about any French wine just by looking up its name in the French laws. That information would include the general vineyard territory for that wine, which grape varieties could possibly be in that wine, and so forth.

If you were to research several French wine names, you'd discover that most of them are the names of places, specifically the vineyard area where the grapes for the wines grow. Vineyard location is the organizational principle behind French wine law and the basis for naming French wines.

The upcoming sections give you an overview of French wine law basics.

## Privileged versus ordinary locales

Not all *terroirs* are equal in the eyes of French wine law. Some vineyards are very privileged locations, whereas others lie in more ordinary territory. The status of the locale determines, to a large extent, the price and prestige of the wine grown there.

Two basic categories of wine zones exist in France:

- Classic wine areas
- Newer grape-growing and winemaking areas

Every vineyard in France lies within one type of wine zone or the other — or sometimes both. Where classic zones and newer areas overlap, a winemaker can use either area's name for the wine, provided she follows the rules governing the production of the wine whose name she uses.

These rules are stricter for vineyards in the classic areas and more flexible in the newer areas. For example, winemakers in a classic zone have less choice of what grape variety to plant. But wines from the classic areas are generally more prestigious.

# Sampling sips in a Paris wine bar

A great selection of wines by the glass can be found in most of Paris's wine bars, as well as tasty light meals that go hand-in-hand with them. Here are a few recommendations for your next trip to the City of Lights:

- **Au Négociant:** The photographer Robert Doisneau came here often, but today a discerning crowd of regulars keep this tiny, hole-in-the-wall wine bar near Montmartre humming. The excellent pates and terrines are homemade and served with fresh, chewy bread.

- **Le Bistrot du Peintre:** Painters, actors, and night crawlers hang out here for the delicious and reasonably priced food and wine, large terrace, and superb Belle Epoque style.

- **La Cloche des Halles:** This tiny bar and café is crowded at lunchtime with people dining on plates of ham or quiche accompanied by a bottle of wine, and maybe the specialty, tarte tatin, for dessert. It's convivial and fun but very noisy, just like the rest of the quarter during the day. If you can't find a seat, you can usually stand at the bar and eat (and drink).

- **Clown Bar:** It's hard to say what gets more attention here — the wine or the clowns from the nearby Cirque d'Hiver who frequent the place. The bar is decorated with a mélange of circus posters and circus-themed ceramic tiles. The wine list features *(quelle surprise!)* an extensive selection of French offerings.

- **Le Griffonnier:** First-rate cuisine and a superb wine cellar make this bistro a standout. Sample specialties such as *confit de canard maison* (duck preserved and cooked in its own fat until it's fall-off-the-bone tender) or a hearty plate of regional meats and cheeses.

- **Mélac:** Owner Jacque Mélac has an excellent selection of wine from nearly all the regions of France and is happy to give you recommendations. The wonderful wall display of regional wines lends a heady ambience.

- **La Sancerre:** Loire wines are the specialty here, including, of course, Sancerre. The manager knows nothing of shyness and will discuss any and all things wine with you, including which of the mouth-watering dishes from his kitchen go best with which wine.

- **La Tartine:** This neighborhood wine bar is relaxed and comfortable — the head waitress will talk to you like you've known each other for years.

- **Willi's Wine Bar:** Since 1980, an upscale crowd of professionals and tourists has sampled more than 250 types of wine while seated at the polished oak bar or dining in the high-ceilinged, oak-beamed dining room.

## Small is beautiful

Where territories overlap, a winemaker generally chooses the name that represents the smallest, most specific *terroir* for which the vineyard is eligible. This is true for several reasons:

- ✔ The smaller area is more exclusive; fewer people can have vineyards there and use that name for their wine.
- ✔ Wines from smaller *terroirs* generally command a higher price than wines named after larger areas.
- ✔ Wines from smaller areas are generally perceived to be of higher quality.

*Note:* An exception to this rule can occur when the name of the larger area is better known and more marketable than the name of the smaller area.

**Book II**

**France:
A Wine
Superstar**

# Understanding a French Wine Label

French words on the labels of French wines indicate whether a wine comes from a classic region or a newer wine area:

- ✔ Wines from classic regions carry the words *Appellation . . . Contrôlée* on the label, in small print under the name of the wine. Between the two words is the name of the place that's the wine's official name.
- ✔ Wines from lesser classic regions carry the words *Vin Délimité de Qualité Supérieure* on the label, below the name of the wine.
- ✔ Wines from newer regions carry the words *Vin de pays de . . .* on their labels. The official name of the area appears at the end of this phrase.

*Appellation Contrôlée* translates as "regulated name." Sometimes, in reading about French wines, you might see the phrase *Appellation d'Origine Contrôlée;* it translates as "regulated place name." The two phrases are used interchangeably and mean the same thing, but the shorter version usually appears on wine labels. People who talk about wine a lot use the abbreviations AC or AOC for these phrases.

*Vin Délimité de Qualité Supérieure* translates as "demarcated wine of superior quality." The abbreviation VDQS applies to these wines. *Vin de pays* translates as "country wine."

At the bottom of the quality ladder is another category, *vins de table,* or table wines. These very inexpensive wines carry no geographic name other than *France* on their labels; they're not vintage dated, and they never carry the name of a grape variety on their labels.

France's overall system of wine laws is called its *AOC laws,* after the name of the highest wine category. These laws went into effect beginning in 1935. Most other wine-producing countries in Europe have used France's AOC laws as a model for their own wine laws.

Currently, France has more than 375 appellations (the highest level), making up over half of the country's wine production. VDQS wines number 10; these are wines from locales that hope to earn AOC status in the future. *Vin de pays* areas number about 140; this relatively new category became effective in 1979.

## Degrees of pedigree within the AOC ranks

AOC is the highest status that a French wine zone can aspire to have, legally speaking. But practically speaking, some AOC zones are more prestigious than others. This extra prestige derives from the following:

- ✔ The size of the locale (the smaller, the better)
- ✔ The quality and distinctiveness of the *terroir* (as expressed in the zones' wines, compared to wines of neighboring areas)
- ✔ The reputation of the appellation in the market (which can vary somewhat over time)

### Are AOC wines better than country wines?

When you buy a bottle of AOC wine, chances are it'll cost more than a bottle of *vin de pays,* or country wine, because it has a higher pedigree. But is it worth the difference in price?

Which type of wine has higher quality depends entirely on what the two wines are; some AOC wines are mediocre, and some country wines are very good — but many AOC wines are far superior to most country wines.

The difference between AOC wines and country wines is one of winemaking mentality and style.

In particular, country wines are often varietal wines; that is, they're labeled with the name of the grape variety that makes the wine. (They still have a place-name, too, but it's in smaller print.) They're made to express the characteristics of that grape rather than the region where the grape grows (which, frankly, can be quite large and not very distinctive). France's country wines are good values if you want a varietal wine, or if you want a simple French wine that's generally a bit fruitier than the classic French wines.

One way of knowing how large or small an AOC appellation is, and how specific its *terroir* is, is to know what type of territory the AOC in question represents. An AOC appellation can represent, in descending size and specificity, any of the following:

- ✔ A region (a fairly large area)
- ✔ A district, that is, an area within the larger region
- ✔ A subdistrict
- ✔ A group of specific villages
- ✔ A single village (also called a *commune*)
- ✔ A single vineyard (the smallest and most specific *terroir*)

**Book II**

**France: A Wine Superstar**

Unfortunately, you can't generally deduce the nature of the AOC territory from the wine's label. The word *villages* as part of the wine name, such as Mâcon-Villages, means that the wine comes from a smaller area than a similar wine without the *villages* appendage on its name. (It comes from a group of specific villages rather than from a larger district.) But most of the time, the label holds no clues.

One fairly reliable standard for determining the precision of the *terroir* of an AOC wine is price. French wineries always charge more for wines from more prestigious appellations than they do for their lesser AOC wines, and this price differential carries down to the shelf price of the wine. Also, French wines are so well-known that most knowledgeable people working in wine shops can help you distinguish between, say, a regionwide AOC and a single-village AOC name. (They can also tell you whether a wine with a technically higher appellation is actually better than another wine with a less-specific appellation; that depends on the producers of each wine.)

The reason that France's appellations lack any sort of uniformity is that the system is decentralized. There's a central governing body, of course; this organization is the INAO. (It almost always goes by the name INAO because its full name — *Institut National des Appellations d'Origine,* or National Institute of Appellations of Origin — is a mouthful.) The INAO rules with a firm hand. But the process of creating an appellation begins with the local grape growers who want their area recognized as an AOC area, and they get to name the area. Because local customs differ from one area to the next, the wine names don't follow any single pattern.

## The French wine label

Labels of AOC wines have one significant difference from those of country wines:

- ✔ For AOC wines, the place-name is the primary name of the wine.
- ✔ For country wines, a grape name is usually the primary name of the wine, with the place-name in smaller print.

The notable exception to this rule is the region of Alsace, where AOC wines are named for their grape variety, followed by the AOC name, Alsace. You could argue that another exception is Muscadet, because that word is used as a synonym for Mélon de Bourgogne, the grape that makes Muscadet wines.

Here are other words or expressions that you may see on French wine labels, along with their meanings:

- ✔ *Millésime,* meaning "vintage year," which is the year the grapes were harvested.
- ✔ *Mis en bouteille au château,* which means "bottled at the château," or *Mis en bouteille au domaine,* which means "bottled at the winery;" it's equivalent to the term "estate bottled."
- ✔ *Vieilles vignes,* meaning "old vines;" this term is unregulated, but it suggests a superior wine because old vines produce fewer grapes and hence a more concentrated wine.
- ✔ *Réserve,* translated as "reserve," is an unregulated term.
- ✔ *Premier cru,* literally meaning "first growth" but more correctly, "first growth vineyard;" this term is used in certain regions to denote superior vineyards that have special AC status.
- ✔ *Grand cru,* meaning "great growth" or "great growth vineyard;" like *premier cru,* this term is used only in certain regions, where it applies to the very best vineyards.
- ✔ *Supérieure,* meaning "superior;" this word appears as part of some AOC names, and it usually connotes a wine with a slightly higher alcohol level than the nonsuperior version of the same wine.

# Chapter 2

# Exploring Bordeaux's Range

*P*erhaps you've noticed that when wine lovers utter the word *Bordeaux,* they say it with a tone of awe and respect. Even if you don't know that a Bordeaux can be a dry or sweet white wine as well as a dry red wine, you probably know that Bordeaux has some mystique about it.

Bordeaux (pronounced bor-doh) can be confusing at first, what with all its districts, subdistricts, and villages — not to mention the classifications of specific properties and the different types of classifications in different districts! Fear not. This chapter not only introduces the region but also tells you about Bordeaux wines from red to white, affordable to elite.

## *Understanding What Makes Bordeaux a Wine Lover's Heaven*

The Bordeaux wine region lies in the southern part of western France, on the Atlantic coast (see Figure 2-1). The Gironde Estuary and its two major rivers, the Dordogne and the Garonne, run through the heart of the region. Almost all of Bordeaux's great wine estates are near the Gironde or one of its tributaries. The city of Bordeaux, France's fourth-largest city, lies in the center of the region.

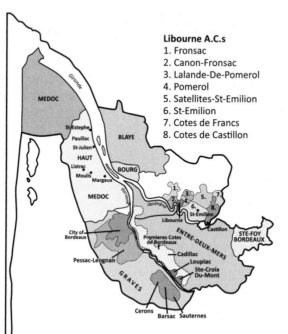

**Libourne A.C.s**
1. Fronsac
2. Canon-Fronsac
3. Lalande-De-Pomerol
4. Pomerol
5. Satellites-St-Emilion
6. St-Emilion
7. Cotes de Francs
8. Cotes de Castillon

**Figure 2-1:**
Bordeaux is a complex region, with many districts.

The Bordeaux area has a maritime climate with damp springtimes, rather hot, fairly dry summers, mild winters, and quite a bit of rain during autumn and winter. When rain occurs in the fall, it often spells trouble for the vintage: Too much rain can turn a promising grape crop into a mediocre one.

Bordeaux's landscape is rather flat in most places, and the soil is quite infertile. Not much else but grapes can grow there. In fact, the Bordeaux wine region — with the exception of the historic town of St.-Emilion — is plain looking. You don't go there for the area's natural beauty.

But the Bordeaux region is a place worth visiting in the eyes of wine lovers, because it's the home of more sought-after and expensive wines than any other region in the world. How has Bordeaux become the world's most prestigious and most renowned wine region? First of all, the *Bordelais,* as the natives of Bordeaux are called, have experience on their side; wine has been made in this region for about 2,000 years. But it's more than that. Other wine regions in Europe have been producing wine just as long and even longer, but they haven't attained Bordeaux's renown.

Bordeaux's superiority derives from the region's very special *terroir,* its unique combination of climate and soil. The wine's quality also benefits from the Bordelaise having figured out which grape varieties grow best in their locale. The varieties that thrive there happen to be among the greatest varieties in the world.

## Seeing (predominantly) red throughout Bordeaux

Bordeaux's reputation as a great wine region rests on its superb reds, legendary wines that can improve for several decades and are made by historic wine estates (called *châteaux*). Seventy-five to 80 percent of Bordeaux's wines are red. (Most of the rest is dry white, and 2 or 3 percent is stunning dessert wine.)

The greatest, most age-worthy red Bordeaux wines start at $30 a bottle retail but can go up to about $2,000 a bottle and more for rare wines, such as a newly released Château Pétrus. Older, fine vintages of the greatest and rarest wines are even more expensive. However, the famous, costly wines make up just 2 to 3 percent of all red Bordeaux.

Many fine Bordeaux reds are available in the $18 to $30 range; these wines are perfect for drinking when they're five to ten years old. And lots of red Bordeaux sell for $8 to $18; these inexpensive wines are made to be enjoyed when they're released at the age of two on up to five or six years of age.

**Book II**

**France:
A Wine
Superstar**

## Recognizing red Bordeaux as a blend of grape varieties

Red Bordeaux is always a blended wine. It's made from two to five so-called black grape varieties, with most wines made from three or four of the five varieties. The percentage of each grape variety used in a particular red Bordeaux wine can change from year to year, depending on the climate and how each variety has fared during the growing season. The percentage also varies from one estate to another.

The five grape varieties of red Bordeaux are

- Cabernet Sauvignon (cab-er-nay saw-vee-nyon)
- Merlot (mer-loh)
- Cabernet Franc (cab-er-nay frahn)
- Petit Verdot (peh-tee vair-doe)
- Malbec (mahl-bec)

Either Cabernet Sauvignon or Merlot is the dominant variety in practically all red Bordeaux wines; Cabernet Franc is the third most utilized variety, followed by Petite Verdot and Malbec. (Actually, Malbec has been rapidly disappearing from most Bordeaux wines, because it hasn't been growing well in the region.)

Red Bordeaux can be quite a different wine depending on whether Cabernet Sauvignon or Merlot is the dominant grape variety.

# The High-Rent Districts for Red Bordeaux

The Bordeaux region is quite large, encompassing more than a quarter-million acres of vineyards, and it produces about 660 million bottles annually (about 10 percent of France's wine, but more than 25 percent of its AOC wine; turn to Chapter 1 in Book II for more on the AOC classification system). Naturally, climate and soil vary across this large area. Four major red Bordeaux districts, each with its own particular *terroir,* exist within the region, along with several minor districts.

Following are the four major districts for red Bordeaux:

- **Haut-Médoc:** The southern — and most important — part of the Médoc peninsula, which occupies the western bank of the Gironde.

- **Graves/Pessac-Léognan:** Pessac-Léognan, the area south of the Médoc, and south of and around the city of Bordeaux, was part of the Graves district until 1987, when it became a separate district. In terms of elite red wines, it's far more important than the Graves district, but the two regions are combined here for historical reasons.

- **St.-Emilion:** A region east of the city of Bordeaux.

- **Pomerol:** Another region east of the city of Bordeaux.

Bordeaux wines with the Haut-Médoc, St.-Emilion, or Pomerol appellations must be red; Graves or Pessac-Léognan wines may be red or white.

Wines from these four districts represent the top of the quality pyramid for red Bordeaux. At the base of the pyramid are the thousands of inexpensive Bordeaux wines made from grapes grown throughout the region, which are entitled to the simple regional appellation Bordeaux AOC (or Bordeaux AC). In the middle are Bordeaux from lesser districts.

Because of certain similarities in the wines, and for historical reasons, these four major districts for red Bordeaux are often grouped as two entities, which are often known as the *Left Bank* and the *Right Bank.* The Médoc peninsula and Graves/Pessac-Léognan make up the Left Bank, because they're situated on the left, or western side, of the Gironde and Garonne rivers as they flow to the sea (as you can see in Figure 2-1). St.-Emilion and Pomerol are Right Bank districts.

The following sections get you acquainted with the specific styles of the Left and Right Banks.

# The villages of the Haut-Médoc

Of the four major districts in Bordeaux, the Haut-Médoc historically has been the most important district during the past two centuries, and it's the origin of many of the most famous Bordeaux wines.

The Haut-Médoc encompasses four villages that rank among the aristocracy of wine names. These four villages are regarded so highly in Bordeaux that, together with two less-renowned villages, they're each official AOC appellations, reflecting a *terroir* more specific than the Haut-Médoc at large. Only red wines may carry the names of these villages on their labels.

The four famous Haut-Médoc wine communes (the term *commune* is synonymous with "village" in French), from south to north, are as follows:

- ✔ **Margaux**
- ✔ **St.-Julien**
- ✔ **Pauillac**
- ✔ **St.-Estèphe**

The two other communes in the Haut-Médoc that have their own AOCs are Listrac and Moulis.

The names of these six villages are an official part of the names of the wines made within these communes. For example, underneath the name of the wine on the label, say, *Château Latour*, are the words, *Appellation Papilla Contrôlée.* Any wines from the Haut-Médoc that don't come from vineyards within these six communes carry the broader appellation *Appellation Haut-Médoc Contrôlée* on their labels.

Each of the four major communes of the Haut-Médoc produces wines of a distinct style, which experienced tasters can identify without knowing the wine's provenance. Here are the different characteristics of the four major communes' wines:

- ✔ **Margaux:** Elegant, medium-bodied, supple wines with complex flavors and a fragrant aroma are typical of Margaux wines. A good example is Château Palmer. Additionally, this commune is home to Château Margaux, one of Bordeaux's most famous wines.

- ✔ **St.-Julien:** This village produces flavorful, rich, medium- to full-bodied wines that are subtle, balanced, and consistent. A typical St.-Julien wine is Château Ducru-Beaucaillou.

- ✔ **Pauillac:** Blackcurrant and cedar aromas are common in Pauillac wines, which tend to be powerful, firm, rich, tannic, full-bodied, concentrated, and very long-lived. A typical Pauillac wine is Château Pichon-Lalande. Additionally, this commune is the home of three famous Bordeaux: Châteaux Lafite-Rothschild, Latour, and Mouton-Rothschild.

- ✔ **St.-Estèphe:** This village produces dark-colored, austere, full-bodied wines that are tannic, acidic, and earthy. Wines from St.-Estèphe are very long-lived and need time to evolve. Château Montrose is a good example of a typical St.-Estèphe wine.

## *The Left Bank style*

The soil on the Left Bank is primarily gravelly, with excellent drainage. Although the area is relatively flat, mounds or terraces of gravel, left by a retreating sea thousands of years ago, exist throughout the Left Bank. Cabernet Sauvignon, which does very well in gravelly soil, is the predominant red grape variety of the Left Bank. A typical Bordeaux from the Haut-Médoc or Pessac-Léognan usually has 60 to 65 percent Cabernet Sauvignon in its blend, with about 25 to 30 percent Merlot.

Generally speaking, the red Bordeaux wines from the Left Bank are quite tannic and austere when they're young (see Chapter 5 in Book I for an explanation of *tannic*), and they have a pronounced blackcurrant aroma and flavor. With age, they develop complex secondary aromas and flavors, such as stewed fruit, leather, earth, and tobacco; their colors lighten and flavors soften as the tannin begins to drop out of the wine.

Left Bank–style wines need ten years or more to come into their own, and the best of them are capable of developing further for decades. The most common mistake regarding Left Bank Bordeaux wines is drinking them when they're less than ten years old: They can taste harsh and bitter at this age, leaving you to wonder what all the fuss is about.

## The Right Bank style

The vineyards of Bordeaux's Right Bank lie east of the city of Bordeaux and the Gironde Estuary, and north of the Dordogne River (as you can see in Figure 2-1). The two major subregions of Bordeaux on the Right Bank are

- St.-Emilion, southeast of the port of Libourne
- Pomerol, northeast of Libourne

Because the Right Bank is farther from the ocean, the soil contains less gravel; it tends to be a mixture of clay, silt, sand, and limestone. In this *terroir*, the Merlot grape variety flourishes and is clearly the Right Bank's dominant grape variety. (Actually, Merlot is the most-planted grape variety in the entire Bordeaux region.)

Cabernet Franc, which ripens faster than Cabernet Sauvignon, is the second-most important variety on the Right Bank. A typical St.-Emilion or Pomerol contains about 70 percent Merlot, with the remainder usually Cabernet Franc and Cabernet Sauvignon — but invariably more Cabernet Franc.

Right Bank Bordeaux reds, such as St.-Emilions and Pomerols, are a good choice for the novice red Bordeaux drinker because they're less tannic and austere, and therefore more approachable, than Left Bank Bordeaux. This difference is particularly noticeable when the wines are young (less than ten years old). The reason for the different style is that the Merlot grape variety has considerably less — and softer — tannin than does Cabernet Sauvignon, which dominates Left Bank Bordeaux. Also, the somewhat richer soil on the Right Bank contributes to a fruitier, softer profile for Right Bank Bordeaux. For this reason, you might drink a Pomerol or St.-Emilion that's less than ten years old, but you'd seldom drink a Left Bank Bordeaux that young.

Although Right Bank red Bordeaux wines are ready to drink sooner than Left Bank Bordeaux, the better examples of these wines can live for many decades — nearly as long as Left Bank Bordeaux, especially in good vintages.

Generally speaking, the wines of Pomerol are the most expensive Bordeaux wines and the most difficult to find — for the simple reason that these wines come from the smallest wine estates of any of the major Bordeaux subregions. For instance, the typical Haut-Médoc wine estate produces about 20,000 to 25,000 cases (12 bottles to a case) of wine annually, whereas the average Pomerol winery makes only 3,000 to 5,000 cases of wine a year.

Book II

France:
A Wine
Superstar

# Classified Information: Ranking Red Bordeaux

Because so many Bordeaux wines are so renowned, many people throughout the years have attempted to rank them according to the wines' merit or quality. These rankings, or *classifications*, have become an important part of the region's lore.

Some classifications of Bordeaux are official, sanctioned by the Bordelais, and others are unofficial, such as personal classifications from wine critics. Various districts of Bordeaux have undertaken official classifications of their wines — but at different times, of course — using different categories to grade the wines. Put all that together and you realize that no one ranking or classification covers all the wines of Bordeaux.

The next few sections alert you to the classifications that apply to Bordeaux's finest reds.

## The 1855 Classification

No classification of Bordeaux wines has created more of an impact than the 1855 Classification of the Great Growths of the Gironde. Devised by Bordeaux merchants in preparation for a visit from Queen Victoria of England, the classification was based on the prices that wines commanded at that time, as well as the wines' track records over the past 100 years.

The 61 red Bordeaux wines that made the cut became known as Classified Growths, or *Grands Crus Classés* wines in French (a *cru* in Bordeaux refers to a wine estate). At that time, the Haut-Médoc subregion dominated the Bordeaux wine trade, and so 60 of the 61 wines were Haut-Médoc wines; one was from the Graves (the part now known as Pessac-Léognan). All of the Right Bank wines were shut out of the famous 1855 ranking.

The 1855 Classification divided the 61 classified growths into five categories, or classes, according to quality. The First Growths ranked at the top, followed by the Second Growths, and so forth. At the time, the First Growth category contained only four wines, but one wine was later added to that rank. These five top wines are

- ✔ Château Lafite-Rothschild

- ✔ Château Latour

- ✔ Château Margaux

- ✔ Château Haut Brion (Graves)

- ✔ Château Mouton-Rothschild (elevated from a Second Growth in 1973)

The 61 classified growths, which account for about 25 percent of the wine production in the Médoc peninsula, have enjoyed more prestige than most other Bordeaux wines over the years. Today, roughly 10,000 wine producers (8,000 of which are wine estates) exist in Bordeaux, but only 61 wines have been blessed or "ordained" by this most renowned of all wine classifications.

The 1855 Classification has remained remarkably accurate. Naturally, a few of the classified wines have declined in quality over the past century and a half, and some wines not classified at that time have improved. Also, some Bordeaux wines of today that weren't around in 1855 might be worthy of inclusion. But for the most part, the classification has held up well.

## The Graves/Pessac-Léognan classification

Wine producers in the Graves district weren't too pleased that only one of their red wines, Château Haut-Brion, was classified in 1855. But it took them almost 100 years to change the situation. Actually, until the Institut National des Appellations d'Origine (INAO) was founded in 1935 and endowed with regulatory power over all AOC wines, the apparatus to make any changes wasn't in place.

In 1953, the INAO officially rated the red wines of the Graves for the first time; the classification was revised in 1959, and this time it included the dry white wines of the district. (The dessert wines from the Graves district, Sauternes and Barsac, had been part of the 1855 Classification.) The 1953 classification named 13 red Graves wines (all in what is now the Pessac-Léognan district) but didn't rank them individually. All the area's top estates — such as Château Haut Brion, Château La Mission-Brion, Domaine de Chevalier, and Château Pape Clément — are classified growths, or *Crus Classés*.

# The St.-Emilion classification

The 1855 Classification completely ignored the wines of the St.-Emilion sub-region, which are all red. (Frankly, St.-Emilion wines weren't very important commercially until the 20th century, even though they have a longer history than the Médoc wines.) The St.-Emilion wines finally received recognition in 1955 when the INAO undertook a classification of these overlooked wines.

In one important way, the St.-Emilion classification is superior to both the 1855 Classification and the Graves classification: It provides for revisions almost every decade. The St.-Emilion classification has been revised (adding some wines and dropping others) in 1969, 1985, and 1996. (Okay, so they missed the 1970s.)

The St.-Emilion classification names wines at three quality levels. From the best to the least, these quality levels are as follows:

- *Premier Grand Cru Classé* (First Great Classified Growth)
- *Grand Cru Classé* (Great Classified Growth)
- *Grand Cru* (Great Growth)

On the bottom tier of the classification are some 200 wines that are entitled to the appellation St.-Emilion Grand Cru. This particular appellation is rather meaningless, because many very ordinary wines (along with a handful of overachievers) are among the 200. Also, the Grand Cru designation is confusing because it sounds similar to the next-highest appellation, St.-Emilion Grand Cru Classé.

The middle tier — with a total of 55 wines — singles out many very good wines, most of which are on par with Fourth and Fifth Growths (Haut-Médoc wines) from the 1855 Classification, and some of which are even better. In fact, at least four wines with the appellation St.-Emilion Grand Cru Classé are now so good that they deserve a promotion to the highest St.-Emilion classification in the near future. The four great Grand Cru Classé wines are

- Château Canon-La-Gaffelière
- Château Pavie Decesse
- Château Pavie Macquin
- Château Troplong-Mondot

Currently, 13 wines hold the highest St.-Emilion ranking, *Premier Grand Cru Classé.* The INAO distinguishes two of the 13 wines — Château Ausone and Château Cheval Blanc — by placing them in Category A of the Premiers Grands Crus Classés. The other 11 Premier Grand Cru Classé wines are in Category B. The two Category A wines are equivalent in quality to the First Growths of the 1855 Classification, and the 11 wines in Category B are roughly comparable to Second and Third Growths of the 1855 Classification.

# Trying Red Bordeaux on a Budget

The elite wines of Bordeaux (listed in the nearby sidebar) have a way of grabbing the spotlight — and rightfully so, because they're among the very finest wines in the entire world. But they don't begin to tell the whole story of the Bordeaux region, where regular people make regular wine for drinking on a regular basis. Literally thousands of Bordeaux wines cost you less than $20 a bottle, and many cost less than $10.

## Bordeaux's best reds

Fancypants French rankings aside, ten wines occupy an elite class of red Bordeaux. They include the five First Growths and one super Second Growth (all from the famous 1855 Classification, which you can read about in the related section in this chapter), as well as the two best St.-Emilion wines and the two best Pomerols. These wines aren't listed in any particular order of preference; they're all great, and each Bordeaux lover has his or her own favorites.

**First Growth**

Château Haut Brion (Pessac-Léognan)

Château Lafite-Rothschild (Pauillac, Haut-Médoc)

Château Latour (Pauillac, Haut-Médoc)

Château Margaux (Margaux, Haut-Médoc)

Château Mouton-Rothschild (Pauillac, Haut-Médoc)

**Second Growth**

Château Léoville-Las Cases (St.-Julien, Haut-Médoc)

**St.-Emilion**

Château Ausone

Château Cheval Blanc

**Pomerol**

Château Lafleur

Château Pétrus

***Note:*** All ten of these wines are very expensive, and a few (Ausone, Pétrus, and Lafleur) are extremely difficult to find. But because Bordeaux is a huge wine region, it offers scores of other great wines nearly as fine (and considerably less costly!) than these ten elite wines.

Besides costing less, these inexpensive red Bordeaux wines have the added advantage of being ready to drink sooner than the classified growths. Instead of waiting ten years or more to appreciate them, you can drink these relatively light-bodied, less tannic, inexpensive wines within a few years of the vintage.

Inexpensive red Bordeaux wines generally fall into three categories:

- ✔ Cru Bourgeois wines from the Médoc peninsula
- ✔ Generic red Bordeaux
- ✔ Red Bordeaux from lesser-known appellations

Frankly, if you're just getting into red Bordeaux, starting at the top is kind of crazy. Trying some inexpensive wines first, and then working your way up the price ladder, provides a context for evaluating and appreciating the finer wines. Even if you're lucky enough to be able to afford a great red Bordeaux every night, you probably won't appreciate it fully without the contrast of drinking lesser wines now and then.

The next sections describe the wines of the various Bordeaux districts that don't get as much (if any) of the spotlight but are still worth tasting, especially for the price.

**Book II**

**France:
A Wine
Superstar**

## Cru Bourgeois wines of the Médoc and Haut-Médoc

The Haut-Médoc is the southern portion of the Médoc peninsula, which is in the northwest part of the Bordeaux region. The northern section, occupying about one-third of the peninsula, was formerly called the Bas-Médoc and is now known simply as the Médoc, just like the peninsula itself. Together, the Médoc and Haut-Médoc are particularly rich sources of good, inexpensive red Bordeaux wines — despite the fact that the Médoc peninsula is also the home of all but one of the elite red wines classified in 1855.

As you can imagine, all of the properties in this area that weren't classified in 1855 felt left out, to say the least. Quite a few of these estates were, and are, making very good wines; in some cases these wines are on par with — or even better than — a few of the classified growths. To remedy the injustice, in 1932, the Bordeaux Chamber of Commerce designated a group of wines in the Médoc peninsula as *Cru Bourgeois*. The Chamber of Commerce let it be known that these châteaux ranked just below the *crus classés* (classified growths) of the 1855 Classification.

The 1932 list featured the wines of about 240 Crus Bourgeois properties; these wines make up about 40 percent of the production of the Médoc peninsula. The list was revised in 1966, and again in 1978, by the Syndicat des Crus Bourgeois, a self-regulatory association of châteaux. The syndicate organized the properties into three categories of wines: *Cru Bourgeois Exceptionnel, Cru Grand Bourgeois,* and *Cru Bourgeois.*

Despite the best of intentions, the Cru Bourgeois classification has its weaknesses. For example, a number of good estates never joined the syndicate — and aren't ranked as a result. A few other estates joined after 1978, which was when the last revision was published, so they aren't ranked either. Yet to some extent, the Cru Bourgeois classification is valid.

Today, nearly 300 *Cru Bourgeois* properties exist — way too many to list here. The following are favorite wines of the Médoc and Haut-Médoc that weren't classified in 1855 — whether they're official Crus Bourgeois or not (a mere 81 wines!). Just think of them as "Crus Bourgeois wines and their friends." Many bear the appellation Médoc or Haut-Médoc, whereas some have specific village appellations. Most retail for $15 to $30, but a few cost $30 to $40. Here they are:

Château d'Angludet (Margaux)
Château d'Arsac (Margaux)
Château d'Agassac (Haut-Médoc)
Château Arnauld (Haut-Médoc)
Château Beau-Site (St.-Estèphe)
Château Beaumont (Haut-Médoc)
Château Bel Air (Haut-Médoc)
Château Bellegrave (Listrac)
Château Le Boscq (Médoc)*
Château Le Boscq (St.-Estèphe)*
Château Branas-Grand Poujeaux (Moulis)
Château Brillette (Moulis)
Château Capbern-Gasqueton (St.-Estèphe)
Château La Cardonne (Médoc)
Château Chasse-Spleen (Moulis)
Château Cissac (Haut-Médoc)
Château Citran (Haut-Médoc)
Château Clarke (Listrac)
Château Clément-Pichon (Haut-Médoc)
Château La Commanderie (St.-Estèphe)
Château Coufran (Haut-Médoc)
Château Le Crock (St.-Estèphe)
Château Duplessis-Hauchecorne (Moulis)

Château Dutrarch-Grand-Poujeaux (Moulis)
Château Fonbadet (Pauillac)
Château Fonréaud (Listrac)
Château Fourcas-Dupré (Listrac)
Château Fourcas-Hosten (Listrac)
Château Fourcas-Loubaney (Listrac)
Château La France (Médoc)
Château du Glana (St.-Julien)
Château Gloria (St.-Julien)
Château Gressier Grand-Poujeaux (Moulis)
Château Greysac (Médoc)
Château La Gurgue (Margaux)
Château Hanteillan (Haut-Médoc)
Château Haut-Beauséjour (St.-Estèphe)
Château Haut-Marbuzet (St.-Estèphe)
Château Hortevie (St.-Julien)
Château Labégorce (Margaux)
Château Labégorce-Zédé (Margaux)
Château Lamarque (Haut-Médoc)
Château Lanessan (Haut-Médoc)
Château Larose-Trintaudon (Haut-Médoc)
Château Larruau (Margaux)
Château Lestage (Listrac)
Château Liversan (Haut-Médoc)

Château Loudenne (Médoc)
Château Malecasse (Haut-Médoc)
Château Malmaison (Moulis)
Château Marbuzet (St.-Estèphe)
Château Maucaillou (Moulis)
Château Mayné-Lalande (Listrac)
Château Meyney (St.-Estèphe)
Château Monbrison (Margaux)
Château Moulin-Rouge (Haut-Médoc)
Château Moulin à Vent (Moulis)
Château Les-Ormes-de-Pez
   (St.-Estèphe)
Château Patache d'Aux (Médoc)
Château Peyrabon (Haut-Médoc)
Château de Pez (St.-Estèphe)
Château Phélan-Ségur (St.-Estèphe)
Château Pibran (Pauillac)
Château Plagnac (Médoc)
Château Potensac (Médoc)
Château Poujeaux (Moulis)

Château Ramage la Batisse
   (Haut-Médoc)
Château Ségur (Haut-Médoc)
Château Sénéjac (Haut-Médoc)
Château Siran (Margaux)
Château Sociando-Mallet
   (Haut-Médoc)
Château Tayac (Margaux)
Château Terrey-Gros-Cailloux
   (St.-Julien)
Château La Tour de By (Médoc)
Château La Tour-de-Mons (Margaux)
Château Tour Haut-Caussan (Médoc)
Château Tour du Haut-Moulin
   (Haut-Médoc)
Château La Tour St.-Bonnet (Médoc)
Château Verdigan (Haut-Médoc)
Château Vieux Robin (Médoc)
Château Villegeorge (Haut-Médoc)
* *Two different châteaux; same
   names.*

**Book II**

**France:
A Wine
Superstar**

# Petits châteaux and generics

Perhaps you just can't dream of spending $20 or more on a bottle of wine, at least not on a regular basis. Does that mean Bordeaux is out of your price range? Au contraire! Many inexpensive Bordeaux wines are produced within every appellation in the region.

Many red Bordeaux wines are available in the $8 to $18 price range. They've never been classified, nor will they ever be; they go by the general name of *petits châteaux* (implying that the proprietors live in a small house as opposed to a large château). These are the wines that the typical French person picks up in his or her supermarket, along with some cheese, on the way home from work. The great advantage of the petits châteaux Bordeaux wines (besides their price) is that you can drink them as soon as you buy them; they don't require aging.

The term *petit château* is somewhat misleading, because it implies that a wine is an estate *(château)* wine; in fact, as the term is used today, it refers to all the least-expensive Bordeaux wines, even those that don't come from a single property. Many of these wines are *generic* Bordeaux, meaning their grapes come from all over the region, and they therefore carry the general Bordeaux appellation. But some carry more specific appellations, such as Médoc, Premières Côtes de Blaye, or St.-Emilion. In other words, not every petit château is a generic Bordeaux, but neither is every petit château a château wine. And don't look for the term *petit château* on the label; it isn't there.

Just like all other Bordeaux, petit château wines are made mainly from a blend of Merlot, Cabernet Sauvignon, and/or Cabernet Franc grape varieties. Literally thousands of such wines exist. To give you an idea of the category of wine, here's a list of a few of the more popular inexpensive red Bordeaux:

- Baron Philippe de Rothschild wines, including Mouton-Cadet, Mouton-Cadet Réserve, and Médoc
- Michel Lynch wines (from the owners of Château Lynch-Bages)
- Château Bonnet (available, and reliable, in both red and white)
- Château Cap de Faugères
- Château de Cruzeau (both red and white)

All petits chateaux Bordeaux, plus the Bordeaux wines from the other Bordeaux appellations in the next section, are at their best when consumed within five or six years of their vintage date; they definitely aren't made for aging.

## Other Bordeaux districts

The Big Four red Bordeaux districts — Haut-Médoc, Graves/Pessac-Léognan, St.-Emilion, and Pomerol — described earlier in this chapter get a lot of attention, but a number of other Bordeaux districts exist on the Right Bank of the Gironde River. These other districts make average to good Bordeaux wines at reasonable prices, for the most part. Following are the other Bordeaux districts (and appellations):

- Fronsac
- Canon-Fronsac
- Côtes de Bourg
- Premières Côtes de Blaye
- Premières Côtes de Bordeaux
- Côtes de Castillon
- Côtes de Francs
- Lalande de Pomerol
- Puisseguin-St.-Emilion
- Lussac-St.-Emilion
- Montagne-St.-Emilion
- St.-Georges-St.-Emilion
- Ste.-Foy Bordeaux

    ✔ Bordeaux Supérieur (a general, regionwide appellation used mainly for Right Bank Bordeaux)

    ✔ Bordeaux (a general, regionwide appellation primarily used for Right Bank Bordeaux)

The wines from these districts are made from the same grape varieties as elsewhere in Bordeaux, with Merlot usually being the dominant variety. With the exception of the relatively more expensive Fronsac and Canon-Fronsac wines, all the other Bordeaux wines in the following sections qualify, price-wise, as petits chateaux wines (see the preceding section for more on petits chateaux wines).

Although you can buy decent red Bordeaux wines from any of these districts or appellations, four of these areas are more important than the others for red wines. These four areas fall neatly into two pairs, because of how they're situated.

**Book II**

**France: A Wine Superstar**

### Fronsac and Canon-Fronsac

When you leave the city of Bordeaux heading east and cross the Dordogne River into the Right Bank region, the very first wine districts you come across on your left are the adjacent areas of Fronsac and Canon-Fronsac. They lie just northwest of Libourne, the town that's the commercial center of the Right Bank Bordeaux districts (see Figure 2-1). Fronsac is three times larger than Canon-Fronsac and surrounds that district.

The word *canon* means "hill" in French. The Canon-Fronsac appellation takes its name from two steep hills that dominate the district. But although this area is hillier than Fronsac, most of the vineyards of both appellations are situated on steep hillsides.

In general, Canon-Fronsac and Fronsac have the highest reputation for quality of the lesser Bordeaux appellations (although Canon-Fronsac has a higher percentage of finer wines), and their prices reflect their reputation. Whereas wines from the other appellations are mainly less than $18 a bottle — with many as low as $10 — the better wines from Fronsac and Canon-Fronsac are in the $18 to $25 range. Another factor affecting price is the size of the wineries: Many wineries in both districts are quite small, making as little as 2,000 to 6,000 cases a year.

Like Pomerol and St.-Emilion, Fronsac and Canon-Fronsac produce only red wines. Merlot is the dominant grape variety in both districts, although Cabernet Franc and Cabernet Sauvignon play a more important role in these two districts than in the other Right Bank appellations. Some properties in the Fronsacs produce a prestige cuvée as well as their regular wine, a practice that's quite unusual for the Bordeaux region.

Some of the better Fronsac and Canon-Fronsac wines include the following:

| | |
|---|---|
| Château Barrabaque (Canon-Fronsac) | Château Fontenil (Fronsac) |
| Château Canon de Brem (Canon-Fronsac) | Château Haut-Carles (Fronsac) |
| Château Canon-Moueix (Canon-Fronsac) | Château Mazeris (Canon-Fronsac) |
| Château La Croix-Canon (Canon-Fronsac) | Château Moulin-Haut-Laroque (Fronsac) |
| Château Dalem (Fronsac) | Château Moulin-Pey-Labrie (Canon-Fronsac) |
| Château La Dauphine (Fronsac) | Château La Rivière (Fronsac) |
| | Château La Vieille-Cure (Fronsac) |

### *Côtes de Bourg and Premières Côtes de Blaye*

Côtes de Bourg and Côtes de Blaye are the two most northerly Right Bank districts. The regions are named after port towns on the Gironde River (see Figure 2-1):

- Blaye is opposite St.-Julien on the Left Bank.
- Bourg, opposite Margaux and south of Blaye, is situated at the confluence of the Gironde into the Dordogne River.

The area known as Côtes de Blaye is much larger than the Bourg district, and confusingly, it actually encompasses several separate AOC appellations. The appellation Côtes de Blaye itself applies to white wines, which historically were more important than the reds; the Premières Côtes de Blaye appellation applies to red wines and some of the area's better whites. White wines from this area can also carry the appellations Blaye or Blayais.

Historically, both the Côtes de Bourg and Côtes de Blaye wine districts, especially Bourg, played an important role in the Bordeaux wine trade. With the emergence of St.-Emilion, Pomerol, and the Left Bank wine districts in the last century, Bourg and Blaye faded into the background, quietly making wines for consumption within France.

Today, both the Côtes de Bourg and the Premières Côtes de Blaye wines (particularly the Côtes de Bourg) are experiencing a resurgence in interest, not only in France but also in other European countries and the United States. The reason is apparent: As prices continue rising at a rapid pace for red Bordeaux wines in the more prestigious districts, consumers are turning to the Bourg and Blaye districts for truly "great value" wines. (Believe it or not, some wines from these districts are in the $8 to $10 price range!)

Red wines predominate in both districts; about 99 percent of Côtes de Bourg wines are red, whereas in the Blaye district, about 90 percent are red. Merlot is the leading grape variety in both Bourg and Blaye red wines, with Cabernet Sauvignon, Cabernet Franc, and sometimes Malbec in the blend.

Both districts make about the same amount of wine annually, around 2.2 million cases. The wines from both regions vary in quality and include

- ✔ Simple, rustic, fruity, but powerful country wines (basically, the $8 to $15 wines)

- ✔ Sophisticated, elegant, complex, age-worthy red wines ($20 and up) that can compare in quality to fine wines from St.-Emilion or the Haut-Médoc, but at half the price

Some of the better Bourg and Blaye wines include the following:

Château de Barbe (Côtes de Bourg)
Château Fougas-Maldoror (Côtes de Bourg)
Château Gigault Cuvée Viva (Premières Côtes de Blaye)
Château Les Grands-Maréchaux (Premières Côtes de Blaye)
Château Haut-Sociando (Premières Côtes de Blaye)
Château Roc de Cambes (Côtes de Bourg)
Château Roland La Garde (Premières Côtes de Blaye)

Château Ségonzac (Premières Côtes de Blaye)
Château Tayac (Côtes de Bourg)*
Château La Tonnelle (Premières Côtes de Blaye)

* *Note that Château Tayca is also the name of a Cru Bourgeois red wine from the Margaux district, but the Château Tayac from the Côtes de Bourg district is probably the better wine of the two.*

**Book II**

**France: A Wine Superstar**

# Drinking Red Bordeaux, the Right Way

Red Bordeaux wine is an extraordinary taste experience, especially when it has fully developed and is mature. That stage varies according to the vintage and the wine. Most better red Bordeaux wines are ready to drink between 10 to 20 years of age, and the best wines, from the best vintages, are mature enough between 20 and 40 years of age. In a few exceptional cases (as with the 1928 and 1945 Bordeaux vintages), the wines take even longer to mature. By consulting vintage charts or seeking the advice of wine experts, and factoring in your own preferences for more youthful or more mature wine, you can determine the optimum period for drinking your red Bordeaux.

Red Bordeaux isn't the easiest wine to match with food. It goes best with simple cuts of red meat, lamb, or venison. It's also fine with hard cheeses, such as Cheddar or Comté, and good, crusty bread.

A fine Bordeaux needs decanting, whether it's young or mature. A young wine will benefit from the extra aeration (at least an hour) that decanting provides. A mature (ten years or older) Bordeaux has sediment, a harmless but disagreeable byproduct, that's removed by careful decanting. Inexpensive Bordeaux wines don't need decanting. (For the basics of decanting, flip to Chapter 4 in Book I.)

Serve red Bordeaux at cool room temperatures, about 63 to 66 degrees Fahrenheit. A fine, large glass (not too wide) is best.

Vintages are very important in the Bordeaux region. The 1982 vintage is the best for red Bordeaux of the last 30 years — actually the best since 1961 — and all 1982s are ready to drink now. Other good vintages are the 1985, 1986, 1988, 1989, 1990, 1995, 1996, 1998, and 2006 (the last one is far from ready to drink). The 2005 looks promising but will need many years to develop.

# Exploring the Range of White Bordeaux

The red wines of Bordeaux cast such a large shadow that one can easily over-look the fact that this region also produces some of the world's finest white wines. The Bordelaise make dry white wine in many districts of the region, including a few wines from the predominantly red-wine Haut-Médoc area. But most of Bordeaux's dry and semidry white wines come from the following three districts:

- ✔ Pessac-Léognan
- ✔ Graves
- ✔ Entre-Deux-Mers

The Pessac-Léognan district is the home of Bordeaux's finest white wines, and most of these wines come from estates that also happen to make fine red wines. The Graves district makes good, dry white wines that are less expen-sive than those of Pessac-Léognan. This area also produces great dessert wines (such as Sauternes, covered later in this chapter).

As you can see in Figure 2-1, Entre-Deux-Mers is a large area that lies east of the Graves and Pessac-Léognan districts and between the Garonne and Dordogne Rivers; its name means "between two seas," a reference to these two rivers. This district is known for its inexpensive dry, off-dry, and sweet white wines, although it also grows reds.

Other white Bordeaux wines, mainly inexpensive versions, come from grapes grown throughout the Bordeaux region rather than in a specific district; these wines simply carry the regionwide appellation, Bordeaux Blanc.

Ironically, the few white wines from the Haut-Médoc and Médoc, which are fairly expensive, must use the same Bordeaux or Bordeaux Blanc appellation as these inexpensive generic white Bordeaux, because no such thing as Médoc Blanc or Haut-Médoc Blanc exists under AOC law.

For the scoop on the grape varieties and great producers that make white Bordeaux, as well as advice on how to enjoy the wine, check out the following sections.

## Two white grapes — and neither is Chardonnay

The Chardonnay grape might rule the world of white wines, but it's not a permitted variety in Bordeaux. In fact, Chardonnay isn't even necessary, because Sauvignon Blanc and Sémillon, which are typically blended together here, have adapted extremely well to the *terroir* of Bordeaux. (A third permitted white grape variety, Muscadelle, plays a minor role in a few wines.)

Sauvignon Blanc (saw-vee-nyon blahnk) is the dominant grape variety (60 to 100 percent) in most of Bordeaux's dry white wines, whereas Sémillon (seh-mee-yohn) dominates the sweeter white wines. The very best dry white wines of Pessac-Léognan contain around 50 percent Sémillon.

Sauvignon Blanc and Sémillon have a fine symbiotic relationship, for the following reasons:

- The Sauvignon Blanc part of the wine offers immediate charm and develops early. It's crisp, lively, herbaceous, and light-bodied.

- The Sémillon part is fuller-bodied, viscous, and honeyed, with lower acidity than the high-acid Sauvignon. It enriches the wine but needs several years to unfold.

Most of the better dry white Bordeaux, which are blends of both varieties, are crisp and lively when they're young but develop a honeyed, fuller-bodied richness with age. In good vintages, they can age a surprisingly long time — often for 30 or 40 years (or more!).

## Top producers of white Bordeaux

Unlike red Bordeaux, the best white Bordeaux wines form a small club. In 1959, the Institut National des Appellations d'Origine (INAO), the regulatory body for French wines, classified the white Bordeaux of the Graves (Pessac-Léognan was then a part of Graves) district. The group named just ten wines, all in Pessac-Léognan.

Here's a list of some top wines, with the provenance of the wine indicated in parentheses. Class One includes the most expensive (from roughly $100 to several hundred dollars); you can come away with a Class Three bottle for around $30 or so.

**Book II**

**France: A Wine Superstar**

**Class One**

Château Haut Brion Blanc
(Pessac-Léognan)
Château Laville-Haut Brion
(Pessac-Léognan)

Domaine de Chevalier Blanc
(Pessac-Léognan)

**Class Two**

Château Couhins-Lurton
(Pessac-Léognan)
Château de Fieuzal Blanc
(Pessac-Léognan)
Château Latour-Martillac Blanc
(Pessac-Léognan)
Château La Louvière Blanc
(Pessac-Léognan)

Château Pape Clément Blanc
(Pessac-Léognan)
Château Smith Haut-Lafitte Blanc
(Pessac-Léognan)
Clos Floridène Blanc (Graves)
Pavillon Blanc du Château Margaux
Bordeaux Blanc (Haut-Médoc)

**Class Three**

Aile d'Argent (Ch. Mouton-
Rothschild) Bordeaux Blanc
(Haut-Médoc)
Blanc du Château Prieuré-Lichine
Bordeaux Blanc (Haut-Médoc)
Blanc de Lynch-Bages Bordeaux
Blanc (Haut-Médoc)
Caillou Blanc de Château Talbot
Bordeaux Blanc (Haut-Médoc)

Château Carbonnieux
(Pessac-Léognan)
Château Larrivet-Haut-Brion
(Pessac-Léognan)
Château Malartic-Lagravière
(Pessac-Léognan)
Château Olivier Blanc
(Pessac-Léognan)
Château Rahoul (Graves)

Eleven lesser-known, but very decent, white Bordeaux wines are worth considering for everyday consumption, because their prices are quite reasonable.
These are mainly the petits châteaux wines of Graves/Pessac-Léognan; most of
them retail from $12 to $14. Here they are, along with their appellations:

Château d'Archambeau Blanc (Graves)
Château Baret Blanc
(Pessac-Léognan)
Château Bonnet (Entre-Deux-Mers)
Château Chantegrive Blanc (Graves)
Château Chantegrive Cuvée Caroline
(Graves)
Château de Cruzeau Blanc
(Pessac-Léognan)

Château Ferrande Blanc (Graves)
Château de France Blanc
(Pessac-Léognan)
Château Haut-Gardère Blanc
(Pessac-Léognan)
Château Pontac-Monplaisir Blanc
(Pessac-Léognan)
Château Rochemorin Blanc
(Pessac-Léognan)

## *Drinking white Bordeaux*

Dry white Bordeaux is a versatile wine, but it's especially nice with
chicken, turkey, veal, and delicate fish entrées. It also goes well
with soft, mild cheeses; goat cheese is particularly fine with white
Bordeaux.

Like most fine white wines, dry white Bordeaux is best when you serve it slightly cool (but not cold!). The ideal serving temperature is in the 58 to 62 degrees Fahrenheit range.

The 1998 vintage is the best white-wine vintage in Graves/Pessac-Léognan in the '90s. Two other very good vintages for dry white wines in these districts were 1994 and 1993. Older vintages to look for — if you can find the wines at this point — are the 1983, 1985, 1987, 1989, and 1990. More recent recommended vintages include 2000, 2005, and 2006. (The least-expensive wines are best young, up to five years of age.)

# Sauternes and Barsac: Appealing to Your Sweet Tooth

Sauternes (saw-tairn) and Barsac (bar-sack) come from the southern part of the Graves district, about 25 miles southeast of the city of Bordeaux. These naturally sweet wines are products of one of nature's great, happy accidents: a fungus called *noble rot.*

In the autumn, mists rise from the Garonne River and its perfectly situated tributary, the Ciron, which runs through the heart of the Sauternes district. When the autumns are warm, dry, and prolonged, these mists enable a fungus called *botrytis cinerea* (boh-*try*-tis sin-eh-*ray*-ah) to grow on the grapes. This fungus makes the grapes ugly and wizened, sort of like raisins with a disease. But it also concentrates the sugars in their juice and contributes certain unusual flavors. These intensely concentrated, sweet grapes retain plenty of acidity, giving the wine made from them a remarkable balance. The acidity in Sauternes and Barsac adds a zest to the wines and prevents them from being cloyingly sweet.

Of course, the greatness of these wines comes at a price.

- ✔ **Production is small.** Each grapevine produces only a little (very concentrated) juice.

- ✔ **Production is very labor intensive.** Workers must go through the vineyards several times to hand-pick only those individual grapes that are sufficiently infected with *botrytis cinerea.*

- ✔ **Weather conditions must be perfect.** Warm or hot summers must be followed by warm, dry, sunny, long autumns for the noble rot to attack the grapes. Rain (especially frequent rains), hail, or frost — all common in a Bordeaux fall — can ruin the vintage for these wines.

Historically, the Sauternes district has averaged just three good vintages of sweet wine per decade. But nature was very good to the sweet wine districts in the 1980s and the second half of the 1990s. Six vintages in the 1980s and five each in the 1990s and 2000s have produced fine sweet wines.

This good fortune didn't come a minute too soon. Economically, the sweet wines of the Bordeaux region had been in dire straits until the 1980s. Numerous issues conspired against the châteaux that produced dessert wines, including a market trend favoring dry wines, the high costs of making these labor-intensive wines, and the infrequency of good vintages. But now things are looking up again, and the sweet wine regions are experiencing a renaissance.

The following sections introduce you to the Sauternes district of Bordeaux, the grapes and producers that make Sauternes and Barsac such renowned dessert wines, and ways to enjoy these wines (and perhaps even find a good bargain to enjoy!).

## Delving into the Sauternes wine district

Five *communes,* or villages, make up the Sauternes district: Barsac, Bommes, Fargues, Preignac, and Sauternes.

The sweet wines from all five of these communes are entitled to the Sauternes appellation. Barsac, the northernmost commune, makes wines that are so distinctive — in general, slightly dryer and lighter-bodied than those of the other communes — that its wines are entitled to a separate Barsac appellation. Each proprietor in Barsac can call its wine either Barsac or Sauternes; most of the better wines proudly use the former.

The Sauterne produced in California (note the difference in spelling; the original French wine has a final *s*) bears absolutely no resemblance to true Sauternes from Bordeaux. California Sauterne is a semisweet, rather ordinary, inexpensive wine made from nondescript grapes; a few of the state's largest producers sell most of it in large 4- or 5-liter bottles.

## Looking at the grape varieties that go into sweet Bordeaux wines

Sauternes and Barsac use the same grape varieties as dry white Bordeaux, but in inverse proportions. Whereas Sauvignon Blanc is the most prominent variety in the dry whites, Sémillon is king of Sauternes. As much as 75 to 80 percent of Sémillon makes up the typical Sauternes or Barsac, with the rest usually Sauvignon Blanc, although a few wineries use a little Muscadelle. Because each vintage brings different weather patterns, different proportions of each grape variety end up in the wine each year, depending on how each variety fared that season.

The golden, thin-skinned Sémillon grape plays the dominant role in these dessert wines because it's the perfect host for *botrytis cinerea*. In contrast, Sauvignon Blanc adds freshness and acidity to the blend. After ten years or so, the characteristics of the two varieties blend together completely and make an outstanding, harmonious dessert wine.

## Breaking down Sauternes and Barsacs by quality and price

At least six superb Sauternes and Barsacs are almost in the same class as Château d'Yquem (the absolute best sweet white Bordeaux). The little-known Château de Fargues, for example, which is owned by Yquem, is almost as good as Château d'Yquem and costs one-third of the price.

Following are six top Sauternes/Barsacs together with their approximate prices

2005 Château de Fargues (Sauternes); $135

2005 Château Climens (Barsac); $125

2005 Château Coutet (Barsac); $70

2005 Château Suduiraut (Sauternes); $100

2005 Château Rieussec (Sauternes); $90

2005 Château Raymond-Lafon (Sauternes); $65

Considering how labor-intensive great Sauternes and Barsacs are, these six wines are all excellent values. In fact, the Sauternes district (and the Barsac commune by association) has been blessed with a rarity — six good vintages in a row — because 1995, 1996, 1997, 1998, 1999, and 2000 are also fine vintages. For more recent years, 2001, 2002, 2003, 2005, 2006, and 2007 look promising.

If the prices of these six wines are a little off-putting, you might be glad to know that several other good Sauternes and Barsacs are out there within the $40 to $50 price range. And as an added bonus, almost all of the following wines (listed in unofficial Class One and Two categories) were ranked as Premier Crus in the 1855 Classification (see the related section earlier in this chapter for more on this important Bordeaux classification):

**Class One**

Château Clos-Haut-Peyraguey (Sauternes)

Château Doisy-Daëne (Barsac)

Château Doisy-Védrines (Barsac)

Château Guiraud (Sauternes)

Château Lafaurie-Peyraguey (Sauternes)

Château Nairac (Barsac)

Château Rabaud-Promis (Sauternes)

Château Sigalas-Rabaud (Sauternes)

Château La Tour-Blanche (Sauternes)

**Class Two**

| | |
|---|---|
| Château d'Arche (Sauternes) | Château de Malle (Sauternes) |
| Château Bastor-Lamontagne (Sauternes) | Château de Rayne-Vigneau (Sauternes) |
| Château Lamothe-Guignard (Sauternes) | Château Romieu-Lacoste (Barsac) |
| Château Liot (Barsac) | Château Suau (Barsac) |

## *Recommending bargain dessert wines*

As good as Sauternes and Barsacs are, they'll always be expensive. Fortunately, other districts in Bordeaux make dessert wines from Sémillon and Sauvignon Blanc as well, and because they're all near the Garonne River, these wines also develop *botrytis cinerea.* None of these wines are as intensely concentrated or as complexly flavored as Sauternes or Barsac, but they're considerably less expensive — retailing for $15 to $25.

---

# Visiting Bordeaux

After you're hooked on Bordeaux, you might want to visit the "mecca" from which these great wines emanate. A visit to the Bordeaux region should certainly include a stop at some of the magnificent châteaux in the Haut-Médoc; Château Margaux and Château Mouton-Rothschild (which has an interesting wine museum) in particular are not to be missed. Other châteaux worth visiting are Château Pichon-Longueville-Baron in Pauillac, with its new, modern winery, and the more traditional Château Palmer in Margaux. All of these châteaux are close to Route D 2, the road that winds its way through the four main villages of the Haut-Médoc. Call ahead for an appointment, and ask for a tasting — or else they might schedule just a tour for you.

In the Pessac-Léognan district, which surrounds and includes the city of Bordeaux, one estate well worth a visit is the First Growth, Château Haut-Brion, located on the outskirts of Bordeaux.

A trip to the southern Graves should certainly include a visit to the great Château d'Yquem, in the village of Sauternes. Write far in advance for an appointment, because Château d'Yquem is one of the most popular wine addresses in the world. The best restaurant in the area — and one of the best in the whole Bordeaux region — is Claude Darroze, in Langon, east of Sauternes. Claude Darroze is also an inn, with comfortable rooms.

St.-Emilion is the most charming, picturesque wine town in Bordeaux, if not in all of France. It's a historic town that was already famous for its wines in the fourth century. St.-Emilion is situated on a hillside overlooking the Dordogne Valley. The two châteaux in St.-Emillion definitely worth seeing are Château Ausone and Château Cheval Blanc, both of which also happen to make the finest wines in the region.

---

The dessert wines of four areas in Bordeaux are especially tasty bargains:

- **Cérons** is a commune within the Graves district, just north of Barsac.
- East of the Garonne River, in the Entre-Deux-Mares district, are the sweet wine areas of **Cadillac, Loupiac,** and **Sainte-Croix-du-Mont.**

These wines are perfect if you find Sauternes and Barsacs too intense, if you prefer a lighter-bodied dessert wine, or if you'd rather spend less money on your dessert wines.

## *Enjoying sweet Bordeaux*

Because Sauternes, Barsac, and other sweet Bordeaux wines are so rich, they go well with foie gras. Sauternes is also perfect after dinner with ripe fruits (such as pears), lemon cake, or pound cake. Not surprisingly, it's an excellent dessert all on its own.

Sauternes, Barsac, and other sweet Bordeaux wines taste best when served cold, at about 52 to 53 degrees Fahrenheit. If a Sauternes or Barsac has some age (15 years or more), it can be served a bit warmer.

# Chapter 3

# Burgundy, Queen of France

Some wine lovers swear that Burgundy is the greatest red wine in the world; others insist that Bordeaux holds that claim. Generally speaking, Burgundies are less reliable than the châteaux wines of Bordeaux's major districts because you often have to try a few red Burgundies before you find a great one. But the search is part of the lure of great Burgundy, and the great wines, when you find them, are nothing short of magical. Nothing quite compares in aroma and flavor to a great red Burgundy. And among white wines, white Burgundies are some of the finest dry whites in the world — when you select them carefully.

Clearly there's a bit of risk involved in loving Burgundy, but rest assured that the reward is so worth it. In this chapter, you uncover the secrets to enjoying the world's most seductive wine.

## The Where, Why, and What of Burgundy

Burgundy (called *Bourgogne* by the French) is a long, narrow wine region in eastern France, southeast of Paris, as you can see in Figure 3-1. It's a slightly fragmented region, consisting of four somewhat contiguous districts and one district that's about 70 miles northwest of the rest of the region. The main part of Burgundy begins just south of the city of Dijon and continues south to the city of Mâcon. Some of the best food and wine in France (and, quite frankly, the world) come from this superb region.

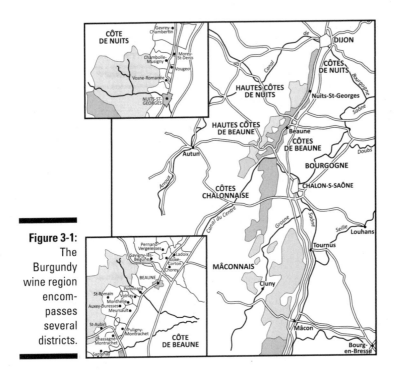

Figure 3-1:
The
Burgundy
wine region
encom-
passes
several
districts.

The next few sections get you familiar with the various factors that give Burgundy its unique flair, as well as the region's wine districts and its AOC system for naming and defining wines.

## A bit about Burgundy: Soil, grapes, and production scale

The soils of Burgundy are extremely varied in their richness, depth, and mineral content. The soils vary not only from one end of the region to the other but also within a single area — for example, from the top of a hill to the bottom, or from one vineyard plot to the next, even if the two are separated only by the breadth of a dirt road. The variation of soils is the most feasible explanation for the enormous range of wines made in Burgundy.

The climate in Burgundy is continental for the most part: cold winters and fairly warm summers, with the constant threat of hail. The region is northerly enough and cool enough that the grapes just about ripen in most years. Not every year is a good vintage; some years bring too much rain or are too cool. Fortunately, the grapes grown in Burgundy are suited to cool climates.

Because of its unique *terroir* — the special growing conditions in the vineyards — the Burgundy region excels in both red and white wines. Nearly all the red wines of the Burgundy region derive from a single red grape variety: Pinot Noir, a variety that's notorious throughout the wine world for being difficult to cultivate because it requires very specific soil and climate parameters to produce its best fruit. Burgundy has that climate and soil. (What's more, the variation in soil throughout the Burgundy region capitalizes on one of Pinot Noir's interesting attributes: that its wines reflect *terroir* differences clearly.) Few would argue that the Burgundy region has more success with this grape than any other wine region, and that red Burgundy wines are the world's finest examples of this challenging but delicious variety.

Chardonnay is the other important variety in the Burgundy region and serves as the basis for the region's most important white wines. Although Chardonnay is a nearly universal variety today, it reaches its height in Burgundy, where it makes complex, masterful wines that can age for decades.

Burgundy's *terroir* and grape varieties make the wines what they are, but they don't tell the whole story of the region. To understand Burgundy, you must also comprehend the intricate scale of the vineyards and the wine production.

Burgundy is a region of small vineyards, mixed ownership of vineyards, and relatively small production. Excluding the Beaujolais district, Burgundy produces a total of about 22 million cases of wine annually. (Beaujolais, which you can read about in Chapter 4 of Book II, is technically part of Burgundy but really a separate type of wine.)

The limited scale of production in Burgundy has three repercussions:

- ✔ The wines are expensive.

- ✔ Multiple brands of any one wine are available.

- ✔ The name of a vineyard isn't a reliable indication of a wine's quality, because every vineyard has several owners and winemakers, who vary in their dedication and ability.

Inconsistent quality from one producer to the next, coupled with high prices, makes buying Burgundies very tricky. Knowing the best Burgundy producers for a type of wine is essential if you plan to buy Burgundy wines on a regular basis. But — Catch-22! — the region has hundreds of producers who make thousands of wines.

If Burgundy is beginning to sound like a labyrinth to you — well, you've grasped the true complexity of the region. But like anything worth having, the reward of a fabulous Burgundy is worth the effort.

## A complex quartet: Burgundy's districts

Burgundy is a complex (some might even say complicated) region that encompasses four distinct wine districts. From north to south, these districts are

- Chablis
- Côte d'Or (a compound district made up of the districts Côte de Nuits and Côte de Beaune)
- Côte Chalonnaise
- Mâconnais

Technically, Burgundy includes another district, Beaujolais, which is south of the Mâconnais. Practically, however, Beaujolais isn't Burgundy; it has its own red grape variety (Gamay) and its own wines that are very different from those produced in the rest of Burgundy. You find out about Beaujolais in Chapter 4 of Book II.

Although the four districts of Burgundy all grow essentially the same two grape varieties, the wines of each district are unique in taste, and, in some cases, naming.

In the early days of winemaking in the United States, wineries borrowed the names of famous European wines — mainly French — for their own (American) wines. These "borrowed" wine names aren't as common as they once were, but they still exist. Real Burgundy and Chablis always have the words *Product of France* or *France* on their labels — and, of course, the phrase *Appellation Contrôlée*.

## The name game: Burgundy's AOC system

Because Burgundy is one of France's classic wine regions, the vast majority of wines produced there are AOC wines. (For more information on France's AOC system of naming and defining wines, turn to Chapter 1 in Book II.)

Burgundy's AOCs fall into four categories, according to the nature of their territory. From the most general to the most specific (and prestigious), these categories are as follows:

- **Regionwide appellations:** The grapes for these wines can grow throughout the Burgundy region.
- **District-specific appellations:** These wines come from grapes grown in a single district of Burgundy or a part of a district.

- **Village-specific appellations:** The grapes for these wines can grow only in the territory of certain villages (also called *communes*) named in the AOC regulations.

- **Vineyard-specific appellations:** The grapes for each of these wines must come from a single vineyard that's recognized in the AOC regulations.

The last category, vineyard-specific appellations, is actually a dual category, encompassing two levels of vineyards:

- **Premier cru vineyards:** 562 of these exist throughout Burgundy.

- **Grand cru vineyards:** AOC law recognizes 31 grand cru vineyards; these are the most prestigious of all the appellations of Burgundy. (This number doesn't include Chablis Grand Cru; the section "Grand Cru Chablis," later in this chapter, explains those wines.)

**Book II**

**France: A Wine Superstar**

One difference between the two levels of vineyard-specific appellations is that premier cru vineyards' names are subsidiary to the village where the vineyard is located. For example, the premier cru vineyard Les Suchots, in the village of Vosne-Romanée, carries the appellation "Vosne-Romanée Les Suchots." Grand cru vineyards, in contrast, are freestanding appellations that carry no village name.

Table 3-1 gives examples of Burgundy wine names that correspond to each category (note that single-vineyard sites are indicated by an asterisk).

| Table 3-1 | The Burgundy AOC System | |
|---|---|---|
| *Type of Appellation* | *Red Wine Example* | *White Wine Example* |
| Regionwide | Bourgogne Rouge | Bourgogne Blanc |
| District-specific | Côte de Nuits-Villages | Mâcon |
| Village-specific | Vosne-Romanée | Puligny-Montrachet |
| Premier cru | Vosne-Romanée Les Suchots* | Puligny-Montrachet Les Combettes* |
| Grand cru | Romanée-Conti* | Montrachet* |

*Single-vineyard site

Regionwide and district appellations account for about 55 percent of all Burgundy wines; these wines range from about $8 to $40 a bottle retail, depending mainly on the prestige of the producer. The most common appellation is Bourgogne, a regionwide appellation that translates simply as *Burgundy*. Some producers name the grape variety, Pinot Noir, on the labels of their Bourgogne Rouge (red Burgundy) wines and mention Chardonnay on the labels of their Bourgogne Blanc (white Burgundy) wines — but for any appellation higher than regionwide, you won't find the grape variety on the label. The regionwide category includes Burgundy's sparkling wine, Crémant de Bourgogne.

Wines with village-specific appellations usually come from several vineyards within the named village, such as Nuits-St.-Georges or Meursault. Village-level Burgundies represent about 34 percent of all Burgundy wines; 53 villages fall into this category. The retail price range for these wines is wide ($20 to $60), according to the prestige of the village and the producer.

A village-level Burgundy sometimes comes from a single vineyard rather than the grapes of several vineyards. In such cases, the name of the single vineyard often appears on the label — and it's easy to confuse this name with a premier cru vineyard name. One key is that the single-vineyard village Burgundy label usually has smaller lettering for the vineyard name than for the village name, and the vineyard name appears on a separate line from the village name. On labels of premier cru Burgundy, the village and vineyard usually appear in the same size print and on the same line.

Premier cru wines make up 10 percent of Burgundy wines. The majority of them carry the name of their premier cru vineyard, but occasionally you can find one that doesn't.

If a wine is made by blending the grapes of two or more premier cru vineyards from the same commune, it can be called a premier cru but can't carry the name of a specific premier cru vineyard. The label of such a wine shows a village name and the words *Premier Cru,* often written as *1er cru.*

Grand cru Burgundies carry only the name of the vineyard on the label, not the name of the village where the vineyard is situated. The 31 grand cru vineyards represent just 1.5 percent of Burgundy's wines.

# Burgundy Royalty: Côte d'Or

Most wine lovers associate the word *Burgundy* specifically with the wines from the Côte d'Or (pronounced coat dor), the heart of the Burgundy region.

The Côte d'Or is the name of a *département,* or county, in the Burgundy region. In wine terms, it's a narrow strip of villages and vineyards that starts just south of the city of Dijon and runs south-southwest about 30 miles to its southernmost major village, Santenay (see Figure 3-1). The Côte d'Or is the northernmost area in the world producing top-notch red wines. All the vineyards of the Côte d'Or are situated on a sunny, east- and southeast-facing slope that's only about a mile and a half wide at its widest point, and less than a quarter mile wide at its narrowest.

The word *côte* refers to this slope; some say that the phrase *d'or* means the slope is golden, because of the quality of wines grown there, but it actually refers to the slope's eastern (Orient) exposure.

Although this section deals with the Côte d'Or as a single district of Burgundy, it's actually two distinct districts in one:

- ✔ **Côte de Nuits:** The more northerly Côte de Nuits, named after its most important commercial town, Nuits-St.-Georges, is renowned for its great red Burgundies. (White Burgundies are a rarity here.)
- ✔ **Côte de Beaune:** The Côte de Beaune is named after Beaune, the major commercial town of the Côte d'Or and the most centrally located place to stay when visiting Burgundy. Côte de Beaune is equally renowned for its white and red Burgundies. Many wine lovers consider Côte de Beaune white Burgundies the world's finest dry white wines.

The Côte d'Or produces all levels of Burgundy wine. District-level appellations that you might occasionally see on wine labels include Côte de Nuits-Villages, Côte de Beaune-Villages, Hautes-Côtes-de-Nuits, and Hautes-Côtes-de-Beaune.

## *The Côte d'Or wine villages*

Although all the wines of the Côte d'Or come from the same grape varieties — Chardonnay (if they're white) or Pinot Noir (if they're red) — the wines are subtly different according to the village near which the grapes grow. And some villages have premier cru or grand cru vineyards that produce wines that are different from the basic village-level wine. These differences occur primarily because of soil variations along the slope.

The main wine villages in the Côte de Nuits are the following:

- ✔ **Marsannay:** Delicate rosés (from Pinot Noir) are its specialty.
- ✔ **Fixin:** This village produces earthy red wines. Its best vineyard is Clos du Chapitre (premier cru).

**Book II**

**France: A Wine Superstar**

- **Gevrey-Chambertin:** Full-bodied, rich red wines come from here, the village that's home to nine grands crus (such as Chambertin and Chambertin-Clos de Bèze).

- **Morey-St.-Denis:** Full, sturdy red wines are its specialty. Grands crus include Clos de la Roche, Clos St.-Denis, Clos de Tart, Clos des Lambrays, and Bonnes Mares (a small part).

- **Chambolle-Musigny:** This village is known for its elegant red wines that have a great deal of finesse. Its grands crus include Musigny and Bonnes Mares (the larger part); it also has superb premiers crus.

- **Vougeot:** Full-bodied red wines come from here, the home of the grand cru Clos de Vougeot.

- **Vosne-Romanée:** This village produces elegant, rich, velvety red wines. Its grands crus include the famous Romanée-Conti, La Tâche, Richebourg, Romanée-St.-Vivant, La Romanée, and La Grande Rue. Very fine premiers crus are also found here.

- **Flagey-Échézeaux:** The grands crus Grands-Échézeaux and Échézeaux are located in this hamlet of Vosne-Romanée.

- **Nuits-St.-Georges:** Sturdy, earthy, red wines are its specialty. This village doesn't have any grand cru vineyards, but it does boast a few excellent premiers crus (such as Les Saints-Georges and Les Vaucrains).

The main wine villages in the Côte de Beaune are as follows:

- **Ladoix:** Inexpensive, medium-bodied red and white wines come from here. The village encompasses part of two grands crus, Corton (red) and Corton-Charlemagne (white).

- **Pernand-Vergelesses:** This village is known for its good-value red and white wines. It encompasses about a quarter of grand cru Corton-Charlemagne (white).

- **Aloxe-Corton:** Full, sturdy wines are its specialty. Aloxe-Corton has several red grands crus vineyards, all of which include the name "Corton." It also has one great white grand cru (Corton-Charlemagne).

- **Chorey-lès-Beaune:** Good-value red wines, plus a few white wines, come from here.

- **Savigny-lès-Beaune:** This village offers mostly red wines that are fine values.

- **Beaune:** This village produces some whites and elegant, medium-bodied reds. It boasts fine premiers crus in both colors.

- **Pommard:** Sturdy, full red wines are Pommard's specialty; it's home to some good premiers crus (such as Rugiens and Épenots).

- ✔ **Volnay:** Elegant red wines with a deal of finesse come from Volnay, which has good premiers crus (such as Caillerets and Clos des Ducs).

- ✔ **Auxey-Duresses, Monthélie, St.-Romain, St.-Aubin:** These four little-known villages produce mainly red, but some white, wines that are excellent values because they're less known.

- ✔ **Meursault:** The first important white Burgundy commune, Meursault produces full-bodied, nutty wines. It's home to some excellent premiers crus (such as Les Perrières, Les Genevrières, and Les Charmes).

- ✔ **Puligny-Montrachet:** Elegant white Burgundies are its specialty, and its grands crus include Montrachet (a part), Chevalier-Montrachet, Bâtard-Montrachet (a part), and Bienvenues-Bâtard-Montrachet. It also has very fine premiers crus.

- ✔ **Chassagne-Montrachet:** A bit sturdier than Puligny, this village encompasses the rest of the Montrachet and Bâtard-Montrachet, plus Criots-Bâtard-Montrachet, grands crus. It produces some earthy, rustic reds.

- ✔ **Santenay:** Light-bodied, inexpensive red wines come from here.

- ✔ **Maranges:** Little-known, mainly red, inexpensive wines are Maranges' specialty.

**Book II**

**France: A Wine Superstar**

If you're struck with the desire to try a Volnay or a Chambolle-Musigny, pause for a bit before running out to buy a Burgundy based on an appellation. Consider choosing a wine according to the producer. You can never overestimate the importance of knowing the producer when you choose Burgundy wines. (Why? Check out the "The name game: Burgundy's AOC system" section earlier in this chapter for an explanation.)

## Côte d'Or wines in the market

The reds and whites of the Côte d'Or are the best that Burgundy has to offer — and they're priced accordingly. If you want to spend about $20 or less, seek out the reds and whites from the Côte Chalonnaise district or the whites from the Mâcon district (information on these wines follows later in this chapter). Or look for a Bourgogne Blanc or a Bourgogne Rouge — wines that can be grown anywhere in Burgundy — from a serious producer who has vineyards in the Côte d'Or; chances are that wine will have plenty of Côte d'Or grapes in it.

Lesser-known Côte d'Or village-level wines are the least expensive Côte d'Or wines; their retail price for both red and white wines can be as low as $20 to $30 per bottle. Village-level wines from the better-known villages are in the $40 to $55 price range.

Premier cru and grand cru Burgundies from the Côte d'Or have vast price ranges, depending upon the producer and the appellation. The less-prestigious premier cru wines, both red and white, can range from $25 to $40 per bottle, but the better-known premier cru Burgundies go from $40 to $150 a bottle.

Prices for grand cru Burgundies, both red and white, start around $70 a bottle but can go up as high as $900 a bottle for a Montrachet (white) from a great producer — or as high as $1,400 (a bottle!) for Romanée-Conti. The grand cru wine Romanée-Conti is normally Burgundy's (if not the world's) most expensive wine, based on the initial price of the wine when it's first released.

So you can spend your Burgundy dollars wisely, abide by the following criteria, listed in order of importance, when choosing your red or white Burgundy wines:

- **The producer's reputation:** Consult recent newsletters, review the list in the following section, or ask a knowledgeable wine merchant to get the scoop on reputable producers.

- **The vintage:** The Burgundy region experiences considerable variation in quality and style from year to year.

- **The appellation:** The name of the village and/or the vineyard, although significant, is invariably less important than the producer or the vintage.

## Côte d'Or producers to buy

Producers named "Domaine" own the vineyards from which they make their wines; those named "Maison" are *négociants* who buy grapes and wine, as well as grow grapes themselves and sell wine made from their various supply sources. *Négociants* are usually larger than grower-producers, and their wines are more readily available.

The following lists show the top producers of Burgundy in the Côte d'Or, first red Burgundy, then white Burgundy. Some producers make wines from two or more villages, and make both white and red wine; those producers are listed under the type for which they're most known.

The top 30 Côte d'Or red Burgundy producers are as follows:

Domaine Bertrand Ambroise (white Burgundy too)
Domaine du Marquis d'Angerville
Domaine Robert Arnoux
Domaine Robert Chevillon

Domaine Bruno Clair (white Burgundy too)
Domaine Claude Dugat
Domaine Dujac
Maison (and Domaine) Faiveley

Maison Bouchard Père et Fils (white Burgundy too)
Domaine Henri Gouges
Domaine Jean Grivot
Domaine Robert Groffier
Domaine Anne Gros
Maison Louis Jadot (white Burgundy too)
Domaine Jayer-Gilles
Domaine Michel Lafarge
Maison Dominique Laurent
Domaine (and Maison) Leroy (white Burgundy too)
Domaine Hubert Lignier

Domaine Méo-Camuzet
Domaine Denis Mortet
Domaine Georges Mugneret / Mugneret-Gibourg
Domaine Jacques-Frédéric Mugnier
Domaine de la Romanée-Conti (also makes Montrachet)
Domaine Joseph Roty
Domaine Georges et Christophe Roumier
Domaine Armand Rousseau
Clos de Tart
Domaine Jean et Jean-Louis Trapet
Domaine du Comte de Vogüé

Other fine red Burgundy producers include

Domaine Amiot-Servelle
Domaine de l'Arlot
Domaine du Comte Armand
Domaine Ghislaine Barthod (also called Barthod-Noëllat)
Domaine Simon Bize (white Burgundy too)
Domaine Jean-Yves Bizot
Domaine Chandon de Briailles (white Burgundy too)
Domaine Chauvenet-Chopin
Domaine du Clos des Lambrays
Domaine Jean-Jacques Confuron
Domaine Edmond et Pierre Cornu
Domaine de Courcel
Domaine Drouhin-Laroze
Maison Joseph Drouhin (white Burgundy too)
Domaine René Engel
Domaine Forey
Domaine Fourrier

Domaine Jean Garaudet
Domaine Antonin Guyon (white Burgundy too)
Domaine Fernand Lécheneaut et Fils
Domaine René Leclerc
Domaine Bernard Maume
Domaine Mongeard-Mugneret
Domaine Albert Morot
Domaine des Perdrix (owned by Maison Antonin Rodet)
Domaine Henri Perrot-Minot
Maison Nicolas Potel
Domaine Jacques Prieur (white Burgundy too; owned by A. Rodet)
Domaine Daniel Rion
Domaine Rossignol
Domaine Emmanuel Rouget
Domaine Christian Sérafin
Domaine Tollot-Beaut (white Burgundy too)

Following are recommended Côte d'Or white Burgundy producers (the asterisk denotes particularly outstanding producers):

Domaine Guy Amiot et Fils
Domaine Bachelet-Ramonet
Domaine Bitouzet-Prieur
Domaine Blain-Gagnard (red
  Burgundy too)
Domaine Jean Boillot (red Burgundy
  too; plus Maison Henri Boillot)
Domaine Jean-Marc Boillot
  (red Burgundy too)
Domaine Bonneau du Martray
  (red Burgundy too)
Domaine Boyer-Martenot
Domaine Louis Carillon & Fils*
Domaine Jean-François Coche-Dury*
Domaine Marc Colin et Fils
Domaine Michel Colin-Déléger
Domaine Arnaud Ente
Domaine Jean-Philippe Fichet
Domaine Fontaine-Gagnard
Domaine Jean-Noël Gagnard
Domaine Génot-Boulanger
Maison Vincent Girardin
  (red Burgundy too)
Domaine Patrick Javillier
Domaine François Jobard
Domaine Rémi Jobard

Domaine des Comtes Lafon*
  (red Burgundy too)
Maison Louis Latour (red
  Burgundy too)
Domaine Latour-Giraud
Domaine Leflaive*
Maison Olivier Leflaive Frères
Château de la Maltroye
Domaine Joseph/Pierre Matrot
Domaine (and Maison) Bernard
  Morey et Fils
Domaine Jean-Marc Morey
Domaine Marc Morey
Domaine Pierre Morey
Maison Morey-Blanc
Domaine Michel Niellon
Domaine Paul Pernot
Domaine Ramonet*
Domaine Roland Rapet (red
  Burgundy too)
Maison Antonin Rodet (red
  Burgundy too)
Domaine Guy Roulet
Domaine Étienne Sauzet*
Maison Verget

# The Côte Chalonnaise: Affordable Burgundies

Shortly after you leave the village of Santenay in the southern end of the Côte d'Or, you enter another Burgundy district called the Côte Chalonnaise (coat shal-oh-naze; check out Figure 3-1). The first town you come across is Chagny, the home of a fine Michelin three-star restaurant and inn, Lameloise. After Chagny, the vineyards begin, and you're in Burgundy wine country once more.

The Côte Chalonnaise district boasts five wine villages that are good sources of very decent, affordable red and white Burgundies — about $15 to $30 a bottle, retail. Côte Chalonnaise Burgundies aren't quite so fine as most Côte d'Or Burgundies; they tend to be a bit earthier and have less complex aromas and flavors. But they're good values and excellent choices in restaurants or for everyday drinking.

## Some tips on serving red Burgundy

Unlike red Bordeaux (see Chapter 2 in Book II), red Burgundy from the Côte d'Or can be consumed when it's relatively young, after five or six years. Why, you ask? Because the Pinot Noir grape contains far less tannin than Cabernet Sauvignon or Merlot (Bordeaux's grape varieties), a fact that makes red Burgundy approachable in its youth.

On the other hand, red Côte d'Or Burgundies from good producers in good vintages are easily capable of aging for 20 years or more, when stored in a cool place. (Red Burgundy is especially vulnerable to heat; flip to Chapter 8 of Book I for advice on properly storing wine.) Red Burgundies from the Côte Chalonnaise should generally be consumed within 10 to 12 years, however.

Serve your red Burgundies slightly cool — about 60 to 62 degrees Fahrenheit in a fine, wide-bowled glass. Do _not_ decant red Burgundies; instead, pour them straight from the bottle. Too much aeration causes you to lose some of your Burgundy's wonderful aromas — one of its greatest qualities.

Recent good red Burgundy vintages include the 1999, 1997, 1996 (especially), 1995, and 1990. Vintages that are worth buying and storing are the 2002 and 2005 vintages.

If you're ordering red Burgundy with food, follow this advice:

- Try a lighter-bodied red Burgundy with chicken, turkey, or ham.
- Drink a full-bodied red Burgundy with beef, game, or game birds (including duck).

Like Côte d'Or whites — and unlike many whites from Chablis or the Mâconnais district (see the "Everyday Whites: The Mâcon" section later in this chapter) — the white wines of the Côte Chalonnaise tend to have smoky, toasty flavors from being fermented or aged in oak barrels. As in the rest of Burgundy, Pinot Noir is the red grape of the Côte Chalonnaise; Chardonnay is the white grape, but the white Aligoté (ah-lee-go-tay) variety happens to be a specialty of the village of Bouzeron.

## Côte Chalonnaise appellations

A new district-level appellation, Bourgogne Côte Chalonnaise, applies to the vineyards in this area. But many grapes grown in this district end up as wines with regionwide appellations, such as Bourgogne Rouge/Blanc or Crémant de Bourgogne.

Five Côte Chalonnaise villages (listed from north to south) boast village-level appellations, and some of them have premier cru vineyards

- Bouzeron
- Rully
- Mercurey
- Givry
- Montagny

The specialty of Bouzeron is Bourgogne Aligoté de Bouzeron, a lively, light-bodied wine with refreshing acidity. Aubert de Villaine (an owner of the great Domaine de la Romanée-Conti in the Côte d'Or) is the best producer; his Bouzeron property is called A&P de Villaine. The A&P de Villaine Bourgogne Rouge and Bourgogne Blanc come mainly from grapes of this area and are good wines.

Rully's production is about half red and half white, but the whites are considerably more interesting. Some Rully vineyards have premier cru status. Antonin Rodet is a leading producer of Rully (and Mercurey) Burgundies.

The best red Burgundies of the Côte Chalonnaise come from Mercurey; in fact, the Chalonnaise district is sometimes even called the *Région de Mercurey*. Mercurey Rouge is equivalent in quality to some of the lesser Burgundies of the Côte d'Or, but at lower prices; the more difficult to find Mercurey whites are also quite good. A whopping 95 percent of Mercurey's production is red, and 5 percent is white; several premier cru vineyards exist in Mercurey.

Givry's red wines, which dominate the village's production and account for about 90 percent of Givry wine, are higher in quality than its whites. They tend to be earthy and rather rustic in style.

The entire production of Montagny, the southernmost Chalonnaise wine village, is white, and some of it is premier cru. The wines offer good value, but generally they aren't quite as good as the more-expensive Rully and Mercurey whites.

# Côte Chalonnaise producers to look for

Look for the following producers of Côte Chalonnaise wines:

Domaine Bertrand (Montagny)

René Bourgeon (Givry Blanc)

Domaine Jean-Claude Brelière (Rully)

Domaine Michel Briday (Rully)

Château de Chamirey (Antonin Rodet — Mercurey Rouge and Blanc)

Château de Rully (Antonin Rodet — both Rully Blanc and Rouge)

J. Faiveley (Mercurey Rouge and Blanc; Rully Blanc; Montagny)

Domaine de la Folie (Rully Blanc; Rouge, especially Clos St. Jacques)

Château Genot-Boulanger (Mercurey)

Domaine Joblot (Givry)

Domaine Michel Juillot (Mercurey Rouge and Blanc)

Louis Latour (Mercurey Rouge; Rully Blanc; Givry Blanc; Montagny)

Olivier Leflaive Frères (Rully Blanc; Mercurey Blanc)

Domaine Thierry Lespinasse (Givry)

Domaine de la Rénarde (Rully)

Domaine Thénard (Givry)

Domaine A & P de Villaine (Bouzeron Aligoté; Mercurey Rouge; Rully Blanc)

**Book II**

**France: A Wine Superstar**

# Chablis, from Chablis, France — A Distant Part of Burgundy

Yes, Virginia, there's a town in France called Chablis (shah-blee). It's a tiny town of less than 3,000 inhabitants, in the center of the Chablis wine district, about a two-hour drive southeast of Paris.

The Chablis district is far from the rest of the Burgundy region, more than 70 miles, and yet it's a part of the region thanks to the Duke of Burgundy, who annexed the area in the 15th century. Chablis has a climate and soil distinctly different from the rest of Burgundy, but it does have a grape variety in common with the other districts: Chardonnay. This northernmost outpost of Burgundy produces 100 percent Chardonnay wines.

Chablis' climate is generally cool, similar to that of the Champagne region to its north (which you can read about in Chapter 6 of Book II). The weather has a particularly strong effect on the wines of Chablis.

✔ The vineyards are prone to spring frosts, and when a frost is severe, it can wipe out half the crop.

✔ Too cool or rainy a year yields lean, ungiving wines that are too high in acidity.

✔ Years that are too warm produce uncharacteristically full-bodied, rich, ripe wines that are too low in acidity.

Chablis is one district for which you must pay particularly close attention to vintages. In a good vintage, Chablis can be magical: pale straw in color with hints of green, turning light gold with age; bone-dry and medium-bodied, with lively acidity that makes the wine great with seafood; concentrated in delicate, minerally aromas and an appley flavor that lingers long after you swallow. A wine with lovely austerity in the best of times, Chablis can have too much acidity in cool, wet vintages. (See the section "Recommended Chablis vintages," later in this chapter, for guidance on good Chablis vintages to buy.)

Read on to find out more about Chablis' distinct naming system and good producers and vintages to watch for.

## Chablis appellations

Chablis has a distinctly different appellation system from the rest of Burgundy. The wines of the Chablis district fall into four separate appellations, listed from least prestigious to most prestigious:

- ✔ Petit Chablis
- ✔ Chablis
- ✔ Chablis Premier Cru
- ✔ Chablis Grand Cru

The Petit Chablis zone, which produces less than 10 percent of Chablis wine, is farthest from the town of Chablis and located in the least interesting part of the district, soil-wise. The wine from this zone is quite forgettable, and very little is exported to the United States.

Most Chablis wines fall into the Chablis appellation; sometimes wine people refer to these wines as Chablis AC (for *Appellation Contrôlée*), to distinguish them from Chablis Grand Cru or Chablis Premier Cru. These basic Chablis wines can be quite decent in good vintages, and they retail in the $16 to $24 price range. Drink Chablis AC wines within five or six years of the vintage.

---

## The lingo of Burgundy

Although the term *Burgundy* technically refers to all the region's wines, most of the time people use the term for red or white Burgundies from the Côte d'Or, or for the regionwide wines, Bourgogne Rouge or Bourgogne Blanc. When people talk about a wine from the Côte Chalonnaise, they usually specify the village, such as Mercurey, or refer to the wine as a Burgundy from the Côte Chalonnaise. For the other districts, common usage is to call the wine by its district or village name, such as Chablis, Mâcon-Villages, or Pouilly-Fuissé, instead of calling it Burgundy.

Chablis is one wine where it pays to upgrade, however. Grand Cru and Premier Cru Chablis are distinctly better wines than the basic Chablis AC wines; they're worth the extra money.

### Grand Cru Chablis

On one slope just north of the town of Chablis lie seven vineyards that have been designated grand cru. The wines made from these grand cru vineyards are the most intensely flavored, concentrated, and longest-lived of all Chablis wines, yet they make up a mere 3 percent of all Chablis wines. The seven grand cru vineyards, listed according to their renown, are

- Les Clos
- Vaudésir
- Valmur
- Grenouilles
- Blanchots
- Les Preuses
- Bougros

**Book II**

**France: A Wine Superstar**

Another small vineyard, La Moutonne, is part of Vaudésir and Les Preuses but doesn't hold grand cru status in its own right. When you see *La Moutonne* on a Chablis label, however, you can consider the wine to be grand cru quality.

Although all seven grand cru Chablis vineyards are capable of producing excellent wines (depending upon the producer and the vintage), three vineyards have the finest reputations: Les Clos and Vaudésir, followed by Valmur.

Most Grand Cru Chablis wines retail in the $45 to $90 price range — not inexpensive but still a bargain, considering their quality and the prices of comparable good white Burgundies from the Côte d'Or (see "Burgundy Royalty: Côte d'Or" earlier in this chapter). In good vintages, Grand Cru Chablis can age and improve for 15 years or more.

### Premier Cru Chablis

The best compromise between the great, but fairly expensive, Grand Cru Chablis and the simple Chablis AC wines are the Premier Cru Chablis. They're a big step up from Chablis AC, yet they're reasonably priced in the $25 to $45 range. And in the hands of a good producer, a Premier Cru (sometimes written as *1er Cru* on the label) Chablis compares in quality to many Grand Crus. It's usually not quite so intensely flavored and a bit lighter-bodied than a Grand Cru, but a Premier Cru in a good vintage can age and improve for ten years or more.

About 40 premier cru vineyards exist, scattered in all directions around the town of Chablis. Some of the best are located right next to grand cru vineyards. Throughout the years, a few of the premier cru vineyards became the best-known (probably because they were the best, quality-wise). Now, lesser-known premier cru vineyards in the proximity of the well-known premier crus are allowed to use the more famous vineyards' names for their wines. Although on the surface this system seems deceptive, the quality of the wines doesn't seem compromised, assuming the producer is good.

The six premier cru names that appear most frequently on Chablis labels are as follows (the first three are the most favorably located):

- Montée de Tonnere
- Mont de Milieu
- Fourchaume
- Vaillons
- Montmains
- Les Forêts (also sold as "La Forest")

## *Good Chablis producers*

Following are some good Chablis producers:

**Class One**

Jean Collet
Jean Dauvissat
René & Vincent Dauvissat
Jean-Paul Droin

Louis Michel & Fils
François & Jean-Marie Raveneau
Verget

**Class Two**

Jean-Claude Bessin
Long-Depaquit
Gérard Duplessis
William Fèvre

Christian Moreau Père et Fils
Domaine Laroche
Billaud-Simon

**Class Three**

Domaine A. & F. Boudin
Jean-Marc Brocard
La Chablisienne (Coopérative)
Jean & Daniel Defaix
Jean Durup
Robert Vocoret et Fils

Jean-Pierre Grossot
Domaine Pinson
A. Regnard & Fils
    (also known as Albert Pic)
Simonnet-Febvre

## Recommended Chablis vintages

A recent classic vintage for Chablis has been 1996. Another very good vintage is 1995 (but these wines are a bit harder and more austere than in '96). If you like a more forward, rich, plush style of wine, then you'll probably enjoy the 1997 vintage.

Older vintages worth buying, if you can find well-stored bottles of Premier or Grand Cru Chablis, are 1992, 1990, 1989, 1986, and 1985. Just about all the Chablis from these vintages are ready to drink; some may be past their best drinking stage.

# Everyday Whites: The Mâcon

The city of Mâcon is an important crossroads in France because it serves as a passageway to Provence, Switzerland, and Italy. It's located at the southern end of the Mâconnais, a wine district that's directly south of the Côte Chalonnaise and north of Beaujolais (see Figure 3-1). As you travel into the Mâconnais, you notice the slight change in climate. The weather becomes warmer and sunnier, more and more Mediterranean-like; palm trees actually grow in Mâcon!

Some of the greatest white wine values in the world come from the Mâconnais district of Burgundy. Where else can you buy a very decent 100 percent Chardonnay wine for $8 to $10?

## Mâcon's appellations and wines

Almost all of the Mâcon wine that's exported is white. About one-third of the wine from the Mâconnais is red, however; it's called Mâcon Rouge, and it comes mainly from the Gamay grape variety, of Beaujolais fame. (After all, Mâcon is adjacent to Beaujolais.) Because Beaujolais is a more successful wine commercially, the production of Mâcon red wine has been declining steadily; it was once more common than white Mâcon.

Bourgogne Rouge, which legally can be made only from Pinot Noir, is also produced in the Mâconnais, as well as an interesting red wine called Bourgogne Passetoutgrains. The colorful name translates roughly as "Burgundy Let All the Grapes In"; the wine is usually two-thirds Gamay and one-third Pinot Noir and is always attractively priced. But white wine is the main game in the Mâconnais district today.

# Enjoying white Burgundy

White Côte d'Or Burgundies are among the most long-lived white wines in the world. In good vintages, the best white Burgundies, such as Corton-Charlemagne or a grand cru Montrachet, can age for 20 years or more. Unlike red Burgundies, the better whites need time, often ten years or more, to really develop and open up. *Remember:* Make sure you decant your serious white Burgundies; they truly benefit from the extra aeration.

The best drinkability periods for other white Burgundies are as follows:

✔ Grand Cru Chablis is at its best after about eight to ten years of aging and can live for at least another five years or more after that.

✔ Premier Cru Chablis needs at least five or six years of aging to develop; it'll still be fine for drinking for another seven or eight years.

✔ Côte Chalonnaise white Burgundies, such as Rully Blanc, can be consumed in their youth, but should last for up to ten years.

✔ All Mâconnais wines are best in their youth; the better Pouilly-Fuissés, however, can age for eight to ten years — although they don't necessarily improve with age.

Serve fine white Burgundies slightly cooler than red ones — about 55 to 58 degrees Fahrenheit. You can't appreciate their wonderful, complex flavors when they're too cold. A wide-bowled glass, just slightly smaller than the one you use for red Burgundies, is perfect for enjoying a good white Burgundy.

Good white Burgundy vintages include the 2006, 2005, 2002, 1999, 1997, 1996 (especially), 1995, 1992, 1989, and 1986. The wines of the last five, 1996, 1995, 1992, 1989, and 1986, are completely developed and ready to drink. (*Note:* Chablis vintages work a little differently because the climate in that region marches to a different drum. See the nearby section "Recommended Chablis vintages" for help buying good Chablis.)

When it comes to pairing white Burgundies with food, try fish, seafood, or poultry; just avoid any fruity sauces, because the wines themselves aren't fruity, and they taste austere against the sauce. Lobster accompanied by a full-bodied white Burgundy is a particularly fine pairing.

The next two sections delve into the specific appellations of Mâcon white wines.

### Mâcon and Mâcon-Villages

Most Mâcon (mah-cawn) white wines carry the appellations Mâcon, Mâcon Supérieur (which contains 1 percent more alcohol), or Mâcon-Villages. Mâcon-Villages (mah-cawn vee-lahj) wines come from 43 specific villages, and they're slightly better than simple Mâcon wines. Also fairly common are wines with one specific village name attached to the word *Mâcon,* such as Mâcon-Viré or Mâcon-Lugny. These last two appellations are common because large *cooperative* wineries (wineries that pool the grapes of private growers) are located in Viré and Lugny. About 90 percent of Mâcon wine is made by cooperatives, in fact; the economy of scale enjoyed by co-ops is one of the main reasons that Mâcon is so reasonably priced.

All of these Mâcon white wines range in price from $8 to $14. They're medium-bodied, fresh, crisp, lively, and almost always made without the use of oak. Drink them when they're young — within three years of the vintage.

### Pouilly-Fuissé and St.-Véran

The best Mâcon wines have more specific appellations. They're all white wines, and they all come from the southernmost part of the Mâconnais, just north of Beaujolais.

The most famous Mâcon wine is undoubtedly Pouilly-Fuissé (pwee-fwee-say), the most full-bodied and, at $18 to $45, clearly the most expensive wine of the Mâconnais. Pouilly-Fuissé wines come from a vineyard area around the villages of Pouilly and Fuissé, and unlike simpler Mâcon white wines, they're usually aged in small oak barrels.

St.-Véran (san-veh-rahn) wines have about half the production (250,000 cases annually) of Pouilly-Fuissé, and at $11 to $17 a bottle, they're far better values. The St.-Véran subdistrict, at the very southern end of the Mâconnais, includes the village of St.-Vérand. These wines are similar to Pouilly-Fuissé but are less full-bodied. A new AOC, Viré-Clessé, established in 1998, now includes some of the better Mâcon white wines from the vicinity of Viré and Clessé.

Book II

France:
A Wine
Superstar

## Mâcon producers to buy

Here's a list of recommended producers of Mâcon, Mâcon-Villages, Viré-Clessé, and St.-Véran wines:

André Bonhomme  
Joseph Drouhin  
Emilian Gillet  
Louis Jadot  
Roger Lasserat  
Louis Latour  

Manciat-Poncet  
Olivier Merlin  
Domaine Jean Thévenet  
Jean-Claude Thévenet  
Domaine Valette  
Verget

If you're looking for a good Pouilly-Fuissé wine to try, check out any of the following recommended producers:

Maniel Barraud

Château de Beauregard

Domaine Robert Denogent

Domaine J.A. Ferrat

Thierry Guérin

Louis Jadot

Roger Lasserat

Louis Latour

Manciat-Poncet

Domaine Valette

Verget

M. Vincent/Château Fuisse

# Chapter 4

# Beaujolais, the Fun Red

. . . . . . . . . . . . . . . . . . . . . . . . . . . . . . . . . . . . . . . . . . . . . . . . .

*In This Chapter*

▶ Exploring the origins of a youthful, unique wine

▶ Splitting Beaujolais's personalities into the main appellations

▶ Knowing who makes Beaujolais and what it costs to get a bottle

. . . . . . . . . . . . . . . . . . . . . . . . . . . . . . . . . . . . . . . . . . . . . . . . .

The Beaujolais region is unique among French wine regions because it makes wines that are happy to please without trying to impress. Sure, some Beaujolais wines are better than others, but even the best wines, such as a good Moulin-à-Vent, don't require contemplative attention. Grapey, unpretentious Beaujolais is for drinking. How refreshing!

## What Makes Beaujolais

Beaujolais (pronounced boh-jhoe-lay) wine is the product of the Beaujolais region and the red Gamay grape variety. (White Beaujolais, or "Beaujolais Blanc" — made mostly from the Chardonnay grape, but Aligoté is permitted — does exist, but it's a relative rarity.) A particular type of winemaking used in the region also shapes the character of Beaujolais wines.

The Beaujolais region lies south of the Mâcon district of Burgundy, extending from the Mâconnais border southward to within a few miles of the city of Lyons. Administratively, Beaujolais is a district of the Burgundy region, but the red wine of Beaujolais is so different from those in the rest of Burgundy — made from a different grape variety grown in different soil and a warmer climate — that Beaujolais can be considered a wine region in its own right, distinct from Burgundy.

The following sections describe the factors that make Beaujolais what it is: *terroir,* Gamay, and carbonic maceration.

## The Beaujolais terroir

To fully appreciate Beaujolais, it helps to have an understanding of the region's *terroir* (its unique combination of climate and soil). Beaujolais is a large wine region by Burgundy's standards: It's about twice the size of Rhode Island and larger than any other Burgundy district. The Monts du Beaujolais (Beaujolais Mountains) form the western border of the region; the terrain descends from these mountains eastward, toward the Saône River Valley. The region encompasses nearly 50,000 acres of vineyards, which extend 34 miles in length and 7 to 9 miles in width. The vineyards are situated on undulating hills in the eastern part of the region.

Beaujolais is near enough to the Mediterranean Sea to experience Mediterranean-like summer weather, which is warm and dry, but the region is also interior enough to experience cold, dry weather from the northeast, including spring frosts. Overall, the climate in the Beaujolais region is temperate.

Soil variations are the most significant factor in defining the character of the region's various wines.

- ✔ In the southern part of the region, south of the town of Villefranche, the soils are either sandstone or a mix of clay and limestone.
- ✔ In the north, the soils are granite or *schist* (crystalline rock) on the upper slopes, with stone and clay soils on the lower slopes.

Just as the soils are different in the north, so are the wines. The sturdiest, firmest Beaujolais wines come from the northern vineyards, whereas the lightest, most supple wines come from the southern vineyards.

## The Gamay grape

Except for a small amount of Chardonnay, 99 percent of the Beaujolais vineyards are covered by a single grape variety: Gamay (pronounced ga-may). All red Beaujolais wine derives entirely from this grape variety.

Gamay exists in a few other places — like in France's Loire Valley and Switzerland — but the Beaujolais region is the true stronghold for this variety. In fact, the finest Gamey wines come from this area. (**Note:** Neither the grape called Gamay Beaujolais in California nor the grape called Napa Gamay is true Gamay.)

The Gamay variety makes wines that are fairly deep in color, with a bluish tinge. Gamey wines tend to have light to medium body, relatively low acidity, moderate tannin, and aromas and flavors of red berries. (Wondering what some of these descriptors are actually describing? Flip to Chapter 5 of Book I for the explanations.)

## The winemaking technique

This book doesn't cover technical issues such as winemaking very much, but for Beaujolais, the topic is unavoidable because a particular winemaking technique that's widely practiced in the region contributes significantly to the style of Beaujolais wines. This technique is known as *carbonic maceration* (because the grapes *macerate,* or soak, in a carbon dioxide–rich environment). It's a fairly simple process in terms of what the winemaker does, but it's more complicated chemically. The effect of the process is a reduction in the wine's tannin and an enhancement of particular fruity aromas and flavors in the wine.

The principal behind carbonic maceration is that when whole grapes are deprived of oxygen, they begin to *ferment* (meaning their sugars convert to alcohol) from the inside; certain other changes occur within the grape berries, such as the formation of particular aroma and flavor compounds. This internal fermentation happens without the help of yeasts; normal fermentation, in contrast, occurs because yeasts come in contact with the juice of crushed grapes.

For the lightest Beaujolais wines — specifically, the style called Beaujolais Nouveau — the fermentation can be as short as three days. Other styles ferment for about ten days, during which time they gain more color and tannin from the grape skins than the lighter styles do.

# From Frivolous to Firm: An Overview of Beaujolais Wines

Not all Beaujolais wine is the same. Soil differences throughout the region and subtle variations in winemaking technique cause the wines to vary considerably in style — from light-bodied, precocious wines at one end of the spectrum to denser, fuller-bodied wines at the other end. However, one characteristic is the same across the board: All Beaujolais wines are dry.

The next few sections provide you with a closer look at the main appellations of Beaujolais. Enjoy!

## Beaujolais and Beaujolais-Villages

The lightest wines, from the southern part of the region, usually carry the region's most basic appellation, Beaujolais. In theory, a wine with a simple Beaujolais appellation can come from anywhere in the region, but in practice, these wines originate almost entirely from the southern third of the region, where the soil is sandy or clayey. They account for about 75 million bottles a year; that's half of the region's total production.

Wines with the simple Beaujolais appellation are generally light-bodied with low tannin and pronounced, youthful, fruity aromas and flavors; they're wines to drink young, in the first year after the harvest. Wines with the appellation Beaujolais Supérieur are basic Beaujolais wines that have a higher minimum alcohol content.

A separate type of Beaujolais comes from grapes grown in the territory of 39 villages in the northern part of the region: Beaujolais-Villages (bo-jhoe-lay vee-lahj). These wines are fuller and more substantial than simple Beaujolais wines, thanks to the schist and granite soils of the north, but they're still fruity, fresh, youthful wines meant to be consumed young (up to the age of two years). Beaujolais-Villages wines account for 25 percent of all Beaujolais production.

## Beaujolais Nouveau

Beaujolais Nouveau (new Beaujolais) is the lightest, fruitiest, most exuberant style of Beaujolais. It differs from other Beaujolais wines not according to where it comes from, but according to how it's made: with minimum aging and maximum personality. Beaujolais Nouveau is designed to be delicious when it's barely two months old.

Beaujolais Nouveau is the first French wine to be released from each year's new crop of grapes. The grapes are harvested in the Beaujolais and Beaujolais-Villages vineyards in late August or September, depending on the weather. (About two-thirds of the wine from these two areas is made into Beaujolais Nouveau.) By mid-November, the wine is already bottled and on its way to market. On the third Thursday of November, the wine becomes legal: Wine drinkers all over the world open bottles to celebrate the harvest.

Some wine lovers like to deride Beaujolais Nouveau, criticizing it for not being a serious wine. Actually, they're right: It's not a serious wine. But it *is* delicious, and it's definitely fun; many wine lovers can't imagine letting November end without drinking a bottle or two of Beaujolais Nouveau. Since when do all wines have to be serious, anyway?

# Cru Beaujolais

The best Beaujolais wines come from ten specific zones in the north. They carry the name of the area where the grapes grow; their official appellations don't use the word *Beaujolais* at all. (Many labels for the U.S. market do carry the words *Red Beaujolais Wine* in small print, however.)

The wines from these ten areas are known as *cru Beaujolais*. (Unlike in Burgundy and Alsace, these top wines are simply crus, not grands crus.) Cru Beaujolais wines are firmer, richer, and more refined than other Beaujolais wines. But generalizations about these wines are problematic, because the cru wines vary in style from one *cru* (wine estate) to another. Some are perfumed and charming in personality; others are dense and relatively powerful in style.

The ten cru Beaujolais, from south to north, are

- ✔ Broadly (broo-yee)
- ✔ Côte de Broadly (coat duh broo-yee)
- ✔ Reggie (ray-nyay)
- ✔ Morgon (mor-gohn)
- ✔ Chiroubles (sheh-roob-leh)
- ✔ Fleurie (flehr-ee)
- ✔ Moulin-à-Vent (moo-lahn-ah-vahn)
- ✔ Chénas (shay-nahs)
- ✔ Juliennes (jool-yay-nahs)
- ✔ St.-Amour (sant-ah-more)

The names of all of these wines are the names of specific villages, with the exception of Brouilly and Côte de Brouilly (named for the volcanic Mont Brouilly) and Moulin-à-Vent (named for a windmill).

Brouilly, Régnié, and Chiroubles tend to be the lightest of the cru wines (although they have more substance than many Beaujolais-Villages wines, described earlier in this chapter). Brouilly, in fact, is the largest of the cru territories. Régnié happens to be the newest cru, recognized in 1988. One of the best — not only of the lighter crus, but of all ten — is Chiroubles, a wine with lovely aromatic delicacy and a perfumed, pretty style; it embodies the very personality of Beaujolais.

In the middle group, stylistically, are Côte de Brouilly, Fleurie, and St.-Amour. Of these three, St.-Amour is generally the lightest, a soft and charming wine with delicious berry flavors. Côte de Brouilly, from a very small area of

**Book II**

**France: A Wine Superstar**

vineyards on the higher slopes of Mont Brouilly, is considerably more concentrated than Brouilly itself. Fleurie is a popular cru that's quite reliable but relatively pricey for a Beaujolais (about $15) because it's popular.

Morgon, Juliénas, Chénas, and Moulin-à-Vent are the fullest of the cru Beaujolais. Chénas is harder to find than the other crus, because many of the wines of Chénas are (quite legally) labeled as Moulin-à-Vent, a recognizable name that's an asset to sales; stylistically, it's fairly substantial, similar to Moulin-à-Vent. Morgon is a full, earthy, wild cherry–scented wine that ages as well as any Beaujolais wine, developing a Burgundian silkiness after about five years. Juliénas is always a wise choice, because the wines are consistently high in quality.

Moulin-à-Vent wines can differ from other Beaujolais wines because some producers age them in small oak casks that give oaky aromas and flavors to the wine, along with extra tannins. These oak-aged Moulin-à-Vents can probably age longer than other cru wines (how long is uncertain because the practice is fairly new) but at the sacrifice of some of the wine's traditional character. You can sometimes identify these wines by the words *fûts de chine* (oak casks) on the label.

# A Look at Beaujolais Producers and Prices

Large *négociant* companies produce most Beaujolais wines; they buy grapes and wine from private growers and then blend, bottle, and sell the wine under their own labels. Many of these companies are Burgundy *négociants,* who also sell a full range of Burgundies; some of them own vineyards in Beaujolais and purchase grapes from growers.

Individual estate Beaujolais wines exist as well. Some are wines of private growers, such as Jacky Janodet, Michel Tête, Domaine Dalicieux, and Jean-Paul Brun. Other estate wines come from *négociants* who segregate certain wines from private estates. Duboeuf, for example, bottles and sells the wines of his best growers separately, as estate wines, when he believes they're distinctive. And the Louis Jadot firm owns the fine Château des Jacques estate in Moulin-à-Vent and sells that wine separately.

WORTH THE SEARCH

Wines from single estates are generally higher in quality and more distinctive than the blended *négociant* wines, but they're also less widely available and usually cost more.

The price of Beaujolais depends on the type, as you can see from this list:

✔ Beaujolais Nouveau costs about $11 a bottle after Thanksgiving; the bottles available the week before Thanksgiving are more expensive because they're shipped by air.

✔ Simple Beaujolais wines sell for $10 to $15.

✔ Beaujolais-Villages wines cost a dollar or two more than simple Beaujolais.

✔ Cru Beaujolais start at about $15, but single-estate wines from the best crus can cost more.

## Enjoying Beaujolais

Beaujolais goes well with a wide range of foods, from poultry and red meats to stews and cheeses (both light and strong). Choose the type of Beaujolais according to the richness of the dish (or vice versa). For example, pair Beaujolais-Villages or a light cru, such as Chiroubles, with poultry and a fuller cru, such as Moron, with stews or game. But don't obsess about the pairings — that would definitely go against the Beaujolais spirit!

*Tip:* The lighter the Beaujolais wine, the more it accommodates chilling. Try drinking Beaujolais Nouveau almost as cool as white wine (about 52 degrees Fahrenheit), Beaujolais and Beaujolais-Villages at cellar temperature (56 to 57 degrees Fahrenheit), and cru Beaujolais at about the same temperature as red Burgundy (60 to 62 degrees Fahrenheit).

Don't forget that Beaujolais is best when it's young (aging causes it to lose its distinctiveness). So what should your Beaujolais mantra be? The lighter the style, the younger the wine. Here are some general guidelines:

✔ **Beaujolais Nouveau:** Drink as young as possible; it'll still be drinkable at one or even two years old, but you sacrifice personality along the way.

✔ **Simple Beaujolais wines:** Ready from their release, about one month after the Nouveau style, to about one year later.

✔ **Beaujolais-Villages:** Drinkable from about March of the year after the harvest until they're about two years old.

✔ **Lighter cru wines:** Drink within three years of the vintage.

✔ **Medium-bodied cru Beaujolais:** Best from one to four years after the vintage.

✔ **The fullest crus:** Drink four to seven years after the vintage, up to ten years for Moulin-à-Vent.

# Chapter 5

# Robust Rhône Reds and Unique Whites

*I*f you're passionate about Bordeaux, Burgundy, and Champagne, Rhône wines might seem an entirely new and alien experience, one divorced from what you know of French wine. The tipping point arrives when you become more accepting of untamed wines that puncture the veil of refinement to offer an animalistic sort of pleasure. You could say that Rhône wines have put wine lovers in touch with their primitive selves. Are you ready to explore the dark pleasures of the Rhône? Then read on!

# Exploring the Rhône Valley: Two Regions in One

The rich wine region known as the Rhône Valley lies in southeastern France, south of Beaujolais. The region takes its name from the Rhône River, which rises in the Swiss Alps and courses westward, then southward through France, emptying into the Mediterranean Sea. The Rhône River runs right through the Rhône Valley wine region for about 120 miles.

In terms of both the terrain and the wines, the Rhône Valley has two distinct parts: the Northern Rhône and the Southern Rhône. The two parts have different grape varieties, different winemaking philosophies, different soils, and, to some extent, different climates. The river, a mighty, continuous presence, is the sultry spirit of the wines and unites the two parts into a single region.

The Rhône Valley produces red, white, rosé, sparkling, and sweet dessert wines, but red wines dominate, representing 91 percent of the region's production. Among its red and white wines, the Rhône Valley makes both inexpensive wines for drinking young and more expensive wines that require aging to reach their prime drinkability. The Rhône Valley makes so much wine — more than 40 million cases a year — that the region is the number-two producer of AOC wine, after Bordeaux. (Flip to Chapter 1 of Book II for the scoop on France's AOC system of naming and defining wines.) This huge quantity encompasses plenty of quality too.

The next two sections familiarize you with the Rhône Valley's distinctly different parts.

## The continental North

The Northern Rhône is a long, narrow wine region that begins 16 miles south of the city of Lyons (called *Lyon* in French) and continues 40 miles southward to just below the town of Valence. It's an area of steep, terraced hills sloping down toward the river from the west, and slightly more open hills facing the river on the east. Vineyards cover these hills in a nearly continuous stretch on the western side of the Valley; vineyards also occupy the river's eastern shore, but they don't continue as far northward as on the western side of the river. Figure 5-1 shows the vineyards of the Rhône Valley.

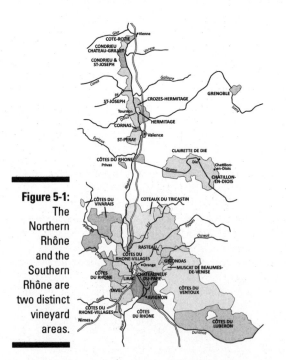

**Figure 5-1:**
The
Northern
Rhône
and the
Southern
Rhône are
two distinct
vineyard
areas.

The Northern Rhône has a *continental* climate: Summers are warm, with lots of sun, and winters are cold. A cold, hurricane-force wind from the north, called the *mistral,* funnels down the narrow river valley, jeopardizing flowering of the vines in the spring and ripening of the grapes in the fall. The slope of the hills and a south-facing orientation for some vineyards help to hasten ripening.

The soils of the Northern Rhône are mainly porous granite and *schist* (crystalline rock), which are generally light, infertile soils. The best vineyard areas, usually found on steep hills, have these soils; where the soil is heavier, in the plain along the river, grapes for lesser wines grow.

REMEMBER

The single red grape variety of the Northern Rhône is Syrah (see-rah), one of the highest-quality red varieties in the world. It's a dark, fairly tannic grape with enormous complexity of flavor. Depending on where it grows, Syrah can make a wine with aromas and flavors that are fruity, floral, spicy, smoky, meaty, and vegetal — quite a range for a single variety! Although Syrah grows in many parts of the world — including Australia, South Africa, California, Washington, and Italy — the Northern Rhône is the one area where Syrah consistently expresses its widest aromatic range.

Several white varieties also grow in the Northern Rhône. They include the following:

✔ **Ligonier:** The most important white variety in terms of the unique character of its wines, Viognier (vee-oh-nyay) has pronounced, but delicate, aromas and flavors that typically include floral notes, as well as peach and apricot.

✔ **Roussanne:** Another high-quality white variety, Roussanne (roos-sahn) has delicate aromas and crisp acidity.

✔ **Marsanne:** A variety that's much easier to grow than Roussanne, Marsanne (mar-sahn) gives more body to its wines despite lacking finesse.

Marsanne and Roussanne typically costar in some of the white wines of the Northern Rhône, but Viognier stands alone in the white wines that feature it.

# The Mediterranean-like South

The main vineyard area of the Southern Rhône begins about 30 miles south of the vineyards of the North, and continues to just south of the city of Avignon (see Figure 5-1). The region is much larger than the Northern Rhône, and it produces much more wine. In fact, about 95 percent of all Rhône Valley wine comes from the Southern Rhône.

The shape and topography of the Southern Rhône are completely different from that of its counterpart: The Southern Rhône is a wide, open area with lots of flat land and some gentle hills. The climate is Mediterranean rather than continental, because the region is quite close to the sea and far less inland than the Northern Rhône. This location means that it's a milder area, with plenty of summer heat to ripen the grapes, but sometimes insufficient rain. The mistral wind from the north blows forcefully through the area, requiring grape growers to take special precautions to protect their vines from damage.

Like the terrain, the assortment of grape varieties in the Southern Rhône is wide open. Numerous red and white varieties grow there, and most Southern Rhône wines are blends of several varieties. Grenache (gren-ahsh), a red variety, is the main grape; in fact, on the strength of its acreage in the Southern Rhône, Grenache is also the main grape variety of the Rhône Valley overall. At low crop levels, this variety makes fairly dense, dark wines with meaty and black pepper flavors; when the crop is large, however, Grenache's color tends to fade, and its flavors become diluted. In order to beef up Grenache's color and tannins, winemakers of the Southern Rhône usually blend it with other varieties grown there.

The other red varieties important in the Southern Rhône are

- **Syrah:** This variety is growing in use among many producers intent on improving the quality of their wines.

- **Mourvèdre:** A deep-colored variety with fruity aromas, Mourvèdre (more-ved'r) is also increasing in use.

- **Cinsault, or Cinsaut:** This grape variety, pronounced san-soh, makes relatively light wines that are soft and perfumed.

Other red varieties of the Southern Rhône include Carignan (a dark, tannic variety of Spanish origin), Picpoul, Terret Noir, Counoise, Muscardin, and Vaccarèse.

White grape varieties hardly figure in the Southern Rhône, because the region's wine production is mainly red. The following white varieties are largely responsible for the few white wines that do exist in the region:

- **Grenache Blanc:** A white version of the red Grenache variety, Grenache Blanc (gren-ahsh blahnk) is soft and full-bodied but short in aroma and flavor.

- **Clairette:** This variety, pronounced kleh-rheht, makes soft, full-bodied whites and is also used in local sparkling wines.

Other white varieties used in Southern Rhône blends include Roussanne, Bourboulenc, Ugni Blanc, Muscat, Marsanne, Picardan, white Picpoul, and Viognier.

# Narrowing the Lens on the Northern Rhône

Most Northern Rhône vineyards occupy dry, scraggy, terraced hillsides rising steeply above small towns perched along the Rhône River. Old, gnarled vines grow in burnt-looking earth; the vineyards look rustic and somewhat primitive.

In a sense, the vineyards reflect the taste of the wines: dry, concentrated, a bit tough, gritty of spirit. The red wines of the Northern Rhône are survivors, born of challenging conditions and enduring for years in the bottle. They vary by degree — some of them are lighter and smoother, whereas others are fuller and more intense — but they're all of the same mold, in part because a single red grape variety, Syrah, is the basis for them all.

White wines come from this region, too, and like the landscape, they're dramatic. As generalizations go, they're full-bodied, dry whites, with intriguing and unusual aromas; some of them need many years of bottle-aging to express themselves best.

Like most French wines, the wines of the Northern Rhône carry the names of the places where their grapes grow. Eight *terroirs* (the unique growing conditions of a vineyard) give their names to wines: two for red wine only, three for red or white wine, and three for white or sparkling wine. Listed roughly from north to south, here are the eight AOC wines:

- **Côte-Rôtie** (coat roe-tee), red
- **Condrieu** (con-drew), white
- **Château Grillet** (sha-tow gree-yay), white
- **Hermitage** (er-mee-tahj), mainly red but also some white
- **Crozes-Hermitage** (crows er-mee-tahj), mainly red but also some white
- **St.-Joseph** (san-jhoe-sef), mainly red but also some white
- **Cornas** (core-nahs), red
- **St.-Péray** (san-peh-ray), mainly sparkling but also some white

Book II

France: A Wine Superstar

The following sections provide a more in-depth look at these appellations of the Northern Rhône.

# Wide-ranging reds

Most of the wine made in the Northern Rhône is red. These red wines fall into two groups:

- ✔ **The most prestigious, expensive, and age-worthy wines:** Hermitage, Côte-Rôtie, and Cornas fall into this category. Of these three, Hermitage and Côte-Rôtie are the real stars.
- ✔ **The less prestigious, less expensive wines for earlier drinking:** St.-Joseph and Crozes-Hermitage are examples.

### Côte Rôtie

The Côte Rôtie ("roasted slope") vineyards are the northernmost of the Rhône, covering nearly 500 acres on the western bank of the Rhône around the village of Ampuis. Because the river runs southwest for 6 miles at this point, the hills above the river face south or southeast rather than east, giving the vines a bonus of sunshine and ripening potential.

The Côte Rôtie vineyards vary in altitude, incline, and soil. The most famous distinction within Côte Rôtie is between the northern vineyards, called the Côte Brune, and the southern vineyards, called the Côte Blonde. The Côte Brune ("brown slope") has an iron-rich, relatively dark, schistous soil, whereas the Côte Blonde has a schist and granite soil that's paler in color. The names of these two areas were born of a legend involving the blonde and brunette daughters of a local lord.

Traditionally, Côte Rôtie wines derived from grapes of both areas blended together, but today a number of producers also make single-vineyard Côte Rôties, which contain the grapes of just one area. These single-vineyard wines command higher prices than most other Côte Rôties and reflect the particular character of their zone. (Côte Blonde wines are elegant, more finesseful, more balanced, and ready-to-drink sooner; Côte Brune wines are more tannic and austere, requiring more time to develop in the bottle.)

Côte Rôtie wine may be made entirely from Syrah, or it may contain up to 20 percent white Viognier grapes; in practice, most producers use less than 5 percent Viognier, if any, in their wines.

One of the most beguiling characteristics of Côte Rôtie wines is their perfume, a fragrant mix of violets, raspberries, green olives, bacon, and underbrush. Although they're full-bodied, dense, tannic, and rustic in the general Rhône model, these wines have finesse and smoothness. They're enjoyable beginning about 5 to 6 years after the vintage (depending on the vintage's quality), but the best wines require 10 to 15 years to mature fully and can age gracefully for 20 years or more.

Côte Rôtie wines sell for about $40 to $75 a bottle, but the most sought-after single-vineyard bottlings cost as much as $150 a bottle or more.

Marcel Guigal has done more to popularize Côte Rôtie than any other producer. Keep an eye out for his firm and these other reliable firms that specialize in Côte Rôtie:

| | |
|---|---|
| Domaine Gilles Barge | E. Guigal |
| Domaine Bernard Burgaud | Domaine Jamet |
| Domaine Champet | Domaine Robert Jasmin |
| Domaine Clusel-Roch | Domaine Michel Ogier |
| Domaine Gentaz-Dervieux | Domaine René Rostaing |
| Domaine Jean-Michel Gerin | Domaine Vidal-Fleury |

Three other reliable producers make Côte Rôtie, but they don't specialize in it: M. Chapoutier, Delas Frères, and Paul Jaboulet Ainé.

### Hermitage

The broad, dramatic Hermitage hill lies on the eastern bank of the Rhône River. The river takes a favorable turn eastward around the town of Tain L'Hermitage, causing the hill and its vineyards to face southward and making Hermitage perhaps the single finest *terroir* of the entire Rhône Valley.

With about 318 planted acres, Hermitage is only two-thirds the size of Côte Rôtie. The soils vary across the Hermitage hill, and the altitude of the vineyards varies, too, creating subtly different wines according to where the vines grow. Unlike in Côte Rôtie, however, single-vineyard Hermitage wines are less common — although many producers do make a super-Hermitage as well as a standard version. La Chapelle, the legendary, nearly eternal Hermitage of the Paul Jaboulet Ainé winery, is perhaps the most famous premium Hermitage.

Quite a few wine critics consider Hermitage to be the greatest Syrah wine on the planet. It's a full-bodied, intense, tannic red with long aging potential. Its aromas and flavors reflect Syrah's full spectrum: spice, cedar, cassis, smoke, meat, leather, and, sometimes, tar. With age, Hermitage becomes soft and slightly sweet, and its aromas grow even more complex. It's truly one of the greatest wines of France.

Technically, Hermitage can contain up to 15 percent of two white varieties, Marsanne and Roussanne, but it rarely contains any. Instead of blending their white grapes into their red Hermitage, producers make a separate white wine, Hermitage Blanc (described later in this chapter).

Hermitage from a great, or even good, vintage (and a good producer) needs many years to develop — at least 10 years from the vintage and as much as 20. If you drink an Hermitage when it's young, you'll probably be impressed by its power and weight, but you won't experience the true majesty of this wine.

Red Hermitage costs from about $40 to $100 per bottle. A few elite, premium, or single-vineyard Hermitages can cost $150 or more.

Hermitage has six particularly outstanding producers. These firms each produce more than one red Hermitage, generally a standard wine and a premium version. These six producers are as follows:

Domaine Jean-Louis Chave
M. Chapoutier
Delas Frères

Paul Jaboulet Aîné
Domaine Marc Sorrel
Domaine Bernard Faurie

### Cornas

Cornas is a very small town on the western bank of the Rhône. The Cornas vineyards are planted entirely with Syrah. Stylistically, Cornas wines resemble Hermitage more than Cote Rôtie: They're dense, powerful wines with aromatic finesse and can take long aging.

Cornas is a tiny area — only 250 acres shared by 38 growers — and is the smallest and southernmost appellation for red wine in the Northern Rhône. Despite its small size, some growers, such as Jean-Luc Colombo, perceive the area to have several distinct *terroirs,* according to the vineyards' altitudes. Because of these perceived differences, some growers bottle single-vineyard Cornas wines.

Traditionally, Cornas wines needed 20 years to reach their best drinking, but today's wines are less ferocious when they're young. Drink them when they're at least 8 years old, up to 20 years or even longer in the best vintages. Because Cornas is a relatively unsung wine, it's a good value; most Cornas wines sell for $30 to $60.

The following eight producers make very good Cornas:

Domaine Guy de Barjac
Domaine Auguste Clape
Jean-Luc Colombo
Domaine Marcel Juge

Paul Jaboulet Aîné
Domaine Robert Michel
Domaine Noël Verset
Domaine Alain Voge

## St.-Joseph

The St.-Joseph vineyards are on the western bank of the Rhône, north of Cornas and across the river from Hermitage. They occupy a fairly large area of hills as well as flatter land above and below the slopes, stretching almost the whole length of the Northern Rhône region. Since the formation of the St.-Joseph appellation in 1956, the territory has expanded considerably, encompassing land that isn't ideal for growing Syrah. Local growers and the AOC committee have now redrawn St.-Joseph's boundaries, but vineyards in the less suitable areas may continue to grow the wine until 2022. As a result of the large area, the quality of St.-Joseph wine is variable according to where the vineyards for a particular wine are situated.

About 90 percent of St.-Joseph wine is red; it may contain up to 10 percent of the white varieties Marsanne and Roussanne. Red St.-Joseph wines are generally the lightest, fruitiest, and most approachable Northern Rhône reds. They're usually medium-bodied and only moderately tannic, with black cherry aromas and flavors.

Most red St.-Joseph wines can be enjoyed within three to five years from the vintage; a few sturdier (and more expensive) ones can age for up to ten years. The price of most St.-Joseph red wines ranges from $14 to $25.

Good producers who specialize in St.-Joseph include the following:

Domaine Louis Chèze        Bernard Gripa
Domaine Courbis        Jean-Louis Grippat
Domaine Pierre Coursodon        Raymond Trollat

## Crozes-Hermitage

The vineyards of Crozes-Hermitage lie on the eastern bank of the Rhône, surrounding the Hermitage hill and stretching far north, south, and east of it. Compared to other Northern Rhône vineyards, the territory is fairly flat and quite large: With about 2,500 acres of vines, it's the largest AOC territory in the Northern Rhône. Naturally for such a large area, the terrain isn't uniform: Soils, slope, and altitude vary; consequently, the wines vary in quality and intensity.

The producers also vary. In addition to established growers and established *négociant* companies (firms that buy grapes and wine from growers and then blend, bottle, and sell the wine under their own labels), the area includes several fairly new growers who've brought fresh energy to Crozes-Hermitage and make some of the area's best wines. Altogether, Crozes-Hermitage producers make almost 12 times as much wine as Hermitage producers.

**Book II**

**France: A Wine Superstar**

Red Crozes-Hermitage wine may legally contain up to 15 percent white grapes, but as for Hermitage itself, the wine is almost always entirely Syrah. Some producers make their wines for early consumption, using methods similar to the carbonic maceration practiced in Beaujolais (see Chapter 4 in Book II for a description of this winemaking technique); these wines are soft and exude grapey Syrah flavor, and they're best within three to four years from the vintage. Other Crozes-Hermitage wines are more traditional: fairly robust and firm wines that evolve slowly over 15 years.

The more forward-styled Crozes-Hermitage wines are usually the least expensive, about $14 to $18, whereas the more traditional wines tend to run about $22 to $28. Good Crozes-Hermitage, in fact, can be one of the best values in French wine today — but choose carefully to avoid a dud producer.

Producers who specialize in Crozes-Hermitage include these four:

Domain Albert Belle
Domain Alain Graillot
Bernard Chave
Domain du Pavilion

You can also find very good Crozes-Hermitage from M. Chapoutier, Delas Frères, Jean-Luc Colombo, and Paul Jaboulet Ainé. Jaboulet's Crozes-Hermitage from the family's Domain du Thalabert estate is consistently fine (and a real value at $23).

## Uncommon whites

White wines make up only a small percentage of the Northern Rhône's production, but they're far from incidental wines that you can basically ignore. The white wines of the Northern Rhône are among the most unusual white wines of the world.

### Condrieu and Château Grillet

The territory of Condrieu runs for 12 miles along the western bank of the Rhône, in the north of the region, just south of Côte Rôtie. The tiny territory of Château Grillet (another, separate AOC wine) lies within the borders of Condrieu.

Both Condrieu and Château Grillet wines derive entirely from the Viognier grape. Because this variety has very small berries that give low juice yields, these two wines are small in production and somewhat rare. Condrieu production is less than 30,000 cases annually, and that of Château Grillet is about 1,000 cases.

A good Condrieu is a fascinating wine — rich in exotic aromas and flavors that suggest peach, flowers, and dried fruits, but dry and quite full in body. The aroma makes one statement (delicacy, finesse), and the wine's body and richness say something else entirely (weight, substance). Château Grillet is similar to Condrieu but generally drier and a bit crisper because it ages for 18 months in oak barrels. (To better understand the impact of oak barrels upon a wine's taste, head to Chapter 1 of Book I.)

Condrieu costs about $45 to $50 a bottle or more, and Château Grillet costs about double. These wines don't age well; drink them no later than three years after the harvest, with very delicately flavored foods, such as light fish or simple chicken dishes (or by themselves), so the wines' delicate aromas aren't overpowered.

Only one winery makes Château Grillet, and that's the Château Grillet estate. The leading producers of Condrieu include the following:

| | |
|---|---|
| Château du Rozay | E. Guigal |
| M. Chapoutier | Paul Jaboulet-Aîné |
| Domaine Clusel-Roch | Domaine Robert Niero-Pinchon |
| Domaine Yves Cuilleron | Domaine André Perre |
| Delas Frères | Domaine Alain Paret |
| Pierre Dumazet | Domaine Georges Vernay |

**Book II**

**France: A Wine Superstar**

### Hermitage Blanc

White Hermitage, or Hermitage Blanc, comes from the same area as red Hermitage, on the eastern bank of the Rhône. The wine is a blend of two varieties, Marsanne and Roussanne. Marsanne, the easier variety to grow, is the main constituent of most Hermitage Blanc wines. However, Roussanne, the finer, more fragrant variety, has gained favor with winemakers; it constitutes an increasing percentage of the blend.

Hermitage Blanc is a statuesque and exotic wine, dry and full-bodied with pronounced honey and floral (and earthy, citrusy, nutty, or marmalade-like) aromas and flavors. It's delicious when it's young, and it's compelling when it's old: richer in texture, its aromas flattened out but its character magnified. In the in-between years — when the wine is about 4 to 15 years of age — disappointment lurks. Like some red wines, but unlike most whites, Hermitage Blanc goes "dumb" and has nothing to say for a period. Eventually it rediscovers its tongue and can be wonderful for decades thereafter. If you have, say, an eight-year-old Hermitage, resist the urge to open the bottle now.

Hermitage Blanc costs about $35 to $55 per bottle, but some wines, such as Chapoutier's Cuvée de l'Orée, sell for more than $100.

Some producers who make red Hermitage also make white Hermitage. Look especially for the Hermitage Blanc from the following producers:

Domaine Jean-Louis Chave
M. Chapoutier
Jean-Luc Colombo
Delas Frères

Jean-Louis Grippat
Paul Jaboulet-Aîné
Domaine Marc Sorrel

Chave and Chapoutier have particularly fine reputations for their Hermitage Blanc; Jaboulet is also worth adding to that elite group.

### Crozes-Hermitage Blanc and St.-Joseph Blanc

Both the Crozes-Hermitage and the St.-Joseph appellations apply to white wine as well as red. In both cases, the whites derive from a blend of Marsanne and Roussanne, but Roussanne (the finer of the two varieties) is more common in Crozes-Hermitage Blanc than in St.-Joseph Blanc.

Crozes-Hermitage Blanc resembles Hermitage Blanc but is somewhat lighter in body and in aromatic intensity, and it can't live as long — nor does it withdraw during its adolescent years. Try Crozes-Hermitage Blanc young, up to about four years of age. St.-Joseph Blanc is lighter yet, charming and quite easy to enjoy during its first four years, which is its best period. Both types of wine generally cost from $14 to $25.

M. Chapoutier, Delas Frères, and Paul Jaboulet Aîné — three good wineries that market a wide range of Rhône wines — all make both Crozes-Hermitage Blanc and St.-Joseph Blanc. Specialists in Crozes-Hermitage Blanc include the same four producers who make red Crozes-Hermitage (see the related section earlier in this chapter for the list).

Top producers of St.-Joseph Blanc include the following:

Domaine Louis Chèze
Domaine Pierre Coursodon
Domaine Yves Cuilleron

Jean-Louis Grippat
André Perret
Raymond Trollat

### St.-Péray

St.-Péray is a town slightly larger than tiny Cornas, situated south of Cornas on the western bank of the Rhône; it's the southernmost AOC area of the Northern Rhône. St.-Péray is the lone appellation of the Northern Rhône that doesn't make red wine. In fact, it makes very little white wine, either: Its production is mainly sparkling.

The sparkling wine called St.-Péray is mainly Marsanne, with some Roussanne and a local grape variety called Roussette (which might or might not be Roussanne). It's made via the traditional method of second fermentation in the bottle. St.-Péray is rather full in body for a sparkling wine, because its vineyards are so southerly. Very little of this wine is available in the United States.

Jean Lionnet produces a very good St.-Péray.

# Spotlighting the Southern Rhône

What a difference 30 miles make! When you drive from the Northern Rhône into the Southern Rhône, the steep, rugged landscape disappears behind you, and a windswept tableau of lavender, olive groves, and cypress trees opens ahead. By the time you reach the heart of the region, you're nearly in Provence. Clearly, such a terrain and such a warm, sunny climate can't produce wines of the same personality as the North (which is far more rugged, as explained earlier in this chapter).

The wines of the Southern Rhône are more generous and approachable than those of the North — they're also more abundant. Largely on the strength of a single type of wine, Côtes du Rhône, the South produces about 19 times more wine than the North.

The wines of the Southern Rhône have place names, but some of the places are very large areas, whereas others are more limited and specific. A total of 18 AOC designations exist in the Southern Rhône or its vicinity. Seven of these are the most important, either for the quantity of wine they produce, the quality of the wine, or their historic standing. These seven AOC areas all produce nonsparkling, dry wines:

- **Côtes du Rhône** (coat dew rone), mainly red but also rosé or white
- **Côtes du Rhône-Villages** (coat dew rone-vee-lahj), a higher-quality Côtes du Rhône
- **Châteauneuf-du-Pape** (shah-toe-nuf-doo-pahp), mainly red but also white
- **Gigondas** (gee-gohn-dah's), mainly red but also rosé
- **Vacqueyras** (vac-keh-rah's), red, rosé, and some white
- **Lirac** (lee-rak), red, rosé, and white wines
- **Tavel** (tah-vell), rosé wine only

Another seven AOCs for still, dry wines are less important. Some of these areas attained AOC status only in the past few years, and their wines are therefore practically unheard of outside France. Others export their wines, which are mainly inexpensive.

Four AOC areas in the Southern Rhône produce either sweet wines or sparkling wines; these wines are

- ✔ **Muscat de Beaumes-de-Venise** (moos-caht deh bohm-deh-veh-nees), sweet white wine from Muscat grapes
- ✔ **Rasteau** (raah-stow), sweet, fortified red wine
- ✔ **Clairette de Die** (clar-et deh dee), sparkling wine
- ✔ **Crémant de Die** (cray-mahn't deh dee), sparkling wine

Although white grape varieties grow throughout the Southern Rhône, red wines are by far the dominant type. One wine — Châteauneuf-du-Pape — stands out both historically and for its quality. Two other wines, Côtes du Rhône and Côtes du Rhône-Villages, account for a huge volume with variable quality, but include some very good wines.

The following sections provide insight on important wines from the Southern Rhône.

## Châteauneuf-du-Pape

The rather large Châteauneuf-du-Pape territory (7,700 acres of vineyards) lies on the eastern bank of the Rhône River, south of the city of Orange. Its name means "new castle of the Pope," a reference to the fact that Pope John XXII constructed a summer residence there in 1318. In wine terms, the area is famous because a local grower, Baron le Roy, developed the idea for France's AOC system in 1923. When France implemented the system in 1935, Châteauneuf-du-Pape was one of France's first AOC wines.

The Châteauneuf-du-Pape territory encompasses a variety of soil types, of which the *galets* — large, smooth round stones — is the most famous. To see vines growing in rocks (no dirt in sight!) is quite amazing. These stones reflect the stored heat of the day onto the vines at night, assisting the ripening of the grapes.

Red Châteauneuf-du-Pape can be made from as many as 13 different grape varieties, including 4 white varieties. These 13 varieties are Grenache (red and white); Syrah, Mourvèdre, Picpoul, Terret Noir, Counoise, Muscardin, Vaccarèse, and Cinsault (all red); Picardan, Clairette, Roussanne, and Bourboulenc (all white). Some producers actually use all 13 varieties, notably the fine Château de Beaucastel.

In modern practice, most Châteauneuf-du-Pape reds come from three or four varieties, all of which are red:

✔ Grenache typically dominates the wine, making up 50 to 70 percent of the blend.

✔ Syrah constitutes from 10 to 30 percent of the blend.

✔ Mourvèdre makes up the balance, sometimes along with Cinsault, Counoise, or Vaccarèse.

Châteauneuf-du-Pape wines can also vary from producer to producer according to how they're made. A few producers *vinify* the grapes (turn them into wine) traditionally to make sturdy, full-bodied, tannic, high-alcohol wines that need several years to develop and can evolve for up to 20 years. Other producers are experimenting with vinification techniques — such as the carbonic maceration method used in Beaujolais (described in Chapter 4 of Book II) — to make wines that are less tannic, fruitier, and easier to drink young. Both styles generally have aromas and flavors that are earthy, herbal, and fruity — especially jammy black cherry or raspberry.

Long-lived Châteauneuf-du-Papes made in the traditional style cost about $40 to $50 a bottle or more; the more modern-styled wines are less expensive, about $25 to $30 a bottle.

More than 120 producers grow and bottle Châteauneuf-du-Pape — not counting the *négociant* brands. The 17 estates in this list all make top-quality, traditional-style red Châteauneuf-du-Pape:

Château de Beaucastel
Domaine de Beaurenard
Henri Bonneau
Les Cailloux
Clos des Papes
Clos du Mont Olivet
Domaine de Mont Redon
Font de Michelle
Château Fortia

Château de la Gardine
Domaine de la Janasse
Domaine de Marcoux
Château la Nerthe
Domaine du Pégau
Château Rayas
Le Vieux Donjon
Domaine du Vieux-Télégraphe

In addition to these estates, Paul Jaboulet Aîné, Jean-Luc Colombo, and M. Chapoutier also make good, reliable red Châteauneuf-du-Pape.

## Châteauneuf-du-Pape Blanc

White Châteauneuf-du-Pape can be made from six white grape varieties: Clairette, Grenache Blanc, Bourboulenc, Picpoul Blanc, Viognier, and Roussanne.

Although it represents only about 7 percent of the zone's production, the quantity of white Châteauneuf-du-Papes is increasing. The quality of the wine has increased as well, thanks to winemaking changes — such as less oak aging and earlier bottling — that help retain the freshness of the wine. At its best, Châteauneuf-du-Pape Blanc is a dry, full-bodied white with aromas and flavors that are earthy, minerally, fruity (pear, pineapple, and melon), and honeylike. Wines from the best producers can age for ten years, but most are at their best at no more than three or four years of age.

Because not every Châteauneuf-du-Pape producer makes a white wine, the following list tells you some of the producers that do make it:

| | |
|---|---|
| Château de Beaucastel | Domaine de Marcoux |
| Les Cailloux | Château de la Nerthe |
| Clos des Papes | Domaine de Nalys |
| Font de Michelle | Château Rayas |
| Château de la Gardine | Domaine du Vieux-Télégraphe |
| Domaine de la Janasse | |

## Côtes du Rhône

The Côtes du Rhône AOC is a regionwide appellation: The grapes can come from anywhere within the Rhône Valley region, including the vineyards of the North. Practically speaking, however, the vast majority of this wine comes from the Southern Rhône. Various vineyard areas in the center of the Southern Rhône region, on both sides of the river, are designated specifically for its production. Together with its sister appellation, Côtes du Rhône-Villages, this area makes a huge amount of wine: almost 28 million cases annually, 2.5 times as much as Beaujolais.

Côtes du Rhône is mostly a red wine; only 2 percent of the production is white, and another 2 percent is rosé. Red Côtes du Rhône is a blend of various grape varieties, which may be combined according to a complicated formula. Since the 2000 harvest, the regulations regarding varieties are as follows:

- ✔ Grenache must represent at least 40 percent of the wine (except in the Northern Rhône, where the wine can be entirely Syrah).

- ✔ Syrah and Mourvèdre are also principal varieties; along with Grenache, they must constitute at least 70 percent of the blend.

- ✔ Secondary red varieties — ten in all, including Carignan and Cinsault — may constitute no more than 30 percent of the wine.

- ✔ White varieties may constitute no more than 5 percent.

Many Côtes du Rhône wines are inexpensive (under $20), soft, fruity, low-tannin reds. They're the everyday wines of the region, tasty reds to enjoy with hamburgers or other casual meals, and the majority of them are for enjoying young. Some producers make a more serious style, however; these better Côtes du Rhônes are as follows:

Coudoulet de Beaucastel, of Château Beaucastel
Château de Fonsalette, of Château Rayas
Domaine Gramenon Côtes du Rhône
Cuvée des Templiers, of Domaine Brusset
Château des Tours Côtes du Rhône

## Côtes du Rhône-Villages

Côtes du Rhône-Villages wines are a higher class of Côtes du Rhônes, made from a more limited vineyard area and fewer grape varieties. That said, the vineyard area isn't all that limited: It encompasses the vineyards of about 70 communities in Southern Rhône. But production is only 13 percent that of Côtes du Rhônes.

Grenache may constitute a maximum of 65 percent of the Côtes du Rhône-Villages blend; Syrah, Cinsault, or Mourvèdre form a minimum of 25 percent, and other local red varieties are no more than 10 percent.

Sixteen of the Côtes du Rhône-Villages communities enjoy special status: They may append their name to the appellation, if the grapes for a wine come specifically from that village. The name of the wine then reads either *Côtes du Rhône-Villages-Cairanne,* for example, or *Cairanne-Côtes du Rhône-Villages.* Other villages of note are Vinsobres, Rasteau, Chusclan, and Laudun.

Côtes du Rhône-Villages wines are slightly more expensive than simple Côtes du Rhônes; expect to pay about $12 to $14 a bottle. Some wines worth seeking out include the following:

Domaine de l'Oratoire-St.-Martin Côtes du Rhône-Villages-Cairanne
Domaine Rabasse-Charavin Côtes du Rhône-Villages-Rasteau
Domaine Marcel Richaud Côtes du Rhône-Villages-Cairanne

Domaine de la Soumade Côtes du Rhône-Villages-Rasteau
Domaine de Ste.-Anne Côtes du Rhône-Villages
Domaine de Deurre Côtes du Rhône-Villages-Vinsobres

**Book II**

**France: A Wine Superstar**

## Gigondas

Until 1971, Gigondas was a village name appended to Côtes du Rhône-Villages, but then the Gigondas area, on the eastern side of the Rhône, became an AOC in its own right. Today Gigondas is a thriving appellation, producing about 30 percent as much wine as the larger Châteauneuf-du-Pape territory.

Gigondas wine is red or rosé only. Grenache constitutes up to 80 percent of the blend; Syrah and Mourvèdre must be at least 15 percent, and other local varieties (excluding Carignan) may represent up to 10 percent of the blend.

Of the Southern Rhône reds, Gigondas wines are considered second in quality only to Châteauneuf-du-Pape. Like that wine, they're made in two styles, a lighter, more approachable style (costing about $20 to $25), and a denser, fuller-bodied style ($30 or more). The lighter-style wines are best up to 6 years of age, whereas the fuller wines usually drink best from 7 or 8 years of age up to 15 years.

Good producers of Gigondas include the following:

Domaine du Cayron                 Domaine Raspail-Ay
Domaine Roger Combe               Domaine Saint Gayan
Domaine de Font-Sane              Domaine de Santa Duc
Domaine Les Goubert

## Vacqueyras

Vacqueyras is a fairly small area directly south of Gigondas, east of the Rhône River. Like Gigondas, Vacqueyras was originally a Côtes du Rhône-Villages area; it was promoted to freestanding AOC status in 1990. Its grape varieties are similar to those of Gigondas, but the wines aren't quite as good, at least not yet. Like Gigondas, most (96 percent) of Vacqueyras wine is red.

Because Vacqueyras is a fairly new appellation, and is therefore not well known, its wines tend to be relatively inexpensive. Good Vacqueyras can cost you as little as $15, although some of the best wines are $20 to $30.

Good producers of Vacqueyras include the following:

Domaine des Amouriers
Domaine Le Clos des Cazaux
Domaine La Fourmone (Roger Combe)
Domaine des Garrigues
Paul Jaboulet Aîné

## *Lirac and Tavel*

Lirac is a sizeable area encompassing four villages on the western banks of the Rhône. Although 80 percent of the wines made there are full-bodied, soft reds (and 4 percent are whites), the area is best known in the United States as a producer of dry rosé wines, along with the neighboring Tavel appellation. Lirac red and rosé derive from Grenache (maximum 40 percent), Cinsault, Mourvèdre, and Syrah, plus Carignan.

The neighboring Tavel AOC covers rosé wines only. These wines derive mainly from Grenache and Cinsault. They're dry, with refreshing berry flavor, and they tend to be quite high in alcohol for rosés, up to 14 percent. Because it's better known, Tavel Rosé is more expensive than Lirac Rosé — about $20 to $25 compared to $15 or less for Lirac.

---

## Enjoying Rhône wines

If you're tempted to run out and purchase a red Rhône wine, it helps to know which vintages are good before plunking down your cash.

✔ Good vintages for Northern Rhône red wines are 1999, 1998, 1997, 1995, 1991 (for Côte Rôtie especially), 1990, 1989 (especially for Hermitage), 1988, and 1985. If you can wait to open the bottle, vintages from 2007, 2006, 2005, 2003, and 2001 are worth picking up.

✔ Good vintages for Southern Rhône red wines are 1999, 1998 (especially), 1995, 1990, and 1989. More recent vintages to look for include ones from 2007, 2006, 2005, 2003, and 2001.

Serve Rhône reds at cool room temperature, about 62 to 64 degrees Fahrenheit. Simple Côtes du Rhône red wines can be served a few degrees cooler. Northern Rhône whites and Châteauneuf-du-Pape Blanc should be only slightly cool, about 58 to 62 degrees Fahrenheit, so you can appreciate their wonderful aromas. Rosé wines are best when served cold — about 50 to 52 degrees Fahrenheit.

Serve your better Rhône wines — both red and white — in a tall glass with an oval-shaped bowl (similar to a Bordeaux or Cabernet Sauvignon glass) that has a minimum capacity of 10 to 12 ounces. (If you want a better understanding of how the glass you use can affect the taste of your wine, check out Chapter 4 in Book I.)

The sturdier Rhône reds are good with roasts of beef or lamb; steaks; stews (especially hearty meat and/or bean stews, such as *cassoulet*); full-flavored game, such as venison; and game birds. The lighter red Rhône wines, such as Crozes-Hermitage, St.-Joseph, and Côtes du Rhône, are good accompaniments to roast chicken, grilled hamburgers, or pizza.

Enjoy Hermitage Blanc and Châteauneuf-du-Pape Blanc with veal or robust poultry dishes. The wines made from the Viognier variety — Condrieu and Château Grillet —are difficult to pair with food; they're really best as apéritifs. Delicate, white fish or simply prepared chicken dishes can work, but any strongly flavored entrée is inadvisable because it'll mask the delicate aromas and flavors of these wines.

Château St.-Roch (produced by Cantegril-Verda), Domaine Pélaquié, and Château de Ségriès are reliable producers of Lirac Rosé. Château d'Aquéria and Domaine Méjan-Taulier are top Tavel producers; the latter also makes a small amount of Lirac Rosé.

## Muscat de Beaumes-de-Venise and Rasteau

Rasteau and Beaumes-de-Venise are 2 of the 16 villages within the Côtes du Rhône-Villages area entitled to append their names to that appellation. But each of these villages also has separate AOC status for a special type of sweet wine, called *Vins Doux Natural,* or VDN (translated as "naturally sweet wines"). VDN wines are made by adding alcohol to grape juice that has fermented only slightly; the alcohol stops the fermentation and fixes the natural grape sugar in the wine.

Rasteau AOC is a VDN from Grenache grapes grown in three villages: Rasteau, Cairanne, or Sablet. The wine can be red or even tawny, depending on the winemaking and aging techniques. It's not common in the United States, but you can occasionally find it for about $18 to $20.

The VDN wine of Beaumes-de-Venise is called Muscat de Beaumes-de-Venise. It comes entirely from the Muscat grape — specifically the best type of Muscat, the Muscat Blanc à Petits Grains. It's a particularly delicious wine, redolent with floral Muscat perfume, yet full-bodied and substantial. It sells for about $18 to $30.

# Chapter 6

# Champagne: The World's Greatest Sparkling Wine

. . . . . . . . . . . . . . . . . . . . . . . . . . . . . . . . . . . . . . . . . . . . . . . .

. . . . . . . . . . . . . . . . . . . . . . . . . . . . . . . . . . . . . . . . . . . . . . . .

*I*s there a better-known, more popular wine in the world than Champagne? When it comes to sparkling wines, the sparkling wine known as Champagne has no peer. Wine lovers can seriously debate what the best red wine, white wine, or dessert wine is, but it's no contest for the best sparkling wine.

What makes Champagne the best of its kind? What are the differences in various types of Champagne? And what are the best Champagnes anyway? You find answers to all of these questions and more in this chapter.

## The Skinny on This Supreme Bubbly

Champagne (pronounced sham-pan-yah) is a white or rosé sparkling wine that starts its life like any other wine — as the fermented juice of grapes. But a subsequent, vital step transforms Champagne, and all the other serious sparkling wines of the world. Bottle the wine with yeast and a little sugar-wine solution, and it undergoes a *second* fermentation; this time, the bottle traps the carbon dioxide (a byproduct of fermentation), so that it takes the form of tiny bubbles in the wine. Voilà! You have Champagne — at least you do if this process takes place in the Champagne region of France. And that's the catch. True Champagne comes only from this one wine region. All other bubbly wines are simply *sparkling wines,* no matter what they choose to call themselves on the label.

But Champagne is more than just the right place and the right process. In almost all cases, Champagne is an extremely complex blended wine — not only a blend of grape varieties but also a blend of wines from various vineyards throughout the region (the blend, called the *cuvée,* combines the strengths of each vineyard). Frequently Champagne is even a blend of wines from different vintages. Geez. For a wine that's so easy to enjoy, Champagne is certainly very difficult to create!

The European Union doesn't permit any of its member countries except France to call their sparkling wines Champagne. And of course, sparkling wines made in French wine regions other than Champagne can't legally be called Champagne either. But, beyond the borders of Europe, many countries continue to cash in on the popularity of the Champagne name — confusing legions of novice wine drinkers in the process — by calling their sparkling wines Champagne. Usually these wines are the least-expensive, mass-produced, poorest quality sparklers; most of the better sparkling wines don't use the word. Just remember: True Champagne always has the word *Champagne* plus *Product of France* or *France* on the label. Anything selling for less than $25 is *not* Champagne!

# Zeroing in on the Champagne Region

The cool, agricultural region called Champagne is roughly 90 miles (or about an hour and a half, if you measure your distances in time spent traveling) northeast of Paris by car or train. Besides hardy grains such as wheat, the region's main crop is grapes, because the soil isn't very fertile and the climate is too forbidding to grow much of anything else. The Champagne vineyards occupy about more than 80,000 acres of the sparsely populated region; vineyards in 321 villages (or *crus*) in the region provide the grapes for Champagne.

Most of the large Champagne *houses* — the name used for producers who make and sell most of the Champagne — are located in the following three communities (see Figure 6-1 for a visual):

- ✔ **Reims**: Champagne's only city, and its capital, Reims is home to 15 of Champagne's most important houses, the Cathedral of Reims (one of the world's most beautiful Gothic churches), and one of France's greatest restaurants, the three-star Michelin restaurant-inn, Boyer Les Crayères.

- ✔ **Épernay:** This town is the geographical center of the Champagne region, and the home of the most Champagne houses (25, to be exact), including the largest, Moët & Chandon. Épernay is about a 20-minute drive south of Reims.

- ✔ **Aÿ:** A small town about ten minutes to the east of Épernay, Aÿ is home to nine Champagne producers. It's also the source of one of the Champagne region's few good red wines (made from Pinot Noir).

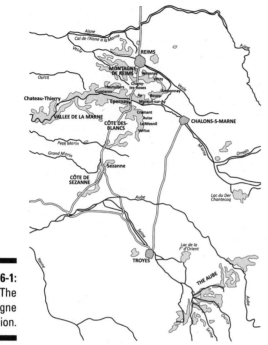

**Figure 6-1:**
The
Champagne
region.

The proximity of these three communities and Champagne's closeness to Paris make a short tour of the region quite feasible for wine lovers interested in checking out its restaurants, inns, and cafés — and, of course, drinking as much Champagne as they desire.

The following sections provide details on the growing conditions that affect Champagne, the grape varieties that go into it, and the four districts where those specific grape varieties are grown.

## A French sparkling wine by any other name

Champagne is by no means the only French region that makes sparkling wines. Many of the other regions use the term *crémant* for their local bubbly, such as Crémant d'Alsace or Crémant de la Loire. This term originally applied to a certain style of Champagne that had lighter carbonation. When the French authorities decided that no other region could use the term *méthode champenoise* to describe the production method of their wines, they granted other regions the right to use *crémant* as a compromise. *Crémant* wines are always made by the Champagne method of second fermentation in the bottle — now called the *traditional method,* or the *classic method.* Alsace, the Loire Valley, and Languedoc-Roussillon (all covered in Chapter 7 of Book II) are three important French regions for sparkling wines.

# Chalking success up to Champagne's climate and soil

The location of the Champagne region really pushes the envelope for grape-growing: It's practically at the northernmost latitudinal limit (a little below 50 degrees latitude) in which vines can be cultivated in the Northern Hemisphere. It's the most northerly wine region in the world, with the exception of two of Germany's minor regions and the vineyards of southern England. The annual mean temperature in Champagne is 50 degrees Fahrenheit — about one-half degree Centigrade above the annual temperature in which grapes can grow.

In most years, wine grapes just about ripen in this marginal growing climate, and (typical of less-ripe fruit) they retain lots of acidity. Even in warmer-than-average years, the grapes are quite acidic. Such high acidity is a real problem for *still* (nonsparkling) wines, but it's an asset to sparkling wines, which need acidity for their palate-cleansing liveliness.

It rains quite a bit in Champagne, even in the summer, but the better vintages have enough sun for the grapes to ripen. The big enemy is late spring frosts, which can wipe out much of a crop.

The chalky soil of Champagne is something special. As you drive through the region, you can actually see mounds of pure white chalk. This soil originated about 65 million years ago, when the region was covered by the sea, which left huge deposits of seashells behind as it receded. This chalky soil is poor for many crops but ideal for wine grapes, which thrive in infertile soils.

The chalk is hundreds of feet deep in most of the best vineyard areas, and the vines' roots dig deep into the earth for nourishment. The chalky subsoil retains enough water for dry spells but is porous enough to prevent the roots from becoming damaged by too much water during rainfalls — essential in this rather rainy region. The chalk also absorbs the heat of the sun during the day and radiates it to the vines during the cool nights.

As a result of the Champagne region's climate and soil, the grapes that grow there tend to be rather tiny, but they have lots of concentrated nutrients. Champagne's cool climate and its chalky limestone soil are undoubtedly the leading factors contributing to the excellence of its sparkling wine.

## Recognizing the grape varieties used in Champagne

Champagne is made mainly from three grape varieties:

- **Pinot Noir,** a red variety
- **Pinot Meunier,** a red variety related to Pinot Noir
- **Chardonnay,** a white variety

Most Champagnes — about 85 to 90 percent of them — are a blend of about two-thirds red grapes and one-third Chardonnay. A few Champagnes (less than 5 percent) are 100 percent Chardonnay (they're called *blanc de blancs*); fewer yet are 100 percent red grapes (those are called *blanc de noirs*). Rosé Champagnes, a small category, are usually, but not always, made from a blend of white and red grapes.

Although Champagne is primarily a white wine, the two red varieties predominate; they make up about 75 percent of the Champagne vineyards. The current percentage of planting of the three grape varieties in Champagne is 33 percent Pinot Noir, 42 percent Pinot Meunier, and 25 percent Chardonnay.

The reason that most Champagnes are blends of Pinot Noir, Pinot Meunier, and Chardonnay is that each grape variety has strengths to contribute to the final blend.

- Pinot Noir adds body, structure, aroma, and a complexity of flavors. This difficult variety likes the cool climate of the region, and it grows well in the chalky limestone soil.
- Chardonnay, a star performer in the Champagne region, gives freshness, delicacy, elegance, and finesse. For this reason, many producers make a blanc de blancs (Chardonnay) Champagne.
- Pinot Meunier contributes fruitiness, floral aromas, and a precocious character (which means the wine is ready to drink sooner).

## Mapping the four grape-growing districts

As it happens, each of the three grape varieties described in the preceding section does best in different areas of the Champagne region, which has four main grape-growing districts. Each district (mapped out in Figure 6-1) specializes in certain varieties. The four districts are

- **Montaigne de Reims:** These chalky hillsides are directly south of the city of Reims, north of Épernay, and north of the Marne River. Pinot Noir is the dominant variety here, but some Chardonnay and a little Pinot Meunier are also grown.

- **Côte des Blancs:** This district, directly south of the town of Épernay, is by far *the* most important vineyard area for Chardonnay. Most of the best blanc de blancs Champagnes use grapes from the villages on the Côte des Blancs; huge deposits of chalk are in the soil here. The Côte de Sézanne prolongs the Côte des Blancs to the south.

- **Valée de la Marne:** As the largest district, located directly west of Épernay, Vallée de la Marne includes Épernay itself and stretches beyond the town of Château-Thierry. Pinot Meunier is the most-planted grape variety by far in this area, but some Pinot Noir and a little Chardonnay also grow here.

- **The Aube:** Also known as the Côte des Bar, this district is well south of Épernay, near the city of Troyes. Pinot Noir is the predominant variety here, although its wine is heavier and not as fine as the Pinot Noir in the Montagne de Reims.

### *The greatest Champagne villages*

Over hundreds of years of grape-growing in the Champagne region, certain villages (or *crus,* as they're called in France) emerged as the best vineyard areas. These crus, numbering 321, started to gain recognition in the second part of the 19th century. The Comate Interprofessionnel du Vin de Champagne (CIVC), a Champagne trade organization formed during World War II that serves as Champagne's regulatory body, now ranks 17 villages as grands crus and another 40 villages as premiers crus. Each cru has an official quality rating on a scale of 100: Grand cru vineyards all rate 100, and premier cru vineyards rank from 90 to 99 points.

The remaining 264 designated Champagne villages rate between 80 and 89. The rating isn't static; the CIVC periodically revises the rankings (the last revision took place in 1985).

If a Champagne is made from all grand cru grapes, it's entitled to use the name *Grand Cru* on its label. Likewise, if it's made from all premier cru grapes, it can use the term *Premier Cru* (or *1er Cru*) on its label. A combination of grand cru and premier cru grapes entitles a Champagne to only a premier cru designation.

Usually only *grower-producers* (grape growers who also make their own Champagne) are small enough to use only grand cru and/or premier cru grapes in their Champagnes. The large houses produce so much wine that they must use grapes from other villages in addition to grand cru or premier cru grapes. The exception for the large houses is their premium Champagnes, which are usually made from only, or mainly, grand cru and/or premier cru grapes. With several exceptions, the large houses usually refrain from using these designations on their Champagnes so they don't denigrate their less-expensive Champagnes in comparison.

The 40 premier cru villages provide about 22 percent of the grapes for Champagne. Most of the premiers crus are in the Montagne de Reims or the Côte des Blancs, but some very good premier cru villages are also in the part of the Vallée de la Marne that's located close to the town of Épernay.

### The best of the best

About 8.6 percent of Champagne's grapes come from grand cru villages. Nine grand crus are in the Montagne de Reims, six in the Côte des Blancs, and two in the Vallée de la Marne. Of the 17 grand cru villages, Aÿ and Verbena are generally regarded as the two best villages for growing the Pinot Noir grape, with Bouzy close behind. Le Mesnil-sur-Oger, Cramant, and Avize, all in the Côte des Blancs, are considered the finest grand cru villages for the Chardonnay grape. Look for these village names on some of the better Champagnes, especially from grower-producers.

# Surveying Champagne Styles

Enormous variation exists among Champagnes. Some Champagnes are sweeter, lighter, or more complex than others, for example. The spectrum of Champagne styles encompasses the following categories:

- Nonvintage, vintage, and prestige cuvée (premium) Champagnes
- Standard, blanc de blancs, blanc de noirs, and rosé Champagnes
- Brut, extra dry, and demi-sec Champagnes

Champagnes also vary in how much body they have, a characteristic that's influenced by the style of the house or grower-producer that makes them. (For help distinguishing between the two, head to the "Selecting a Bottle of Bubbly" section later in this chapter.) The following sections explain the intricacies of these different Champagne styles to aid you in purchasing the Champagne that will be most in line with your tastes.

# Translating years and quality into Champagnespeak

When you understand what distinguishes a nonvintage, vintage, and prestige cuvée Champagne, you can tell them apart from one another fairly easily. The challenge is that the labels don't give you a clue as to which type a Champagne is. To help you out, here's a bite-size description of each:

- ✔ **Nonvintage Champagne:** The most common style by far, *nonvintage* Champagnes are blends of wines from several years, and no vintage date appears on the label. These wines are called nonvintage because they don't derive from just *one* vintage. Such Champagne is also known as *classic* and is the least expensive type (with a few exceptions).

- ✔ **Vintage Champagnes:** These wines are made from grapes of a single year, which is usually, but not always, a better-than-average year; the vintage year is always on the label of vintage Champagnes.

- ✔ **Prestige cuvées:** The producers' best Champagnes are considered prestige cuvées. These wines are mainly vintage Champagnes but can be nonvintage.

For the full scoop on each of these three styles, refer to the following sections.

### Nonvintage Champagnes

Nonvintage Champagnes make up 85 to 90 percent of all Champagnes produced today. They're the foundation of the Champagne business by necessity. Because of the region's marginal climate, not every year can be a perfect "vintage" year. If producers didn't blend the wines of several years together, evening out the faults of one year with the virtues of another, they would've been out of business a long time ago.

Nonvintage Champagnes are also referred to as *classic* Champagnes because they were the original type of Champagne. Some producers prefer the term *multivintage*. Sometimes *classic* appears on the label, but *nonvintage* never does, because Champagne producers believe this term is disparaging.

Nonvintage Champagnes are the least-expensive Champagnes, mainly $20 to $45 per bottle. Every Champagne producer makes a nonvintage Champagne, which is always her biggest-selling wine. (The one exception is a small house, Salon, which produces only a vintage blanc de blancs; to find out what makes a blanc de blancs, see the section "Recognizing the grape varieties used in Champagne" earlier in this chapter.)

Most nonvintage Champagnes are made from approximately two-thirds red grapes (Pinot Noir and Pinot Meunier) and one-third white grapes (Chardonnay). A large part of each year's nonvintage blend is made up of wines from the current harvest. Then, older wines (known as *reserve* wines) are added to the blend. Most producers use between 5 and 25 percent reserve wines in their nonvintage blends. A few high-quality producers, such as Charles Heidsieck and Krug, use even higher percentages of reserve wines, up to 45 or 50 percent.

Although vintage Champagnes are generally superior to nonvintage Champagnes, there's absolutely nothing wrong with the quality of most non-vintage Champagnes. And they're generally $10 to $15 less expensive per bottle than standard vintage Champagnes.

**Book II**

**France: A Wine Superstar**

### *Vintage Champagnes*

Vintage Champagne comes from the grapes of one year only, which means 100 percent of the grapes must be from the vintage stated on the label.

Standard vintage Champagnes (those that aren't prestige cuvées, which are described in the next section) make up a small part of the Champagne market — less than 10 percent of production and sales. This fact is ironic, because vintage Champagnes usually represent the best value in Champagne. Yes, they average about $45 to $60 a bottle (which is $10 to $15 more than nonvintage Champagnes), but they're invariably higher in quality because

- ✔ They're made from better grapes, usually from better vineyards. As a result, vintage Champagnes are richer and more concentrated than non-vintage Champagnes.

- ✔ They're aged for two to three years longer by the producer; the extra aging adds more complexity and maturity.

- ✔ Most producers use only the two finest grape varieties, Pinot Noir and Chardonnay, for vintage Champagnes; the quicker-maturing Pinot Meunier is used mainly in nonvintage Champagnes.

- ✔ They're made from the grapes of at least a good, and sometimes a superb, vintage.

Producers normally make vintage Champagnes only when the weather has been warm and dry, especially in the autumn, near harvest. On average, about five or six years each decade are good enough for vintage Champagnes to be produced. But each producer decides whether she'll make a vintage Champagne in any given year. Some vintages have been so good — such as 1982, 1985, 1988, 1989, 1990, 1995, and 1996 — that just about every producer made a vintage Champagne. The 2002 and 2004 vintages will be ready to drink down the road.

### Prestige cuvées

The best Champagne a producer makes is usually considered her *prestige cuvée* — also known as *premium Champagnes*— although you won't find any of these words on the label. The way that you normally identify a Champagne as a prestige cuvée is by its price, which starts at about $70 a bottle and can go well over $100.

Most prestige cuvées are also vintage Champagnes, but a few are nonvintage. Almost every large Champagne house, and most of the smaller ones, makes at least one prestige cuvée; some houses make two prestige cuvées, a white and a rosé.

The most famous prestige cuvées are as follows:

- Moët & Chandon Cuvée Dom Pérignon (the largest-selling prestige cuvée in the world)
- Louis Roederer Cristal
- Perrier-Jouët Fleur de Champagne (the renowned "flower bottle")

Other well-known prestige cuvées include the following:

| | |
|---|---|
| Dom Ruinart Blanc de Blancs | Pommery Louise |
| Krug Grande Cuvée | Salon Le Mesnil |
| Laurent-Perrier Cuvée Grand Siècle | Taittinger Comtes de Champagne |
| Pol Roger Cuvée Sir Winston Churchill | Veuve Clicquot La Grande Dame |

When you're spending quite a bit of money on a bottle of Champagne, you want to know that you're getting your money's worth. In the case of prestige cuvée Champagne, rest assured that you are, for two reasons. First, prestige cuvées are made from the finest grapes from the very best locations, usually from grand cru or a blend of grand cru and premier cru vineyards (see "The greatest Champagne villages" earlier in this chapter for more on these distinctions). Second, they're aged longer in the producer's cellars than any other Champagnes (typically from five to eight years). Both of these factors ensure high quality.

Following is a rundown of how prestige cuvées differ from other Champagnes:

- Their bubbles are finer, very tiny and delicate.
- Their aromas and flavors are more complex, more elegant, and more intense.

> ✔ They have greater length on the palate (meaning their flavors persist longer) than other Champagnes.
>
> ✔ They have greater longevity than other Champagnes; they're usually at their best 15 or more years from the vintage date.

And of course there's the status value of a prestige cuvée. When you want to impress someone, nothing works quite like a prestige cuvée Champagne.

## Highlighting the nontraditional Champagnes

More than 90 percent of all Champagnes are traditional, or *standard,* Champagnes — a blend of at least two grape varieties (Pinot Noir and Chardonnay), but usually all three, that's white in color. However, three other types of Champagne exist, all of which are made in small quantities:

> ✔ *Blanc de blancs* Champagne is white and made solely from Chardonnay.
>
> ✔ *Blanc de noirs* Champagne is golden-white and produced from one or two red grapes.
>
> ✔ *Rosé* Champagne is pink and made from one or more grape varieties.

### Blanc de blancs Champagne

In the 1920s, Eugène-Aimé Salon started selling a Champagne made exclusively from Chardonnay; this was the first commercial *blanc de blancs* (literally, "white from white") Champagne. Today Salon Champagne still exists, but it's an expensive (over $100) prestige cuvée made in small quantities and difficult to find.

Blanc de blancs Champagnes didn't really catch on internationally until 1957, when Taittinger, a large, family-owned house, released its first blanc de blancs Champagne: the 1952 Comtes de Champagne prestige cuvée. Now, a good many houses and grower-producers make a blanc de blancs. Regardless of who makes them, blanc de blancs are always *brut* (very dry) Champagnes.

Blanc de blancs Champagnes can be nonvintage, vintage, or prestige cuvée Champagnes (see the earlier related sections for descriptions of these three styles). Because the Chardonnay grape is so suited to the cool climate and chalky soil of the Champagne region, the quality of these wines is quite high.

Most, but not all, blanc de blancs Champagnes are lighter-bodied, more acidic, and more elegant than other Champagnes. Many have vibrant, tart lemony flavors. They tend to be slightly more expensive than other Champagnes, but they also age extremely well.

Following are some of the most famous blanc de blancs Champagnes:

| | |
|---|---|
| Billecart-Salmon Blanc de Blancs | Pol Roger Blanc de Chardonnay |
| Deutz Blanc de Blancs | Dom Ruinart Blanc de Blancs |
| Mumm de Cramant | Taittinger Comtes de Champagne |

### Blanc de noirs Champagnes

Blanc de noirs are the rarest type of Champagne, especially among the larger Champagne houses; only a few grower-producers make one. Blanc de noirs, typically golden in color, are made from the red grapes Pinot Noir and/or Pinot Meunier, but most are 100 percent Pinot Noir. This is the fullest-bodied type of Champagne and can accompany main courses at dinner very nicely. Like blanc de blancs, blanc de noirs are always *brut* (very dry) Champagnes.

### Rosé Champagnes

About 97 percent of all Champagne is white. That leaves only 3 percent for rosé Champagnes, which come in all different hues of pink, from the palest salmon or onion-skin to the deepest rose. Rosé Champagnes are always Brut Champagnes and are therefore always dry. They get their color from a little Pinot Noir wine added for that purpose (or, in a few cases, the grape juice remains in contact with the dark skins of Pinot Noir and/or Pinot Meunier during the first fermentation).

Rosé Champagnes are usually blends of Pinot Noir and Chardonnay, but sometimes Pinot Meunier makes it in there, too. In a few cases, rosés are 100 percent Pinot Noir, but unlike blanc de noirs Champagnes, rosés are always some shade of pink.

Most houses make at least one rosé Champagne. Like blanc de blancs, rosés can be nonvintage, vintage, or prestige cuvée; and they're usually slightly higher in price than other Champagnes. The majority of rosé Champagnes have aromas and flavors of wild strawberries, and like blanc de noirs Champagnes, rosés are more full-bodied than most other Champagnes, which makes them a good companion for main courses at the dinner table.

A few popular rosé Champagnes, all of which happen to be nonvintage, are the following:

Billecart-Salmon Brut Rosé
Gosset Grand Rosé Brut
Laurent-Perrier Cuvée Rosé Brut
Pommery Brut Rosé

# Categorizing Champagne from dry to sweet

Most Champagnes benefit from a *dosage,* a wine-sugar solution added as a final adjustment to the wine after its second fermentation and aging; the dosage balances the wine's high acidity and makes the wine more palatable. Depending on the amount of sugar added, and the amount of counter-balancing acidity in the wine, you might or might not perceive the sweetness.

The French nomenclature for categorizing Champagnes on a dryness versus sweetness scale can be quite confusing. For instance, Extra Dry Champagne isn't that dry at all! And *Demi-Sec* (medium-dry) Champagne is rather sweet. (Strangely, no one wants to admit that anything is sweet, including Champagne producers.)

**Book II**

**France: A Wine Superstar**

Technically, six different levels of dryness are permitted in Champagne, but practically speaking, you tend to see only three types: Brut, Extra Dry, and Demi-Sec. Table 6-1 shows the six categories of dryness/sweetness, the amount of residual sugar expressed in grams per liter, and the real meaning of the dryness categories.

| Table 6-1 | Dryness-Sweetness Levels in Champagne | |
|---|---|---|
| *Category* | *Residual Sugar (grams/liter)* | *Description* |
| Extra Brut (bone dry) | 0–6 | From totally dry (0) to extremely dry |
| Brut (very dry) | 0–15 | From totally dry (0) to fairly dry |
| Extra Sec (extra dry) | 12–20 | From fairly dry to off-dry |
| Sec (dry) | 17–35 | Medium dry |
| Demi-Sec (medium dry) | 35–50 | Quite sweet |
| Doux (sweet) | 50+ | Very sweet |

Actually, more than 95 percent of all Champagne produced today — regardless of whether it's nonvintage, vintage, rosé, and so forth — is labeled *Brut.* But the term *Brut* is somewhat of a misnomer, because many so-called Brut Champagnes, those whose residual sugar is close to the maximum 15 grams per liter, aren't really all that dry.

The following sections provide some specifics on the three categories of dryness versus sweetness that you're most likely to encounter in Champagnes at your local wine shop.

### Brut Champagnes

Brut Champagnes constitute the largest category of Champagnes, but it's not a uniform category: The only way to determine how dry or sweet a Brut Champagne actually is, within the range allowed by law, is to know the producer's style.

Most Brut Champagnes are in the 10- to 15-gram category. The following six major Champagne houses make Brut Champagnes that have *less than* 10 grams of sugar. If you crave truly dry Champagnes, check out these houses:

| | |
|---|---|
| Bollinger | Krug |
| Gusset | Bruno Paillard |
| Jacquesson | Salon |

### Extra Dry and Demi-Sec Champagnes

Extra Dry Champagnes are on the dry side but tend to be somewhat sweeter than Brut Champagnes. This category is really marketed only in the United States. In fact, one brand, Moët & Chandon's White Star (an Extra Dry Champagne) is the country's best-selling Champagne.

Although Extra Dry Champagnes are sweeter than Bruts, they aren't sweet enough for dessert. The only Champagne that has enough sweetness for after dinner and/or dessert is Demi-Sec Champagne. Demi-Sec Champagnes aren't very common, but at least four houses (Moët & Chandon, Veuve Clicquot, Laurent-Perrier, and Louis Roederer) still make this style.

## Selecting a Bottle of Bubbly: Knowing Producers and Their Styles

In the Champagne region, a *négociant house* is a firm that buys grapes from growers, makes and blends the wines, ages and bottles them, and sells them under the company's own label; most *négociant* houses also own some vineyards as well. The French term for these *négociant* houses is *négociant-manipulant* (look for the initials *NM* on the labels of *négociant* Champagnes).

Many of the *négociant* houses are huge, such as Moët & Chandon, Mumm, and Veuve Clicquot. The Champagne region's 261 *négociant-manipulants* dominate Champagne sales with a 71 percent share of the total market. (Outside of Europe, they're responsible for a whopping 97 percent of all Champagne sales!)

About 2,000 of the region's 15,000 grape growers actually make Champagne themselves. Another 3,000 have it made for them, from their own grapes, at their local cooperative, where the wine is bottled with their own label. These 5,000 grower-producers account for 22 percent of all Champagne sales (mostly within France itself). The prices of grower-producers' wines (by the way, the initials *RM* are on the bottom of the front labels of their wines) are comparable to those of the big *négociant* brands, except at the prestige cuvée level, where the grower-producer Champagnes represent better value.

Cooperatives account for the remaining 7 percent of all Champagne sales. Champagnes from grower-producers and cooperatives combined account for just 3 percent of Champagne sales outside of Europe; this fact proves that, with a few exceptions, almost all of the Champagne sold in the United States is made by *négociant* houses. But sales by grower-producers and cooperatives have risen over the years.

The increasing prosperity of the larger grower-producers has given them the means to start exporting their Champagnes. This development is excellent for wine lovers, who now not only have a larger group of Champagnes from which to choose but who also have the opportunity to buy prestige cuvée Champagnes at reasonable prices.

Of course, knowing the difference between a Champagne house and a grower-producer is all well and good. But how can you tell the difference between their styles of Champagne so you know which one you want to pick up? Check out the next two sections for a little help.

## *Matching the houses and their styles*

The following lists classify 25 major Champagne houses into three categories according to their house styles: light and elegant, medium-bodied, or full-bodied. The house styles of the producers are most evident in their nonvintage Brut (and Extra Dry) Champagnes, which they produce every year and which make up the largest part of their production. (Although producers try to express their house styles in their vintage Champagnes, the influence of the climate in a particular vintage year can sometimes mask the house style.)

**Light, Elegant Style**

| | |
|---|---|
| Billecart-Salmon | Bruno Paillard |
| Henriot | Perrier-Jouët |
| Jacquesson | Piper-Heidsieck |
| Lanson | Pommery |
| Laurent-Perrier | Ruinart |
| G.H. Mumm | Taittinger |

**Medium-Bodied Style**

Cattier

Deutz

Charles Heidsieck

Moët & Chandon

Philipponnat

Pol Roger

**Full-Bodied Style**

Bollinger

Gosset

Alfred Gratien

Krug

Louis Roederer

Salon

Veuve Clicquot Ponsardin

# Figuring out the styles of the best grower-producer Champagnes

Grower-producer Champagnes generally offer more individualistic flavors than Champagnes of the large *négociant* houses. The reason is simple: The grapes of grower-producers usually come from the vineyards of just one village, whereas most of the *négociant* Champagnes (excepting their prestige cuvées) typically are made from a blend of grapes from many villages throughout the region. Also, most of the better grower-producers — those who export their Champagnes — own vineyards in grand cru and/or premier cru villages, so they have access to superior raw material even for their least-expensive Champagnes.

The following list divides these grower-producers according to the style of their Champagnes and includes the village and district where each grower-producer is situated:

**Powerful, Pinot Noir-Dominated**

Paul Bara (Bouzy, Montagne de Reims)

Henri Billiot (Ambonnay, Montagne de Reims)

Egly-Ouriet (Ambonnay, Montagne de Reims)

Tarlant (Oeuilly, Vallée de la Marne; a balance of all three grape varieties)

**Rich, Chardonnay-Dominated**

J. Lassalle (Chigny-les-Roses, Montagne de Reims)

Vilmart & Cie (Rilly-la-Montagne, Montagne de Reims)

**Full, Rich Blanc de Blancs**

Guy Charlemagne (Le Mesnil-sur-Oger, Côte des Blancs)

Diebolt-Vallois (Cramant, Côte des Blancs)

Larmandier-Bernier (Vertus, Côte des Blancs)

Pierre Peters (Le Mesnil-sur-Oger, Côte des Blancs)

Alain Robert (Le Mesnil-sur-Oger, Côte des Blancs)

# Buying, serving, and storing Champagne

Champagne is a fascinating topic — and one that's hard to talk about without getting thirsty! When you're looking for a bottle to enjoy with friends, be sure to buy Champagne either in a standard 750-milliliter bottle or in a *magnum* (a 1.5-liter bottle); magnums are best because they age longer. And unless you know they're fresh, don't buy half-bottles (375 milliliters) or, worse, quarter-bottles (187 milliliters, known as *splits*); all wines age faster in small bottles, and Champagnes are particularly vulnerable to premature aging. The slower turnover of smaller-sized bottles in wine shops and restaurants increases the odds that the Champagne won't be fresh. Be wary, too, of bottles larger than magnums — again, because of the turnover issue. Also, the really large bottles are far more difficult to pour!

Even though Champagne producers encourage you to drink your Champagne right away (they insist it's ready to drink when you buy it), don't be afraid to age it in the proper storage conditions (described in Chapter 8 of Book I) to allow the blended wines more time to marry and add complexity and maturity to your wine. Vintage Champagnes and prestige cuvées don't really start developing until about 10 years from the vintage date, and they can age for 15 to 20 years or more in good vintages. Blanc de blancs Champagnes age particularly well (15 to 20 years or more), whereas rosés and blanc de noirs Champagnes are usually best consumed within 10 years. Even nonvintage Champagnes improve with two or three years of aging; properly stored nonvintage Champagnes should last at least four or five years without any signs of deterioration.

Good Champagne glasses are crucial for maximum enjoyment of your bubbly. The glass should be tall and slender, with a long stem (so you don't hold the glass by the bowl and warm up your Champagne). Tulip-shaped glasses (about 9 to 10 inches tall, including the stem) can be used for all Champagnes; the wider tulip shape benefits the wine's aromas.

To prepare your Champagne for serving, chill it to the desired temperature (provided in Chapter 4 of Book I) with at least four hours in the fridge, or a half hour in a tall ice bucket (with half ice and half cold water). When serving, pour the Champagne slowly into the glass so the fizziness has time to settle down; doing so ensures you won't shortchange your guests with a tiny pour. Fill the glass about two-thirds of the way and refill it when just a little bit of Champagne remains in the glass. After pouring your first round of Champagne, put the bottle into an ice bucket or back into the refrigerator. And if you have any Champagne left over, simply close the bottle with a Champagne stopper and put it back into the fridge. It should keep well there for up to three days.

If pairing Champagne with food is your major concern, you'll be glad to know you can go all kinds of ways with this versatile beverage. Champagne pairs well with pasta or risotto (but not pasta with tomato sauce), most vegetables, and fish and seafood dishes. Champagne also works well with all kinds of poultry, game birds, veal, and pork. Be careful with desserts, though; most Champagnes are too dry and acidic to accompany desserts. However, you can try a Demi-Sec Champagne, which is fairly sweet, with a dessert that's not too sweet, such as pound cake, shortcake, or a lemon tart.

**Book II**

**France: A Wine Superstar**

# Chapter 7

# Other Wine Regions of France

Sparkling wine brings the three regions in this chapter together — all of them produce some doozies — but each region has a unique claim to fame that sets it apart:

✔ Alsace is a world within the wine world of France, growing a number of grape varieties all its own.

✔ The Loire Valley is an often-overlooked haven for white wine production and a temperate, gorgeous locale.

✔ The south of France is not only the country's oldest wine-producing area but also its most prolific, boasting more than 40 percent of France's wine production.

This chapter gets you up close and personal with all three regions and the wines they're known for.

## Alsace: Location, Location, Location

The location of the Alsace region has everything to do with the type of wines the region makes. Besides dictating the *terroir* (flip to Chapter 1 in Book II for more on this important concept), Alsace's location also has cultural and historical implications that influence the style of the region's wines. Alsace is situated in northeastern France, across the Rhine River from Germany. The Alsace region, along with the Lorraine area northwest of Alsace, was formerly part of Germany, time and again. Most recently, France regained possession of Alsace in 1919, as a result of World War I.

## Picture-perfect traveling

If you enjoy visiting wine regions, put Alsace at the top of your list. The region is dotted with beautiful medieval towns that are so charming, you might suspect they're not for real (but of course, they are). Each of the old towns has its own personality, as well as plenty of history. The vineyards come right to the edges of town. Apart from the region's beauty, the food (and, of course, the wine!) is terrific.

Today, many of the French who live in Alsace have Germanic names, as do the towns there, but the region is decidedly French — no doubt about it. (Cross any bridge over the Rhine River from Germany to Alsace, and the dramatic change in scenery, from industrial highway on one side to quaint, flower-bedecked towns on the other side, tells you immediately that you've arrived at a new place.) And yet Alsace wines have been shaped by Germany. Like German wines, Alsace wines are

- ✔ Predominantly white wines
- ✔ Predominantly unblended wines (each made from a single grape variety)
- ✔ Usually without oaky flavor

Also, their grape varieties are the same as some of those used in Germany. The winemakers of Alsace have even adopted the German practice of naming their wines according to the grape variety used to make the wine.

Despite these conceptual similarities, however, Alsace wines don't taste at all like German wines because growing conditions in Alsace are very particular.

The most important factor in the Alsace landscape is actually not the Rhine River (and Germany on the other side of it) but the Vosges Mountains, which flank Alsace's vineyard area on the west. The mountains are important because they block rain from the west. Their foothills also provide slopes that are ideal for vineyards and a variety of soil types, which creates diversity in the wines.

In terms of climate, the Vosges Mountains cut the Alsace region off from any Atlantic influence by blocking moisture and storms that blow eastward from the ocean. As a result, Alsace enjoys an unusually dry, sunny climate — the driest of any classic French wine region. (Colmar, the main city in the southern part of Alsace, is the second-driest city in France, with an annual rainfall of only about 19 inches, compared to 37 inches in Bordeaux, for example.) Because the mountains are lower in the north, and less effective in blocking rain and clouds, the northern part of Alsace tends to be moister and less sunny than the south, although it still has a fairly dry climate.

# Surveying the grapes of Alsace

Compared to many other French wine regions, Alsace grows a real hodge-podge of grapes: Nearly a dozen varieties in all are permitted in the production of AOC wines, and all but one grape variety is white.

Four noble white varieties (check out Chapter 1 of Book I to discover noble grapes) enjoy special status: They're entitled to be used in the production of *grand cru* wines, a special, high-level category of Alsace wine. These four varieties are as follows:

- **Riesling:** Pronounced *reese*-ling, Riesling is one of the two best white grape varieties in the world (the other is Chardonnay), and by general consensus, it's the finest variety grown in Alsace. It's also the single most-planted grape variety in Alsace, populating about a quarter of the vineyard acreage. Because Riesling is the latest variety to ripen, it particularly benefits from the long, sunny Alsace autumns.

- **Gewürztraminer:** This grape, pronounced geh-*vairtz*-trah-mee-ner, is Alsace's third most-planted variety, covering nearly 18 percent of the vineyard land. Of all the wine regions of the world that grow this highly aromatic variety, Alsace undoubtedly is the most suitable, in view of how excellent Alsace's Gewürztraminer wines can be.

- **Pinot Gris:** Representing about 10.5 percent of Alsace's grape plantings, some people consider Pinot Gris (pee-noh gree) the number two grape after Riesling in terms of the quality of wine it makes in Alsace.

- **Muscat:** Although it's considered one of the four noble grapes of Alsace, Muscat (moos-caht) is a minor variety quantitatively, covering less than 2.5 percent of the vineyard land. And that small amount of acreage is actually divided between two distinct varieties: Muscat d'Alsace (elsewhere known as the Muscat à Petits Grains, or small-berried Muscat) and Muscat Ottonel. Usually the two Muscats are blended together and the wines are labeled simply *Muscat.*

Beyond these four white varieties, a few others are important locally, for various reasons:

- **Pinot Blanc:** The second most-planted variety after Riesling, Pinot Blanc (pee-noh blahnk) covers 21 percent of the vineyards. Some of this quantity actually isn't Pinot Blanc at all, however; it's another variety called Auxerrois, which looks similar to Pinot Blanc except that its grapes are more greenish when they're ripe. The two varieties are usually blended together, and the wines are labeled *Pinot Blanc.* Pinot Blanc is a fairly undistinguished variety, with shy aroma and flavor, but in the right vineyard, it can be very good.

✔ **Pinot Noir:** Alsace's only red grape variety, Pinot Noir (pee-noh nwahr) makes the region's only red wines. It covers nearly 9 percent of the vineyard land, an amount that's slowly rising.

✔ **Sylvaner:** Pronounced sihl-*vah*-ner, Sylvania represents nearly 14 percent of Alsace's production, although wines bearing this name are rarely seen on the shelves of U.S. wine shops. This variety is important to grape growers because it ripens early and can produce a large crop, but plantings are in decline.

# Examining the region's range of wines

Because of the varying terrain and soil types in the region and the variability in the protection the Vosges Mountains offer, Alsace wines run the gamut of styles within the white wine category. The lower-altitude vineyards, for example, tend to produce light-bodied, fresh white wines, whereas the hillside vineyards make intense, concentrated wines. As another example, the northern vineyards supply most of the grapes for sparkling wine because the rainier climate results in less-ripe grapes of the sort that are suitable for sparkling wine production.

Alsace's wine production encompasses the following styles:

✔ Sparkling white and rosé wines, ranging from dry to semidry

✔ Off-dry, light-bodied, fruity white wines

✔ Dry white wines, light-bodied to full-bodied, with varying degrees of richness

✔ Sweet dessert wines from late-harvested grapes

✔ Light-bodied red wines

Nonsparkling *(still)* whites are the largest category. (In fact, Alsace produces 18 percent of France's entire still white wine production.) Sparkling wines account for 14 percent of production. Dessert wine production generally represents only a tiny portion of Alsace's wines.

The following sections introduce you to the prominent style of Alsace wines, the three standard appellations for Alsace wines, and the additional categories that denote ripeness.

### Bowing down to the dominant style and its variations

The majority of Alsace wines are dry, medium-bodied white wines with pronounced aromas and flavors that derive from the grapes and the land as opposed to winemaking techniques. For example, Alsace whites don't have smoky, toasty aromas and flavors from oak barrels.

A slight trend has developed toward greater richness in Alsace Riesling, Gewürztraminer, and Pinot Gris: Some wines have very ripe fruit flavors and aren't fully dry. The majority of Alsace's wines, however, are dry.

### Giving AOC names to Alsace wines

The laws governing the naming and labeling of Alsace wines are just about the easiest to understand of all French wine laws — but they do have a few particular wrinkles of their own.

All the wines of Alsace can be divided into just three AOC names:

- **Cremant d'Alsace:** This is the region's sparkling wine. Pinot Blanc usually forms the base of the wine, with various other grape varieties blended in. Only six varieties may be used to make Crémant d'Alsace: Pinot Blanc, Pinot Gris, Riesling, Auxerrois, Chardonnay, and Pinot Noir.

- **Alsace AOC:** Most of the wines made in Alsace carry the Alsace AOC appellation, which has existed since 1962. Each varietal wine must be made entirely from the grape whose name it carries.

- **Alsace Grand Cru:** Varietal wines made from any of the four noble Alsace varieties — Riesling, Gewürztraminer, Pinot Gris, and Muscat — grown in a grand cru vineyard can carry on their label the name of that vineyard and the appellation Alsace Grand Cru. As a quality measure, the law requires that the vines bear a 25 percent smaller crop than those for Alsace AOC. Alsace Grand Cru wines are typically higher in quality and more expensive than basic Alsace AOC wines; they also have great aging potential. These wines represent about 5 percent of Alsace's production.

### Measuring ripeness with the VT and SGN categories

Alsace has two more categories of wine that cut across both the Alsace AOC and Alsace Grand Cru appellations. These categories aren't based on where the grapes grow, but on how ripe the grapes are when they're harvested. Such distinctions are common in Germany, where grape ripeness (rather than vineyard location) is the principle behind the wine laws, but they're unheard of in France — outside of Alsace, that is.

In Alsace, when the grapes attain an unusually high concentration of sugar, often with the help of *botrytis cinerea* (noble rot), the wine can be labeled as *Vendange Tardive,* which means "late harvest." The extra sugar concentration in the grapes translates into extra richness in the wine; often, but not necessarily, VT wines — the shorthand for *Vendange Tardive* — are sweet or medium-sweet.

When the grapes are extraordinarily ripe and infected with *botrytis cinerea,* the wine can be labeled as *Sélection de Grains Nobles,* which roughly means "choice berry harvest." The desiccated grape berries make an extremely rich, concentrated, sweet dessert wine that's as delicious as it is rare. Only the very finest vintages give producers the opportunity to make SGN wines, as they're known, and the wines are quite expensive — more than $60 for a 375-milliliter half bottle.

Only four grape varieties may make VT or SGN wines, and these are the same varieties that can be used for Alsace Grand Cru wines: Riesling, Gewürztraminer, Pinot Gris, and Muscat.

## Appreciating Alsace's wine gems

One of the virtues of Alsace is that the region makes so many terrific wines, each suitable for different tastes or different levels of experience. As an added bonus, Alsace wines are among the world's most versatile wines for food. In fact, some classic wine-unfriendly foods actually are friendly to Alsace wines. Take tomatoes and sauerkraut, for example. The former is surprisingly good with Gewürztraminer, and the latter can complement Pinot Gris without a problem.

Read on to find out more about some of Alsace's true wine superstars.

### Riesling

The Riesling wines of Alsace tend to have the following characteristics:

- Aromas and flavors of citrus (especially grapefruit), citrus peel, apple, or peach, along with definite mineral accents, such as steeliness or flintiness; these characteristics vary according to the soil of the vineyard.

- Medium body with a firm backbone of acidity, although some wines have such weight that they cross the line into full-bodied; Alsace Rieslings are fuller than most Rieslings from other regions.

- Alsace Rieslings that aren't harvested late range from bone-dry to sweet; the majority of them taste dry, either because they *are* dry (their sugar was completely fermented into alcohol) or because their high acidity counterbalances any sweetness in the wine and creates an impression of dryness.

At their best, Alsace Rieslings are regal wines, with great depth, length, and complexity. They have so much to say, but so unobtrusively, that tasting them thoughtfully can stun you into reverent silence.

Alsace Rieslings need age. You can drink them at least 3 years after the vintage date, but you're better off waiting 8 to 15 years from the vintage. With age, their acidity is less noticeable, and they're therefore a bit softer and less austere than when they're young.

One Trimbach wine — Riesling Clos Ste Hune — is the greatest of all Alsace Rieslings; its production is quite small (never more than 700 cases per year), and the wine is quite expensive (about $150 per bottle when it's first released; often more if you buy older vintages at auction).

Another tremendous Trimbach Riesling is Cuvée Frédéric Emile, the winery's third Riesling up the quality ladder, after its basic Riesling and its Réserve Personnelle Riesling. In the typical Trimbach style, the wine is bone-dry; it has ripe apple and peach flavors that make a compelling contrast to the wine's dry, firm structure. Cuvée Frédéric Emile costs about $40 when it's first released.

**Book II**

**France: A Wine Superstar**

### Gewürztraminer

Close your eyes and imagine the fragrant aromas of lychee fruit, roses, and spice: That's Gewürztraminer. You might expect a wine that smells so floral and fruity to be sweet, but when you taste it, you find it surprisingly dry. The wine's rather full body and slight undercurrent of earthy bitterness provide yet more contrast to the heady aromas and flavors. Fascinating!

Gewürztraminers have a touch of sweetness more frequently than Rieslings do — similar to the sweetness of many California Chardonnays, for example, which everyone classifies as a dry wine. The low acidity of Gewürztraminer reinforces this impression of sweetness.

Gewürz — a nickname that's widely used in wine circles — doesn't age as remarkably as Riesling, but it lasts surprisingly long for such a fruit-driven wine. In general, drink Gewürztraminer when it's three to ten years old.

To capture the full Gewürztraminer experience, try one from an Alsace producer who favors a rich style of wines, such as Hugel. (Hugel's Jubilee Gewürztraminer, his top bottling, is a great example.) A basic Gewürztraminer from most producers will cost you about $13 a bottle; reserve-level wines are $20 to $30, and the top bottlings, such as Alsace Grand Cru wines, run from $40 to $60.

### Pinot Blanc

The Pinot Blanc grape is the personality opposite of Gewürztraminer: Its aromas and flavors are so mild that they're often described as neutral. In Alsace, though, Pinot Blanc wines do have some character, generally a minerally and delicately floral aroma and delicate flavors of pear and citrus.

Of the Alsace wines that are usually available on export markets, Pinot Blanc is the lightest-bodied, mildest, and least expensive (about $10 to $15 a bottle). That's not to say it can't be a very good wine. Producers such as Paul Blanck, Josmeyer, and Mark Kreydenweiss make stunning Pinot Blancs.

If you visit Alsace, you might see wines labeled *Clevner* or *Klevner;* these are local synonyms for Pinot Blanc, and they're rarely used on bottles for export markets. (Klevner, with only two *e*'s, isn't the same as Klevener de Heiligenstein, a Gewürztraminer-like wine.)

If you've never had an Alsace wine, try a Pinot Blanc as an introduction to the area. And drink it as young as you want to; most Pinot Blancs are best from when you buy them to about four years of age.

### Tokay-Pinot Gris

Fifteen years ago, a rumor claimed that the producers of Alsace would be required to drop the word *Tokay* from the name of Tokay-Pinot Gris wine to prevent confusion with Hungary's classic Tokaji wines. The hyphenated name was still in use by some companies until about 2006 and finally disallowed in 2007.

Whatever they're called, the Pinot Gris wines of Alsace are unique. They have concentrated flavors of peach — more precisely, the part of a cling peach that surrounds the pit — and sometimes citrus (lime, lemon, tangerine, and orange peel) or even tropical fruit such as mango; some typical Alsace mineral character usually accompanies this fruitiness. (In general, these wines are less interesting aromatically than Rieslings, however.) Alsace Pinot Gris wines are rich but solid wines with good firmness. They're typically dry, but of course some producers make them in a very rich style.

You can find Alsace Pinot Gris wines at $14 to $18 for a producer's basic quality tier, up to $70 for Grand Cru wines; these wines are best from about four years of age to ten years. Because Pinot Gris is relatively susceptible to noble rot, VT and SGN styles of Pinot Gris are more common than similar styles of Riesling and cost about $30 to $60 for a half bottle.

## Highlighting top Alsace producers

The average quality of winemaking in Alsace is among the highest in France. The finest wines are magnificent, but even the ordinary-quality wines are well made and worth drinking.

Alsace is a region of small producers. Approximately 1,000 wine producers (and another 5,000 grape growers, who supply grapes to some of the producers) make 160 million bottles a year, for an average production of fewer than 14,000 cases per winery — what would be considered "boutique" level in the United States. Naturally, some of these producers are larger than others: 230 producers account for 85 percent of the region's production.

As in most other wine regions, Alsace wine producers vary in nature.

- ✔ Some sell only the wine they make from their own vineyards; these are the smallest producers.
- ✔ Others are grower-*négociants,* who own vineyards but also purchase grapes and wines.
- ✔ Others are cooperative wineries, where dozens of growers pool their grapes.

This list of recommended producers features growers and grower-*négociants.* Some of these brands are widely available outside of France, whereas others are hard to find but worth the search. Here are the producers, sometimes with a few comments thrown in:

Jean-Baptiste Adam
Domaine Lucien Albrecht
Jean Becker
Léon Beyer (true varietal character and very good quality)
Paul Blanck (high-quality dry wines with strong *terroir* character)
Bott-Geyl
Albert Boxler
Ernest Burn
Marcel Deiss (a top-quality producer in all categories)
Dopff & Irion
Dopff au Moulin
Hugel (impressively rich wines, especially the Jubilee tier)
Josmeyer (fine-tuned, elegant wines of very high quality)
Roger Jung
André Kientzler
Domaine Klipfel
Marc Kreydenweiss (a fine, small producer making dry but rich wines)
Kuentz-Bas

Gustave Lorentz (makes terrific Gewürztraminer)
Domaine Julien Meyer
Mittnacht-Klack
Muré/Clos St.-Landelin (reliable wines, and a very good Pinot Noir)
Domaine Ostertag
Preiss-Henny
Rolly Gassmann
Charles Schleret
Domaine Schlumberger (great Grand Cru wines)
Albert Seltz
Pierre Sparr (very good *crémant* and a full line of fairly rich wines)
Trimbach (very dry, sleek, well-concentrated wines)
Domaine Weinbach (rich wines with ripe fruit character)
Willm (particularly good Gewürztraminer)
Domaine Zind-Humbrecht (a celebrated producer making some of the richest of all Alsace wines)

# Touring the Loire Valley and Its Unique Wines

The Loire Valley (shown in Figure 7-1) is the longest and most rural wine region in France. It follows the path of the Loire River, France's greatest waterway. The region begins in north-central France, a little to the south of Paris, and stretches about 250 miles across northwest France to the port city of Nantes, where the Loire empties into the Atlantic Ocean. The region boasts tremendous beauty, yet it's still unspoiled and not overrun by tourists. The Loire Valley is truly France's secret gem.

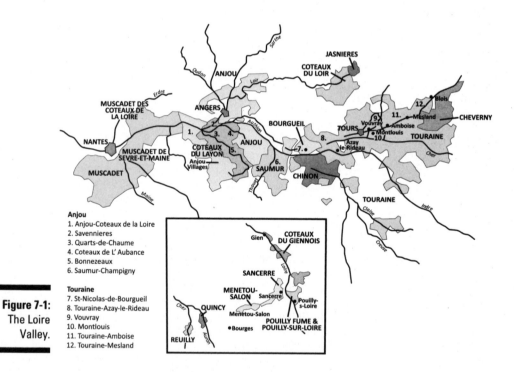

**Figure 7-1:**
The Loire
Valley.

**Anjou**
1. Anjou-Coteaux de la Loire
2. Savennieres
3. Quarts-de-Chaume
4. Coteaux de L' Aubance
5. Bonnezeaux
6. Saumur-Champigny

**Touraine**
7. St-Nicolas-de-Bourgueil
8. Touraine-Azay-le-Rideau
9. Vouvray
10. Montlouis
11. Touraine-Amboise
12. Touraine-Mesland

The Loire Valley makes white, rosé, red, sparkling, and dessert wines, but white wines, both dry and sweet, are the main attraction. White wine represents 55 percent of the region's production, compared to 24 percent red wine, 14 percent rosé wine, and 7 percent sparkling wine. A total of 40 AOC wines are produced across the Loire Valley; in a typical vintage, they account for about 32 million cases of wine.

Influenced by both the Atlantic Ocean and the Loire River, the climate is generally temperate throughout the Valley, with fairly warm but not hot summers, and winters that are never intensely cold. Summers have some rain, but most rain falls in the autumn and winter. As wine regions go, it's a rather cool area — and the closer to the ocean, the cooler and damper the growing season is.

The cool weather dictates the types of wines that the Valley produces. The Loire Valley specializes in crisp, white wines, because white wine grapes need less heat and sun than red wine grapes. The red wines from the Loire Valley tend to be light-bodied and fairly low in alcohol, reflecting their struggle to ripen in the northerly Loire latitude.

Of the Loire Valley's various soils, the most significant soil is chalky limestone, especially in the Upper Loire (the eastern part of the region, near Paris), around the towns of Sancerre and Pouilly-sur-Loire. The slopes of Vouvray in the Central Loire are rich in limestone and *tuffeau* (which is like soft limestone), soil extremely favorable for the Chenin Blanc grape, the dominant variety of the Vouvray district. In the Lower Loire (the western part, near the Atlantic Ocean), the hills are mainly sand and gravel — soils that exist throughout the rest of the Valley as well.

**Book II**

**France: A Wine Superstar**

## The Upper Loire: Sauvignon Blanc's spiritual home

The Upper Loire district is the extreme eastern part of the Loire Valley region, situated roughly in the center of France. This area is much closer to parts of Burgundy — it's only about 60 miles from Chablis — than it is to the opposite end of its own region. In fact, it shares a grape variety with Burgundy: the red Pinot Noir. But it doesn't grow Chardonnay, the grape of Chablis; instead, the white wines of the Upper Loire come mainly from Sauvignon Blanc.

Because the Upper Loire district is the most interior part of the Loire Valley, its climate is dryer and more continental than that of the rest of the region — but it's still a cool climate. Dry white wines dominate, although a fair amount of red and rosé wines also come from here.

The following sections describe the Upper Loire's important wines, as well as its leading wine producers.

### Sancerre and Pouilly-Fumé

Wines of the Upper Loire, primarily Sancerre (sahn-sehr) and Pouilly-Fumé (pwee-foo-may), are likely the world's finest interpretations of the Sauvignon Blanc variety. They're less intensely herbaceous than New Zealand and Italian Sauvignon Blancs but more assertive than most South African versions. They're more concentrated than Bordeaux's Sauvignon Blanc–based whites and racier than Bordeaux's richer whites, which are often blended with Sémillon. The Loire Valley's versions are also the most food-friendly.

Of the more than one million cases of Sancerre produced annually, about 80 percent is white, made entirely from Sauvignon Blanc. The other 20 percent is dry rosé and red Sancerre, from Pinot Noir; both are pleasant enough, but not of the quality of white Sancerre.

Across the river from the Sancerre vineyards, the town of Pouilly-sur-Loire is the center of another vineyard area for a similar white wine. Called Pouilly-Fumé, this wine is also 100 percent Sauvignon Blanc, but its production is only about half of Sancerre's.

The Pouilly-sur-Loire vineyards also produce another white, simply called Pouilly-sur-Loire. It's made from Chasselas, the principal variety of Swiss white wines. Unfortunately, Chasselas makes less distinguished wines in the Upper Loire than in Switzerland; Pouilly-sur-Loire is decent enough and inexpensive, but it's not of the quality of Pouilly-Fumé.

Sancerre and Pouilly-Fumé wines are more similar than different. They're light- to medium-bodied, crisp, and lively, with spicy, herbaceous, green-grass, mineral, and citrus aromas and flavors. Additionally, they're usually unbaked. The herbaceous aromas are usually more pronounced in Sancerre, whereas Pouilly-Fumé wines often have a distinct flinty, mineral aroma. Also, Pouilly-Fumés are slightly fuller, rounder, and less spicy than Sancerres — which tend to be livelier and a bit lighter-bodied.

Price-wise, Sancerre and Pouilly-Fumé wines are both good values. Most of them retail in the $15 to $25 range, but a few of the best examples of Pouilly-Fumé can cost more than $50.

Sancerre and Pouilly-Fumé, typical of most wines made entirely from Sauvignon Blanc, are best when they're consumed within one to four years of the vintage — with two or three years being their optimum age. They can live longer in some cases, but they begin to lose their freshness and liveliness, two of their most endearing characteristics.

### Other wines of the Upper Loire

The Upper Loire Valley is the home of three other fairly important AOC vineyard areas:

- Quincy
- Reilly
- Ménétou-Salon

In terms of white wines, all three produce dry, crisp whites based entirely on Sauvignon Blanc that are stylistically fairly similar to Sancerre and Pouilly-Fumé.

Of the three, Ménétou-Salon — from an area southwest of the town of Sancerre and near the ancient city of Bourges — is the most available in the United States and the most comparable to Sancerre and Pouilly-Fumé in style, flavor, and overall quality. Because none of these three are well-known wines, they tend to be good values; some white Ménétou-Salon wines retail for less than $15, despite the fact that production is only about 40,000 cases annually.

Although the white wines of Quincy and Reilly — not to be confused with Rully, a Burundian wine made from Chardonnay — are also well-priced, they tend to be lighter-bodied and more herbaceous than Sancerre and Pouilly-Fumé (described in the preceding section).

Whereas Quincy makes only white wine, Reuilly and Ménétou-Salon also make red and rosé wines. In Reuilly, half the production is red or rosé wine, with the red made from Pinot Noir and the rosé made from Pinot Gris, a white variety with fairly dark skin. About 40 percent of the production of Ménétou-Salon is rosé or red, from Pinot Noir. Most of the dry rosé and light-bodied red wines of Ménétou-Salon and Reuilly are also light in flavor and color. These wines are pleasant enough to accompany a warm-weather lunch, but they have no aging capacity; you should drink them within two or three years of their vintage date — the younger, the better. Nevertheless, Ménétou-Salon's rosés and reds tend to be more interesting than those of Sancerre.

Another AOC area of the Upper Loire is Coteaux du Giennois, the newest AOC zone of the district. Thirty percent of its production is white wine from Sauvignon Blanc; the balance is mainly light red wine from Gamay or Pinot Noir, as well as some rosé. These wines are even more obscure than Quincy, Reuilly, and Ménétou-Salon.

### Leading Upper Loire producers

Sancerre producers to look for include the following:

| | |
|---|---|
| Bailly-Reverdy et Fils | Domaine Alphonse Mellot |
| Domaine Henri Bourgeois | Domaine Paul Millerioux |
| Domaine Lucien Crochet | Domaine de Montigny |
| Domaine Vincent Delaporte | Domaine Roger Neveu |
| Cotat Frères | Gitton Père et Fils |
| Pascal Jolivet (also, Château du Nozay) | Domaine Vincent Pinard |
| | Bernard Reverdy |
| Comte Lafond (also spelled Lafon) | Jean-Max Roger |
| Château de Maimbray | Domaine Vacheron |

Top Pouilly-Fumé producers are listed here (note that the first two producers' best Pouilly-Fumés cost more than $50):

Domaine Cailbourdin
Jean-Claude Chatelain
Didier Dagueneau
Domaine Serge Dagueneau
De Ladoucette (especially Baron de L)
Masson-Blondelet

Michel Redde (best wine, "La
Moynerie")
Domaine Guy Saget
Tinel-Blondelet
Château de Tracy

## The Central Loire: A duo of diverse districts

The Central Loire is by far the largest and most diversified wine area of the Loire Valley. All kinds of wines are made in the Central Loire: dry white, sweet white, rosé, red, and sparkling.

The Central Loire area has two main districts:

- ✔ The Touraine
- ✔ Anjou-Saumur

These two districts share the same grape varieties — mainly Chenin Blanc (shen-in-blahnk) for white wine and Cabernet Franc (cab-er-nay frahn) for the reds — but both districts encompass numerous wine zones.

### Touraine's (too) many AOCs and Vouvray, the district's star

The historic city of Tours is the focal point of the Touraine district; it also gives the district its name. The Touraine is a large area producing red, white, rosé, and sparkling wines, as well as dry, off-dry, and sweet wines (in other words, it makes everything under the sun). The climate varies from the eastern part, which is warmer and dryer, to the western part, which has more maritime influence. Soils also vary across the breadth of the district.

The Touraine is a particularly confusing district because it makes so many different wines (many of which are fairly minor and are seldom seen in wine shops). Some of the vineyards grow wines with the districtwide AOC, Touraine. Other vineyards are in smaller, more-precise AOC zones named for specific communities, such as Vouvray and Chinon. Still other vineyards grow grapes for wines that share their AOC name with vineyards from the Anjou district, such as Rosé de la Loire.

Ouray — clearly the Touraine's most famous wine — comes from a vineyard area just east of Tours. The AOC zone includes the village of Vouvray and seven other villages; the grape variety is Chenin Blanc. Along with areas within the Anjou district, the Vouvray area produces the world's best Chenin Blanc wines. Wines made from Chenin Blanc hail from California, South Africa, and other places, but it is only in Vouvray, on the north bank of the Loire, and in the Anjou district, that Chenin Blanc rises to noble heights.

Ouray's production is more than a million cases a year — but those million cases represent several styles of wine. Vouvray can be still or sparkling. The still versions of Vouvray can be dry, semidry, or fairly sweet. The dry and semidry styles often have floral and/or nutty flavors along with fruity character; they can be quite rich in texture, and yet they have refreshing, high acidity. They generally need four or five years to soften and can live far longer; even the dry Vouvray wines can age and improve for 15 to 20 years or more. The *moelleux,* or sweet, style of Vouvray is considered the best. It's also the most long-lived; these rich, mellow wines can develop for 50 years or more, taking on flavors of apples and honey and becoming more complex with age.

Among sparkling Vouvray wines, two different versions exist: *pétillant* (slightly sparkling) and *mousseux* (fully sparkling). Both are made by the classic method of second fermentation in the bottle. Drink bubbly Vouvrays within three years of the vintage if they're vintage dated; if they're nonvintage bubblies, drink 'em soon after you buy 'em.

Most dry and semidry styles of still Ouray start at $15 a bottle, but wines from a few of the best producers (Gaston Huët-Pinguet and Domaine du Clos Naudin, to name two) are in the $20 to $40 range. Most of the *moelleux* Vouvrays are in the $20 to $50 price range (often for a 500-milliliter bottle, rather than the standard 750-milliliter size); a few of the finest sweet Vouvrays cost $75 to $90. Sparkling Vouvrays run about $15 to $20.

Some of the best producers of Ouray wines are the following (note that Class One producers are considered a cut above Class Two producers by those in the know):

**Class One**

Domaine des Aubuisières

Domain Le Haut Lieu, of Huët-Pinguet

Domaine du Clos Naudin, of Philippe Foreau

**Class Two**

Domaine Allias (aka Clos du Petit Mont)

Clos Baudoin, of Prince Poniatowski

Domaine Bourillon-D'Orléans

Marc Brédif

Domaine de la Fontainerie

Château Gaudrelle, of Monmousseau

François Pinon

# Montlouis, a cheaper 100 percent Chenin Blanc option than Vouvray

Montlouis is a wine village across the Loire from Vouvray, on the south bank of the river. The wines of Montlouis, also 100 percent Chenin Blanc, are similar in most ways to those of Vouvray; you can find all the same styles: dry, semidry, sweet, and sparkling. Montlouis wines tend to be softer, a bit lighter-bodied, and less concentrated than Vouvrays. They're also ready sooner and not as long-lasting. Montlouis is a bit less expensive than Vouvray, especially the *moelleux* (sweet) Montlouis wines, which are about $20 to $45. Montlouis production is roughly 200,000 cases annually — only about 20 percent that of Vouvray. About half of Montlouis wines are sparkling wines.

*Tip:* Five good Montlouis producers are as follows:

Domaine François Chidaine
Domaine Olivier Délétang
Alain Lelarge
Claude Levasseurr
Dominique Moyer

## *Touraine's best red wines*

About 25 miles west of Tours is the one area in the Loire Valley known for its *red* wine. This area encompasses three AOC zones whose wines are named after their villages:

- Chinon, south of the Loire River

- Bourgueil, north of the river

- Saint-Nicolas-de-Bourgueil, also north of the Loire

Cabernet Franc is the main grape variety for all three of these wines. This variety ripens earlier than Cabernet Sauvignon and is therefore more suited to cool climates. Nevertheless, in 1996, French wine authorities allowed up to 10 percent Cabernet Sauvignon in these wines, and in 2000, the maximum amount rose to 25 percent. Apparently, this law was introduced in an effort to beef up these frequently light-bodied wines.

The Chinon vineyards produce about 700,000 cases a year, more than those of the other two red wines combined. Chinon (shee-nohn) is light- to medium-bodied, fruity, and lively, and often has aromas and flavors of raspberries and/or wild strawberries. It's the most elegant and generally the finest of the Touraine's three red wines. Chinon can be good when it's young and exuberant, but some Chinons can age quite well in the best vintages. You can find it in two styles:

- The light-cherry red, light-bodied (and inexpensive) style for immediate enjoyment.

- The dark red, medium-bodied style, with some tannin; this style will age for a decade or so in good vintages.

Despite its occasional aroma of violets, Bourgueil (boor-guh'y) is more rustic and earthy than Chinon and needs about four or five years of aging. Saint-Nicolas-de-Bourgueil (san-nee-co-lah-deh-boor-guh'y), lighter-bodied than Bourgueil, is ready to drink sooner.

All three of Touraine's red wines have fairly high acidity, which makes them refreshing, especially in warm weather. None of the three is a particularly long-term wine. With the possible exception of the fuller-styled Chinons, enjoy their fruitiness and berrylike flavors in their adolescence.

Like Sancerre, these three red wines, especially Chinon, are quite popular in France; you can find them in most of Paris's wine bars and bistros. These three reds are also good values; retail prices range between $12 and $20.

Following are Chinon producers to look for (note that the first two Chinon producers are especially fine):

| | |
|---|---|
| Philippe Alliet | Château de la Grille |
| Domaine Bernard Baudry | Charles Joguet |
| Couly-Dutheil | Olga Raffault |

Recommended Bourgueil producers include Pierre-Jacques Druet, Domaine de la Lande, and Domaine des Ouches. Saint-Nicolas-de-Bourgueil producers to look for are Domaine Joël Taluau and Cognard-Taluau.

### The dry and the sweet of Anjou-Saumur

You can't categorize Anjou-Saumur. Every type of wine — dry white, semidry white, sweet white (of varying types), rosé (both dry and semidry), dry red, and sparkling — has a strong presence in this wine district, which lies east of the Touraine district.

Anjou and Saumur are separate towns within the district. Saumur is nearly on the eastern edge of the district, and Anjou is about 20 miles to the west. This district is close enough to the Atlantic Ocean that its climate is maritime, reflecting the cool and rainy influence of the ocean.

The next two sections break down the details of Anjou and Saumur's distinctly different wines.

#### Saumur's sparkling and still wines

The town of Saumur is surrounded by vineyards, and its major business is sparkling wine production. Saumur, in fact, is the leading sparkling wine producer of the Loire Valley. It annually produces up to 3 million cases of mainly traditional-method sparkling wine (made by second fermentation in the bottle), primarily from Chenin Blanc but with some Cabernet Franc thrown in. (Other permitted varieties include Chardonnay, Sauvignon Blanc, Cabernet Sauvignon, Malbec, Gamay, Grolleau, Pinot d'Aunis, and Pinot Noir.) A rosé version also exists; it's made from the red varieties permitted in the white bubbly.

Saumur AOC sparkling wine comes from grapes grown in 93 communities. Another sparkling wine, Crémant de Loire (white and rosé), is also made in Saumur, but the grapes for that wine can originate anywhere within the Anjou-Saumur or Touraine districts. Permitted varieties for Crémant de la Loire are Chenin Blanc, Cabernet Franc, Cabernet Sauvignon, Grolleau, Pinot d'Aunis, Pinot Noir, Chardonnay, and Arbois. Both Saumur and Crémant de la Loire sparkling wines are a good deal, retailing for $10 to $15.

Recommended sparkling Saumur producers are the following:

Ackerman-Laurance
Veuve Amiot
Bouvet-Ladubay
Domaine de Gabillière

Gratien & Meyer, of the Champagne
   Alfred Gratien firm
Langlois-Château
Château de Passavant

Saumur also makes a small amount of still white wine, mainly from Chenin Blanc; rosé wine, called Cabernet de Saumur; and Saumur Rouge, a fairly light red wine based on Cabernet Franc, Cabernet Sauvignon, and Pineau d'Aunis grapes.

Saumur's best still wine (and in fact the best red wine in the entire Anjou-Saumur district) is the red known as Saumur-Champigny. It's a great value in the $10 to $18 range and derives from Cabernet Franc grapes grown in the vineyards around Saumur and the nearby village of Champigny. At its best, the wine is quite dark in color, fairly low in tannin, and easy to drink — without any aging needed. Saumur-Champigny resembles the wines of nearby Chinon, but it's also similar to a light-bodied Bordeaux. Recommended Saumur-Champigny producers are as follows:

Domaine Filliatreau
Domaine des Roches Neuves
Clos Rougéard

Château de Targé
Château de Villeneuve

### Anjou's varied offerings

Most of the Anjou portion of the Anjou-Saumur district is on the southern banks of the Loire River, south of the city of Angers. Anjou produces more different kinds of wine than any other Loire Valley district, but its largest production is its rosé wines, which are the wines most wine drinkers associate with the term *Anjou.*

Anjou producers make three different kinds of rosé wines:

- **Rosé d'Anjou:** The highest production, this semidry wine is made from Gamay, Malbec, and a local variety called Grolleau (or Groslot).
- **Cabernet d'Anjou:** Also semidry, this more serious rosé is made from Cabernet Franc and Cabernet Sauvignon. It's capable of aging for several years, which is unusual for a rosé.
- **Rosé de la Loire:** Mainly Cabernet Franc, this dry rosé's production area extends into the Touraine district.

Rosé d'Anjou and Cabernet d'Anjou fall into the broad appellation Anjou, which also includes red and white wines. Some other wines of the Anjou appellation include

Book II

France: A Wine Superstar

- **Anjou Rouge:** Made mainly from Cabernet Franc, along with Cabernet Sauvignon, Pineau d'Aunis, and Malbec, Anjou Rouge is a simple, fruity wine.
- **Anjou Gamay:** This wine is made entirely from the Gamay grape variety.
- **Anjou Blanc:** These mainly dry (but sometimes sweet) white wines are made from Chenin Blanc, with Chardonnay and Sauvignon Blanc also permitted.
- **Anjou-Coteaux de la Loire:** Made from Chenin Blanc, these wines are off-dry and sweet.

Another AOC wine is Anjou-Villages, a red wine from Cabernet Franc and Cabernet Sauvignon grapes grown in 46 communities within the Anjou region. All Anjou wines are excellent values (in the $10 to $18 price range) and fine choices as everyday wines — when you choose a good producer.

Recommended producers of Anjou AOC and Anjou-Villages AOC are as follows:

Château de Fesles
Château de la Genaiserie
Domaine de Montgilet
Domaine Ogereau

Château Pierre-Bise
Domaine Richou
Domaine des Rochelles

Of course, the best wines of Anjou are white wines — both dry and sweet — from two limited AOC zones. Arguably the greatest dry Chenin Blanc wines in the world come from the Savennières area of the Anjou portion of the district. Savennières (sah-ven-yair) wines are concentrated and intensely flavored, with intriguing mineral notes to their aroma and flavor that give them more character than other dry Chenin Blanc wines. Despite their wonderful floral, honeyed aromas, they're totally dry.

Two special vineyards within the Savennières AOC hold cru status: Coulée de Serrant and Roche aux Moines. Nicolas Joly, the sole owner of Coulée de Serrant vineyard and part owner of Roche aux Moines, is a standout producer in the Savennières area. The wines from these two Savennières crus can age and improve for 15 to 20 years or more in good vintages.

Considering its quality, Savennières is very reasonably priced, because it hasn't truly been discovered yet. It starts in the $18 to $20 range and can go up to about $60 for the finest examples. Recommended Savennières producers are as follows:

Domaine des Baumard

Domaine du Closel

Clos de Coulaine

Clos de la Coulée de Serrant,
   of Nicolas Joly

Château d'Epiré

Domaine Laffourcade

Clos des Perrières

The other great white wine of the Anjou, produced on the southern banks of the Loire, is Coteaux du Layon (coat-toe doo lay-awn). The wines of this area are naturally sweet, made from overripe Chenin Blanc grapes that are often affected by noble rot, as in Sauternes (see Chapter 2 in Book II for details). Like Sauternes, the Coteaux du Layon wines possess that wonderful balance between sweetness and acidity that prevents them from being cloying. These wines really improve with at least ten years of aging. As they mature, Coteaux du Layon wines take on aromas of apricots, peaches, honey, and spice.

Coteaux du Layon is a rather large zone, and within it are two areas so special that they have separate AOC status: Quarts de Chaume (cahr deh show'm) and Bonnezeaux (bon-zoe). Like Coteaux du Layon, these are sweet wines from grapes affected by noble rot. They need *at least* five or six years to develop — better yet, ten years — but then they can age and improve for 20 years or more in good vintages. Prices range from about $20 up to $75, with a few extraordinary bottles costing more than $100. Many of these wines come in a 500-milliliter bottle.

Recommended Coteaux du Layon, Quarts de Chaume, and Bonnezeaux producers include the following:

Patrick Baudouin

Domaine des Baumard

Château de Bellerive

Château du Breuil

Domaine Cady

Domaine Delesvaux

Château de Fesles

Domaine des Forges

Château de la Genaiserie

Domaine Laffourcade

Moulin-Touchais

Domaine Ogereau

Domaine du Petit Val

Château Pierre-Bise

Domaine Pithon

Château de Plaisance

Château des Rochettes

Domaine de la Sansonnière

Château Soucherie

Domaine de Terrebrune, of René
   Renou

Another appellation making good sweet white wine is the small Coteaux de l'Aubance area, named for the Aubance River; it's just south of Angers and close to Coteaux de Layon.

# *The Western Loire: Makers of Muscadet*

Brittany, the French province that faces the Atlantic Ocean and is known for its fishing, is the home of the Pays Nantais wine district. The Pays Nantais is the western end of the Loire Valley. Because it's close to the Atlantic Ocean, the weather is cooler and damper than in other parts of the Loire Valley wine region.

This district, named for the city of Nantes, is the home of Muscadet (moos-cah-day), a dry, light-bodied white wine made from the Melon de Bourgogne grape variety, which is also known as Muscadet. This variety thrives in the cool but mild climate of the Pays Nantais, where it produces a light, dry, pleasant white wine that's always well priced.

The simplest form of Muscadet is simply Muscadet AOC. Three other AOCs must come from lower-yielding vineyards, and therefore are generally higher in quality:

- ✔ **Muscadet de Sèvre-et-Maine:** Named for two local rivers, this is the largest production area, and it usually makes the best wines.

- ✔ **Muscadet des Coteaux de la Loire:** This northern area produces just one-fifth as much as the preceding AOC, making the wine more difficult to find.

- ✔ **Muscadet Côtes de Grand Lieu:** This newest AOC area in the southwest just gained that status in 1996.

If you choose a good producer from a recent vintage, Muscadet is one of the great bargains in the wine world. But don't buy or drink this wine if it's any older than three years — in fact, the younger, the better. When it's properly fresh and crisp, Muscadet is a perfect warm-weather white wine, especially with shellfish. Retail prices for Muscadet range from $6 to $12.

Recommended Muscadet producers are

| | |
|---|---|
| D. Bahuaud | Domaine de l'Ecu, of Guy Bossard |
| Chérau-Carré | Domaine de la Fruitière |
| Domaine Chiron | Marquis de Goulaine |
| Château du Cléray, of Sauvion et Fils | Domaine de la Haute-Févrie |
| Domaine des Dorices | Domaine Les Hautes Noëlles |

*(continued)*

Domaine des Herbauges
Domaine de la Louvetrie
Château de la Mercredière
Louis Métaireau
Domaine Pierre Luneau-Papin

Château de la Preuille
Domaine la Quilla
Château de la Ragotière
Domaine de la Tourmaline

# Discovering Wines from the South of France

The south of France claims two superlatives among French wine regions: It's the country's oldest wine-producing area, as well as the area that produces the most wine. The Greeks made wine in Provence — one of the wine regions of southern France — as long ago as the sixth century B.C., well before the Romans conquered Gaul. And Languedoc-Roussillon, a dual wine region, boasts 38 percent of France's vineyards and more than 40 percent of its wine production! The world didn't always pay much attention to these wines, but now these old wine regions are hot, especially Languedoc-Roussillon. Much of the experimental work in France's vineyards is taking place there. This warm area of France is mainly red wine country, but these regions also produce rosés, sparkling wine, and some interesting whites, as well as dessert wines. The best part is that wines from southern France are still very affordable.

The following sections give you a guided tour of the Languedoc-Roussillon and Provence wine regions and the wines that come from them.

## Languedoc-Roussillon: The mother wine region of France

The south of France is teeming with wine. Languedoc-Roussillon, also known as the *Midi,* is the most prolific wine region not only in France but also in the world. It produces more than three times as much wine as Bordeaux. In fact, one of every ten bottles of the world's wine comes from Languedoc-Roussillon.

Roussillon and Languedoc are two adjoining ancient regions that stretch along the Mediterranean shores of south-central France, from the Pyrénées Mountains (France's border with Spain) eastward to the Rhône River (check out Figure 7-2). Languedoc, the eastern region, is by far the larger of the two.

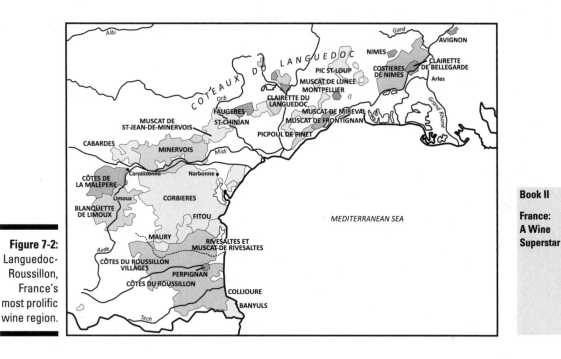

**Book II**

**France:
A Wine
Superstar**

**Figure 7-2:**
Languedoc-
Roussillon,
France's
most prolific
wine region.

Almost all of Languedoc-Roussillon — with the exception of a few areas in the northern foothills — has a Mediterranean climate: dry, sunny, and warm. Rain seldom falls during the vines' growing season, but winds from the mountains often bring refreshing, cool weather. Roussillon is the sunniest and driest part of France (with Languedoc close behind). Actually, the area is so dry and sunny that drought can occur.

More than 90 percent of the wine grown in Languedoc-Roussillon is red. Carignan, Grenache, and Cinsault are the traditional red grape varieties of the area, but as the quest for quality has grown among wine producers, so have the plantings of Syrah, as well as Mourvèdre. In recent decades, even Cabernet Sauvignon, Merlot, and other popular grape varieties have become big players in Languedoc-Roussillon.

Like other French wine regions, Languedoc-Roussillon has many AOC wine zones. But unlike most other regions, Languedoc-Roussillon has a significant production of commercially successful wines in the *vins de pays,* or country wine, category; 85 percent of French vins de pays come from this region. (Chapter 1 in Book II explains the difference between the AOC and vins de pays categories of French wine.) These wines are mainly varietal wines from well-known French grape varieties, such as Chardonnay, Cabernet Sauvignon, Syrah, and so forth. The largest vins de pays district is Vins de Pays d'Oc, an area that covers the entire Languedoc-Roussillon territory.

The Languedoc-Roussillon quality movement began on a smaller scale when Aimé Guibert founded a wine estate in a cool microclimate in the northern Languedoc in the 1970s; he called his estate Mas de Daumas Gassac. (*Mas* is the local name for *Domaine*.) Guibert was convinced that "foreign" varieties, such as Cabernet Sauvignon, could make successful wines in certain parts of southern France, and he set out to prove his point. He released his first wines in 1978 and over the years won critical acclaim for his efforts. Mas de Daumas Gassac became the forerunner of many other serious, small Languedoc-Roussillon wine estates that make fine wines from non-native varieties. (Mas de Daumas Gassac's red wine is a long-lived Bordeaux-type blend, made mainly from Cabernet Sauvignon. The property also has a dry rosé, as well as an aromatic white wine from the Viognier grape variety. All three wines bear the humble designation, *Vin de Pays de l'Hérault.*)

The largest AOC zone of Languedoc is Coteaux du Languedoc, an area that covers most of the Hérault *département* (county) from the town of Narbonne in the west, extending almost to the Roman town of Nîmes in the east. Much of the area is plains, but it also includes some foothills. The wines include good-value blended reds from Grenache, Lladoner Pelut (a local variety similar to Grenache), Syrah, and Mourvèdre, with Carignan and Cinsault now limited to 40 percent of the blend. There are also light, dry rosés, and some interesting dry white wines — made mainly from Grenache Blanc, Bourboulenc, Picpoul, and Clairette (all Southern Rhône varieties).

Besides Coteaux du Languedoc, the Languedoc-Roussillon region has numerous other AOC areas. The following is a roundup of the region's principal AOC wine districts and their important wines:

- ✔ **Corbières:** This large area in the Pyrénées foothills of southwestern Languedoc, consisting of 11 subdistricts, is perhaps the region's most well-known and most important red wine area. Dense, dark, full-bodied, spicy, dry red wines are the specialty. Carignan is the dominant grape variety, but Syrah and Mourvèdre are increasingly being planted; Cinsault is also used. White Corbières (cor-bee-air) wine derives from ten local varieties.

- ✔ **Minervois:** This old Roman wine area is in western Languedoc, north of Corbières. Its red wines are generally softer and more supple than those of Corbières but capable of aging for several years. In an effort to upgrade the wine, AOC regulations have reduced Carignan to no more than 40 percent of the blend, with Grenache, Syrah, Mourvèdre, and other local varieties making up the balance. White Minervois (mee-ner-vwah) wines, from six local varieties, also exist.

- ✔ **Fitou:** This entirely red wine district is situated on the Mediterranean coast of Languedoc between Corbières and the Roussillon subregion. The best wines come from the slopes of the Pyrénées, farther inland. Fitou is dominated by wine cooperatives, not private estates. Carignan and Grenache are the main varieties in the medium- to full-bodied, rustic, dry red wines, but more and more Syrah and Mourvèdre are being used.

✔ **Faugères:** The mainly red wines of this Languedoc district come from the slopes of the Cévennes Mountains northeast of the Minervois area. They're full-bodied, spicy, rustic, dry, fruity wines; the previously omnipresent Carignan is now limited to 40 percent in Faugères's red wine blends, with Syrah, Grenache, and Mourvèdre becoming more important; Cinsault and Lladoner Pelut are also allowed.

✔ **St.-Chinian:** This Languedoc area located between Minervois and Faugères, in the foothills of the Cévennes, makes very full-bodied, dry red wines, plus some dry rosés. Carignan and Cinsault are gradually being replaced with Syrah, Grenache, and Mourvèdre.

✔ **Clairette du Languedoc:** This tiny but longstanding AOC area makes only white wines from the Clairette Blanche grape variety.

✔ **Clairette de Bellegarde:** Another tiny AOC area making whites entirely from Clairette; it's located southeast of Costières de Nîmes.

✔ **Costières de Nîmes:** This is the easternmost district of the Languedoc, separated from the southern Côtes-du-Rhône vineyards by the Rhône River. It shares the soil (including the stones) and climate of the Côtes-du-Rhône, and the major variety of the Southern Rhône, Grenache, is also dominant here. But Syrah is slowly replacing Carignan in the blend and becoming a major factor in the wines. About 75 percent of the wines are medium-bodied reds, but some powerful, dry rosés and a small amount of white wines also exist. The whites are based on Clairette, Grenache Blanc, Bourboulenc, and Ugni Blanc.

✔ **Côtes du Roussillon:** Located in the Pyrénées, next to the Spanish border, this is the most southerly appellation zone in France; it covers the lower two-thirds of the Roussillon region. Naturally, the district has a strong Spanish influence. The wines are mainly big, spicy reds made primarily from Carignan, with at least 40 percent from a blend of varieties in which Syrah and Mourvèdre must make up half; Grenache, Lladoner Pelut, and Cinsault are also permitted. This area makes some fruity dry rosés, as well as floral, robust, dry whites made from the Spanish Maccabéo variety, Grenache Blanc, and other grapes. Château de Jau is a major producer.

✔ **Côtes du Roussillon-Villages:** This appellation area makes up the northern part of the Côtes du Roussillon zone (the upper third of Roussillon) and is located south of Corbières and Fitou. It's an all-red wine zone consisting of 28 villages. The wines derive from basically the same varieties as the red wines of the Côtes du Roussillon, but production requirements are more stringent, and the wines are generally higher in quality. Four villages can append their names to the Côtes du Roussillon-Villages appellation: Caramany, Latour de France, Lesquerde, and Tautavel. Their production is limited but generally powerful and of high quality.

- **Banyuls:** Named after the picturesque town of Banyuls, this area of terraced hillside vineyards sits on the Mediterranean coast, north of the Spanish border and at the southwest corner of Roussillon. It's France's leading district for production of *vins doux naturels* (sweet, fortified wines known, in short, as VDNs). Banyuls (bahn-yule) can be red, rosé, tawny, or white; the red is the richest and most acclaimed, but the white, which turns old-gold in color with aging, is the most commonly produced. Grenache is the dominant grape variety in Banyuls. Dr. Parcé is *the* renowned producer of Banyuls wines; his wines are in the $55 to $60 price range.

- **Collioure:** This seaside village in the Banyuls district has a separate appellation; from this area comes a rich, spicy, high-alcohol (up to 15 percent) red wine made from over-ripe grapes. Mourvèdre, Syrah, and Grenache are the main varieties. Collioure (coh-lee-or) wines are technically dry, but the very ripe flavors give the impression of sweetness. Look for Dr. Parcé's Collioure wines, in the $35 to $40 price range.

- **Muscat de Frontignan:** Frontignan is a village on the Mediterranean coast, just past the port town of Sète, in the Languedoc region. Of various fortified, sweet, spicy Muscats made in Languedoc-Roussillon, Muscat de Frontignan (moos-cah deh fron-tee-nyahn) is the most renowned; it's a VDN made solely from the Muscat Blanc à Petit Grains (also known as Muscat of Frontignan), the most popular Muscat variety.

- **Blanquette de Limoux:** The zone for this sparkling wine is in southwest Languedoc, west of Corbières; the small town of Limoux is in the heart of the zone. This area has a distinctly cool microclimate, high in the Pyrénées foothills and away from any Mediterranean influence. Blanquette de Limoux (blahn-ket deh lee-moo) is a good-value, white sparkling wine made from a minimum of 90 percent Mauzac (known locally as Blanquette), sometimes with Chardonnay and Chenin Blanc.

## Provence: The beautiful home to eight AOC zones

Provence is perhaps France's most beautiful region — it's certainly the country's most fashionable and touristy area (outside of Paris). Provence is located in southeastern France, east of Languedoc-Roussillon, southeast of the Southern Rhône, just south of the Alps, and west of northern Italy. The region's southern border is the Mediterranean Sea. Provence is home to the Riviera, Nice, Cannes, and the bustling seaport of Marseilles, France's second-largest city.

The climate of Provence is classic Mediterranean: very warm summers, mild winters, and little rainfall. The famous wind that sweeps down from the north, the *mistral*, minimizes the threat of diseases to the vineyards; on the other hand, vines must be planted in protected areas to avoid destruction by the fierce wind. Many of the best vineyards are near the seacoast, where cool breezes minimize the effects of sometimes harsh and brutally hot weather.

The soil is so variable throughout Provence that generalizations are difficult. One significant pattern is pockets of limestone and shale in the hillsides; in the Cassis AOC zone on the Mediterranean, for example, the chalky clay of the hillside vineyards is perfect for the cultivation of white grape varieties.

Provence has always been known for its rosé wines (all the rave among tourists at beachside cafés), which still dominate production — despite the fact that many Provençal rosés are quite mild. But more producers are now making good red wine, for which the climate is well suited. Over one-third of Provençal wines are now red, and there's a small amount of white wine, including some interesting ones.

Provence has eight AOC wine zones, which are responsible for most of its wines. Following are a few details on each one:

- ✔ **Côtes de Provence:** This huge area of 85 communes and 400 producers is the largest in Provence, accounting for about 75 percent of the region's wine production. Eighty percent of Côtes de Provence's wines are rosé (with 15 percent being red and 5 percent being white); red wine production, however, is increasing. A favorite producer is Domaine Richeaume, for its red and excellent rosé wines.

- ✔ **Coteaux d'Aix-en-Provence:** This AOC zone, the second largest in Provence, occupies the western and northwestern part of the region; it covers about 50 villages, including the beautiful town of Aix-en-Provence. The wines are generally of a higher level than Côtes de Provence wines, and the emphasis on red wines is greater: 60 percent of the production is red, 35 percent is rosé, and 5 percent is white. Grenache, Cinsault, and Mourvèdre are the dominant varieties in the red and rosé wines, but Cabernet Sauvignon is making inroads; in fact, the reds are permitted to be as much as 60 percent Cabernet Sauvignon. A superb producer is Château Vignelaure, which makes a Bordeaux-style red wine based on Cabernet Sauvignon. Château Calissane and Château Revelette make excellent wines, with prestige cuvées produced from Syrah and Cabernet Sauvignon.

- ✔ **Les Baux-de-Provence:** This district, in the northwest corner of Provence, was until recently a part of Coteaux d'Aix-en-Provence. Now it's an independent AOC zone. Red wines dominate production (80 percent), most of which are deeply colored and full-bodied; the remaining 20 percent of production is dry, mainly full-bodied rosé wine. Grenache, Mourvèdre, and Syrah, which must make up at least 60 percent of the AOC red wine blends, are the primary red varieties. The best and most-renowned wine estate here is Domaine de Trévallon, which makes a non-AOC wine of the same name composed of 60 percent Cabernet Sauvignon and 40 percent Syrah. Two other top wine estates in the Les

Baux-de-Provence district are Mas de la Dame and Domaine des Terres Blanches.

✔ **Coteaux Varois:** This district is named after the Var *département* (county), in which the main part of Provence lies. The Coteaux Varois AOC zone is situated in hilly central Provence, between Côtes de Provence and Coteaux d'Aix-en-Provence. Rosés dominate the district's production, along with one-third red and a little bit of white wine. Grenache, Syrah, Cinsault, Mourvèdre, Cabernet Sauvignon, and Carignan are all used in varying proportions for red and rosé wines. From Coteaux Varois, look for the good-value wines of Château Routas.

✔ **Bandol:** This AOC district has the greatest reputation of all Provence's appellations — especially when it comes to its red wines. Located in southeastern Provence bordering the Mediterranean Sea, the area's stony, silica-limestone soil and the warm climate are perfect for the late-ripening Mourvèdre variety, which thrives here. Red Bandol AOC wines must be at least half Mourvèdre; Grenache and Cinsault are two other important components, for both red and rosé wines. Bandol is mainly red, but rosés represent about a third of the wines; a little bit of white wine also exists. The reds are dark, rich, intense, and complex, with black fruit flavors; they require at least ten years to fully develop. The leading producer of red Bandol is the renowned Domaine Tempier, clearly one of Provence's finest wine estates. Mas de la Rivière and Domaine de Pibarnon are two other fine red wine producers. Bandol is also home for Domaines Ott, famous for its rosés and earthy whites.

✔ **Cassis:** This wine has no relation to the blackcurrant liqueur of the same name. Cassis is the one AOC district in Provence where white wines dominate, with more than 75 percent of the production devoted to them. Cassis is a small district on the coast, 10 miles west of Bandol and close to the city of Marseilles. The white wines, grown in limestone soil, are made mainly from Clairette and Marsanne, with some Ugni Blanc and Sauvignon Blanc; they're full-bodied, dry, low-acid, herbal-scented wines that are great with the local specialty, *bouillabaisse.* In fact, the wine is so popular locally — especially in summer — that the rest of the world, unfortunately, sees little of it. Domaine de La Ferme Blanche is a major producer.

✔ **Bellet:** This small AOC district is located in southeastern Provence, in the hills above the city of Nice. Equal parts of red, white, and rosé wines are made, but the fresh, fragrant whites, made from Rolle (Italy's Vermentino), Roussanne, Chardonnay, and Clairette, are Bellet's best wines. Sadly, most Bellet wines never leave the *Côte d'Azur.*

✔ **Palette:** East of the town of Aix-en-Provence, Palette is Provence's smallest AOC district; in fact, most of its vineyards, which are on limestone soil, are owned by one wine estate, Château Simone. This estate produces rich, long-lived reds, rosés, and white wines. The red and rosé — made mainly from Grenache, Mourvèdre, and Cinsault — resemble Southern Rhône wines, as does the white, which is made chiefly from Ugni Blanc.

# Book III
# Italy: Small but Mighty

"Well, I'm enough of a wine expert to know that if the boat were sinking, there'd be several cases of this Nebbiolo that would go into a lifeboat before you would."

# In This Book . . .

Thanks to the popularity of Italian restaurants, most people have frequent opportunities to enjoy best-selling Italian wines such as Pinot Grigio, Soave, Valpolicella, and Chianti. But Italy makes other wines, too — many of them among the greatest wines on the planet. And just about every one of Italy's thousand-something wines is terrific with food, because Italian wines are made specifically to be enjoyed during a meal.

This book takes you through Italy's most renowned wine areas and introduces you to some of the other Italian regions whose wines you're likely to find in your local wine shop or *ristorante*.

Here are the contents of Book III at a glance:

# Chapter 1

# The Big Picture of Italian Wine

*In This Chapter*
▶ Exploring the many kinds of Italian wine
▶ Identifying the major grapes of Italy
▶ Understanding an Italian wine label

*W*hen most people think of Italy, they think of food. (History, art, or fast cars might be other associations, but food is definitely near the top of the list.) As central as food is to Italy's personality, so is wine. For most Italians, wine *is* food, no less essential to every meal than bread or family. Wine, in fact, *is* family — and community — because nearly every Italian either knows someone who makes wine or makes wine himself.

## Diverse Conditions, Diverse Wines

The Italian peninsula, with its fanlike top and its long, bootlike body, has the most recognizable shape of any country on earth. But its recognition exceeds its actual size. Italy is a small land; the whole country is less than three-quarters the size of California.

Despite its small size, Italy's role in the world of wine is huge.

  ✔ Italy produces more wine than any other country on earth, in many years. (When Italy isn't the world's number one wine producer, it's number two, behind France.) Italy's annual wine production is generally about 1.5 billion gallons, the equivalent of more than 8 billion bottles! Nearly 30 percent of all the world's wine comes from Italy.

  ✔ Italy has more vineyard land than any other country except Spain. Vines grow in every nook and cranny of the peninsula and the islands.

  ✔ Italy boasts dozens of native grape varieties, many of which are successful only in Italy.

Although the land called Italy has a long, proud history, the country became a unified nation only in 1861, and it has existed in its present form only since 1919, when the Austro-Hungarian Empire ceded certain northern territories to Italy after World War I. Politically, Italy today consists of 20 regions, similar to states — 18 on the mainland and 2 islands; these 20 political regions are also Italy's wine regions. (Figure 1-1 shows Italy's 20 wine regions.) Because of the country's relative youth, diverse cultures exist in different parts of the country, and regional pride runs stronger than national pride. Italy's wines reflect these diverse cultures.

**Figure 1-1:**
Italy's 20 wine regions.

The following sections introduce you to Italy's diverse landscape, as well as the styles and range of wines that land produces.

## Getting the lay of the wine land

Italy starts in the Alps but ends fairly close to Africa; it has a long, long seacoast but very little flat land; it has three major mountain ranges dividing it from other countries and segregating its regions from one another. Altogether, Italy has everything in a small package of disjointed pieces that's isolated from everything else around it.

The mountain ranges are the Alps in the northwest, separating Italy from Switzerland and France; the Dolomites, actually part of the Alps, separating northeastern Italy from Austria; and the Apennines, starting in the northwest and running like a spine down the Italian boot, separating the regions of the east coast from those of the west.

Italy's major expanse of flat land is the Po River Valley, which begins in western Piedmont and extends eastward until the Po empties into the Adriatic Sea just north of Emilia-Romagna's border with the Veneto (refer to Figure 1-1). Most of Italy's rice, grain, maize, and fruit crops come from this area; the rest of the country grows olive trees, garden vegetables, and, of course, grapes. In most of Italy, you can't travel 5 miles without seeing vines.

What makes Italy an ideal and unique territory for growing grapes is its improbable combination of natural conditions.

- ✔ The range of latitudes creates a wide variety of climatic conditions from north to south.

- ✔ The foothills of the mountains provide slopes ideal for vineyards, as well as higher altitudes for cool climate grape-growing.

- ✔ The varied terrain — seacoast, hills, and mountains — within many regions provides a diversity of growing conditions even within single regions.

- ✔ The segregated nature of the regions has enabled local grape varieties to survive in near isolation.

In terms of wine production, Italy's odd situation is a formula for variety (and a formula for confusion on the part of the people trying to master Italian wines). Different grape varieties make different wines in different regions. And the same grape variety makes different wines in different parts of a single region.

**Book III**

**Italy: Small but Mighty**

# Describing modern Italian wine styles

Wine is so universally accepted within Italy, and so present everywhere, that most Italians traditionally took it for granted. This casual attitude has changed somewhat in recent years, but it has taken its toll: Although Italy has some really great wines, these wines haven't enjoyed nearly the prestige of France's top wines. (That situation is slowly changing though.) And, considering how many wines Italy makes, only a small percentage are widely available in U.S. wine shops. The silver lining is that some of Italy's wines are still fairly inexpensive.

Italian wine producers today are more serious about their wine than they've ever been, and the quality of Italian wine is at an all-time high. (Recent excellent vintages have only helped.) As producers experiment with new techniques in their vineyards and wineries, new styles of Italian wine are emerging, and the traditional styles are improving. As a result, Italian wines today are more varied than ever.

The fundamental style of Italian wine derives from the fact that Italians view wine as a mealtime beverage — a wine's first responsibility is to go well with food. The prototypical Italian red or white wine has the following characteristics:

- ✔ High acidity, which translates as crispness in the whites, and firmness in the reds (high-acid wines are very food friendly)

- ✔ No sweetness

- ✔ Fairly subdued, subtle aromas and flavors (so as not to compete with food)

- ✔ Light to medium body (although many full-bodied wines do exist)

When you imagine such a wine, you can understand that it's a wine without illusions of grandeur, a straightforward beverage that might not win a wine competition but is a welcome dinner companion.

Variations on this prototype in recent years have included some of the following characteristics:

- ✔ More concentrated flavor and slightly fuller body due to greater ripeness in the grapes (thanks to improved vineyard practices)

- ✔ Smoky or toasty aromas and flavors from small oak barrels

- ✔ Fruitier aromas and flavors — although the wines are still much less fruity than the typical Californian or Australian wine

## Exploring the reds, the whites, and beyond

About two-thirds of all Italian wine is red. Every region makes red wine, even the cool northern regions and especially the warmer southern regions. But Italy makes plenty of white wine too, particularly northeast and central Italy. Rosé wine is only a minor category.

Italy's production of sparkling wine is considerable, especially in the North. Italian sparkling wines include sweet styles, such as Asti, and fully dry styles. Dessert wines are a serious specialty of some regions. These sweet wines include wines from grapes dried after the harvest (to concentrate their sugar); wines from late-harvested grapes affected with *noble rot* (a fungus that dehydrates the grapes and concentrates their sugar); and wines that are fortified with alcohol to preserve their natural sweetness.

# Italy's Curious Grape Varieties

An astounding number of wine grape varieties grow in Italy. Besides varieties that are indigenous to Italy, Italian vineyards grow most of the world's major red grapes and many of the world's major white grapes. To a large extent, the vast diversity of Italian wines is a result of the enormous range of grapes that grow throughout the peninsula and the islands.

**Book III**

**Italy: Small but Mighty**

## Unveiling the native talents

Most of the grape varieties that make Italian wines are native Italian varieties that don't grow much, or don't grow well, outside of Italy. Like most wine grape varieties, they have multisyllabic, foreign, difficult-to-pronounce names — and their names are all the more foreign to wine drinkers because they generally don't appear on wine labels. (Most Italian wines are named for the places where the grapes grow rather than for the grapes that make them; the later "Grasping an Italian Wine Label" section explains Italy's wine-naming protocol.)

Some of Italy's native varieties, such as Sangiovese, Barbera, and Trebbiano, grow more or less throughout the country. But many varieties occupy vineyards only in certain parts of Italy or are limited to a single region. For example,

- Nebbiolo grows only in certain parts of Piedmont and Lombardy, in northwestern Italy.
- Verdicchio grows mainly in the Marche region.

✔ Lambrusco is a specialty of the Emilia area of Emilia-Romagna.

✔ Negroamaro and Primitivo grow almost exclusively in Puglia.

✔ Nero d'Avola grows mainly in Sicily.

## Checking out the immigrants and migrants

Besides native Italian varieties, Italy also grows many French varieties, as well as a few varieties that are native to Germany, Austria, and Spain. Some of these nonindigenous varieties have grown in parts of Italy for more than 100 years. Cabernet Sauvignon, Merlot, Cabernet Franc, the Pinot family of grapes (Pinot Noir, Pinot Gris, and Pinot Blanc), and Riesling are among these varieties.

Italy also has some varieties that are relative newcomers, introduced into the country by a few progressive wineries in the spirit of experimentation; Viognier and Syrah are examples. This group of grape varieties is small, however, because Italian winemakers can find plenty of means for experimentation within their own country.

What has happened in the past quarter century or so — rather than the mass importation of internationally famous grape varieties into Italy — is a migration of major varieties from one part of Italy to another. Cabernet Sauvignon, for example, has been a major player in two northeastern regions, Trentino-Alto Adige and Friuli-Venezia Giulia, for generations; now it also figures prominently in many Tuscan wines. Similarly, Chardonnay has grown in northeastern Italy for several decades but now appears all over Italy.

The migration of Cabernet Sauvignon and Chardonnay within Italy is indicative of another trend: the increasing importance of internationally known varieties. This trend exists for two reasons:

✔ Italian producers have sought to validate themselves and earn recognition by making wines from grape varieties that the outside world considers prestigious.

✔ In an effort to win critical acclaim from foreign critics, Italian producers have increasingly made wines with characteristics that appeal to international tastes, such as deep color and rich mouthfeel; many internationally known varieties have these characteristics.

Ironically, most of these internationally recognized varieties existed in Italy all along.

# Meeting Italy's Major Grapes

Because growing conditions and local traditions vary so much throughout Italy, the country's grape varieties vary tremendously from one region to the next. The country as a whole grows red varieties more than white varieties, and many of its red grapes are top-notch varieties that make superior wine. However, a few white varieties do excel in Italy as well.

## Reds aplenty

Four of Italy's 21 major red grape varieties are especially important, either for the quality of wine they produce or for their dissemination throughout the country. The following sections describe these big four according to their relative importance.

### Sangiovese

The indigenous Sangiovese (san-joe-*vay*-say) is the most-planted red variety in Italy's vineyards. It's the lifeblood of red wine production in the central Italian regions of Tuscany and Umbria, and it also grows in several other regions. Sangiovese is the major grape of Chianti and Vino Nobile di Montepulciano, and it's the only variety in Brunello di Montalcino. Many critically acclaimed super-Tuscan wines also derive largely from Sangiovese. Common blending partners for Sangiovese include the native Canaiolo (can-eye-*oh*-lo) grape, Cabernet Sauvignon, and Merlot.

Dozens of *clones,* or subvarieties, of Sangiovese exist, some finer than others. (This variety changes in response to its grape-growing environment, which accounts for its diversity.) One family of clones responsible for many of the best Sangiovese wines is called Sangiovese Grosso ("large Sangiovese"). Some Tuscan producers call Sangiovese Grosso "Sangioveto," but this term isn't an official name.

The characteristics of Sangiovese include medium color intensity, high acidity, firm tannin, and aromas and flavors of cherries and herbs. Most wines made from Sangiovese are lean in structure; they're generally medium-bodied, but some are light-bodied or full-bodied, depending on where the grapes grow. The more serious wines based on Sangiovese can develop forest-floor aromas and a seductive smoothness and harmony with age.

### Nebbiolo

The Nebbiolo (nehb-be-*oh*-loh) variety is a specialty of the Piedmont region. This native Italian grape makes two of Italy's very greatest red wines, Barolo and Barbaresco, as well as several less-exalted wines.

**Book III**

**Italy: Small but Mighty**

Nebbiolo produces full-bodied, characterful wines with high acidity and marked tannin but generally only medium color intensity. Nebbiolo's aromas and flavors vary according to the vineyard site, but they cover a wide spectrum, from fruity (strawberry) to herbal (mint, camphor, and anise) to earthy (mushrooms, white truffles, and tar) to floral; these aromas can be very vivid and pure. The finest Nebbiolo-based wines take many years to develop and can live for decades, but many approachable, young-drinking wines from Nebbiolo also exist. Nebbiolo usually isn't blended with other varieties; when it is, Barbera and Bonarda are predictable partners.

### Barbera

Until Sangiovese dethroned Barbera sometime in the past 30 years, Barbera (bar-*bae*-rah) was the most-planted red variety in all of Italy. It still grows in many parts of the Italian peninsula, but its finest wines come from Piedmont, Barbera's home turf.

Barbera is a very unusual red variety because it has almost no tannin. It has deep color and high acidity, as well as spicy and red-fruit aromas and flavors that are vivid in young wines. The combination of high acid, low tannin, and vivid flavor makes Barbera wines particularly refreshing. The finest expressions of Barbera are unblended, but many blended wines containing Barbera do exist.

### Aglianico

The unsung native variety Aglianico (ahl-*yahn*-ee-co) is the pride of the Campania and Basilicata regions in southern Italy, where it makes Taurasi (tow-*rah*-zee) and Aglianico del Vulture (ahl-*yahn*-ee-co del *vul*-too-rae), respectively. Aglianico came to southern Italy from Greece millennia ago. Today it grows as far north as Lazio; in the southern portion of Italy, it also grows in Molise, Puglia, and Calabria.

At its best, Aglianico makes dark, powerful, high-quality red wines, but its production is relatively small. In many cases, the variety is merely part of a blend with other southern varieties. Nevertheless, it's one of Italy's finest red varieties and has excellent potential.

## Overachieving whites

Of Italy's 17 major varieties for white or sparkling wine production, 5 are key; their descriptions follow, roughly in their order of importance.

### Trebbiano

If any single factor is to blame for the lackluster quality of the white wine category in Italy, it's the Trebbiano grape. Trebbiano (trehb-bee-*ah*-noh), known as Ugni Blanc in France, can make characterful white wines when it's grown carefully, but to a population that takes wine as casually as the Italians do, this variety is a cheap ticket to bland, neutral-tasting, light-bodied, crisp wines.

Trebbiano is the most common (in both senses of the word) white variety in Italy, grown almost everywhere but particularly prevalent in the central regions. It has several clones, of which Trebbiano Toscano is probably the most planted; other clones include Trebbiano di Romagna, Trebbiano d'Abruzzo (which might actually be Bombino Bianco), Trebbiano Giallo, Trebbiano di Soave, and the relatively fine Procanico. In one manifestation or another, it's the backbone of numerous classic Italian white wines, such as Frascati.

The main aroma and flavor descriptor of Trebbiano-based wines is "vinous" — a fancy way of saying that they smell and taste winey. These wines are usually dry and high in acid, but in recent years, many producers have started making them with some sweetness, which eliminates their one virtue — their crisp, refreshing, food-friendly style — without improving the wines' quality one iota.

### Pinot Grigio

Pinot Grigio (pee-noh *gree*-joe) is the Italian name for the French variety Pinot Gris. Like other varieties of French origin, Pinot Gris immigrated to northeastern Italy more than a century ago; however, its production has increased since the late 1970s because its wines have found such commercial success.

Because of high crop levels and popular taste in Italy, Pinot Grigio most often makes light-bodied, pale, high-acid wines. Some producers make more characterful styles with concentrated flavors of peach or mineral, but none as rich as Alsace Pinot Gris wines (see Chapter 7 in Book II). The best Pinot Grigios come from Friuli-Venezia Giulia.

**Book III**

**Italy: Small but Mighty**

### Verdicchio

Verdicchio (ver-*deek*-kee-oh) excels in the Marche region, on the Adriatic coast. It has far more potential for flavor and character than Trebbiano does, making wines with medium body, crisp acidity, and aromas of lemon and sea air. It's used mainly for unoaked wines that are *varietally labeled* (meaning they're named after the grape and not the land where the grape is grown).

### Vernaccia

Two distinct white Italian varieties go by the name Vernaccia (ver-*nahtch*-cha), one in Tuscany and the other in Sardinia. (You can also find a red Vernaccia from Marche!) The Tuscan Vernaccia is the finer of the two whites. Although its wines have the trademark Italian high acidity and light to medium body, the best examples show depth and character, with mineral nuances. Vernaccia usually makes unoaked wines, but it can sometimes age quite nicely in oak barrels.

### Tocai Friulano

Although Pinot Grigio gets the lion's share of attention, many fans of Friulian wines favor the Tocai Friulano (toh-*kye* free-oo-*lah*-no) grape, which is the most widely planted white variety in Friuli. Tocai makes light- to medium-bodied with crisp acidity; the best of them have a rich, thick texture and are more flavorful than the Italian norm.

These wines used to be known as Tocai Friulano, but the European Union required producers to desist from using the name Tocai by 2007, to avoid confusion with Hungary's classic wine zone, Tokaj-Hegyalja (which produces the world-class dessert wine Tokaji Azsu, described in Chapter 4 of Book VI).

# Grasping an Italian Wine Label

Some people say that Italian wine labels are the most difficult wine labels of all to understand, which is true (to some extent). Italy's wine names are unfamiliar to most wine drinkers — after all, Italy has so many (very long) wine names! Factor in the Italian propensity for getting around official regulations, and you end up with some very confusing labels. Never fear though. The sections that follow help you understand how Italian wines are named and translate some of the other Italian label lingo you might encounter.

## The name game

*Terroir* is a French concept that says the place where grapes grow (the climate, soil, altitude, and so forth) shapes the quality and character of the wine made from those grapes. What does that have to do with Italian wines? Well, France's wine laws — which identify wines according to *terroir* — were the model for most other European countries' wine laws. Hence, Italy's wine laws are also based on the concept of *terroir,* even if some Italian winemakers have never heard the word.

Wine laws based on the *terroir* concept split hairs. If you can show that your climate, soil, or other natural condition (including human factors, such as tradition) is different from that of a nearby area, then you presumably make a different type of wine than that other area, so, upon request, the authorities can give you a unique, official name for your type of wine. In Italy, this process has occurred more than 300 times, resulting in more than 300 official wine names. These names are all names of places, because vineyard location is the fundamental issue, but sometimes they also include a grape variety name.

### Valuing pedigree: DOC and DOCG wines

Italy has two official wine names:

- ✔ **DOC:** The DOC abbreviation stands for *Denominazione di Origine Controllata,* which translates as "controlled (or protected) place-name." This long Italian phrase appears on the wine label.

- ✔ **DOCG:** The DOCG abbreviation stands for *Denominazione di Origine Controllata e Garantita,* which translates as "controlled and guaranteed place-name." This even longer Italian phrase appears on the labels of DOCG wines.

Every DOC or DOCG wine comes from a specific place that's defined by law, is made from specific grapes stipulated by the law (although sometimes the law gives producers a lot of leeway in their choice of grapes), is aged for a certain length of time, and so forth. In the end, a wine that carries a DOC or DOCG name should taste more or less the way the law says that wine should taste, although the official taste descriptions are loose. For example, the law might say that a particular wine should taste "dry, crisp, harmonious, and slightly tannic." A lot of room for interpretation there, don't you think?

Using a DOC or DOCG name for their wine somewhat restricts producers, but, in exchange, using an official name gives the wine a pedigree of sorts.

### Rejecting authority: IGT and vino da tavola wines

Not every Italian wine has to have a DOC or DOCG name, but it does have to carry the name of a place where the grapes grow, because that's the ultimate law. Producers who renounce a DOC/G name for their wine have two choices: to state a less precise area than the DOC/G area (for example, a broad, regional name) or to state only the country of origin, namely Italy. Wines with broad geographic designations are called *IGT wines,* and a wine with no geographic designation other than the country of origin is called a *vino da tavola.*

IGT stands for *Indicazione Geografica Tipica,* which translates as "typical place-name" and appears on the label in Italian. *Vino da tavola* translates as "table wine"; it might appear on the label in Italian or in English.

U.S. regulations define "table wine" as "grape wine having an alcoholic content not in excess of 14 percent by volume." Most DOC/G and IGT wines are table wines by the U.S. definition, and they might also carry the words *Table Wine* in English on their labels. The labels on DOC/G and IGT wines also include the Italian words indicating which Italian category they fall into, as well as the name of the place where the grapes were grown (other than just *Italy*).

**Book III**

**Italy: Small but Mighty**

At this moment, 120 broad territories of Italy are official IGT zones. (Yes, even these less formal names are still official.) Wines with IGT names can come from grapes grown anywhere within the broad territory of the zone, such as Toscana or Veneto, and can come from any of a large list of grape varieties approved for that area. The IGT designation, in other words, gives producers more freedom of expression than a DOC/G designation does.

On the other hand, the vino da tavola designation deprives producers of certain privileges. For example, they can't put a vintage year on the wine, and they can't name the grape variety that made the wine.

Because the IGT category is not yet even 20 years old, and because some IGT territories are very new, you can still find Italian wines whose labels predate the existence of an available IGT territory. These wines are considered vini da tavola — but if they carry a geographic designation smaller than Italy itself, they're the equivalent of IGT wines. Older vintages of super-Tuscan wines fall into this category, for example.

## Putting faith in the DOC

Knowing the legalese of wine categories helps you determine which category of wine you're buying — but, in the end, does it really matter? When you buy a DOC/G wine, do you have a better wine than if you buy an IGT wine or a vino da tavola?

The DOC/G system isn't really about quality; it's about authenticity. When you buy a DOC/G wine, you're buying the real thing, and it might or might not be as high quality as another wine with an IGT or even a vino da tavola designation. Ultimately, any wine's quality boils down to how carefully the winemaker grew the grapes and how talented the winemaker is, not to the political and legal technicalities of wine categories. But with DOC/G wines, at least you know which fairly restricted, fairly classic vineyard areas the wines came from, and which grape (or grapes) made the wines.

Italy created its wine laws in 1963 — 28 years after France established its AOC wine law system — and recognized the first DOC wines in 1966. But the process of recognizing wine zones as DOCs is ongoing. The traffic has gotten particularly heavy in recent years as Italy tries to bring a higher percentage of its wines into the DOC/G category. (In the European Union, having a high percentage of your wine production in the top category earns you bragging rights as a high-quality wine-producing nation; Italy has historically had a relatively small percentage of its wines in the top category.) The number of DOC/G wines has increased by about 10 percent, to a current total of 316 — assuming *that* number hasn't already changed!

DOCG wines number more than 20. These wines are officially the elite of Italy, and some of them are Italy's top wines — such as Barolo, Barbaresco, Brunello di Montalcino, and Chianti Classico. But some of them are elite in title only, not in their quality or renown — such as Albana di Romagna and Ghemme. The number of DOCG wines will increase as producers in DOC zones petition the authorities to elevate their zones to the higher status.

## More label lingo

Besides their official place-name and the name of the producer, most Italian wines carry other names on their labels, too. The most common extra names are the following:

✔ A proprietary name, sometimes a *fantasy* name (one pulled from the winemaker's imagination and having nothing to do with the wine itself) that a producer creates for a particular wine

✔ The name of a grape variety (DOC/G wines can carry a grape name only if their individual regulation permits; IGT wines may carry a grape name)

✔ The name of an individual vineyard where the grapes grew (somewhat common) or an official subzone of the DOC/G territory (unusual)

Other words and phrases, along with their meanings, that you may see on Italian wine labels are

✔ *Abboccato,* meaning "semidry."

✔ *Annata,* translated as "vintage."

✔ *Amabile,* meaning "semisweet."

✔ *Azienda agricola, vinicola,* and *vitivinicola,* which all refer to the producer.

✔ *Bianco,* translated as "white."

✔ *Cantina sociale,* often abbreviated as C.S. and meaning "cooperative winery."

✔ *Chiaretto,* translated as "rosé."

✔ *Classico,* which indicates that the grapes came from the original and finest part of the wine's DOC zone.

✔ *Consorzio,* meaning "voluntary trade association of producers."

✔ *Dolce,* translated as "sweet."

✔ *Fattoria,* meaning "estate."

✔ *Frizzante,* translated as "fizzy" or "slightly sparkling."

**Book III**

Italy: Small but Mighty

- *Imbottigliato all'origine,* meaning "estate-bottled."

- *Liquoroso,* meaning "a wine fortified with alcohol."

- *Novello,* referring to "a young wine (usually red) that's released early."

- *Passito,* meaning "sweet wine made from dried grapes."

- *Produttore,* translated as "producer."

- *Riserva,* which indicates a wine that has aged longer at the winery than a non-riserva version of the same wine. This term implies that the wine is of a higher-than-average quality and is therefore worthy of that additional aging.

- *Rosato,* meaning "rosé."

- *Rosso,* translated as "red."

- *Secco,* meaning "dry."

- *Spumante,* translated as "sparkling."

- *Superiore,* which indicates that a wine has a higher minimum alcohol content than the non-superiore version of the same wine.

- *Tenuta,* meaning "estate."

- *Vendemmia,* translated as "vintage."

- *Vigna* and *Vigneto,* which both mean "vineyard."

- *Vino,* translated as "wine."

- *Vitigno,* meaning "grape variety."

# Chapter 2

# Perusing Piedmont's Wines

· · · · · · · · · · · · · · · · · · · · · · · · · · · · · · · · · · · · · · · · · ·

· · · · · · · · · · · · · · · · · · · · · · · · · · · · · · · · · · · · · · · · · ·

*P*iedmont is remote from the rest of mainland Italy; this remoteness has helped to preserve local traditions, local cuisine, and local wine styles. And not just in the sense of quaint local color: Some of the wines from north-western Italy are among Italy's very greatest wines — period.

# Drinking In the Majesty of Piedmont

Piedmont, Italy's northwestern-most region, has something majestic about it. The feeling comes from the people, the place itself, and certainly the wines — especially Barolo and Barbaresco. The food is majestic, too. Piedmontese cuisine ranks among the finest in Italy, if not the world, its specialty being the numerous *antipasto* dishes that precede the pasta and main course.

True to its name, Piedmont — "foot of the mountain" — is surrounded by mountains on three sides. The mighty Alps separate it from France to the west and from Switzerland (and the tiny Aosta Valley region) to the north, while the Apennines separate it from the region of Liguria to the south. Only Piedmont's eastern border, facing Lombardy and Milan, offers easy, mountain-free (and, frankly, visually boring) access.

Piedmont's capital city, Turin, in the center of the region, is one of Italy's largest cities and the home of Fiat. Turin is situated in the Po River Valley, the plains area of Piedmont — not the area to find top vineyards and wineries. Most of Piedmont's best wines come either from the foothills of the Apennines in the south or the foothills of the Alps in the north. Although Piedmont is Italy's second-largest region, good vineyard land is scarce and very expensive: The mountains and the Po River Valley occupy most of the region, leaving only 30 percent of the land suitable for hillside vineyards.

Piedmont generally has a continental climate: cold winters and mainly dry, hot summers. The mild autumns, with heavy fog especially in southern Piedmont, are extremely beneficial for late-ripening grape varieties, such as Nebbiolo — Piedmont's finest variety.

The following sections introduce you to the red wines and grape varieties of the impressive Piedmont region.

## *The wines of Piedmont*

In Italy, only Tuscany rivals Piedmont for the greatness of its red wines. Piedmont — specifically the Barolo and Barbaresco districts — was the first region in Italy to recognize the importance of making separate wines from exceptional vineyards, a concept that Burgundy and other regions of France had practiced for some time. Producers such as Vietti and Prunotto began making single-vineyard Barolos and Barbarescos in 1961.

In volume, Piedmont makes more *DOC/G wine* (pedigreed wine that comes from specific regions and adheres to specific guidelines) than any other region in Italy; the region also boasts the highest number of DOC/G wine zones, 50, and the most DOCG wines, seven. In fact, Piedmont is the only region in Italy (so far) that has created a network of DOCs that in effect covers practically all the wines grown there. Upwards of 84 percent of Piedmont's wine production is DOC or DOCG. (See Chapter 1 for more information on the DOC and DOCG designations.)

About 90 percent of Piedmont's wine comes from the southern part of the region (see Figure 2-1). This production roughly falls into the following two areas:

- ✔ The Alba area, in south-central Piedmont, which includes the Langhe Hills area and the Roero area
- ✔ The Asti/Alessandria area, in southeastern Piedmont, extending south of the Po River to the border with Liguria and including the Monferrato Hills

Additionally, wine comes from two separate parts of northern Piedmont and from a few wine zones in the pre-Alpine, western part of the region.

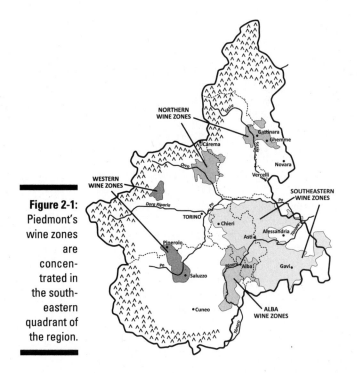

**Figure 2-1:**
Piedmont's
wine zones
are
concen-
trated in
the south-
eastern
quadrant of
the region.

# *The grapes of Piedmont*

Piedmont boasts three major red grape varieties and two major white varieties.
These varieties are

- **Nebbiolo:** Pronounced nehb-be-*oh*-loh, Nebbiolo is a noble but difficult,
  late-ripening red variety that doesn't grow as well anywhere else in the
  world or make such superb wine (when conditions are right) as it does
  in the Langhe hills around the town of Alba.

- **Barbera:** Pronounced bar-*bae*-rah, Barbera is a native red Piedmontese
  variety that, until a few decades ago, was Italy's most-planted red variety.
  In Piedmont, it grows mainly in the Asti and Alba areas, making serious, as
  well as everyday, wines.

- **Dolcetto:** A spicy red variety seldom seen outside Piedmont, Dolcetto
  (dohl-*chet*-toh) is widely grown in the Alba and southeastern areas of the
  region.

- **Moscato:** A world-renowned white grape with floral aromas and flavors,
  Moscato (mo-*scah*-toh) is a specialty of the Asti area.

- **Cortese:** Pronounced cor-*tae*-sae, Cortese is a grape that makes delicately
  flavored dry white wines; it's a specialty of the Gavi area.

The vineyards of Piedmont grow numerous other native varieties, such as the white Arneis, Favorita, and Erbaluce, and the red Grignolino, Freisa, Malvasia Nera, Pelaverga, Bonarda, Croatina, Vespolina, and several more. Internationally famous varieties include Chardonnay, Sauvignon Blanc, Cabernet Sauvignon, and Merlot.

# Sampling the Wines of the Alba Area

The Alba wine zone consists of two areas in south-central Piedmont, the Langhe hills and the Roero, which surround the town of Alba. This fairly small area is Piedmont's major vineyard territory in terms of the quality of the wines produced there. The area encompasses 11 DOC/G zones, including Barolo and Barbaresco, Piedmont's — and northern Italy's — two greatest red wines.

A prosperous town of about 30,000 inhabitants, Alba is surrounded by hills — the Roero hills to the north and west, and the Langhe hills to the south and east. The Tanaro River, which flows from the Apennine Mountains in the south, cuts through the town; it separates the hills of the Roero from those of the Langhe. Alba's wealth comes from its many industries: clothing, hazelnuts, chocolate and other confections, and, of course, food and wine. Perhaps Alba's greatest gastronomic treat is its white truffles, which grow in the ground on local hillsides and are harvested in the fall. (The sidebar, "Restaurants of Piedmont's pride and joy, the Alba-Asti area," lists many excellent restaurants in this area, certainly among the finest in Italy.) And then there's the wine.

## Barolo

A well-made Barolo (bah-*roh*-loh) from a good vintage is one of the greatest red wines in the world. It's powerful and full-bodied, with all sorts of intriguing aromas and flavors — ripe strawberries, tar, mint, eucalyptus, licorice, camphor, tobacco, chocolate, roses, spices, vanilla, and white truffles — and it only gets better with age. Often referred to as "the king of wines," Barolo is austere and tannic in its youth, and it usually requires many years of aging before it's ready to drink — and even then, decanting and aerating the wine help soften it. Barolo's longevity is foreshadowed by its production regulations: The wine must age a minimum of three years before release (five for *riservas,* or specially aged, premium wines). Along with Italy's other two big "B" wines — Barbaresco and Brunello di Montalcino — Barolo was among the first Italian wines granted DOCG status in 1980.

Barolo's vineyard district is in the Langhe hills, just a few miles southwest of the town of Alba. Barolo is also the name of one of the 11 communities that grow the wine (5 of which are really important).

Barolo must be made entirely from Nebbiolo, which is both a blessing and a curse. The blessing is that the Nebbiolo variety expresses itself brilliantly in the Barolo and Barbaresco zones of the Langhe hills. The marly clay soil is alkaline enough to tame the fiercely high acidity of Nebbiolo. In most years, the area gets enough warmth from the sun and just enough rain; most importantly, the mild, foggy autumns provide enough time for the notoriously late-ripening Nebbiolo to slowly complete its growth. The Tanaro River, which flows through the Barolo and the Barbaresco areas, tempers the summer heat and fosters the mild and misty autumns. Nebbiolo normally ripens in late October in the Langhe hills areas, long after other varieties have been picked; it has ripened as late as mid-November.

The curse of Nebbiolo is that weather conditions don't always allow it to ripen sufficiently — in which case Nebbiolo's tannin and acidity can be too great, making harsh wine. Fortunately, global warming or good fortune in recent years has brought many excellent vintages for both Barolo and Barbaresco: 1989, 1990, 1996, 1997, 1998, and 1999 are all outstanding. More recent vintages that show promise are 2001, 2004, 2006, and 2007. In general, Barolo has never been better than in the past 20 years.

### *The intricacies of a tiny DOCG zone*

The Barolo wine zone isn't large compared to other famous wine areas. Physically, it extends a little more than 7 miles southwest of Alba and is about 5 miles wide at its widest point. (Actually, it seems a *lot* larger when you travel up and down the steep Langhe hillsides to visit Barolo producers.) The entire annual production of Barolo amounts to only a little over half a million cases — a small amount compared to Burgundy and a tiny fraction of the amount of Bordeaux produced annually. Production is small not only because the zone is tiny but also because the Nebbiolo grape is extremely choosy as to where it grows well (generally only on hillsides facing south or southeast).

Basically, five communities produce most Barolo (not to mention most of the *best* Barolo):

- ✔ La Morra
- ✔ Barolo
- ✔ Serralunga d'Alba
- ✔ Castiglione Falletto
- ✔ Monforte d'Alba

**Book III**

**Italy: Small but Mighty**

Not counting the producers' individual imprints, two different types of Barolo exist, according to the location of the vineyards:

- ✔ The Barolo wines of the Serralunga (eastern) Valley — which includes the communities of Serralunga d'Alba, Castiglione Falletto, and Monforte d'Alba — tend to be more austere, powerful, and long-lived; they're more tannic and more full-bodied than other Barolos, generally have more extract (solid grape matter) and alcohol, and require long aging — 12 to 15 years — to develop and mature.

- ✔ The Barolo wines of the Central (western) Valley — basically the largest community, La Morra, which accounts for about one-third of all Barolo wine, and part of the community of Barolo — often have more perfumed aromas, such as white truffles; they're typically more elegant and have a velvety texture, are less full-bodied, and are less tannic than the Barolos of the Serralunga Valley. They're usually ready to drink sooner — often within eight to ten years of their vintage date.

Vineyards in the commune of Barolo itself, which extend into both valleys, make both styles of Barolo wine — depending on their location and, to some extent, the wine producer.

Bear in mind that a winemaker's own style can override the style of his vineyard area to some extent. For example, Giuseppe Rinaldi makes some Barolo from the Brunate vineyard in La Morra. But his very traditional style of winemaking is such that his Barolo wines resemble those from the Serralunga Valley more than the typical, softer La Morra Barolo. Conversely, Paolo Scavino's "Bric del Fiasc" Barolo from Castiglione Falletto is much less tannic and more approachable than traditionally made Barolos from Castiglione Falletto, such as those of Giuseppe Mascarello.

### Recommended Barolo producers

Barolo is similar to red Burgundy in that you have to search for the best producers if you want a true representation of these fine wines. When choosing a Barolo (or a Barbaresco, for that matter), take this approach:

- ✔ Select the producer first, based on his reputation.
- ✔ Consider the relative excellence of the vintage.
- ✔ Look for the name of a well-known single vineyard on the label.
- ✔ Check the name of the commune, such as La Morra or Castiglione Falletto (in the case of Barolo); it gives you an indication of the style of the wine.

Following are Barolo producers listed in two classes along with the communes where most, or all, of their vineyards are located. The producers in Class One are favorite producers; but all of the producers in Class Two are excellent producers, as well. The wines in this list start at $35 to $40 retail and can go to well over $100 for single-vineyard wines.

### Class One

Giacomo Conterno (Serralunga d'Alba)

Gaja (Serralunga d'Alba; La Morra) — through the 1995 vintage

Bruno Giacosa (Serralunga d'Alba; Castiglione Falletto)

Bartolo Mascarello (Barolo)

Giuseppe Mascarello (Castiglione Falletto; Monforte d'Alba)

Giuseppe Rinaldi (Barolo; La Morra)

Luciano Sandrone (Barolo)

Paolo Scavino (Castiglione Falletto)

Vietti (Castiglione Falletto)

### Class Two

Elio Altare (La Morra)

Giacomo Borgogno (Barolo)

Brovia (Castiglione Falletto)

Tenuta Carretta (Barolo)

Cavalotto (Castiglione Falletto)

Ceretto, also known as Bricco Rocche (Castiglione Falletto)

Michele Chiarlo (La Morra)

Clerico (Monforte d'Alba)

Elvio Cogno (Novello)

Podere Colla (Monforte d'Alba)

Aldo Conterno (Monforte d'Alba)

Conterno-Fantino (Monforte d'Alba)

Cordero di Montezemolo (La Morra)

Corino (La Morra)

Luigi Einaudi (Barolo)

Fontanafredda (Serralunga d'Alba)

Elio Grasso (Monforte d'Alba)

Silvio Grasso (La Morra)

Manzone (Monforte d'Alba)

Marcarini (La Morra)

Marchesi di Barolo (Barolo)

Oddero (Serralunga d'Alba)

Parusso (Monforte d'Alba)

Pio Cesare (Serralunga d'Alba)

E. Pira & Figli (Barolo)

Luigi Pira (Serralunga d'Alba)

Prunotto (Monforte d'Alba)

Renato Ratti (La Morra)

Francesco Rinaldi (Barolo)

Rocche Costamagna (La Morra)

Rocche dei Manzoni (Monforte d'Alba)

Seghesio (Barolo)

Gianni Voerzio (La Morra)

Roberto Voerzio (La Morra)

**Book III**

**Italy: Small but Mighty**

## Barbaresco

The other great red wine of the Langhe hills, Barbaresco (bahr-bah-*res*-co), also a DOCG wine, is very similar to Barolo, with most of its virtues and few of its faults. The reasons for the similarities between Barolo and Barbaresco are that they're both made entirely from Nebbiolo, they share similar soils and climate (because they're within 10 miles of each other), and many producers make both wines, using similar production methods.

Barbaresco is a sturdy, austere, powerful wine, generally only slightly less full-bodied than Barolo: Its minimum alcohol content is slightly less (12.5 percent, compared to 13 percent for Barolo), and its minimum aging at the winery (two years minimum, four for *riservas*) is one year less than Barolo's.

The Barbaresco zone is a few miles northeast of the town of Alba and about a 20-minute drive from the Barolo zone. It's a slightly smaller area than Barolo, covering only three communities: Barbaresco itself, Neive, and Treiso. All three villages are high in the Langhe hills. The Tanaro River cuts through the northwestern part of the Barbaresco zone, and the zone's closeness to the flatter Tanaro Valley helps make the Barbaresco area slightly warmer and drier than the Barolo zone. As a result, the Nebbiolo grape ripens earlier here than in the Barolo area and generally has less tannin.

The aromas and flavors of Barbaresco wines are very much the same as those of Barolo (see the "Barolo" section earlier in this chapter). But Barbaresco is more elegant, typically less austere, and more accessible in its youth, making it generally a better choice in restaurants, especially when most of the available wines are from recent vintages. As with any generalization, however, you can find exceptions. The very traditional producer Bruno Giacosa, for example, makes powerful, tannic Barbarescos from the Neive area that require many years of aging before they're ready to drink — just like Giacosa's Barolos.

Barbaresco's annual production is only about 2.5 million bottles, which is 35 percent of Barolo's production — one reason why top producers, such as Bruno Giacosa, Angelo Gaja, Ceretto, and Marchesi di Gresy, have no trouble selling their limited supply of rather expensive Barbarescos. (Barbaresco prices are about the same as Barolo, ranging from $35 to well over $100 a bottle.)

Because Barbaresco has fewer producers than Barolo, in a smaller, more consistent territory, it's a more consistently reliable wine, generally speaking. About 200 producers make Barolo, quite a few of which aren't very good. On the other hand, you seldom come across a poor Barbaresco producer.

### Vineyard and winemaking styles in the Barbaresco zone

The soils of the vineyards around the three villages where the grapes for Barbaresco grow are more uniform than those of the Barolo communities; consequently, you don't see such striking differences among Barbaresco wines as you do among Barolos. But some differences do exist among Barbarescos according to their vineyard areas (note that winemaking style can camouflage the characteristics of the vineyard area, however). Here are some of the differences:

- ✔ **Barbaresco:** Many of the best vineyards are here, as well as many of the largest, most renowned wineries (although no Barbaresco winery is very large), such as Angelo Gaja, Ceretto's Bricco Asili, Produttori del Barbaresco (perhaps the most respected wine cooperative in the world), and Marchesi di Gresy, owner of the entire, renowned Martinenga vineyard. In general, the wines of the Barbaresco area tend to be a bit lighter in color and lighter-bodied than those of Neive, but they're known for their perfumed aromas and their structure.

✔ **Neive:** Located on the next hill east of Barbaresco, this community produces the most full-bodied, tannic Barbarescos in the region. Neive is the home of the great Bruno Giacosa, as well as Fratelli Cigliuti and the historic Castello di Neive.

✔ **Treiso d'Alba:** Also called Treiso, this community south of Barbaresco is the least known of the three areas; some of the Barbaresco zone's highest hills are here. Treiso's Barbarescos tend to be lighter-bodied than the others, and they're known for their finesse and elegance.

In general, Barbaresco tends to be drinkable sooner than Barolo, but many exceptions exist. Both Bruno Giacosa's and Angelo Gaja's single-vineyard wines (Gaja's, as of the 1996 vintage, are actually called Nebbiolo Langhe DOC rather than Barbaresco) easily last for 20 or more years in good vintages.

### Recommended Barbaresco producers

The following is a list of favorite Barbaresco producers in two classes along with the communes where most, or all, of their vineyards are located. Many Barolo producers also make good Barbarescos; if a producer's primary wine is Barolo, you'll find it only under the earlier "Recommended Barolo producers" section. Barolo producers whose Barbarescos are of greater or equal importance — such as Gaja, Bruno Giacosa, and Ceretto — appear on both lists. The producers in Class One are favorite producers, but all of the producers in Class Two are good producers as well.

#### Class One

Ceretto, also known as Bricco Asili (Barbaresco)
Fratelli Cigliuti (Neive)
Angelo Gaja (Barbaresco)
Bruno Giacosa (Neive)
Marchesi di Gresy (Barbaresco)

Luigi Bianco (Barbaresco)
Ca' Romé (Barbaresco)
Castello di Neive (Neive)
Giuseppe Cortese (Barbaresco)
De Forville (Barbaresco)
Moccagatta (Barbaresco)

#### Class Two

Fiorenzo Nada (Treiso)
Sorì Paitin, also known as Secondo Pasquero-Elia (Neive)
Parroco di Neive (Neive)
Pelissero (Treiso)
I Vignaioli Elvio Pertinace (Treiso)
Produttori del Barbaresco (Barbaresco)

Roagna, also know as I Paglieri (Barbaresco)
Albino Rocca (Barbaresco)
Bruno Rocca (Barbaresco)
La Spinetta (Neive)
La Spinona (Barbaresco)

# Barbera, Dolcetto, and Nebbiolo of Alba

The town of Alba gives its name to three red varietal wines, each made entirely from its named grape: Barbera d'Alba (bar-*bae*-rah *dahl*-bah), Dolcetto d'Alba (dohl-*chet*-toh *dahl*-bah), and Nebbiolo d'Alba (nehb-be-*oh*-loh *dahl*-bah).

Of these three, Barbera d'Alba is generally the finest and most serious wine — despite the fact that Nebbiolo is the most serious of the three grape varieties. In fact, Barbera in the Alba zone is about as good as Barbera gets — except for parts of the Asti zone, where it can be at least as good, but subtly different. (See the section "Barbera d'Asti" later in this chapter.)

### Barbera d'Alba

Barbera is a strange variety. It has a lot of pigmentation and very high acidity, but almost no tannin in its skins and seeds; as a result, its wines are dark in color but crisp and refreshing, rather like white wines, instead of being firm and mouth-drying like most reds — but its berry-cherry and spicy flavors are red wine all the way. When you taste most Barbera d'Albas, you find a red wine more mouthwatering and refreshing than most other reds; this wine goes amazingly well with food.

In many parts of Italy, Barbera wines are only average in quality because the farmers grow too large a crop, or because the climate doesn't let the grapes ripen optimally. But in the Alba area, the growers respect Barbera, and the grapes return the favor by making rich, flavorful wines with intense fruity and spicy flavors.

When the grapes are especially good, some winemakers age some of their Barbera d'Alba for a short time in small barrels of French oak, which gives the wine some of the tannin the grapes themselves lack and brings the wine closer in style to other red wines. The oaked styles generally cost more, about $22 to $45 rather than $12 to $20 for the unoaked wines.

The Barbera d'Alba territory is a fairly large area that encompasses the Langhe hills as well as the Roero; this area includes the production zone for both Barolo and Barbaresco. Many of the best wines come from vineyards within Barolo territory, which are some of the best vineyards of the entire area.

Barbera d'Alba is enjoyable both young and with age, up to about 15 years — although as it ages beyond about 8 years, it loses its spicy vibrancy and becomes a more normal red wine. Simple, inexpensive Barbera is great with pizza, but the best examples of this wine are really too good for such casual food. Barbera is terrific with pasta with tomato sauce, spicy foods, bitter greens, and hearty dishes.

Following are some top producers of Barbera d'Alba to watch for:

| | |
|---|---|
| Elio Altare | Bartolo Mascarello |
| Elvio Cogno | Giuseppe Mascarello |
| Aldo Conterno | Moccagatta |
| Giacomo Conterno | Prunotto |
| Gaja | Giuseppi Rinaldi |
| Manzone | Paolo Scavino |
| Marcarini | Vietti |

## Dolcetto d'Alba

Dolcetto d'Alba comes from vineyards in the Langhe hills but not from the Roero area. It's made entirely from Dolcetto grapes, which ripen earlier than other red varieties of the area. Dolcetto d'Alba is also earlier maturing as a wine than either Barbera or Nebbiolo, and in meals, it's usually served before Barbera — to accompany the five or six antipasto courses of a typical Piedmontese meal.

Dolcetto has lower acidity than Barbera, but it's still acidic, as any self-respecting Italian wine should be; its acid suits it well to food. Dolcetto is more tannic than Barbera — a dry, medium-bodied, rich-textured wine with aromas and flavors of black pepper and ripe berry fruit.

Dolcetto is the featured variety in seven Piedmontese DOC zones. The Alba zone, whose Dolcettos are the easiest to find in the United States, is one of the top two areas in terms of the quality of the wines, along with Dogliani (which you can find out more about later in this chapter). Dolcetto is a relatively inexpensive wine to drink young and isn't a serious wine for aging. Most Dolcettos taste like ripe Dolcetto fruit instead of having the smoky, toasty nuances of oak.

**Book III**

**Italy: Small but Mighty**

Drink Dolcetto with some of the same kind of foods as Barbera: pizza, somewhat spicy dishes, and earthy vegetarian foods. It's also terrific with casual meals, such as chef salads, cold cuts, sandwiches, or turkey burgers. Dolcetto d'Alba costs about $12 to $20 per bottle and is best when it's no more than three years old. Many Barolo producers also make Dolcetto d'Alba; look for the following producers:

| | |
|---|---|
| Elio Altare | Marcarini |
| Clerico | Ratti |
| Elvio Cogno (a specialty) | Sandrone |
| Giacomo Conterno | Vietti |
| Conterno-Fantino | |

### Nebbiolo d'Alba

Nebbiolo d'Alba is a well-made wine in most cases, but it lacks the intensity and flair of Barolo and Barbaresco. It's just a good, medium-bodied, firm red wine with delicate flavors of tar, red fruits, and herbs.

The grapes for Nebbiolo d'Alba grow in certain parts of the Langhe hills and in the entire Roero. Although many Barolo and Barbaresco producers make Nebbiolo d'Alba, their wine is never a declassified Barolo or Barbaresco, because the Nebbiolo d'Alba vineyard area doesn't overlap with those of the two great DOCG wines. Some Barolo and Barbaresco producers source their grapes for Nebbiolo d'Alba from vineyards across the river, in the Roero.

Nebbiolo d'Alba is a relatively light style of Nebbiolo for drinking young; the wine must age only one year before release. Its best drinkability period is three to seven years from the vintage. Its price is also to its advantage; Nebbiolo d'Alba is relatively inexpensive — generally about $15 to $18 a bottle. One Barolo producer who makes a specialty of producing fine Nebbiolo d'Alba is Tenuta Carretta.

# Roero and Roero Arneis

The Roero (roh-*eh*-roh) is an area north of the city of Alba, across the Tanaro River from the Barolo and Barbaresco zones. It's a hilly area, but the hills are lower than on the other side of the river. The soils are also lighter, for the most part, than in the Barolo and Barbaresco zones, with a high percentage of sand, although parts of the Roero have a richer, calcareous clay soil similar to that found in the hills south of the river.

The Roero territory has several overlapping or partially overlapping DOC zones, including parts of the Barbera d'Alba and Nebbiolo d'Alba zones. Growers here have traditionally cultivated both Nebbiolo and Barbera for these two wines. Part of the Langhe DOC zone (described in the next section) falls into part of the Roero, too. But the real excitement in the Roero these days is wine made with the DOC Roero, a relatively new appellation created in 1985.

Roero Rosso is a red wine that's almost entirely Nebbiolo; a token 2 to 5 percent of the local white Arneis (ahr-*nase*) variety may also be used. What's different about this wine compared to Barolo and Barbaresco, in theory, is that it's a lighter wine — in practice, the difference is the avant garde attitude with which many producers approach the wine. Free of any accountability to tradition, they readily employ modern winemaking methods designed to produce concentrated wines with intense fruity character framed by the taste and structure of French oak. Producers whose vineyards are in the part of Roero with the richest soils, such as the northern area around Canale, have the best resources for making such wines. You can also find some lighter Roero wines.

The following producers are on the front line of high-quality Roero Rosso:

| | |
|---|---|
| Cascina Ca' Rossa | Funtanin |
| Tenuta Carretta | Filippo Gallino |
| Cascina Chicco | Malvirà |
| Cornarea | Monchiero Carbone |
| Matteo Correggia | Angelo Negro e Figli |
| Deltetto | |

The Roero DOC also covers a white wine called Roero Arneis, made entirely from the Arneis grape variety. Roero Arneis is a medium-bodied white wine with pronounced aromas and flavors that suggest fresh grass, flowers, and ripe, white fruits. It's usually dry, although some producers make it slightly off-dry, and it sometimes has a refreshing prickle of carbon dioxide in its rich texture. Arneis is best enjoyed young, within three years of the harvest. Some producers of note are

| | |
|---|---|
| Ceretto | Bruno Giacosa |
| Matteo Correggia | Malvirà |
| Deltetto | Vietti |
| Funtanin | |

## Five other Alba DOCs

Depending on exactly where their vineyards are situated, producers in the Alba area have another five DOC designations at their disposal. Three of these apply to wines made entirely from Dolcetto:

Book III

Italy: Small but Mighty

- ✔ **Dolcetto delle Langhe Monregalesi:** Pronounced dohl-*chet*-toh del-lae *lahn*-gae mahn-rae-gah-*lae*-see, this territory spans both sides of the Tanaro River upstream (south) from the Barolo district, where the river runs north-south; the wine is somewhat lighter than Dolcetto d'Alba.

- ✔ **Dolcetto di Diano d'Alba:** Pronounced dohl-*chet*-toh dee dee-*ah*-no *dahl*-bah, this area is also called just Diano d'Alba. It's a small area, specifically the hilly part of the commune of Diano d'Alba, which nestles between the Barolo and Barbaresco zones.

- ✔ **Dolcetto di Dogliani:** This zone (pronounced dohl-*chet*-toh dee doh-*l'yah*-nee) begins about where the Dolcetto d'Alba, Nebbiolo d'Alba, and Barbera d'Alba zones end (to their south) and takes its name from the small town of Dogliani. Some of the Dolcetto wines here are very good; they're more concentrated than those of the Alba zone and need a bit more time to develop. Because this is a traditional Dolcetto area, that grape earns the best vineyard sites, which is one theory as to why these wines can be more intense than Alba Dolcettos. Seek out the Dolcetto of Luigi Einaudi and the brilliant wines of Quinto Chionetti.

# Restaurants of Piedmont's pride and joy, the Alba-Asti area

The region around Alba and Asti, where most of the great Piedmont wines are made, is one of the finest restaurant areas in Italy, if not the world. If you happen to visit the area between October and December, you'll assure yourself ample shavings of the special treat of this region — pungent white truffles — on your pasta, soups, meat courses, and anything else you desire. But any time of the year, the restaurants perform their magic for you. (Bear in mind that it does get rather hot in this area during July and August.) To accompany your Barolo or Barbaresco, try beef braised in wine, roast pork, rabbit (all local specialties), game, game birds, and aged hard cheeses.

All the restaurants in the list that follows are relatively inexpensive to moderate in price compared to their equivalents in major European cities, and the wines are downright bargains:

✔ **Guido di Costigliole (Da Guido)** (Relais San Maurizio, phone 0141 841900): Probably the most renowned restaurant in Piedmont and one of the best in Italy; superb food and service; astounding wine list, for both Italian and French wine; located in the Langhe area of Piedmont

✔ **Da Cesare** (Albaretto della Torre, phone 0173 520141): The chef-artist, Cesare Giaccone, rivals Da Guido with his brilliant, typically Piedmontese cuisine; a local favorite; located in a high hill town in the Alta Langhe, south of Alba

✔ **La Pergola** (Vezza d'Alba, phone 0173 65178): Northwest of Alba, this fine restaurant offers the largest, most complete Piedmontese wine list in the world (ten pages of Barolo alone!)

✔ **Ristorante La Contea** (Neive, phone 0173 67126): Very typical Piedmontese fare; a great prelude to the region; Tonino Verro is host, and his wife, Claudia, is the excellent chef; has a few rooms

✔ **Giardino da Felicin** (Monteforte d'Alba, phone 0173 78225): Restaurant-inn in the heart of Barolo country; host-owner Giorgio Rocca speaks English and acts as your guide to the wine region, if you're fortunate enough to get a room (in the busy season, it's booked a year in advance)

✔ **Hotel Belvedere** (La Morra, phone 0173 50190): Traditional and very fine restaurant in Barolo country, with a better chance of getting rooms than in Giardino da Felicin; also fabulous views

✔ **Il Cascinalenuovo** (Isola d'Asti, phone 0141 958166): A hotel with a swimming pool and tennis court; very fine restaurant with an excellent wine list; northeast of Barbaresco

✔ **Gener Neuv** (Asti, phone 0141 557270): Asti's leading restaurant; fine wine list

✔ **Vincafè** (Alba, phone 0173 364603): Best wine bar in Alba; 240 wines on the list, 70 wines open by the glass every day; local cheeses; lunch available; in the heart of town

✔ **Ristorante Enoclub** (Alba, phone 0173 33994): Good, casual restaurant in downtown Alba; very good wine list

✔ **La Ciau del Tornavento** (Treiso, phone 0173 638333): Beautiful country restaurant-inn in Barbaresco country; some rooms available

✔ **Le Torri** (Castiglione Falletto, phone 0173 62849): Hotel-restaurant in the center of this old hill town; some rooms have a fine view of Barolo country

✔ **Locanda nel Borgo Antico** (Barolo, phone 0173 56355): Fine restaurant in the town of Barolo

✔ **Trattoria Marsupino** (Briaglia, phone 0174 563888): Excellent country restaurant about 12 miles south of the town of Dogliani; a few rooms

✔ **La Carmagnole** (Carmagnola, phone 011 9712673): A private home converted into a small, charming restaurant; excellent food; proprietor treats you like a guest in his home; the town is off the *autostrada* on the road north to Turin

✔ **Al Rododendro** (Boves, phone 0171 380372): Even though Boves is a bit distant — about an hour's drive south of Alba — Al Rododendro is one of Italy's finest restaurants, on the level of Da Guido; outstanding food, wine, and service; rooms available

A new DOC wine, since 1995, is Verduno Pelaverga (ver-*doo*-no pel-ah-*ver*-gah). It's made primarily from the local red Pelaverga grape mainly in the community of Verduno, one of the fringe areas of the Barolo zone west of Alba. This wine is medium-bodied and vibrant with red fruits and spicy flavors (and, according to local legend, it's an aphrodisiac).

The final additional DOC zone of the Alba area — called simply Langhe (*lahn*-gae) DOC — is the largest of all. It covers approximately the territory of all the DOC/G zones in this chapter and extends eastward into the Asti DOCG area (which you find out about later in this chapter). The Langhe DOC came into existence in the 1990s, basically as a catchall for wines that producers were categorizing as *vino da tavola*. These include wines whose grapes (or blends) don't conform to the various other DOC/G regulations of the area — as well as wines of the other DOC/G zones that producers wanted to declassify (for example, to make a Nebbiolo in the Barolo zone with less than the three years of aging required for Barolo).

Six varietal wines fall under the Langhe DOC (each one deriving 100 percent from its named grape): Nebbiolo, Dolcetto, Freisa, Favorita, Arneis, and Chardonnay. The Langhe name also applies to two very important nonvarietal wines, a Rosso and a Bianco.

Langhe Nebbiolo can be declassified Barolo, Barbaresco, Nebbiolo d'Alba, or Roero Rosso, or Nebbiolo grown in other parts of the zone. Langhe Freisa comes from the local red Freisa (*frae*-sah) grape variety, which makes an exceptionally lively, vibrant red wine with high acid and high tannin, often vinified in a *frizzante* (lightly bubbly or fizzy), slightly sweet style that's popular locally. Some producers now successfully make Freisa as a dry, oak-aged wine. Three Langhe Freisas to seek out are Giacomo Conterno's, G. Mascarello's Vigna Toetto, and Varaldo's.

**Book III**

**Italy: Small but Mighty**

Langhe Favorita comes from the local white Favorita variety, which makes dry, crisp wines with delicate flavors that are slightly floral or citrusy. Langhe Rosso and Langhe Bianco are wide-open designations in terms of the varieties permitted: Each may be made from any one or more locally grown grape varieties of the appropriate color.

The Langhe Rosso designation is particularly noteworthy for stunning, modern wines that are nontraditional blends of Nebbiolo, Barbera, and/or Cabernet Sauvignon. These wines include Altare's Vigna Arborina, Clerico's Arte, Conterno-Fantino's Monprà, and Rocche dei Manzoni's Vigna Big.

# Exploring the Wines of Southeastern Piedmont

The Alba wine zone is small in comparison to the wine-producing areas of southeastern Piedmont (refer to Figure 2-1). These areas make more wine than any other part of the region because they have a greater concentration of hilly land for grape-growing.

Alba's wine zones, for example, lie within the province of Cuneo, a large province occupying the southwestern quarter of Piedmont — most of which is either too mountainous for vineyards or so flat that it's better suited to growing kiwis and maize. But the provinces of Asti, east and north of the Alba area, and Alessandria, east of Asti, are mainly hilly. This is the area of the Monferrato Hills, which extend from the Po River south to the Apennines. The name Monferrato appears as part of many wine names, as does Asti, the province — but oddly enough, Alessandria doesn't.

Nebbiolo recedes in importance in Asti and Alessandria, and Barbera comes strongly to the foreground — along with a minor red variety called Grignolino, the red Malvasia, the white Cortese grape, and, above all, Moscato.

## Asti DOCG

Asti (*ahs*-tee) is a famous name around the world, even to those who've never visited the city. The reason is the DOCG wine called Asti, Italy's flagship — and distinctive — sparkling wine. Asti is made entirely from the Moscato grape, specifically the Muscat à Petits Grains type, the best Muscat variety of all. It's a sweet and absolutely delicious bubbly with rich floral, peachy flavors and a lot of acidity to balance its sweetness.

The vineyard area for Asti is quite large, extending beyond the province of Asti itself into limited parts of the Alba area to the west and the Alessandria province to the east. Asti is made using a particular process whereby the juice begins fermenting, then stops, then begins again. This process, which is repeated several times, makes a low-alcohol wine (only about 8 percent) that retains the grapes' fresh flavors.

When Asti is about two or three years old, it starts to taste richer and some-what heavy — still tasty, but no longer at its best. To complicate the matter, however, Asti doesn't carry a vintage date, so you don't know how old a particular bottle really is. Purchase Asti from a store that sells a lot of it and pick a brand that sells well, because the turnover assures freshness. Look for Fontanafredda, Martini & Rossi, and Cinzano, but freshness is even more important than which brand you choose. And make sure the wine is genuine Asti; imitations do exist!

A companion wine to Asti — made from the same grapes in the same vine-yard areas and covered under the same DOCG — is Moscato d'Asti (mo-*scah*-toh *dahs*-tee). This wine is quite similar to Asti except that it's just *frizzante* rather than sparkling, and its flavors are more delicate than Asti's. It's also even lower in alcohol — generally from 5 to 7.5 percent. (In some states, that's technically too low to be considered wine!) Freshness is even more crucial for Moscato d'Asti than it is for Asti, but fortunately, these wines are vintage-dated. Buy the youngest vintage possible and never buy any vintage that's more than two years old.

Moscato d'Asti has a real following among some wine lovers in the United States. In New York, for example, you can find it offered by the glass as a dessert wine in some restaurants. But you don't have to relegate this wine to after dinner just because it's sweet. It's particularly refreshing on a lazy summer afternoon.

Moscato d'Asti is actually more expensive than Asti, the sparkling version. Asti generally runs from $10 to $12 at retail, whereas Moscato d'Asti tends to cost about $12 to $15. Check out Moscato d'Asti Cascinetta, made by Vietti. La Spinetta is a well-regarded brand, but the wine is slightly less delicate. Other good brands are Ceretto's Santo Stefano, Piero Gatti, Dante Rivetti, and Paolo Saracco.

## Barbera d'Asti

The Barbera grape is thought to have originated around Asti, in the Monferrato Hills; the province of Asti (like the Alba wine area) has grown

Book III

Italy: Small but Mighty

Barbera for more than 200 years. The DOC production zone for Barbera d'Asti is large, covering most of the Asti province and extending into Alessandria.

Barbera d'Asti wines are typically lighter and leaner than Barbera d'Alba wines. The Asti zone is a larger area than Alba's Barbera zone, and it includes some parts where the grape makes racy wines with tart fruit flavors and very pronounced acidity. But some parts of the zone grow superior grapes from old vines that make the finest Barbera wines anywhere: rich, dark, ripe, and spicy.

Barbera d'Asti ranges in price from about $10 for the lightest wines to about $45 for the richer, *barrique*-aged wines (those aged in small, French oak barrels). Excellent producers of Barbera d'Asti are

| | |
|---|---|
| Cascina La Barbatella | Prunotto |
| Bava | Scarpa |
| Boffa | Scrimaglio |
| Braida | Tenuta La Tenaglia |
| Michele Chiarlo | Trinchero |
| Coppo | Vietti |
| Franco Martinetti | |

## Other varietal wines

Much of the wine production of Asti and Alessandria is varietally labeled wine, mainly red but also white. With the exception of Barbera d'Asti, most of these wines aren't particularly outstanding in quality, or of significant commercial importance in the United States, although some gems are among them, as you find out in the following sections.

### Dolcetto

The Dolcetto grape variety is widely dispersed in southeastern Piedmont. In addition to the five DOC Dolcetto wines produced in the Alba area, another three (all 100 percent varietal) come from the provinces of Asti and Alessandria.

- **Dolcetto d'Asti:** Fairly light, Dolcetto d'Asti (dohl-*chet*-toh *dahs*-tee) is made from vineyards in the southern part of the Asti province.

- **Dolcetto d'Acqui:** The Acqui zone lies in the province of Alessandria and takes its name from the town of Acqui Terme. Dolcetto d'Acqui (dohl-*chet*-toh *dah*-kwee) is noted for its floral perfume.

- **Dolcetto di Ovada:** The Ovada zone is in the very south of Piedmont, just west of the Gavi zone. Dolcetto is ingrained here; Dolcetto di Ovada (dohl-*chet*-toh dee oh-*vah*-dah) is fuller-bodied and more tannic than other Dolcettos and ages nicely.

## Freisa

The unusual and ancient Piedmontese grape variety known as Freisa is a local specialty in two additional zones besides Langhe DOC (covered earlier in this chapter). These two other wines are

- ✔ **Freisa d'Asti:** A dry or sweetish red wine, Freisa d'Asti (*frae*-sah *dahs*-tee) comes from a zone that covers practically the whole province of Asti. Coppo makes an excellent dry Freisa d'Asti called Mondaccione, which, unusually enough, ages in small oak barrels.

- ✔ **Freisa di Chieri:** The Chieri area is actually in the province of Torino, in the western Monferrato hills, east of the city of Turin. Freisa di Chieri (*frae*-sah dee key-*ae*-ree) wine can be dry or sweetish; the sweeter style is labeled *amabile*. Production is small.

## Grignolino

If Freisa is mainly a local specialty, Grignolino is even more so; it holds little interest for wine lovers outside of Piedmont. This native variety makes rather pale, fairly light-bodied but tannic red wines with delicate flavors of tart red fruits and what the official regulations describe as a "pleasantly bitterish aftertaste." Actually, Grignolino can be refreshing in the heat of summer, and it goes well with many antipasto dishes. Following are two DOC Grignolinos:

- ✔ **Grignolino d'Asti:** Pronounced gree-n'yoh-*lee*-no *dahs*-tee and mainly from Grignolino with a small amount of Freisa, its production zone is an area roughly centered around the city of Asti.

- ✔ **Grignolino del Monferrato Casalese:** A small amount of Freisa is optional in this wine, which is pronounced gree-n'yoh-*lee*-no del mahn-fer-*rah*-toh cah-sah-*lae*-sae and produced in the northern Alessandria province in the hills south of the Po River, east of the town of Casale Monferrato — a classic Grignolino area.

**Book III**

**Italy: Small but Mighty**

## Malvasia

In any discussion of Italian wines, most references to the Malvasia grape mean the white Malvasia. But, like the Muscat grape, Malvasia also exists in red form, called Malvasia Nera in Italy. In Piedmont, this red grape makes two of its most unusual wines:

- ✔ **Malvasia di Casorzo d'Asti:** This wine (pronounced mahl-vah-*see*-ah dee cah-*sort*-zoh *dahs*-tee) grows in a small zone mainly in the Asti province; it's a spritzy, sweet, pale red with fragrant, fruity aroma and flavor; a sparkling version is scarce.

- ✔ **Malvasia di Castelnuovo Don Bosco:** From a Malvasia Nera variant, sometimes with a bit of Freisa, Malvasia di Castelnuovo Don Busco (mahl-vah-*see*-ah dee cahs-tel-*n'woh*-voh don *bos*-coh) is a sweet, spicy, *frizzante* (or *spumante*) red from a small zone in northern Asti province.

### Brachetto, Cortese, and Ruché

The three varieties you find in this section are all Piedmont specialties. Cortese is the most famous because it's the variety that makes Gavi, Piedmont's renowned still white wine (described in the next section). But Brachetto is the variety whose star seems to be on the rise, because its wine is now DOCG. The three varietal wines from these grapes are as follows:

- **Brachetto d'Acqui:** Sometimes called just Acqui, this wine (pronounced bra-*ket*-toh *dah*-kwee) derives entirely from the Brachetto grape variety. It's a sweet red that's most often seen as a sparkling wine, with pronounced fruity and floral flavors that might remind you of Moscato or even Lambrusco. Banfi (of Montalcino fame) produces a Brachetto d'Acqui in its Piedmont winery that sells for $22 to $24.

- **Cortese di Alto Monferrato:** A dry, delicate white, Cortese di Alto Monferrato (cor-*tae*-sae dee *ahl*-toh mahn-fer-*rah*-toh) is made from Cortese grapes grown in a fairly large zone of the Alto Monferrato (high Monferrato hills), in the southern Asti and Alessandria provinces, over-lapping several other DOC zones.

- **Ruché di Castagnole Monferrato:** A dry or slightly sweet, medium-bodied red with pronounced aromas, this wine (pronounced roo-*kae* dee cahs-tah-*n'yoh*-lae mahn-fer-*rah*-toh) is made mainly from the local Ruché grape variety in a fairly small zone northeast of the city of Asti.

# Gavi DOCG

The Gavi (*gah*-vee) district is in the southernmost Alessandria province, close to Liguria. This area has been a wine production zone for more than 1,000 years, but that wine was traditionally red and made from Barbera and Dolcetto grapes, usually blended. The local white grape, Cortese, was grown to make a base wine for sparkling wines — for which it was ideal, because of its high acidity and subtle flavors. In the post-World War II period, however, one local grower, La Scolca, commercialized Cortese as a still wine. Today, the area's still white wine, Gavi (or Cortese di Gavi) DOCG, is considered among Italy's best whites.

Gavi isn't an easy wine to appreciate. The high acidity of the Cortese grape — with not a lot of alcohol to counterbalance it — makes the wine crisp and austere rather than soft; also, Cortese's flavors are subtle rather than pronounced.

Writing off Gavi as just another crisp, white Italian wine is easy. When Gavi is made by a good producer, however, it has delicate but complex aromas of ripe apple, grapefruit, honey, flowers, or minerals, and it can develop for a few years. In ripe vintages such as 1997 or 2000, it can be particularly fine. Gavi is generally an unoaked white, but some producers are aging their Gavis partially in oak, and that style can also be good, although those wines tend to taste heavier and less fresh. Wines labeled Gavi di Gavi come from vineyards around the town of Gavi itself — which locals consider as a sort of "classico" area — as opposed to other areas of the DOCG zone.

Gavi costs from $12 to $18 a bottle for the basic wines, with premium wines such as La Scolca's Black Label running about $35. Recommended Gavi producers include

| | |
|---|---|
| Nicola Bergaglio | La Scolca |
| Broglia "La Meirana" | La Toledana |
| Castellari Bergaglio | Morgassi Superiore |
| La Chiara | Villa Sparina |
| La Giustiniana | |

## Other wines of Piedmont's southeast

A new but significant DOC designation of southeastern Piedmont is Monferrato (mahn-fer-*rah*-toh), a large area extending throughout most of the combined Asti and Alessandria provinces. Like Langhe DOC, this appellation is a catchall DOC for wines that otherwise would fall between the DOC/G cracks. Its most flexible wines are Monferrato Bianco and Monferrato Rosso, each made from one or more locally grown varieties. Like Langhe Rosso, Monferrato Rosso is a useful "home" for serious wines that are orphaned by the requirements of other DOC zones; La Spinetta's Pin and Martinetti's Sul Bric are two fine examples.

Monferrato DOC also features a Dolcetto and a Freisa; Monferrato Casalese Cortese, made mainly from Cortese grapes grown in a subzone around Casale Monferrato, in the south; and Chiaretto (also called Ciaret), a rosé or light red wine that derives primarily from any or all of nine red varieties (Barbera, Bonarda, Cabernet Franc, Cabernet Sauvignon, Dolcetto, Freisa, Grignolino, Pinot Nero, and Nebbiolo).

The maze of DOCs in southeastern Piedmont includes another six wines, which are

- **Albugnano:** A dry or semidry red or rosé, Albugnano (ahl-boo-*n'yah*-no) is made mainly from Nebbiolo (85 percent), with Freisa and/or Barbera and/or Bonarda; it's made in the northern part of Asti province.

- **Barbera del Monferrato:** Piedmont's third original zone for Barbera, along with the Alba and Asti zones, this large area (pronounced bar-*bae*-rah dell mahn-fer-*rah*-toh) lies partly in the province of Asti and partly in Alessandria, but most of the wines come from Alessandria.

- **Loazzolo:** A sweet, still wine from the Moscato variety, Loazzolo (loh-ahtz-*zoh*-lo) is grown in a small part of the Asti province that's possibly Piedmont's smallest DOC zone. The grapes are dried and, in some cases, affected by noble rot; the resulting wine is rich, high in alcohol (15.5 percent), and delicious. Borgo Maragliano and Forteto della Luja are two good producers.

✔ **Gabiano:** A dry, medium-bodied red from the Barbera, Freisa, and Grignolino varieties, this wine (pronounced gah-bee-*ah*-no) is grown in a small part of northern Alessandria province with distinct, clayey soils.

✔ **Rubino di Cantavenna:** A dry red wine made mainly from Barbera, with Grignolino or Freisa, this wine (pronounced roo-*bee*-no dee cahn-tah-*vain*-nah) is from the first hills of Alessandria rising above the Po Valley — roughly the same area as Gabiano.

✔ **Colli Tortonesi:** The Tortona Hills are in the very east of southern Piedmont, north of Gavi and bordering Lombardy. The Colli Tortonesi (*coh*-lee tor-toh-*nae*-see) DOC covers a Dolcetto and a Barbera, each at least 85 percent from that variety, and a Cortese deriving entirely from that variety; it also covers a Bianco, Rosso, and Chiaretto (rosé) made from locally grown grapes.

# Getting to Know Northern Piedmont's Various Offerings

Northern Piedmont is the only other area in the world, besides the Langhe region in southern Piedmont and the Valtellina region in northern Lombardy, where the Nebbiolo grape variety makes good red wines. The Nebbiolo wines of northern Piedmont — such as Carema, Gattinara, and Ghemme — resemble Barolo and Barbaresco mainly in their aromas; however, their structures are quite different. The cooler temperatures and higher altitudes (in the case of Carema) of northern Piedmont make for lighter-bodied, less tannic, and often more acidic Nebbiolo wines than the Barolo and Barbaresco wines of the Langhe region.

One advantage that these less tannic northern Nebbiolo wines have is that they're ready to drink sooner. And in most cases, the Nebbiolo wines of northern Piedmont are about half the price.

The next sections get you up to speed on the wine zones of northern Piedmont.

## Carema and Caluso

The Carema DOC zone is in northwestern Piedmont, around the village of Carema; it's the last Piedmontese village before the border with the Valle d'Aosta region (refer to Figure 2-1). The stunningly dramatic Carema (cah-*rae*-ma) vineyards perch on the very steep, eastern slopes of the Alps at altitudes of over 1,000 to nearly 2,000 feet.

The thin, acidic soil of Carema, combined with the elevation of the vineyards, yields light- to medium-bodied, elegant wines made entirely from Nebbiolo. The high acidity of Carema helps to guarantee fairly long-lasting wines. Unfortunately, the difficult task of making a living in Carema's vineyards — plus the availability of jobs in the city of Ivrea, about 7 miles south of Carema — has led to a serious decline in Carema's production; fewer than 10,000 cases are made per year. Part of the challenge for producers is that DOC regulations require that Carema be aged for four years before it can be sold — a hardship for small producers in need of ready cash.

Only two producers have Carema available for sale outside the area: Luigi Ferrando and Produttori Nebbiolo di Carema. Fortunately, both of these producers do an excellent job with this increasingly difficult-to-find wine. Look for Luigi Ferrando's black-label Carema Riservas (in New York, at Rosenthal Wine Merchant, phone 212-249-6650); they're especially fine. The Cantina dei Produttori Nebbiolo di Carema is a very fine cooperative whose Carema, especially its best wine, Carema Carema, is usually top-notch. Because Carema can be too lean and acidic in lesser vintages, buy Carema only in good vintages. (Your wine merchant can guide you toward notable vintages.)

Erbaluce di Caluso, or simply Caluso (cah-*loo*-so), is a fairly large vineyard area in the hills of a glacial basin south and east of the city of Ivrea; Caluso is one of the 32 communities within the zone. Erbaluce (ehr-bah-*loo*-chae) is a white grape variety used locally for centuries; in the Middle Ages, it made golden or amber dessert wines from semidried grapes, called Caluso Passito. Today, the *passito* style and the fortified sweet wine called Caluso Passito Liquoroso are rarities. As a dry white wine, Erbaluce di Caluso is crisp with pronounced acidity that can be too severe in the hands of a mediocre producer; you can also find a sparkling style. Like Carema, Caluso wines are now difficult to find. Look for the following producers: Vittorio Boratto, Colombaio di Candia, Luigi Ferrando, and Orsolani.

A third DOC zone of this area is Canavese (cah-nah-vae-sae), the largest of the three. It encompasses the Caluso zone and features five types of wine: a Nebbiolo and a Barbera; Canavese Bianco, entirely Erbaluce; Canavese Rosso (in normal or *novello* styles), made at least 60 percent from Nebbiolo, Barbera, Bonarda, Freisa, and Neretto, singly or together; and a Rosato, from the same grapes.

**Book III**

**Italy: Small but Mighty**

# Vercelli and Novara hills wines

The Vercelli and Novara provinces occupy the whole northernmost part of Piedmont (refer to Figure 2-1). Their alpine hillsides sit in a favorable microclimate right between the Po River basin to the south and the Alps and Lake Maggiore to the north. The Sesia River flows south from the Alps, separating the two provinces. Three red-only wine zones, including Gattinara, are in Vercelli, to the west; four red wine zones, including Ghemme, are in Novara, the eastern province. (All seven zones are east of Carema, at about the same latitude, but considerably lower in altitude, as Carema is in the Alps, not just the foothills.) Two other DOC zones for red and white wine have also been designated, one in each province, bringing the total number of wine zones in this area to nine.

The seven totally red wine zones all feature Nebbiolo — called "Spanna" in these two northern provinces; you sometimes see Spanna as part of the name of wines from these parts. Gattinara is clearly the standout wine of the area, followed by Ghemme. None of these seven wine zones could be called dynamic, however. Only about 80,000 cases of wine are produced annually from the seven zones, about half of which is Gattinara.

Nevertheless, a well-made Gattinara, Ghemme, or any other of the Nebbiolo-based DOC wines from northern Piedmont is a more accessible wine than Barolo or Barbaresco, at about half the price. (For the best wines, choose one from the recommended producers listed later in this section.) The fact that these wines are lighter in body and color than Barolo or Barbaresco doesn't mean they're short-lived; their tannin and pronounced acidity allow these wines — particularly Gattinara and Ghemme — to continue developing and maturing for 20 years or more, especially in good vintages.

## Gattinara

Gattinara (gah-tee-*nah*-rah), a DOCG wine, is the most renowned wine of northern Piedmont. Its vineyard area is the hillside north of the community of Gattinara. The wine must be at least 86 percent Nebbiolo, with Bonarda and Vespolina permitted, and it must age for at least three years, or four years for *riservas*. Like other Nebbiolo wines, Gattinara's color turns garnet with age, and the wine develops a penetrating bouquet of violets and tar, characteristic of the finest Piedmontese Nebbiolos. Antoniolo, Nervi, and Travaglini are three leading producers of Gattinara; all of these producers' Gattinaras are widely distributed in the United States.

## Ghemme

Ghemme (*gae*-mae), from a vineyard area across the Sesia River from Gattinara, around the town of Ghemme, is often mentioned in the same breath as Gattinara and is also a DOCG wine. It's quite similar to Gattinara and just as long-lasting — if not even longer-lasting — but Ghemme is generally less fine than Gattinara, perhaps because less Nebbiolo is required in its blend. Ghemme must be 65 to 85 percent Nebbiolo, with 10 to 30 percent of the local Vespolina, and up to 15 percent Bonarda Novarese. The minimum aging requirement for Ghemme is four years. Antichi Vigneti di Cantalupo is the leading Ghemme producer.

## Other wines of the Novara-Vercelli hills

The following seven DOC wines also come from the hills of the Vercelli and Novara provinces:

- **Lessona:** The Lessona (lehs-*soh*-nah) DOC zone is in the hillsides around the community of Lessona, west of Gattinara. Like all Nebbiolo-based wines, the austere Lessona needs time to develop its violet aromas, but it's generally ready to drink before Gattinara or Ghemme. Nebbiolo constitutes at least 75 percent of Lessona, and Vespolina and Bonarda are optional. One producer, Sella, dominates the zone; Sella makes two single-vineyard Lessona wines as well as a standard Lessona.

- **Bramaterra:** The Bramaterra (bra-ma-*ter*-rah) zone encompasses seven communities between Gattinara and Lessona; Bramaterra is the name of the area. The wine is 50 to 70 percent Nebbiolo and 20 to 30 percent Croatina, with up to 20 percent Bonarda and/or Vespolina. Bramaterra is drinkable sooner than either Gattinara or Lessona. Its two leading producers are Sella and Luigi Perazzi.

- **Boca:** The Boca (*boh*-cah) area is the northernmost of the seven Nebbiolo zones. Boca is 45 to 70 percent Nebbiolo and 20 to 40 percent Vespolina, with up to 20 percent Bonarda; minimum aging is three years. Antonio Vallana, known for his Spanna (Nebbiolo) wines, is a leading producer of Boca.

- **Sizzano:** The Sizzano (sitz-*zah*-no) zone is south of the town of Ghemme. The wine derives 40 to 60 percent from Nebbiolo and 15 to 40 percent from Vespolina, with up to 25 percent Bonarda. Having less Nebbiolo in the blend, Sizzano is lighter-bodied and drinkable sooner than Ghemme, Gattinara, and Lessona. Giuseppe Bianchi is the leading producer.

- **Fara:** The southernmost DOC area of the seven Nebbiolo zones, Fara (*fah*-rah) is also the lightest-bodied of the seven wines. It contains only 30 to 50 percent Nebbiolo in its blend, along with 10 to 30 percent Vespolina, with up to 40 percent Bonarda Novarese. The well-known wine house, Dessilani, is the leading producer of Fara, making two Fara wines: Caramino and Lochera.

- **Colline Novaresi:** This large zone, pronounced co-*lee*-nae no-vah-*rae*-see, encompasses 26 communities throughout Novara province. It makes five varietal wines — Spanna (Nebbiolo), Bonarda, Barbera,

Vespolina, and Croatina — as well as a blended dry red called Colline Novaresi Rosso (at least 30 percent Nebbiolo, up to 40 percent Bonarda, and up to 30 percent Vespolina and/or Croatina) and a dry white called Colline Novaresi Bianco, made entirely from Erbaluce. Cantalupo and Dessilani are two fine Colline Novaresi producers. The wines are good values, retailing for as low as $10.

✔ **Coste della Sesia:** The newest DOC in northern Piedmont and similar to Colline Novaresi, Coste della Sesia (*cose*-tae del-lah *sae*-see-ah) is in the Vercelli province, where it covers 18 communities. Four varietal wines may use this DOC name: Spanna (Nebbiolo), Bonarda, Vespolina, and Croatina. Another three wines include Coste della Sesia Rosso (a dry, blended red made at least 50 percent from Nebbiolo, Bonarda, Vespolina, or Croatina, with the optional addition of other red varieties; a *Novello* is also made); Coste della Sesia Rosato (a dry rosé from the same varieties as the Rosso); and Coste della Sesia Bianco (a dry white, made 100 percent from Erbaluce). Two producers are Antoniolo and Nervi.

### Recommended Novara-Vercelli wine producers

Look for the following recommended northern Piedmont producers (note that the producer is listed first, followed by his recommended wines):

Antichi Vigneti di Cantalupo: Ghemme; Colline Novaresi
Antoniolo: Gattinara; Coste della Sesia Nebbiolo
Giuseppe Bianchi: Sizzano; Ghemme
Le Colline: Gattinara (Monsecco); Ghemme
Dessilani: Fara; Gattinara; Ghemme; Colline Novaresi Spanna

Umberto Fiore: Gattinara
Nervi: Gattinara; Coste della Sesia Spanna
Luigi Perazzi: Bramaterra
Sella: Lessona; Bramaterra
Travaglini: Gattinara
Antonio Vallana: Boca; Spanna
Villa Era: Spanna

# Other Piedmont Wines

Three DOC zones of Piedmont are off the beaten track. One is in the province of Cuneo — in the foothills of the Alps, in the west of the region, about an hour's drive from Alba. The other two are also in the Alpine foothills but farther north, mainly in the Torino province. These three zones are

✔ **Colline Saluzzesi:** This area (pronounced co-*lee*-nae sah-lootz-*zae*-see), straddling the Po River in the western part of Cuneo province, is named after the town of Saluzzo, the last sizeable town before the roads climb toward the mountain resorts. This area makes a varietally labeled Pelaverga (a supposed aphrodisiac) that may be dry or sweetish; a

Quagliano, a pale, full-bodied, but sweetish red from a local variety of the same name that can be still or sparkling; and a Colline Saluzzesi Rosso that's at least 60 percent Pelaverga and/or Barbera.

✔ **Pinerolese:** This area (pronounced pee-neh-ro-*lae*-sae) north of the Colline Saluzzesi zone overlaps it somewhat. Its wines are all red, except for a rosé, and they include five varietal wines (Barbera, Bonarda, Freisa, Dolcetto, and Doux d'Henry). In this area, you can also find a Pinerolese Rosso (made at least 50 percent from Barbera, Bonarda, Nebbiolo, and Neretto, singly or together), a Rosato (from the same varieties as the Rosso), and Pineroloese Ramie (a red from a two-village subzone that's blended from 30 percent Avana, at least 20 percent Neretto, and at least 15 percent Averengo, with up to 35 percent of other local grapes permitted).

✔ **Valsusa:** Made a DOC zone in 1997, Valsusa (vahl-*soo*-sah) is known as the Susa Valley and is located in Torino province. It produces only a red wine made at least 60 percent from Barbera, Dolcetto, Neretta, or Avana, together or alone — this wine is a dry, moderately tannic red; also *Novello.*

The final DOC of Piedmont is, literally, Piemonte. From its name, you'd think this appellation covers the entire region, but, in fact, it applies specifically to vineyards in Asti, Alessandria, and Cuneo (which are most of Piedmont's vineyards). It's a multipurpose designation, providing a fallback DOC for producers making Barbera, Grignolino, Brachetto, Cortese, Moscato, or Chardonnay in other parts of these three provinces — if their wines somehow don't precisely fit the DOC requirements for their zone, or if they choose not to use their local DOC for whatever reason. The following types of wines may be Piemonte DOC:

✔ A *spumante* made from Chardonnay, Pinot Bianco, Pinot Grigio, and Pinot Nero, in any combination or singly; and varietally labeled Spumante wines from any of these grapes other than Chardonnay

✔ Five varietal wines: Cortese, Chardonnay, Barbera, Bonarda, and Grignolino

✔ A varietally labeled Brachetto from a limited subzone, and from the same area, a still or *frizzante* Moscato or a Moscato *passito,* from dried grapes

**Book III**

**Italy: Small but Mighty**

# Chapter 3

# Finding Sparkling Wines and More in North-Central Italy

Lombardy, a large, scenic region in north-central Italy, is more famous as the home of Milan — the fashion capital of the world and the business-industrial center of Italy — than as a wine-producing region. It's also renowned as a tourist mecca, thanks to the fabulously beautiful Lake Como and Lake Garda, plus the majestic Alps that cover Lombardy's northern third. But Lombardy is also the home of most of Italy's best sparkling wines and interesting reds made from Piedmont's famed Nebbiolo variety.

Emilia-Romagna is really two regions joined at the hip. The Emilia sub-region is often called the gastronomic capital of Italy; it's the home of Bologna, Modena (renowned for balsamic vinegar, among other delicacies), Parma, and the Reggiano district (is there a better cheese than Parmegiano Reggiano?). But, enough about food! Emilia is also the home of one of Italy's most famous wines: Lambrusco.

## *Lombardy Has It All*

In many ways, Lombardy is the most fortunate region in Italy — and a pretty darn good place to live. It has everything going for it. The mighty Po River, Italy's largest, which forms most of the region's southern border, has created a vast fertile plain for cultivating rice and wheat. Lombardy's beautiful lakes spread across the center of the region and are crowned by the Alps in the north. Thriving cities such as Milan, Bergamo, and Brescia provide a high quality of life for their residents, including great wine and food.

Lombardy is directly south of Switzerland, east of Piedmont, north of Emilia-Romagna, and west of Veneto and Trentino-Alto Adige. It's the fourth-largest region in Italy and the most highly populated. It's also the wealthiest.

Because of the incredibly varied climate and terrain of the region, Lombardy produces diverse wines. But *cool* is the operative climatic descriptor for all of Lombardy's wine areas. The region's far northern wine zone is the Valtellina — which makes one of Lombardy's two DOCG wines. Here, the Nebbiolo grape has found a second home. The wines certainly don't resemble the more muscular Nebbiolo wines — Barolo and Barbaresco — of warmer, southern Piedmont (see Chapter 2 in Book III for more on these wines), but they're interesting, nevertheless, and a lot less expensive than their famous Piedmont cousins.

The most renowned wines of Lombardy are its sparkling wines. In fact, two distinct sparkling wine zones exist: Oltrepó Pavese, in the region's south-west corner, and Franciacorta (the region's other DOCG wine), in the hills west of Brescia, around breezy Lake Iseo (in central Lombardy; see Figure 3-1). Most of Italy's best sparklers are made in Franciacorta. Several wine zones are scattered throughout the rest of Lombardy, producing light- to medium-bodied red, rosé, and white wines, many of which are consumed on the Riviera del Garda. The most famous Lake Garda wine is a white wine called Lugana.

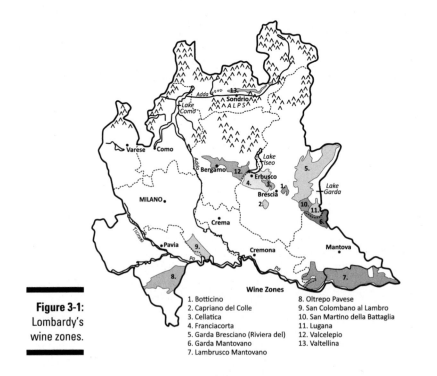

**Figure 3-1:**
Lombardy's
wine zones.

**Wine Zones**

1. Botticino
2. Capriano del Colle
3. Cellatica
4. Franciacorta
5. Garda Bresciano (Riviera del)
6. Garda Mantovano
7. Lambrusco Mantovano
8. Oltrepo Pavese
9. San Colombano al Lambro
10. San Martino della Battaglia
11. Lugana
12. Valcelepio
13. Valtellina

# The Valtellina: Nebbiolo's most austere face

In the northernmost part of Lombardy, just east of Lake Como, the Adda River and its valley cut through the steep slopes of the Alps, from west to east. This isolated alpine terrain is one of the unlikeliest places in the world to find vineyards — yet here they are.

Along a dramatic 30-mile stretch called the Valtellina (vahl-tel-*lee*-nah), Nebbiolo grapevines flourish in south-facing vineyards on the sunny banks of the Adda River. The steep Alps on both sides protect the valley from harsh, cold weather and also trap heat; the stony soil retains this heat at night. These conditions provide the long growing season that Nebbiolo (locally called Chiavennasca, pronounced key-ah-ven-*nahs*-cah) needs to ripen properly. In fact, the Valtellina is the only major production zone of Nebbiolo outside of Piedmont.

The steep vineyards must be tended by hand, a laborious and costly procedure, which is one reason why wine production in the Valtellina has declined over the past few decades to only about a half-million cases annually.

Several types of Valtellina wine exist, differentiated primarily according to where the grapes grow. Simpler wines, labeled with the Valtellina DOC, come from grapes (mainly Nebbiolo) grown anywhere in the Valtellina district. Wines with the better Valtellina Superiore DOCG designation (about one-third of Valtellina's wines) come from riper grapes grown in a smaller area that includes four specific subzones. Valtellina Superiore wines must age a minimum of two years, and those that are aged four years are called Valtellina Superiore Riserva. Almost all Valtellina wines are light- to medium-bodied reds.

**Book III**

**Italy: Small but Mighty**

### Taking a look at the Valtellina Superiore subdistricts

The four Valtellina Superiore subzones, from west to east, are Sassella, Grumello, Inferno, and Valgella. Wines made from grapes grown in one of these four areas carry the name of the area on their labels.

Of these four wines, Sassella is generally the finest and the longest lasting (although Valtellina wines — with one exception noted later — usually don't age well beyond seven or eight years), followed by Grumello and then Inferno, with Valgella definitely the lightest wine of the four. The Valgella subzone is the largest of the four; it produces the most wine, although it's generally not *riserva*-grade. The Inferno area is quite rocky, and it's the warmest area in the Adda Valley — hence its name!

### Checking out sturdy Sfursat

Valtellina has a stronger brother in Sfursat (s'foor-sat), also known as Sforzato. Sfursat is made with semidried, extra-ripe grapes. The resulting wine is high in alcohol (14.5 percent minimum), sturdy, full-bodied, and concentrated. Sfursat can easily last up to 20 years or more and is great with cheeses (such as Parmesan or Asiago), beef dishes, and stews. Sfursat needs about four hours of aeration in a decanter to soften (see Chapter 4 in Book I for more on decanting and aerating wine).

### Enjoying Valtellina wines

With the exception of Sfursat, Valtellina wines are light red in color (typical of Nebbiolo), and they turn garnet with about six years of aging. They have pronounced Nebbiolo aromas (tar, violets, and strawberries) and are very dry, even austere, with high acidity and tannin. Unlike Piedmont's major Nebbiolo wines (Barolo and Barbaresco; see Chapter 2 in Book III for more on these wines), Valtellina wines are delicate and elegant and are best in their youth. They go well with pasta dishes, risotto, and light meat dishes, such as chicken.

Wine drinkers in the United States see only two Valtellina producers on a consistent basis: Nino Negri, whose wines retail for $15 to $18 a bottle (excellent Sfursats for $30 to $40), and Rainoldi, whose wines are in the $8 to $15 range.

## Oltrepó Pavese: Sparkling wines and more

Pavia is a town and a province in southwestern Lombardy, directly south of Milan. The part of the province south of the Po River is known as Oltrepó Pavese (ohl-trae-*poh* pah-*vae*-sae), meaning "Pavia across the Po" (refer to Figure 3-1). More than half of Lombardy's wine — and two-thirds of its DOC wine — is produced here, where the plains of the Po Valley give way to the foothills of the Apennine Mountains to their south. Oltrepó Pavese (once a part of Piedmont, its neighbor to the west) provides Milan with much of its (mainly red) everyday wines and provides all of Italy with sparkling wines.

### The wines of Oltrepó Pavese

The Oltrepó Pavese area produces white, rosé, red, and sparkling wines. The main type of red is a blended wine called simply Oltrepó Pavese Rosso and made from Barbera, Croatina, and Uva Rara (a typical local trio), along with Vespolina and Pinot Nero grapes. Aged two years, this blended wine becomes *riserva.* The same varieties make a rosé as well as two reds from specific zones within the district; these reds are Buttafuoco (boo-tah-*fwoh*-coh, meaning "fire-thrower") and Sangue di Guida (*sahn*-gwae dee *jew*-dah, meaning "Judas' blood"). Buttafuoco is dry or lightly sparking *(frizzante),* and Sangue di Guida is usually made in a *frizzante,* slightly sweet style.

Other Oltrepó Pavese reds can also be varietal wines from Barbera, Croatina (locally called Bonarda), or Cabernet Sauvignon. Barbera is Oltrepó's leading red variety and a best-selling wine; it can be *frizzante,* as the Bonarda often is. When made as a *frizzante,* Bonarda — less acidic than Barbera — goes well with sausages and other fatty meats.

Nine varietal Oltrepó Pavese white wines are Welschriesling (labeled as *Riesling Italico*), Riesling (labeled *Riesling Renano*), Cortese, Moscato, Malvasia, Pinot Grigio, Chardonnay, Sauvignon, and Pinot Nero (vinified as a white wine). Most of these wines come in both still and fizzy styles. Moscato has two additional variations: Moscato *liquoroso,* a dry or sweet fortified style, and Moscato *passito,* a sweet style from dried grapes.

The best white or rosé sparkling wines with the Oltrepó Pavese designation carry the words *metodo classico* (classic, or Champagne, method) and derive mainly from Pinot Nero, with up to 30 percent Pinot Bianco, Chardonnay, and/or Pinot Grigio.

Nearby — but on the Milan side of the Po River — a DOC zone called San Colombano (sahn coh-lohm-*bah*-noh), makes only one type of wine, a dry red mainly from Croatina, Barbera, and Uva Rara.

### A few leading Oltrepó Pavese producers

Historically, the Frecciarossa estate (which makes the wine with the red arrow on its label) has been the most famous Oltrepó Pavese wine estate. Other top producers from the area include Lino Maga, La Muiraghina, Tenuta Mazzolino, and Doria for still wines; Fontanachiara for sparkling wine; and Anteo and Monsupello for both sparkling and still wines.

## Franciacorta: Sparklers with style

Just northwest of the city of Brescia lies the greatest sparkling wine zone in Italy (and one of the best anywhere outside of Champagne, France). This region is called Franciacorta (frahn-cha-*cor*-tah), and it's the home of the two most prestigious sparkling wine houses in Italy: Ca'del Bosco and Bellavista. Chardonnay and Pinot Bianco are the main grapes of Franciacorta sparklers, with a maximum of 15 percent Pinot Nero. A rosé style, however, requires a minimum of 15 percent Pinot Nero in its blend. A *crémant* style (a gentler wine with lower carbon dioxide pressure) may contain no Pinot Nero and is a specialty of Franciacorta; the wines in this style carry the trademarked name Satèn. Some of the district's very best sparklers, such as Ca'del Bosco's Satèn, are made in this style.

### Seeing Franciacorta then and now

Conditions are ideal for grape-growing in the Franciacorta zone thanks to the area's stony, well-drained soil and nearby Lake Iseo, which has a moderating effect on the climate. Local growers have produced red and white still wines for centuries. But Franciacorta has emerged as a major wine zone only in the past 50 years — since a young enologist named Franco Ziliani convinced the Berlucchi estate to plant Pinot Nero and make *méthode champenoise* sparkling wines (sparkling wines made via the traditional method of conducting the second fermentation in the individual bottles).

Now the producers of Franciacorta are firmly committed to sparkling wine. In 1995, when Franciacorta was elevated to DOCG status, the producers of Franciacorta spun off their still wine production into a separate DOC appellation called Terre di Franciacorta. These white wines are made from the same varieties as the sparkling wine — Chardonnay, Pinot Blanc, and Pinot Noir — together or singly, but they aren't varietally labeled. A creative formula for Terre di Franciacorta Rosso allows plenty of stylistic freedom to individual producers: a minimum of 25 percent Cabernet Franc and Cabernet Sauvignon, with a minimum of 10 percent each of Barbera, Nebbiolo, and Merlot.

### Exploring some other Franciacorta estates

Although many of Italy's sparkling wines are made by very large companies from purchased grapes or wine, small private estates (that make wine from their own grapes) are the standard in Franciacorta. Your best bets for high-quality sparkling wines are the following:

- **Bellavista:** This beautiful estate, which is now also home to the Michelin three-star Gualtiero Marchesi Restaurant and inn, is clearly one of the area's two quality leaders (along with Ca'del Bosco), and its prices reflect that status. Its least-expensive sparkler, the Cuvée Brut NV, is a relative bargain at about $27 retail; the Vintage Grand Cuvée goes for $40; and the excellent, top-of-the-line Riserva Vittorio Moretti will cost you $90. Bellavista also makes a fine Chardonnay, a Cabernet Sauvignon-Merlot blend called Solesine, and a Pinot Nero called Casotte — all in the $40 to $45 price range.

- **Ca'del Bosco:** Mauizio Zanella, who founded this estate about 40 years ago, is Lombardy's most respected wine producer. His winery is state of the art, and all of his wines, both still and sparkling, are superb. The basic Brut NV goes for $40; the Vintage Brut Zero is in the $52 to $55 range; the classic Vintage Satèn is $60; and the premium Cuvée Annamaria Clementi Vintage Brut is $65 to $70. Ca'del Bosco's Chardonnays and its Bordeaux-style red, Maurizio Zanella, are first-rate.

- **Cavalleri:** Giovanni Cavalleri makes very good sparkling *bruts* as well as some of the best Chardonnays in the district. His Brut NV retails for $27 to $30, his Satèn is $32 to $35, and his Vintage Brut and Rosé are about $40.

- ✔ **Cornaleto:** A small but very good producer, this estate produces not only a high-quality Franciacorta but also a fine Rosso made primarily from Cabernet Franc.

- ✔ **Enrico Gatti:** Another small winery, this estate produces an impressive Franciacorta, a still Bianco (mainly Chardonnay), and a fine Rosso.

- ✔ **Monte Rossa:** This estate is the leader in the Corte Franca area, east of Erbusco and closer to Brescia. The soils here are more fertile than in the Erbusco area; thus Monte Rossa's *bruts* are rather full-bodied. The Satèn is a standout.

- ✔ **Ricci Curbastro:** This small, quality estate produces a fine Satèn Brut that retails for $45 to $50; its Rosso Vigna Santella is $30.

- ✔ **Uberti:** This small family winery makes fine sparkling *bruts* and white wines, along with a good Cabernet called Rosso dei Frati Priori.

## Lake Garda: Fresh lake wines

Lake Garda is a great tourist attraction from spring through fall. The charming village of Sirmione and the famous wine village of Bardolino are located on the eastern, or Veneto, side of the lake. On the western shores, you find three Lombardy wine districts.

### Riviera del Garda Bresciano

Along the western shores of the lake lies the Riviera del Garda Bresciano zone. This area makes delicious wines to quaff while sitting around Lake Garda — or any surrogate lake — in the summer. A standout summer wine is Chiaretto (kee-ah-*reht*-toh), a term that applies to several dry, Italian, deep-colored rosé wines. In this area, Chiaretto is made mainly from the local Gropello grape, with Sangiovese, Barbera, and Marzemino (another local grape), and sometimes other varieties. This rosé is fresh, completely dry, and low in alcohol, with a slight bitterness in the finish. Chiaretto is best when it's young and cool.

The Rosso from Riviera del Garda Bresciano is very similar to the Chiaretto, the difference being that the Rosso is darker and fuller-bodied. The Gropello is a straight varietal wine, full-bodied, rich, and tannic. The local Bianco derives from Riesling or Welschriesling, together or singly.

Three Riviera del Garda producers to look for are Cascina La Pertica, Comincioli, and Costaripa. As you can imagine, the best places to find these wines are hotels and restaurants around Lake Garda — which makes for a good excuse to visit this lovely area!

### Lugana

Lugana is a white wine area along the southern shores of Lake Garda, a small part of which extends eastward into the Veneto region. Lugana is made from a particular subvariety of Trebbiano called Trebbiano di Lugana. It's a dry, medium-bodied wine with good fruitiness and somewhat rich texture that can actually age for a few years — unlike other Trebbiano-based wines. It's perfect with lake fish.

The two finest producers are Visconti and the Ca'dei Frati estate. Ca'dei Frati's Lugana retails for $14 to $15, and its single-vineyard Lugana Brolettino is about $17 to $18 — a great value.

### Other Garda DOCs

San Martino della Battaglia (sahn mar-*tee*-no del-lah baht-*tah*-l'yah) is a white wine made mainly in Lombardy, but like Lugana, its territory encroaches into Veneto. It derives from the Friulano grape variety — unusual for Lombardy — and is a dry wine of decent quality; a *liquoroso* style also exists.

Colli Morenici Mantovani del Garda (*coh*-lee more-ae-*nee*-chee mahn-toh-*vah*-nee del *gar*-dah), also called Garda Colli Mantovani, is a Bianco blended from Trebbiano and Garganega, a Rosso, a Rosato made from Molinara (a variety from nearby Veneto), and a Merlot.

# Emilia-Romagna: One Region, Two Identities

Italians who live in the Emilia-Romagna region tell you they're from Emilia or Romagna — never both. Emilia, the larger, western part of the region, identifies with northern Italy and Milan. Romagna, the southeastern third, looks toward Tuscany and central Italy; it even shares two of Tuscany's main grape varieties, Sangiovese and Trebbiano. In Emilia, Lambrusco is the reigning king. Even with these differences, Emilia and Romagna *do* have some things in common:

- The Apennine Mountains (the spine of Italy, which starts in southern Piedmont and Liguria in the northwest and ends in southern Italy) occupy much of the region's southern flank.

- The plains of the Po Valley account for half the region's area.

- Cooperatives, such as Emilia's gigantic Riunite, dominate both halves of the region, accounting for 70 percent of Emilia-Romagna's wine production and contributing to the region's rank as Italy's fourth-largest wine producer.

The plain between Piacenza in the northwest corner of Emilia and Bologna in the east is known as the Val Padana. This area grows more than two-thirds of Emilia's wines — much of which is Lambrusco, a bubbly dry or sweet red from the Lambrusco grape variety. In the Apennine foothills south of Piacenza, Parma, and Bologna are some vineyard areas, such as Colli Piacentini, Colli di Parma, and Colli Bolognesi, where you can find some more serious wines (see Figure 3-2).

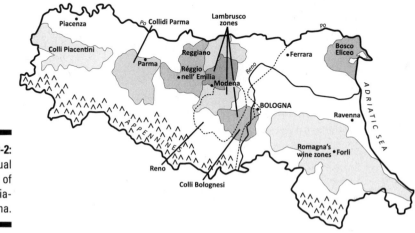

**Figure 3-2:**
The dual region of Emilia-Romagna.

**Book III**

**Italy: Small but Mighty**

## *Emilia's beloved Lambrusco wines*

During the 1970s and early 1980s, Lambrusco (lam-*brews*-coh) was the biggest-selling imported wine in the United States — from any country. Almost all of it was semisweet and slightly sparkling. As wine drinkers turned to dryer wines at the end of the 20th century, Lambrusco sales decreased. But Emilians love their Lambrusco. The wine's bubbles and the high acidity of the dry style help cut through the rich local cuisine, built around salami, sausage, pasta, prosciutto, cheese, cream, and butter.

Quite a lot of Lambrusco is DOC level, from four zones in the provinces of Reggio Emilia and Modena. The names of three of these zones are also, confusingly, the names of clones of the Lambrusco grape variety. These four types of Lambrusco are

✔ **Lambrusco Reggiano:** Lambrusco Reggiano (rej-gee-*ah*-noh) is the largest zone for production and exports. Most of the Lambrusco grapes from the plains around the town of Reggio nell'Emilia are turned into light-bodied, *frizzante,* and semisweet wines. This area is the seat of the huge cooperative Cantine Riunite, whose wines have been extremely successful in the United States. In higher vineyards toward the south of the province, small producers, such as Venturini & Baldini, Medici, and Moro, make fuller-bodied, dry, deep-colored Lambrusco.

✔ **Lambrusco di Sorbara:** The most highly regarded Lambrusco subvariety, or *clone,* Lambrusco di Sorbara (dee sor-*bah*-rah) grows in the plains north of Modena, around the village of Sorbara. The wine ranges from ruby to purple in color and has fragrant, grapey aromas and flavors reminiscent of violets; like all Lambruscos, it can be dry or semisweet. Fine producers, such as Cavacchioli (with its Vigna del Cristo) and Francesco Bellei make fresh, fruity, flamboyant Lambruscos — dry (for domestic sales) and semisweet (mainly for the export market).

✔ **Lambrusco Salamino di Santa Croce:** This wine (pronounced sah-lah-*mee*-noh dee *sahn*-tah *croh*-chae) comes from vineyards around the village of Santa Croce, which is about 7 miles west of Sorbara. Wines with this name contain at least 90 percent of the Salamino clone, which is similar to the Sorbara subvariety but usually makes wines that are a bit lighter in color and body. The *frizzante* wines are dry or semisweet.

✔ **Lambrusco Grasparossa di Castelvetro:** The smallest of the four Lambrusco DOC zones, this zone (pronounced grahs-pah-*rohs*-sah di cas-tel-*vae*-troh) is located 10 miles south of Modena, in the foothills of the Apennines, near the village of Castelvetro. Here, small producers, such as Vittorio Graziano, Villa Barbieri, and Enzo Manicardi, make serious Lambrusco — deep purple-red, dry, and full-bodied. You might have to visit Modena or Bologna to find a bottle, though. Wines are at least 85 percent from the Grasparossa clone. They also come in semi-sweet styles.

Most of the Lambrusco shipped to the United States carries the designation IGT Emilia. The wines with this designation, bearing brand names such as Riunite and Giacobazzi, sell for $5 per 750-milliliter bottle. Dry Lambruscos, many of which are DOC, and some of which are *spumante,* are difficult to find outside of Emilia. Another DOC wine from the Emilian plains is Montuni del Reno, a dry or semisweet white, still or fizzy, from the local Montù grape variety.

## The hillside wines of Emilia

Four DOC zones in the Apennine foothills of Emilia grow numerous grape varieties, but most wines here are made in the style Emilians seem to prefer: *frizzante* and *amabile* (semisweet). Perhaps nowhere else in the world can you find a sweet, sparkling Cabernet Sauvignon or Merlot!

## Colli Piacentini

Like Oltrepó Pavese to its west, Colli Piacentini (*coh*-lee pee-ah-chen-*tee*-nee) was once a part of Piedmont. All of its vineyards are in the hills south of Piacenza; in fact, the zone's name translates as "Hills of Piacenza." Most of the wines that head to Bologna or Milan, whether white or red, are slightly bubbly and slightly sweet. But some estates now make dry, still wines for export.

Colli Piacentini is the most renowned wine district in Emilia — a fact that's no great wonder because it's a vast district making 17 different wines. These wines include varietally labeled reds (Barbera, Croatina — called Bonarda here — Cabernet Sauvignon, and Pinot Nero) and varietal whites (Chardonnay, Malvasia, Ortrugo, Pinot Grigio, and Sauvignon), all at least 85 percent from the named grape, except Ortrugo (which is at 90 percent). The white or rosé Colli Piacentini Pinot Spumante is mainly Pinot Nero, with Chardonnay. Two different Vin Santo wines (from dried grapes) also exist. A *novello* wraps up the repertoire; it's a still or spritzy young red mainly from Pinot Nero, Barbera, or Croatina, singly or together.

Four more Colli Piacentini wines come from subzones within the district and carry the name of the zone where the grapes grow:

- **Gutturnio:** This red wine (pronounced goot-*tour*-nee-oh) is made 55 to 70 percent from Barbera, with the rest from Croatina; it comes in dry and semidry styles, *frizzante* or still. *Riserva* is an aged, still type.

- **Trebbianino Val Trebbia:** A dry or semidry white made from the local Ortrugo, the aromatic Malvasia di Candia, Moscato Bianco, Trebbiano Romagnolo, Sauvignon, and others, Trebbianino Val Trebbia (treb-bee-ah-*nee*-no vahl *treb*-bee-ah) can be *frizzante* or *spumante.*

- **Valnure:** This white wine (pronounced vahl-*noo*-rae) is similar in composition to Trebbianino, except with more Malvasia and no Moscato.

- **Monterosso Val d'Arta:** Similar to Trebbianino, Monterosso Val d'Arta (mohn-tae-*rohs*-so vahl *dar*-tah) has less emphasis on Ortrugo and requires more Sauvignon in its blend.

Four wine estates in Colli Piacentini are noteworthy. At La Stoppa, charming owner Elena Pantaleoni has a fine, elegant, dry Cabernet Sauvignon called Stoppa, a good Pinot Nero called Alfeo, a Barbera-Croatina blend called Macchiona (all about $23 to $25 per bottle) and a Barbera (about $30). La Tosa makes a very good Gutturnio called Vignamorello ($28 to $30), a great Cabernet Sauvignon called Luna Selvatica ($37 to $39), and a fine Sauvignon Blanc ($20 to $22). The experimental estate of Vigevani makes not only standard DOC reds and whites but also many non-DOC wines and dry sparkling wines. Finally, Fugazza boasts an excellent Gutturnio.

### Colli di Parma

The Colli di Parma (*cohl*-lee dee *par*-mah) DOC zone occupies hillsides south of Parma. With their world-renowned *prosciutto* ham, Parma locals prefer Malvasia, their elegant, fragrant white wine. It's made dry *(secco)* or semisweet *(amabile);* the dry wine can be still, fizzy, or sparkling, although the sweet style is only fizzy or sparkling. The aromatic Malvasia di Candia variety is the backbone of this wine, with up to 15 percent Moscato. Colli di Parma Sauvignon is a dry white made entirely from Sauvignon Blanc, in still, *frizzante,* or sparkling styles. Colli di Parma Rosso is a dry red made mainly from Barbera (60 to 75 percent), with Croatina and/or Bonarda Piemontese; it can be still or *frizzante.*

Three notable estates in the Colli di Parma zone are

- ✔ **Calzetti:** Makes two fine *frizzante* wines, a Malvasia named Conventino and a Sauvignon, as well as a fine Colli di Parma Rosso
- ✔ **Lamoretti:** Makes an excellent Malvasia, fine Rosso, and Sauvignon
- ✔ **Monte del Vigne:** Produces a good Rosso and an interesting non-DOC, oak-aged red called Nabucco made from Barbera and Merlot

### Colli Bolognesi

The Colli Bolognesi (*cohl*-lee boh-lon-*yay*-see) district lies southwest of Bologna. Producers in this area may make nearly 50 different wines — varying according to grape variety and vineyard location — all under the umbrella of the Colli Bolognesi name. The majority of these wines are varietally labeled whites and reds from the following grapes: Barbera, Cabernet Sauvignon, Merlot, Sauvignon, Pinot Bianco, Welschriesling, Pignoletto (a fragrant local white variety making dry, semidry, *frizzante,* or sparkling wines), and Chardonnay (still or sparkling). These wines derive 85 to 100 percent from the named variety, depending on which part of the district appears on the label. Seven subzones may use this area's name on their labels: Colline di Riosto, Colline Marconiane, Zola Predosa, Monte San Pietro, Colline di Oliveto, Terre di Montebudello, and Serravalle. A blended white wine, Colli Bolognesi Bianco, derives mainly from Albana.

Three leading Colli Bolognesi estates are

- ✔ **Terre Rosse:** Offers Cuvée Enrico Vallania Rosso (Cabernet Sauvignon) and the late-harvest Welschriesling named Elisabetta Vallania
- ✔ **Tenuta Bonzara:** Leads Emilia — as well as all of Italy — in Cabernet and Merlot quality and offers a rich Cabernet Sauvignon Bonzarone ($28 to $30), a good-value Merlot Rosso del Poggio ($14 to $15), and a premium Merlot Rocca di Bonacciara ($28 to $30)
- ✔ **Vallona:** Offers great Cabernet Sauvignons and Chardonnays, as well as a fine Pignoletto

## The wines of Romagna

All of Romagna's better wines come from its southern part, southeast of Bologna, in the hillsides it shares with Tuscany, its neighbor to the south. Romagna also shares Tuscany's (and Italy's) most-planted red grape variety, Sangiovese, although Romagna has its own clone.

One of Romagna's rather obscure DOC wines, Albana, became the first DOCG white wine in Italy in 1987. Albana di Romagna (ahl-*bah*-nah dee roh-*mah*-nyah) comes in dry, semidry, sweet, and *passito* (sweet, from dried grapes) styles, all produced from the thick-skinned Albana variety. The best style is slightly sweet, with soft aromas and flavors sometimes suggestive of peaches; it must be consumed when it's young. Albana also makes a DOC sparkling wine called Romagna Albana Spumante.

Romagna has the following eight other DOC wines:

- ✔ **Sangiovese di Romagna:** This dry red is made from the Romagna clone of Sangiovese (san-joe-*vay*-say). Although this clone isn't as highly regarded as Tuscany's, in the hands of a few of Romagna's best producers, its wines can rival Tuscany's.

- ✔ **Trebbiano di Romagna:** Romagna's everyday dry white (also *frizzante* or sparkling) is made from the Romagnolo clone of Trebbiano (trehb-bee-*ah*-noh).

- ✔ **Cagnina di Romagna:** A somewhat tannic, purple, full-bodied red mainly from Refosco grapes, Cagnina (cah-*n'yee*-nah) di Romagna is made in the Forli province and around Ravenna, near the Adriatic Sea.

- ✔ **Pagadebit di Romagna:** One of Italy's colorful wine names, Pagadebit (pah-gah-*day*-beet) means "pays the bills." Its name is an allusion to cash-poor growers who used this once easy-to-sell wine to stay out of debt. It's a dry or semidry white wine from the Bombino Bianco variety, native to Puglia.

- ✔ **Bosco Eliceo:** A blended, light-bodied white made from Trebbiano Romagnolo, Sauvignon, and Malvasia, Bosco Eliceo (*bos*-co eh-lee-*chae*-oh) is also a varietal Sauvignon, Merlot, and Fortana (a local red variety, tannic but grapey). The two whites can be dry or semidry, still or *frizzante*.

- ✔ **Colli di Rimini:** This wine (pronounced *coh*-lee dee *ree*-mee-nee) can be a blended, dry white (mainly Trebbiano Romagnolo); a blended red (mainly Sangiovese); a Cabernet Sauvignon; a Biancame (a local white); and a Rébola, a white made mainly from Pignoletto, which can be dry, semisweet, sweet, or *passito*.

- **Colli di Imola:** This recognized DOC area (pronounced *coh*-lee dee *ee*-mo-la) encompasses hillsides around the town of Imola.

- **Colli di Faenza:** The Colli di Faenza (*coh*-lee dee fa-*en*-za) DOC area encompasses the hillsides around the town of Faenza.

Romagna's leading wine producers are as follows:

- **Castelluccio:** Produces a very good Sangiovese di Romagna

- **Umberto Cesari:** Huge winery producing cleanly made, widely available wines, including Albana and Sangiovese (which retail for $7 to $8) and Laurento Chardonnay (which retails for about $15)

- **Fattoria Paradiso:** Produces a fine single-vineyard Sangiovese di Romagna Vigna delle Lepri and a Barbarossa, both about $25

- **Fattoria Zerbina:** Makes two noteworthy wines — the Marzieno Ravenna Rosso (Sangiovese-Cabernet Sauvignon blend) and the Albana di Romagna Passito called Scacco Matto (a honeyed, almond beauty that might be *the* best Albana)

- **Stefano Ferrucci:** Produces fine Sangiovese di Romagna and Albana di Romagna

- **Tenuta La Palazza:** Makes two fine reds, a Cabernet Sauvignon (Magnificat) and Sangiovese di Romagna, plus a top Chardonnay

- **Tre Monti:** Produces good wines at reasonable prices, including a Colli d'Imola Cabernet Sauvignon Turico, which retails for about $16, and a Colli d'Imola Boldo, which is a Sangiovese-Cabernet blend that retails for about $18 to $20

# Chapter 4

# Northeastern Italy: Where Whites Rule

*I*n the strange — er, different — country of Italy, northeastern Italy is the most different part of all. In one region, Alto Adige, you hear and see more German than Italian. In another region, the eastern part of Friuli-Venezia Giulia, Italian competes with Serbo-Croatian and German as the native language.

Another way in which northeastern Italy is different than the rest of the country is in wine: In all the rest of Italy, red wine dominates, but the cool Northeast, with its Austrian and Slovenian influences, is the most important part of Italy for white wine. Northeastern Italy is also particularly scenic, thanks to the splendor of the Dolomite Alps, for example, and the incomparable canals of Venice. This chapter covers three regions: Trentino-Alto Adige, Veneto, and Friuli-Venezia Giulia.

## Trentino-Alto Adige: One Region, Two Cultures

The strikingly beautiful dual region of Trentino-Alto Adige, Italy's northern-most area, is entirely located in the branch of the eastern Alps known as the Dolomites. Austria forms its northern border, Friuli-Venezia Guilia the east, Veneto the south, and Lombardy the west; a small northwestern part borders Switzerland. Trentino, named after the regional capital, Trento, is the south-ern part of the region; the northern part is Alto Adige. Figure 4-1 depicts this dual region.

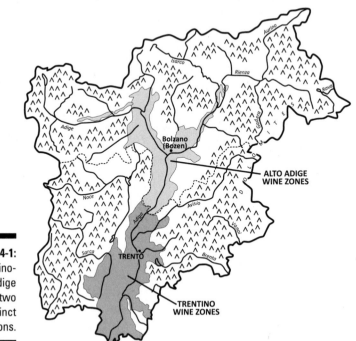

**Figure 4-1:**
Trentino-
Alto Adige
is really two
distinct
subregions.

The Adige River, Italy's second largest, descends from an alpine lake high in the Dolomites, near the Austrian border, and travels south through the center of Trentino-Alto Adige, creating the Valdadige — the Adige Valley, where most of the region's inhabitants live. This valley is one of the few things that Alto Adige and Trentino have in common. The natives of Alto Adige and Trentino have two distinct cultures, as well as two distinct wine zones.

Alto Adige, also known as the South Tyrol, encompasses the Bolzano province of the Trentino-Alto Adige region. It was part of Austria until World War I; in 1919, Austria ceded the South Tyrol (in German, *Südtirol* and pronounced *sood-tee-rohl*) to Italy, but most of the German-speaking Austrians stayed in the region. Today, German remains the primary language, with Italian the second language. All street signs are in two languages. The capital city is Bolzano, or Bozen — take your choice of languages.

Alto Adige is quite mountainous. In the northernmost part, the mountains are very steep, but they gradually become somewhat lower and less steep toward the south. Many of the grapevines grow on south- or east-facing slopes on the western hillsides. Only 15 percent of the land is cultivable. The climate is continental, with fairly hot summers and cold winters. (The city of Bolzano, in the valley's basin, is one of Italy's hottest places in July.) The hillsides are very cool at night during the growing season; the day-night temperature contrast heightens the aromas and flavors in Alto Adige wines.

Trentino, in contrast, is typically Italian; the only way you might hear German spoken is by visiting South Tyroleans. The mountains of Alto Adige exist here as well, but much of Trentino's wine comes from grapes grown in fertile, lowland areas. The region also has some fine wine estates with hillside vineyards and one of Italy's best sparkling wine houses — Ferrari.

Despite their widely disparate cultures, Alto Adige and Trentino *do* have some similarities that apply to their wines: Wine cooperatives dominate both subregions (co-ops account for 75 percent of wine production in Trentino and more than 60 percent in Alto Adige); both areas grow native and international grape varieties; and both subregions used to make considerably more red wine than they do now. Today, thanks to the increased popularity of Pinot Grigio and Chardonnay, white wines account for about 40 percent of the region's wine production — and this percentage is growing. Altogether, this region produces the equivalent of 11.7 million cases of wine annually.

Eighty-one percent of Trentino-Alto Adige's wine is DOC — which was the highest percentage in Italy until recently, when Piedmont surpassed it. But the region has the potential to make higher-quality wine than it does now. The crop levels in both subregions — except at the finest estates — are among the highest in Italy (an average of about 5 tons per acre regionwide), which compromises the quality and intensity of the wines. Wineries find selling their wines to hordes of Austrian, German, and Swiss tourists too easy, and the larger cooperatives, especially those in Trentino, have too ready a market for their mass-produced Pinot Grigios and Chardonnays abroad. The region's non-DOC wines have four IGT designations: Vigneti delle Dolomiti, Mitterberg, Mitterberg tra Cauria and Telor, and Vallagarina delle Venezie. (You can find out the details about DOC, non-DOC, and IGT wines in Chapter 1 of Book III.)

The following sections fill you in on the various DOC zones of Trentino-Alto Adige and the wines that come from them.

## *Introducing the wines of Trentino*

For a long time, the only winery in Trentino internationally known for its quality wines was Ferrari, founded in 1902 and one of Italy's finest sparkling wine houses. Growers were content to sell their grapes to the huge cooperatives, such as Cavit in Trento and MezzaCorona in Mezzocorona. As in Veneto to the south, growers planted mainly on the fertile valley floor; in the hands of the co-ops, the large crops from these vineyards made a huge amount of rather ordinary, inexpensive wine.

But a number of wine estates and small wine houses have emerged and are helping to change Trentino's image. Also, a truly superb cooperative, La Vis (in the town of Lavis, north of Trento) is raising the bar for co-ops with its excellent wines. Now Trentino is known not only for mass-produced Chardonnays and Pinot Grigios but also for some fine red wines made from its local variety, Teroldego (pronounced teh-*rohl*-dae-go and very similar to Alto Adige's Lagrein), and from Cabernet Sauvignon and Merlot — as well as some good-quality white wines.

Trentino has six DOC zones. The Trentino (tren-*tee*-noh) DOC is an umbrella appellation that applies to wines made in 72 communities in the Trento province. It covers 24 types of wine: 11 white wines, 10 reds, a rosé, a late-harvest white, and a Vin Santo.

Trentino DOC whites include a blended white (Trentino Bianco, made from 80 percent Chardonnay and/or Pinot Bianco) and ten varietally labeled whites: Chardonnay, Pinot Bianco, Sauvignon, Pinot Grigio, Moscato Giallo, Müller-Thurgau, Riesling, Welschriesling, Gewürztraminer, and Nosiola. The reds include Trentino Rosso (a blend of Cabernet Franc and/or Cabernet Sauvignon with Merlot) and nine varietally labeled wines: Cabernet Franc, Cabernet Sauvignon, Cabernet, Lagrein, Pinot Nero, Merlot, Moscato Rosa, Rebo, and Marzemino.

Many of the best wines of the Trentino province carry the Trentino DOC, and some of Trentino's best producers — Foradori, Pojer & Sandri, Roberto Zeni, Conti Martini, Guerrieri Gonzaga, Gaierhof, La Vis, Maso Poli, Baroni a Prato, and the Instituto Agrario Provinciale — use this appellation for their white varieties and Pinot Nero. Zeni makes an intriguing Pinot Grigio rosé wine called Cru Fontane ($20 to $22), which is excellent with antipasto.

Trentino's five other DOC zones include the following:

- ✔ **Trento:** A geographically large DOC, the Trento DOC applies only to sparkling wines, either white or rosé, from Chardonnay, Pinot Bianco, Pinot Nero, and Pinot Meunier, together or singly.

- ✔ **Teroldego Rotaliano:** Campo Rotaliano, a plain around the town of Mezzolombardo, surrounded by the Dolomites, is the home of Teroldego Rotaliano (teh-*rohl*-dae-go roh-tah-lee-*ah*-noh) wine; Teroldego, Trentino's best red variety, is the grape. At its best, sturdy Teroldego makes dark, robust, spicy, tannic red wines, most of which need several years to develop. A basic red, a *superiore* version (which includes a *riserva* for wines aged at least two years), and a rosé style exist under this DOC. Perhaps the best wines come from Foradori, with its basic 1998 Teroldego Rotaliano ($16 to $18) and its more serious 1997 Sgarzon (more than $50). Foradori's red wine, called Granato ($45 to $48), is an excellent non-DOC blend based on the Teroldego grape. Other good Teroldego Rotaliano producers include Conti Martini, Cantina Cooperativa Rotaliana, Barone de Cles, and Roberto Zeni.

✔ **Sorni:** The Sorni (*sor*-nee) zone is a small area named for a hamlet outside of Lavis in northern Trentino. The zone produces just two wines, a white and a red. Sorni Bianco consists of Nosiola, Müller-Thurgau, Silvaner, Pinot Bianco, Pinot Grigio, and Chardonnay, together or singly. Sorni Rosso comes from Teroldego, Schiava, and Lagrein, together or singly. The La Vis co-op and Maso Poli are two leading producers.

✔ **Casteller:** The narrow, hilly Casteller (cah-*stel*-ler) zone found along the Adige River, north and south of Trento, produces light red, quaffable, dry or semisweet wines, which are mainly consumed locally. The wines are based on Schiava and a local (raggedy-leaved) type of Lambrusco, blended with Teroldego, Lagrein, and/or Merlot.

✔ **Valdadige:** Sometimes called Etschtaler, this inter-regional DOC (pronounced vahl-*dah*-dee-jhae) covers vineyards in Alto Adige, Trentino, and the Veneto, all in the Adige Valley — but most of the vineyards are in Trentino. This DOC's seven types of wine, all basically inexpensive styles, include three blended wines: Valdadige Rosso (a dry or semisweet red blend of Schiava, local Lambrusco, Merlot, Pinot Nero, Lagrein, Teroldego, and Negrara); Bianco (a dry or semisweet white blended from up to nine varieties); and Rosato (a dry or semisweet rosé from the same grapes as Rosso). The varietal wines are Pinot Grigio, Pinot Bianco, Chardonnay, and Schiava.

Two other Trentino wineries are noteworthy. The fine Tenuta San Leonardo estate (also known as Guerrieri Gonzaga, the family's name), located just north of the Veneto, produces the finest Cabernet Sauvignon in Trentino. The 1997 San Leonardo Cabernet retails in the $45 to $48 range; the estate's 1997 Merlot ($16 to $18) is also quite good. The huge Concilio winery is the second noteworthy Trentino winery; its basic (but very decent) wines sell for $10, and the wines in its Reserve Collection go for $15.

**Book III**

**Italy: Small but Mighty**

---

# Sparklers with quality and value

The top sparkling wines of Ca'del Bosco and Bellavista in Lombardy's Franciacorta zone might be finer (they're definitely more expensive!), but *no* winery in Italy has a better all-around line of sparklers for the price than Trento's Ferrari house. Ferrari is one of Italy's largest sparkling wine houses, with an annual production of 3 million bottles. Its entire line, from its Brut Non-Vintage ($16 to $18) and Brut Rosé NV ($19 to $20), to its 1994 and 1995 Vintage Perlé Brut ($20 to $22), to its top-of-the-line 1990 and 1991 Giulio Ferrari Riserva Brut ($34 to $38), offers excellent value. The Giulio Ferrari Riserva, in particular, one of Italy's best sparkling wines, is a true steal at that price.

Another real deal in sparkling wines is Rotari Brut, made by MezzaCorona, offering excellent quality for its $12 to $15 price. It has a bright orange label (perhaps borrowed from a famous Champagne with the initials VC?).

# Getting to know the wines of Alto Adige

White wine production seems to be the future of Alto Adige, but the most popular grape variety by far is a red one. It's a variety that few people outside the region — except perhaps German-speaking tourists from the North — have ever heard of, and it's called Schiava (skee-*ah*-vah), more commonly known in the South Tyrol by its German name, Vernatsch (vehr-*nahtsh*). This high-yielding variety presently accounts for more than 60 percent of Alto Adige's wines; it's the basis of locally popular, light-bodied red wines. Yet some of the world's finest Pinot Bianco, Sauvignon, Pinot Grigio, Müller-Thurgau, and Gewürztraminer wines come from Alto Adige today.

## Italy's monster DOC

Recent changes in DOC regulations have resulted in one general appellation — Alto Adige, or Südtiroler — which now encompasses most of the DOC wines in Alto Adige, including six subzones that formerly were separate DOCs. The general Alto Adige DOC is an umbrella appellation covering 51 wines: 31 whites, 16 reds, 3 rosés, and 1 sparkling wine.

The general Alto Adige DOC appellation covers Alto Adige's finest white wines, such as those from the house of Alois Lageder, clearly a leader in the area, with its single-vineyard Pinot Bianco Haberlehof, its Pinot Grigio Benefizium (both $16 to $18), and its Chardonnay Löwengang ($27 to $30), among other wines. The best reds carrying this appellation are those from the native Lagrein (lah-*gryne*) grape, from Cabernet Sauvignon, Cabernet Franc, Merlot, and Pinot Nero. (The red Lagrein wines, dark-colored and full-bodied, are among the great, underrated red wines of the world.)

The six subzone wines of the Alto Adige DOC come from vineyards in the northern and central part of the larger appellation. The following list includes the Italian names as well as the German ones:

- **Santa Maddalener (St. Magdalener):** Hillside vineyards north of Bolzano grow Santa Maddalener (*sahn*-tah mah-dahl-*lae*-ner), Alto Adige's most beloved Schiava-based wine (with Lagrein and/or Pinot Grigio optional). This wine is a bit deeper in color, fuller, and fruitier than the other popular Schiava-based wine, Lago di Caldaro.

- **Meranese di Collina (Meraner Hügel):** The historic Meranese di Collina (mer-ah-*nae*-sae dee coh-*lee*-nah) vineyards around the town of Merano, about 20 miles northwest of Bolzano, are the home of the region's fullest and most aromatic Schiava wine, which is made entirely from that grape. The vineyards are high on the hillsides.

✔ **Terlano (Terlaner):** The Terlano (ter-*lah*-noh) area extends many miles north and south of Terlano, a town 6 miles west of Bolzano. The area is best known for its Sauvignon Blanc, Pinot Bianco, and Chardonnay. Lageder's fine Sauvignon Lehenhof ($17 to $18) comes from this area. Other Terlano wines are Riesling, Riesling Italico, Müller-Thurgau, Sylvaner, and Terlano Bianco (a dry white or *spumante,* meaning fully sparkling, wine made mostly from Pinot Bianco).

✔ **Colli di Bolzano (Bozner Leiten):** Colli di Bolzano (*coh*-lee dee bol-*zah*-noh) is the hillside area around Bolzano. Winemakers produce a light-bodied, spritzy, Schiava-based wine here.

✔ **Valle Isarco (Eisacktaler):** High up in the Alps, along the Isarco River, about 30 miles northeast of Bolzano, is Valle Isarco (*vah*-lae ee-*sahr*-coh), a fine area for mainly German varieties: Sylvaner, Müller-Thurgau, Gewürztraminer, Ruländer (the German name for Pinot Grigio), Kerner, and Veltliner. This zone's one red wine is called Klausner Leitacher and is made from at least 60 percent Schiava, with Blauer Portugieser (an Austrian variety) and/or Lagrein. Perhaps the best winery in this zone is the Abbazia di Novacella, an authentic, working Augustinian abbey. Its wines retail in the $15 to $20 price range.

✔ **Valle Venosta (Vinschgau):** Alto Adige's most isolated vineyard area, in the extreme northwest, near the Swiss and Austrian borders, Valle Venosta (*vah*-lay veh-*nohs*-tah) is best known for its Rieslings, but it also makes Chardonnay, Pinot Bianco, Pinot Grigio, Müller-Thurgau, Kerner, and Gewürztraminer, as well as Pinot Nero and Schiava.

Other than Alto Adige/Südtiroler, the subregion's only other DOC is Lago di Caldaro (*lah*-go dee cahl-*dah*-roh), or just Caldaro (also called Kalterer or Kaltersee, its German names). This very large vineyard area in the southern part of Alto Adige takes its name from Lake Caldaro, about 10 miles south of Bolzano. The region's oldest DOC area, it makes a pale, highly quaffable red wine from the Schiava grape, with Lagrein and/or Pinot Grigio optional.

**Book III**

**Italy: Small but Mighty**

## *Notable Alto Adige producers*

Any good rundown of Alto Adige producers starts with Alois Lageder, the area's leading producer. The J. Hofstätter estate, Lageder's only real, local winemaking rival, makes two of the finest wines in Italy, the country's best Pinot Nero, called Villa Barthenau Sant'Urbano ($50 to $55), and a Gewürztraminer called Kolbenhof ($24 to $25) from vineyards near Termeno (Tramin, in German), the birthplace of the Traminer grape variety and its variant, Gewürztraminer. Hofstätter also makes an excellent Lagrein (about $45). Another fine house, Castel Schwanburg, makes a Cabernet blend that's one of the best wines of its kind in Alto Adige.

J. Tiefenbrunner is another Alto Adige winery of note. Tiefenbrunner produces what has to be the world's best Müller-Thurgau (admittedly, not a great white variety), called Feldmarschall, from one of the world's highest vineyards, nearly 3,000 feet in altitude. The wine retails for about $27 to $30 and is an excellent value. Other notable producers in Alto Adige include Josef Brigl, Kettmeir, Peter Zemmer, Josef Niedermayr, Hirshprunn, Hans Rottensteiner, Baron von Widmann, Franz Haas, and Wilhelm Walch. In addition, the excellent San Michele Appiano cooperative, with wines under the Castel San Valentino label, makes fine white wines.

# The Veneto: Verona to Venice

The Veneto is the largest and most populous of the three regions in northeastern Italy. Friuli-Venezia Guilia and the Adriatic Sea are to its east, Emilia-Romagna is south (across the Po River), and Trentino-Alto Adige lies west and north. Part of Austria shares the Veneto's northern border, and the Alps cover the northern third of Veneto. The region's wines come from the southwestern and east-central zones — made up of both hillsides and plains (see Figure 4-2). The climate ranges from mild in the coastal area (influenced by the Adriatic Sea), to hot in the central plains, to mild and cool in the Verona area.

Veneto is Italy's third-largest wine producer, after Apulia and Sicily, with a volume of more than 77 million cases of wine a year. Twenty-nine percent of that production is DOC wine, a quantity that makes Veneto one of the largest producers of DOC wines. Two-thirds of these wines come from the province of Verona and are mainly the prolific Veronese trio of Soave, Bardolino, and Valpolicella, plus the up-and-coming Bianco di Custoza. Much of the rest of Veneto's large production is Pinot Grigio, some of which are labeled with the Veneto IGT and others with one of the region's eight other IGTs. (See Chapter 1 in Book III for the specifics on the IGT designation.)

Veneto wine production features many traditional local varieties, such as the red Corvina and the white Garganega (grown for centuries in the Verona province), as well as Merlot and both Cabernets (also grown for a long time), and popular white varieties, such as Chardonnay, Pinot Grigio, Pinot Bianco, and Sauvignon.

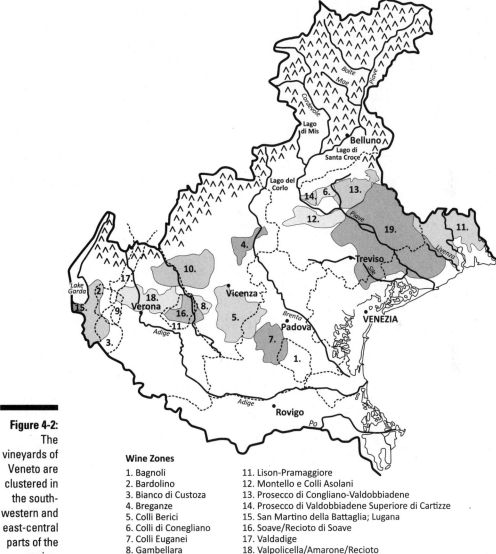

**Figure 4-2:**
The
vineyards of
Veneto are
clustered in
the south-
western and
east-central
parts of the
region.

**Wine Zones**

1. Bagnoli
2. Bardolino
3. Bianco di Custoza
4. Breganze
5. Colli Berici
6. Colli di Conegliano
7. Colli Euganei
8. Gambellara
9. Garda
10. Lessini Durello
11. Lison-Pramaggiore
12. Montello e Colli Asolani
13. Prosecco di Congliano-Valdobbiadene
14. Prosecco di Valdobbiadene Superiore di Cartizze
15. San Martino della Battaglia; Lugana
16. Soave/Recioto di Soave
17. Valdadige
18. Valpolicella/Amarone/Recioto
19. Vini del Piave

## *Tasting Verona's major wines*

Verona's four main wines — Bardolino, Bianco di Custoza, Valpolicella, and Soave — take their names from the province's four important DOC wine zones. Although all of these wines are mass-produced today, you can still find handcrafted examples of each by seeking out the wines that appear in the following lists of recommended producers. ***Note:*** IGT wines from Verona carry the designation Veronese or Provincia di Verona.

### *Bardolino*

The *classico* zone, the original vineyard area for Bardolino (bar-doe-*lee*-no), consists of the hillsides around the town of Bardolino and nearby villages, located on the eastern shores of beautiful Lake Garda, Italy's largest lake. Grapes from this area make Bardolino the DOC's best wine: a light-bodied, pale-ruby, delicate wine with lively aromas and flavors reminiscent of cherries, a slightly tart aftertaste, and a perfect balance of acidity.

DOC regulations allow grapes for Bardolino to be grown north and south of the *classico* zone (extending into the Bianco di Custoza area in the south) and farther east of the lake area. Outside of the *classico* zone, the wine tends to be thinner and more neutral in character, especially when it's made by large, industrial wineries. Check out the list of recommended producers at the end of this section for help in choosing your Bardolino wines.

The four main grape varieties that make up Bardolino, all of which are native to Verona, are Corvina (35 to 65 percent), Rondinella (10 to 40 percent), Molinara (10 to 20 percent), and Negrara (up to 10 percent). Corvina is the finest of the four, and the best Bardolino wines use high percentages of Corvina.

A dry rosé version of Bardolino, called Chiaretto (key-ah-*ret*-toh), is delightful in the summer when served chilled. You can also find a sparkling Bardolino and a Bardolino *novello* (sold a few months after the harvest, just like France's Beaujolais Nouveau [see Chapter 4 in Book II]), a specialty of the Lamberti house. Both the red and Chiaretto versions of Bardolino are light-bodied enough to accompany fish and seafood, as well as light meat entrées, pasta, and pizza.

Drink Bardolino when it's young and fresh, definitely within three years of the vintage — but younger if possible. Retail prices for Bardolino range from less than $10 for the basic wines up to $15 for single-vineyard versions.

Look for wine with the DOC Bardolino Classico or Bardolino Classico Superiore (a bit fuller, with one more degree of alcohol) from the following producers:

Bertani

Cavalchina Corte Gardoni's Le Fontane

Le Fraghe

Guerrieri-Rizzardi (especially its
   Tacchetto)

Lamberti

Le Vigne di San Pietro

Santa Sofia

Masi's La Vegrona

Fratelli Zeni

### Bianco di Custoza

Bianco di Custoza (b'*yahn*-co dee coos-*toh*'t-zah) is a dry, light-bodied, somewhat characterful white wine named for Custoza, a village southeast of Lake
Garda and southwest of Verona. The standard quality of Bianco di Custoza is
surprisingly high for such an inexpensive white wine (retailing for $10 to $12),
making it one of the really good white wine values in Italy. It has been called
the white version of Bardolino, and like its Lake Garda neighbor, it's best when
consumed within two or three years of the vintage. Its main grape varieties are
Trebbiano Toscano (35 to 45 percent), the native Garganega (20 to 40 percent),
and Tocai Friulano (5 to 30 percent). A sparkling style also exists.

Keep your eyes peeled for the following producers of Bianco di Custoza:

Cavalchina

Corte Gardoni

Lamberti

Montresor

Santa Sofia

Santi

Le Tende

Le Vigne di San Pietro

### Valpolicella and Amarone

Valpolicella (vahl-poh-lee-t'*chell*-ah) and its sturdier brother, Amarone
della Valpolicella, are the two most important red wines in the Veneto area.
Like Bardolino, the best Valpolicella wines come from the original *classico*
zone — in this case, the western part of the steep, terraced Monti Lessini
hillsides north of Verona, the area historically known as Valpolicella.
Valpolicella-Valpantena identifies wines whose grapes come from the
Pantena Valley.

Valpolicella is made from three of the same varieties as Bardolino, in slightly
different percentages: Corvina (40 to 70 percent), Rondinella (20 to 40 percent), and Molinara (5 to 25 percent). Valpolicella has similar aromas and
flavors to Bardolino (tart cherry fruit, with a slightly bitter aftertaste), but
it tends to be a bit darker in color and slightly more full-bodied. At 4 million
cases annually, Valpolicella's production is twice that of Bardolino, so finding
a good Valpolicella is easier than finding a good Bardolino.

The fact that the quality of both Valpolicella and Bardolino has suffered from
overproduction on the part of industrialized wineries and cooperatives is no
secret. But you can find increasingly good examples of these wines, primarily
from quality-conscious, family-owned wineries. For example, Allegrini, one

of the leaders in the Valpolicella quality revival, makes a fine, well-balanced Valpolicella Classico (about $11 to $12). But Allegrini has abandoned the Valpolicella DOC for its other wines in order to have more freedom in blending (the wines now carry the designation IGT Veronese). The outstanding single-vineyard wine called La Grola, a wine well worth its $18 price tag, contains some Merlot and Syrah, for example, and La Poja is made entirely from the best Veronese red grape variety, Corvina. Considered one of Italy's best red wines, La Poja retails for about $60. (It was less than half that price before it was "discovered.")

In good vintages, some of the grapes for Valpolicella are set aside to make the two special wines of the district: the dry Amarone (ah-mah-*roe*-nae) della Valpolicella and the sweet Recioto (reh-*cho*-toh) della Valpolicella. Especially ripe bunches of grapes, primarily Corvina, are spread out on mats in cool, dry rooms for three to four months, where they become partially shriveled and their juice becomes very concentrated. The grapes are fermented until the wine is dry to make Amarone, the far more popular style. It's a rich, heady, robust red wine that's 14 to 16 percent alcohol and needs about 10 years to mature (although it can age for 20 years or more). For the sweet Recioto, fermentation is stopped so that natural sweetness remains in the wine; this style can also be sparkling. Hearty Amarone is definitely a wine for the wintertime; accompany it with full-flavored roasts, game, or mature, hard cheeses, such as Asiago or Parmesan.

Amarone is a labor-intensive wine and, consequently, a good one is never inexpensive. Prices range from about $30 to $75 for wines from the best producers, with most between $45 and $60. If you see an Amarone priced at $20 or less, avoid it; it won't be a true example of this fine wine.

Another variation of Valpolicella is a group of wines made by the *ripasso* method; these wines are actually just beefed-up Valpolicellas. In the *ripasso* process, regular Valpolicella undergoes a second fermentation in contact with the deposits from the fermentation of Amarone; the resulting wine develops deeper color, more glycerine, richer texture, and more tannin. *Ripasso* is a winemaking technique, not a legal designation; the word generally appears only on a wine's back label, if it appears at all (see Chapter 3 in Book I for help figuring out which label is the back one). Three fine examples of *ripasso* wines are Masi's Campo Fiorin, Bertani's Catullo, and Allegrini's Palazzo alla Torre — all from the Valpolicella area but not Valpolicella DOC wines.

The following favorites for both Valpolicella and Amarone show up in classes, with those in Class One nosing ahead of the wines in Class Two:

**Class One**

| | |
|---|---|
| Allegrini | Masi |
| Bertani | Quintarelli |
| Bolla (Valpolicella Classico Le Poiane) | Le Ragose |
| Brigaldera | Tommasi |
| Dal Forno | |

**Class Two**

| | |
|---|---|
| Stefano Accordini | Angelo Nicolis e Figli |
| Brunelli | Pasqua |
| Ca'del Monte | Santa Sofia |
| Campagnola | Santi |
| Michele Castellani | Fratelli Speri |
| Corte Rugolin | Fratelli Tedeschi |
| Corte Sant'Alda | Venturini |
| Ferrari | Zenato |
| Guerrieri-Rizzardi Montresor | Fratelli Zeni |

## *Soave*

Rounding out Verona's major DOC wines is Soave (so-*ah*-vae), Italy's most famous white wine (along with Pinot Grigio, of course). Soave wines from the *classico* zone, in the hills above the towns of Soave and Monteforte d'Alpone (east of Verona), offer the highest quality. Most other Soaves reflect the neutral, insipid style that has cheapened the name of Soave and caused it to be frequently maligned. At its best, Soave is a fruity, very dry, fresh, straw-colored wine with class and character; in the hands of a fine producer, such as Gini, Pieropan, or Anselmi, it's one of Italy's best inexpensive white wines. (Most good Soave wines retail in the $10 to $15 range; a few single-vineyard Soaves cost a bit more.)

Soave's main grape variety is the local Garganega; up to 15 percent of Trebbiano di Soave, Chardonnay, Pinot Bianco, and/or Trebbiano Toscano is also permitted. A sweet Recioto di Soave (which recently became Veneto's only DOCG wine), is made from partially dried grapes in either still or sparkling form. Like Bardolino and Valpolicella, most Soave is at its best when young, within three years of the vintage. (The best producers' Soave wines can last much longer, however.)

Two incredible Soaves, both probably 100 percent Garganega, are Gini's La Froscà and Pieropan's La Rocca. Both retail in the $18 to $21 range and are well worth that price.

**Book III**

**Italy: Small but Mighty**

Soave is now a huge wine zone (producing up to 6 million cases annually), so take care when choosing a producer. Look for Soave Classico or Soave Classico Superiore wines from the following producers (note that the first three producers are in a class by themselves; the remaining producers make up Class Two):

**Class One**

| | |
|---|---|
| Anselmi | Pieropan |
| Gini | |

**Class Two**

| | |
|---|---|
| Bertani | Masi |
| Bisson | Montresor |
| Bolla (Soave Classico Tufaie) | Pasqua |
| Campagnola | Umberto Portinari |
| La Cappuccina | Pra |
| Ca' Rugate | Santa Sofia |
| Guerrieri-Rizzardi | Santi |
| Inama | Suavia |
| Lamberti | |

### Other Verona-area DOC wines

A relatively new DOC zone called Durello lies in the eastern Lessini hills, north of the Soave region. Durello is a dry wine, with quite high acidity, made primarily from a local grape variety called Durella. It's also made in *frizzante* (slightly sparkling) and fully sparkling styles.

A new DOC area, called Garda Orientale, extends slightly into Lombardy, south of Lake Garda. The wines are mainly varietals: reds are Cabernet (from both Cabernet varieties), Cabernet Franc, Cabernet Sauvignon, Merlot, Pinot Nero, Marzemino, and Corvina; whites are Garganega (still or fizzy), Pinot Bianco, Pinot Grigio Chardonnay, Trebbianello, Riesling, Welschriesling (dry or semidry and labeled Riesling Italico), Cortese, and Sauvignon. Garda Orientale Spumante is a sparkling wine from Pinot Bianco, Chardonnay, and Riesling.

## Sampling the wines of the Central Hills

The Central Hills area of the Veneto is east of Verona and west of Venice, in the provinces of Vicenza and Padua. This area has five DOC zones, of which Breganze is the most important.

### Breganze

The Breganze (breh-*gahn*-zae) district, north of the city of Vicenza, occupies foothills sheltered by the Asiago plateau (part of the Alps) to the north, with a river on each side. It has a mild climate and produces well-structured red wines along with fine whites.

Breganze Bianco, the basic white, is mainly (at least 85 percent) Friulano, and Breganze Rosso is mainly Merlot. In addition to these basics, the Breganze DOC covers four varietal reds (Cabernet made entirely from both Cabernet varieties, Cabernet Sauvignon, Pinot Nero, and Marzemino) and four white varietals (Pinot Bianco, Pinot Grigio, Chardonnay, and Sauvignon). It also covers Vespaiolo, a white wine made from Vespaiola, which is a local, aromatic white variety. Torcolato is a dessert wine made from semidried Vespaiola grapes.

Fausto Maculan, one of Italy's best wine producers, dominates the Breganze district. Maculan makes an array of internationally styled and traditional red and white wines, as well as two of Italy's finest dessert wines. His Breganze Bianco DOC, called Breganze di Breganze (about $15), is clean, fresh, and dry, with hints of peach aromas and flavors. Maculan's Brentino di Breganze (also $15) is a traditional Breganze Rosso. His most impressive dry wines are his three Cabernets: the single-vineyard Fratta (an old-vines blend of both Cabernets, with some Merlot), the single-vineyard Cabernet Sauvignon Palazzotto, and the Cabernet Sauvignon Ferrata (all retailing for $47 to $50).

Maculan also makes two Chardonnays, a Merlot, and several other dry wines, but his pride and joy are his two acclaimed dessert wines, Torcolato and Acininobili. The Torcolato comes in half-bottles and sells for $27 to $30. The wine is aged in small barrels until it's golden colored, with intense aromas and flavors of honey and dried fruit, such as apricots. The even richer Acininobili is made similarly, but its grapes are affected with *botrytis cinerea* (noble rot), as in Sauternes. The resulting wine, which comes in half-bottles and retails for $85 to $90, compares favorably to a great Sauternes.

### Gambellara

Gambellara (gahm-bel-*lah*-rah) is very similar to Soave, which is no big surprise, because the DOC zone is located just east of Verona's Soave zone and uses the same white grape varieties: Garganega, with up to 20 percent Trebbiano di Soave and/or Trebbiano Toscano. But because this wine isn't well known outside the Veneto, it retails for only about $7 or $8! The Gambellara zone also produces a sweet Recioto di Gambellara, a still or sparkling wine made from semidried or dried grapes, and a Vin Santo di Gambellara, a golden-colored dessert wine.

Two producers to look for are Zonin (Italy's largest private wine company, whose headquarters are in the town of Gambellara) and the La Biancara winery, which makes two Gambellara Classicos, Sassaia and I Masieri — both excellent values.

### Colli Berici

Colli Berici (*coh*-lee *beh*-ree-chee) is a large, historic vineyard area south of Vicenza whose wines are virtually unknown outside the region. Its two main wines are the dry white Garganega and a curious, dry red varietal wine called Tocai Rosso (sometimes called Barbarano when the grapes are more than minimally ripe), whose ripe raspberry flavors suggest that the grape is related to Grenache. This DOC covers four other white varietal wines (Tocai Italico, Sauvignon, Pinot Bianco, and Chardonnay), a Cabernet, and a *spumante.* Producers to look for are Conti da Schio, Villa dal Ferro, and Ca'Bruzzo.

### Colli Euganei and Bagnoli

These two wine zones are in the vicinity of the city of Padua — Colli Euganei (*coh*-lee ae-yu-*gah*-nae), which is southwest of Padua, and Bagnoli (bahn-*yo*-lee), which is south of it.

Vineyards in the beautiful Euganei hills make semisweet and bubbly wines. The whites are a Bianco made mainly from Garganega, Prosecco, Tocai Friulano, and Sauvignon; a Fior di Arancio (meaning "orange blossom") made from Moscato Giallo, which also has a *passito* style, from dried grapes; and six varietals, which are Chardonnay, Moscato, Pinello, Pinot Blanc, Tocai Italico, and Serprino (Prosecco). Red wines are a basic Rosso (from Merlot, the two Cabernets, Barbera, and Raboso Veronese grapes), a Rosso *novello,* a Cabernet, a Cabernet Franc, a Cabernet Sauvignon, and a Merlot.

Vignalta is the leading producer. Look for its Colli Euganei Rosso, made mainly from Merlot. Also worth trying are the Fior d'Arancio of La Montecchia, Ca'Lustra, and Borin, as well as Borin's dry white, Colli Euganei Bianco.

Bagnoli, or Bagnoli di Sopra (meaning "Upper Bagnoli"), is a newly created DOC zone located directly east of the Colli Euganei area. It covers nine wines. Except for three — a varietal Merlot, a dry red called Friularo (from the Raboso Piave variety), and Bagnoli Cabernet (from Cabernet Franc, Cabernet Sauvignon, and Carmenère, together or singly) — the wines are blends with complicated formulas.

## Exploring the wine offerings on all sides of Venice

Venice itself is surrounded by marshland, but north, west, and northeast of this magical city are alluvial plains and hillsides covered with vines. The two main wines of this area are Pinot Grigio and Prosecco (a wonderful, inexpensive sparkling wine). Merlot and both Cabernets (Franc and Sauvignon) are also important wines here. Five DOC wine zones are located mainly in the two provinces of Treviso and Venezia. IGT wines from eastern Veneto can carry the designation Veneto Orientale.

### Prosecco di Conegliano-Valdobbiadene

Prosecco di Conegliano-Valdobbiadene (pro-*sae*-co dee co-nael-*yah*-no vahl-doh-bee-*ah*-deh-nae) takes its tongue-twisting name from two towns north of the Piave River and south of the Alps: Valdobbiadene, in the cooler, hillier west, and Conegliano, in the east, near the Adriatic Sea. Both areas are sheltered by the Alps, making the climate ideal for the Prosecco vines that proliferate between and around the towns.

Prosecco sparkling wine, which comes in both *frizzante* and *spumante* styles, is at its crispest, most refined best in the cooler hills around Valdobbiadene. (Usually Prosecco labels list only one of the two towns as part of the DOC name.) Wines from a small area of steep hills around Valdobbiadene are entitled to the designation Superiore di Cartizze, or just Cartizze (cahr-*teet*-zae) — theoretically the finest Prosecco.

Most Prosecco nowadays is dry, fully sparkling, and made by the tank fermentation method rather than the Champagne or bottle fermentation method (see Chapter 6 of Book II for an explanation of these two production methods). The shorter tank process is preferable in this case because it preserves the freshness and flavor of the grape. Variations include a small amount of dry, still Prosecco and a sweeter (*amabile* or *dolce*) style of sparkling Prosecco. Prosecco is generally soft more than crisp and has aromas and flavors that are floral, slightly peachy, and somewhat reminiscent of almonds. Look for Prosecco that's labeled *Extra Dry* or *Extra Brut* if you want the driest version. Most Prosecco retails in the $10 to $15 range.

Give these recommended Prosecco producers a try:

| | |
|---|---|
| Adami | Col Vetoraz |
| Astoria Vini | Nino Franco |
| Desiderio Bisol & Figli | Gregoletto |
| Bortolomiol | Mionetto |
| Canevel | Ruggeri & C. |
| Carpenè Malvolti | Zardetto |
| Le Case Bianche | Zonin |

### Montello e Colli Asolani

Montello e Colli Asolani (mon-*tel*-lo ae *coh*-lee ah-so-*lah*-nee) is a wine zone south of the Piave River and northwest of the city of Treviso. The zone's best area is on the slopes of Il Montello. Even though this DOC applies to Prosecco in all forms — dry or semi-dry, still, *frizzante,* or fully sparkling — the specialties are red wines. The three reds are a blended Rosso (minimum of 85 percent Merlot, Cabernet Franc, and/or Cabernet Sauvignon), Cabernet, and Merlot. Besides Prosecco, other white wines of the area are Chardonnay and Pinot Bianco (both made as still or sparkling wines) and Pinot Grigio.

The zone's most renowned wine estate is Venegazzù, owned by the Loredan Gasparini family. The estate makes primarily Cabernet blends, including one called Venegazzù, which retails for about $25. A winery to watch is Serafini e Vidotto; its acclaimed Bordeaux blend, Il Rosso dell'Abazia (about $35), is one of the best wines of its kind in Italy.

### Piave

The Piave (pee-*ah*-vae) DOC sometimes goes by the name Vini del Piave. The Piave River cuts through the center of this very large district, and most of the zone is the plains of the river basin, with some vineyards in the hills. Piave's three most distinctive wines — the vivid, intense red varietal Raboso and the two lively varietal whites, Verduzzo and Tocai Italico — are gradually giving way to seven international varietals: the red Cabernet Sauvignon, Cabernet, Merlot, and Pinot Nero, and the white Chardonnay, Pinot Bianco, and Pinot Grigio. A leading producer in this zone is Ornella Molon Traverso, whose husband-wife team, Ornella Molon and Giancarlo Traverso, make a fine Piave Cabernet and Piave Merlot.

### Lison-Pramaggiore

The Lison-Pramaggiore (*lee*-sohn prah-mahj-*joh*-rae) zone is in the easternmost part of the Veneto, near the Adriatic Sea, extending slightly into the Friuli region. It has 12 DOC wines, but it's most renowned for one wine — Pinot Grigio — and one wine house — Santa Margherita. The Santa Margherita name has become synonymous with Pinot Grigio, and the brand is greatly responsible for the popularity of the Pinot Grigio category.

The Lison-Pramaggiore name covers seven varietally labeled white wines (Tocai Italico, Pinot Bianco, Chardonnay, Pinot Grigio, Riesling Italico, Sauvignon, and Verduzzo). It also covers varietal Merlot, Cabernet Franc, Cabernet Sauvignon, Cabernet, and Refosco. Technically, any of these wines may be vinified as sparkling wines.

# Friuli-Venezia Giulia: The Great White Way

Tucked away in the northeastern corner of Italy, Friuli-Venezia Giulia (*free*-oo-lee veh-*net*-zee-ah *jhoo*-lee-ah) was once part of the Venetian Republic, and its eastern sections were part of the Austro-Hungarian Empire until after World War I. Because this region is situated at the crossroads of Slavic countries, Germanic countries, and the rest of Italy, it has been influenced by many cultures. Its best wines are white — in fact, the wines in this area are indisputably the best white wines in Italy!

Friuli-Venezia Giulia is usually simply called Friuli. (The name Venezia Giulia happens to be the region's only IGT designation.) All of Friuli's vineyards are in the southern half of the region; the Alps take up its entire northern section (see Figure 4-3). The Veneto is to the south and west, the Adriatic Sea is also to the south, Austria is to the north, and Slovenia is to the east. Friuli produces the equivalent of about 12.2 million cases of wine each year, about 62 percent of which is DOC, a percentage third only to Piedmont and Trentino-Alto Adige in Italy. But, most tellingly, Friuli's grape yields per acre (about 3.5 tons, on average) are much lower than either Trentino-Alto Adige or Veneto and are in fact among the lowest in Italy, especially in the region's eight DOC zones. Friuli is a quality-conscious wine region, yet most Friulian wines retail in the $14 to $24 price range — excellent prices for the quality.

Friuli is considered the birthplace of modern white wine in Italy. In the 1960s, producers in this region were pioneers in fermenting the juice of white grapes without the grape skins, thereby creating cleaner, fresher, lighter-colored white wines that didn't oxidize rapidly. Surprisingly though, red wine still accounts for 40 percent of Friuli's DOC wine production because Merlot predominates in the largest DOC zone — the vast, gravelly plains of western Friuli. But in Friuli's two best wine zones, Collio Goriziano (usually known as Collio) and Colli Orientali del Friuli, well over two-thirds of the DOC wines are white.

**Book III**

**Italy: Small but Mighty**

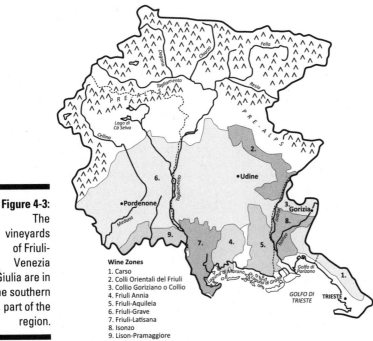

**Figure 4-3:**
The vineyards of Friuli-Venezia Giulia are in the southern part of the region.

**Wine Zones**
1. Carso
2. Colli Orientali del Friuli
3. Collio Goriziano o Collio
4. Friuli Annia
5. Friuli-Aquileia
6. Friuli-Grave
7. Friuli-Latisana
8. Isonzo
9. Lison-Pramaggiore

Friuli now has eight DOC wine zones. Also, a small part of the Lison-Pramaggiore DOC zone of the Veneto (covered in the previous section) extends into the Pordenone province in southwestern Friuli.

The following sections take you on a tour of Friuli's DOC zones, describing the characteristics of the wines produced there and recommending some producers you should try.

## The wines of Collio and Colli Orientali del Friuli

Of the eight Friuli wine zones, Collio and Colli Orientali del Friuli — often abbreviated as Colli Orientali — are the most important.

### Collio

The Collio (*coh*-lee-oh) or Collio Goriziano (*coh*-lee-oh go-ree-zee-*ah*-no) zone is in the province of Gorizia in southeastern Friuli. Across Friuli's eastern border is Slovenia, and many of Collio's vineyards extend into that country, mindless of the political border. (As a result, you can actually find the name *Collio* on bottles of Slovenian wine.) Most of Collio's best vineyards are located around the town of Cormons, where an ideal, temperate microclimate exists. This area is in the pathway between the cool breezes from the Adriatic Sea and the sheltering foothills of the Alps to the north, and the soil in the hills around Cormons is great for grape-growing. This is the finest white-wine area not only in Friuli but in all of Italy; Collio makes five times as much white wine as red wine.

Collio's wines are quite rich and full-bodied for Italian white wines. Among white varieties, the rich Tocai Friulano excels here, but Pinot Bianco, Pinot Grigio, Sauvignon Blanc, Chardonnay, and two local varieties, Ribolla Gialla (ree-*bo*-lah *jhal*-lah) and Malvasia Istriana (mahl-vah-*see*-ah ees-tree-*ah*-nah), also do well. (All of these varieties are produced as varietal wines under the Collio DOC.) Cabernet Franc and Merlot are the leading red varieties; Collio Rosso, a blend of Merlot, Cabernet Franc, and/or Cabernet Sauvignon, is a popular red wine.

Other Collio DOC wines are the following: Bianco (dry white, from 45 to 55 percent Ribolla Gialla, 20 to 30 percent Malvasia Istriana, 15 to 25 percent Tocai Friulano, and eight other white varieties optional); Müller Thurgau; Picolit (semidry or sweet white); Riesling; Welschriesling; Traminer Aromatico; Cabernet; Cabernet Sauvignon; and Pinot Nero. Varietal wines from Collio derive completely from the named grape.

## Colli Orientali del Friuli

Colli Orientali del Friuli (*coh*-lee or-ee-en-*tah*-lee del *free*-oo-lee) is north and west of Collio. Almost all the vineyards are in the southern part of this DOC zone, directly north of Collio; thus, the two zones share similar climate and soil, for the most part. As a result, Friulano, Pinot Bianco, Pinot Grigio, Sauvignon, and Chardonnay all do well here. But subtle differences in micro-climate and customs exist. Among white varieties, Ribolla Gialla is more important here, as are two varieties quite the specialty of Colli Orientali: Picolit, which makes a famous dessert wine, and Verduzzo, which makes dry, semidry, and sweet styles of wine. The three grapes produce varietal wines under the Colli Orientale de Friuli DOC.

Red varieties are more important here than in Collio, as well. (White wine production outnumbers red by only a two-to-one ratio.) Besides making heartier, varietally labeled versions of Merlot and both Cabernets, Colli Orientali winemakers specialize in one regional favorite red wine — the traditional, sturdy Refosco, made from the grape of the same name — and two red wines from varieties indigenous to Colli Orientali, the elegant Schiopettino (also known as Ribolla Nera) and the once almost-extinct Pignolo, which makes a dark-colored, aromatic, tannic, intensely fruity, dry wine.

Colli Orientali del Friuli also has three distinct subdistricts; wines made from grapes grown in these subdistricts may use the subdistrict names on their labels. The three subdistricts are as follows:

- **Ramandolo:** In the extreme northern part of Colli Orientali, Ramandolo (rah-*mahn*-doh-loh) is renowned for its sweet dessert wine, Verduzzo di Ramandolo. Two leading producers in this area are Giovanni Dri and Fratelli Coos.

- **Cialla:** In the central part of the zone, the Cialla (*chal*-lah) district specializes in sweet or semisweet Picolit, dry Ribolla Gialla, and Verduzzo (dry, semidry, and sweet). Other wines that can carry the Cialla appellation are Cialla Bianco (a dry white that can be made from one or more white varieties of the zone), Cialla Rosso (a dry red that can be made from one or more red varieties of the zone), Cialla Refosco dal Peduncolo Rosso, and Cialla Schiopettino. Ronchi di Cialla is a leading producer in the Cialla zone.

- **Rosazzo:** In the south, the Rosazzo (roh-*sahtz*-zoh) area is especially identified with Ribolla Gialla. In fact, this variety is thought to have originated in the vineyards of the historic abbey, Abbazia di Rosazzo, more than 1,000 years ago. Other wines that carry the Rosazzo appellation are Rosazzo Bianco (a dry white that can be made from one or more white varieties of the zone); Rosazzo Rosso (a dry red that can be made from one or more red varieties of the zone); Rosazzo Picolit (a semidry or sweet white); and Rosazzo Pignolo (a dry red). Abbazia di Rosazzo and Livio Felluga are two leading wineries that have vineyards in Rosazzo.

### *Recommended producers of Collio and Colli Orientali wines*

The following recommended producers of Collio and Colli Orientali del Friuli wines are listed in two categories (Class One notes the standout producers):

**Class One**

Giralamo Dorigo (Colli Orientali)
Livio Felluga (Collio; Colli Orientali)
Gravner (Collio)
Jermann (Collio)
Le Due Terre (Colli Orientali)
Miani (Colli Orientali)
Ronco dei Rosetti, of Zamò (Colli Orientali)

Ronco dei Tassi (Collio)
Russiz Superiore, of Marco Felluga (Collio)
Mario Schiopetto (Collio)
Venica & Venica (Collio)
Villa Russiz (Collio)

**Class Two**

La Boatina (Collio)
Bastianich (Colli Orientali)
Borgo Conventi (Collio)
Borgo del Tiglio (Collio)
Ca' Ronesca (Collio)
Paolo Caccese (Collio)
La Castellada (Collio)
Castello di Spessa (Collio)
Collavini (Colli Orientali)
Conte Attems (Collio)
Conte D'Attimis-Maniago (Colli Orientali)
Conti Formentini (Collio)
Fratelli Coos (Colli Orientali)
Giovanni Dri (Colli Orientali)
Marco Felluga (Collio)
Walter Filliputti, at Abbazia di Rosazzo (Colli Orientali)
Gradnik (Collio)
Livon (Collio)
Ascevi-Luwa (Collio)
Francesco Pecorari (Collio)

Perusini (Colli Orientali)
Petrucco (Colli Orientali)
Pighin (Collio)
Isidoro Polencic (Collio)
Prà di Pradis (Collio)
Doro Princic (Collio)
Puiatti (Collio)
Radikon (Collio)
Rocca Bernarda (Colli Orientali)
Paolo Rodaro (Colli Orientali)
Roncada (Collio)
Ronchi di Cialla (Colli Orientali)
Ronchi di Manzano (Colli Orientali)
Ronco delle Betulle (Colli Orientali)
Ronco del Gnemiz (Colli Orientali)
Specogna (Colli Orientali)
Torre Rosazza (Colli Orientali)
Tenuta Villanova (Collio)
La Viarte (Colli Orientali)
Vigne dal Leon (Colli Orientali)
Volpe Pasini (Colli Orientali)
Zamò & Zamò (Colli Orientali)

## *The wines of Isonzo and Carso*

Like Collio and Colli Orientali, the Friuli Isonzo (*free*-oo-lee ee-*sohn*-zoh) — or Isonzo del Friuli — and the Carso (*car*-so) DOC zones are in the eastern part of Friuli, specifically the southeast (see Figure 4-3). The Isonzo zone is directly south of Collio. The northwest part, closest to Cormons, is the best vineyard area. Isonzo has a number of good producers and is a prime source of good white and red wines. The best Isonzo whites are Sauvignon; Chardonnay; fine, dry Malvasia Istriana; Friulano; and Pinot Bianco. Merlot is Isonzo's best red wine. All varietal wines in this zone are 100 percent of the named variety.

The Carso wine zone is in the extreme southeastern part of Friuli. Its claim to fame, wine-wise, is its unique grape variety, the red Terrano, which is related to Refosco. In a specific subzone of Carso, Terrano makes wines of piercing acidity that are quite popular with the locals in Trieste, who enjoy it with Slavic and other hearty cuisine. ***Note:*** This wine is definitely an acquired taste.

Vie di Romans is the standout producer in the Isonzo zone. Other producers of Isonzo and Carso wines to watch out for include

Borgo San Daniele (Isonzo)  Pierpaolo Pecorari (Isonzo)
Castelvecchio (Carso)  Ronco del Gelso (Isonzo)
Mauro Drius (Isonzo)  Sant' Elena (Isonzo)
Edi Kante (Carso)  Tenuta di Blasig (Isonzo)
Eddi Luisa (Isonzo)  Gianni Vescovo (Isonzo)
Masut da Rive (Isonzo)  Vie di Romans (Isonzo)
Lis Neris-Pecorari (Isonzo)

## Other Friuli DOC wines

Four Friuli wine zones are in the central and western part of the region: Grave del Friuli (*grah*-vae del *free*-oo-lee), Friuli Aquilea (ah-kwee-*lae*-ah), Friuli Latisana (lah-tee-*sah*-nah), and Friuli Annia (*ahn*-nee-ah). Known collectively as the Adriatic Basin zones, they're located in the plains, where the alluvial soil consists primarily of sand and gravel. Pordenone, in the western part of Grave del Friuli (which is Friuli's largest DOC zone by far), is the major city.

The wines of the Adriatic Basin zones are made from the same varieties as the wines in the other Friuli DOC zones, but they're lighter in body and have less finesse. More red wines come from these four zones than the eastern zones, especially wines made from Merlot. Cabernet Franc, Cabernet Sauvignon, Cabernet, and the local Refosco are also popular. Most of the white wines are varietally labeled: Tocai Friulano, Pinot Bianco, Pinot Grigio, Chardonnay, Verduzzo (in dry, semidry, and sweet forms), and others (often in *frizzante* or even *spumante* styles). Varietal wines are 90 percent from the named variety in the Friuli Annia and Friuli Latisana zones and 85 percent in the other two zones.

Here are the recommended producers from the Adriatic Basin zones:

Borgo Magredo (Grave del Friuli)

Emiro Cav. Bortolusso (Annia)

Ca' Bolani (Aquileia)

Cabert (Grave del Friuli)

Forchir (Grave del Friuli)

Mangilli (Grave del Friuli)

Mulino delle Tolle (Aquileia)

A. Vicentini Orgnani (Grave del Friuli)

Pighin (Grave del Friuli)

Plozner (Grave del Friuli)

Tenuta Beltrame (Aquileia)

Vistorta (Grave del Friuli)

# Chapter 5

# Tuscany: Checking Out Chianti and Other Tuscan Reds

*I*f you were to poll wine lovers regarding their favorite Italian regions, Tuscany would probably rank first. Besides making Italy's most famous wine — Chianti — Tuscany is home to one of Italy's most prestigious wines, Brunello di Montalcino, and the exciting category of super-Tuscan wines. Tuscany is also tourist heaven. With the famous cities of Florence, Siena, and Pisa; quaint medieval towns such as San Gimignano and Montalcino; storybook castles; and the stirringly beautiful hills of the Tuscan countryside, Tuscany is one of Europe's best destinations for art, architecture, history, natural beauty, great food, and fine wine.

## Taking In the Big Picture of Tuscany

One particular church in Florence contains the graves of Amerigo Vespucci, Dante, Galileo, Verrazzano, Machiavelli, and Michelangelo — enduring testimony to Tuscany's leadership in the realms of science, politics, world discovery, art, and literature during the Middle Ages. In the realm of wine, Tuscany is no less a leader. Italy's most recent wine renaissance began in Tuscany in the early 1970s, when producers of Chianti decided to show the world once and for all that Tuscan wines deserve to be taken seriously; their quality movement changed the face of wine all over Italy.

Tuscany (including its seven islands) is Italy's fifth-largest region, covering a territory slightly smaller than New Hampshire. It sits on Italy's western coast, surrounded by Emilia-Romagna to the north, Umbria to the east, and Lazio to the south. Except for a small border with Liguria in the northwest, Tuscany's entire western border is the Tyrrhenian Sea, which is part of the Mediterranean.

The Apennine Mountains separate Tuscany from Emilia-Romagna in the north, and smaller mountains line the region to the west and south, but Tuscany is more hilly than mountainous. The region's interior is particularly hilly, and some areas of high elevation also exist near the coast. The altitude of the hills tempers the summer heat, which can otherwise be sweltering. (An air-conditioned hotel and mosquito repellent are absolute requisites for a summertime stay in Florence.)

Tuscany has plenty of vineyard land: In all of Italy, only Sicily and Puglia have more acres planted with vines. But seven regions of Italy produce more wine than Tuscany does. Winegrowers focus Tuscany's hillside vineyards and poor soils on quality rather than quantity of production. In terms of volume, Tuscany produces more DOC wine than any other region except Piedmont and Veneto, and many of Tuscany's IGT-level wines are extremely high in quality (see Chapter 1 in Book III for more on the DOC and IGT aspects of Italy's wine-classification system).

About 50 percent of Tuscany's wine production is DOC or DOCG. Tuscany has 6 DOCG wines and 29 DOCs; the vast majority (80 percent) of this classified-level production is red wine. Figure 5-1 depicts Tuscany's DOC/G zones.

Sangiovese is the main red grape variety of Tuscany, not just quantitatively but also qualitatively speaking. Many clones of Sangiovese exist; in addition to the broad families of Sangiovese, such as the top-quality Sangiovese Grosso and the ordinary Sangiovese di Romagna, numerous local clones have evolved in response to local conditions in each of the districts where the grape has traditionally grown. Sangiovese's many mutations explain why it has several different names or nicknames in Tuscany, such as Brunello, Prugnolo Gentile, and Morellino.

The next most important red variety in terms of quality is Cabernet Sauvignon. This variety has grown in the region for at least 250 years, but it has become especially popular since the late 1970s. Numerous other red varieties exist, including native varieties, such as Mammolo, Canaiolo, Malvasia Nera, and Colorino, and international varieties, such as Merlot (like Cabernet, Merlot is increasingly popular with growers), Pinot Noir, and Syrah.

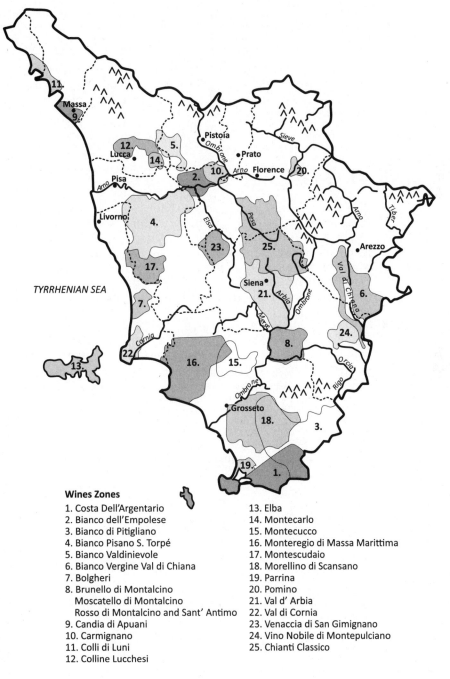

**Book III**

**Italy: Small but Mighty**

**Wines Zones**

1. Costa Dell'Argentario
2. Bianco dell'Empolese
3. Bianco di Pitigliano
4. Bianco Pisano S. Torpé
5. Bianco Valdinievole
6. Bianco Vergine Val di Chiana
7. Bolgheri
8. Brunello di Montalcino
   Moscatello di Montalcino
   Rosso di Montalcino and Sant' Antimo
9. Candia di Apuani
10. Carmignano
11. Colli di Luni
12. Colline Lucchesi
13. Elba
14. Montecarlo
15. Montecucco
16. Monteregio di Massa Marittima
17. Montescudaio
18. Morellino di Scansano
19. Parrina
20. Pomino
21. Val d' Arbia
22. Val di Cornia
23. Venaccia di San Gimignano
24. Vino Nobile di Montepulciano
25. Chianti Classico

**Figure 5-1:**
Tuscany's
wine zones.

Trebbiano is the leading white variety of the region in terms of acreage planted — and the main reason why Tuscan white wines are far less exciting than the reds. But Vermentino, an increasingly popular variety that's full of character, is common in Tuscany's coastal areas, in blends and alone. The highest-quality white wines derive from the Vernaccia grape, grown around San Gimignano, and Chardonnay, which is an international variety that has grown in Tuscany for about 150 years but has been particularly fashionable in the past three decades.

# Exploring the Land of Chianti

Chianti (key-*ahn*-tee) isn't just Tuscany's most famous wine — it's Italy's most famous wine, and one of the most famous wines in the entire world. But Chianti isn't just one type of wine, either. The name embodies wines from several subzones, which vary quite a lot in richness and quality — it covers wines for drinking young and age-worthy wines, as well as inexpensive wines ($8 a bottle) and pricey ones ($60). What these wines have in common is that they're all red, and they're all based on the Sangiovese grape.

The collective Chianti zone is by far the largest classified wine zone in Tuscany. It's situated mainly in the central part of the region, with one sub-zone (Chianti Colli Pisane) extending farther west, toward the sea. The collective territory produces about 8 million cases of Chianti wine per year, along with various white wines, other types of red wine, and dessert wine. Some of these other wines are DOC wines from zones that overlap the Chianti area, such as Pomino, and others are IGT-level wines, such as the so-called super-Tuscan wines.

The next sections give you an in-depth look at Tuscany's world-famous Chianti wines and the areas responsible for creating them.

## The range of Chianti wines

Two separate DOCG designations apply to Chianti wines today: Chianti Classico DOCG is for wines from the area between Florence and Siena, and Chianti DOCG is for all other Chianti wines. The Chianti DOCG includes wines from six subzones, which carry the name of their subzone on their labels, as well as wines *not* from a specific subzone, whose labels simply read *Chianti*.

Since 1996, both Chianti and Chianti Classico are 75 to 100 percent Sangiovese, with up to 10 percent Canaiolo and up to 6 percent of two white varieties (Trebbiano and Malvasia); other red varieties may constitute up to

15 percent of the blend. In practice, Chianti can be entirely Sangiovese, or it can be entirely from red varieties; adding as much as 15 percent Cabernet Sauvignon — popular with Sangiovese — or Merlot is entirely legal.

The flexibility that wine producers have in their grape variety selection is one of the reasons why Chianti wines vary in weight and intensity. Simple, inexpensive wines for drinking young are likely to have some white grapes in their blend, whereas richer wines are made entirely from red grapes; the richest wines are mainly Sangiovese, often with Cabernet Sauvignon, and come from the finest vineyard areas.

# Chianti Classico

Not only is Chianti Classico the heartland of Tuscany — the original Chianti area, situated at the very center of Tuscany — but it's also the emotional heart of the region. The zone is populated by serious and skilled winemakers who care deeply about their land and their wines, and who infect wine lovers all over the world with their passion.

An area of approximately 100 square miles, Chianti Classico is situated between the cities of Florence and Siena. It encompasses four communes, or communities, in their entirety — Greve, Radda, Gaiole, and Castellina — as well as portions of five others. More than 700 grape growers farm the 24,700 acres of vineyards in this area.

Although this region isn't a tremendously large area, the diversity of its climate and soil — together with the flexibility regarding grape varieties that the DOCG regulation provides and varying winemaking styles — creates a stunning array of wines.

Most Chianti Classico wines are medium-bodied rather than full-bodied, firm rather than soft, with a medium amount of dry tannin and medium to high acidity. Tart cherry or ripe cherry are the main aroma/flavor descriptors, sometimes with delicate floral or nutty notes. One characteristic of Chianti that surprises many is that the wines are fairly inexpressive in the front of the mouth; all of their action happens in the middle and rear. They're completely different from most New World reds, whose richness is evident as soon as you put them in your mouth.

Vintages also vary quite a lot in Chianti Classico, but variations in soil and microclimate throughout the zone can offset some vintage variations. (Vineyards in warmer areas can do well in cool years, for example.) Years that are unusually warm and dry bring greater ripeness to the grapes and atypical weight and richness to the wines.

In good vintages, most producers make a *riserva* version of their Chianti Classico; *riserva* wines are generally made from a producer's best grapes, and they must age for at least 27 months at the winery, as well as have at least 12.5 percent alcohol compared to the minimum 12 percent for regular Chianti Classico. *Riservas* are capable of aging longer after they're released, too. A Chianti Classico Riserva from a good producer in a good vintage can be very enjoyable even 15 years from the vintage date, although a basic Chianti Classico is best consumed within 10 years.

In addition to making both *riserva* and regular styles, many producers make single-vineyard Chianti Classicos that are usually *riserva* level. These single-vineyard wines are generally the most expensive Chianti Classicos of all: They range from $35 to $60, compared to $25 to $45 for *riservas* and $15 to $30 for basic Chianti Classico wines.

Most Chianti Classico producers are wine estates — fairly small operations that own vineyards and make wines from their own grapes; each estate typically makes two or three Chianti Classico wines — a basic version, a *riserva,* and a single-vineyard, for example. The names of these estates often begin with *castello* ("castle"), *fattoria* ("farm"), or *podere* ("property"). Most bottles of Chianti Classico carry a neckband with a black rooster on it, the trademark of a voluntary consortium that has promoted the region's wines since 1924.

Some large producers who own vineyards in the zone also make wines from purchased grapes; these wines are usually less expensive than estate-bottled wines. Some large producers own several estates and make wines at each of them (Ruffino, for example, owns estates in Greve, Panzano, and Castellina, and bottles the production of some of them separately). These large producers also make wines that are blended from their holdings throughout the *classico* zone (Antinori's Tenute Marchesi Antinori Riserva is an example of a blended Chianti Classico).

The average quality level of Chianti Classico wines is quite high. The following favorite producers are listed in two groups, with the top-tier picks in Class One; the producers in each group are listed with the name of the commune where they're located.

**Class One**

Barone Ricasoli, formerly Castello di Brolio (Gaiole)

Castellare di Castellina (Castellina)

Castello dei Rampolla (Panzano)

Castello di Ama (Gaiole)

Castello di Fonterutoli (Castellina)

Castello di Volpaia (Radda)

Fattoria di Felsina (Castelnuovo Berardegna)

Fontodi (Panzano)

Isole e Olena (Barberino Val d'Elsa)

Marchesi Antinori (San Casciano Val di Pesa)

La Massa (Panzano)

Monsanto (Barberino Val d'Elsa)

Podere Il Palazzino (Gaiole)

Ruffino (various estates)

San Giusto a Rentennano (Gaiole)

**Class Two**

Agricoltori del Chianti Geografico (Gaiole)

Badia a Coltibuono (Gaiole)

La Brancaia (Castellina)

Carpineto (Greve)

Castell'in Villa (Castelnuovo Berardegna)

Castello d'Albola (Radda)

Castello di Cacchiano (Gaiole)

Castello di Gabbiano (Mercatale Val di Pesa)

Castello di Lilliano (Castellina)

Castello di Querceto (Greve)

Castello di Verrazzano (Greve)

Le Corti (San Casciano Val di Pesa)

Dievole (Castelnuovo Berardegna)

Machiavelli (San Casciano Val di Pesa)

Melini (Poggibonsi)

Nittardi (Castellina)

Nozzole (Greve)

Poggerino (Radda)

Poggio al Sole (Tavarnelle Val di Pesa)

Querciabella (Greve)

Riecine (Gaiole)

Riseccoli (Greve)

Rocca di Castagnoli (Gaiole)

San Fabiano Calcinaia (Castellina)

San Felice (Castelnuovo Berardegna)

Vecchie Terre di Montefili (Panzano)

Vignamaggio (Greve)

Villa Cafaggio (Panzano)

Cecchi-Villa Cerna (Castellina)

Viticcio (Greve)

# *Chianti*

The Chianti DOCG designation applies to all Chianti wines other than those made from grapes grown in the Chianti Classico area. This appellation covers wines from six specific subzones, as well as wines from peripheral areas. Wines from individual subzones may carry the name of that subzone on their labels; wines from the other areas, or wines combining grapes from more than one subzone, simply carry the appellation Chianti DOCG. Chianti Superiore is another designation within the Chianti DOCG; it applies to wines made from grapes grown within the provinces of Florence or Siena but not within the Chianti Classico area.

**Book III**

**Italy: Small but Mighty**

The best Chianti wines are those made in these six specific subzones:

- **Chianti Colli Pisane:** Pronounced *coh*-lee pee-*sah*-nae; the westernmost part of the zone, in the province of Pisa

- **Chianti Colli Fiorentini:** Pronounced fee-or-en-*tee*-nee and literally meaning "Florentine hills"; the area north of Chianti Classico, in the province of Florence

- **Chianti Colli Senesi:** Pronounced seh-*nae*-see; the Siena hills, the southernmost part of the zone

- **Chianti Colli Aretini:** Pronounced ah-rae-*tee*-nee; the Arezzo hills, the eastern part of the zone

- **Chianti Montalbano:** Pronounced mon-tahl-*bah*-no; the northwestern part of the zone

- **Chianti Rufina:** Pronounced *roo*-fee-nah; the northeastern part of the zone

Of these areas, the Rufina zone probably ranks highest for the quality of its wines — it's also the one area whose wines are generally available in the United States. (Rufina is also the area whose name most confuses wine drinkers; Rufina, the zone, has nothing to do with Ruffino, the wine producer.) Traditionally, most Chianti Rufina is relatively light-bodied and made to be enjoyed young, but since the mid-1980s, producers have also made richer, more serious, and more age-worthy Chianti Rufina wines. Some Rufina wines, such as the best of Selvapiana and Frescobaldi, are among the finest of all Chiantis.

If the Rufina zone has any competition within the Chianti DOCG, it comes from Chianti Colli Senesi. This is a large area — the largest of the six subzones — extending west and south of the *classico* zone. It encompasses vineyards around San Gimignano, Montalcino, and Montepulciano, among others. Each of these areas is famous for other wines (Vernaccia di San Gimignano, Brunello di Montalcino, and Vino Nobile di Montepulciano, all described later in this chapter), but some producers make Chianti Colli Senesi there as well. The warmer microclimate of the southern part of Colli Senesi enables producers to make relatively full-bodied Chianti wines.

The most common Chianti DOCG wines on the U.S. market are inexpensive ($6 to $12), fairly light-bodied wines under the basic Chianti appellation. Producers in the *classico* zone purchase less expensive grapes (or wine) from beyond the Chianti Classico borders specifically to make these competitively priced wines.

Because Chianti Classico truly dominates the export market for all types of Chianti, the following list of recommended Chianti DOCG producers is short (note that the producers are listed with their subzones in parentheses):

Fattoria di Basciano (Rufina)          Castello di Farnatella (Colli Senesi)
Fattoria di Manzano (Colli Aretini)    Marchesi de' Frescobaldi (Rufina)
Fattoria di Petrolo (Colli Aretini)    Chigi Saracini (Colli Senesi)
Tenuta di Capezzana (Montalbano)       Fattoria Selvapiana (Rufina)

## Pomino, San Gimignano, and other Chianti neighbors

Certain areas within the Chianti zone have their own DOC/G designations for other types of wine. These wines are actually distinct wines that have nothing to do with Chianti itself, except that their vineyards lie in the Chianti area.

### Vernaccia di San Gimignano

San Gimignano (sahn gee-me-*n'yah*-no) is a charming medieval town famous for its towers. The vineyards east of San Gimignano lie within the Chianti Colli Senesi area, but the local pride is the DOCG white wine, Vernaccia (ver-*nahtch*-chah).

Vernaccia di San Gimignano is Tuscany's finest type of white wine and has been for seven centuries. It derives at least 90 percent from the Vernaccia grape variety, which is famous only in this area. Generally, Vernaccia is a fairly full-bodied, dry, soft white, with honey, mineral, and earthy flavors, but sometimes it can be quite fruity.

The wine varies quite a lot in style according to its winemaking: Some producers ferment or age the wine in small French oak barrels, which gives the wine a toastiness or a creaminess that it doesn't otherwise have; other producers make the wine unoaked so the mineral aromas and flavors shine through more clearly. Some producers make more than one Vernaccia wine, each a different style.

If you want to try Vernaccia di San Gimignano, seek out bottles from any of the following producers:

| | |
|---|---|
| Baroncini | Palagetto |
| Casale-Falchini | Giovanni Panizzi |
| Vincenzo Cesani | Fattoria Il Paradiso |
| Fattoria di Cusona (or Guicciardini Strozzi) | San Donato |
| | Fattoria San Quirico |
| La Lastra | Signano |
| Melini | Teruzzi & Puthod |
| Montenidoli | Fratelli Vagnoni |
| Mormoraia | |

### Pomino

Pomino (po-*mee*-no) is a tiny enclave within the Chianti Rufina area. This hilly zone, with its sandy soil and particularly benevolent climate, is a stronghold of French grape varieties in Sangiovese land. Vittorio degli Albizi, whose family came from Auxerre in France's Chablis region, planted Chardonnay, Merlot, and other French varieties here in the mid-1800s. His heirs later married into the Frescobaldi family, and Frescobaldi — a major producer in the Chianti Rufina zone — is now the main landowner in Pomino.

In the 1960s, some Pomino vineyards were replanted with typical Tuscan varieties; DOC regulations therefore permit both nationalities of grapes. Pomino Rosso derives from Sangiovese, Canaiolo, Cabernet Sauvignon, Cabernet Franc, and Merlot, with other varieties (for example, Frescobaldi uses Pinot Nero); a *riserva*-level Pomino Rosso requires three years' aging. Pomino Bianco comes mainly from Pinot Bianco, Chardonnay, and Trebbiano grapes, with other varieties, such as Pinot Grigio. You can also find Pomino as a Vin Santo — dry, medium-sweet or sweet, white or red.

The white wines of Pomino are full-bodied and rich and among the best white wines of Tuscany. In addition to Frescobaldi, another fine producer of Pomino is Fattoria Petrognano, which is owned by the owner of Selvapiana, another good Chianti Rufina producer. Expect to pay $18 to $27 for Pomino.

### Vin Santo

Vin Santo (vin *sahn*-toh) di Chianti Classico is the DOC name for a traditional Tuscan dessert wine made within the Chianti Classico zone; however, several Vin Santos exist, DOC and not, from different parts of Tuscany and elsewhere in Italy.

Winemakers create Vin Santo (which means "holy wine") by drying grapes for several months to concentrate their sugar before pressing them. Then they age the wine from these grapes in small barrels for several years, which sometimes results in the wine's refermenting and developing characteristics of oxidation, such as a nutty aroma and an amber color. Vin Santo wines range from dry to sweet, depending on the individual wine. If red grapes are part of the blend, the wine is sometimes pink.

Vin Santo di Chianti Classico must come mainly from Trebbiano and Malvasia, but other grapes, red or white, are allowed; the wine ages in barrels for at least three years, or four years for *riserva*. Many producers make it, but they do so in small quantities.

# Monumental Montalcino

In terms of international renown, the Montalcino (mon-tal-*chee*-no) area is Tuscany's second most important wine zone, after Chianti Classico. In terms of quality, however, it's Tuscany's shining star.

Montalcino is a small medieval town that perches at 1,850 feet altitude atop a hill in the province of Siena. This isolated community stands apart from the cosmopolitan parts of Tuscany in both space and spirit.

The Montalcino wine district is a hilly, densely wooded area surrounding the town, which sits slightly northeast of the district's geographic center. The area's climate is generally warmer and dryer than Chianti Classico's, and it has few extremes because of the tempering influence of the sea to the southwest and the sheltering effect of Mount Amiata, Tuscany's highest peak, to the southeast. Soils are varied from one end of the district to the other and from lower-altitude vineyards (490 feet) to higher ones (up to 1,640 feet). The particular climate, soils, altitudes, and hillside aspects of the vineyards combine to create a singular effect: Montalcino is the finest location on earth for the Sangiovese grape.

Montalcino's signature wine is Brunello (brew-*nel*-lo) di Montalcino, a hefty red wine that, according to production regulations, must be made entirely from Sangiovese. (Brunello is the local, but unofficial, name for Sangiovese.)

In the isolated hills of Montalcino, the Sangiovese grape ripens more and better than elsewhere in Tuscany, giving its wines in this area more color, body, extract, tannin, and richness than other wines based on the same variety.

However, other Sangiovese wines aren't necessarily based on exactly the same grapes. The various clones of Sangiovese that grow in Montalcino are believed to be distinct from those that grow elsewhere in Tuscany, because they evolved in response to the conditions of Montalcino. In the mid-1800s, a local man named Clemente Santi isolated the clones most suited to making a high-quality, age-worthy, 100 percent Sangiovese wine, in an age when easy-to-drink, blended wines were the norm in Montalcino. The wines of his grandson, Ferruccio Biondi-Santi, and a handful of other producers became celebrated during the second half of the 19th century and affirmed the special synergy that Brunello and Montalcino share.

Today, about 200 grape growers — mostly small farmers — exist in Montalcino, and Brunello di Montalcino is considered one of Italy's two best wines (the other is Barolo, which you can find out more about in Chapter 2 of Book III). It was the first wine to earn DOCG status (in 1980), and it's generally among Italy's most expensive wines. But production is small: Only about 333,000 cases of Brunello di Montalcino are made each year.

**Book III**

**Italy: Small but Mighty**

Although the Montalcino district is small, the wines aren't uniform in style. The grapes ripen in very different ways in different parts of the zone. For example, compared to grapes grown in the southern and western parts of the zone, grapes grown in the northern and eastern vineyards ripen more slowly because of the area's north-facing hillsides, higher altitude, more rain, and/or cooler temperatures. Wines from these areas can also be more perfumed, a bit lighter in body, and harder than the wines from the southern areas, where warmer temperatures, intense sunlight, and maritime breezes enable the grapes to produce richer wines with riper and more intense aromas and flavors. But this wine zone is even more complex than this example implies.

In addition to its flagship Brunello di Montalcino, this zone has three other DOC wines today: Rosso di Montalcino, Moscadello di Montalcino, and Sant'Antimo. The authorized vineyard zone for these three wines is precisely the same as that of Brunello di Montalcino, but the wines differ from Brunello either because of their grape varieties or their aging. Moscadello di Montalcino, for example, is a sweet white wine made from the Muscat grape. This type of wine was traditional in the area for many years, but it had all but disappeared until Castello Banfi revived the style by planting Muscat grapes in Montalcino in the early 1980s.

# Brunello di Montalcino

Since its earliest conception, Brunello di Montalcino has been a wine for aging. Some wines from good vintages not only can age for 50 years or more but also absolutely *need* a couple of decades to lose the fire of youth and become harmonious. The DOCG regulations echo the wine's potential by requiring that Brunello age for four years before it can be released — the longest minimum aging period for any wine in Italy; Brunello di Montalcino Riserva, made from a producer's best wines in very good vintages, must age five years before its release. For at least two of these four or five years, the wine must age in oak barrels or casks.

Although traditionally minded producers age their wine for three years or more in large, old casks, which produces more austere wines, the most avant-garde producers age some of their Brunello in small barrels of French oak (and practice other nontraditional winemaking techniques) to fix a certain fruitiness in their wine. In either case, almost every Brunello is best with *at least* ten years of age from the vintage.

Despite the privileged climate of Montalcino, vintage differences do exist. Since World War II, the Montalcino zone has averaged about five very good to outstanding vintages per decade. The Brunellos from the 1990s that were released in 2004 exceeded the historical average, with three outstanding vintages 1990, 1995, and 1997.

Tasting wines from these great vintages carries a price, however. For instance, Brunello from the 1995 vintage costs about $40 to $75 a bottle at retail, and 1995 *riservas* cost up to $100 or more.

Check out the following producers of Brunello di Montalcino for a good introduction to this impressive wine:

| | |
|---|---|
| Altesino | Cerbaiona |
| Argiano | Ciacci Piccolomini |
| Castello Banfi | Col d'Orcia |
| Fattoria dei Barbi | Costanti |
| Biondi-Santi (expensive) | Fattoria del Casato |
| Camigliano | Tenuta Friggiali |
| Campogiovanni | Fuligni |
| Canalicchio di Sopra | La Gerla |
| Capanna | Gorelli |
| Tenuta Caparzo (especially, the single-vineyard La Casa) | Il Greppone Mazzi |
| | Lisini |
| Casanova di Neri | Il Marroneto |
| Case Basse of Soldera (very expensive) | Mastrojanni |
| Castelgiocondo | Tenute Silvio Nardi |

Siro Pacenti

Pertimali di Angelo Sassetti

Pertimali di Livio Sassetti

La Pieve di Santa Restituta

La Poderina

Poggio Antico

Poggio Salvi

Il Poggiolo

Il Poggione

Salvioni-La Cerbaiola

Talenti-Pian di Conte

La Torre

Uccelliera

Val di Suga

## *Rosso di Montalcino*

Rosso di Montalcino is linked to tradition only in that its existence (since 1984) has helped preserve the traditional long aging of Brunello di Montalcino by giving producers an outlet for wines that they prefer not to age so long. In other words, Rosso di Montalcino is a baby Brunello, made from the same grape variety (100 percent Sangiovese) grown in the same territory, but aged less than Brunello is (with a minimum of one year rather than four years). Rosso di Montalcino is similar to Brunello in its aromas and flavors, but it's fresher, lighter-bodied, and easier to enjoy young. Of course, the diminutive of a blockbuster can still be substantial, and some Rosso di Montalcino wines are fairly serious wines; others, however, are lighter.

Producers can grow grapes specifically to make Rosso di Montalcino (using their younger vines, for example), or they can relegate grapes originally intended for Brunello to the Rosso category when a vintage is less than ideal. They can even decide at some point during the aging period to bottle their Brunello-in-waiting early, as Rosso. In effect, Rosso di Montalcino enables producers to declassify grapes or wines that they believe are unsuitable for Brunello for whatever reason; it also lets them make a younger, more approachable wine, if that's their goal. Rosso di Montalcino was the first DOC wine to give producers such a flexible, viable alternative to their traditional wine.

Rosso di Montalcino doesn't command the price or prestige that Brunello does. But Rosso isn't cheap, either: Prices range from $20 to $30 at retail. Nevertheless, it's a great means of experiencing what Sangiovese can do in Montalcino. The vast majority of Brunello producers (some good ones are listed in the preceding section) make a Rosso, at least in some vintages. Depending on the vintage, Rosso di Montalcino is at its best three to ten years from the vintage date.

## *Sant'Antimo*

Since the late 1970s, some producers in the Montalcino area — like their counterparts elsewhere in Tuscany — have grown Cabernet, Merlot, and other internationally famous varieties for the production of super-Tuscan wines (see the "Super-Tuscan Wines — The Winds of Change" section later

**Book III**

**Italy: Small but Mighty**

in this chapter). In 1996, Italian authorities approved a new DOC designation called Sant'Antimo for these wines and similar wines not made from the traditional Sangiovese grape.

Sant'Antimo wines take their name from a beautiful local abbey reputedly built by Charlemagne in the ninth century. The wines include a Bianco and a Rosso, as well as varietally labeled wines: Chardonnay, Sauvignon Blanc, Pinot Grigio, Pinot Nero, Cabernet Sauvignon, and Merlot.

Producer Castello Banfi uses the Sant'Antimo appellation for its varietal wines, as well as for its two flagship blended red wines from the Montalcino zone: Summus (a blend of Sangiovese, Cabernet, and Syrah) and Excelsus (Merlot and Cabernet). On the other hand, Frescobaldi doesn't use the Sant'Antimo DOC for its Lamaione Merlot, preferring to designate that wine as IGT Toscana instead.

# The "Noble Wine" of Montepulciano

The second red Tuscan wine to attain DOCG status in 1980, Vino Nobile di Montepulciano (*vee*-no *no*-bee-lae dee mahn-tae-pul-chee-*ah*-no), has a proud history dating back to the 17th century, when the local wine of the Montepulciano territory was dubbed "noble" because it was a favorite of noblemen. In more recent times, the producers of the Montepulciano zone have worked hard to maintain an elite image for their wine, especially in the face of stiff competition from both Chianti Classico and Brunello di Montalcino. But Vino Nobile's day might finally have come (again): The Montepulciano zone now seems to have attained a critical mass of serious producers, and the wines today are finer than they were in the past 40 years.

The Montepulciano district is a small area around the ancient town of Montepulciano, in southeastern Tuscany (see Figure 5-1). It's an area of fairly open hills crowned by the old town, which sits at an altitude of 1,968 feet. Vineyards occupy slopes down to 820 feet in altitude, the soils of which vary from sandy to clay to rocky, depending on the precise location within the territory. The variety of altitudes and soils provides built-in diversity for the wines; local authorities have, in fact, identified 20 distinct (but unofficial) subzones within the district.

Despite the fact that the Montepulciano area is quite inland, the climate is strongly influenced by the sea; breezes keep the air dry and the grapes healthy. The grapes in question are mainly Prugnolo Gentile (prew-*n'yoh*-lo jen-*tee*-lae), a local clone of Sangiovese, which constitutes 80 to 100 percent of the wine. Up to 20 percent of other recommended varieties of the area are also allowed. Traditionally, the soft Canaiolo and the perfumed Mammolo were the blending partners, but these days producers are increasingly using international varieties such as Cabernet or (especially) Merlot.

Just like Chianti Classico, Vino Nobile di Montepulciano has reinvented itself since the mid-1980s. The wine has changed from a multifaceted blend (of Sangiovese, Canaiolo, Mammolo, and other red and white varieties) to a straightforward red wine based largely on Sangiovese. Renovation of some of the vineyards has resulted in riper grapes that make a darker, richer wine. And changes within the wineries — notably the use of French oak barrels — have further beefed up the wines' intensity.

Vino Nobile is still in transition. Some wines today are soft, rich wines with creamy, plumlike fruit flavors and toasty oak notes, yet others are relatively lean but smooth with firm tannin and gentle almond and red fruit flavors. In general, they range in price from about $18 to $30, with some single-vineyard wines costing slightly more.

Rosso di Montepulciano is a DOC wine from the same territory and the same grape varieties as Vino Nobile, but this wine can age in as little as five months before release from the winery. As in the Montalcino zone (described earlier in this chapter), some producers make their Rosso from specific vineyard sites, whereas others make Rosso from whichever grapes or wines they deem unsuitable for Vino Nobile. Rosso di Montepulciano tends to sell for $12 to $15.

Vin Santo di Montepulciano is the third DOC that applies to the same territory. It's a white — actually gold or amber — dessert wine (see the "Vin Santo" section earlier in this chapter for more on this type of wine) made at least 70 percent from Malvasia, Grechetto, and/or Trebbiano grapes, with other local whites permitted. An amber-red style, called Occhio di Pernice (pronounced *oke*-kee-oh dee per-*nee*-chae and meaning "eye of the partridge") contains at least 50 percent Sangiovese. The white must age for three years (or four, to be considered *riserva*); the red wine must age for eight years.

The most famed and sought-after Vin Santo, not only of Montepulciano, but of all of Tuscany as well, is that of Avignonesi. Its bouquet, complexity of flavors, and length on the palate are truly remarkable; unfortunately, it's made in minute quantities and is expensive.

Keep an eye out for the following favorite producers of Vino Nobile di Montepulciano and Rosso di Montalcino:

| | |
|---|---|
| Avignonesi | Lodola Nuova |
| Poderi Boscarelli | Poliziano |
| La Braccesca | Redi |
| La Calonica | Massimo Romeo |
| Contucci | Salcheto |
| Dei | Tenuta Trerose |
| Fassati | Tenuta Valdipatta |
| Fattoria del Cerro | Villa Sant'Anna |
| Il Macchione | |

# Tuscany's "Hot" Coast

The central hills of Tuscany have been *the* scene of the wine action for generation upon generation, but Tuscany's coastal areas have emerged as major production zones for fine wine, too. Wine producers from Tuscany's interior and from other regions of Italy have invested in vineyards and wineries along the coast, and wineries that already existed there have hired famous winemaking consultants to help them improve the quality of their wines.

If you were to travel through Tuscany in the company of winemakers, you'd hear a lot of talk about an area called Maremma. Technically, Maremma is a stretch of land that extends from 6 miles north of the town of Bolgheri southward into the region of Latium. The name is still used to refer to that whole coastal area, but increasingly, in wine terms, Maremma refers only to the province of Grosseto — Tuscany's southernmost province, where Maremma Toscana is an IGT designation.

The next sections introduce you to the wine zones along Tuscany's coast.

## Bolgheri

The Bolgheri DOC (*bohl*-gheh-ree) zone sits about in the middle of the Tuscan coast, in the province of Livorno, and takes its name from the small, walled town of Bolgheri. The original super-Tuscan wine, Sassicaia (sas-ee-*kye*-ah), is made here in vineyards of the Tenuta San Guido estate, which is owned by Marchese Incisa della Rochetta, cousin of the Antinori brothers (see the "Super-Tuscan Wines — The Winds of Change" section later in this chapter for more on this quirky wine category). These vineyards are an official subzone of Bolgheri, specifically Bolgheri-Sassicaia DOC. Sassicaia, a blend of Cabernet Sauvignon and Cabernet Franc, was first made in 1944 and commercialized in 1968.

Bolgheri is a fairly small wine zone with fewer than 1,000 acres of vineyards. Although the coast itself is flat, the land quickly rises into hills, where the vineyards are located; sea breezes create a particular microclimate for these hills. The Bolgheri DOC covers a range of wines, including blended whites from Trebbiano, Vermentino, and Sauvignon; a varietal Vermentino (Antinori has a good one) and Sauvignon; reds and rosés from Cabernet, Merlot, and Sangiovese; and a pink Vin Santo. Many Bolgheri wines are unremarkable, but the finest are quite good.

Apart from the Tenuta San Guido estate, which makes Sassicaia, other Bolgheri properties of note are Ornellaia, which is owned by Lodovico Antinori (who makes a first-rate blended red under the estate name, a block-buster Merlot called Masseto, and a thoroughly enjoyable Sauvignon called Poggio alle Gazze); Tenuta Guado al Tasso, which is owned by the Piero

Antinori family (whose top wine is a Cab/Merlot blend called Guado al Tasso); Grattamacco; and Ca'Marcanda, a new property built by Angelo Gaja of Piedmont.

## Val di Cornia

Other coastal DOC wines in the province of Livorno come from an area called Val di Cornia (vahl dee *cor*-nee-ah), situated south of Bolgheri where the land juts into the sea. The distinction between DOC and super-Tuscan wines is still a bit blurry in this area because DOC is a fairly new designation here — but some of the wines can be impressive, however you categorize them. The Val di Cornia DOC applies to light- and medium-bodied whites made mainly from Trebbiano, with Vermentino and other white varieties, including Pinot Grigio and Pinot Bianco; rosés and reds almost entirely from Sangiovese, with Cabernet Sauvignon, Merlot, and other varieties; and a *riserva*-level red, aged for three years. Four of the major subzones of Val di Cornia — whose names appear on their wines' labels — are Suvereto, San Vincenzo, Campiglia Marittima, and Piombino.

Val di Cornia's recommended producers include the following:

| | |
|---|---|
| Tua Rita | Lorella Ambrosini |
| Gualdo del Re | Montepeloso |
| Villa Monte Rico | Jacopo Banti |
| Le Volpaiole | Azienda Agricola Rigoli |
| Podere San Michele | |

## Grosseto

Eight DOC wines hail from Grosseto, Tuscany's southernmost and largest province. Monteregio di Massa Marittima (mahn-tae-*rae*-gee-oh dee *mahs*-sah mah-*reet*-tee-mah) is a very hilly area extending inland from the coast in the northern part of the Grosseto province; Massa Marittima is one of the towns in this area. DOC regulations provide for a Vermentino and a Rosso, regular or *riserva,* that's 80 percent Sangiovese. In the future, producers hope to reduce Sangiovese to 50 percent to enable more use of varieties such as Cabernet, Merlot, or Syrah.

Partially overlapping the Monteregio di Massa Marittima zone and extending farther inland is the Montecucco (mahn-tae-*kook*-coh) DOC zone (established in 1998). This area makes a varietal Vermentino and Sangiovese, as well as a blended white (60 percent Trebbiano) and a blended red (60 percent Sangiovese). Two even newer DOCs are Capalbio and Sovana. Capalbio (cah-*pahl*-bee-o) features a varietal Vermentino, Sangiovese and Cabernet Sauvignon, a blended white (at least half Trebbiano), and a blended red (at least half Sangiovese). Sovana (so-*vah*-nah) is a red wine zone with varietal wines from Sangiovese, Cabernet Sauvignon, Merlot, and Aleatico, as well as a blended Rosso that's half Sangiovese.

Another DOC area, Costa dell'Argentario (*cohs*-tah del-lar-jen-*tah*-ree-oh), occupies islands and an adjoining coastal area just north of the border with Latium. The wine from this resort area is a soft, dry, varietally labeled white from the Ansonica grape variety (a grape that's very big in Sicily, where it's called Inzolia). The tiny Parrina (pah-*ree*-nah) zone lies just north of the Costa dell'Argentario zone; it makes a white wine based mainly on Trebbiano, Ansonica, and/or Chardonnay, as well as red and rosé wines based mainly on Sangiovese and a *riserva*-level red that requires three years of aging.

Morellino (moh-rael-*lee*-no) is the name winemakers use for the Sangiovese grape in the hilly vineyard area around the town of Scansano (scahn-*sah*-no), in the central part of the Grosseto province. The dry, fragrant wine, Morellino di Scansano, derives from this grape variety; a *riserva*-level, with two years aging, also exists. Although Morellino di Scansano isn't a new DOC zone, the wine here is somewhat in transition because of all the new action in Grosseto in general. For example, Jacopo Biondi-Santi is selling a high-end Scansano, which is made at his new Castello di Montepo property, for $45 a bottle — making an emphatic quality statement. Other Morellino di Scansano wines, such as Moris Farms and Cantina del Morellino di Scansano, sell in the $12 to $15 range. Le Pupille and Massa Vecchia are two other good producers from this area whose wines are available in the United States.

Overlapping the eastern half of the Morellino di Scansano zone and extending south and eastward to Latium is the DOC zone of Bianco di Pitigliano. This soft, dry white variety derives 50 to 80 percent from Trebbiano grown on volcanic soil, along with numerous other grapes such as Greco, Malvasia, Verdello, Grechetto, Chardonnay, Sauvignon Blanc, Pinot Blanc, and Welschriesling.

# Super-Tuscan Wines — The Winds of Change

The category of so-called super-Tuscan wines is a mixed bag of wines from all over Tuscany, mainly red but also white. It's a completely unofficial category; in fact, according to how wines are normally classified in Italy, the category of super-Tuscans doesn't even exist. But for about 30 years now, wine lovers and wine professionals have used the term to refer to certain wines from Tuscany.

What are super-Tuscan wines? They're expensive wines ($45 and up) of small production, usually internationally styled (with fairly pronounced fruitiness and a lot of oak flavor), usually made from grape varieties or blends that aren't traditional in Tuscany, and usually labeled with fanciful names. When winemakers began fashioning super-Tuscan wines in the late 1970s and early 1980s, these wines had another thing in common — they were all technically only *vini da tavola* with no geographic designation smaller than Tuscany. (Chapter 1 of Book III explains the significance of *vini da tavola.*) They weren't DOC wines, and the IGT designation didn't yet exist.

To grasp exactly what super-Tuscan wines are, you need to consider their origins. Thirty years ago, Chianti had to contain at least 10 percent of white varieties in its blend, and Sangiovese could be no more than 70 percent of the wine. Chianti's image was low, and its market was depressed. Some producers felt they could make a better wine (and receive a higher price for it) by using unconventional grape varieties (or blends) and winemaking methods that they borrowed from places that produce high-quality wines, such as Bordeaux. These new wines didn't qualify as DOC Chianti, so they were labeled as *vino da tavola di Toscana.* The most common of these new wines were blends of Sangiovese and Cabernet Sauvignon, or wines that were entirely Cabernet or entirely Sangiovese.

The trend of super-Tuscan wine production spread beyond the borders of Chianti Classico to every corner of Tuscany as winemakers sought to show off their talent and make profitable wines. (Actually, the first super-Tuscan wine didn't come from the Chianti zone but from the Bolgheri zone, near the Tuscan coast; however, the movement gained its impetus in Chianti.) It even spread to other parts of Italy, where today you can find a few super-Veneto wines, for example, or super-Piedmont wines — although they're never really called that.

The super-Tuscan trend accomplished a huge amount of good for Tuscany, and for Chianti Classico, because it forced wine professionals around the world to take Tuscan wines seriously. It also forced modifications to the Chianti and Chianti Classico regulations (in 1984 and 1996) so that outdated practices, such as using white grapes in the blend, are no longer required.

Under today's DOCG regulations, many of the super-Tuscan wines from within the Chianti Classico zone can actually qualify as DOCG Chianti Classico. As a result, some producers are bringing their wines back under the Chianti umbrella, but others aren't. (The entire production of the excellent producer Montevertine, for example, is still all non-DOC.) But all super-Tuscan wines today are now IGT-level wines because Tuscany is an official IGT designation.

You won't find an official or even complete listing of all super-Tuscan wines, but you will find a lot of confusion over what is and isn't a super-Tuscan wine today, because some of the original super-Tuscan wines, such as Sassicaia, are now DOC wines. (See the earlier "Bolgheri" section for more on Sassicaia.) This confusion is a part of having an unofficial category.

Until a complete list comes along, here are some favorite super-Tuscan wines (some of which are now DOC wines) with their grape blend; the producer's name is in parentheses:

Brancaia — Sangiovese-Merlot (La Brancaia)

Cabreo Il Borgo — ⅘ Sangiovese and ⅕ Cabernet; La Pietra — Chardonnay (Ruffino)

Camartina — Cabernet-Sangiovese; Batàr — Chardonnay (Querciabella)

Cepparello — Sangiovese (Isole e Olena)

Cerviolo — 40-30-30 percent Sangiovese-Merlot-Cabernet (San Fabiano)

Flaccianello della Pieve — Sangiovese (Fontodi)

Fontalloro — Sangiovese (Fattoria di Felsina)

Grattamacco — Sangiovese, Malvasia Nera, Cabernet (Grattamacco)

Lamaione — Merlot (Marchesi de' Frescobaldi)

Masseto — Merlot (Tenuta dell'Ornellaia)

Ornellaia — mainly Cabernet Sauvignon, some Merlot, Cabernet Franc (Tenuta dell'Ornellaia)

Il Pareto — Cabernet (Nozzole)

Percarlo — Sangiovese (San Giusto a Rentennano)

Le Pergole Torte — Sangiovese (Montevertine)

Prunaio — mainly Sangiovese (Viticcio)

Sammarco — ⅘ Cabernet and ⅕ percent Sangiovese (Castello di Rampolla)

Sassello — Sangiovese (Castello di Verrazano)

Sassicaia — 75-25 percent Cabernet Sauvignon-Cabernet Franc (Tenuta San Guido)

I Sodi di San Niccolò — mostly Sangiovese, some Malvasia Nera (Castellare di Castellina)

Solaia — 80-20 percent Cabernet-Sangiovese (Antinori)

Tignanello — 80-20 percent Sangiovese-Cabernet (Antinori)

La Vigna di Alceo — mainly Cabernet, some Petite Verdot (Castello di Rampolla)

# Chapter 6

# Getting Acquainted with Central Italy's Wines

* * * * * * * * * * * * * * * * * * * * * * * * * * * * * * * * * * * * * * * * *

### In This Chapter

▶ Discovering Umbria, the only region bordered completely by Italy

▶ Finding Verdicchio in the Marche region

▶ Checking out rugged Abruzzo and its Montepulciano

▶ Exploring the region that surrounds Rome

* * * * * * * * * * * * * * * * * * * * * * * * * * * * * * * * * * * * * * * * *

Many of the wines of central Italy, both red and white, are particularly good values. Some of the white wines — such as Orvieto, Verdicchio, and Frascati — are old friends to wine drinkers. However, even these old friends are new, in a sense, because they're better made today than they've ever been — particularly Verdicchio. Other wines of central Italy are new to wine lovers; for example, Sagrantino di Montefalco, a red DOCG wine from Umbria, is practically unknown in the United States, despite the fact that it's a pretty terrific wine. (Now you know that insider tidbit — good thing you picked up this book, eh?)

## Umbria: The Inland Region

Umbria (*oom*-bree-ah) has the distinction of being Italy's only region that's surrounded entirely by Italy. Most other regions manage to touch a sea or — in the case of a few northern regions — another country. But Umbria lies in the center of Italy. Tuscany is Umbria's neighbor to the northwest, and Rome is a two-hour drive southwest from Umbria's southern border (see Figure 6-1). The region's eastern border is entirely occupied by Abruzzo.

Other than its capital — the busy, industrial city of Perugia, home of one of Italy's finest universities — Umbria is sparsely populated. The Apennine Mountains take up much of the land. But tourists do flock to the town of Assisi, near Perugia, where St. Francis of Assisi, friend of animals and nature, once lived.

**Figure 6-1:**
The five
regions of
central Italy
and their
wine zones.

**Umbria Wine Zones**
1. Colli Altotiberini
2. Colli Perugini
3. Torgiano DOCG
4. Montefalco
5. Orvieto

**Marche Wine Zones**
6. Bianchello del Mentauro
7. Verdicchio dei Castelli di Jesi
8. Rosso Conero
9. Verdicchio di Matelica
10. Vernaccia di Serrapetrona

**Abruzzo Wine Zones**
11. Montepulciano d'Abruzzo
12. Trebbiano d'Abruzzo

**Latium Wine Zones**
13. Frascati
14. Marino

**Molise Wine Zones**
15. Biferno
16. Pentro

Wine-wise, Umbria is in Tuscany's shadow. Many of its grape varieties are the same as Tuscany's, but no matter how good the wines are, they simply can't compete with Tuscany's international recognition. (Chapter 5 in Book III covers Tuscan wines.) Umbria's main claim to wine fame is the historic hilltop town of Orvieto — and the white wine of the same name. But even in Orvieto, large Tuscan producers, such as Antinori and Ruffino, make much of the wine.

Umbria is blessed with a similar climate to Tuscany's: warm and dry but cool enough for the grapes to grow well, thanks to the Tiber River and its tributaries that flow through the region. The soil is mainly calcareous clay and sand, with plenty of limestone, which is always good for vines. Considering its natural resources, Umbria hasn't nearly realized its potential as a wine region. But in the last decade, Umbria has made significant progress. The region's most well-known red wine — Rubesco Riserva, the Torgiano Rosso Riserva DOCG of Lungarotti, which was Umbria's first family of wine — continues to draw admiration throughout the world. And lately, Umbria's other DOCG wine, the red Sagrantino di Montefalco, is receiving some belated attention beyond the borders of Umbria.

Umbria has always been known as a white wine region. Twenty-three percent of its wines are DOC or DOCG, and a high percentage of this wine is white — mainly Orvieto — and made by large wineries or cooperatives. But more and more of Umbria's wines are red.

With the debut of 3 new DOCs in the past few years, Umbria now has 11 DOC wines, in addition to its 2 DOCG wines. (The majority of these wines hail from the province of Perugia, which occupies the northern two-thirds of Umbria.) But many fine Umbrian wines, especially reds, carry the designation IGT Umbria because that name has strong recognition. (Umbria's other IGT zones are Allerona, Bettona, Cannara, and Spello.)

# Orvieto

The town of Orvieto (or-vee-*ae*-toh) arises from a rocky hill and is also the name of Umbria's most famous white wine. The Orvieto wine zone is a large area in southwestern Umbria that extends north to the border of the Perugia province and south into the Latium region. The original *classico* subzone, where the best Orvieto originates, is the middle third of the area; wines from this part of the zone are named Orvieto Classico. The special chalky limestone soil (called *tufa*), which dominates in the *classico* area, along with ancient remnants of volcanic soil, gives Orvieto Classico wines a unique character.

---

## Umbria's aristocracy

If you'd like living proof of the potential of southern Umbria as a wine zone, look no further than the wines of Antinori's Castello della Sala winery, an ancient castle north of Orvieto that has been in the Antinori family for generations.

The winery's two specialties are the dry white Cervaro della Sala (about $38), a very good, age-worthy, barrel-fermented wine made from Chardonnay with some Grechetto, and a white dessert wine called Muffato della Sala (about $40 to $42 for a 500-milliliter bottle), made from Sauvignon and other varieties affected by noble rot. This winery also makes an attractive Chardonnay and a Sauvignon (both about $11 to $12) as well as a Pinot Nero — all of which carry the Umbria IGT designation. Antinori's Orvieto Classico Campogrande DOC (less than $10) comes from the same winery.

---

In the Middle Ages, Orvieto was a sweet, golden-colored wine; only in the past 60 years or so has most Orvieto been made *secco* (dry). As recently as the 1970s, Italians urged visitors to try the real Orvieto — Orvieto Abboccato (or-vee-*ae*-toh ahb-boh-*cah*-toh), a semidry style that was popular in Italy. DOC regulations still permit the production of sweet or semisweet Orvieto; besides the *secco* style, the wine can be *abboccato, amabile* (semisweet), and *dolce* (sweet).

Orvieto is a blended wine that's at least 60 percent Grechetto (considered the zone's best variety), with up to 15 percent Trebbiano (known locally as Procanico), plus some other local white varieties, including Verdello, Canaiolo Bianco, and Malvasia. This formula enables producers to make the wine in varying degrees of richness. Some producers use as much Grechetto as possible in their wine to give it fruitiness and weight, for example. The quality of Orvieto has improved quite a bit in recent years, thanks to grape-growing and winemaking experimentation and the work of Umbrian enologists Riccardo and Renzo Cotarella.

As evidence of Umbria's new red wine direction, Orvieto now has a companion DOC red wine, Rosso Orvietano (*rohs*-so or-vee-ae-*tah*-no), made in a very large area that includes the entire Orvieto zone. This new DOC covers a blended Rosso plus eight varietally labeled wines. The Rosso derives at least 70 percent from any or all of nine varieties — Aleatico, Cabernet Franc, Cabernet Sauvignon, Canaiolo, Ciliegiolo, Merlot, Montepulciano, Pinot Nero, and Sangiovese — with Barbera, Cesanese, Colorino, and Dolcetto optional.

## *Torgiano*

Torgiano (tor-gee-*ah*-no) is a town on the east bank of the Tiber River, across from Perugia. In the northern hills of Torgiano, which have a rather warm microclimate, both red and white grape varieties grow to make a DOCG and several DOC wines.

Torgiano owes its popularity as a quality wine zone to one producer: Lungarotti. The late Giorgio Lungarotti made his Cantine Lungarotti not only Umbria's most renowned winery but also one of the most prestigious wineries in all of Italy. Lungarotti wines are popular worldwide; of the nearly 220,000 produced annually, more than half are exported. Thanks to Lungarotti, Torgiano earned DOC status in 1968.

In 1990, one Torgiano wine, the Rosso Riserva, received the unusual honor of being singled out for DOCG status. The Torgiano Rosso Riserva DOCG is basically just one wine, Lungarotti's Rubesco Riserva della Vigna Monticchio, the brand's flagship wine. Torgiano Rosso Riserva is mainly Sangiovese with a small amount of Canaiolo; Trebbiano, Ciliegiolo, and/or Montepulciano are optional. It must age at least three years — but Lungarotti's wine is released ten years after the vintage. In good vintages, Lungarotti's Rubesco Riserva has the complexity, finesse, and aging ability of top classified-growth Bordeaux wines selling for twice the price or more.

Torgiano DOC wines number nine (not counting its one DOCG), of which the blended Rosso and Bianco are the most popular. Torgiano Rosso is basically the same blend as the Rosso Riserva, except that it ages for a minimum of 18 months. It's best known in the form of Lungarotti's Rubesco, a fine value at $14 to $15 retail. Torgiano Rosato, a dry rosé, has the same blend. Torgiano Bianco is mainly a mix of Trebbiano and the local Grechetto. (Lungarotti's version, called Torre di Giano, is a dry wine full of character and made from 70 percent Trebbiano and 30 percent Grechetto; it retails for $11 to $12.) Torgiano varietal wines are Chardonnay, Cabernet Sauvignon, Pinot Nero, Pinot Grigio, Riesling Italico, and a Spumante made from Chardonnay and Pinot Nero.

**Book III**

**Italy: Small but Mighty**

# Sagrantino di Montefalco

About 12 miles south of Torgiano, the town of Montefalco is enjoying a revival — and its leading grape variety, Sagrantino (sah-grahn-*tee*-no), is following its lead. This native variety has made red wine locally since the Middle Ages, but the wine was traditionally a sweet wine. In its revived form, it's now mainly a dry, full-bodied wine, and it has won enough acclaim to receive DOCG status.

Purplish-ruby Sagrantino is a robust wine that can take some aging. Some producers still make a sweet *passito* version. But the dry Sagrantino di Montefalco is gaining renown, as producers begin to make it a specialty; retail prices range from $23 to $28.

From the same area also come the Montefalco DOC wines. Rosso di Montalfalco is mainly Sangiovese, with some Sagrantino and up to 15 percent other varieties; it retails for $10 to $20. Less available in the United States is the dry white Montefalco Bianco, which is made mainly from Grechetto and Trebbiano; Adanti's Montefalco Bianco sells for a mere $10 to $11.

### Recommended Umbrian wineries

Look for the following recommended wine producers of Umbria:

Fratelli Adanti
Antonelli
Barberani-Vallesanta
Bigi
Arnaldo Caprai-Val di Maggio
La Carraia
Castello della Sala
Cantina Sociale dei Colli Amerini
Còlpetrone
Co.Vi.O. (also known as Cardeto)

Decugnano dei Barbi
La Fiorita-Lamborghini
Cantine Lungarotti
Cantina Monrubio (formerly Vi.C.Or.)
Pieve del Vescovo
Rocca di Fabri
Tenuta di Salviano
Fratelli Sportoletti
Tilli
Tenuta Le Velette

# Marche on the Adriatic

Marche, pronounced *mahr*-kae and also known as the Marches region, is in east-central Italy, and its rather long eastern border runs along the Adriatic Sea. Umbria is Marche's neighbor to the west, Emilia-Romagna is north, and Abruzzo is south (see Figure 6-1). Marche's most important city and its capital is the seaport of Ancona, located in the central part of the coastline.

The Apennine Mountains occupy about two-thirds of Marche, including the entire western part. The rest is mainly hillsides, ideal for grapevines. The weather between the Adriatic Sea and the Apennines is nearly perfect most of the time, sunny and mild with pleasant breezes. Several rivers course through the hillsides, exerting a tempering effect on the climate on their way to the sea.

Marche has 11 DOC zones and one IGT designation, Marche. Its most famous wine is the white varietal wine, Verdicchio (ver-*deek*-kee-oh). The region's two most renowned reds are Rosso Cònero (*rohs*-so *coh*-nae-ro) and Rosso Piceno (*rohs*-so pee-*chae*-no). The fact that many people outside of Marche still haven't heard of these two fine reds is evidence that Marche has quite a way to go in promoting its wines.

The following sections bring you up to speed on Marche's top wines and recommend some producers to seek out if you're interested in trying them.

## Tasting Verdicchio

Marche has two DOC Verdicchio wines:

- **Verdicchio dei Castelli di Jesi:** Mainly from the province of Ancona, by the sea, this wine is pronounced ver-*deek*-kee-oh dae cahs-*tel*-ee dee *yae*-see.

- **Verdicchio di Matelica:** From an inland area in the province of Macerata, this wine is pronounced ver-*deek*-kee-oh dee mah-*tae*-lee-cah.

In terms of production, Verdicchio dei Castelli di Jesi is clearly the most important DOC wine in Marche. The vineyard area is mainly in the hills west of the city of Jesi on both sides of the Esino River. The best, or *classico* area, is west of Jesi in a hilly area 12 to 18 miles from the Adriatic. The soil here is calcareous clay with sand, remnants of fossils, and minerals. Wines from the *classico* subzone are generally the best Verdicchio wines.

Although producers may blend up to 15 percent Malvasia and/or Trebbiano into their Verdicchio wines, many of them make a 100 percent Verdicchio for quality reasons. Most also make single-vineyard Verdicchios or special *cuvées* (blends). Verdicchio is an unusual white wine for this part of Italy because it's capable of aging, and you can find *riserva* versions, although it offers fruity freshness and liveliness when it's young. The wine is totally dry with fresh apple or lemon flavors and sometimes a slightly tangy character suggestive of salty sea air. DOC regulations also permit the production of a sparkling and a sweet *passito* version.

The Matelica wine zone is in an isolated valley in the foothills of the Apennines in western Marche. The climate here, away from the Adriatic, is more continental, resulting in a somewhat different style of Verdicchio. With fresh, delicate aromas in its youth and good acidity, Verdicchio di Matelica is fuller-bodied and longer lasting than the easy-drinking Verdicchio dei Castelli di Jesi. Wine drinkers seek out Verdicchio di Matelica because its production is only one-tenth that of Verdicchio di Castelli di Jesi.

**Book III**

**Italy: Small but Mighty**

The grape variety requirements for Verdicchio di Matelica are the same as those of Verdicchio di Castelli di Jesi, and the permitted Trebbiano and Malvasia are seldom used. Verdicchio di Matelica comes in regular, *riserva*, sparkling, and *passito* versions.

## *Sampling Rosso Cònero and Rosso Piceno*

Rosso Cònero is the premium red wine of Marche, made only in a limited area: the hillsides of Monte Cònero, a dramatically beautiful area that provides a striking backdrop to the seaport of Ancona. In this area,

Montepulciano is clearly the best red variety, and Rosso Cònero derives at least 85 percent from this grape (up to 15 percent Sangiovese is permitted but seldom used).

Rosso Cònero might just be the best relatively unknown red wine of Italy; if this wine were from a high-profile region, such as Tuscany or Piedmont, it would've been granted DOCG status long ago. Rosso Cònero has pronounced herbal and black cherry aromas and flavors, is quite tannic and full-bodied, and improves with age. Yet it retails for only $15 to $20, which makes it one of Italy's finest red wine values.

Rosso Piceno, Marche's other important red, has a much larger production than Rosso Cònero; in fact, it's Marche's largest-volume red wine, second only to Verdicchio dei Castelli di Jesi in total volume. The Rosso Piceno wine zone is the largest in Marche, extending from the Abruzzo border in the south into all of Ascoli Piceno province except the Apennine Mountains, through both Macerata and Ancona provinces — but excluding the small Rosso Cònero and Lacrima di Morro d'Alba zones. The best part of the zone is a limited hillside area of 13 communities east of the provincial capital, Ascoli Piceno, that extends to the coast.

Rosso Piceno is at least 60 percent Sangiovese, with up to 40 percent Montepulciano and up to 15 percent of two white varieties, Trebbiano and Passerina. The wine is at its best when producers use a full 40 percent of the lower-cropping Montepulciano. Rosso Piceno can be decent, but Rosso Cònero is generally the far superior wine.

## The comeback wine of the decade

Verdicchio first gained fame in the 1950s when the Fazi-Battaglia winery bottled it in a green amphora-shaped bottle and promoted it as the ideal wine with fish — which it is. The wine caught on, and it was a big success for a couple of decades.

The vast increase in sales unfortunately had a downside. The wine slipped badly in quality, and by the late 1970s, you couldn't give it away to the more wine-savvy customers who replaced the less sophisticated wine drinkers of the '50s and '60s.

In the 1980s, Verdicchio producers, led by Fazi-Battaglia, moved to improve the quality of their wines, starting with replanting the vineyards. Fazi-Battaglia hired one of Italy's top wine consultants, Franco Bernabei, to oversee the project. The results have been nothing short of remarkable. Today, Verdicchio is better than ever, and it's selling retail for $8 to $9! It's crisp, full of flavor, unoaked, and quite delicious — a natural with fish and seafood.

## Suggesting some Marche wine producers

The wines of Marche are still great values because producers of this region — with the exception of Fazi-Battaglia and Umani Ronchi, both Verdicchio producers — haven't really marketed their wines around the world. The three best wines to look for are the two Verdicchio wines and the excellent red, Rosso Cònero. Bear in mind that ten times as much Verdicchio dei Castelli di Jesi exists than Verdicchio di Matelica — making the latter more difficult to find. Here are some recommended wine producers of the Marche region:

Belisario (Cantina Sociale di Matelica)
Bisci
Boccadigabbia
Bonci
Brunori
Fratelli Bucci
Le Caniette
Casalfarneto
Tenuta Cocci Grifoni
Colonnara
Fattoria Coroncino
Attilio Fabrini
Fazi Battaglia
Fiorini
Garofoli
Lanari
Conte Leopardi
Mario Lucchetti

Stefano Mancinelli
Fattoria Mancini
Marchetti
Enzo Mecella
La Monacesca
Monte Schiavo
Moroder
Saladini Pilastri
San Biagio
Santa Barbara
Sartarelli
Anzillotti Solazzi
Tavignano
Le Terrazze
Terre Cortesi Moncaro
Umani Ronchi
Velenosi
Villa Pigna
Villamagna

# Mountainous Abruzzo

Like Marche, the Abruzzo region is in east-central Italy with the Adriatic Sea as its eastern border. Along with Molise, its neighbor to the south, the Abruzzo region is one of Italy's most mountainous regions — and perhaps the most isolated. (Officially, Abruzzo is 65 percent mountains, 35 percent hills, and 100 percent rugged.) Until recently, the very high, formidable Apennines — which reach about 9,000 feet here, their tallest point in mainland Italy — kept Abruzzo separate from the rest of the country, especially the northern and western parts. Thus, Abruzzo historically had little contact with Latium and Rome to the west, and Marche to the north (see Figure 6-1). As for mountainous Molise to the south, that region might be even more isolated than Abruzzo!

Isolated or not, Abruzzo's warm, sunny hillsides provide ideal conditions for grapevines. Unfortunately, with the exception of a handful of producers, quantity rather than quality is the goal in Abruzzo's hillsides: Abruzzo's average crop size (almost 8 tons per acre) is the highest in Italy, a country known for some large grape crops! To illustrate the point, Abruzzo has only 38 percent as much vineyard land as Tuscany, but it usually makes half as much wine. Just as in many southern regions of Italy, cooperatives make most of the wine (two-thirds), and they sell much of it in bulk to other producers and co-ops outside of the region.

Of the 45 million cases produced in Abruzzo annually, only 17 percent is DOC, and most of that is Montepulciano d'Abruzzo or Trebbiano d'Abruzzo, both inexpensive commercial wines commonly sold as jug wines. (Abruzzo's small DOC production explains why the region has so many IGT designations — nine in all.) Even so, the potential for quality does exist. In the hands of a great producer, such as Edoardo Valentini, these two DOC wines can reach uncommon heights of nobility. Like many other regions of Italy that never before focused on producing quality wines from low-yielding vines, Abruzzo has begun its renaissance. Look forward to better wines coming from this rugged region in the future.

Most of Abruzzo's vineyards are planted on hillsides, where calcareous clay predominates. The hillsides face the Adriatic, whose breezes ventilate the vineyards during the warm, dry summers. Wine is made throughout Abruzzo's four provinces, but the northern two, Teramo and Pescara, have the most favorable hillside sites, climate, and soil for quality wines. The southern province of Chieti, known for its quantity of wine, is the fifth-largest wine-producing province in Italy. Little wine is made in the totally mountainous L'Aquila province, home of the regional capital of the same name; Cerasuolo (cher-ah-*swo*-lo), a dry rosé wine made from Montepulciano, is the main wine from the few hillsides in L'Aquila that produce wine.

The next sections introduce you to a few of Abruzzo's better-known wines and list some producers worth looking for.

## *Montepulciano d'Abruzzo*

Montepulciano (mon-tay-pul-*cha*-noh), the reigning grape variety of Abruzzo, has absolutely no relation to Vino Nobile de Montepulciano, the DOCG wine from the town of Montepulciano in Tuscany (see Chapter 5 in Book III for more on Tuscan wines). At its best, the Montepulciano grape makes a dark, fragrant, tannic, sturdy, age-worthy red wine with naturally low acidity. It's a prolific variety that grows throughout central Italy and is, in fact, Italy's fifth most-planted red variety — after Sangiovese, Barbera, Merlot, and Puglia's Negroamaro.

Montepulciano d'Abruzzo (mon-tay-pul-*cha*-noh dah-*brewtz*-zoh) is one of Italy's most popular red wines, primarily because much of it retails for the equivalent of less than $5 a 750-milliliter bottle, plus it's of decent quality. Although it's produced in all four provinces, most of it comes from the prolific vineyards of the warm Chieti province in southern Abruzzo; most of the better (and somewhat more expensive) Montepulciano d'Abruzzo comes from the Teramo and Pescara provinces in the north. Much of the dry, deep, cherry-pink version, Cerasuolo, comes from L'Aquila.

Montepulciano d'Abruzzo and Cerasuolo must be at least 85 percent Montepulciano, with Sangiovese (or other red varieties of the region) optional. In Abruzzo, Montepulciano is far superior to Sangiovese, and many producers use it exclusively. A third version of Montepulciano d'Abruzzo, called Colline Teramane (cohl-*lee*-nae ter-ah-*mah*-nae), is made from grapes grown only in Teramo and 30 other communities in Teramo province. It must have a minimum of 90 percent Montepulciano, with up to 10 percent Sangiovese permitted.

## Trebbiano d'Abruzzo

The other leading wine of Abruzzo is the dry white Trebbiano d'Abruzzo (trehb-bee-*ah*-no dah-*brewtz*-zoh). The name of the wine is the same as the name of a local clone of the Trebbiano grape, which is considered finer than Tuscany's Trebbiano grape. Some wines made from Trebbiano d'Abruzzo are so good and so uncharacteristic of Trebbiano (especially in their low acidity) that some people don't believe the grape is really a Trebbiano at all, but possibly the Bombino Bianco of Puglia. In any case, DOC regulations permit Trebbiano d'Abruzzo wine to be made at least 85 percent from Trebbiano d'Abruzzo and/or Trebbiano Toscano varieties. Most of the mass-market Trebbiano d'Abruzzo wines are so Trebbiano-like in character — pale and crisp, with neutral, modest flavors — that they probably rely heavily on Trebbiano Toscano.

One producer who most certainly doesn't rely on the pale, modest Trebbiano Toscano is the "Lord of the Vines," as he's called locally. Edoardo Valentini makes clearly the world's greatest wine from the Trebbiano variety (if that's what it is). Two other Abruzzo producers of note are Masciarelli and Emidio Pepe, both known for their Montepulciano d'Abruzzo and Trebbiano d'Abruzzo. Pepe, a throwback from another time, is renowned for still crushing his grapes by foot (a method still used for some Porto wine in Portugal's Douro Valley, but practically nowhere else) and for aging his wines entirely in bottles — you won't find a barrel in sight at his winery, and as a result, the sediment in his bottles is awesome!

Although Trebbiano d'Abruzzo wine is made in all four provinces, most of it comes from the southern Chieti province. Like Montepulciano d'Abruzzo, however, the best Trebbiano wines are made in the two northern provinces, Termano and Pescara.

**Book III**

**Italy: Small but Mighty**

## Controguerra

The newest DOC wine in Abruzzo is Controguerra (cohn-tro-*gwer*-rah), which comes from five communities near the Marche border, including Controguerra, whose colorful name means "antiwar." This DOC designation permits a whole slew of wine styles: a dry, blended Rosso (at least 60 percent Montepulciano and at least 15 percent Merlot and/or Cabernet, with up to 25 percent of other red grapes); a *novello* from the same grapes (at least 30 percent of which must undergo *carbonic maceration,* a technique that produces a dark, grapey, low-tannin wine for drinking young); and a blended, dry Bianco (at least 60 percent Trebbiano Toscano and at least 15 percent Passerina, with up to 25 percent other white varieties). Varietal wines are Cabernet (Franc and/or Sauvignon), Ciliegiolo, Merlot, Pinot Nero, and Chardonnay.

The ambitious Controguerra producers also make two bubbly wines and two dessert wines: a dry *frizzante* from the same grape varieties as the Bianco; a dry *spumante* (at least 60 percent Trebbiano Toscano, at least 30 percent Chardonnay, and/or Verdicchio, and/or Pecorino, and other white varieties); a sweet Bianco *passito* from semidried grapes of the same varieties as the *spumante;* and a Rosso *passito,* a fairly sweet red made mainly from semidried Montepulciano grapes.

## Abruzzo wine producers worth supporting

The main action in Abruzzo is its native grape, Montepulciano d'Abruzzo, and some of the fine wines made from this variety. But if you can find Valentini's Trebbiano d'Abruzzo, buy it! Also, Cataldi Madonna's Cerasuolo is the best dry rosé in the region.

If you think Abruzzo wines might strike your fancy, keep your eyes peeled for these recommended producers:

| | |
|---|---|
| Casal Thaulero | Monti |
| Cataldi Madonna | Camillo Montori |
| Barone Cornacchia | Emidio Pepe |
| Illuminati | Cantina Tollo |
| Marramiero | Valentini |
| Masciarelli | Zaccagnini |

# Latium: Rome's Region

Latium, an Italian region that has been a famous wine area since Roman times, is located in west-central Italy, where the Mediterranean Sea forms its rather long western border. At the center of Latium, called Lazio in Italian, is its capital, Rome, the Eternal City. Tuscany and Umbria are north of Latium, Abruzzo is to the east, and Campania is to the south (see Figure 6-1). With more than 5 million people, Latium ranks third in population among Italy's regions, after Lombardy and Campania. The region has plenty of cultivable land for wine because the Apennines occupy only its eastern part; most of the region is hilly, and about one-fifth is made up of plains.

The high-volume production of inexpensive, neutral-tasting white wines in the post–World War II era has tarnished Latium's image. The most renowned wine of the region, Frascati, has often been the victim of overproduction. But, as in many other regions of Italy, a quality movement is building steam here.

Latium has traditionally been a white wine region; well over 80 percent of its wines, and more than 95 percent of its DOC wines, are white. (Malvasia and Trebbiano Toscano dominate this white wine production.) But the region's dry, warm weather, combined with the volcanic terrain throughout much of the region, is ideal for red wines. Fortunately, some wine producers have realized the area's potential and are making interesting new red wines. At this point, Latium ranks sixth among Italian regions in wine production with an annual output of about 35 million cases — 17 percent of which is DOC wine. As quality becomes more important in Latium, total wine production will probably decrease, but red wine production will increase.

In the past two decades, the number of Latium's DOC wine zones has jumped from 14 to 26. These zones fall into the following four general wine areas:

✔ The Castelli Romani and Colli Albani hills, south of Rome

✔ Northern Latium

✔ The southern coast

✔ The hills of southeastern Latium

## The hills south of Rome

The most important wine area in Latium comprises two sets of hills south of Rome. The Castelli Romani hills are closer to the city; the Albano hills, named for Lake Albano, are slightly farther south and east. These two districts have nine DOC zones, producing 80 percent of Latium's DOC wine, almost all white. This area is the home of Frascati, Marino, and other zones that have supplied the citizens of Rome (and the rest of the world!) with oceans of inexpensive wine for the past few decades.

Some producers of both Frascati and Marino have reacted against the colorless, industrial-style wines bearing these names by making more intensely flavored, golden-colored Frascati and Marino that are quite interesting.

### Frascati

Frascati (frah-*skah*-tee), one of Italy's most popular white wines, is made from vineyards around the hill town of Frascati and three other Castelli Romani communities. Frascati is at least 70 percent Malvasia di Candia and/or Trebbiano, up to 30 percent Greco and/or Malvasia del Lazio, and up to 10 percent other varieties. Although Frascati is usually dry (labeled *secco* or *asciutto*), it can also be made fairly sweet *(amabile)* or sweet *(canellino)*; it's also made in *novello* and *spumante* versions. Wines exported to world markets — such as the Fontana Candida and Gotto d'Oro brands — are usually inexpensive, light-bodied, and fairly dry.

### Marino

The Marino zone is adjacent to the Frascati area to its west. Marino (ma-*ree*-no) is made on the western slopes of Castelli Romani, which extend to the southern outskirts of Rome. It derives up to 60 percent from Malvasia Bianca di Candia, 25 to 55 percent from Trebbiano (any of three clones), 15 to 45 percent from Malvasia del Lazio, and up to 10 percent from Bonvino and/or Cacchione. It can be dry *(secco)*, semidry *(abbocato)*, semisweet *(amabile)*, or sweet *(dolce)*; it can also be *spumante*.

When Marino is mass produced, it looks and tastes very much like Frascati — colorless and insipid. But in the hands of a quality producer such as Paola Di Mauro, the wine shows how full-bodied and complex it can be. Check out her Marino, called Colli Picchioni Oro, for a full-bodied example.

### Colli Albani

A third important DOC zone of this area, in terms of production, is Colli Albani (*co*-lee ahl-*bah*-nee), the second-largest source of wine in Latium after Frascati. Most Colli Albani wine is inexpensive, dry white wine made in large co-ops from up to 60 percent Malvasia di Candia, 25 to 50 percent various clones of Trebbiano, and 5 to 45 percent Malvasia del Lazio, with up to 10 percent other white grapes; it can be made in various sweeter versions as a *spumante* or *novello*.

### Other DOC zones near Rome

The remaining six DOC zones of this area are the following, arranged roughly in the order of their proximity to Rome, from closest to farthest:

- **Castelli Romani:** An umbrella DOC, Castelli Romani (kah-*stehl*-ee roh-*mah*-nee) covers all of Castelli Romani and Colli Albani, Rome, and parts of Latina province to the south. The Bianco in this DOC is mainly Malvasia and Trebbiano and can be *secco, amabile, frizzante,* or *novello*; the Rosso and Rosato are at least 85 percent Cesanese and/or Merlot and/or Montepulciano and/or Sangiovese and/or Nero Buono. Both wines can be dry, sweet, or *frizzante,* and the Rosso can also be *novello*.

- ✔ **Montecompatri Colonna:** This small area (pronounced mon-tae-com-*pah*-tree co-*lohn*-nah) adjoins Frascati on the east, around Montecompatri, Colonna, and other communities. The wine may carry the name Montecompatri, Colonna, or both. It's very similar to Frascati, made from Malvasia Bianca di Candia and/or Malvasia del Lazio with at least 30 percent Trebbiano and up to 10 percent Bellone or Bonvino optional. It can be *secco, amabile, dolce,* or *frizzante.*

- ✔ **Colli Lanuvini:** From vineyards on the southern slopes of the Colli Albani area, stretching south to the Aprilia zone (described in the "Latium's southern coast" section of this chapter), this wine (pronounced *co*-lee lah-nu-*vee*-nee) is a dry white made mainly from Malvasia di Candia and/or Malvasia del Lazio, with at least 30 percent various clones of Trebbiano, and up to 10 percent other white grapes. Colli Lanuvini can also be a semisweet *(amabile)* wine.

- ✔ **Zagarolo:** From vineyards northeast of Castelli Romani, Zagarolo (zah-gah-*ro*-lo) is a dry or semisweet white wine from the same varieties used in the Montecompatri Colonna zone; it's made in small quantities.

- ✔ **Genazzano:** East of Zagarolo, Genazzano (jeh-nahtz-*zah*-no) is one of Latium's newest DOC wines. The zone produces a dry white as well as a dry red wine. The Bianco is mainly Malvasia di Candia, Bellone, Bombino, Trebbiano Toscano, and Pinot Bianco; the Rosso is mainly Sangiovese and Cesanese.

- ✔ **Velletri:** In the southeastern slopes of Colli Albani, the Velletri (vehl-*leh*-tree) wine zone produces both dry and sweet white and red wines. Velletri Bianco is from the same varieties as Montecompatri Colonna and can be a dry, semisweet, or sweet wine, as well as a dry or sweet sparkling wine; a dry or semisweet Rosso is 20 to 45 percent Sangiovese, 30 to 35 percent Montepulciano, at least 15 percent Cesanese, and up to 10 percent Bombino Nero and/or Merlot and/or Ciliegiolo.

**Book III**

**Italy: Small but Mighty**

## *The hillsides and coastal regions of northern Latium*

The Tiber River, flowing from Umbria in the north on its way to Rome and the Mediterranean, cuts northern Latium in two; not much wine is made east of the Tiber in mountainous Rieti province. Most wine in this area is produced around the lakes of Viterbo province in the north and along the coastline of Roma province, north of Rome. Northern Latium has eight DOC wines, the most well-known of which is Est! Est!! Est!!! di Montefiascone (mon-tae-fee-ahs-*co*-nae). (*Est* is Latin for "It is," or "This place rocks.") In any case, the modest, dry white wine of Montefiascone has never lived up to all those exclamation marks. It's made in the volcanic hillsides around the craterous lake Lago di Bolsena, from 65 percent Trebbiano, 20 percent Malvasia Bianca, and 15 percent Rossetto (also known as Trebbiano Giallo). It's also made in an *abboccato* (semidry) style.

In a nutshell, most of the wines of the remaining DOCs of northern Latium are light-bodied whites from Malvasia and Trebbiano, although a few red wines exist, too. The remaining seven northern Latium DOCs are

- **Aleatico di Gradoli:** This sweet red, varietal dessert wine (pronounced ah-lae-*ah*-tee-co dee *grah*-doh-lee) comes from the northwestern hillsides of Lago di Bolsena. This wine zone carries over into the Est! Est!! Est!!! di Montefiascone DOC zone.

- **Colli Etruschi Viterbesi:** Several blended wines and ten varietally labeled wines come from this large zone, which encompasses most of northern Latium and is pronounced *co*-lee ae-*true*-ski vee-ter-*bae*-see. The blended wines are Rosso, Rosso *novello,* and Rosato (all from Sangiovese and Montepulciano — in dry, sweet, and *frizzante* versions) and Bianco (from Trebbiano Toscano, or Procanico, as it's called locally, and Malvasia — in dry, sweet, and *frizzante* styles). The ten varietals are Procanico, Grechetto, Rossetto (dry or sweet), Moscatello (dry or sweet), Moscatello Passito, Sangiovese Rosato (dry or sweet), Greghetto, Montepulciano, Canaiolo, and Merlot. Many of these come in *frizzante* and *novello* versions.

- **Vignanello:** Wineries in the Vignanello (veen-yah-*nel*-lo) area make Rosso and Rosato from Sangiovese and Ciliegiolo, Bianco from Trebbiano and Malvasia, varietal Greco, and a Greco *spumante.*

- **Cerveteri:** A long, narrow wine zone, Cerveteri (cher-veh-*teh*-ree) includes the northern outskirts of Rome and six communities north of Rome along the coast, including Cerveteri itself, a coastal resort where the dry white Cerveteri Bianco is quite popular. The wines are Bianco *secco,* Bianco *frizzante,* and Bianco *amabile* (all made from Trebbiano Toscano and/or Trebbiano Giallo, Malvasia di Candia and/or Malvasia del Lazio, with other white varieties permitted), as well as Rosso *secco,* Rosso *novello,* Rosso *amabile,* and Rosato (all made from Sangiovese and/or Montepulciano, Cesanese, and other red varieties).

- **Tarquinia:** Another broad DOC zone, Tarquinia (tar-*kee*-nee-ah) encompasses 30 communities in Latium's two northern provinces. The types of wine and grape varieties of the Tarquinia DOC wines are exactly the same as those of the Cerveteri zone.

- **Bianco Capena:** Bianco Capena (bee-*ahn*-coh cah-*pae*-nah) is a dry or *abboccato* white wine made in the hills north of Rome from three Malvasia clones, three Trebbiano clones, and up to 20 percent Bellone and/or Bombino.

- **Colli della Sabina:** A DOC on the eastern side of the Tiber River, Colli della Sabina (*co*-lee del-lah sah-*bee*-nah) includes a dry white Bianco, *spumante,* and *frizzante,* which are at least 40 percent Trebbiano and at least 40 percent Malvasia; a Rosso, Rosso *frizzante,* Rosso *novello,* Rosso *spumante,* Rosato, and Rosato *frizzante,* which are made from 40 to 70 percent Sangiovese and 15 to 40 percent Montepulciano, with other red varieties.

## *Latium's southern coast*

The southern coast of Latium includes three DOC wines: Aprilia, Cori, and Circeo. With the exception of Cori, the northernmost part of the area, the southern coast of Latium is less blessed with favorable grape-growing conditions than the cooler Castelli Romani and Colli Albani hills to the northeast. However, some exciting wines, both red and white (many of which are non-DOC), are being made from low-yielding vines, especially at the Casale del Giglio winery in Aprilia. The following zones are located on Latium's southern coast:

✔ **Cori:** This small area (pronounced *coh*-ree) is closest to the Colli Albani hills, and its wines resemble those of the neighboring Velletri. Cori Bianco (up to 70 percent Malvasia di Candia, up to 40 percent Trebbiano Toscano, and up to 30 percent Trebbiano Giallo and/or Bellone) can be dry, *amabile,* or *dolce.* The more distinctive Cori Rosso is a dry red with 40 to 60 percent Montepulciano, 20 to 40 percent of the local Nero Buono di Cori, and Cesanese.

✔ **Aprilia:** The Aprilia (ah-*pree*-lee-ah) wine zone, between the Colli Albani area to the north and the Mediterranean to the south, is one area of Latium's wine renaissance. Aprilia has three varietal wines, each of which must derive at least 95 percent from its named grape: Aprilia Trebbiano, Merlot, and a dry rosé called Sangiovese.

✔ **Circeo:** The Circeo (cher-*chae*-oh) wine zone along the coastline covers six types of wine: Circeo Bianco (dry or *amabile,* made from at least 60 percent Trebbiano Toscano and up to 30 percent Malvasia di Candia, with up to 30 percent other white varieties); Circeo Rosso and Rosato (both of which can be dry, *amabile,* or *frizzante,* made from at least 85 percent Merlot); Circeo *novello* (from the same grapes as the Rosso, but made only as a dry wine); and three varietal wines — Trebbiano, Sangiovese (still or *frizzante*), and Sangiovese Rosato (still or *frizzante*).

## *The Ciociaria hills of southeastern Latium*

The Ciociaria hills of southeastern Latium have been producing red wines from the local Cesanese (chae-sah-*nae*-sae) grape for some time; the three DOC wines of the area all derive 90 percent from this variety. Traditionally, these wines were sweet and bubbly, but the trend has shifted to dry wines. Much of the area's sparse population has left grape-growing in favor of opportunities in industry; as a result, two of the three red wines — Cesanese di Affile (ahf-*fee*-lae) and Cesanese di Olevano (oh-lae-*vah*-no) — have practically disappeared. The third, Cesanese di Piglio (*pee*-l'yoh), is the best of the three, but the grapes are difficult to cultivate in the mountainous territory. Look for the Cesanese del Piglio of Massimi Berucci.

The DOC Atina (ah-*tee*-nah) holds more promise — or so some people say. This DOC, located in the southern part of inland Latium, includes a Rosso made mainly from Cabernet Sauvignon with some Merlot and a Bianco made from Sauvignon Blanc, and possibly Sémillon, Malvasia, and Vermentino. Producer Giovanni Palumbo is a leader in making these red and white Bordeaux-style blends.

## Latium's top wine producers

Even though large cooperatives dominate Latium, independent wine producers have made a name for themselves with quality wines in recent years, and they've begun to restore the image of this historic region. Also, some of the large wineries and co-ops have begun making smaller lots of finer wine. For example, the huge Fontana Candida winery, which exports 625,000 cases of wine annually, is making an excellent Frascati Superiore, called Santa Teresa, in small quantities.

Following are Latium's top wine producers:

| | |
|---|---|
| Massimi Berucci | Gotto d'Oro |
| Cantina Cooperativa di Cerveteri | Casale Marchese |
| Colacicchi | Mazzioti |
| Colle Picchioni-Paola Di Mauro | Mottura |
| Falesco | Giovanni Palombo |
| Fiorano | Castel de Paolis |
| Fontana Candida | Tenuta Le Quinte |
| Casale del Giglio | Villa Simone |
| Cantina Oleificio Sociale di Gradoli | Conte Zandotti |

# Chapter 7

# Southern Italy: "The Land of Wine"

**S**outhern Italy has a proud wine history. The area has produced wine for more than 4,000 years; in 2000 BC, when Phoenician traders arrived in what is today the region of Puglia, a local wine industry was already thriving! The Greeks later dubbed southern Italy "the Land of Wine," and the Romans delighted in the wines of the Campania region.

But that was then. In more recent history, southern Italy has been perhaps the world's prime example of an underachieving viticultural area. The old bugaboo, overproduction — along with indifference plus political and criminal corruption — conspired to keep southern Italy from achieving wine greatness. In the past, most of the area's huge production of dark, high-alcohol, low-acid wine was sold in bulk, as blending wine, to wineries in northern Italy, France, and Germany. Only within the past two decades has this area begun its long-awaited wine renaissance, producing fine wines from quality-conscious producers. The future now looks rosy in the land of wine.

## Campania: Revival Begins

The region of Campania in many ways embodies southern Italy. It's the home of Naples, Italy's third-largest city and the most bustling metropolis south of Rome. With its famous bay, Naples — or Napoli (*nah*-po-lee) as the Italians call it — is one of the world's great seaports, not to mention the birthplace of pizza! As in the rest of Italy's southern regions, the weather in Campania is generally warm, at least in the low altitudes. Flavorful vegetables, fruits, and grains crowd the countryside, along with grapevines.

Campania sits along Italy's western coast, on the Tyrrhenian Sea; the region is south of Latium and Molise, west of Puglia and Basilicata, and north of

Calabria (see Figure 7-1). Campania has Italy's second-largest population, thanks to thriving Naples, and it boasts one of the most beautiful coastlines in the world; the Amalfi Coast and the Sorrento Peninsula, with the nearby isle of Capri, are just some of the renowned coastal attractions.

**Figure 7-1:**
Southern
Italy — "the
Land of
Wine."

**Wine Zones**

**Basilicata**
1. Aglianico del Vulture

**Calabria**
2. Cirò
3. Donnici
4. Savuto

**Campania**
5. Asprinio di Aversa
6. Campi Flegrei
7. Capri
8. Castel San Lorenzo
9. Cilento
10. Costa d'Amalfi
11. Falerno del Massico

12. Fiano di Avellino
13. Gallucio
14. Greco di Tufo
15. Ischia
16. Lacryma Christi del Vesuvio
17. Penisola Sorrentina
18. Sant 'Agata dei Goti
19. Solopaca
20. Taurasi

**Puglia**
21. Alezio
22. Brindisi
23. Cacc'e mmitte di Lucera
24. Castel del Monte
25. Copertino

26. Gioia del Colle
27. Gravina
28. Levorano
29. Lizzano
30. Locorotondo
31. Martina
32. Matino
33. Moscato di Trani
34. Nardò
35. Orta Nova
36. Ostuni
37. Primitivo di Manduria
38. Rosso Canosa
39. Rosso di Cerignola
40. Salice Salentino
41. San Severo
42. Squinzano

Campania is so gifted in terms of its climate, soil, and topography that it could be one of the great wine regions of Italy — and perhaps someday it will be. The Romans clearly favored Campania for wine. And yet, not 20 short years ago, more than half of the region's DOC wine came from *one* producer! That producer, Mastroberardino, is still the leader in DOC wine production, but today several others have finally joined the ranks of quality-conscious firms willing to tap Campania's tremendous potential. One of this region's key assets is a red grape variety, Aglianico (ahl-*yahn*-ee-co), which has proved to be one of the great noble grapes of Italy; also, two white varieties, Fiano and Greco di Tufo, make some of the very best, long-lived white wines in the country. In a few years, Campania will most certainly be regarded as one of Italy's hot wine regions.

More than half of Campania's terrain consists of hillsides. The Apennines run along the central and eastern parts of the region; other mountains and hills are in and near the western coastline, including several volcanoes — some of which aren't extinct (namely the famous Mount Vesuvius). The climate is mainly hot and dry near the sea, but it can be cool and rainy, especially in the autumn, in the inland Apennines.

Campania produces about 23 million cases of wine annually, only about 8 percent of which is DOC/G wine. (But give the region credit for its progress: Twenty years ago, less than 2 percent of Campania's wine was DOC/G, the lowest percentage in Italy.) Campania now has one DOCG wine (in 1993, Taurasi was awarded DOCG status), along with 18 DOC wines, which are scattered throughout the region's five provinces. These 19 wines can be grouped geographically into the following four areas:

**Book III**

**Italy: Small but Mighty**

- ✔ The Irpinia hills of Avellino, in central Campania

- ✔ The coastal hills and islands around Naples

- ✔ Southern Campania

- ✔ The northern hills of the region

## *Meeting the wines of Avellino*

Campania's three greatest wines come from the Irpinia hills around the city of Avellino (the capital of the Avellino province): the red Taurasi, and two DOC whites, Fiano di Avellino and Greco di Tufo.

### *Taurasi*

Mastroberardino's 1968 Taurasi Riserva won so much acclaim worldwide that it brought this massive red wine — and its noble grape variety, Aglianico — attention it had never before received. Taurasi (touw-*rah*-see) is a wine that demands aging, not unlike the other great Italian reds (Barolo, Barbaresco, and Brunello). In good vintages, this complex, powerful, and tannic wine is at its best after 15 to 20 years.

Taurasi's vineyard area is located in the hills around the community of Taurasi and 16 others northeast of Avellino. Taurasi wine must be at least 85 percent Aglianico, with up to 15 percent other red varieties, but in practice, most of the better Taurasi wines are 100 percent Aglianico. Taurasi must age for at least three years before being released, including at least one year in wood; Taurasi Riservas must age for at least four years, including at least 18 months in wood. Taurasi wines retail in the $32 to $40 price range. Mastroberardino's finest Taurasi is the single-vineyard Radici; other good Taurasi wines are made by Feudi di San Gregorio and Terredora.

### Fiano di Avellino

At its best, Fiano di Avellino is southern Italy's top dry white wine — and one of the best in the entire country. It's a delicately flavored wine with aromas of pear and toasted hazelnuts, which become more pronounced with age. Unlike most dry white wines, Fiano di Avellino is best with at least 5 or 6 years of aging and will be fine for up to 15, in good vintages.

The DOC zone for this wine is located in the hills around Avellino and 25 other communities, a few of which are in the Taurasi DOCG zone; the best Fiano vineyards are in the hills around Lapio. Fiano di Avellino must have at least 85 percent Fiano grapes, with the rest being Greco and/or Coda di Volpe and/or Trebbiano Toscano. Fiano di Avellino wines retail for about $18 to $24. Wines to look for include Terredora's single-vineyard Terre di Dora, Mastroberardino's single-vineyard Vignadora or Radici, and Feudi di San Gregorio's Pietracalda.

### Greco di Tufo

The name Greco di Tufo (*greh*-co dee *too*-foh) applies to both a white grape variety and a DOC wine. The Greeks introduced the Greco variety to Italy more than 2,000 years ago. It flourishes in many parts of Italy, but the particular clone (called Greco di Tufo) that grows around the hillside village of Tufo and seven other communities directly north of Avellino is undoubtedly the best. *Tufa* or *tufo* is the name of a type of calcareous rock deposited by springs or lakes; the tufaceous and volcanic soil of the Tufo area creates a favorable environment for this grape.

Greco di Tufo is a far more prolific grape than the difficult-to-grow Fiano. Even though the wine's DOC zone is about one-third the size of Fiano di Avellino's, much more Greco di Tufo is made — in fact, it's Campania's largest-production DOC wine. Greco di Tufo is similar to Fiano di Avellino.

The differences are that Greco di Tufo wines are more intensely fruity and crisper, whereas Fiano di Avellino wines are subtler and a bit softer. Greco di Tufo also ages well, but not quite as long as Fiano; Greco di Tufo is usually ready to drink after 3 or 4 years, but it can age for at least 10 to 12 years. Greco di Tufo wines must derive at least 85 percent from Greco, with the rest being Coda di Volpe. Greco di Tufo retails for about $17 to $23. Look for the Greco di Tufo wines of Feudi di San Gregorio, Mastroberardino — especially the single-vineyard Vignadangelo — and Terredora.

## Checking out wines of the coastal hills and islands around Naples

When hundreds of thousands of uncritical tourists descend on your shores every year and buy up all of your wine, you don't have to aim for greatness. Perhaps this fact explains why the coastal hills and islands around Naples haven't made much high-quality wine in the past. Certainly the area has the right ingredients: a warm, dry climate and soil rich in tufa and volcanic ash. (Actually, these conditions favor red wine production more than white, but the vacationing tourists favor cool, white wines, which is why this style has predominated the area.) Some producers are joining the quality-wine movement, despite their two nemeses: Naples' urban sprawl and the easy tourist *euro* (dollar).

The area around Naples has seven DOC wines. Three of them, Ischia, Capri, and Vesuvio, are longstanding. Ischia (*ees*-key-ah) actually became Italy's second DOC wine in 1966. And that's not the only history this wine has going for it: The Greeks planted the grapes that make Ischia on this island in 770 BC. Not much wine is made today, but white wines dominate production, with D'Ambra Vini d'Ischia making the island's best. Ischia Bianco is mainly Forastera, with Biancolella and other white grapes; the same varieties also make a Bianco *spumante,* and each of these two grapes makes a varietal wine. Ischia Rosso is a dry red mainly from Guarnaccia (in the Grenache family) and Piedirosso (known locally as Pér'e Palummo); Piedirosso also makes a varietal wine and a *passito.*

Capri (*cah*-pree), the island at the end of the Sorrento Peninsula, is such a wealthy tourist mecca that vineyards and winemaking don't get much attention here. Capri's extremely limited vineyards are on terraced slopes with calcareous soil, and they overlook the sea. Capri has two wines: Capri Bianco (mainly Falanghina and Greco, with up to 20 percent Biancolella) and Capri Rosso (mainly Piedirosso).

Lacryma Christi del Vesuvio (*lah*-cree-mah *chree*-sti de veh-*soo*-vee-oh), also called Vesuvio, comes from vineyards on the slopes of Mount Vesuvius, east of Naples and overlooking the Bay of Naples. The area has great volcanic soil, but it had very little quality wine until Mastroberardino came along. Vesuvio's wines can be white, red, or rosé. The basic wines, with less than 12 percent alcohol, carry the simpler Vesuvio DOC; the white, red, or rosé wines from riper grapes are Lacryma Christi ("tears of Christ") del Vesuvio. The Bianco is mainly Verdeca and Coda di Volpe, with up to 20 percent Greco and/or Falanghina; the Rosso and Rosato are mainly Piedirosso and Sciascinoso, with up to 20 percent Aglianico. All three Lacryma Christi wines can also be *spumante*.

Since 1990, four new DOC wine areas have joined the original three:

- **Campi Flegrei:** The Campi Flegrei (*cahm*-pee *fleh*-grae) zone includes parts of the city of Naples, the coastal town of Pozzuoli, and four other communities situated around (hopefully) extinct volcanoes near Naples. Of Campania's newer DOC zones, this area has the most promise — if Naples doesn't gobble it up. Campi Flegrei Bianco is a dry white made mainly from the Falanghina, Biancolella, and Coda di Volpe grape varieties; Campi Flegrei Falanghina is a dry white varietal — or a *spumante* — derived at least 90 percent from that variety. Campi Flegrei Rosso is a dry red (or *novello* style) made mainly from Piedirosso, Aglianico, and Sciascinoso grapes. Campi Flegrei Piedirosso — dry or *passito* — must contain at least 90 percent of this variety.

- **Costa d'Amalfi:** The hills above the Costa d'Amalfi (pronounced *cohs*-tah dah-*mahl*-fee and translated as "Amalfi Coast") in Salerno province are the striking setting for vineyards that now produce better wine than ever, doing justice to their newly awarded DOC status. Wines from vineyards in three subzones — Furore, Ravello, and Tramonti — can add these names to their labels. One exceptional producer for both red and white wines in the Furore and Ravello subzones is Marisa Cuomo. The Costa d'Amalfi DOC features Bianco, Rosso, and Rosato wines. The Bianco is at least 60 percent Falanghina and Biancolella; the Rosso and Rosato are at least 60 percent Piedirosso and Sciascinoso.

- **Penisola Sorrentina:** The Penisola Sorrentina zone (pronounced *peh*-nee-so-lah sor-ren-*tee*-nah and translated as "Sorrento Peninsula") juts out at the southernmost part of the Naples province and borders the Amalfi Coast to the south. Parts of the area can name their wines with a subzone name; these include two villages on the northern side of the peninsula, Lettere and Gragnano (for dry red wines), as well as the town of Sorrento (for red and white wines). Both Lettere and Gragnano were once known for their fizzy red wines but have lost many of their vineyards because of Naples' expansion. Penisola Sorrentina Bianco is mainly Falanghina, Biancolella, and/or Greco; the Rosso and Rosso *frizzante naturale* are mainly Piedirosso, Sciascinoso, and/or Aglianico.

> ✔ **Asprinio di Aversa:** This wine zone, pronounced ahs-*pree*-nee-oh dee ah-*vehr*-sa and located in the plains north of Naples, makes a dry white wine from at least 85 percent Asprinio grapes. In its more popular form, Asprinio di Aversa is a dry *spumante,* from 100 percent Asprinio grapes. Aversa has been a declining wine area with hopes that the blessing of DOC status can revive it.

## Sampling in southern Campania's two DOC zones

The rugged, rocky hills of southern Campania are known as the Cilento Hills, which include an unspoiled area (with remnants of ancient Greek towns), a spectacular coastline extending to the neighboring region of Basilicata, and mountains (part of the Apennine chain) preserved as a national park. In this beautiful, natural setting, robust red grapes, such as Aglianico, thrive, along with the white Fiano and Moscato varieties. (Luigi Maffini makes fine varietal Fiano wines in this area under the Paestum IGT.)

Southern Campania boasts two formal wine zones that make a total of ten wines. Cilento (chee-*len*-toh) is Campania's largest DOC zone; it occupies the region's southern coastal area and extends well inland. Four types of Cilento wine exist: a dry Rosso (60 to 75 percent Aglianico, 15 to 20 percent Piedirosso and/or Primitivo, and 10 to 20 percent Barbera); a dry Rosato (70 to 80 percent Sangiovese, 10 to 15 percent Aglianico, and 10 to 15 percent Piedirosso and/or Primitivo); a Bianco (60 to 65 percent Fiano, 20 to 30 percent Trebbiano Toscano, and 10 to 15 percent Greco Bianco and/or Malvasia Bianca); and an Aglianico.

Castel San Lorenzo (*cahs*-tel sahn lo-*ren*-zo) is a new DOC zone inland from the Cilento area that has three blended wines and three varietals. Castel San Lorenzo Rosso and Rosato are dry wines (80 percent from Barbera and Sangiovese); the Bianco is a dry white (80 percent from Trebbiano Toscano and Malvasia Bianca). The three varietal wines are Barbera, a sweet Moscato Bianco, and a Moscato *spumante.*

**Book III**

**Italy: Small but Mighty**

## Scoping out the most established zones of Campania's northern hills

Northern Campania is dominated by the Apennine Mountains and their foothills; it includes some historic wine districts, such as Falerno del Massico, on the coastline, which dates back to Roman times, and some newer, developing wine areas. The climate varies considerably. The coastal area of Falerno is warm and produces plump, fruit-scented wines; wine zones farther inland have a cooler Apennine-influenced climate, which produces more austere wines. Northern Campania now has nearly 20 DOC wine zones; the following 6 are the most established of the group:

- **Falerno del Massico:** The Falerno del Massico (fah-*ler*-no del *mah-see*-co) vineyards occupy the slopes of Monte Massico, near the Latium border to the north. The name Falerno goes back to the Romans, who revered the white wine of this area. Today, three styles of Falerno del Massico exist: a Bianco (most likely made from a different variety than the one winemakers used 2,000 years ago), a Rosso, and a Primitivo (one of the rare varietal Primitivo wines found outside of Puglia). The Bianco is a dry white made entirely from Falanghina, the area's best white variety; the Rosso is a dry red made primarily from Aglianico, with 20 to 40 percent Piedirosso and up to 20 percent Primitivo and/or Barbera; and the Primitivo has up to 15 percent Aglianico and/or Piedirosso and/or Barbera. Villa Matilde and Fontana Galardi are two leading wineries.

- **Gallucio:** The Gallucio (gahl-*loo*-cho) wine zone in northern Campania, on the Latium border, is directly north of Falerno but farther inland, where the climate is cool and the terrain is hilly. Gallucio's vineyards occupy the hills around an extinct volcano, where the soil is rich in minerals. The wines are similar to Falerno's but tend to be a bit lighter and have more aromatic finesse. Gallucio wines include a Rosso and Rosato based mainly on Aglianico, as well as a Falanghina Bianco.

- **Solopaca:** The Solopaca wine zone (pronounced so-lo-*pah*-cah and named for the village of Solopaca) in north-central Campania is in a valley between two mountain ranges. Six types of wine carry the Solopaca DOC: a Rosso, a Rosato, a Bianco, two varietal wines, and a *spumante*. Solopaca Bianco is a dry white made from Trebbiano Toscano, Falanghina, Coda di Volpe, Malvasia Toscana, and Malvasia di Candia, with other white varieties optional; the Rosso and Rosato are dry wines made from Sangiovese and Aglianico, with up to 30 percent Piedirosso and/or Sciascinoso and other varieties optional. The varietals are a red Aglianico and a white Falanghina; the *spumante* is at least 60 percent Falanghina.

- **Taburno:** Named after the Taburno mountain range, south of Solopaca, the Taburno (tah-*bur*-no) DOC has a varietal Aglianico (Rosso or Rosato); Falanghina, Greco, and Coda di Volpe (all whites); and Piedirosso. Blended wines include a dry Bianco, 70 percent from Trebbiano Toscano and Falanghina; a Rosso, 70 percent from Sangiovese and Aglianico; and a dry *spumante,* mainly from Coda di Volpe and/or Falanghina.

✔ **Sant'Agata dei Goti:** This DOC zone's production area (which is pronounced sahnt-*ahg*-ah-tah dae *go*-tee) is located west of Taburno. This DOC produces a Bianco, a Rosso, a *novello,* and a Rosato — all from the same grape varieties. Those varieties are Aglianico and Piedirosso, both reds (other nonaromatic red varieties may be added); the Bianco is made using only the colorless juice of the grapes, not their red skins. Five varietal wines include two dry reds (Aglianico and Piedirosso), two dry whites (Greco and Falanghina), and one sweet white (Falanghina *passito*), all of which are at least 90 percent of the named variety.

✔ **Guardiolo:** Vineyards in the Guardiolo (gwar-dee-*oh*-lo) DOC zone are in high hills around the village of Guardia Sanframondi, within the eastern part of the Solopaca area. Guardiolo Bianco is a dry white made mainly from Malvasia Bianca di Candia and Falanghina; the DOC also includes a Rosso and a Rosato, which are mainly Sangiovese. Guardiolo Aglianico is a dry red made from at least 90 percent of Aglianico grapes; Guardiolo Falanghina is a 90 percent varietal dry white, with Malvasia Bianca and/or other white grapes; a *spumante* is a dry sparkling wine made from the same varieties as the Falanghina.

IGT wines from Campania can carry the following regional names, depending on where in the region their vineyards are located: Beneventano, Colli di Salerno, Dugenta, Epomeo, Irpinia, Paestum, Pompeiano, Roccamonfina, and Terre del Volturno.

## Listing the Campania producers to know

If you want to start exploring the wines of Campania, seek out any of the offerings from these producers:

| | |
|---|---|
| Antonio Caggiano | Michele Moio |
| Cantina Grotta del Sole | S. Molettieri |
| La Caprense | Montevetrano |
| Marisa Cuomo | Mustilli |
| D'Ambra Vini d'Ischia | Ocone |
| De Concilus | San Giovanni |
| De Lucia | Terredora |
| Feudi di San Gregorio | Antica Masseria Venditti |
| Galardi | Villa Matilde |
| Luigi Maffini | Villa San Michele |
| Mastroberardino | |

# Puglia: Italy's Wine Barrel

Puglia (*poo*-l'yah), as the Italians call it — or Apulia, as you might also see it — is truly Italy's wine lake, producing between 100 and 130 million cases of wine annually. About 80 percent of Puglia's wine is red, but less than 4 percent of it is DOC; most of Puglia's wine is unremarkable and made by large-volume cooperatives who ship it north in bulk to improve the less robust red wines of cooler climes.

One of the reasons why Puglia produces so much wine — besides its wine-friendly, sunny, dry climate — is its lack of mountains (as you can see in Figure 7-1). It's the only southern region that's practically mountain free. In fact, it's Italy's flattest region, consisting mainly of fertile plains plus some hills and plateaus.

Puglia's three major grape varieties are Negroamaro, Primitivo, and Malvasia Nera — all red grapes. These grapes grow mainly on the Salento Peninsula, and most of the wines of that area are made from one, or a blend, of them. Negroamaro and Primitivo, in fact, are Italy's fourth- and sixth-most-planted red grape varieties — even though they grow mainly in Puglia. The Malvasia Nera used in Puglia is mainly two particular clones, Malvasia Nera di Lecce and Malvasia Nera di Brindisi.

Puglia has 25 DOC wine zones, one of which — Aleatico di Puglia — extends across all five provinces (but, in actuality, the Aleatico di Puglia wine grows almost entirely in the Gioia del Colle district, south of Bari). This historic specialty is a sweet, high-alcohol red dessert wine made from the Aleatico variety, with up to 15 percent other grapes (Negroamaro, Primitivo, and Malvasia Nera). A *liquoroso* version also exists.

Puglia's 24 other DOC zones fall into four general groups, according to their location. From south to north, these areas are

- ✔ The Salento Peninsula, the most important area for quality
- ✔ The Trulli district, north of the Salento Peninsula
- ✔ Central Apulia, including Castel del Monte, a quality zone
- ✔ The northern plains

IGT wines from Puglia can carry the following place-names, depending on where their vineyards are located and what their producers prefer: Daunia, Murgia, Puglia, Salento, Tarantino, or Valle d'Itria.

# *The Salento Peninsula*

With its flat, arid plains, palm trees, and cactus plants, the Salento Peninsula resembles a desert area in many places; if not for the cool breezes from the Adriatic Sea, this area would be unbearably hot, especially in the summer. Vines grow in a red soil atop primarily calcareous rock that's particularly ideal for red grapes. Some vineyards bear very small crops of Negroamaro, Primitivo, and Malvasia Nera — particularly small compared to typical crop sizes in the rest of Puglia — which reflects the advanced thinking of many local producers and results in intensely flavored wines.

The Salento Peninsula is Puglia's major wine district; its 11 DOC wines include the renowned Salice Salentino and Primitivo di Manduria. Most of its wines are dark and robust, with ripe flavors and rather high alcohol content. They're made mainly from Negroamaro and/or Primitivo, with Malvasia Nera the third most important grape. (But Aglianico, Campania's noble red grape — one of the best red varieties in southern Italy — is an emerging presence in the peninsula, either for varietal or, more commonly, blended red wines.)

### Salice Salentino

Salice Salentino (*sah*-lee-chae sah-len-*tee*-no) is Puglia's wine ambassador: It's the one Puglian wine that many wine drinkers abroad have tasted, or at least heard of. It's a dark, robust wine of the South, with all the warm, ripe, even slightly baked, flavors of sun-drenched grapes. It's made mainly from Negroamaro, with up to 20 percent Malvasia Nera.

Today, at Agricole Vallone, enologist Severino Garofano not only makes a fine Salice Salentino but also has come up with Puglia's answer to Amarone (see Chapter 4 in Book III for info on Amarone) — Graticciaia, a blackish, concentrated, high-alcohol red from late-harvested Negroamaro and Malvasia Nera grapes. Basic Salice Salentino retails for $10 to $11, but special, single-vineyard versions run anywhere from $12 to $30. Graticciaia costs about $35.

**Book III**

**Italy: Small but Mighty**

Although the main type of Salice Salentino is a red wine, various other styles exist: a *novello;* a refreshing, dry rosé; a Rosato *spumante* (all from the same grape varieties as the Rosso); and even white and sweet versions. Salice Salentino Bianco is 70 percent Chardonnay, and Salice Salentino Pinot Bianco (still or *spumante*) combines Pinot Blanc with up to 15 percent Chardonnay and Sauvignon. The traditional sweet, high-alcohol red wine of Puglia, Aleatico Dolce (or *liquoroso*), is another style of Salice Salentino.

### Primitivo di Manduria

Primitivo di Manduria (pre-meh-*tee*-vo dee mahn-*doo*-ree-ah) is the name of both a DOC wine and a grape. Of the various types of Primitivo grapes, this is the one many people think is genetically the same as Zinfandel. Surely, Primitivo di Manduria wines share certain characteristics with Zinfandel: They're dark in color (although some red American Zins are made in a lighter style), they're usually high in alcohol, and they're rich and opulently fruity. If anything, Primitivo seems to make wines that are bigger in every way than most Zinfandels, starting with their deep purple color (which is partly because the juice of the grapes is dark, not colorless).

Primitivo di Manduria wine always comes 100 percent from that grape. (What other variety could compete with it?) It's rich, ripe, and explosively fruity; its *minimum* alcohol content is 14 percent but usually higher. Although this wine can age for a few years, it's best young.

The Perucci brothers — who make wine under the Pervini, Felline, and Sinfarosa brands — are greatly responsible for the improvement of wines in this DOC zone. Formerly, the wines were rough and rustic — like some rowdy relative you enjoy but try to avoid introducing to polite company. But lately, Primitivo di Manduria wines have taken on an elegance — relatively speaking, since high-alcohol reds trade on power rather than subtlety or finesse — that they didn't previously have. You can find Primitivo di Manduria retailing for $9 to $12 — although Sinfarosa makes one called Zinfandel, which sells for $20. Primitivo di Manduria also comes in three dessert styles: *dolce naturale* (minimum alcohol, 16 percent); *liquoroso dolce naturale* (minimum alcohol, 17.5 percent); and *liquoroso secco* (minimum alcohol, 18 percent). With two glasses of these wines, you'll eat the whole cake.

### Other Salento Peninsula wines

The nine other Salento Peninsula DOC wines are as follows:

- **Brindisi:** Named after the coastal town of Brindisi (*breen*-deh-see), this is a dry, rich red wine (or a rosé) that's mainly Negroamaro, with up to 30 percent Montepulciano and/or Malvasia Nera and/or Susumaniello (a Croatian variety), and Sangiovese. Cosimo Taurino's greatest wine, Patriglione, mainly Negroamaro, is Brindisi's finest wine. Agricole Vallone also makes good Brindisi wines.

- **Copertino:** The dry red and rosé Copertino (co-per-*tee*-no) wines are mainly Negroamaro, with up to 30 percent Malvasia Nera and/or Montepulciano, plus up to 15 percent Sangiovese. The great enologist of the Salento Peninsula, Severino Garofano, consults at wineries in Copertino, so quality is high here. The vineyards are directly south of the Salice Salentino zone.

- **Squinzano:** At one time, this area near the coast, south of Brindisi, was just a source of bulk wines. Now Squinzano (skwin-*zah*-no) has a higher profile thanks to Antinori's Vigneti del Sud, a new 1,250-acre estate that grows mainly Negroamaro. Squinzano's two wines are a dry Rosso and a Rosato, both from the same varieties — mainly Negroamaro, with Malvasia Nera and Sangiovese.

- **Levorano:** Levorano (leh-vo-*rah*-no) Rosso and Rosato are Negroamaro with up to 35 percent Malvasia Nera and/or Sangiovese and/or Montepulciano, and up to 10 percent Malvasia Bianca. Levorano Bianco (which became Salento's first white DOC wine in 1980) is at least

65 percent Malvasia Bianca, with Bombino Bianco and/or Trebbiano Toscano. This small zone is located east of Copertino and Salice Salentino.

✔ **Nardò:** Nardò (nar-*doh*) Rosso and Rosato are mainly Negroamaro, with Malvasia Nera and/or Montepulciano. Vineyards are on the western coast of the peninsula, north of Gallipoli.

✔ **Alezio:** The dry Alezio (ah-*leh*-zee-oh) Rosso (or Rosato) is mainly Negroamaro, with Malvasia Nera, Sangiovese, or Montepulciano, together or singly. This small zone is east of coastal Gallipoli. The leading winery is Calò's Rosa del Golfo, which makes one of Italy's best dry rosés, from Negroamaro and Malvasia Nera.

✔ **Matino:** Salento's earliest (1971) and southernmost DOC zone, Matino (mah-*tee*-no) makes two dry DOC wines, a Rosso and Rosato, both of which are mainly Negroamaro, with up to 30 percent Malvasia Nera and/or Sangiovese.

✔ **Lizzano:** Lizzano (leet-*zah*-no) boasts the most varied range of wines in the Salento Peninsula. They include a dry Rosso and Rosato (still or *frizzante*) and a Rosato *spumante,* all mainly from Negroamaro, with some Malvasia Nera, and other varieties, including Montepulciano, Sangiovese, and Pinot Nero optional. A dry white Lizzano Bianco (also *frizzante*) and Bianco *spumante* are made mainly from Trebbiano and/or Chardonnay and/or Pinot Bianco, with Sauvignon and other varieties optional. Varietals are Negroamaro (Rosso or Rosato) and Malvasia Nera (from either the Lecce or Brindisi clones, or both) The Lizzano zone borders the Gulf of Taranto and overlaps the western part of the Primitivo di Manduria zone.

✔ **Galatina:** This zone, pronounced gah-lah-*tee*-nah, is the newest and smallest DOC zone in Puglia, situated south of Copertino and west of the coastal town of Otranto. It produces a Rosso and Rosato wine based primarily on Negroamaro.

# The Trulli district

The Trulli district, south of the city of Bari, is an area of valleys and gorges carved by the Itria River. Unique to this area are the unusual, conical-roofed, triangular-shaped stone dwellings, called *trulli,* built to counteract the sometimes harsh heat of the area. Ironically, considering the heat, two of the four DOC wines of the district are white — they grow in a belt where the clashing currents of the Adriatic and Ionian seas bring cool breezes and summer rain.

Puglia's most renowned white wine is Locorotondo (lo-co-ro-*tohn*-doh). It's a dry white made mainly from Verdeca with 35 to 50 percent Bianco di Alessano, and Fiano and/or Bombino Bianco and/or Malvasia Toscana optional. A *spumante* style also exists. Martina Franca (or Martina) is the other white DOC wine of the Trulli district. It's very similar to Locorotondo, made from exactly the same grape varieties. Martina Franca, the community at the center of this wine zone, is a dramatic, *trulli* hill town, 5 miles south of Locorotondo.

Vineyards around the ancient town of Ostuni (oh-*stew*-nee), northwest of the coastal city of Brindisi, make Ostuni Ottavianello — a dry, light-bodied, cherry-red wine made from Ottavianello (France's Cinsault variety) — and Ostuni Bianco, a dry white made mainly from the local Impigno and Francavilla.

The Gioia del Colle (*joy*-ah del *co*-lae) name applies to six wines made in a fairly large area south of the city of Bari. This area is the northernmost zone in Puglia producing a Primitivo DOC wine, a 100 percent varietal. Primitivo is also the main variety (50 to 60 percent) in Gioia del Colle Rosso and Rosato; these two wines also contain Montepulciano and/or Sangiovese and/or Negroamaro, with Malvasia Nera optional. Gioia del Colle Bianco is a dry white made from Trebbiano and other white varieties of the zone. Besides Aleatico di Puglia — which is made primarily in the Gioia del Colle area — two Gioia del Colle Aleaticos are Aleatico *dolce,* a sweet red, and Aleatico *liquoroso dolce.*

# Central Puglia

Castel del Monte is the most important DOC wine in the Bari province of central Puglia; four other DOC wines are also located in this province, either wholly or partly in the Bari area.

The rather large wine zone of Castel del Monte lies northwest of Bari. Its reddish soil, the temperate climate, and the altitude of this dry plateau favor grapevines, especially red varieties.

Castel del Monte can be a blended Rosso, Rosato, or Bianco wine, or one of seven varietal wines. The Rosso is a dry red mainly from Uva di Troia and/or Aglianico and/or Montepulciano, with up to 35 percent other red varieties. The dry Rosato derives from Bombino Nera and/or Aglianico and/or Uva di Troia, and up to 35 percent other red varieties. The Bianco is a dry white mainly from Pampanuto (an indigenous variety) and/or Chardonnay and/or Bombino Bianco, with up to 35 percent other white varieties. Six of the Castel del Monte varietal wines must derive at least 90 percent from the named variety: Pinot Bianco, Chardonnay, Sauvignon, Pinot Nero, Aglianico, and Aglianico Rosato. The seventh varietal, Pinot Bianco da Pinot Nero, is a dry white made from Pinot Nero, with up to 15 percent Pinot Bianco.

Castel del Monte's best producer is Rivera, a longstanding leader whose Rosso Riserva Il Falcone is internationally renowned. The area has attracted outside investment, such as Tuscany's Antinori firm, which, under the name Vigneti del Sud, purchased 250 acres of land here (plus 1,250 acres in the Salento peninsula).

The four other central Puglia DOC wines are

- **Moscato di Trani:** This rare, traditional golden dessert wine, pronounced mohs-*cah*-toh dee *trah*-nee, is one of southern Italy's best sweet wines; it's made from at least 85 percent Moscato di Trani or Moscato Reale grapes, with other Moscato varieties. A sweeter *liquoroso* style also exists. The wine zone is located around the coastal town of Trani, north of Bari.

- **Rosso Barletta:** This dry red wine, produced around the coastal town of Barletta (north of Trani and Bari) and pronounced *rohs*-so bar-*let*-tah, is made primarily from the native Uva di Troia, with Montepulciano, Malbec, and/or Sangiovese.

- **Rosso Canosa:** The dry, difficult-to-find Rosso Canosa (*rohs*-so cah-*no*-sah) comes from a small zone around the community of Canosa di Puglia, just south of the Castel del Monte zone. This red wine is very similar to Castel del Monte Rosso; it's mainly Uva di Troia, with Montepulciano and Sangiovese.

- **Gravina:** Another little-known DOC wine, Gravina (grah-*vee*-nah) is a delicate, dry white (which can also be *amabile* or *spumante*) made from Malvasia del Chianti, with Greco di Tufo and/or Bianco di Alessano, and Trebbiano and/or Bombino Bianco and/or Verdeca optional. The zone is located near the Basilicata border in the west, around the town of Gravina-in-Puglia.

**Book III**

**Italy: Small but Mighty**

## The northern plains

The northern plains area in the province of Foggia, known as La Capatanata, is Puglia's least-important wine district. The red wines in this area are made mainly with Montepulciano and Sangiovese grapes, and Bombino Bianco and Trebbiano dominate the whites.

The district's leading DOC zone, not to mention its most prolific zone, is San Severo (sahn seh-*veh*-ro), which is located in the northernmost part of Puglia, around the community of San Severo. The Rosso and Rosato wines made here are both dry and come mainly from Montepulciano, with some Sangiovese; the Bianco is a dry white made from Bombino Bianco and Trebbiano, with up to 20 percent Malvasia Bianca and/or Verdeca; a *spumante* also exists.

Other DOC wines of the northern plains include the following:

- **Cacce'e Mmitte di Lucera:** A simple red wine meant to be enjoyed young, Cacce'e Mmitte di Lucera (*cah*-chae-ae *meet*-tae dee loo-*cher*-ah) comes from a zone south of San Severo. It's made from the local Uva de Troia, with Montepulciano and/or Sangiovese and/or Malvasia Nera, and 15 to 30 percent of white varieties (Malvasia del Chianti and/or Bombino Bianco).

- **Orta Nova:** This zone lies south of the provincial capital of Foggia, around the community of Orta Nova (*or*-tah *no*-vah). A dry Rosso and Rosato are primarily Sangiovese, with up to 40 percent Uva di Troia and/or Montepulciano, with Lambrusco Maestri and/or Trebbiano optional.

- **Rosso di Cerignola:** The Cerignola zone is located south of Orta Nova. Rosso di Cerignola (*rohs*-so dee cheh-ree-*n'yoh*-lah) is a rather scarce, dry red made primarily from Uva de Troia, with Negroamaro and up to 15 percent Sangiovese and/or Barbera and/or Malbec and/or Montepulciano and/or Trebbiano.

## Recommended Puglia producers

Almost all of Puglia's best wines are red, and a large majority of them come from the Salento Peninsula. Most of them (except for the Primitivo wines) are based on Negroamaro, Puglia's leading grape variety. Here are some top Puglia wine producers to watch for:

Botromagno
Michele Calò
Candido
Cantele
Cantina del Locorotondo
Cantina Sociale Copertino
D'Alfonso del Sordo
Felline
Leone de Castris
Lomazzi & Sarli
Masseria Monaci
Nugnes
Masseria Pepe

Pervini
Rivera
Rosa del Golfo (also known as Giuseppe Calò)
Sinfarosa
Cosimo Taurino
Torrevento
Agricole Vallone
Valle dell'Asso
Vigneti del Sud (Antinori)
Vinicola Savese
Conti Zecca

# Mountainous Basilicata

Basilicata (see Figure 7-1) is a paradox: Here in southern Italy, "the Land of Wine" mind you, Basilicata produces only 5 million cases of wine annually, one of the country's lowest totals, and it has one of the lowest grape yields per hectare of any of Italy's regions. Basilicata's topography — mostly mountains — and its cool, harsh climate seem to be too much for the vines. The region's one DOC wine, Aglianico del Vulture (ahl-*yahn*-ee-co del *vool-too-rae*), amounts to less than 3 percent (about 140,000 cases) of Basilicata's annual production.

Aglianico del Vulture is made from vineyards around the extinct Monte Vulture volcano, in northwest Basilicata, near Campania's border. Other than Aglianico, the Monte Vulture region produces some IGT-level Moscato and white Malvasia, both mainly sweet and sparkling. In the eastern plains area, around Matera, and in the Ionian plains area in the southeast, some robust, red, IGT-level wines are made from Montepulciano, Sangiovese, Aglianico, Primitivo, and Bombino Nero grapes. All of these IGT wines carry the designation IGT Basilicata.

*TIP*

If it weren't for Aglianico del Vulture, you could skip right over Basilicata. But Aglianico del Vulture is a serious wine worth trying. It's mainly a dry, powerful red. *Amabile* and sweet *spumante* versions are also made, but they're rarely exported.

*WARNING!*

Aglianico del Vulture derives entirely from the austere, tannic Aglianico grape variety, and like all Aglianico-based wines, it requires aging. When its black-red color starts to turn to ruby and its blackberry aromas begin to evolve, usually after about five years, you can begin to enjoy the wine.

Basic Aglianico del Vulture ages a minimum of one year at the winery, but wines labeled *vecchio* (old) age for at least three years, and those labeled *riserva* age for at least five years before their release. Aglianico del Vulture wines, especially the *vecchio* and *riservas*, improve for ten years or more, especially in good vintages. Most Aglianico del Vulture wines retail for $16 to $20.

*TIP*

Look for the following leading producers of Aglianico del Vulture (basically the only exported Basilicata wine): Basilium, D'Angelo, Armando Martino, Paternoster, and Francesco Sessa.

**Book III**

**Italy: Small but Mighty**

# Rugged Calabria

As you can see in Figure 7-1, Calabria is the "ball" and "toe" of Italy's boot, as well as the southernmost region of the Italian mainland. The Ionian Sea is on its eastern border, the Tyrrhenian Sea is to the west, the island of Sicily is to the southwest, across the narrow Straits of Messina, and Basilicata is across the Apennine Mountains to the north.

Calabria is a poor region that has lost many of its inhabitants to emigration, primarily to the United States and Argentina. Here wine is a minor product, less important in the region's economy than olive oil, produce, and grains.

The climate along both coastlines is hot and dry, but winters are cold and harsh in the interior mountains, especially in northern Calabria. Most of the region's wines come from the central part of both the eastern and western coasts.

Almost 90 percent of Calabria's annual wine production of nearly 11 million cases is red wine. Only 4 percent of Calabria's wine has DOC status. In fact, only a few independent producers and cooperatives even bottle their wine; much of Calabria's sturdy, high-alcohol wine is sold in bulk to wineries in northern Italy and nearby countries.

Although 12 DOC wine zones now exist in the region, only one, Cirò, located on the east-central coast, has gained any recognition outside of Calabria; most of the other wines are consumed locally. The dominant red variety throughout Calabria is Gaglioppo (gah-l'yee-*oh*-po), possibly a native grape but probably of Greek origin. Greco is the major white variety.

The Cirò (chee-*roh*) wine zone is in the eastern foothills of the Sila Mountain range (part of the Apennines) and extends to the eastern Ionian coastline; the Cirò Classico area, the best section, is located around the communities of Cirò and Cirò Marina in the northern part of the zone. Vines grow in calcareous, marly soil that also contains lots of clay and sand; summers are hot and dry, but winters are mild, thanks to the influence of the Ionian Sea.

Ciró comes in red, white, and rosé styles, but the red is the area's best wine. Cirò Rosso and Rosato are dry wines made from at least 95 percent Gaglioppo, with Trebbiano and/or Greco Bianco optional. A good Cirò Rosso is full-bodied, powerful, tannic, fruity, and soft; it's at its best when consumed within three or four years of the vintage. Cirò Bianco is a dry white made from at least 90 percent Greco Bianco, with Trebbiano optional. The *classico* designation is for Cirò Rosso only.

To say that Cirò is spearheading a Calabrian wine resurgence would be overstating the case. Most of Cirò is still bound to the past — many common technological winemaking practices, such as temperature-controlled fermentation, have barely arrived in Calabria. But two Cirò wineries — Librandi and Fattoria San Francesco — have employed enologists and are taking the necessary steps to make quality wine. The basic Cirò Rosso from these wineries retails for a mere $10 to $11; their *riservas* cost $15 to $16.

Much of Calabria's limited production of bottled wines never leaves the region. The following three private wineries and two cooperatives are the progressive quality leaders in the region today: Fattoria San Francesco, Librandi, and Odoardi; and Cantine Lamezia Lento and Caparra & Siciliani (both co-ops).

# Chapter 8

# Sicily and Sardinia: Focusing on Quality

*In This Chapter*

▶ Discovering the new, higher-quality side of Sicily

▶ Tasting Vermentino, Cannonau, and other wines in Sardinia

S icily and Sardinia, the two largest islands in the Mediterranean Sea, have more in common than size. Both islands have a wine culture that dates back a long time — to the eighth century BC for Sardinia, and 4,000 years for Sicily. Both islands have been dominated by foreigners for much of their history, up until the 19th century. Both islands also have their own language besides Italian (Sicilian and Sardo), and inhabitants of both islands are fiercely independent — so much so that they don't like to be compared. (Sorry about that!)

In terms of wine, both Sicily and Sardinia were primarily suppliers of bulk and jug wines until about 20 years ago. Inexpensive wines are still a big business, but a quality movement has definitely taken shape on both islands. With their wonderful climates and terrains, both Sicily and Sardinia are sure to be prime sources of fine wine in the near future.

## Sicily Leaves the Past Behind

Sicily is not only the largest island in the Mediterranean but also Italy's largest region. It has the fourth-largest population in the country — practically tied with Latium for third. In most years, Sicily vies with Puglia as Italy's largest producer, with an average annual production of more than 100 million cases, about one-sixth of Italy's total wine production. Actually, Sicily has more vineyards than Puglia, but its recent emphasis on quality has reduced crop size and, therefore, the amount of wine produced from those vineyards. That being said, one province in western Sicily, Trapani, is the volume leader of Italy's 94 provinces.

Cooperatives make 75 percent of Sicily's wine, but smaller, private producers are on the rise. For instance, just 20 years ago, co-ops made 90 percent of Sicily's wine. Until the mid-1980s, when Italy's wine revival reached across the Straits of Messina into Sicily (or, more likely, flew in by jet from Turin and Florence), Sicilian producers still emphasized quantity rather than quality.

Besides quantity, Sicily's focus over the past 100 years had been its dessert and fortified wines, such as Marsala. These types of wine are still important, but in the past two decades, high-quality dry whites and reds have become more of the emphasis. White wine exceeds red wine production by nearly three to one — another tradition in this warm island where fish and seafood play a leading role in the local cuisine — but more producers are beginning to concentrate on dry reds.

Sicily clearly has a Mediterranean climate: hot and dry on the coasts, temperate and moist in the interior. About 85 percent of Sicily is mountainous or hilly; the Apennine Mountains of mainland Italy extend into Sicily and are especially high in the northeastern part, where Mount Etna is located. (At 10,705 feet, Mount Etna is the highest active volcano in Europe.) Most of Sicily's wines are made around the coast, where the majority of the people live; Figure 8-1 shows Sicily's wine zones.

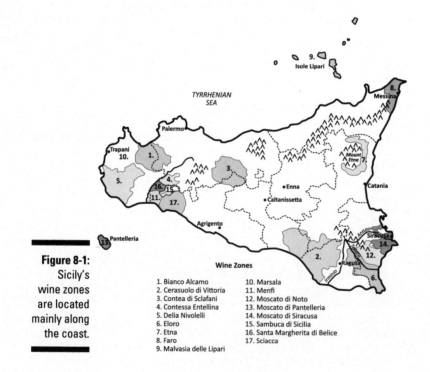

**Figure 8-1:**
Sicily's
wine zones
are located
mainly along
the coast.

**Wine Zones**

1. Bianco Alcamo
2. Cerasuolo di Vittoria
3. Contea di Sclafani
4. Contessa Entellina
5. Delia Nivolelli
6. Eloro
7. Etna
8. Faro
9. Malvasia delle Lipari
10. Marsala
11. Menfi
12. Moscato di Noto
13. Moscato di Pantelleria
14. Moscato di Siracusa
15. Sambuca di Sicilia
16. Santa Margherita di Belice
17. Sciacca

A white grape variety, Catarratto Bianco, is by far Sicily's most-planted grape, covering more than 40 percent of its vineyards; it's especially prominent in western Sicily. Catarratto Bianco, in fact, is Italy's third-most planted variety, after Trebbiano and Sangiovese. Other white varieties popular in Sicilian vineyards are Trebbiano Toscano, Grillo, and the indigenous Inzolia (also known as Ansonica).

Nero d'Avola (*nae*-ro *dahv*-oh-lah) is the main red variety and the primary grape in Sicily's best red wines. The indigenous Perricone (also known as Pignatello) is Sicily's second-most popular red variety, but it's mainly used for blending. Nerello Mascalese is starting to be recognized as Sicily's other fine red variety, along with Nero d'Avola.

The DOC concept has come slowly to Sicily. Its wines are about 98 percent non-DOC — and most of the remaining 2 percent is Marsala. But, like dry wines and fine wines, DOC wines are increasing in Sicily. In fact, the number of DOC wines has risen from 9 to 19 over the past 20 years. Even so, Sicily's most famous wine for the past 200 years has been Marsala. The following sections introduce you to Marsala and Sicily's other wine offerings.

## Marsala, far from "just cooking wine"

Until its recent revival, which began in the mid-1980s, the word *Marsala* stirred up images of cheap cooking wine for most people. Marsala was prized for its culinary versatility — it does wonders for that custardy dessert, *zabaglione,* and it's the backbone behind the classic dish, *vitello marsala* (veal sautéed in a buttery Marsala sauce) — but no one would dream of actually drinking the stuff! What made Marsala's image even worse were the imitation Marsala wines that other countries, such as the United States, produced. Marsala producers themselves — especially major firms, such as Florio, Rallo, and Pellegrino — made sure that much stricter production regulations went into effect in 1986; commercial flavored styles, such as Egg Marsala, are no longer legal, and the wine's average quality has improved. But it's still a confusing type of wine, because it comes in numerous color, sweetness, and age styles.

The vineyard area for Marsala is the entire province of Trapani in western Sicily — excluding Alcamo (another DOC zone) — and various islands off the western coast. Marsala can have three hues: *oro* (light golden), *ambra* (amber-yellow), and *rubino* (ruby red). The *oro* and *ambra* hues derive mainly from two white varieties, Grillo and Catarratto, with Inzolia and Damaschino also permitted; aging turns the wines to deep gold and deep amber. The *rubino,* a far smaller category, derives from red varieties — Pignatello and/or Nero d'Avola and/or Nerello Mascalese — with up to 30 percent of the white varieties that go into *oro* and *ambra* Marsala.

## Sicily's most famous winery

The name Duca di Salaparuta would probably draw a blank stare from most wine buyers, but the name Corvo brings quick recognition. Corvo is the brand name of wines from the gigantic, ultra-modern Duca di Salaparuta winery, about 10 miles east of Palermo. This winery is one of Italy's largest, producing 10 million bottles of wine annually. Just about every wine shop and Italian restaurant in the United States carries Corvo White (made from Inzolia, Trebbiano, and Catarratto grapes) and Corvo Red (made from Nerello Mascalese, Perricone, and Nero d'Avola); both retail for about $12. The winery makes a very good premium Corvo White named Colomba Platina, which costs $15 to $16. Under the Duca di Salaparuta label, the winery's top-of-the-line wine, and possibly Sicily's best dry red, is the powerful, complex Duca Enrico (entirely Nero d'Avola), which costs about $60.

Most Marsala is also made in three different sweetness levels: *secco* (dry), *semisecco* (semidry), and *dolce* (sweet). Finally, Marsalas are categorized by their aging. The following types are made:

- **Fine:** Aged at least one year
- **Superiore:** Aged at least two years
- **Superiore Riserva:** Aged at least four years
- **Vergine, Soleras, or Vergine Soleras:** Aged at least five years
- **Vergine Soleras Stravecchio, Vergine Soleras Riserva, Soleras Stravecchio, or Soleras Riserva:** Aged at least ten years

The last two types are only dry. These styles are the two most serious types of Marsala, consumed very much like dry Sherry — as apéritif wines or with consommé. Retail prices for Marsala (Sicilian Marsala, that is!) range from $10 up to $40 for the *Vergine* or *Soleras* versions. Pellegrino, Rallo, and Florio are all reliable Marsala producers. De Bartoli is a smaller producer who specializes in *Vergine* and *Soleras* Marsalas.

## *Sicilian dry (though sometimes sweet) wines*

The provinces of Trapani, Palermo, and Agrigento, in the western part of Sicily, contain 9 of the 17 DOC zones in the region and make 80 percent of the quality wine in Sicily — whether it's DOC, IGT, or vino da tavola level. (The latter two categories include many fine wines as well the inexpensive wines you'd expect to see with those designations because many Sicilian producers, typically independent, have abdicated DOC status for their wines.) In eastern Sicily, the 7 DOC zones produce small quantities.

Only one formal wine zone exists in mountainous central Sicily — Contea di Sclafani — and although this is a new DOC area, it's important for the quality of wine produced there. The Contea di Sclafani zone is home to the acclaimed Regaleali winery, owned by the equally renowned Tasca d'Almerita family. The late Count Giuseppe Tasca d'Almerita proved to the world that excellent dry red, white, and rosé wines can be made in Sicily, thanks to the temperate to cool microclimates of the family vineyards, which are located on mountain slopes of 1,500 to 2,000 feet in altitude.

Typical of newly legislated DOC zones, central Sicily produces a wide range of wine, including three blended wines (a white, red, and rosé) and 15 varietally labeled wines. Contea di Sclafani Bianco is a dry white that's at least 50 percent Catarratto and/or Inzolia and/or Greganico, with the optional use of other white varieties. The Rosso is a dry red made from at least 50 percent Nero d'Avola and/or Perricone, with the optional addition of other red varieties; the Rosato is a dry rosé from at least 50 percent Nerello Mascalese. The 15 Contea di Sclafani varietal wines include 7 whites and 8 reds. The whites are Inzolia, Catarratto, Chardonnay, Grecanico, Grillo, Pinot Bianco, and Sauvignon Blanc. The red varietal wines are Cabernet Sauvignon, Merlot, Nerello Mascalese, Nero d'Avola, Perricone, Pinot Nero, Sangiovese, and Syrah. All the white wines can also be made as *dolce* (sweet) wines and *vendemmia tardiva* (late-harvest) wines; the white or rosé wines can be *spumante* (sparkling); and the reds can be made in *novello* versions.

Other Sicilian wine zones that specialize in dry wines, from west to east, are as follows:

- **Alcamo (or Bianco Alcamo):** This wine zone, pronounced *ahl*-cah-mo, located in northwestern Sicily, west of Palermo, produces a dry, light-bodied white wine that's at least 80 percent Catarratto, with Trebbiano Toscano and/or Damaschino and/or Grecanico optional. Rapitalà is a leading winery in the zone.

- **Delia Nivolelli:** This new wine zone, pronounced *dae*-lee-ah nee-vo-*lel*-lee, is located in southwestern Sicily, within the Marsala area. Some varietal wines carry this DOC designation, but most of the local dry white and red wines aren't DOC wines (yet).

- **Menfi:** The Menfi (*men*-fee) wine zone is found along the coast of southwestern Sicily. Menfi Bianco is a dry white, 50 to 70 percent Inzolia and 25 to 50 percent Grecanico, Catarratto, and Chardonnay, with other white varieties optional. Three white varietals, all at least 90 percent from the named grape, are Chardonnay, Grecanico, and Inzolia. Two wines, a white and a red, come from specific Menfi subzones: Feudi dei Fiori is a dry white from 50 to 75 percent Inzolia and 25 to 50 percent Chardonnay, with other varieties optional; Bonera is a dry red from 50 to 70 percent Nero d'Avola and 25 to 50 percent Sangiovese and/or Cabernet Sauvignon and/or Frappato di Vittoria, with other varieties optional. The Settesoli cooperative is the predominant winery of the area.

✔ **Contessa Entellina:** Ten DOC wines take their unusual name from the village of Contessa Entellina (con-*tehs*-sah en-tel-*lee*-nah). These wines include seven dry varietals: the white Inzolia, Chardonnay, Grecanico, and Sauvignon; and the red Cabernet Sauvignon, Merlot, and Pinot Nero. Blended wines include a dry Bianco (at least half Inzolia, with seven or more optional white grapes) and a dry Rosso and Rosato (both at least half Nero d'Avola and/or Syrah). This area is north of the Menfi zone and is dominated by the Donnafugata winery (owned by the Rallo family of Marsala fame).

✔ **Santa Margherita di Belice:** Five of the seven local wines in this zone (which is pronounced *sahn*-tah mar-geh-*ree*-tah dee beh-*lee*-chae) are varietals: Catarratto, Grecanico, Inzolia, Nero d'Avola, and Sangiovese. A dry Bianco is 50 to 70 percent Grecanico and/or Catarratto and 30 to 50 percent Inzolia, with other varieties optional; a dry Rosso is 50 to 80 percent Sangiovese and/or Cabernet Sauvignon and 20 to 50 percent Nero d'Avola, with other varieties optional. All of these wines come from a small area in southwestern Sicily, between the Contessa Entellina and Menfi zones.

✔ **Sambuca di Sicilia:** The fairly new DOC wines in this zone, pronounced sahm-*boo*-cah dee see-*chee*-lee-ah, come from southwestern Sicily, from an area overlapping part of the Menfi zone, and take their name from the town of Sambuca di Sicilia — not from Italy's anise-flavored liqueur! They include a blended white, red, and rosé, along with a varietal Chardonnay and Cabernet Sauvignon. The dry Bianco is mainly Inzolia, with 25 to 50 percent Catarratto and/or Chardonnay, and other varieties optional; the dry Rosso and Rosato are mainly Nero d'Avola, with 25 to 50 percent Nerello Mascalese and/or Cabernet Sauvignon, and/or Sangiovese, with other varieties optional. A peculiarity of the DOC regulations for these wines is that they explicitly forbid the use of Trebbiano Toscano, the mainland's uninspiring white grape that has gained a foothold in Sicily. Planeta winery has achieved quite a reputation for its varietal wines.

✔ **Sciacca:** A DOC zone in southwestern Sicily, around the coastal town of Sciacca, in the Agrigento province, Sciacca's (*shock*-cah) wines are similar to those of nearby Menfi.

✔ **Faro:** Faro (*fah*-ro) is a dry red wine from the extreme northeast corner of Sicily, around the slopes of the city of Messina. Its historic vineyard area is now attempting a revival after decades of desolation caused by phylloxera (the louse that wiped out many of Europe's vineyards more than 100 years ago). A few wineries make Faro, but production is a fraction of what it once was. Faro is mainly Nerello Mascalese, with Nerello Cappuccio, some Nocera, and Nero d'Avola, Gaglioppo, and/or Sangiovese optional. The definitive Faro is made by Palari, whose concentrated, limited-production wine retails for about $55. This winery is in the village of Palari, between Messina and the beautiful hilltop town of Taormina, which is a must-stop for every tourist in Sicily.

- **Etna:** Etna's (*eht*-nuh) vineyards on the volcanic slopes of Mount Etna in northeastern Sicily — as high as 2,300 feet — are the coolest vineyards in Sicily. (Ironically, they overlook Catania, on the east-central coast, often Italy's hottest city.) Like the vineyards of Faro, Etna's vineyards are a shell of what they were a century ago, having never recovered from the phylloxera blight. Yet a few valiant winemakers struggle on, as do some 80-year-old vines. Etna Bianco is a dry wine that's mainly Carricante, with Catarratto and/or Trebbiano and/or Minella Bianca; the delicately perfumed Carricante variety is especially suited to volcanic soil. A dry Rosso and Rosato are mainly Nerello Mascalese, with Nerello Cappuccio and white varieties optional. Benanti is a leading Etna winery; its Rosso Rovitello retails for about $22.

- **Cerasuolo di Vittoria:** The powerful, dry red from this zone (which is pronounced cher-ah-*swo*-lo dee veet-*tor*-ee-ah) in southeastern Sicily has a fairly light cherry color that belies its strength (at least 13 percent alcohol); it's best when young. The wine is 40 percent Frappato and up to 60 percent Nero d'Avola, with Grosso Nero and/or Nerello Mascalese optional. Valle dell'Acate is a leading producer; its Cerasuolo di Vittoria is about $20.

- **Eloro:** The Eloro (eh-*loh*-ro) zone is in the extreme southeast corner of Sicily. Eloro wines are all red or rosé and include three varietals: Nero d'Avola, Frappato, and Pignatello, all at least 90 percent from the named variety. Eloro Rosso and Rosato are dry wines from the same three grapes, with other varieties optional. A Rosso Pachino, from the Pachino subzone, also derives from the same varieties, but with emphasis on Nero d'Avola; it's an intensely flavored, dry red that's the area's most renowned wine.

## Sweet DOCs in Sicily

Sicily also boasts four sweet DOC wines that derive either from Moscato or the white Malvasia varieties. (If ever there were a place for good dessert wines, it's Sicily, where you can find some of the best pastries and desserts in the world!)

Moscato di Pantelleria (mohs-*cah*-toh dee pan-tel-leh-*ree*-ah) comes from the volcanic island of Pantelleria, about 25 miles southwest of the main island of Sicily — actually closer to Tunisia in North Africa. The hot African winds and blazing sun make grape-growing difficult, to say the least, but the hardy Zibibbo (Muscat of Alexandria) manages to survive these conditions and makes a concentrated, rich, peach-tasting dessert wine that's one of Italy's best. Two broad types of Moscato di Pantelleria exist: Moscato Naturale, which can be *dolce, spumante,* or *liquoroso,* and the exotic Passito di Pantelleria. The high sugar content of the *passito's* dried grapes produces a wine with 14.5 percent alcohol, but the wine can also be made in a *liquoroso*

style, which is at least 21.5 percent alcohol; when the wine is labeled *Extra,* it must be 23.9 percent alcohol. Marco De Bartoli, the Marsala producer, makes a superb Moscato Passito, called Bukkuram, which retails for about $50; other good Pantelleria wines sell for as little as $20.

The coastal hills around the ancient Greek city of Siracusa, in southeastern Sicily, make up the territory in which you find the renowned Moscato di Siracusa (mohs-*cah*-toh dee sir-ah-*coo*-sah), which is made from partially dried Moscato grapes. This dessert wine has an old-gold, slightly amber color, and at least 16.5 percent alcohol. This wine almost disappeared 20 years ago, but an increase in interest for dessert wines has caused a revival of sorts. Another sweet wine from southeastern Sicily is Moscato di Noto, from the hills south of the Moscato di Siracusa zone. Moscato di Noto Naturale is a dessert wine from Moscato Bianco grapes — quite similar to Moscato di Siracusa; it's also made as a sweet *spumante* and as a powerful (22 percent minimum alcohol) *liquoroso.*

Sicily's final dessert wine is a Malvasia from the Lipari Islands, including the volcanic island of Stromboli, located in the Straits of Messina, about 25 miles north of northeastern Sicily's mainland. One man, the late Carlo Hauner, revived the wine business on the islands and preserved one of the most haunting, captivating dessert wines in the world: Malvasia delle Lipari (mahl-vah-*see*-ah del lae *lee*-pah-ree). This wine, which is mainly Malvasia with 5 to 8 percent of the red Corinto Nero, takes on unique characteristics from the volcanic soil of the islands. This wine, light-bodied, with just a touch of sweetness, has almost indescribable floral and herbal aromas, combined with hints of dried or ripe apricots and dried figs. A sweeter *passito* version and a rarer, fortified *liquoroso* version also exist. Hauner Malvasia delle Lipari retails for about $36 or $37; Hauner *passito* costs about $45. Another good producer is Colosi, whose Malvasia delle Lipari retails for $22 to $23.

## A Sicilian wine shopping list

Look for these recommended Sicilian wine producers when browsing at your local wine shop:

| | |
|---|---|
| Abbazia Sant'Anastasia | Duca di Salaparuta (Corvo) |
| Benanti | Firriato |
| Cantine Torrevecchia | Florio |
| Colosi | Hauner |
| Cooperativa Interprovinciale Elorina | Morgante |
| COS | Salvatore Murana |
| D'Ancona | Palari |
| De Bartoli | Pellegrino |
| Donnafugata | Planeta |

| | |
|---|---|
| Pupillo | Settesole |
| Rallo | Spadafora |
| Rapitalà | Valle dell'Acate |
| Regaleali (Tasca d'Almerita) | Vitivinicola Avide |

# Sardinia Stands Alone

If you ask a native of Sardinia what her nationality is, she'll reply, "Sardinian" — not Italian. Although this scenario might play out similarly with citizens of many of Italy's independent-minded regions, nowhere would the answer be more emphatic than in Sardinia. But who can blame Sardinians for feeling independent? Sardinia is the most remote, isolated part of Italy. The nearest point of mainland Italy is 111 miles east, across the Mediterranean Sea. Ironically, the closest land is French-owned Corsica, 7 or 8 miles north.

Sardinia, like Sicily, was invaded by most of the major Mediterranean powers at some time during the past 3,000 years (even the Piedmontese!), but it was never truly conquered. It has been a part of Italy only since 1860. Although the island has Italy's longest coastline, most of the people of Sardinia remain in the hills to farm, tend sheep, and log, instead of moving to the coast to fish.

Wine plays a role in the Sardinian life and economy, but not nearly as large a role as you'd expect considering the sunny, dry climate that much of the island enjoys and the predominantly hilly terrain. Sardinia, the second-largest island in the Mediterranean after Sicily, is Italy's third-largest region (see Figure 8-2), but it produces only 2 percent of Italy's wine — about 11 million cases annually, which is only one-tenth of Sicily's total output!

Ironically, considering Sardinia's small wine production, the island's wine producers had focused on quantity rather than quality until recently. The change started slowly when Sella & Mosca, a winery that's a Sardinian institution, began its own revival in the early 1970s. When enologists such as Giacomo Tachis, the dean of Italian wine consultants, started working in Sardinia, wine connoisseurs knew it would only be a matter of time before this region began producing quality wines.

Sardinia makes slightly more white wine than it does red; it still has a few excellent dessert wines, but, like in Sicily, a declining market for sweet wines has decreased production. Sardinia's most-planted variety — occupying about one-third of all the vineyards — is the prolific white grape Nuragus (noo-*rah*-goos), which makes rather bland, neutral-tasting wine. But Vermentino (ver-men*tee*-noh), a grape of Spanish origin that's now a distant second to Nuragus in white grape plantings, is on the increase.

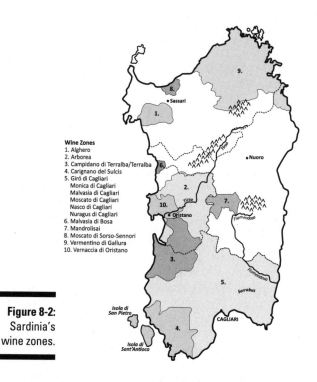

**Wine Zones**
1. Alghero
2. Arborea
3. Campidano di Terralba/Terralba
4. Carignano del Sulcis
5. Giró di Cagliari
   Monica di Cagliari
   Malvasia di Cagliari
   Moscato di Cagliari
   Nasco di Cagliari
   Nuragus di Cagliari
6. Malvasia di Bosa
7. Mandrolisai
8. Moscato di Sorso-Sennori
9. Vermentino di Gallura
10. Vernaccia di Oristano

**Figure 8-2:**
Sardinia's
wine zones.

The Spanish occupation of Sardinia in the Middle Ages brought more than just Vermentino to the island. The Spaniards planted three of their native red varieties, which together account for 40 percent of Sardinia's plantings and most of its best red wine. Those grapes are Cannonau (cahn-no-*now*), which is Spain's Garnacha (and France's Grenache); Carignano (cah-ree-nyahno), the Spanish Carignan, a variety now more common in France than in Spain; and Monica (moh-nee-cah). Cannonau has become especially popular as an inexpensive but pleasant Sardinian varietal wine — the red equivalent of Vermentino.

The structure of Sardinia's wine zones is somewhat different from those of other Italian regions. Sardinia has five regionwide DOCs, whose territories cover the whole island; six province-wide DOCs, whose territories cover the entire province of Calgari in the south; and eight other, more specific DOC wine zones. DOC/G wines account for about 14 percent of Sardinia's total production.

The next sections get you acquainted with Sardinia's numerous wines and share the names of some producers whose wines are worth seeking out.

## *Sardinia's regionwide DOC wines*

Two of Sardinia's five islandwide DOC wines are red varietals, and three are white varietals. Cannonau di Sardegna (cahn-no-*now* dee sar-*daen*-yah) is the star performer of the group and Sardinia's leading red wine. It's now made almost exclusively as a dry wine, but sweet and fortified Cannonau wines were common in the past. Grapes grown in the vineyards of three subzones (the best areas for Cannonau) may carry the subzone name on their labels: Oliena (or Nepente di Oliena) and Jerzu in the eastern hills of Nuoro province or Capo Ferrato in the Calgari province. Cannonau is best within a few years of its vintage date. A Cannonau Rosato also exists, as well as increasingly rare, dry, fortified *(liquoroso secco)* and sweet, fortified *(liquoroso dolce naturale)* Cannonau.

The Monica grape variety makes a softer, lighter-bodied red wine than does Cannonau. Although the grapes for Monica di Sardegna (moh-nee-cah dee sar-*daen*-yah) can grow anywhere on the island, they grow mainly in the Campidano plains in western Sardinia. The wine is usually dry (whereas Monica di Cagliari is typically sweet) — but it can be *amabile* (semisweet) or *frizzante* (spritzy). Most Monica wines, including the Cagliari version, stay on Sardinia.

Vermentino di Sardegna is a dry white wine made mainly in northern Sardinia. *Amabile* and *spumante* versions also exist. Vermentino from Sardinia is a fairly distinctive and characterful wine that's blessedly inexpensive; it very well might become a big success story for Sardinia. However, because of the large crops that DOC regulations generously allow Vermentino di Sardegna, it's seldom as good as the DOCG Vermentino di Gallura, unless it comes from the Alghero area, as Sella & Mosca's does.

The windswept Gallura hills in northeastern Sardinia have grown Vermentino for centuries; cool breezes from the Adriatic Sea and the rocky, granitic soil create an ideal environment for Sardinia's first DOCG wine (granted in 1996). Considering that only about 40 DOCG wines exist in Italy (as of this writing), the elevation of Vermentino di Gallura to DOCG is quite an honor for this remote outpost in the middle of the Mediterranean.

Vermentino di Gallura is at least 95 percent Vermentino. Restricted crop levels, plus a fine group of wineries in the area, assure the excellence of this wine; it's generally richer and more concentrated than most Vermentino di Sardegna. And this fine DOCG white retails for around $10! Producers to look for are Cantina del Vermentino, Cantina Gallura, and Tenute Capichera.

An obscure white variety called Semidano, seldom found outside of Sardinia, makes Sardegna Semidano (sar-*daen*-yah seh-mee-*dah*-no), which is usually a dry, soft, flavorful white wine. Sardegna Semidano can also be *amabile, dolce,*

**Book III**

**Italy: Small but Mighty**

or *passito* (from semidried grapes). The subzone name Mogaro applies to Semidano wines whose grapes grow around the village of Mogaro in western Sardinia.

The final wine in the regional category, Moscato di Sardegna, is a sweet *spumante* that's at least 90 percent Moscato Bianco. Very little of this delicately flavored bubbly is made, with most of it coming from the Anglona and Gallura hills in the north; Tempio Pausania (or Tempio) and Gallura are Moscato subzones in the Gallura hills.

## The copious wines of Cagliari, Sardinia's capital

Cagliari (*cah*-l'yah-ree), on the southern coast of Sardinia, is the region's capital and one of Italy's hottest cities in the summer months. The Cagliari province occupies the southern third of Sardinia. This entire area, plus a part of Oristano province on the west-central coast, is the vineyard territory for five wines, most of which have been traditionally sweet and/or fortified.

Four of these wines are unblended varietals that come in a similar range of styles: Their prevalent form is as a *dolce naturale* (sweet) wine, but they can also be made as a *secco* (dry) wine, and sometimes they're fortified to make a *liquoroso dolce* or *liquoroso secco* style. These four wines include two reds (Girò di Cagliari, from another Spanish variety, and Monica di Cagliari) and two whites (Malvasia di Cagliari and Nasco di Cagliari, from an indigenous variety). The fifth wine, Moscato di Cagliari, is a sweet *(dolce naturale)* or sweet, fortified *(liquoroso dolce naturale)* white wine made from Moscato Bianco. The Campidano di Cagliari area, in the Oristano and Cagliari provinces, is the main vineyard zone.

Cagliari's sixth wine is the largest-production wine in Sardinia and the one most consumed throughout the island. Its zone extends into villages in a third province, Nuoro, in east-central Sardinia. Nuragus di Cagliari is mainly a dry, light, rather neutral-tasting white wine made entirely from the Nuragus grape variety; it's also made *amabile* and *frizzante*.

## Other Sardinian wines

Many other Sardinian wines come from eight vineyard zones of more restricted sizes, mainly along the island's western coast. The fairly small but prolific Alghero (ahl-*gae*-ro) zone in northwestern Sardinia was approved for DOC wines in 1995, thanks basically to the work of one exceptional winery,

Sella & Mosca — a leader for its modern viticultural practices, state-of-the-art-winery, and research. Sella & Mosca proved that it's possible to make a fine Vermentino di Sardegna by controlling crop size. Sella & Mosca's La Cala is the wine of choice at the nearby coastal resort, Costa Smeralda, and is doing well on international markets as well. Another exceptional Alghero winery, Santa Maria La Palma, was responsible for draining local marshlands to make the Alghero zone suitable for vineyards.

Alghero Bianco, Rosso, and Rosato are dry, still wines that can be made from any of the authorized varieties in the Sassari province (a whole range of local and international varieties). The latitude that producers have in choosing their grapes extends to the styles of wines they make: The Bianco can be *frizzante, spumante,* or *passito;* the dry Rosato can be *frizzante;* and the Rosso can be *frizzante, novello,* or *liquoroso.* You may be wondering whether this zone produces any varietal wines. As a matter of fact, it does — seven of them. These varietal wines are Torbato and Torbato Spumante, which can be dry, *amabile,* or *dolce* (Torbato, a rare grape brought in from Spain, but probably French in origin, is considered Sardinia's finest dry white variety); Sauvignon; Chardonnay and Chardonnay Spumante, which can be dry, *amabile,* or *dolce;* Vermentino Frizzante, which can be dry or *amabile;* Sangiovese; Cagnulari (or Cagniulari, a dry red); and Cabernet (made from Cabernet Franc and/or Cabernet Sauvignon and/or Carmenère).

Sardinia's remaining DOC wines are limited in the scope of styles made as well as in their production zones. The seven remaining DOC wines are the following:

- **Moscato di Sorso-Sennori:** Pronounced mohs-*cah*-toh dee *sor*-so-sehn-*no*-ree, this wine's name can use Sorso, Sennori, or both. It's a sweet wine (or fortified *liquoroso dolce*) made entirely from Moscato Bianco grapes in the small wine zone around the communities of Sorso and Sennori on the northwest coast, north of the Alghero zone.

- **Malvasia di Bosa:** A real rarity, Malvasia di Bosa (mahl-vah-*see*-ah dee *boh*-sah) is made around the village of Bosa on Sardinia's western coast, between Alghero in the north and Oristano. Made entirely from Malvasia di Sardegna grapes, it can be *secco* (the most prized form, resembling a fine, dry Madeira), *dolce naturale, liquoroso secco,* or *liquoroso dolce.*

- **Vernaccia di Oristano:** Besides Malvasia di Bova, this wine, pronounced ver-*nahtch*-cha dee oh-ree-*stah*-no, is the other great apéritif/dessert wine of Sardinia, once very popular, but now falling out of favor. It's made entirely from Vernaccia di Oristano, probably an indigenous variety not related to any other Vernaccia. This dry, Sherry-like wine is best as an apéritif wine, like Sherry; it's also made as a *liquoroso* wine, either *secco* or *dolce.*

- **Mandrolisai:** The Mandrolisai (mahn-dro-lee-*sye*) zone lies in the barren center of Sardinia. Mandrolisai is a dry Rosso or Rosato made from Bovale Sardo (another Spanish red variety), Cannonau, and Monica, with other grapes.

- **Campidano di Terralba:** Terralba (ter-*rahl*-ba) is a dry red wine made mainly from the Bovale Sardo and/or Bovale di Spagna grape varieties, with up to 20 percent Pascale di Cagliari and/or Greco Nero and/or Monica. This large zone is in the Campidano plains in southwestern Sardinia. Try as you might, you can only buy the wine locally.

- **Arborea:** Arborea (ahr-bo-*rae*-ah) is a large zone in the Oristano province that makes light Sangiovese Rosso and Trebbiano (still or *frizzante*).

- **Carignano del Sulcis:** This zone, pronounced cah-ree-*n'yah*-no dee *suhl*-chees, is located in extreme southwestern Sardinia, including two islands off the southwest coast, in the Cagliari province. The zone produces dry Rosso and Rosato Carignano as varietal wines; it also makes *novello* and *passito* versions of the Rosso. One good producer, Santadi, makes a soft, fleshy Rosso with enough richness to outweigh Carignano's tough tannin; it sells for about $13.

## Sardinian producers to watch for

Keep your eyes peeled for the following recommended Sardinian wine producers:

Argiolas
Tenute Capichera
Giovanni Cherchi
Attilio Contini
Cantine Dolianova
Giuseppe Gabbas
Cantina Gallura

Antici Poderi Jerzu
Pala
Santadi
Santa Maria La Palma
Sella & Mosca
Cantina del Vermentino

# Book IV

# California and Elsewhere in North America

# In This Book . . .

When it comes to the wines of North America, one area stands apart. That area, of course, is sunny California, which produces outstanding wines in several styles.

The number of wineries in California has exploded to more than 2,000, and the map of wine regions has expanded to include pockets of vineyard land that were literally off the map only 15 years ago. What's more, California now grows dozens of grape varieties beyond its traditional Big Six fine-wine mainstays (Chardonnay, Sauvignon Blanc, Cabernet Sauvignon, Merlot, Pinot Noir, and Zinfandel).

This book takes you into the stunning, welcoming wines of California and also shows off winning wines produced in Oregon, Washington, New York, and Canada.

Here are the contents of Book IV at a glance:

# Chapter 1

# Introducing California Wines

*A*ll 50 American states make wine — mainly from grapes, but in some cases from berries, pineapple, or other fruits. Equality and democracy end there. California stands apart from the rest of the pack for the quantity of wine it produces (almost 90 percent of American wine), the international reputation of those wines, and the degree to which wine has permeated the local culture. To say that in the United States, wine *is* California wine isn't a huge exaggeration.

If you want to begin finding out about American wine, the wines of California are a good place to start. If you're already a wine lover, chances are California's wines still hold a few surprises worth discovering.

## Covering the Bases in Wine Production

Wine, of course, isn't just wine. The shades of quality, price, color, sweetness, dryness, and flavor among wines are so many that you can consider *wine* a whole world of beverages rather than a single product. Can a single state possibly embody this whole world of wine? California can and does.

Whatever your notion of wine is — even if that changes with the seasons, the foods you're preparing, or how much you like the people you'll be dining with — California has that base covered.

### The color and type spectrums

California makes a huge amount of white wine and red wine — the split's about even these days — and yet one of California's best-selling types of wines is actually pink, or *rosé*. That would be the wine called White Zinfandel, and yes, that name *is* illogical. California also produces plenty of rosé wines besides White Zinfandel.

*Sparkling* wine — wine with bubbles in it — and really sweet like-dessert-in-a-glass wines are two classic types of wine beyond regular *still* (nonsparkling), *dry* (not sweet) wines. California's sparkling wines range in price from super-affordable to elite; in quality, they range from decent to world-class. They also encompass a range of styles, from sweet and easy-to-enjoy to classically dry and complex. Sweet dessert wines are one of California's smallest wine categories, but nevertheless, you can score if dessert wines are what tickle your fancy. Your options range from delicious red Port-style wines (*fortified* wines, made by adding extra alcohol) to rich, seductive, golden-colored wines made from grapes that shriveled into an extra-sweet state.

## The wallet spectrum

For some wine drinkers, love of wine is colorblind as long as the price is right — and the wine producers of California are completely obliging. At their most affordable, California's wines cost as little as $2 for the equivalent of a standard bottle. (The volume of a standard wine bottle is 750 milliliters, which is a little more than 25 ounces.) And a few elite wines boast prices of up to $750 a bottle. Yes, that's $1 per milliliter, or $30 an ounce.

In terms of the dollar value of sales, the booming segment of the market is in the $15-and-up wines. But a greater quantity of wine sells in the under-$8 price tier. Bottom line: plenty of wine at whatever price you choose.

## The packaging spectrum

For several generations, California specialized in making red, white, and pink wines that sold in large juglike bottles at very affordable prices. These were easy wines for everyday life, with screw-off caps so you could pour two glasses and then close up the bottle for the next day. You can still find these California *jug wines* in most places where wine is sold, although their sales have declined.

Today's large-volume, easy-open option is the 3-liter box with a collapsible bag of wine inside and a spigot attached to the bag for easy serving. Some California wines even come in *Tetra-Pak* packages, which are compact, plasticized paper containers like you see for cooked tomatoes, generally about 1 liter in size — 33 percent bigger than a standard wine bottle. They don't require a plastic bag inside them to hold the wine, and they're super portable, not to mention eco-friendly and a great value. California certainly isn't the only place packaging wine in such innovative ways, but California's wine repertoire definitely includes plenty of wines in this category.

User-friendly wine options from California now also include premium wines — the good stuff — in regular-size wine bottles that are sealed with screw-off caps. Some winemakers, concerned that the screwcaps might confuse wine drinkers because of California's long tradition of making inexpensive jug wines with that type of closure, aren't embracing screwcaps for fine wine the way that Australian and New Zealand winemakers are. But some are, so California has that too.

# Leading the Market in Popularity

The Golden State makes more wine than all other U.S. states combined. Not only that, its wine production is huge even on a world scale. The United States as a whole ranks fourth for the quantity of wine it produces. But California owns that number-four spot all by itself, producing 7 percent of the world's wine — more than Argentina, Chile, Australia, Germany, and every other country except for Italy, France, and Spain.

In 2007, California made almost 566 million gallons of wine. That's equivalent to more than 2.8 billion standard-size bottles.

All of that production reflects a big demand for California wine. Two out of every three times someone in the United States grabs a bottle of wine to take home, points to a wine name on a restaurant wine list, or clicks an Internet link to buy wine, that wine comes from California.

A driving force behind the popularity of California wine is the way the wines taste. California wines are very fruity (that is, they have aromas and flavors that suggest fruits) and very flavorful (those fruity flavors are intense and easy to notice when you taste the wine), and these characteristics appeal to the typical American palate. When Americans taste California wines, they like them, and they come back to them again and again. Well, two out of three times, anyway.

Another factor feeding the popularity of California wines is the smart marketing practiced by the wineries. Winemakers in California understand what people want and make wines that fill those needs. That's why California wines run the gamut of styles and types: Wine drinkers themselves run the gamut in taste and price preferences. Whether you're a glass-of-Chardonnay-at-the-bar drinker, a fine wine collector, or a passionate Pinot Noir hobbyist, California makes wines that can appeal to you.

**Book IV**

**California and Elsewhere in North America**

Of course, quality also plays a role. Starting in the 1970s, California pioneered many winemaking innovations that improved wine quality. Flaws that used to exist in wines all over the world are now rare because the highly trained winemakers of California discovered how to prevent them, and other winemakers followed suit. In terms of fundamental quality, California wines are among the most reliable in the world.

# Golden Resources in the Golden State

Could the success story of California wines have happened anywhere, or is there something about the state itself that's an integral part of the picture?

Actually, the place itself is always part of the picture when you talk about wine. Wine is an agricultural product: The grapes that provide the raw material for wine come from vineyards that possess certain growing conditions — certain soil fertility, certain moisture, certain sunshine and heat, and so forth. These growing conditions affect the quality and, to some extent, the style of the final wine. If California makes quality, flavorful wines, that's due in no small part to the place called California.

The following sections offer a bit more insight into what makes California such an ideal winemaking locale.

## California climate

Of the various factors that influence vineyard regions and determine their suitability for growing wine grapes, one of the most important is climate. *Climate* is the general meteorological pattern of a large area. *Microclimate,* a term you hear frequently in wine circles, is the particular meteorological pattern of a smaller area, such as a certain hillside.

In wine terms, what matters is having a good, long stretch of months with temperatures above 50 degrees Fahrenheit, not-excessive amounts of rain, and few (if any) frosts or hailstorms. Beyond those basic requirements, winemakers look for special characteristics, such as fog or winds that moderate high temperatures, long sunshine hours, or abundant winter rains that supply groundwater. Every nuance in a microclimate affects the grapes that grow there. Even if California wines are generally very fruity and flavorful, nuances of taste occur as the result of differences in climate — and these differences are part of the reason California makes wines in every conceivable style.

The French use the word *terroir* to describe the combination of climate and soil factors that affect the grapes and thereby influence the style of an area's wines. California's winemakers also sometimes use this term.

### Rainfall and the need for irrigation

California has a Mediterranean-type climate, which means that rains fall in the winter but not during the summer growing season.

To supply the water grapevines need, most California wineries rely on irrigation. Generally they use *drip irrigation,* a system that feeds drops of water to each vine through a small hose that stretches along the base of the vines. These days, irrigating the vines is a complex balancing act between conserving water and giving the vines enough to thrive.

Some vineyards, particularly those on steep slopes where irrigation installations are difficult, survive solely on the water held in the ground. California has these *dry-farmed* vineyards, but they're the exception rather than the rule.

### Hot but cool, cool but hot

Apart from their common lack of growing-season rain, California's winemakers face many differences in weather patterns, depending on where in the state their vineyards are situated. For example, in the huge Central Valley, which lies mainly south of the state capital of Sacramento, the temperatures can be very high all summer. In contrast, the vineyards in Napa and Sonoma Counties that lie across the San Pablo Bay north of San Francisco experience many mornings that are so cool and foggy you might forget it's summer.

More than 60 years ago, two eminent scientists in California devised a method for categorizing the climate of various wine regions according to the average monthly temperatures from April through October. They defined five temperature bands, calling the coolest Region I and the warmest Region V. Different *heat summation regions,* as they're called, are appropriate for growing grapes to make different types of wines. California's finest wines come from the cooler regions, Regions I and II.

### Ocean breezes, elevation, and other influences on climate

Picture what California looks like on a map. (If you're having trouble, turn to Chapter 2 in Book IV for a map of California's wine regions.) With its long coastline, mountains, and deserts, the state has an amazing range of altitudes and other features that influence temperature, humidity, and rainfall patterns. The Pacific Ocean to the west provides a moist, cooling influence, whereas the deserts that occupy the state's eastern border, adjacent to Nevada and Arizona, provide a hot, dry weather influence.

**Book IV**

**California and Elsewhere in North America**

In California, one of the key determinants of local climate isn't how northerly or southerly a vineyard is but how close it is to the Pacific Ocean. Ocean breezes and fog moderate the temperature downward. Interior vineyard areas experience no moderating influence from the ocean, except in special cases when a mountain range funnels ocean air far inward or through some such anomaly.

California also boasts a wide range of altitudes, from Death Valley, which lies at 282 feet below sea level, to Mount Whitney, which rises 14,505 feet above sea level. You won't find any wineries or vineyards at either extreme, of course, but the state's diversity of altitudes has an impact on its wines nonetheless.

Altitudes vary even within a single wine region of California. For example, Napa Valley — California's most famous wine region — has vineyards on flat, low-lying land close to the Napa River; on hillsides that rise gently to the west and east of the river; and on mountains that rise above the hills. And that's just one of California's wine regions, of which there are dozens!

## Soil matters

In grape-growing circles, not all dirt is equal. The particular soil that a vineyard has is an important element in the ecosystem of that vineyard, affecting the availability of water and nutrients to the vines, the depth to which the roots grow, the rate of vine growth, and so forth.

Different soils can require different irrigation treatments, different pruning techniques, or different *rootstocks* (the rooting part of the vine, which, through grafting, is usually a different species from the part of the vine that produces the fruit). Subtly or not-so-subtly, the soil affects the way the grapes grow and therefore the wine that the grapes make.

In California, many of the least-expensive wines come from grapes grown in fertile soils, and plenty of the fine wines come from grapes grown in soils of medium or poor fertility. Mountain vineyards in particular tend to have poor soils, resulting in grapes that are concentrated in color and flavor.

California's winemakers tend to place less emphasis on soil than many European winemakers do, but that doesn't mean soil variations are nonexistent throughout the state. In Napa Valley alone, scientists have documented more than 30 types of soil.

# *The human factor*

Another element in California's unique combination of wine resources is its people. Even if Californians joke that very few of them were actually born in the state, the fact is that California's climate and lifestyle have attracted an impressive pool of winemaking talent. Or to be perfectly correct, California has attracted the people, and its universities have nurtured the winemaking talent.

California boasts two major universities that specialize in teaching wine-making and *viticulture* (that's *grape-growing* to the rest of us). The two schools are the California State University at Fresno (www.csufresno.edu) and the University of California at Davis (www.ucdavis.edu), both of which are known in wine circles by just the location name. A high percentage of California's winemakers have launched their careers by studying at these universities.

Davis, in particular, is world famous. Seldom will you visit wine regions in Europe — even the most established, elite winemaking regions — without meeting a winemaker who studied at Davis. The stellar reputation of the university's technical wine programs has made Davis a destination of choice for winemakers of the present and future who could go anywhere in the world.

Besides studying in California, winemakers from abroad often spend time working in California's wineries, particularly when they're young and just getting started in their families' wine businesses. This is a boon for everyone involved, because the sharing of traditions and winemaking philosophy that results enriches California winemakers' experience as much as it does the visitors'.

# Chapter 2

# California's Major Wine Regions: An Overview

*W*ine grapes flourish throughout much of California — as far north as Mendocino County in the upper third of the state, as far west as the edge of the Pacific Ocean, and as far east as the city of Fresno. Napa Valley and Sonoma County, both north of San Francisco, are world-famous wine destinations. But the past 30 years have also witnessed the emergence of Santa Barbara and Monterey along the state's central coast and Anderson Valley in Mendocino County — to mention just a few of the new hot spots for California wine. This chapter gives you an up close and personal look at them all.

## Location Matters

Like the differences in growing conditions, the differences in wines from region to region can be subtle or dramatic. California's wine producers didn't always take the issue of regional differences, or *terroir,* as seriously as they do today. However, those who make fine wine all over California now have real respect for the individual distinctions that make one vineyard different from the next and that make every wine region unique. Grape growers and wineries in specific regions have banded together, funded research, and shared their experiences to better define and understand the intricate nature of their own region's *terroir.*

Although plenty of California wines come from the grapes of multiple regions rather than from the grapes of a specific region (the labels of these wines simply state the wines' origins as *California*), a wine's region of production is an increasingly important consideration in buying fine wine from the Golden State. Figure 2-1 depicts California's main wine regions.

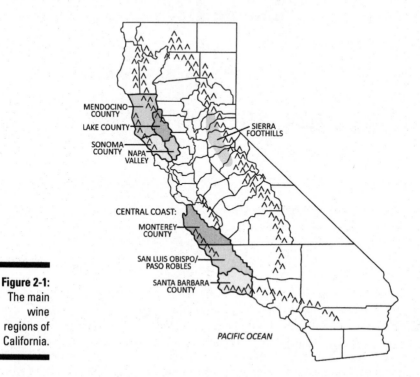

**Figure 2-1:**
The main
wine
regions of
California.

# *Napa Valley: Wine Country's Hollywood*

When someone utters the words *Napa Valley,* the first image that springs to most people's minds is of wine. Napa Valley is by far the best-known, most prestigious wine region in the New World. And yet only about 4 percent of California's wine comes from the very expansive vineyard lands of Napa Valley!

Today, nearly 400 wineries produce wine from about 47,000 acres of vineyards in Napa Valley. The wine boom here is a relatively recent phenomenon: Only 25 wineries existed in Napa Valley in 1960. Most of Napa Valley's wineries are small operations, although a few large wineries, such as Robert Mondavi Winery, Beringer, and Sutter Home, are based in Napa County.

Many Napa Valley wineries own large vineyards, which surround their properties like gorgeous manicured lawns. Other wineries don't own vineyards but instead buy their grapes from independent grape growers or buy juice or bulk wine from other wine producers. And some Napa Valley wine producers (including some winery names that you see on very expensive bottles of wine) surprisingly don't have their own wineries; they bring their grapes to *custom-crush* wine facilities, which they rent — all for the distinction of making "Napa Valley wine."

Reading about Napa Valley and its wines can be confusing at times because the name *Napa* actually applies to three entities:

- ✔ The political entity is Napa County.

- ✔ The city of Napa, situated at the southern end of the county, is the county seat.

- ✔ Napa Valley is the name of the AVA — that is, the official American Viticultural Area within Napa County (an *AVA* is a registered vineyard area within the United States).

For all practical purposes, the territory within the Napa Valley AVA is the same as that within Napa County. (The AVA doesn't encompass Lake Berryessa in the eastern part of the county, for example, but no one could grow grapes there, anyway.)

The following sections help you get more familiar with Napa Valley and the wine styles it's famous for.

## *Mapping Napa Valley*

Napa Valley isn't large: It's about 30 miles long and 5 miles wide at its widest point — about one-eighth the size of France's famous Bordeaux wine region (which you can read all about in Chapter 2 of Book II).

In addition to the broad Napa Valley AVA and the even broader (six-county) North Coast AVA, Napa Valley has 14 distinct viticultural areas that are considered subappellations of the Napa Valley AVA itself. (An additional subappellation, Calistoga, is pending.) The following are the standing Napa Valley AVAs, which you can also see in Figure 2-2:

- ✔ Mount Veeder; Spring Mountain District; Diamond Mountain District

- ✔ Oak Knoll District; Yountville; Oakville; Rutherford; St. Helena

- ✔ Howell Mountain; Stags Leap District; Atlas Peak

- ✔ Chiles Valley District

- ✔ Wild Horse Valley

- ✔ Los Carneros

## The United States' official grape-growing areas

The United States has registered vineyard areas, just like Europe does. These are called *American Viticultural Areas,* commonly abbreviated as AVAs. Because most American wines are named for their grape variety rather than their origin, American regulations defining viticultural areas are less all-encompassing than most European regulations. They define the boundaries of the territory in question but don't dictate grape varieties that growers can use, how they can grow the grapes, or how the winemakers can make the wine. In the Land of the Free, grape growers and winemakers are free to decide those issues for themselves.

The agency that regulates registered viticultural areas in the United States is the Alcohol and Tobacco Tax and Trade Bureau of the U.S. Department of the Treasury (the agency usually goes by TTB). Right off the bat, the U.S. regulations recognize every state, and every county within every state, as geographic designations that may be used on wine labels. All other areas must go through an approval process with the TTB to become official AVAs.

California had 104 AVAs as of the summer of 2008. Some of these AVAs are world famous, but others are still fairly obscure, even to wine lovers who live in the United States and perhaps even to wine lovers who live in California!

Despite its fairly small size, Napa Valley has an enviable range of soil types and climatic differences. Mountains surround Napa Valley on both sides — the Mayacamas Mountains to the west and the Vaca Mountains to the east — and the Napa River runs north-south through the valley. Soils vary according to how close to the river a vineyard is or how far into the hills or mountains it is, among other factors.

The climate in Napa Valley is generally warm and dry, but a dominant feature of the region is the combination of cool winds and fog that sweep up the valley from the San Pablo Bay in the south. Summer weather in the southern part of the Valley, in wine districts such as Los Carneros, Yountville, and Oakville, for example, can be distinctly cooler than that of the Calistoga area at the north end.

Napa Valley sits next to Sonoma County. The Mayacamas Mountains separate the two counties from each other for most of their length, but in the south, the terrain is open and flatter, and driving from one county to the other is easier. The two counties even share a wine district, Los Carneros, at their southern ends.

**Figure 2-2:**
Napa Valley
and its
AVAs.

# Discovering Napa's key wines

Napa Valley certainly benefits from its range of growing conditions.
Winemakers of the region produce every major type of California wine, along
with some of the lesser-known whites and reds. The next few sections show
you how Napa Valley's wines compare in terms of production.

**Book IV**

**California
and
Elsewhere
in North
America**

### Cabernet Sauvignons, Napa Valley's top wines

Napa Valley's best wines are its Cabernet Sauvignons (cab-er-nay saw-vee-nyons) and Cabernet blends. The generally warm, dry climate of Napa Valley suits the Cabernet Sauvignon grape variety just fine. Even though Cabernet Sauvignon wines are produced in many regions throughout the world, only France's Bordeaux region and Napa Valley have achieved world-class status for wines made from this popular variety.

### Other important reds

Merlot (mer-loh) remains Napa Valley's second most produced red wine after Cabernet Sauvignon. When not made as a varietal wine, Merlot is invariably blended into Cabernet Sauvignon (in small quantities, such as 10 percent) or blended into other Napa Valley red wines.

Pinot Noir (pee-noe nwahr) is Napa Valley's third most produced varietal red wine — a fact that was true even before the film *Sideways*. Although this award-winning movie definitely increased Pinot Noir wine production in California, the effect in Napa Valley was limited by the land: In Napa Valley, Pinot Noir grows primarily in Los Carneros, the Valley's coolest district.

Zinfandel — the original red version, pronounced *zihn*-fuhn-dehl — is Napa Valley's fourth largest red varietal wine in production, although as with Pinot Noir, Sonoma is more renowned than Napa Valley for Zinfandel. (**Note:** White Zinfandel, which is really pink, comes primarily from California's inland Central Valley.)

Blended wines have become increasingly popular in Napa Valley. Three of Napa Valley's elite reds — Opus One, Rubicon, and Dominus — are red wine blends (although all are primarily made from Cabernet Sauvignon). Most Napa Valley blended wines use the grape varieties famous in France's Bordeaux region: Cabernet Sauvignon, Cabernet Franc (frahn), Merlot, and sometimes Petit Verdot (peh-tee vair-doe) and/or Malbec (mahl-bec).

## Sonoma and Napa: Crossing from county to county

The easiest way to get from Napa Valley to Sonoma Valley (and vice versa) is to head to the southern end of either valley (the Los Carneros district) and cross over along the Sonoma Highway (California 12/121). From Napa to Sonoma, the trip takes about 20 minutes, assuming you don't encounter any traffic. Another option is to take the Oakville Grade (also known as Trinity Road) over the Mayacamas Range, which links Oakville in Napa with Glen Ellen in Sonoma. It's an extremely steep and windy road, but it can be a real timesaver if you're headed to the northern end of either valley.

Getting to Northern Sonoma is a snap from Sonoma Valley. Just follow Highway 12, which runs north to south and connects Sonoma Valley's towns, north to get to Santa Rosa. From there, jump on Highway 101 north and exit at the town of your choice.

### Napa Valley's whites

Chardonnay (shar-dohn-nay) continues to be Napa Valley's most popular white wine by a good margin, and Sauvignon Blanc (pronounced saw-vee-nyon blahnk and sometimes labeled Fumé Blanc) is Napa Valley's second favorite white. Newcomers such as Pinot Grigio/Gris (pee-noe *gree*-joe/gree) and Viognier (vee-oh-nyay) are beginning to make inroads into the dominance of these two wines, however.

## Getting to and staying in Napa Valley

San Francisco and Oakland are the entry cities via air for Napa Valley, which is about 60 miles northeast of these cities. The drive from both cities over the Oakland Bay Bridge or the Golden Gate Bridge is about 90 minutes.

For touring Napa Valley, a more luxurious (albeit costlier) alternative to a car rental is limousine service; this option is an especially good one if you don't have a designated driver with you and you're splitting the cost among a group of four to six people.

You have tons of places to choose for lodging, ranging from grandiose, posh resorts to chain hotels and motels. If you want to treat yourself, two upscale (more than $500 a night) destinations provide luxury accommodations in the Valley:

✔ **Auberge du Soleil:** This "Inn of the Sun" is one of the oldest (and still one of the best) inns in Napa Valley. A resort that's part of the Relais et Chateaux group, Auberge du Soleil has a wonderful location in the hillsides east of Rutherford village and an outstanding view from its excellent French restaurant.

✔ **Meadowood Resort:** This is a huge facility east of St. Helena, with many private cottages tucked into the woods. It also has a very fine restaurant.

Five comfortable, fine inns extend from the city of Napa in the southern part of the Valley northward to the town of St. Helena (note that Harvest and Villagio are generally more than $400 a night; the other three are less than $300 a night):

✔ **Harvest Inn:** Harvest Inn is just off Route 29 as you enter St. Helena from the south. It has modern, well-appointed rooms and cabins, and it's quite luxurious.

✔ **Napa River Inn:** Right in downtown Napa on the Napa River, this inn offers peaceful accommodations at reasonable prices.

✔ **Rancho Caymus:** Rancho Caymus is centrally located and is designed in the Spanish architectural motif. It's in Rutherford on Route 29, close to Beaulieu Vineyard Winery.

✔ **Villagio Inn:** Located in Yountville, close to Domaine Chandon winery, Villagio offers large rooms, top service, and an excellent breakfast.

✔ **Wine Country Inn:** Just north and a bit east of St. Helena sits the Wine Country Inn with its rustic charm.

*Note:* Whatever your lodging tastes or budget requirements, you can easily find a hotel or inn that meets your needs by doing some research online.

As with the blended red wines, most Napa Valley blended white wines use grape varieties famous in Bordeaux — in this case, Sauvignon Blanc and Sémillon (pronounced seh-mee-yohn).

# Sonoma County: Hardly an Also-ran!

Sonoma County is on California's North Coast, directly north of San Francisco and about an hour's drive from the majestic Golden Gate Bridge. It borders Napa Valley to the east but extends farther north. Sonoma is more than twice as large as Napa, and the wineries found here are more spread out. You have to allow more driving time when visiting Sonoma's wineries, which now number more than 250.

Sonoma (see Figure 2-3) has three general American Viticultural Areas (AVAs) and 11 specific AVAs, in addition to being part of the huge North Coast AVA, which encompasses six counties north of San Francisco. Here are Sonoma's general AVAs:

- Sonoma County

- Northern Sonoma (an area that includes Russian River Valley, Alexander Valley, Dry Creek Valley, and Knights Valley, along with other territory)

- Sonoma Coast, an elongated area in western Sonoma (along the Pacific coast) that's particularly known for its Pinot Noir

Sonoma differs from Napa in climate, in the wines that do best, and in attitude:

- **Climate:** In general, much of Sonoma is cooler than Napa, especially in Sonoma's coastal areas.

- **Top wines:** The cooler areas of Sonoma, such as Russian River Valley, Green Valley, and the Sonoma Coast, produce some of California's finest Pinot Noirs, Chardonnays, Zinfandels, and sparkling wines. (Napa's generally warmer climate provides an especially suitable environment for Cabernet Sauvignon, that county's most renowned wine.)

- **Attitude:** Sonoma doesn't have the glitz and glamour of Napa Valley; it's more laid-back. One of the great benefits of this is that fewer tourists visit Sonoma's wineries. Except during rush hour, you don't find the traffic problems that you can find in Napa Valley, especially in the summer.

Sonoma also has more than its share of some of California's largest and most famous wineries, such as Gallo Family Wineries, Kendall-Jackson, Korbel, Simi, Sebastiani, Jordan, and Gloria Ferrer, to name a few. Serious wine lovers could easily spend a week each in both Sonoma and Napa, just visiting some of the top wineries.

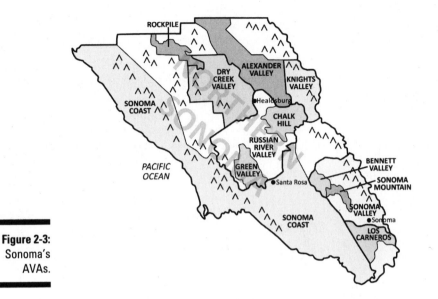

**Figure 2-3:**
Sonoma's
AVAs.

The sections that follow note some of the highlights of Sonoma County, as well as the region's top wine styles and its more diverse offerings.

## An idyllic wine region

In many ways, Sonoma is the most charming wine region in California. It has a little bit of everything, from Old World charm to modern wineries and fine restaurants. Going from the southern part of Sonoma to the north, some of its highlights include the following wineries, cities, and towns:

- ✔ **Gloria Ferrer Winery:** In windswept western Los Carneros, Gloria Ferrer is part of Spain's Freixenet — the largest sparkling wine producer in the world. The winery is an architectural wonder, and its sparkling wines are among the best in California.

- ✔ **Buena Vista Winery:** Also in Los Carneros, the dramatically beautiful Buena Vista is California's oldest continually operating winery (since 1857). Guided and self-guided tours are available. Wines are reasonably priced.

- ✔ **Town of Sonoma:** Dominated by its huge plaza, this fascinating old Spanish mission town is a must-see. Many fine wineries are nearby, including Ravenswood (the great Zinfandel specialist) and Hanzell (one of California's finest Chardonnay producers). Great cheese shops (try the Sonoma Jack) and bread shops offer their wares for picnickers.

**Book IV**

**California and Elsewhere in North America**

- ✔ **Village of Glen Ellen:** Just north of the town of Sonoma and south of Santa Rosa, this beautiful little village of about 1,000 residents was the home of one of America's great authors, Jack London, and one of its greatest food writers, MFK Fisher. Benziger Family Winery is also in Glen Ellen.

- ✔ **Santa Rosa:** In the center of the county, Santa Rosa is the largest city in Napa/Sonoma wine country, with lots of hotels and fine restaurants.

- ✔ **Healdsburg:** In Northern Sonoma, the town of Healdsburg is ideally located for winery visits because it's surrounded by three great Sonoma wine regions: Alexander Valley, Dry Creek Valley, and the Russian River Valley. Simi Winery is also in Healdsburg. The town has great restaurants, such as Cyrus and Bistro Ralph, plus lots of fine hotels and bed and breakfast inns.

## Sonoma's signatures: Pinot Noir and Zinfandel

Sonoma County succeeds with many diverse wines, but its two most renowned wines are Pinot Noir and Zinfandel.

Many wine critics believe that the United States' best Pinot Noirs come from Sonoma's Russian River Valley. Other wine regions also have a Pinot following: Los Carneros and the Sonoma Coast, in Sonoma County (with Los Carneros extending into Napa Valley); Santa Barbara; Santa Lucia Highlands; Mendocino's Anderson Valley; and Oregon's Willamette Valley. But Russian River Pinot Noirs have a combination of richness, voluptuousness, balance, and elegance that's hard to beat.

Zinfandel is truly California's wine. Even though the grape's genetic origin has been traced to Croatia, most of the world's Zinfandels, red and pink, are Californian. And most wine experts agree that a majority of the best *Zins* (as they're called for short) hail from Sonoma. Dry Creek Valley is particularly famous for red Zinfandel (the only color of Zin that Zin fanatics recognize). Russian River Valley and other Sonoma AVAs also produce fine Zinfandels, but in Dry Creek Valley, delicious, spicy Zinfandel is a real specialty.

## Sonoma's wines: Something for everyone

Sonoma's vineyards and wineries extend from Los Carneros in the south to Alexander Valley in the north — a much larger area than Napa Valley's (see the earlier section on Napa). Because Sonoma is so large, and because it has both coastal and interior wine districts, its climate varies from one wine district to another more than Napa's climate does.

In fact, the varied climate and soils of Sonoma offer more different types of wine than any other wine region in California. For example, the vineyard areas of Alexander Valley and Geyserville (in the north) and the Sonoma Mountain area (farther south) can be quite warm and dry, and they're ideal growing regions for Cabernet Sauvignon. The cooler regions, such as the Russian River Valley, Green Valley, Forestville, and the Sonoma Coast, produce excellent Pinot Noirs, Chardonnays, and sparkling wines. Temperate areas in Sonoma grow Zinfandel, Syrah, Merlot, Sauvignon Blanc, and Petite Sirah, to name a few of the more prominent varieties. But many more exist.

A short drive from one of Sonoma's viticultural areas to another can be a revelation: Each area seems to specialize in different wines. Following are the 11 distinct AVAs in Sonoma County (see Figure 2-3 for a visual), listed approximately from south to north, and the wines that are most renowned there:

- **Los Carneros (partly in Napa Valley):** Pinot Noir, Chardonnay, Merlot, sparkling wine

- **Sonoma Valley:** Chardonnay

- **Sonoma Mountain:** Cabernet Sauvignon

- **Bennett Valley:** Chardonnay, Sauvignon Blanc, Merlot

- **Green Valley (within Russian River Valley):** Sparkling wine, Chardonnay, Pinot Noir

- **Russian River Valley:** Pinot Noir, Chardonnay, sparkling wine, Zinfandel

- **Knights Valley:** Cabernet Sauvignon, Sauvignon Blanc

- **Chalk Hill (within Russian River Valley):** Chardonnay, Sauvignon Blanc

- **Dry Creek Valley:** Zinfandel, Cabernet Sauvignon

- **Alexander Valley:** Cabernet Sauvignon, Chardonnay, Sauvignon Blanc

- **Rockpile:** Zinfandel, Cabernet Sauvignon, Syrah, Petite Sirah

# More Key Wine Regions

Napa Valley and Sonoma County might be California's most famous wine regions, but they're only part of today's wine story in the Golden State. North, east, and south of Napa and Sonoma, vineyards grow all sorts of grape varieties for producing all kinds of wines. The following sections first head north, to idyllic Mendocino and Lake Counties, before covering the rest of the major wine regions in California.

# Up the North Coast to Mendocino and Lake Counties

California's majestic redwood sequoia trees, some 2,000 years old, are among the oldest living things on Earth. If you follow the giant redwoods — which begin in the Muir Woods just north of San Francisco — up the coastline through Sonoma County, you find forests full of them into Mendocino County and beyond, all the way north to Oregon. You don't find too many wine tourists in the region, even in the summer, and wineries genuinely welcome visitors up here.

The old town of Mendocino, on the coast, is a fantastic place to stay when visiting the wineries of Mendocino County. The place resembles a New England coastal town in the architectural style of its houses much more than a typical California town. There used to be a standing joke that Mendocino was populated mainly by old beatniks from the '50s and hippies from the '60s. There's still something a bit wild about Mendocino, but nowadays you also find a lot of fine little restaurants and interesting places to stay.

If you want an even quainter locale, try the hamlet of Boonville; it's located in the heart of cool Anderson Valley — Mendocino's prime grape-growing district. Anderson Valley is ideal for Pinot Noir, Chardonnay, Gewürztraminer (geh-*vairtz*-trah-mee-ner), Riesling (*reese*-ling), and some of the country's best sparkling wines, including those of the renowned Roederer Estate winery (see Chapter 3 in Book IV).

## Staying in Healdsburg

The town of Healdsburg is a popular place to stay in Northern Sonoma. Keep in mind that during the high season — between June and November — most hotels charge peak rates and sell out completely on weekends; many have a two-night minimum. Always ask about discounts. For more lodging options, check sonoma.com and winecountry.com.

**Les Mars Hôtel** 27 North St. (at Healdsburg Ave.), Healdsburg, CA 95448; Phone 877-431-1700 or 707-433-4211; Web site www.lesmarshotel.com

Staying at Northern Sonoma's most luxurious inn feels more like staying at a rich friend's home than a hotel. The 16 individually decorated rooms feature hand-selected 18th and 19th century European antiques, a canopy bed with Italian linens, a large TV and DVD player, a marble bathroom with a whirlpool soaking tub and walk-in shower, and personal touches at every turn. Each morning, guests are treated to a continental breakfast in the wood-paneled library, and during evenings they have easy access to the region's finest restaurant, Cyrus, which adjoins the hotel. *16 units. $495–$995 double. Rate includes continental breakfast. AE, DISC, MC, V.*

**Hotel Healdsburg** 25 Matheson St. (at the square), Healdsburg, CA 95448; Phone 800-889-7199 or 707-431-2800; Web site www.hotelhealdsburg.com

This home away from home across the street from the plaza is a visitor favorite because not only does it have spacious, comfortable rooms adorned with country-chic furnishings but it also has amenities associated with a true hotel, such as a spa, a heated pool, and the refined Dry Creek Kitchen restaurant. Rooms are minimalist-refined (think Pottery Barn) with angular, modern, dark-wood furnishings; big fluffy beds; oversized bathrooms with glass walk-in showers (some with soaking tubs); and, in many cases, balconies. Each floor has a computer with Internet access that's free to use. *55 units. $250–$495 double, $425–$790 junior and one-bedroom suites. Rates include a "country harvest" breakfast. AE, MC, V.*

**Honor Mansion** 14891 Grove St., Healdsburg, CA 95448; Phone 800-554-4667 or 707-433-4277; Web site www.honormansion.com

Guests who stay at this small luxury inn don't want to leave their rooms. Maybe that's due to the fluffy featherbeds, winter and summer bathrobes, or delicious toiletries. If you're in one of the particularly splendid units boasting a claw-foot tub, cozy gas fireplace, or a private deck with a Jacuzzi, you may only get up to help yourself to the decanter of sherry placed in each room. In addition to a decadent two- to three-course breakfast, Honor Mansion boasts bocce

and tennis courts, a huge lap pool, a croquet lawn, afternoon wine and cheese, a 24-hour self-serve espresso and cappuccino machine in the main building, and a never-ending supply of cookies. *$190–$325 double, $300–$550 suite. Rates include full breakfast and evening wine and cheese. DISC, MC, V.*

**Best Western Dry Creek Inn** 198 Dry Creek Rd., Healdsburg, CA 95448; Phone 800-222-5784 or 707-433-0300; Web site www.drycreek inn.com

It's not exactly a romantic wine country getaway, but anyone looking for a wonderfully clean and affordable place to crash after a day of wining and dining will be very happy here — especially considering all the extras. Along with basic motel-style rooms, you'll find a complimentary bottle of Sonoma wine upon check-in, a small fridge for chilling your Chardonnay and picnic items, and even a tiny fitness room for working off the pounds you're inevitably putting on. Add to that coffeemakers, free high-speed Internet access, and the great promotions featured on the Web site, and you've found one of wine country's best bargains. *103 units. $69–$239 double. Rates include breakfast. AE, DISC, MC, V.*

The other major wine district in Mendocino County lies in the eastern, somewhat warmer part of the county. Redwood Valley is home of Fetzer Vineyards, one of California's largest wineries, with its organic winery affiliate, Bonterra Vineyards. This area of Mendocino is best known for its Syrah, Petite Sirah, and Zinfandel.

Directly north of Napa County lies the smallish, off-the-beaten path Lake County, dominated by Clear Lake, California's largest natural lake. Here you find Lake County's best-known vineyards: Guenoc Vineyards and its sister winery, Langtry Estate. You also find a number of smaller wineries, many of which have sprung up in the past ten years or so. Cabernet Sauvignon is the leading varietal wine in Lake County, and Sauvignon Blanc is Lake County's most important white wine.

**Book IV**

**California and Elsewhere in North America**

# Down the Central Coast

California's so-called Central Coast is a huge area that extends from San Francisco to Santa Barbara. This area is actually a collection of separate wine districts, each with its own identity (see Figure 2-4). From north to south, these areas are

- Livermore Valley and Santa Clara Valley
- Santa Cruz Mountains
- Monterey, Carmel, and the Santa Lucia Highlands
- Paso Robles (San Luis Obispo County)
- Edna Valley (San Luis Obispo County)
- The Santa Maria and Santa Ynez Valleys

The following sections describe these different wine districts in greater detail.

## Livermore Valley and Santa Clara Valley

East and south of San Francisco, large tracts of vineyards used to exist. Now urban sprawl, from the cities of Palo Alto to San José (California's Silicon Valley), has usurped most of the vineyards in Livermore Valley, which is east of San Francisco, and Santa Clara Valley, which runs south of San Francisco.

But 39 wineries still exist in Livermore Valley, including two major operations: Wente Family Estates and Concannon Vineyard, both historic wineries. Livermore Valley has always been known for its Sauvignon Blanc and Sémillon, as well as Chardonnay, although Concannon's signature wine is Petite Sirah. Three other popular Livermore Valley wineries are Murrieta's Well, Page Mill, and Tamás Estates, the latter known for its *Cal-Ital varietals* (varietal wines made from native Italian grapes, such as Sangiovese and Barbera, grown in California).

Santa Clara Valley includes the Santa Cruz Mountains district, but the wines there are so distinct (see the next section) that it can be considered its own wine zone. The area of Santa Clara that's east of Santa Cruz Mountains, around San José, still has two major wineries: J. Lohr and Mirassou Vineyards. The latter is now part of the Gallo wine empire. Chardonnay, Cabernet Sauvignon, and Merlot are the three major wines in this part of the Santa Clara Valley.

**Figure 2-4:**
The Central
Coast's
wine
regions.

### *Santa Cruz Mountains*

Only an hour's drive south of San Francisco, the rugged, isolated Santa Cruz Mountains seem to be a world apart from urban life. Although Pinot Noir and Chardonnay grow well on the cooler, ocean side of the mountains, most of the district's more than 80 wineries — including California stalwarts such as Ridge (with its renowned Monte Bello Vineyard) and Mount Eden Vineyards — are located on the San Francisco Bay side. Magnificent Cabernet Sauvignon grows up here, as does Chardonnay.

**Book IV**

**California
and
Elsewhere
in North
America**

### Monterey County

Monterey County has a wealth of attractions, including its beautiful coastline, the Monterey Bay, Pebble Beach golf course, a wildlife refuge, and the chic town of Carmel. Additionally, the rugged beauty of Big Sur, a wilderness area, lies just south of Carmel on Route 1.

Monterey County now has about 85 wineries. But the vineyards of the Monterey peninsula serve an even larger population of wineries. As much as 80 percent of the wine grapes grown in Monterey County are purchased by non-Monterey wineries.

The weather in Monterey County is extremely variable. The northern part, closer to the town of Monterey and the Bay, is quite cool and breezy, with winds blowing in from the Pacific Ocean. As you travel south and farther inland, you can experience warm, even hot days but cool evenings in the summer. Riesling, Pinot Noir, and Chardonnay grow successfully in northern Monterey, especially near the coast, and Cabernet Sauvignon, Syrah, and Zinfandel do well in warmer southern Monterey.

A particularly special part of Monterey wine country is the Santa Lucia Highlands. This remote region, sheltered from the Pacific by the Santa Lucia Mountains, has vineyards up to 1,400 feet in altitude, where they rise into the sunshine above the morning fog line and enjoy cool breezes from Monterey Bay. Most of the wineries up here are small and new, but they're creating considerable fanfare among Pinot Noir lovers for their lush, rich style of wines.

Monterey's wineries offer something for everyone, as you can see from the following:

- **Large wineries:** Estancia Estates and Chateau Julien produce good value wines. Chateau Julien, in the Carmel region, is known for its reasonably priced Merlot.

- **A midsized winery:** Bernardus Winery in Carmel makes midpriced varietal wines from Cabernet Sauvignon, Merlot, and other varieties. It also offers first-rate lodging.

- **Smaller, more upscale wineries:** These wineries include

  - Chalone Vineyard, master of Chardonnay and Pinot Blanc (pee-noh blahnk).

  - Morgan Winery, renowned for its Pinot Noir and Chardonnay.

  - Robert Talbott Vineyards, known mainly for its Chardonnay and lately for its Pinot Noir. (*Note:* This is the same Robert Talbott who designs and produces very classy men's ties.)

- **Great views:** Smith & Hook/Hahn Estates Winery and Paraiso Vineyards, both in the Santa Lucia Highlands, offer sheer dramatic beauty. You can sip Paraiso's super Pinot Noir in the tasting room while taking in its view of the Pacific Coast from the edge of a cliff.

# Monterey County AVAs

Like most California wine regions, Monterey County has been changing rapidly since the 1980s, and now, in addition to the general Monterey County AVA, nine distinct AVAs exist here. Here they are, listed approximately from north to south, as well as the most renowned wines in each one:

| AVA | Description/Location | Wines |
|---|---|---|
| Monterey | Largest AVA in vineyard acreage | Pinot Noir, Chardonnay, Riesling in the north; Cabernet Sauvignon, Merlot, Syrah, and Chardonnay in the south |
| Carmel Valley | High in the Santa Lucia Mountains, near the coast | Cabernet Sauvignon and Merlot |
| Santa Lucia Highlands | In the Santa Lucia Mountains, close to the Pacific | Pinot Noir and Chardonnay |
| Chalone | In the Gavilan Mountains, to the east | Chardonnay, Pinot Blanc, Pinot Noir |
| Arroyo Seco | In the Santa Lucia foothills | Chardonnay, Riesling, and Zinfandel in the warmer part |
| San Bernabe | In the central part of the county | Merlot, Syrah, Chardonnay |
| San Lucas | Warmer AVA south of Salinas Valley | Cabernet Sauvignon, Merlot |
| San Antonio Valley | Warm AVA south of Santa Lucia Mountains | Cabernet Sauvignon, Petite Sirah, Syrah |
| Hames Valley | Southernmost tip of the county | Syrah, Rhône varietals |

## *San Luis Obispo: Paso Robles, Edna Valley, and Arroyo Grande*

The Big Sur wilderness in the southern part of Monterey County separates the northern districts of the Central Coast from those in the south. The southern part of the Central Coast begins in San Luis Obispo County. San Luis Obispo County resembles Monterey County in that the climate varies a great deal from north to south (see the preceding section on Monterey). In this case, most of the northern part — the hilly Paso Robles region north of the town of San Luis Obispo — is quite warm, and the southern parts — Edna Valley and Arroyo Grande, both near the coast — are distinctly cooler.

The Paso Robles vineyard area is the true center of the Central Coast (it's about equidistant from San Francisco and Los Angeles). The sunny, dry Paso

Robles climate makes this region primarily red wine country, with Cabernet Sauvignon, Merlot, Syrah, and Zinfandel the leading wines.

Paso Robles is one of California's fastest-growing wine regions; in 2006, the region had more than 90 wineries. Today, Paso Robles has nearly 170 wineries — and probably more by the time you read this. Some of the leading wineries in Paso Robles are Eberle, Justin Vineyards, Meridian Vineyards, Rabbit Ridge Vineyards, Tablas Creek, Treana, and Wild Horse Winery.

Paso Robles has two AVAs: the general Paso Robles AVA and York Mountain AVA. York Mountain is a small area in the southwestern part of the Paso Robles region that specializes in Cabernet Sauvignon. Because York Mountain is only 7 miles from the Pacific Ocean and is 1,500 feet in altitude, it's considerably cooler than the main, eastern part of Paso Robles — thus its need for a separate AVA. That said, the western part of the Paso Robles AVA is itself a fairly cool area.

The cool Edna Valley, south of Paso Robles, and the Arroyo Grande region, farther south, feature Pinot Noir and Chardonnay as their signature wines. But some wineries also grow Rhône varieties, such as Viognier, Syrah, Grenache, and Roussanne; others have Riesling, Pinot Grigio/Gris, Cabernet Sauvignon, and Zinfandel. Paragon Vineyard, one of California's best Pinot Noir vineyards, is in Edna Valley.

Fewer than 20 wineries are located in Edna Valley and Arroyo Grande, most of them in Edna Valley. The leading wineries are Alban Vineyards (Viognier specialists), Claiborne & Churchill (sounds like a law firm, but this winery makes good Riesling), Corbett Canyon, Edna Valley Vineyard (Pinot Noir/ Chardonnay specialists), Laetitia (sparkling wine and Pinot Noir), Saucelito Canyon (Zinfandel), and Talley Vineyards (Chardonnay and Pinot Noir).

### Santa Barbara County: Santa Maria, Santa Ynez, and Los Alamos Valleys and Sta. Rita Hills

Although Spanish missionaries planted vineyards in what is now Santa Barbara County more than 200 years ago, Firestone Vineyard, the County's first major winery, didn't open until 1975. Today, more than 110 wineries are operating throughout Santa Barbara. The fact that Santa Barbara County was the setting of the film *Sideways* certainly didn't hurt. Pinot Noir is Santa Barbara's poster child, for sure, but Chardonnay, Sauvignon Blanc, Riesling, and Syrah thrive there as well.

Santa Barbara has three official AVAs (Santa Maria Valley, Santa Ynez Valley, and Sta. Rita Hills) and one unofficial one (Los Alamos Valley) that's still pending official recognition. All four wine regions are north of the city of Santa Barbara and share a cool, unique climate, thanks to the positions of the Valleys.

Three Valleys (Santa Maria, Santa Ynez, and Los Alamos) run east to west — whereas most of California's coastal valleys run north to south — and are open to the cool breezes of the Pacific Ocean that channel through the Valleys. And so the southern latitude of Santa Barbara matters little; the position of the Valleys is what determines the climate, making all the Santa Barbara wine regions quite cool (the average temperature in Santa Maria Valley during the growing season is 74 degrees Fahrenheit), ideal for Pinot Noir and Chardonnay.

Here's a rundown of the three Santa Barbara Valleys:

- ✔ **Santa Maria:** Santa Maria Valley, the northernmost AVA, is particularly renowned for Pinot Noir; in fact, its Pinot Noir grapes are sought out by many wineries outside of Santa Barbara. Of the Santa Barbara AVAs, the foggy, windswept Santa Maria Valley area is the most influenced by the Pacific Ocean; Pinot Noir and Chardonnay are true standouts here.

- ✔ **Santa Ynez:** Santa Ynez Valley, in the southern part of the County and closest to the city of Santa Barbara, has the largest concentration of wineries. The western part, nearer the Pacific Ocean, grows Pinot Noir; the warmer, eastern end of the Valley features Syrah and other Rhône varieties.

  Sta. Rita Hills AVA, at the western end of Santa Ynez Valley, has a climate quite similar to that of Santa Maria Valley; Chardonnay and Pinot Noir do well here.

- ✔ **Los Alamos:** Los Alamos Valley, which lies between the Santa Maria Valley to the north and the Santa Ynez Valley to the south, uses the general Santa Barbara County AVA for its wines at present. Not as cool as Santa Maria Valley but cooler than Santa Ynez, Los Alamos's most important wines are Chardonnay and Pinot Noir.

Santa Barbara wine is typically enjoyable when it's young, within its first five years. The region's Pinot Noir has its own distinctive characteristics: Primarily, it exhibits intense strawberry fruit, with herbal notes.

Santa Barbara has many great wineries. A partial list includes Au Bon Climat, Babcock, Byron, Cambria, Cottonwood Canyon, Daniel Gehrs, Fess Parker, Fiddlehead Cellars, Foxen, Gainey, Hitching Post, Lane Tanner, Qupé, Sanford, Santa Barbara, and Zaca Mesa.

# Southern California

Although Southern California saw the very beginnings of California wines, not much wine exists there today. One reason is apparent: Too many people

**Book IV**

**California and Elsewhere in North America**

and too many houses occupy the land. Another reason is that vintners found regions more suitable for fine wine farther north, in central California, especially near the coast. But some wineries do still exist in Southern California.

One winery worth noting is in the Los Angeles area. Located in Moraga Canyon, Moraga Vineyards sits about 600 to 800 feet in altitude in the Bel Air hills. Tom and Ruth Jones, the proprietors, discovered that the area's soil resembled that of part of France's Bordeaux region in that it has gravelly beds, limestone, and fossils — a result of being submerged under the ocean millions of years ago. Tom Jones planted Cabernet Sauvignon, Merlot, and Sauvignon Blanc. He makes about 1,000 bottles a year of Moraga Red (80 percent Cabernet Sauvignon, 20 percent Merlot) and a little bit of Moraga White (all Sauvignon Blanc). The red sells for $125, the white for $65.

The Temecula Valley, about an hour's drive north of San Diego, near the city of Oceanside, is blessed with cool breezes that funnel in from the Pacific Ocean and create an environment suitable for fine wine grapes. At present, the Temecula Valley has 24 wineries. No one grape variety seems to predominate; Merlot and Syrah are the popular reds, whereas Chardonnay and Sauvignon Blanc are the dominant whites. Many dessert wines come from this area as well, generally from Muscat and late-harvested Zinfandel grapes. The two best-known wineries, both founded in 1969, are Callaway Coastal Winery and Mount Palomar Winery. Both wineries purchase a large part of the grapes for their wine production from Central Coast vineyards, however, partially due to an infestation of the root louse phylloxera that devasted the area in the late 1990s.

# Inward and upward

California's coastal regions get the lion's share of critical acclaim, but the state's wine economy owes a debt to the vast, interior vineyard areas. California's largest source of wine production is the huge Central Valley, located smack in the middle of the state. Another interior region, the Sierra Foothills, banks more on charm than on volume of production.

## Central Valley

More than 50 percent of all California wine is made in the Central Valley — which is the general name for San Joaquin Valley, Sacramento Valley, and surrounding areas. This huge valley in the middle of California extends from the city of Bakersfield at its southern end (near coastal Santa Barbara) all the way up and beyond Yuba City at its northern end (at a similar latitude to coastal Mendocino). It encompasses the state capital of Sacramento; the cities of Stockton and Fresno; and the wine towns of Lodi, Woodbridge, Modesto, Madera, and Clarksburg, among others.

## Sierra Foothills

If you want to experience a wine region that has a romantic history and has changed little over time, take a trip into the past and visit the charming wineries in the Sierra Foothills. The region has a rustic charm that you can't find anywhere else in California. Life is still simple here, so don't expect to find any fancy restaurants. But the people are friendly, and the wines are good — and reasonably priced!

The largest wine businesses in California have their principal wineries, or at least part of their operations, in the Central Valley. These businesses include E. & J. Gallo Winery, Constellation Wines, Robert Mondavi-Woodbridge (owned by Constellation), Bronco Wine Company, R.H. Phillips, Cribari, Paul Masson, Mariposa (part of Kendall-Jackson, headquartered in Sonoma), Delicato, Almaden, and Franzia. Three prominent smaller wineries are Bogle Vineyards, Quady, and Ficklin (the latter two are dessert wine specialists).

Climate in the Central Valley is generally warm and dry in the summer and temperate in the winter. Most of the state's grape varieties grow here. Three varieties that thrive in this climate are Zinfandel, Petite Sirah, and Chenin Blanc. The Central Valley specializes in producing inexpensive, large-production wines, helping make it the foundation of California's wine business.

# Central Valley AVAs

Unlike other California wine regions, the huge Central Valley has no regional AVA that encompasses the entire Valley. It does, however, have 17 specific AVAs spread throughout the Valley. Here they are, listed alphabetically:

- Alta Mesa
- Borden Ranch
- Capay Valley
- Clarksburg
- Clements Hills
- Cosumnes River
- Diablo Grande
- Dunnigan Hills
- Jahant
- Lodi
- Madera
- Merritt Island
- Mokelumne River
- River Junction
- Salado Creek
- Sloughhouse
- Tracy Hills

**Book IV**

**California and Elsewhere in North America**

One of the most memorable events in California's history was the Gold Rush of 1849. With the discovery of gold in Sutter Creek, in the foothills of the Sierra Nevada Mountains, this previously isolated area was forever changed. Besides prospectors and miners, others arrived there, and some of them decided to plant vineyards. By 1870, the Sierra Foothills boasted 100-plus wineries, more than Napa and Sonoma combined at the time! One of the varieties planted there, Zinfandel, eventually gave the region its most renowned wine. Most of the oldest grapevines in the United States — some even more than 100 years old — can be found in the Sierra Foothills.

The Sierra Foothills is a rather large region east and southeast of Sacramento. Most of the wineries are in Amador, El Dorado, or Calaveras Counties, or a little north or south of them. The Shenandoah Valley and Fiddletown are the two major viticultural areas, and many of the wineries are located in one of these two areas. Some major wine towns (where you can find accommodations) are Plymouth, Placerville, Sutter Creek, and Amador City.

In addition to the general Sierra Foothills AVA, five specific AVAs exist:

- California Shenandoah Valley (there's also a Virginia Shenandoah Valley AVA)
- El Dorado
- Fiddletown
- Fair Play
- North Yuba

Most of the vineyards in the Sierra Foothills are about 1,500 to 2,000 feet in altitude, some even higher. Much of the soil is decomposed granite or crushed volcanic rock, both very good for growing wine grapes.

Besides red Zinfandel, which dominates the region, other leading grape varieties in the Sierra Foothills include Syrah, Cabernet Sauvignon, Barbera, Petite Sirah, and Sauvignon Blanc.

After being practically wiped out by Prohibition in the 1930s, more than 100 wineries are in business today. Some of the leading Sierra Foothills wineries are Monteviña (now known as Terra d'Oro), Renwood, Shenandoah Vineyards, Amador Foothill, Boeger, Sierra Vista, Karly, Renaissance Vineyard, and Sobon Estate. Just about every winery here specializes in Zinfandel (and many produce true Old Vines Zinfandels), but many wineries also make Syrah and Barbera.

# Chapter 3

# Chardonnay, Sauvignon Blanc, and Sparkling Wines

. . . . . . . . . . . . . . . . . . . . . . . . . . . . . . . . . . . . . . . . . . . . .

## In This Chapter

▶ Tasting California Chardonnay and listing some of the best by price

▶ Checking out the styles of California Sauvignon Blanc and noting some wines to try

▶ Savoring California's premium bubbly, whether French or American owned

. . . . . . . . . . . . . . . . . . . . . . . . . . . . . . . . . . . . . . . . . . . . .

Chardonnay has been a staple of California wine production since the very first days when producers began naming wines after their dominant grape variety, and the style of California's Chardonnays has varied quite a lot over those 40 or so years. But stylistic changes haven't dampened California Chardonnay's popularity. It's the single best-selling type of wine that the state has — red or white (or pink).

Sauvignon Blanc is Chardonnay's perpetual sidekick in California. Its production is much smaller than Chardonnay's, and its appeal is much less universal among wine drinkers. Nonetheless, Sauvignon Blanc is California's number two white varietal wine — for many good reasons.

California's top sparkling wines, often referred to as *sparkling bruts* because most are made in the *brut* (very dry) style, are generally excellent and deserve more attention than they receive. The best of them are among the best sparkling wines in the world; only some true Champagnes, from France, stand above them in quality — but of course you pay a hefty price for most Champagnes today!

In this chapter, you find out about all three of these winners from the West Coast, including recommendations.

# Chardonnay: The Wine that California Made Famous

For all practical purposes back in the 1960s, wines named Chardonnay didn't exist! California had a few of them, but hardly anybody knew the wines. Chardonnay's trajectory from unknown entity to the biggest-selling wine in the United States is truly spectacular. The following sections give you a taste test of California Chardonnay and explain how the wine's taste is in part related to its price.

The Chardonnay grape traces its origins back to the Burgundy region in eastern France, where it was cultivated as early as the 1100s. It's the primary — and practically the only — variety used in making Chablis and the other iconic white wines of Burgundy (which you can read about in Chapter 3 of Book II). Also, Chardonnay is one of the major varieties in Champagne and other sparkling wines.

## The taste of California Chardonnay

The Chardonnay grape variety brings little aroma or flavor to its wines. In cooler regions, its wines often have hints of apple aromas and flavors; in warmer regions, they suggest tropical fruits, particularly pineapple. In some regions (such as Chablis, France), the wines have a distinctive mineral character, such as flintiness. These characteristics hold true in California's cooler and warmer wine regions. But because the state has more warm wine regions than cool ones, California Chardonnays tend to gravitate toward tropical fruit flavors, as well as ripe lemon.

Because of the wine's fairly limited aromas and flavors — and because Chardonnay juice is particularly compatible with oak — California winemakers ferment and/or age most of their better Chardonnays in oak barrels. Lower-priced Chardonnays typically obtain oaky aromas and flavors from oak planks, oak chips, or oak powder that soaks in the wine while it's in stainless steel vats. (Oak barrels are expensive!)

California Chardonnays made using any form of oak can smell and taste toasty, spicy, and/or smoky, with aromas and flavors of vanilla or butterscotch. *Note:* All of these aromas and flavors come from oak, not from the grape. Oaked Chardonnays can also have some tannin that comes from the oak. If the wine is actually fermented in oak barrels, which is common practice for pricier Chardonnays, it can have a special richness of texture as a result. But many California Chardonnays today, even cheap brands, have a thick, viscous texture not from oak but as the result of very high alcohol content; this characteristic is positive, unless you have a low threshold for alcohol and therefore taste a hard, burning character along with the rich texture.

Some critics have taken issue with the way California Chardonnay is made. Too many Chardonnays have been too high in alcohol, too sweet, and too oaky. A few producers make Chardonnays without using any oak, or even more commonly, with few or no new oak barrels. (Used barrels, depending on their age, give little or no oaky flavor to the wine.) The trend in California seems to be moving slowly away from heavily oaked Chardonnays toward more lightly oaked styles.

## For richer or for value

Some wine drinkers believe that California Chardonnays are too expensive. In fact, some of the most celebrated brands cost upward of $100 a bottle. But California Chardonnays exist at all price levels: You can even find one for $3 a bottle.

The taste of a California Chardonnay does vary according to price, as you can see from the following:

- ✔ The least-expensive wines tend to be quite sweet. You can sense their sweetness — a combination of residual sugar in the wines, in some cases, and the sweetness of high alcohol levels — as soon as you put the wine in your mouth. This sweetness counterbalances the edgy, sharp burn that overly high alcohol brings to a wine.

- ✔ Midpriced wines, especially those that cost about $15 to $20 a bottle, seem a bit less overtly sweet.

- ✔ The highest-priced wines vary a lot from brand to brand. In the best wines, you can sense a real concentration of flavor, and those flavors remain along the whole length of your tongue instead of stopping short midway.

You find great Chardonnays at each price level in the later section titled "Recommending Top Chardonnay Producers."

**Book IV**

**California and Elsewhere in North America**

# Where Chardonnay Grows in California

Chardonnay is somewhat of a workhorse grape variety: It can grow productively in all kinds of climates. But as California wine producers discovered in the last decades of the 20th century, Chardonnay does best in cool, coastal regions — such as Los Carneros, the Russian River Valley, and the Sonoma Coast — where the soil is usually quite poor and the vines don't grow prolifically. Figure 3-1 shows the Russian River Valley, a key Chardonnay region.

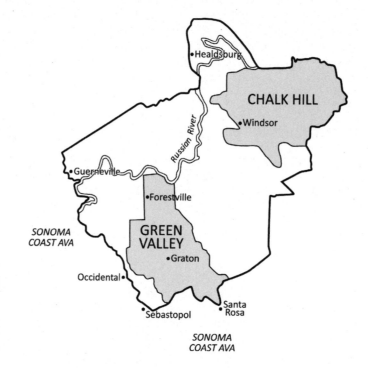

**Figure 3-1:**
The Russian
River Valley.

Chardonnays produced in the cool, coastal places can be quite expensive, but if you want to pay $15 or less, rest assured that lots of Chardonnay is made in this price range. The majority of inexpensive Chardonnays come from California's warmer regions, such as the Central Valley, where the soil is more fertile and grape-growing is more bounteous. Instead of having specific regional names on their labels, most of these wines simply carry the wider geographic designation of *California*.

The sections that follow clue you in to the premium spots for Chardonnay growing in both cool and warm regions of California.

# Cool, coastal, classic regions

Most of California's best Chardonnays come from its coolest growing areas, which are near its coastline and/or located at high altitudes. Many of these regions are in the coastal and northern parts of Sonoma County, such as the Russian River Valley and its even cooler subregion, Green Valley. The newest area that's gaining acclaim for Chardonnay is the Sonoma Coast, which is really pushing the envelope with its marginal growing conditions: It's a very cool area with poor soil, and both of these factors challenge the grapevines to perform.

Los Carneros, a region that's partly in Napa and partly in Sonoma, is another classic Chardonnay region. Although Los Carneros is in the southern part of both counties, the cool ocean breezes coming through San Pablo Bay in the south create ideal growing conditions for Chardonnay.

Santa Barbara County, although quite southerly, has valleys open to Pacific Ocean breezes and is generally an excellent region for Chardonnay. In particular, Santa Maria Valley, in the northwestern part of Santa Barbara County, is one of Santa Barbara's coolest districts because of its ocean breezes, and it's a fine area for growing Chardonnay.

Other cool regions that are perfect for Chardonnay include coastal Monterey County and the Chalone region in Monterey's Gavilan Mountains. Monterey County makes lots of Chardonnay, and most of it is fairly inexpensive. Mendocino County's Anderson Valley, along California's North Coast, is another cool location suited to making top-flight Chardonnays.

# Warm regions for everyday Chardonnays

California's gigantic Central Valley produces most of the state's inexpensive Chardonnays. You find some of these wines carrying appellations of origin such as *Lodi, Woodbridge, Modesto,* and *Madera* on their labels — but most of them simply carry the *California* designation. Growing conditions such as warm, sunny days, fertile soil, and irrigation enable grape growers here to produce huge crops of Chardonnay that find their way into many of the mass-market, value-priced brands.

**Book IV**

**California and Elsewhere in North America**

# Recommending Top Chardonnay Producers

California is the largest producer of varietal Chardonnay wines in the world. At least 2,000 different brands of California Chardonnay exist. This section names just a few of these brands to guide you toward some of the best California Chardonnays available at various price levels.

The text in parentheses after each wine indicates the American Viticultural Area (AVA) or other location where the grapes for that wine are grown.

### Moderately Priced Chardonnays, $12–$20

Alma Rosa Winery (Santa Barbara County)

Bernardus Winery (Monterey County)

Cambria Winery, Katherine's Vineyard (Santa Maria Valley)

Franciscan Oakville Estate (Napa Valley)

Freemark Abbey (Napa Valley)

Gainey Vineyard (Sta. Rita Hills)

Kendall-Jackson, Grand Reserve (Monterey/Santa Barbara Counties)

Markham (Napa Valley)

Sebastiani Vineyards (Sonoma County)

Wente Vineyards, Riva Ranch Reserve (Arroyo Seco, Monterey)

### Moderate-Plus Chardonnays, $20–$50

Anderson's Conn Valley Vineyards, Fournier Vineyard (Los Carneros, Napa Valley)

Arrowood Vineyards (Sonoma County)

Au Bon Climat, "Nuits-Blanchesau Bouge," Bien Nacido Vineyard (Santa Maria Valley)

Beringer Vineyards Private Reserve (Napa Valley)

Byron Vineyard (Santa Maria Valley)

Chalk Hill Estate (Chalk Hill)

Chalone Vineyard (Chalone, Monterey County)

Chappellet (Napa Valley)

Chasseur Wines (both in Sonoma Coast and Russian River Valley)

Chateau Montelena (Napa Valley)

Dehlinger (Russian River Valley)

Domaine Alfred, Chamisal Vineyards, "Califa" (Edna Valley)

Ferrari-Carano, "Tre Terre" (Russian River Valley)

Foley Estate (Sta. Rita Hills)

Forman Vineyard (Napa Valley)

Gallo Family Vineyards, Laguna Ranch (Russian River Valley)

Gary Farrell Vineyards, Russian River (Russian River Valley)

Grgich Hills Estate (Napa Valley)

The Hess Collection, Su'skol Vineyard (Napa Valley)

Jordan Vineyard (Russian River Valley)

Long Vineyards (Napa Valley)

Lynmar Winery, Quail Hill Vineyard (Russian River Valley)

Marimar Torres, Don Miguel Vineyard (Green Valley, Russian River Valley)

Mayacamas (Mt. Veeder, Napa Valley)

Morgan, "Metallico" (Monterey)

Nickel & Nickel, Searby Vineyard (Russian River Valley)

Patz & Hall, Dutton Ranch (Russian River Valley)

Ramey Wine Cellars, Russian River Valley, or Sonoma Coast (Sonoma)

Ridge Vineyards, Estate (Santa Cruz Mountains)

Robert Talbott Vineyards, Sleepy Hollow Vineyard (Monterey)

Saintsbury, Carneros Estate (Los Carneros, Napa Valley)

Sonoma-Cutrer (Russian River Ranches and Sonoma Coast)

Stag's Leap Wine Cellars, Karia Vineyard (Stags Leap District, Napa Valley)

Stony Hill Vineyard, Estate (Napa Valley)

Talley Vineyards, Rincon Vineyard (Arroyo Grande)

Trefethen Vineyards, Estate (Oak Knoll District, Napa Valley)

## High-End Chardonnays, Mostly $50–$100

Aubert Wines, Ritchie, Lauren, or Quarry Vineyard (Sonoma Coast); over $100

Brewer-Clifton, Seasmoke Vineyard (Sta. Rita Hills)

Dumol (Russian River Valley)

Far Niente (Napa Valley)

Fisher Vineyards, Whitney's Vineyard (Sonoma)

Flowers Vineyard (Sonoma Coast)

Hanzell Vineyards (Sonoma Valley)

Hyde De Villaine (HDV) Los Carneros (Los Carneros, Napa Valley)

Kistler Vineyards, Dutton Ranch (Russian River Valley); over $100

Kistler Vineyards, Kistler Vineyard (Sonoma Valley); over $100

Marcassin Vineyard, Zio Tony Ranch (Sonoma Coast); over $200

Marcassin, Marcassin Vineyard (Sonoma Coast); over $200

Mount Eden Estate (Santa Cruz Mountains)

Newton, "Unfiltered" (Los Carneros, Napa Valley)

Pahlmeyer (Napa Valley)

Paul Hobbs (Russian River Valley)

Peter Michael, Ma Belle-Fille (Knights Valley, Sonoma)

J. Rochioli Vineyards, Estate (Russian River Valley)

Rudd Estate, Bacigalupi Vineyard (Russian River Valley)

Williams Selyem, Allen Vineyard (Russian River Valley)

Book IV

California and Elsewhere in North America

# Six top-value Chardonnays

These six Chardonnays, all selling for about $12 or less, are consistently reliable:

✔ Acacia Winery, A by Acacia (California)

✔ Chateau Julien, Barrel Select (Monterey County)

✔ Chateau St. Jean (Sonoma County)

✔ Estancia, Pinnacles Ranches (Monterey County)

✔ Guenoc Winery (Lake County)

✔ J. Lohr, Riverstone (Arroyo Seco, Monterey County)

# Sauvignon Blanc: Always a Bridesmaid, Never a Bride

Sauvignon Blanc is California's second most popular white wine, but it's far behind Chardonnay in production and sales. In fact, Italian Pinot Grigio outsells California Sauvignon Blanc in the United States. Although some California winemakers have been passionate about Sauvignon Blanc, quite a few wineries, particularly in Napa Valley, gave up on Sauvignon Blanc — either because their winemakers weren't satisfied with their version of the wine or because the wine didn't sell well enough.

One of the main reasons for Sauvignon Blanc's failure to compete with Chardonnay is that in the early days of its history in California, Sauvignon Blanc didn't have a distinct identity. During the 1970s and part of the 1980s, producers often planted Sauvignon Blanc grapes in areas similar to where they planted Chardonnay and gave Sauvignon Blanc wine the same oak treatment as Chardonnay. And guess what? It tasted like Chardonnay.

But within the past decade, things have been changing in California for Sauvignon Blanc. Producers have been identifying the best regions to plant the grape, and many winemakers are now using little or no oak in the fermentation and aging process. As a result, California Sauvignon Blanc is slowly gaining a distinct identity and, in some cases, new respect among wine drinkers.

Many wine critics believe, however, that Sauvignon Blanc still hasn't hit its stride in California. Common complaints are that the high alcohol of many Sauvignon Blanc wines (sometimes combined with residual sugar in the wines) creates a sweetness that's discordant with the raw, bitter flavors that high alcohol can extract from the grapes.

The following sections introduce you to California Sauvignon Blanc styles you may encounter and explain why the wine is such a value.

## Three styles of California Sauvignon Blanc

The Sauvignon Blanc grape variety has always made wines of different styles in different wine regions. Depending on how ripe the grape gets, it can express herbal and vegetal aromas and flavors (when it's less ripe) or fruity aromas and flavors (when the grapes are riper). In some regions, particularly the Loire Valley in France, the wines can have a distinct mineral flavor.

The grape typically brings high acidity to its wines, which results in a fresh-ness and vibrancy in the wine unless a winemaker masks these characteristics with oak or by blending with another variety, typically Sémillon.

One of Sauvignon Blanc's identity problems in California is that the wines don't exhibit any one style. Often, you don't know what to expect when you buy a bottle. In this sense, Sauvignon Blanc is the antithesis of Chardonnay: Each brand is as different from the next as each brand of Chardonnay is similar to the next.

Today, California Sauvignon Blanc seems to fall into three main styles:

- **Grassy, herbaceous:** Sauvignon Blanc wines in this style have aromas and flavors that suggest freshly mown grass, fresh herbs, and/or green vegetables such as asparagus and bell peppers; these aromas can be more or less intense, depending on the wine. These wines are generally crisp and vibrant, with high acidity, but lately some of them are soft rather than crisp in texture. Sauvignon Blancs made in the grassy, herbaceous style usually ferment and age in stainless steel tanks, with little or no use of oak, which would diminish the vivid flavors of the grape.

- **Fruity:** Sauvignon Blancs in this style emphasize fruity aromas and flavors — melon, fig, citrus, passion fruit, and/or pear. These wines, generally crisp and lively but sometimes soft, are fermented and aged mainly or totally in stainless steel tanks, with little or no use of oak — just like wines in the herbaceous style. To tone down Sauvignon Blanc's grassy, herbal tendencies, winemakers either blend in other varieties, particularly Sémillon, or ensure that their grapes are ripe enough to prevent any underripe herbaceous or vegetal notes.

- **Oak-influenced:** This style, formerly the predominant type of Sauvignon Blanc in California, is closest to the style in which Chardonnays are made — although these days, most wines in this style have much less overt oaki-ness than most Chardonnays do. Typically, winemakers barrel-ferment and barrel-age these Sauvignon Blancs, which results in a more richly textured, somewhat fuller-bodied wine with toned-down aromas and flavors from the grape and gentle vanilla notes from the oak. Oak-influenced Sauvignon Blancs usually have Sémillon in the blend. The closest model for the oak-influenced style is white Bordeaux from the Graves and Pessac-Léognan districts in France (see Chapter 2 in Book II).

Today in California, the grassy, herbaceous style and the fruity style have overtaken the oak-influenced style in popularity. But you can still find all three styles of Sauvignon Blanc. What's hard to find, however, is a truly dry Sauvignon Blanc. Whether from high alcohol or from actual residual sugar in the wines, almost every California Sauvignon Blanc tastes a bit sweet.

**Book IV**

**California and Elsewhere in North America**

Sauvignon Blanc complements many foods, such as fish, shellfish, many chicken entrees, and Asian cuisine. And most California Sauvignon Blancs are ready to drink when you buy them; they don't need extra aging. Drink these wines well-chilled, because a low temperature enhances their vibrancy and diminishes the perception of any sweetness in the wine.

## Taste trumps price

One of the great aspects of California Sauvignon Blanc is that most cost less than $20. Some retail in the $20 to $30 range, and just a handful sell for more than $30. Sauvignon Blanc wines from California are much more affordable than California Chardonnays for two reasons:

- ✔ Chardonnay is still in much more demand, and therefore the grapes themselves, as well as the wines, cost more.
- ✔ Most Sauvignon Blanc producers use little or no expensive new French oak barrels for fermenting and aging their wines.

# Regions for Sauvignon Blanc

Nowadays, many of the best Sauvignon Blancs come from California's cooler American Viticultural Areas (AVAs), especially sites in Sonoma and Santa Barbara but also in Napa Valley's cooler regions, such as Los Carneros and mountainous regions within Napa County.

Napa Valley makes sense as a region for producing Sauvignon Blanc because Cabernet Sauvignon shines in Napa Valley, and Sauvignon Blanc performs well in Bordeaux, where Cabernet Sauvignon also excels. In fact, Sauvignon Blanc is genetically one of the parents of the Cabernet Sauvignon grape, along with Cabernet Franc.

Many of the early fine examples of Sauvignon Blanc wines came out of the Napa Valley. Although these Napa Valley wineries still produce good Sauvignon Blancs, today's epicenter for California Sauvignon Blanc might be switching to cooler Sonoma County and, to a lesser extent, Santa Barbara.

In the following sections, you find out about the main wine regions in California that produce Sauvignon Blanc wines and discover favorite California Sauvignon Blancs.

# Napa originals

Three Napa wineries that continue to be standard bearers for Sauvignon Blanc are as follows:

- **Frog's Leap:** This was one of the first California wineries to specialize in Sauvignon Blanc; today, Sauvignon Blanc comprises half of the winery's 50,000-case Rutherford AVA production.

- **St. Supéry:** Here's another one of the rare Napa Valley wineries that feature Sauvignon Blanc, not Chardonnay, as the primary white wine. In fact, St. Supéry makes two Sauvignon Blancs: its standard Sauvignon Blanc, which sells for less than $20, and an excellent single-vineyard Sauvignon Blanc, Dollarhide Ranch, which costs $30 to $35.

- **Voss Vineyards:** This winery, which grows its Sauvignon Blanc grapes in Napa Valley's Rutherford district, champions the grassy, herbaceous style of Sauvignon Blanc (one of three styles described earlier in this chapter). Voss is also one of the few California producers using a screw-cap rather than a cork on its Sauvignon Blanc bottles (although other California wineries are switching over to screwcaps as fast as they can). Voss Vineyards' Sauvignon Blanc retails for about $16.

Seven other Napa Valley wineries known for their Sauvignon Blancs are Flora Springs, which calls its wine Soliloquy; Selene (whose grapes come from Los Carneros's Hyde Vineyard); Cakebread Cellars; Grgich Hills; Honig; Rudd Estate; and Mayacamas. Spottswoode is another Napa Valley winery making a fine Sauvignon Blanc, but production is small and the wine is difficult to find.

Mayacamas Vineyards is an old-time (for California) mountain winery known for its long-lasting wines. Mayacamas's history dates back to 1889. Its present owner, Bob Travers (along with his son, Chris), produces only 600 cases or so of Sauvignon Blanc every year; the style is crisp, lively, assertive, and has excellent citrus and mineral notes. Mayacamas Sauvignon Blanc is one of the truly long-lived Sauvignon Blancs made in California; in a good vintage, it'll age for ten years or more. The current vintage sells for $30.

Another iconic Sauvignon Blanc is the "I Block" Fumé Blanc Reserve of Robert Mondavi Winery. This limited-production wine, from the To-Kalon Vineyard, costs about $75 a bottle. If that sounds pricey for a Sauvignon Blanc, well, it can seem like a bargain when you taste how complex and compelling the wine is after several years of age. Another good one to try is the Robert Mondavi Winery Fumé Blanc Reserve, which also comes from the To-Kalon Vineyard but costs a lot less — only about $35 to $40.

**Book IV**

**California and Elsewhere in North America**

A positive sign for Sauvignon Blanc in California is that a few wineries have begun making varietal Sauvignon Blanc for the first time. For example, Napa Valley's prestigious Franciscan Estate has released its first Sauvignon Blanc ever with its 2007 vintage. And it's a good one, made in a combined fruity and herbal style with a bit of ingratiating sweetness. It sells for $16 to $17.

## Sonoma takes on Sauvignon

With the stylistic preference for California Sauvignon Blancs gradually switching from oak-influenced to fruity and grassy, herbaceous styles, the cooler AVAs in Sonoma County are now producing many of California's most sought-after Sauvignon Blancs. The Russian River Valley, in particular, and the cooler parts of Dry Creek Valley — the district's western vineyards, near the Russian River Valley — excel with Sauvignon Blanc today.

### Russian River Valley

Sonoma's cool Russian River Valley (mapped out in Figure 3-1) has already proven to be an excellent location for Pinot Noir and Chardonnay wines, but lately it has become known as a fine source of Sauvignon Blancs as well.

Leading the way for Sauvignon Blancs in the Russian River Valley is J. Rochioli, a winery known for its Pinot Noirs. Rochioli's Sauvignon Blanc is a lively, crisp wine made in the fruity style, with lots of citrus notes; a small amount of oak fermentation rounds out the wine's texture and gives the wine weight. At $33 to $34, it's a bit pricey for a Sauvignon Blanc — but worth it.

Another Russian River Valley winery, Sauvignon Republic, is (as its name suggests) devoted exclusively to Sauvignon Blanc. Sauvignon Republic's Russian River Valley Sauvignon Blanc, made in the grassy, herbaceous style, sells for $15 to $16.

Hanna Winery also makes its Russian River Sauvignon Blanc ($14 to $16) in the grassy style. Other top Russian River Valley Sauvignon Blancs include Adler Fels, Chateau St. Jean, Dutton Estate, Gary Farrell, Paradise Ridge, and Rodney Strong.

### Dry Creek Valley

Although Dry Creek Valley is best known for its terrific Zinfandels and its Cabernet Sauvignons, Sauvignon Blanc now joins its list of very good varietal wines. At Dry Creek Vineyard, in fact, Sauvignon Blanc is the flagship white. Dry Creek Vineyard produces three Fumé Blancs, as they're called at this winery. Its Sonoma County Fumé Blanc, about $14, is in a restrained grassy, herbaceous style. Dry Creek Vineyards' two fine single-vineyard Fumé Blancs — its Estate DCV 3 and its Taylor's Vineyard Musqué, both about $25 — are in the fruity style.

Fritz Winery is also a champion of Sauvignon Blanc in Dry Creek Valley. Its Estate Sauvignon Blanc, about $20, is crisp and lively, with pronounced fruity flavors but also with a touch of grassiness.

Other fine Dry Creek Valley Sauvignon Blancs include those of Adobe Road, a small, new winery producing two Sauvignons (one from Dry Creek Valley and one from Russian River Valley); Dutcher Crossing; Handley Cellars; Lambert Bridge; Mill Creek; and Quivira Vineyards.

## Top Sauvignon Blancs from other regions

Two important Sauvignon Blanc producers are in Santa Barbara County:

- ✔ **Babcock Winery and Vineyards:** Babcock is in the Sta. Rita Hills, an AVA known for its Chardonnay and Pinot Noir. Although Babcock produces good examples of these other wines, it has become well-known for its assertive Sauvignon Blanc (made in the grassy, herbaceous style), which sells for about $20.

- ✔ **Brander Vineyard:** In the Santa Ynez Valley AVA, this winery is arguably the greatest Sauvignon Blanc specialist of any winery in California — no, make that the entire United States. Although Brander does make other wines, its most important wine is Sauvignon Blanc. Brander produces an amazing five different Sauvignon Blancs — in all styles and with prices ranging from $15 to $30. Brander ferments and ages most of its Sauvignon Blanc wines in stainless steel tanks and avoids new oak at all costs.

The Santa Ynez Valley, an inland area of Santa Barbara County, is in fact a prime source for Sauvignon Blancs, despite the fact that it's warmer than other parts of Santa Barbara County. Besides Brander, some top Santa Ynez Valley producers of Sauvignon Blanc include the Ojai Vineyard, Fiddlehead Cellars, Lincroft Vineyards, Firestone Vineyard, and Gainey Vineyard.

Other California Sauvignon Blancs to try include Greenwood Ridge Vineyards in Anderson Valley (Mendocino) and Bernardus in Monterey County.

# Names to Trust in Sauvignon Blanc

Many producers make two Sauvignon Blanc wines, a midpriced one that ferments and ages in stainless steel and a more expensive one that often — but not always — ferments and/or ages at least partially in French oak. Sometimes the costlier Sauvignon Blanc simply comes from a better vineyard site, occasionally a specific single vineyard, and has been produced without oak.

*Note:* A few Sauvignon Blancs on the following lists include the term *Musqué* in their names; this word refers to a variant of the Sauvignon Blanc grape variety that produces particularly rich, aromatic wines. Also, when the producer calls its wine *Fumé Blanc,* you find that name in the list.

### Moderately Priced Sauvignon Blancs, $12–$25

Adler Fels (Russian River Valley)
Babcock Vineyards (Sta. Rita Hills)
Bernardus Winery (Monterey)
The Brander Vineyard
    (Santa Ynez Valley)
Cain Cellars, Musqué (Monterey)
Chateau Potelle (Napa Valley)
Chateau Souverain (Alexander
    Valley, Sonoma)
Chateau St. Jean Fumé Blanc, "La
    Petite Etoile" (Russian River
    Valley)
Dry Creek Vineyard Fumé Blanc
    (Sonoma County)
Duckhorn Vineyards (Napa Valley)
Dutcher Crossing Winery
    (Dry Creek Valley)
Dutton Estate (Russian River Valley)
EOS Estate (Paso Robles)
Ferrari-Carano Fumé Blanc
    (Sonoma County)
Flora Springs "Soliloquy"
    (Napa Valley)
Franciscan Estate (Napa Valley)
Fritz Winery (Dry Creek Valley and
    Russian River Valley)
Frog's Leap (Napa Valley)
Gainey Vineyard (Santa Ynez Valley)
Gary Farrell (Russian River Valley)
Greenwood Ridge Vineyards
    (Anderson Valley)

Groth Vineyards (Napa Valley)
Handley Cellars (Dry Creek Valley)
Hanna Winery, Slusser Road
    (Russian River Valley)
Honig Vineyard (Napa Valley)
Justin Vineyards (Paso Robles)
Kunde Estate, "Magnolia Lane"
    (Sonoma Valley)
Mason Cellars (Napa Valley)
Matanzas Creek (Sonoma County)
Mill Creek Vineyards (Dry Creek
    Valley)
Quivira Vineyards, "Fig Tree
    Vineyard" (Dry Creek Valley)
Robert Mondavi Winery, Fumé Blanc
    (Napa Valley)
Robert Pecota Winery, "L'Artiste"
    (Napa Valley)
Rodney Strong Vineyards, Charlotte's
    Home (Sonoma County)
Silverado Vineyards, Miller Ranch
    (Napa Valley)
St. Supéry (Napa Valley)
Stag's Leap Wine Cellars (Napa
    Valley)
Voss Vineyards (Napa Valley)
Whitehall Lane (Napa Valley)
Wildhurst Vineyards Reserve
    (Lake County)

### Moderate-Plus Sauvignon Blancs, mostly $25–$50

Adobe Road (Russian River Valley,
    and Dry Creek Valley)
Araujo Estate (Eisele Vineyard, Napa
    Valley); $75 to $90; very scarce
The Brander Vineyard, "Au Naturel"
    (Santa Ynez Valley)

Cakebread Cellars (Napa Valley)
Chalk Hill Estate (Chalk Hill, Sonoma)
Dry Creek Vineyard Fumé Blanc,
    "DCV3," and "Taylor's Musqué"
    (Dry Creek Valley)

Fiddlehead Cellars, "Goosebury," (Santa Ynez Valley)

Grgich Hills Fumé Blanc (Napa Valley)

Mayacamas Vineyards (Napa Valley)

The Ojai Vineyard, Westerly Vineyard (Santa Barbara County)

Robert Mondavi Winery, Fumé Blanc Reserve (Napa Valley)

J. Rochioli Vineyards (Russian River Valley)

Rudd Estate (Napa Valley)

Selene Wines, Hyde Vineyard (Los Carneros)

St. Supéry, Dollarhide Ranch (Napa Valley)

Spottswoode Winery (Napa Valley)

Sonoma Coast Vineyards, Hummingbird Hill Vineyard (Sonoma Coast)

# Presenting California's Sparkling Wines

California producers make sparkling wines in every major category: *nonvintage* bruts (bubblies blended from wines of several different years), rosé bubblies, *blanc de blancs* (from white grapes only), *blanc de noirs* (white or pink sparkling wines made entirely from red grapes), and vintage-dated bruts and rosés. You can even find California sparkling wines labeled *Spumante* that are sweet, flavorful wines in the style of Italy's famous sparkling wine, Asti. However, California's top sparkling wine producers use the varieties used in France's Champagne region — Pinot Noir and Chardonnay — as their main grape varieties. (**Note:** Pinot Blanc and Champagne's third important grape, Pinot Meunier, are minor components in a few California sparkling wines.)

## Top-value Sauvignon Blancs

These 12 Sauvignon Blancs, all available for $12 and under at nationwide average retail prices, are consistently reliable:

- Benziger Family Winery (Sonoma Mountain)
- Estancia Estates (Monterey County)
- Firestone Vineyard (Santa Ynez Valley, Santa Barbara)
- Geyser Peak (California)
- Guenoc (Lake County)
- Kendall-Jackson (California)
- Kenwood Vineyards (Sonoma County)
- Murphy-Goode (Alexander Valley, Sonoma)
- Robert Pepi Winery (Napa County)
- Pedroncelli, East Side Vineyards (Dry Creek Valley, Sonoma)
- Simi (Sonoma County)
- Wente Vineyards (Livermore Valley)

All the better California sparkling bruts are made by the same method used in Champagne, called *méthode champenoise* or *classic method*. In this method, the wine's second fermentation, which gives the wine its bubbles, takes place in the bottle that you buy. However, some sparkling wines from larger wineries are the product of more economical methods, such as large-batch second fermentations in tanks or even the injection of gas directly into a wine. Labels of wines made using large-batch fermentation usually carry the term *charmat method;* wines made by the injection of carbon dioxide gas must be labeled as *carbonated* wines. Price can also be a guide: Wines costing less than $8 are generally made by using either of these two shortcut methods.

The following sections help you get acquainted with California sparkling wines in terms of taste, ownership of the different brands, and wines worth trying.

## Characterizing California bubbly

California's different climates, soils, and other variables make the state's sparkling wines different from France's Champagnes and all other sparkling wines in the world. Because California's bubblies tend to be made with riper grapes than those of Champagne and many other regions, they taste fruitier than these other wines. Also, California generally ages most of its sparkling wines a shorter time than the historic French region, Champagne, does; as a result, California bruts usually lack the toastiness or biscuity character that you can find in some aged Champagnes.

The fruitiness, exuberance of bubbles, and frothiness of California bubblies makes them perfect for less-formal settings, such as parties, outdoor events, and casual eating. However, more and more serious, longer-aged, complex California sparkling wines are now available from such producers as Iron Horse and Schramsberg.

## Looking at the French- and California-owned brands

Many of California's top sparkling wine companies are French owned. Producers from the region of Champagne opened wineries in California for two reasons: They were running out of vineyard land in their home region, and they knew Americans were very loyal to their own brands. (Even today, almost 70 percent of all wines sold in the United States are domestic, and most of them are from California.)

## Roederer Estate, the ultimate California bubbly

When French Champagne producers realized they were running out of vineyard land back home, many started buying vineyards in California and building wineries there. Most of these new operations were in Napa Valley or Sonoma. But Jean-Claude Rouzaud, the crafty boss of Champagne Louis Roederer (producers of the sublime *Cristal*) knew that top sparkling wine demanded a very cool climate, and in 1982 he found it 125 miles north of San Francisco, in Mendocino's Anderson Valley.

Roederer Estate debuted its first sparkling *brut* (a dry sparkling wine) in 1988, followed shortly by a delicately colored brut rosé. Both wines have been the critics' darlings since their introduction. In 1993, Roederer Estate introduced a premium vintage sparkling wine, L'Ermitage, which, vintage after vintage, vies for honors as the best sparkling wine in the world made outside of Champagne. Recently, a vintage L'Ermitage Rosé joined the line. If you shop around, you can find the nonvintage Roederer Estate sparkling brut for less than $20, the brut rosé for about $25, the L'Ermitage for about $40, and the low-production, harder-to-find L'Ermitage Rosé for about $50.

Moët & Chandon, located in the town of Epernay in France, started the Champagne foray into California in 1973 when it opened Domaine Chandon — today the second-largest sparkling wine producer in California after Korbel. Other French producers from Champagne followed: G. H. Mumm (which founded Mumm Napa), Taittinger (which owns Domaine Carneros), and Louis Roederer (owner of Roederer Estate).

Other top California wineries producing sparkling wines are American owned. These include Iron Horse, Schramsberg, J Wine Company, Laetitia Estate, and Korbel. The one exception to French or American ownership is Gloria Ferrer, owned by huge Spanish producer Freixenet.

## *Recommending some of California's sparkling wines*

The following recommended California sparkling wines — including rosés, blanc de blancs, and vintage bubblies — are divided into three price categories, according to their typical prices in wine shops:

**Moderately Priced Sparkling Wines, under $30**

Domaine Carneros Vintage Brut (Los Carneros)

Domaine Chandon Brut Classic and Blanc de Noirs (Napa Valley)

Gloria Ferrer Vintage Blanc de Blancs and Royal Cuvée (Los Carneros)

Handley Cellars Vintage Brut and Brut Rosé (Anderson Valley)

*(continued)*

*(continued)*

Iron Horse Vintage Brut and Blanc de Blancs (Green Valley, Sonoma)

J Vineyards Brut, "Cuvée 20" (Russian River Valley)

Korbel Vintage Brut "Natural" (Russian River Valley)

Laetitia Estate Brut (Central Coast)

Laetitia Estate Vintage Brut Rosé (Arroyo Grande Valley)

Mumm Napa Brut Prestige, Blanc de Noirs, "Cuvée M," and Vintage Blanc de Blancs (Napa Valley)

Piper Sonoma Brut Cuvée and Blanc de Blancs (Sonoma County)

Roederer Estate Brut and Brut Rosé (Anderson Valley)

Scharffenberger Brut (Anderson Valley)

Schramsberg Vintage Blanc de Blancs and Blanc de Noirs (North Coast)

### Moderate-Plus Sparkling Wines, $30–$50

Domaine Carneros Vintage Rosé Brut (Los Carneros)

Étoile Brut and Étoile Brut Rosé, Domaine Chandon (Napa Valley)

J Vineyards Vintage Brut and Brut Rosé (Russian River Valley)

Mumm Napa, Vintage "DVX" (Napa Valley)

Roederer Estate Vintage Brut "L'Ermitage" (Anderson Valley)

### High-End Sparkling Wines, over $50

Domaine Carneros, Le Rêve Vintage Blanc de Blancs (Los Carneros)

Gloria Ferrer, Carneros Cuvée (Los Carneros)

Iron Horse Vintage Blanc de Blancs "Late Disgorged" (Green Valley, Sonoma)

Iron Horse, Joy! magnum only (Green Valley, Sonoma); $147

J Vineyards, Vintage "Late Disgorged" Brut (Russian River Valley)

Roederer Estate Vintage Brut Rosé "L'Ermitage" (Anderson Valley)

Schramsberg Vintage Brut "Reserve"

J. Schram Vintage Brut (North Coast)

J. Schram Vintage Brut Rosé (North Coast); $125

# Chapter 4

# California's Standout Red Wines

*I*n 2006, a proposed ruling to declare Zinfandel the official wine of California made its way around legislative circles in Sacramento, the state capital. Although Zinfandel has impressive family ties to the soil and the people of California, Cabernet Sauvignon might have been as wise a choice for California's official wine. Cabernet Sauvignon is the wine that proved to the world California's stellar standing in the red wine universe.

Where there's Cabernet Sauvignon, there's Merlot — often coexisting in the bottle, regardless of which grape gets official billing on the label. California's Merlot wines have a shorter history than the state's Cabernets, and they've had a tougher time establishing a reputation for greatness. But from the right vineyard, they're great.

When the two grapes come together, is the whole greater than the sum of the parts? In other words, do California's nonvarietal Cabernet-Merlot blends outshine varietal Cabernets and Merlots? Sometimes yes, sometimes no. One thing you can be sure of is this: California Cabernet, Merlot, and their blends together offer terrific drinking. This chapter gives you the lowdown on California's major red wines, including Pinot Noir, which has joined Zinfandel, Cabernet Sauvignon, and Merlot only recently, and after a rough start, but now is well-established and earning high marks.

# Hailing the California Cab, a World-Class Red

Cabernet Sauvignon is California's leading red grape variety in terms of quantity produced — a fairly recent occurrence. For many years, Zinfandel topped the statistics (although, of course, most of the wine made from those Zinfandel grapes was pink rather than red). Now that Cabernet Sauvignon is number one, it can probably expect to have a long reign as the king of California's reds, because except for Zinfandel, nothing else is close. The following sections describe the taste that brought Cabernet Sauvignon its place at the top, explain how California's Cabernets relate to Bordeaux, and present some of the best California wines made from the Cabernet Sauvignon grape.

## Tasting California Cabernet

Cabernet Sauvignon grapes (like all grape varieties) grow differently and develop different taste characteristics in different wine regions. For instance, when Cabernet Sauvignon grapes grow in very cool climates, the flavor of the wine can run toward vegetal notes, such as green bell peppers. In very warm climates, the wine's flavors can suggest baked fruit rather than fresh fruit.

In general, however, wines from the Cabernet Sauvignon grape are deep in color and medium- to full-bodied, with firm tannin, lean structure, and a relatively simple aroma/flavor profile that includes blackcurrant, mint, tobacco, and cedar. Some Cabernets are slightly sweet, with flavors that suggest candied fruit; others are dry, with flavors of dark fruits and sometimes earthy notes.

Given California's fairly warm climate, the Cabernet wines produced there tend to be rather full-bodied and high in alcohol, with many containing 14 percent alcohol and upward. The richest wines have dense, velvety texture as well as a considerable amount of tannin (a characteristic of wine described in Chapter 5 of Book I) that shows itself in the back of your mouth as you taste the wine. The lightest wines are fairly smooth in texture with a medium to small amount of tannin.

The majority of California's Cabernets are dry wines that have noticeable tannin. That tannin is just a fact of life for Cabernet Sauvignon, although today's winemakers are adept at softening the tannin so it doesn't taste bitter. And frankly, a meal with meat or cheese generally mellows that tannin right out of the wine's taste. (For tips on pairing wine with food, flip to Chapter 6 in Book I.)

California's winemakers make Cabernet Sauvignon wines to suit different consumer tastes, and those wines taste different depending on the price tier. Elite Cabernets, costing $50 a bottle or double (and sometimes more than quadruple), for example, are powerful red wines with a serious amount of firm tannin from aging in small, new barrels of French oak. In contrast, Cabernets that sell for about $10 or less are often medium-bodied, easy-to-drink, very fruity red wines with a bit of sweetness and very little tannin to speak of.

## Making a California original from a Bordeaux grape

To understand the taste of California Cabernets, comparing them to red Bordeaux wines (covered in Chapter 2 of Book II) is quite helpful. The Bordeaux region of western France produces the world's most legendary wines based on the Cabernet Sauvignon grape.

The red wines of a particular part of Bordeaux, known as the Left Bank, are the most Cabernet Sauvignon–dominant Bordeaux wines; they typically contain about 60 to 65 percent Cabernet Sauvignon. Connoisseurs and collectors revere some Left Bank Bordeaux wines that have maintained the highest standards of quality over decades and sometimes centuries. The best Left Bank Bordeaux wines can age for many decades, developing complex, compelling aromas and flavors of leather, tobacco, and cedar and becoming soft in texture and nearly sweet from their aged tannins.

California's Cabernets are different from Cabernet Sauvignon–based Bordeaux reds, even comparing the best wines from each region. California's Cabs tend to

- ✔ Be fruitier and therefore more enjoyable when they're young
- ✔ Be fuller in body
- ✔ Have sweeter, riper fruit flavors and less earthy flavor
- ✔ Have higher alcohol content
- ✔ Have softer, denser texture

Most of Bordeaux's least-expensive wines are heavily based on Merlot rather than Cabernet Sauvignon, which makes comparisons at the lowest price levels meaningless. At midprice levels, however — say about $25 a bottle — the general differences between Bordeaux and California Cabs do ring true: California's wines are fruitier and fuller-bodied, with riper fruit flavors, less earthiness, and less vegetal suggestion in their flavor than Bordeaux wines.

The California style of Cabernet Sauvignon (midpriced and higher, that is) is so unique, in fact, that it has redefined Cabernet Sauvignon wine. California's top Cabernets have become role models for winemakers all over the world, who emulate their ripe fruit character, relatively soft tannins, and rich texture.

**Book IV**

**California and Elsewhere in North America**

# Listing favorite Cabernets

Cabernet Sauvignon needs a warm, dry climate with a fairly long growing season because it's a late-ripening grape. In terms of quality, the three most important regions for Cabernet Sauvignon wines and Cabernet-based blended wines are Napa Valley, Sonoma County, and the Santa Cruz Mountains.

### Napa Valley Cabernet Sauvignons

Napa Valley has the most Cabernet Sauvignon acreage in the state and clearly the largest number of wineries producing Cabernet Sauvignon wines. Probably about two-thirds of California's best Cabernets come from Napa Valley grapes.

Even though Napa Valley is quite small, it has 14 distinct American Viticultural Areas (AVAs; see Chapter 2 of Book IV for the listing), all of which — even cool, windy Los Carneros — grow Cabernet Sauvignon. Cabernet grows on the valley floor and the benchlands leading up to the mountains, as well as in the mountains themselves: the Mayacamas Mountains to the west and Vaca Mountains to the east. This diversity of growing areas leads to interesting comparisons between mountain Cabernets (which are generally more tannic and have more acidity and concentrated fruit character) and valley floor Cabernets (which are usually broader in structure, with riper, more generous fruit character).

Eleven of Napa Valley's 14 AVAs are most important for Cabernet Sauvignon. Here they are, listed from south to north within each bullet point:

- **Valley floor/benchland:** Oak Knoll District, Yountville, Oakville, Rutherford, and St. Helena

- **Mayacamas Mountains:** Mt. Veeder, Spring Mountain District, and Diamond Mountain District

- **Vaca Mountains:** Atlas Peak, Stags Leap District (hillside), and Howell Mountain

Los Carneros is certainly an important AVA in Napa (and Sonoma), but only a few wineries make Cabernet Sauvignon in that cool region.

Each Napa Valley AVA produces distinctly different Cabernet Sauvignons. For example, Stags Leap District and Oak Knoll District (typified by the Cabernets of Stag's Leap Wine Cellars, Clos du Val, and Trefethen Vineyards) are known for their elegant, finesseful wines, whereas Diamond Mountain and Howell Mountain (typified by the Cabernets of Diamond Creek and Dunn Vineyards) are known for powerful, tannic, full-bodied wines requiring considerable aging before they're ready to drink.

Napa Valley Cabernet Sauvignons are by far the most expensive wines in California. Witness the recommendations that follow, which include only one moderately priced ($12 to $20) wine and, at the opposite extreme, 40 high-end ($50 to $100) Cabs (a fourth category, luxury Cabernets, covers the many over-$100, well-regarded Napa Valley Cabernet Sauvignons).

The info in parentheses after each wine indicates the AVA or other area where the grapes for that wine are grown.

### Moderately Priced Napa Valley Cabernet Sauvignon, $12–$20
Joseph Carr Cellars (Napa Valley)

### Moderate-Plus Napa Valley Cabernet Sauvignons, $20–$50
Anderson's Conn Valley, "Prologue" (Napa Valley)
Beaulieu Vineyard, "Rutherford" (Napa Valley)
Chappellet, "Signature" (Napa Valley)
Charles Krug, "Yountville" (Napa Valley)
Chimney Rock, "Stags Leap" (Napa Valley)
Clos du Val (Napa Valley)
Cuvaison, "Mt. Veeder" (Napa Valley)
Dyer Vineyard, "Estate" (Diamond Mountain, Napa Valley)
Flora Springs Vineyards (Napa Valley)
Franciscan, "Oakville Estate" (Napa Valley)
Frog's Leap, "Napa Valley" and "Rutherford" (Napa Valley)
Heitz Wine Cellars (Napa Valley)
Hess Collection, "Estate" (Mt. Veeder, Napa Valley)
Joseph Phelps (Napa Valley)
La Jota Vineyard (Howell Mountain, Napa Valley)
Mount Veeder Winery (Mount Veeder, Napa Valley)
Newton Vineyard, "Unfiltered" (Napa Valley)
Pine Ridge (Rutherford, Napa Valley)
Ramey Wine Cellars (Napa Valley)
Robert Mondavi (Napa Valley)
Silverado Vineyards (Napa Valley)
Snowden Vineyards, "The Ranch" (Napa Valley)
Smith-Madrone (Spring Mountain, Napa Valley)
St. Clement (Napa Valley)
Swanson Vineyards, "Alexis" (Oakville, Napa Valley)
Terra Valentine (Spring Mountain, Napa Valley)
Tom Eddy, "Elodian" (Napa Valley)
Trefethen Vineyards (Oak Knoll District, Napa Valley)
Truchard Vineyards (Los Carneros, Napa Valley)
Turnbull Cellars (Oakville, Napa Valley)
Vineyard 29, "Cru" (Napa Valley)
Whitehall Lane (Napa Valley)

### High-End Napa Valley Cabernet Sauvignons, $50–$100
Altamura Winery (Napa Valley)
Anderson's Conn Valley, "Estate Reserve" (Napa Valley)
Beaulieu Vineyard, "Georges de Latour Private Reserve" (Napa Valley)
Bennett Lane (Napa Valley)
Beringer Vineyards, "Private Reserve" (Napa Valley)
Cakebread Cellars (Napa Valley)
Caymus Vineyard (Napa Valley)
Charles Krug, "Vintage Selection" (Napa Valley)
Chateau Montelena (Napa Valley)

Clark-Claudon Vineyards (Napa Valley)

Clos du Val, "Stags Leap" (Napa Valley)

Corison Winery (Napa Valley)

Duckhorn, Estate (Napa Valley)

Dunn Vineyards, "Napa Valley" and "Howell Mountain" (Napa Valley)

Etude (Napa Valley)

Fisher Vineyards, "Coach Insignia" (Napa Valley)

Forman Vineyard (Napa Valley)

Freemark Abbey, Bosché and Sycamore Vineyards (Napa Valley)

Grgich Hills (Napa Valley)

Groth Vineyards (Napa Valley)

Hartwell Vineyards (Stags Leap District, Napa Valley)

Heitz Wine Cellars, Bella Oaks and Trailside Vineyard (Napa Valley)

Hoopes Vineyard (Oakville, Napa Valley)

J. Davies (Diamond Mountain, Napa Valley)

Jarvis Winery (Napa Valley)

Kuleto Estate (Napa Valley)

Mayacamas Vineyards (Mt. Veeder, Napa Valley)

Nickel & Nickel, all single-vineyard Cabernet Sauvignons (Napa Valley)

Palmaz Vineyards (Napa Valley)

Paradigm (Oakville, Napa Valley)

Pine Ridge, "Oakville" and "Stags Leap District" (Napa Valley)

Pride Mountain (Napa Valley)

Ramey Wine Cellars, Larkmead Vineyard (Napa Valley)

Robert Craig Winery, "Mt. Veeder" and "Howell Mountain" (Napa Valley)

Saddleback Cellars (Napa Valley)

Shafer Vineyards, "One Point Five" (Napa Valley)

Silver Oak Cellars "Napa Valley" (Napa Valley)

Silverado Vineyards, "Solo" (Stags Leap, Napa Valley)

Stag's Leap Wine Cellars, S.L.V. and Fay Vineyard (Stags Leap District, Napa Valley)

Tom Eddy (Napa Valley)

### Luxury Napa Valley Cabernet Sauvignons, over $100

Araujo Estate, Eisele Vineyard (Napa Valley); $300+

Chappellet, Pritchard Hill (Napa Valley); $120/$130

Chateau Montelena, "Estate" (Napa Valley); $100+

Diamond Creek, Gravelly Meadow, Red Rock Terrace, and Volcanic Hill Vineyards (Napa Valley); $160

Far Niente, "Oakville" (Napa Valley); $115

Fisher Vineyards, Lamb Vineyard (Napa Valley); $125

Heitz Wine Cellars, Martha's Vineyard (Napa Valley); $150

Joseph Phelps, Backus Vineyard (Napa Valley); $250

M by Michael Mondavi (Napa Valley); $200

Nickel & Nickel, Martin Stelling Vineyard (Oakville, Napa Valley); $125

Ramey Wine Cellars, Pedregal Vineyard (Oakville, Napa Valley); $150

Robert Mondavi "Reserve" (Napa Valley); $125

Spottswoode Estate (Napa Valley); $130

Staglin Family Vineyard, Estate (Rutherford, Napa Valley); $155

# The Mondavi legacy

When Constellation Brands, the world's largest wine company, purchased Robert Mondavi Corporation and all of its brands in 2004, many Mondavi fans wondered what would become of the family. Five years later, all seems to be going well with Robert Mondavi Winery, judging by its latest vintages. And Robert Mondavi's two sons and daughter — Michael, Tim, and Marcia — now have Napa Valley Cabernet Sauvignon–based wines of their own. The two wines (Tim and Marcia are partners in producing one of them) are different, but both are exceptional.

In 2005, the families of Tim Mondavi, Marcia Mondavi, and the late Robert Mondavi joined forces to produce a wine, appropriately named Continuum, from grapes grown in Oakville vineyards and vineyards in the Stags Leap District that the Robert Mondavi family had cultivated for decades. The 2005 Continuum is a Bordeaux-style blend: 58 percent Cabernet Sauvignon, 23 percent Cabernet Franc, and 19 percent Petit Verdot. The blend can change with each vintage, according to what Tim Mondavi and his winemaking team deem best. The 2005 Continuum (about $150) is quite impressive. It's a cross between fine Bordeaux and elegantly styled Napa Cabernet, with firm acidity and lots of finesse. Oh yeah, and it's rather hard to find: Tim made just 1,500 cases of this wine.

Even at this early stage, 2005 Continuum tastes as if it'll be one of the great Mondavi family wines. Production will increase a bit, but Tim wants to keep it small and high quality, not more than several thousand cases a year.

The impressive 2005 M by Michael Mondavi (about $200) is entirely Cabernet Sauvignon, sourced from an Atlas Peak vineyard owned by Michael and his wife, Isabel. M is more typical of a top Napa Valley Cabernet Sauvignon than Continuum is; it's richer and fleshier but with the restraint and balance that typifies the Mondavi Cabernet style. Still a baby now, the 2005 M will join the ranks of California's finest red wines. Only 600 cases of the 2005 exist, and Michael says that no more than 1,200 cases will be produced in future vintages. The wine will sell primarily in fine restaurants and resorts.

With these two impressive wines, the Mondavi family's legacy is in good shape.

## Sonoma Cabernets

About twice as large as Napa Valley, Sonoma County has more-diverse microclimates (refer to Chapter 1 in Book IV for more on microclimates); only the warmer areas of Sonoma — such as Alexander Valley, parts of Dry Creek Valley, and smaller areas such as Sonoma Mountain and parts of Sonoma Valley — are known for their Cabernet Sauvignon wines.

Most of Sonoma's Cabernet Sauvignons come from five AVAs:

- **Alexander Valley:** Cabernet Sauvignon is the leading variety in this huge valley in Northern Sonoma.
- **Dry Creek Valley:** This AVA is just west of Alexander Valley. Cabernet Sauvignon is the leading variety here, followed by Zinfandel.

> ✔ **Knights Valley:** The warmest Sonoma AVA, Knights Valley is bordered by Alexander Valley in the west and Napa County in the east. Cabernet Sauvignon reigns supreme here.
>
> ✔ **Sonoma Mountain:** Cabernet Sauvignon is the dominant grape variety in this AVA, which is situated within the larger Sonoma Valley AVA.
>
> ✔ **Sonoma Valley:** Sonoma Valley is a huge AVA in southern Sonoma. Among red wines, Cabernet rules here, followed by Zinfandel and Syrah.

The following lists include recommended Sonoma Cabernet Sauvignons in three price categories: moderately priced, moderate-plus, and high-end.

### Moderately Priced Sonoma Cabernet Sauvignons, $12–$20

B. R. Cohn, "Silver Label" (Sonoma County)

Benziger Family Winery (Sonoma County)

Souverain (Alexander Valley)

Foppiano Vineyards (Russian River Valley)

Frei Brothers, "Reserve" (Alexander Valley)

Louis M. Martini (Sonoma County)

Ravenswood (Sonoma County)

St. Francis (Sonoma County)

Sebastiani Vineyards (Sonoma County)

### Moderate-Plus Sonoma Cabernet Sauvignons, $20–$50

Arrowood Vineyards (Sonoma County)

B. R. Cohn, Olive Hill Estate (Sonoma Valley)

Beringer Vineyards (Knights Valley)

Chalk Hill Estate (Chalk Hill)

Clos Du Bois, "Briarcrest" (Alexander Valley)

Dry Creek Vineyard (Dry Creek Valley)

Ferrari-Carano (Alexander Valley)

Gundlach Bundschu, Rhinefarm Vineyard (Sonoma Valley)

Hanna Winery (Alexander Valley)

Jordan Vineyard (Alexander Valley)

Kendall-Jackson Highland Estates, "Hawkeye Mountain" (Alexander Valley)

Kenwood Vineyards, Jack London Vineyard (Sonoma Valley)

Laurel Glen, "Counterpoint" (Sonoma Mountain)

Louis M. Martini (Alexander Valley)

Martin Ray Winery (Sonoma Mountain)

Rodney Strong Vineyards, "Alexander Valley" and Alexander's Crown Vineyard (Alexander Valley)

Sbragia Family Vineyards, Monte Rosso Vineyard (Sonoma Valley)

Schrader Cellars, Double Diamond Mayacamas Range Estate Vineyard (Sonoma County)

Scherrer Winery (Alexander Valley)

Schug Carneros Estate (Sonoma Valley)

Sebastiani Vineyards (Alexander Valley)

Simi Winery (Alexander Valley)

Stonestreet (Alexander Valley)

Stuhlmuller Vineyards (Alexander Valley)

Trentadue Winery, "Estate" (Alexander Valley)

**High-End Sonoma Cabernet Sauvignons, $50–$100**

Kendall-Jackson Highland Estates,
"Trace Ridge" (Knights Valley)

Kenwood Vineyards, "Artist Series"
(Sonoma County)

Laurel Glen, "Estate"
(Sonoma Mountain)

Louis M. Martini, Monte Rosso
Vineyard (Sonoma Valley)

A. Rafanelli (Dry Creek Valley)

Sebastiani Vineyards, "Cherryblock"
(Sonoma Valley)

Silver Oak (Alexander Valley)

## Santa Cruz Mountain Cabernet Sauvignons

The rugged terrain of the Santa Cruz Mountains AVA, about an hour's drive south of San Francisco, spreads out over Santa Clara, Santa Cruz, and San Mateo counties. The isolation, lack of modern conveniences, and thin mountain soil are just some of the challenges that face grape growers and wineries there, and yet the AVA has more than 80 wineries, including some of the best in the state. Even though the Santa Cruz Mountains area seems large, it encompasses fewer than 1,500 acres of vines.

Microclimates vary widely, depending on which side of the mountain range a vineyard is situated (Pacific Ocean or San Francisco Bay) and what its elevation is. The three leading varietal wines produced in the Santa Cruz Mountains are Chardonnay, Pinot Noir, and Cabernet Sauvignon, in that order. Most of the wineries specializing in Cabernet Sauvignon are on the warmer San Francisco Bay side of the mountain range, but they're high enough in elevation to avoid coastal fog.

## Laurel Glen Estate, a Sonoma star

One of California's consistently finest Cabernet Sauvignons comes not from Napa Valley but from Sonoma, and it costs but a mere $55! The wine is Laurel Glen Estate Cabernet, made from grapes sourced high on Sonoma Mountain, above the fog line.

What's owner-winemaker Patrick Campbell's secret (besides a great site for Cabernet Sauvignon)? First of all, he chooses only the best vineyard blocks for his Laurel Glen Estate Cabernet Sauvignon; the remainder goes into a second Cabernet called Counterpoint (about $30). Second, Campbell's winemaking philosophy favors balanced, complex Cabernet Sauvignon that ages well; he's not interested in producing the sort of ripe, jammy, powerful Cabs that attract big scores from some wine critics. And he insists on charging what he considers to be a fair price for his wines. Wouldn't it be nice if there were more people in the wine business like Patrick Campbell?

For fun, Campbell makes an everyday red called Reds — usually a blend of 60 percent 70-year-old-vine Zinfandel, 30 percent Carignan, and 10 percent Petite Sirah — which sells for about $9 to $11. It happens to be one of the best under-$12 red wines in California.

**Book IV**

**California and Elsewhere in North America**

Ridge Vineyards is undoubtedly the most renowned winery in the Santa Cruz Mountains. Ridge's acclaimed Monte Bello Cabernet Sauvignon is one of the finest Cabernets produced anywhere in the world.

Here are recommended Santa Cruz Mountain Cabernet Sauvignons in four price categories.

### Moderately Priced Santa Cruz Mountain Cabernet Sauvignon, $12–$20

Clos La Chance, "Ruby Throated" (Santa Cruz Mountains)

Moderate-Plus Santa Cruz Mountain Cabernet Sauvignons, $20–$50

Cinnabar Vineyard (Santa Cruz Mountains)

Martin Ray Winery (Santa Cruz Mountains)

Mount Eden Vineyards, "Saratoga Cuvée" and Estate (Santa Cruz Mountains)

Ridge Vineyards, Santa Cruz Mountains Estate (Santa Cruz Mountains)

### High-End Santa Cruz Mountain Cabernet Sauvignon, $50–$100

Kathryn Kennedy Winery, "Small Lot" (Santa Cruz Mountains)

Luxury Santa Cruz Mountain Cabernet Sauvignons, over $100

Kathryn Kennedy Winery, Estate (Santa Cruz Mountains); $140

Ridge Vineyards, "Monte Bello" (Santa Cruz Mountains); $145

## *Noting other California Cabernets*

Although Napa Valley and Sonoma County are the prime regions for Cabernet Sauvignon (with a nod to the Santa Cruz Mountains as a small but excellent source), the state's leading red varietal wine also comes from many other regions. Paso Robles in San Luis Obispo County, for example, is known for its Cabernet Sauvignons. On the other hand, very few wineries in Santa Barbara County produce Cabernet Sauvignons; it's just not warm enough there for Cabernet, a variety that needs a long, warm growing season.

In this section, you find recommended Cabernet Sauvignons from other regions throughout California in two price categories: moderately priced and moderate-plus. Make sure you also check out the nearby sidebar for some reliable California Cabs that retail for $15 or less.

### Other Moderately Priced Cabernet Sauvignons, $12–$20

Bonterra Vineyards, "Organically Grown" (North Coast)

Clayhouse Vineyard (Paso Robles, San Luis Obispo County)

Eberle Winery (Paso Robles, San Luis Obispo County)

Guenoc Winery, "Lake County" (Lake County)

Lolonis Vineyards (Redwood Valley, Mendocino County)

Rabbit Ridge Vineyards (Paso Robles, San Luis Obispo)

Shannon Ridge (Lake County)

Wild Horse Winery (Paso Robles, San Luis Obispo County)

**Other Moderate-Plus Cabernet Sauvignons, $20–$50**

Beckmen Vineyards (Santa Ynez Valley, Santa Barbara)

Justin Vineyards (Paso Robles, San Luis Obispo County)

Langtry Estate, Tephra Ridge Vineyard (Lake County)

Lava Cap Winery, "Reserve" and "Stromberg" (Sierra Foothills)

Paul Dolan Vineyards, "Organically Grown" (Mendocino County)

Renaissance Vineyard (Sierra Foothills)

# Merlot, Sometimes a Contender

The Merlot grape, like Cabernet Sauvignon, hails from the Bordeaux region of France. Genetic testing has proved that Merlot is the offspring of Cabernet Franc and therefore is related to Cabernet Sauvignon, which also originated from Cabernet Franc. Today, Cabernet Sauvignon plantings worldwide exceed those of Merlot, but not by much. In California, however, a big gap exists: Cabernet Sauvignon claims 62 percent more acreage than Merlot does. The following sections introduce you to California Merlot wine, characterize its style, and suggest several ones to try.

## Merlot's up, down, and Sideways reputation

Merlot in California is a bundle of contradictions. Merlot grapes are fairly easy to grow and therefore are very popular with grape growers, yet only in a few places in California do the grapes grow well enough to make seriously good wine. California's Merlot wines have mass appeal with wine drinkers, and yet many connoisseurs dismiss them. (You might recall the sentiments toward "[expletive deleted] Merlot" expressed by Miles Raymond, the main character in the film *Sideways*.) Yet some excellent California Merlots do exist.

As a varietal wine, Merlot got off to a late start in California. The first varietal Merlot wines were those of Sterling Vineyards and Louis M. Martini Winery, which both produced varietal Merlot from the 1968 vintage.

Merlot today is the number three red grape variety in California in terms of tons harvested, after Cabernet Sauvignon and Zinfandel. Merlot wine began an impressive ascent in popularity in the mid-1990s, racking up sales growth of almost 35 percent each year, on the average, from 1995 to 1999. During that period, many wine drinkers were shifting to red wines from white and blush wines, and Merlot became a popular choice. Since then, growth in Merlot sales has slowed to more reasonable levels — particularly in 2005,

**Book IV**

**California and Elsewhere in North America**

as the impact of *Sideways* made itself felt. Still, Americans drank 21.4 million cases of California Merlot in 2006, proving that Merlot is alive and well in California.

One of California's top Merlot producers, Swanson Vineyards (in Napa Valley) promoted Merlot heavily with wine journalists and restaurant wine buyers in the wake of the *Sideways* backlash against Merlot. The reason Merlot is so popular with some wine drinkers and yet so scorned by others, the winery representatives theorized, is that Merlot vines need certain vineyard conditions — a relatively cool climate; well-drained soils, generally clay; and sites conducive to slow, even growth and ripening — to produce grapes capable of making great wine. When grown in less-than-optimal conditions, the grapes produce wines that are thin and lacking in flavor concentration. Such wine can be appealing to those who want an easy-to-drink red wine whose tannins are soft, but they fall short of Merlot's potential.

## The taste of California Merlot

Imagine a deeply colored red wine — a full-bodied, dry wine with soft, velvety tannin and aromas and flavors of ripe, dark plums, a hint of chocolate, and a slight toasty note of oak. It fills your mouth with its fleshy texture and its plump, fruity flavors, yet it's not too soft; it has enough firmness to give it definition. If you had to associate it with a shape, you'd say it tastes "round." That's the experience of California Merlot at its best. And who wouldn't love such a wine? Its plumpness, richness, and softness are why Merlot became popular in the first place.

---

## Seventeen top-value Cabernet Sauvignons

These 17 California Cabernet Sauvignons, all under $15, are consistently reliable:

- Blackstone, California (California)
- Chateau Julien (Monterey)
- Chateau St. Jean (California)
- De Loach, California (California)
- Edna Valley Vineyard (San Luis Obispo)
- Esser Vineyards (California)
- Estancia (Paso Robles)
- Fetzer Vineyards, Valley Oaks (California)
- Gallo of Sonoma, Estate (Sonoma County)
- Hahn Estates (Central Coast)
- Hawk Crest (California)
- Hess (California)
- J. Lohr Vineyards, Seven Oaks (Paso Robles)
- Jekel Vineyards (Central Coast)
- Lockwood Vineyard (Monterey)
- Kenwood Vineyards (Sonoma County)
- Red Truck (California)

---

To capture the experience of a plump, rich, and soft Merlot, expect to pay at least $20 a bottle in a wine shop. When you pay less than $20 for Merlot, you get less plump-fruit impression, and you might find aromas and flavors of tea or other herbal notes, as well as a thinner, less velvety texture. You still get the deep color, full body, and soft tannin, however.

Either way, you find that Merlot's *intensity* of aroma and flavor (how pronounced the aromas and flavors are) is fairly low-key, especially compared to a wine such as Pinot Noir (see the later section in this chapter). Merlot has that characteristic in common with Cabernet Sauvignon; what's appealing about these types of wine is their structure (mouthfeel, body, texture, and depth) at least as much as their flavors.

Because Merlot isn't an intensely flavorful wine, it's a good accompaniment to food. It lets the food's flavors take center stage and doesn't compete with them.

Just as Cabernet Sauvignon producers often blend in a bit of Merlot to give their wines softness, Merlot producers often take advantage of their "25 percent other grapes allowed" option to blend in some Cabernet Sauvignon. The more Cabernet that a Merlot wine has, the firmer and less "round" the wine is. Some winemakers say that Merlot can taste a bit hollow — or they describe it as seeming to have a hole in the middle of its taste — unless the wine includes some Cabernet. Unfortunately, the label rarely tells you whether a wine contains any Cabernet Sauvignon.

## Regions that excel with Merlot

About one-third of California's Merlot vineyards is in the very warm Central Valley, where conditions aren't optimal for this variety. Another one-third, approximately, is in Napa Valley and Sonoma County together, and most of the state's best Merlots hail from these areas.

Just as for Cabernet Sauvignon, Napa Valley is the leading region for varietal Merlots. One main difference from Cabernet Sauvignon, however, is that the cool Los Carneros AVA, which extends from Napa into Sonoma County, is a prime region for Merlot in Napa Valley. Merlot grows quite well in fairly cool microclimates such as Los Carneros because it ripens earlier than Cabernet Sauvignon.

The Paso Robles AVA in San Luis Obispo boasts the third-largest production of Merlot, apart from Napa and the statewide California AVA. Sonoma County is also a prime region for Merlot: Sonoma's microclimates vary so widely that Merlot finds many areas throughout the county in which to thrive. Other important regions in California for Merlot are Monterey and Santa Barbara counties.

**Book IV**

**California and Elsewhere in North America**

The following sections suggest some Merlots to try from Napa Valley and other wine regions in the Golden State.

### Reliable Napa Valley Merlots

Napa Valley has the largest contingent of renowned Merlot producers. Unlike Napa Cabernet Sauvignons, varietal Napa Valley Merlots haven't developed cult followings; this is fortunate for wine drinkers, because it means that there are no $100-plus Merlots! Here are recommended Napa Valley Merlots in three price categories, from moderate to high-end.

#### Moderately Priced Napa Valley Merlots, $12–$20

Beringer Vineyards (Napa Valley)

Franciscan, "Oakville Estate" (Napa Valley)

Joseph Carr Cellars (Napa Valley)

Markham Vineyards (Napa Valley)

#### Moderate-Plus Napa Valley Merlots, $20–$50

Chappellet Winery, Estate (Napa Valley)

Charles Krug Winery (Napa Valley)

Clos du Val (Napa Valley)

Duckhorn Vineyards (Napa Valley)

Flora Springs Winery (Napa Valley)

Frog's Leap Winery (Napa Valley)

Grgich Hills (Napa Valley)

Havens, "Napa Valley" and "Reserve Carneros" (Napa Valley)

MacRostie Winery (Los Carneros, Napa Valley)

Merryvale, Beckstoffer, Las Amigas Vineyard (Los Carneros, Napa Valley)

Newton Vineyards, "Unfiltered" (Napa Valley)

Neyers, Neyers Ranch, Conn Valley (Napa Valley)

Paradigm, Estate (Oakville, Napa Valley)

Pine Ridge, "Crimson Creek" (Napa Valley)

Robert Mondavi (Napa Valley)

Rubicon Estate (Napa Valley)

Selene, Frediani Vineyard (Napa Valley)

Shafer Vineyards (Napa Valley)

Silverado Vineyards (Napa Valley)

Stag's Leap Wine Cellars (Napa Valley)

Swanson Vineyards (Oakville, Napa Valley)

Trefethen Family Vineyards, "Estate" (Oak Knoll District, Napa Valley)

Turnbull Wine Cellars (Oakville, Napa Valley)

#### High-End Napa Valley Merlots, over $50

Cakebread Cellars (Napa Valley)

Duckhorn Vineyards, Three Palms Vineyard (Napa Valley)

Nickel & Nickel, Suscol Ranch and Harris Vineyard-Oakville (Napa Valley)

Pahlmeyer (Napa Valley)

### Other California Merlots

If it's not from Napa Valley, a recommended Merlot in the following lists is most likely from Sonoma County.

**Other Moderately Priced Merlots, $12–$20**

Benziger Family Winery
(Sonoma County)

Clos du Bois (Sonoma County)

Dry Creek Vineyard
(Dry Creek Valley)

Lolonis Winery, Redwood Valley
(Mendocino County)

Murphy Goode (Alexander Valley)

Ravenswood (Sonoma County)

St. Francis Winery (Sonoma County)

Wild Horse Winery (Paso Robles)

**Other Moderate-Plus Merlots, $20–$50**

Arrowood (Sonoma County)

Bargetto Winery, Reserve
(Santa Cruz Mountains)

Ferrari Carano (Sonoma County)

Matanzas Creek
(Bennett Valley, Sonoma)

Schug Carneros Estate, "Sonoma
Valley" and "Carneros Estate"
(Sonoma)

Thomas Fogarty Winery, Razorback
Vineyard (Santa Cruz Mountains)

# The Secret's in the Bordeaux Blend

The wines of France's Bordeaux region are the role models for most of the world's Cabernet Sauvignon and Merlot wines, and yet most of those wines rarely contain 75 percent of either grape variety — the minimum amount required to make a varietal wine in the United States. Some California producers have decided to follow the Bordeaux model more closely and forego a varietal name for their wine in order to have more leverage in blending Cabernet Sauvignon and Merlot. While they're at it, they might throw in other so-called Bordeaux grape varieties, such as Cabernet Franc, Petit Verdot, or Malbec. Such red wines are loosely called California's *Bordeaux blends*.

Some of these blended wines might be named Meritage or be described on their labels as *Meritage wines*. The Meritage Association (www.meritage wine.org) permits its members to call a red wine Meritage if no single variety makes up more than 90 percent of the blend and if the grapes include at least two of eight permitted grape varieties. (Besides the five classic Bordeaux varieties — Merlot, Cabernet Sauvignon, Cabernet Franc, Petit Verdot, and Malbec — the others are St. Macaire, Gros Verdot, and Carmenère, which are minor varieties in the Bordeaux region.) But not every winery that makes a so-called Bordeaux blend is a member of the Meritage Association, so you don't always find this term on wine labels.

The following sections explain the purpose behind California's Bordeaux-style blends and recommend the best ones you should try.

**Book IV**

**California
and
Elsewhere
in North
America**

## Combining strengths

The point behind blending Cabernet Sauvignon, Merlot, and other Bordeaux varieties isn't to change the nature of the dominant grape, but to create a harmonic whole that goes beyond the sum of its parts. This is possible because of the similarities among the various grape varieties rather than their differences.

Cabernet Sauvignon, Cabernet Franc, and Merlot are genetically related. All three red varieties make wines that have fairly subtle aromas and flavors and strong structural character — meaning that the experience of tasting them is more about how they feel in your mouth than it is about specific flavors that you can perceive. (However, Cabernet Franc is the fruitiest and most flavorful of the three, especially in California.) All three varieties have aromas and flavors of dark fruits and a tendency toward herbal or vegetal notes, especially when the grapes aren't fully ripe. Additionally, all three can develop tobacco notes with age.

Petit Verdot — a minor variety compared to the other three but one that's becoming increasingly popular with winemakers around the world and especially in California — has the characteristics of a darker, more concentrated, and more tannic Cabernet Sauvignon. Malbec, to some extent, suggests a more rustic Merlot.

## Eighteen top-value Merlots

These 18 Merlots, all under $15, are consistently reliable and top values for the money:

- Beringer, Third Century (North Coast)
- Blackstone (California)
- Bonterra Vineyards (Mendocino)
- Chateau Julien (Monterey)
- De Loach (California)
- Esser Vineyards (California)
- Estancia (Paso Robles)
- Fetzer Vineyards, Valley Oaks (California)
- Foppiano Vineyards (Russian River Valley)
- Gallo of Sonoma, Estate (Sonoma County)
- Hawk Crest (California)
- J. Lohr Vineyards, Los Osos (Paso Robles)
- Jekel Vineyards (Central Coast)
- Kenwood Vineyards (Sonoma County)
- Raymond Vineyard, R Collection (California)
- Red Truck (California)
- Sebastiani Vineyards (Sonoma County)
- Taft Street Winery (Sonoma County)

In a blend incorporating some or all of these varieties, you ideally can't recognize any one variety. The Merlot rounds out the linear structure of the Cabernet Sauvignon, for example; the Petit Verdot (usually only a small part of the blend, if used at all) contributes some color and spiciness; and the Cabernet Franc brings a bit of fruitiness. Each variety completes the others for a harmonious whole.

Many wines that are Bordeaux-style blends mention the grape varieties and the percentage of each on the bottle's back label, but some wines don't reveal the blend on the label — frustrating, huh? Sometimes, you find a wine that could be labeled as a varietal Cabernet Sauvignon or a varietal Merlot because one of those varieties accounts for at least 75 percent of the wine. But the percentages of each variety can and do change from one vintage to the next, and the winemaker chooses a nonvarietal name for the wine so he has the flexibility to use less than 75 percent of a dominant variety if desired.

## Selecting key brands of Bordeaux-style blends

Many California wine producers who make varietal Cabernet Sauvignon also produce at least one blended red wine. In most of these blends, Cabernet Sauvignon is the dominant variety, although Merlot or even Cabernet Franc occasionally plays a primary role. For example, the prestige blend of HdV Wines is mainly Merlot, and Dalla Valle's prestige blend (Maya) is often more Cabernet Franc than Cabernet Sauvignon.

California's Bordeaux-style blended wines vary widely: Some use only Cabernet Sauvignon and Merlot or Cabernet Franc; some use all three of these varieties; and a few — such as the wines called Cain Five and Cinq Cépages — use all five of the major Bordeaux varieties, including Petit Verdot and Malbec. The percentage of each variety usually varies each year, depending on the nature of the vintage and/or the tastes of the winemaking team.

Here are two recent trends in Bordeaux-style red blends:

✔ **Petit Verdot is becoming an increasingly important part of many wines.** This late-ripening variety adds color, tannin, and blueberry and violet aromas and flavors to the blend. Petit Verdot generally grows better in many parts of California than it does in Bordeaux. The wine called V from Viader Winery is a Bordeaux blend that's primarily Petit Verdot, with a bit of Cabernet Sauvignon and Cabernet Franc.

**Book IV**

**California and Elsewhere in North America**

> ✔ **Carmenère and especially Syrah are showing up more and more in California's Bordeaux-style red wine blends.** The late-ripening Carmenère, an almost-forgotten Bordeaux variety that's achieving new fame in Chilean wines, brings texture and berrylike aromas and flavor, especially blueberries, to blends. Syrah — a classic Rhône variety — adds color, tannin, and its own spicy aromas and flavors. As long as the blended wine doesn't call itself Meritage (see "The Secret's in the Bordeaux Blend" section earlier in this chapter for why), Syrah is a perfectly permissible addition to California blends.

Frequently, a producer's blended red wine is its top wine. It can often be the winery's most expensive wine and is sometimes made in small quantities, especially in vintages when the weather has been difficult.

The following lists name some top picks for red California blends based on the Bordeaux grape varieties:

### Moderate-Plus Bordeaux-Style Blends, $20–$50

Alexander Valley Vineyards, "Cyrus" (Alexander Valley)

Archipel (Sonoma/Napa Valley)

Bernardus, "Marinus" (Carmel Valley)

Chateau St. Jean, "Cinq Cépages" (Sonoma County)

Clos du Bois, "Marlstone" (Alexander Valley)

Dry Creek Vineyard, "Meritage" and "The Mariner" (Dry Creek Valley)

Murrieta's Well, "Meritage" (Livermore Valley)

Ramey Wine Cellars, "Claret" (Napa Valley)

Ravenswood, Pickberry Vineyard (Sonoma Mountain)

### High-End Bordeaux-Style Blends, $50–$100

Anderson's Conn Valley Vineyards, "Eloge" (Napa Valley)

Benziger Family Winery, "Tribute" (Sonoma Mountain)

Flora Springs, "Trilogy" (Napa Valley)

HdV Vineyards, "HdV Red" (Los Carneros, Napa Valley)

Justin Vineyards, "Isosceles" (Paso Robles)

Mount Veeder Winery, "Reserve Red" (Napa Valley)

St. Supéry, "Élu" (Napa Valley)

Stonestreet, "Legacy" (Alexander Valley)

Turnbull Cellars, "Black Label" (Oakville, Napa Valley)

Viader Vineyards, "Viader Red" (Howell Mountain) and "V" (Napa Valley)

### Luxury Bordeaux-Style Blends, over $100

Cain Cellars, "Cain Five" (Napa Valley); $125

Continuum (Oakville); $150

Dalla Valle, "Maya" (Oakville, Napa Valley); $400

Dominus Estate, "Dominus" (Napa Valley); $110

Harlan Estate (Napa Valley); $700 to $900

Joseph Phelps, "Insignia" (Napa Valley); $200

Moraga Vineyards, "Bel Air Estate Red" (California); $125

Opus One (Napa Valley); $190

Pahlmeyer, Red (Napa Valley); $120

Peter Michael, "Les Pavots" (Knights Valley); $175

Quintessa Estate, "Quintessa" (Rutherford, Napa Valley); $130

Rubicon Estate, "Rubicon" (Rutherford, Napa Valley); $115

Rudd Estate, "Oakville Estate" (Oakville); $125

Stag's Leap Wine Cellars, "Cask 23" (Napa Valley); $180

Vérité Winery, "La Joie," "La Muse," and "Le Désir" (Sonoma County); $150 each

# Zinfandel: Big, Bold, and Berry

Zinfandel is California's third most important grape variety, after Chardonnay and Cabernet Sauvignon, in terms of the quantity of grapes grown. Cabernet Sauvignon ranks higher than Zinfandel by only a fraction of a percentage point.

Red wines from the Zinfandel grape boast a unique combination of ripe berry flavors that give an impression of sweet fruitiness and a firm, dry texture that adds a spicy energy to play against that sweet fruitiness. The wines have plenty of flavor, but their appeal isn't just flavor: They balance that flavor with firm structure and a sturdy character that make the wines particularly satisfying.

Zinfandel wines are typically said to have flavors of *bramble berries* — berries from plants that contain thorns, such as blackberries and loganberries. They often have a distinctive spicy black-pepper note as well, which usually comes from blending in some Petite Sirah. Some winemakers even assign a chocolate note to Zinfandel's taste.

Compared to Cabernet Sauvignon or Merlot wines, Zinfandel wines are generally fruitier and more flavorful, and they have a personality that's slightly wild and untamed — the opposite of sedate and proper. Compared to Pinot Noir wines, Zins are less seductive in their fruity aromas and flavors, and they're leaner in structure, giving less of an impression of "roundness" in your mouth.

The sections that follow cover the characteristics of Zinfandel, California's best Zinfandel regions, and the best California Zins out there just waiting to be tasted.

**Book IV**

**California and Elsewhere in North America**

## Surveying the spectrum of Zin styles

Although Zinfandel is truly delicious and compelling, its following isn't huge. Some winemakers theorize that what holds Zinfandel back from broader sales is that when you buy a bottle, you can't be sure which style you're going to get. That's because Zinfandel wines cover a range of styles, from lean and relatively restrained to rich, opulent, and high in alcohol, resembling Portugal's Port wines. (*Port* is an alcohol-added dessert wine; find out more about it in Chapter 2 of Book VI.)

Many factors contribute to this diversity of style, including the usual suspects — winemaking techniques and climate differences in the vineyards — as well as Zinfandel's special issue of vine age. The old vineyards produce small crops of flavorful, concentrated grapes, so Zinfandels made from old vines taste more concentrated and less fruity than other Zins.

Wine lovers used to speak of *claret-style* Zinfandels, which were leaner, trimmer, dry wines somewhat in the style of Cabernet Sauvignon. (*Claret* is the term that the British traditionally use for Cabernet-dominant wines from Bordeaux, France.) Today, the wave of super-ripeness that has swept through California's red-grape vineyards has brought Zinfandel wines that are richer and fuller than ever, and few truly claret-style Zins exist. Nevertheless, some Zinfandel wines today are dry and relatively trim and lean in style. Examples include Green and Red Vineyard, A. Rafanelli, Nalle, Frog's Leap, and The Terraces.

Many Zinfandel wines today are made from extremely ripe grapes and are therefore very ripe, sweet, and high in alcohol, containing more than 16 percent alcohol in many cases. Often these wines have Port-like flavors of sun-baked fruit and raisins. Wine literature sometimes refers to the most extreme wines in this style as *late-harvest* Zins. Then there are the many Zins that occupy the middle ground: They're medium- to full-bodied wines that have perceptible sweetness but technically qualify as dry, with firm tannin and exuberant, but not excessive, fruity flavor.

When choosing a Zinfandel, pay particular attention to the alcohol level listed on the label. The higher the alcohol, the higher the odds that the wine will be sweet, jammy, and powerfully rich.

## *Venturing into Zinfandel country*

Zinfandel grows all over California, and the style of the wine varies according to the wine region and the specific location of the vineyard, as well as the age of the vines for any particular wine. In general, the following holds true:

- ✔ The cooler areas, which include many of the coastal counties, tend to produce spicier, leaner, and more refined wines.
- ✔ The interior regions tend to make richer, lustier, more powerful Zinfandel wines.

The Central Valley is responsible for a big chunk of Zinfandel production, but most of those grapes make White Zinfandel or go into inexpensive blended red wines. Other areas — specific AVAs and certain California counties — specialize in growing the grapes for red Zinfandel wines, or they boast specific wineries that are renowned as Zinfandel specialists.

Specialist Zinfandel wineries often source grapes from vineyards in several different AVAs and make several vineyard-specific wines. One example is Ravenswood, which makes five Zins under single-county appellations (Sonoma, Napa, Lodi, Amador, and Mendocino) and eight single-vineyard Zinfandels in addition to producing a large quantity of "Vintners Blend" Zinfandel under the California state appellation. Another example is Rosenblum Cellars, which makes a California-appellation "Vintner's Cuvée" Zinfandel and 18 or more additional Zins under specific AVAs, reserve labels, or single-vineyard-designated labels.

The Dry Creek Valley AVA in Northern Sonoma is a major region for Zinfandel, known for making fine Zins that are firm and structured. Other key Sonoma County AVAs for Zinfandel include the Russian River Valley, the Alexander Valley, and Sonoma Valley. Generally speaking, these areas make spicy Zinfandels with black pepper, blackberry, and black cherry aromas and flavors.

To find out about the characteristics of Zinfandels from various growing areas, consult the *Resource Guide to Zinfandel* available from ZAP, the Zinfandel Advocates & Producers organization. (To access it, head to www. zinfandel.org, hold your mouse over the About Zinfandel button at the top of the page, and click the Resource Guide link.) The descriptions tend to focus on the aromas and flavors of the wines from each area instead of describing the wines' weight, structure, alcohol levels, and so forth, but the array of descriptors will make your mouth water and perhaps inspire you to begin some firsthand research.

## *Recommending California's best Zins*

Most of the Zinfandels in the following lists fall into the two lower-priced categories: moderate (under $20 in wine shops) and moderate-plus ($20 to $50); just a couple of the wines are high-end (over $50). These lists exclude wines that are available only in California, although some of the recommended wines do have limited availability nationally.

**Book IV**

**California and Elsewhere in North America**

## Moderately Priced Red Zinfandels, under $20

Alexander Valley Vineyards, "Sin Zin" (Alexander Valley)

Bonny Doon, "Cardinal Zin" (California)

Cline Cellars, "Ancient Vines" (Contra Costa County)

Dry Creek Vineyard, "Heritage Clone" (Dry Creek Valley)

Fife Vineyards, "Mendocino Uplands" (California)

Francis Coppola, "Diamond Series" (California) and "Director's Cut" (Dry Creek Valley)

Fritz Winery (Dry Creek Valley)

Gravity Hills, "Tumbling Tractor" (Paso Robles)

Kunin Wines, "Westside" (Paso Robles)

Lake Sonoma Winery (Dry Creek Valley)

Lolonis Winery (Redwood Valley, Mendocino)

Marietta Cellars (Sonoma County)

Mia's Playground, "Old Vines" (Dry Creek Valley)

Peachy Canyon Winery, "Westside" (Paso Robles)

Pezzi King Vineyards, "Old Vines" (Dry Creek Valley)

Quivira Vineyards (Dry Creek Valley)

Renwood Vineyards, "Old Vine" (Amador County)

Rodney Strong Vineyards, "Knotty Vines" (Sonoma County)

Sausal Winery, "Family Old Vines" (Alexander Valley)

Scott Harvey, "Mountain Selection"; "Old Vine" (Amador)

Sebastiani Vineyards (Dry Creek Valley)

Seghesio Family Estates (Sonoma County)

Starry Night (Lodi)

Trentadue Winery (Sonoma County)

Wente Vineyards, "Smith Bench Reserve" (Livermore Valley)

## Moderate-Plus Red Zinfandels, $20–$50

Carol Shelton Wines, "Wild Thing" (Mendocino); "Monga," Lopez Vineyard (Cucamonga Valley); "Karma" (Russian River Valley); "Rocky Reserve," Rockpile Vineyard (Rockpile)

Chateau Montelena, Estate (Napa Valley)

Cline Cellars, Live Oak and Big Break Vineyards (Contra Costa County)

Dashe Cellars (Dry Creek Valley)

De Loach, "OFS" and "Forgotten Vines" (Russian River Valley)

Dry Creek Vineyard, "Old Vines" (Dry Creek Valley)

Eberle, Steinbeck/Wine Bush Vineyards (Paso Robles)

Edmeades, all single-vineyard Zins (Mendocino County)

Elyse Winery, Korte Ranch and Morisoli Vineyard (Napa Valley)

Frank Family Vineyards (Napa Valley)

Frog's Leap Winery (Napa Valley)

Gravity Hills, "The Sherpa" (Paso Robles)

Green & Red Vineyard, "Chiles Mill Estate" (Napa Valley)

Grgich Hills Cellar (Napa Valley)

Hartford Family Wines (Russian River Valley)

Hendry Winery, Hendry Vineyard, "Block 7" (Napa Valley)

Kenwood Vineyards, Jack London
Vineyard and "Reserve"
(Sonoma Valley)

Michael-David Winery, "Earthquake"
(Lodi)

Mill Creek Vineyards (Dry Creek
Valley)

Nalle Winery (Dry Creek Valley)

Neyers Vineyards, "High Valley" and
Tofanelli Vineyard (Napa Valley);
Pato Vineyard (Contra Costa
County)

Papapietro Perry Winery
(Russian River Valley)

Peter Franus Wines, Brandlin Ranch
(Mt. Veeder) and "Napa Valley"
(Napa Valley)

Peachy Canyon Winery, Snow
Vineyard (Paso Robles)

Preston of Dry Creek, "Old Vines"
(Dry Creek Valley)

Quivira Vineyards, Wine Creek Ranch
and Anderson Ranch (Dry Creek
Valley)

A. Rafanelli (Dry Creek Valley)

Ravenswood, Old Hill (Sonoma
Valley) and all other single-
vineyard Zinfandels

Renwood Vineyards, "Grandpère,"
"Grandmère," and "Fiddletown
Vineyards" (Amador County)

Ridge Vineyards, Lytton Springs and
East Bench (Dry Creek Valley);
Ponzo Vineyard (Russian River

Valley); Pagani Ranch (Sonoma
Valley); York Creek (Napa Valley);
Dusi Ranch (Paso Robles); "Three
Valleys" (Sonoma County)

Robert Biale Vineyards, Aldo's
Vineyard, "Napa Ranches," Old
Cranes, Grande Vineyard, Black
Chicken (Napa Valley); Monte
Rosso Vineyard (Sonoma Valley)

Rosenblum Cellars, Monte Rosso
Vineyard and "Maggie's Reserve"
(Sonoma Valley) plus all other
single-vineyard Zins

Rubicon Estate, "Edizione Pennino"
(Napa Valley)

Saucelito Canyon (Arroyo Grande)

Sausal Winery, "Private Reserve" and
"Century Vine" (Alexander Valley)

Seghesio Family Estates, Home
Ranch and Lorenzo Vineyard
(Alexander Valley); Cortina and
Rockpile (Rockpile); "Old Vines"
(Sonoma County)

St. Francis Winery, "Old Vines"
(Sonoma County)

Storybook Mountain, "Mayacamas
Range" (Napa Valley)

The Terraces Winery (Napa Valley)

Trentadue Winery, "La Storia"
(Alexander Valley)

Turley Wine Cellars, Dusi Ranch,
"Juvenile" and "Old Vines"
(California); Duarte Vineyard
(Contra Costa County)

**High-End Red Zinfandels, over $50**

Martinelli Winery, Giuseppe & Luisa
and Jackass Vineyards (Russian
River Valley)

Williams Selyem Winery, Baciagalupi,
Feeney, and Forchini Vineyards
(Russian River Valley)

Book IV

California
and
Elsewhere
in North
America

## Twenty top-value Zinfandels

These 20 red Zinfandels, all under $15, are super values:

- Alexander Valley Vineyards, "Temptation" (Alexander Valley)
- Bogle Vineyards, Old Vines (California)
- Cartlidge & Browne (California)
- Cline Cellars (Sonoma County)
- De Loach (Russian River Valley)
- Gnarly Head, Old Vine (Lodi)
- Jessie's Grove, "Earth, Zin & Fire" (Lodi)
- Kendall-Jackson, Vintner's Reserve (California)
- Kenwood Vineyards (Sonoma County)
- Peachy Canyon, "Incredible Red" (Paso Robles)
- Pedroncelli Winery, "Mother Clone" (Dry Creek Valley)
- Pepperwood Grove, Old Vine (California)
- Rabbit Ridge Vineyards (Paso Robles)
- Rancho Zabaco, "Dancing Bull" (California)
- Ravenswood "Vintners Blend" (California)
- Renwood Winery, "Sierra Series" (Sierra Foothills)
- Robert Mondavi "Private Selection" (Central Coast)
- Shenandoah Vineyards, "Special Reserve" (Amador County)
- Sobon Estate, "Rocky Top" and "Old Vine" (Amador County)
- Terra d'Oro (Amador County, Sierra Foothills); *formerly Monteviña*

# California Pinot Noir: From Obscurity to Overnight Fame

Pinot Noir has had a fitful history in California. Some evidence exists that Sonoma's Buena Vista Winery grew this variety as early as 1858. But before the 1970s, not many Pinot Noir vineyards existed in California — and many of those were in the wrong location, such as warm sites in Napa Valley, which can be fine for Cabernet Sauvignon but not for the more delicate Pinot.

Pinot Noir is now a hot commodity in California and throughout the world. Wine producers in the Golden State have been planting Pinot Noir at a frenzied pace, and today more than 200 California wineries make Pinot Noir wine.

Unfortunately, many of the Pinot Noirs rushed to the market haven't been of very high quality. Wine drinkers therefore have to be more careful than ever when selecting Pinots.

Never fear though. In addition to explaining the style variations of Pinot Noir, the following sections provide numerous recommendations of Pinot Noirs worth seeking out at your local wine shop.

## The general style

Pinot Noir wines can be light to deep ruby red in color. Most California Pinot Noirs tend to be darker rather than paler; however, because of the grape's light pigmentation, Pinot Noir wines are generally lighter in color than other popular red wines.

Structure-wise, Pinot Noir can range from medium-bodied to full and rich. The fuller-bodied examples are typically deeper in color and riper in flavor than the lighter-bodied Pinot Noirs. In general, Pinot Noir wines are high in alcohol (most of today's California Pinots contain more than 14 percent alcohol). They have medium to high acidity and a low to medium amount of tannin (although wines aged in new oak barrels have more tannin). At its best, the texture of Pinot Noir wines feels silky or satiny.

Pinot Noir's aromas and flavors are definitely a strong point. They can range from an assortment of berries — mainly raspberries and/or strawberries and cherries — to earthy, woodsy, and mushroomy. In some wines, the aromas and flavors can give the impression of very pure fruit. The richest, darkest wines tend to be oaky in aroma and flavor. Most California Pinot Noirs express fruity rather than earthy, woodsy aromas and flavors.

The delicacy of aroma and flavor in Pinot Noir wines allows variations in vintages and in vineyard sites to become evident, much more so than in other wines. This transparency to site accounts for wide differences in Pinot Noir wines between one producer and another. Because of the wine's delicate, pure aromas, Pinot Noir is, in its classic examples, rarely blended with other grapes.

Some of California's Pinot Noirs have real finesse: They're fragrant, elegant, and well balanced, with great purity of fruit expression. But too many Pinots suggest excessive ripeness of the grapes: They're too sweet, rather clumsy, and too high in alcohol. These heavy-handed excesses blur the delicacy and elegance a good Pinot Noir wine should possess. Other Pinots, especially many of the inexpensive (under $15) ones, are just too light, with candied fruit aromas and flavors as well as perceptible sweetness.

**Book IV**

**California and Elsewhere in North America**

---

# The four Rs of Zinfandel

Four wineries are at the head of the class in red Zinfandel renown, and coincidentally, all of their names begin with the letter *r*. Here's another factor all four have in common: Almost all of their Zinfandels come from Sonoma County. In alphabetical order, these wineries are

✔ **A. Rafanelli:** Rafanelli's Winery is in Dry Creek Valley, and all of David Rafanelli's Zinfandels — intensely flavored with great balance — are textbook examples of Dry Creek Zinfandel at its best.

✔ **Ravenswood:** Joel Peterson of Ravenswood, whose winery is in Sonoma Valley, makes about eight single-vineyard Zins, all but one from vineyards in Sonoma.

✔ **Ridge Vineyards:** Paul Draper of Ridge Vineyards makes one of the most famous Zinfandel-based wines of all, Geyserville. (Technically it can't be called Zinfandel because it's a blend of what grows in the Geyserville vineyard — about 70 percent Zinfandel along with Carignan, Petite Sirah, and Mataro/Mourvèdre.) Apart from Geyserville, Ridge also makes about seven wines actually labeled as Zinfandel.

✔ **Rosenblum Cellars:** Kent Rosenblum, a former veterinarian, makes about 19 single-vineyard Zinfandels from all over California in any given vintage, but his best Zins come from Sonoma.

---

## *Local styles*

California's unique climate and soil situations have spawned styles of Pinot Noir wine distinctly different from those of Burgundy, New Zealand, Chile, and even nearby Oregon; however, no such thing as "the typical California Pinot Noir" exists. If you were to line up, say, an Au Bon Climat Pinot Noir from Santa Barbara County, a Calera from Mount Harlan in San Benito County, a Saintsbury from Napa Valley's Los Carneros AVA, and a Williams Selyem from Sonoma's Russian River Valley — all iconic California Pinot Noirs — you might be able to recognize all of them as Pinot Noirs, but they'd be four very different wines.

The following list gives you some general notions about Pinot Noir styles from various regions of California (for more on these regions and specific wine recommendations, please see the next section):

✔ **Los Carneros:** Los Carneros Pinot Noirs are renowned for their tight structure, herbal aroma nuances, and spicy berry flavors, mainly strawberry and black cherry. Some Los Carneros wineries are maintaining an elegant, herbal style that put them on the Pinot Noir map in the first place; however, many winemakers are now making darker, weightier

Pinot Noirs, in keeping with the general California trend toward bigger, riper, fruitier, and higher-alcohol Pinot Noirs.

✔ **Santa Maria Valley:** The classic Pinot Noir style of Santa Maria Valley encompasses aromas and flavors of cherries, plums, spices, and sometimes a tomato-like character. High acidity and purity of fruit expression also characterize these wines.

✔ **Russian River Valley:** Classic Russian River Valley Pinot Noirs have always emphasized cherry and berry fruit — primarily raspberry and strawberry — in their aromas and flavors, which are concentrated and focused. They typically have been medium-bodied and medium to dark ruby in color, with a good amount of acidity and a reputation for aging ten years or more. This classic style still exists (in such wineries as Hartford Court, Littorai, Mueller Winery, Rochioli Vineyards, and Williams Selyem), although the newer, bigger style has been making serious inroads.

✔ **Anderson Valley:** Classic Anderson Valley Pinot Noirs are characterized by crispness and natural acidity. As a group, they tend to be somewhat leaner in style and exhibit more earthiness than the plusher, fruitier Russian River Valley Pinots. Some critics talk about a *red-fruit style* of Anderson Valley Pinot Noir — medium-bodied, with aromas and flavors of red berries and cherries — and a *black-fruit style* — fuller-bodied, with aromas and flavors of black cherries, plums, and blackberries.

✔ **Sta. Rita Hills:** Generalizing about a Sta. Rita Pinot Noir style is difficult because the region is so new. Many of the Sta. Rita Pinot Noirs from new wineries have been very dark in color and quite full-bodied, with lots of ripe, concentrated black cherry and other black-fruit flavors.

✔ **Santa Lucia Highlands:** These Pinot Noirs are typically rich and full-bodied rather than elegant, with rich, black cherry aromas and flavors.

✔ **Sonoma Coast:** In style, Sonoma Coast Pinot Noir wines somewhat resemble Pinot Noirs from their neighbor, the Russian River Valley. They sport lush red- and black-fruit aromas and flavors, especially black cherry but sometimes also red cherry, along with forest and mushroom aromas and a spiciness typical of cool-climate wines. They also tend to have higher acidity than Pinot Noirs from other regions.

## California's Pinot Noir regions

Over the years, through trial and error, California wine producers have found their best areas for growing Pinot Noir — or at least the best areas so far. One characteristic that all of these regions have in common is a relatively cool climate. The upcoming sections describe the five classic Pinot Noir regions in California and offer recommendations for standout wines.

**Book IV**

**California and Elsewhere in North America**

*Note:* Some of the Pinot Noirs in this chapter are small-production wines that have only limited national distribution. Check www.wine-searcher.com to find retail stores where the wine is available and to comparison shop for the lowest prices.

### Mount Harlan, San Benito County

Calera Wine Company's single-vineyard Pinot Noirs, especially Selleck, Jensen, and Reed, are known for their ability to age and improve with age. In a good vintage, they need at least ten years of aging to reach their peak of development.

Besides the single-vineyard wines, Jensen makes a moderately priced Mt. Harlan Cuvée Pinot Noir, which contains grapes from his various estate vineyards. He also makes a Central Coast AVA Pinot Noir, from purchased grapes, which retails for $21 to $24. (Mount Harlan is one small part of the much larger Central Coast AVA.)

Following are recommended Mount Harlan AVA Pinot Noirs, all from Calera Wine Company:

- ✔ Calera Mills Vineyard and Ryan Vineyard (Mount Harlan, San Benito County); $37 to $40

- ✔ Calera Mt. Harlan Cuvée (Mount Harlan, San Benito County); $29 to $30

- ✔ Calera Selleck Vineyard, Jensen Vineyard, and Reed Vineyard (Mount Harlan); $50 to $70

### Los Carneros

Carneros Creek Winery, founded by Francis Mahoney in 1973, was Los Carneros's (often referred to simply as *Carneros*) first winery focused on Pinot Noir. Mike Richmond opened Acacia Winery and Kent Rasmussen began his self-named winery in Carneros in 1979. The Carneros Pinot Noir movement was spurred further by Dick Ward and David Graves in 1981, when they started Saintsbury, perhaps *the* iconic Carneros winery specializing in Pinot Noir today.

Currently, 37 wineries are in Carneros (almost all of which make Pinot Noir), and lots of wineries in other regions use Pinot Noir grapes from Carneros for their wines. Of the 37 wineries, more than a dozen have earned national acclaim for their Pinot Noirs. A few of these — such as Domaine Carneros, Artesa (formerly Codorniu Napa), and Gloria Ferrer — began as sparkling wine houses.

Bouchaine Vineyards, with a long history in Carneros, is experiencing a revival with its Pinot Noir, now under the direction of winemaker/general manager Mike Richmond, formerly of Acacia. And Buena Vista Carneros Estate, the oldest continually operating winery in California (founded in 1857 by Hungarian emigrant Count Agoston Haraszthy), is still going strong with its Pinot Noir and other wines.

Here are three recommended Carneros Pinot Noirs for under $20:

- ✔ **Acacia Winery, "A by Acacia" (California):** This is the reliable second wine of the prestigious Acacia Pinot Noir of Carneros. "A by Acacia" is widely distributed throughout the United States, and it's a real value at $17 to $18.

- ✔ **Saintsbury "Garnet" (Carneros):** Light, fresh, fragrant, and totally delicious, with lots of berry and cherry flavor. Unfortunately, "Garnet," which retails for $16 to $18, sells out quickly each year after it's released. Your best bet might be to order it directly from the winery if your state allows that.

- ✔ **Jacuzzi Family Vineyards (Carneros):** Jacuzzi Family Vineyards (of the same family that invented the Jacuzzi whirlpool bathtub) is less well-known than Saintsbury — and is therefore more readily available and surprisingly good for its price ($17 to $19). It has herbal and cherry aromas and flavors, and it's quite elegant and well balanced. A winner!

If you feel like spending a little more on your Pinot Noir, try one of these wines in the moderate-plus price range:

**Moderate-Plus Carneros Pinot Noirs, $20–$50**

Acacia Winery, Carneros (Carneros)
Artesa Winery, Carneros (Carneros)
Bouchaine Vineyards, Carneros (Carneros)
Buena Vista Carneros Estate (Carneros)
Cuvaison Winery, Estate Selection (Carneros)
Domaine Carneros, Estate (Carneros)
Domaine Chandon, Carneros (Carneros)
Gloria Ferrer, Carneros (Carneros)
Kent Rasmussen, Carneros (Carneros)

MacRostie Winery, Carneros (Carneros)
Mahoney Vineyards, Estate (Carneros)
Robert Mondavi Carneros (Carneros)
Saintsbury Carneros (Carneros)
Schug Carneros Estate, Carneros, and "Heritage Reserve" Carneros (Carneros)
Toad Hall Cellars, Lavender Hill Vineyard and Willow Pond Vineyard (Carneros)
Truchard Vineyards (Carneros)

### Santa Barbara County

Wine production in Santa Barbara County really didn't get going commercially until 1975, when Firestone Vineyards opened. By the early 1980s, Santa Barbara County had 13 operating wineries. From the beginning, Pinot Noir was a major player, especially in the northwestern part of the county, where Santa Maria Valley is situated. More than 30 wineries are located within Santa Maria Valley, and another 50 wineries source grapes from this region.

**Book IV**

**California and Elsewhere in North America**

---

# Saintsbury: Classic Carneros Pinot Noir

Saintsbury Winery has been foremost in establishing Carneros as a fine region for Pinot Noir. Currently, Saintsbury is trying to bring Carneros back into the public eye in the face of stiff competition from places such as Sta. Rita Hills in Santa Barbara and Monterey's Santa Lucia Highlands.

Saintsbury's Pinot Noirs will never be like the powerful blockbusters coming out of the newer regions. Not that Saintsbury's Pinots are wimpy — except for their least-expensive Pinot Noir (the lighter-bodied "Garnet"); Saintsbury's six other Pinot Noirs range from medium-bodied to quite full-bodied. But they're well balanced, elegant, and consistently Carneros in style, and they don't approach the 15 percent-plus alcohol of many newer California Pinots.

Saintsbury's flagship wine, its Carneros Estate, is the quintessential Carneros Pinot Noir: crisp and lively, medium-bodied, with aromas and flavors of tart cherries. It retails in the $28 to $32 range.

---

Santa Maria Valley is the home of a great Pinot Noir site: the renowned Bien Nacido Vineyard. Many of Santa Barbara's best producers buy Pinot Noir grapes from Bien Nacido's owners.

In the southern part of Santa Barbara County, just north of the city of Santa Barbara, lies the huge Santa Ynez Valley, which runs east-west. Many grape varieties do well in the eastern end, which is the warmest part of the Santa Barbara wine region. The western end of Santa Ynez Valley, nearer the Pacific, is much cooler. Because of its obvious climatic differences from the eastern end, this part of Santa Ynez Valley became a separate AVA in 2001: Sta. Rita Hills.

Here's a rundown of the great Pinot Noirs from Santa Barbara County:

### Moderate-Plus Santa Barbara Pinot Noirs, $20–$50

Alta Maria Vineyards, Bien Nacido Vineyards (Santa Maria Valley)

Au Bon Climat (Santa Barbara County)

Au Bon Climat, "La Bauge Au-Dessus" (Santa Maria Valley)

Byron Vineyard, Santa Maria Valley, Nielson Vineyard and Bien Nacido Vineyard (Santa Maria Valley)

Cambria Winery, Julia'a Vineyard and Bench Break Vineyard (Santa Maria Valley)

Foley Estate, Santa Maria Hills Vineyard (Santa Maria Valley)

Foxen Winery (Santa Maria Valley)

Hartley-Ostini Hitching Post Winery, "Cork Dancer" (Santa Barbara County)

Kenneth Volk Vineyards, Santa Maria Cuvée (Santa Barbara County)

Lane Tanner Winery, Santa Barbara County and Bien Nacido Vineyard (Santa Maria Valley)

Summerland Winery, Bien Nacido Vineyard (Santa Maria Valley)

Tantara Winery, Bien Nacido and Solomon Hills Vineyards (Santa Maria Valley)

Whitcraft Winery, Bien Nacido Vineyard–N Block (Santa Maria Valley)

### High-End Santa Barbara Pinot Noir, $50–$75

Foxen Winery, Bien Nacido Vineyard–Block Eight (Santa Maria Valley)

## Russian River Valley

The huge Russian River Valley AVA, about 198 square miles, is in the central part of Sonoma County and encompasses two smaller AVAs, Green Valley and Chalk Hill. However, Chalk Hill, in the extreme northeastern part of the Russian River Valley, is too warm for Pinot Noir. Russian River Valley's largest city is Santa Rosa, at its southeastern end, about 55 miles north of San Francisco; however, its wine center is the rapidly growing town of Healdsburg, in the northern part of the Valley.

Depending on the location of their vineyards, Russian River Valley Pinot Noirs can carry either Russian River Valley or Green Valley AVAs on their labels. Although many of the recommended wines in this section actually come from Green Valley grapes, the producer often chooses to use the better-known Russian River Valley AVA on the wine's label.

The recommended Russian River Valley Pinot Noirs are sorted into three price categories: moderately priced, moderate-plus, and high-end.

### Moderately Priced Russian River Valley Pinot Noirs, under $20

De Loach Vineyards, Estate
  (Russian River Valley)
Kenwood Vineyards
  (Russian River Valley)

Rodney Strong Vineyards (Russian
  River Valley)

In the picks for moderate-plus Pinot Noirs, you'll notice that Dutton Ranch vineyard appears three times. Warren Dutton planted Pinot Noir in 1964, and today Dutton Ranch is one of California's celebrated vineyards for Chardonnay and Pinot Noir, selling its grapes to many elite wineries as well as making its own wines. As for other notable names, the family of the legendary late Joseph Swan — perhaps the first person to make great, long-lived Russian River Valley Pinot Noirs (and Zinfandels) — makes a couple of the wines on the moderate-plus list.

### Moderate-Plus Russian River Valley Pinot Noirs, $20–$50

Chasseur (Russian River Valley)
Davis Bynum Winery, Moshin
  Vineyards (Russian River Valley)
De Loach Vineyards, Green Valley
  and "O. F. S."
  (Russian River Valley)
Dutton-Goldfield Winery, Dutton
  Ranch (Russian River Valley)
Freeman Vineyard
  (Russian River Valley)

Frei Brothers (Russian River Valley)
Gary Farrell Vineyards
  (Russian River Valley)
Inman Family Wines, Olivet Grange
  Vineyard (Russian River Valley)
Iron Horse Vineyards, Estate
  (Green Valley)
"J" Vineyards (Russian River Valley)

**Book IV**

**California and Elsewhere in North America**

*(continued)*

*(continued)*

Joseph Swan, Great Oak and Trenton Estate Vineyards (Russian River Valley)

La Crema Winery (Russian River Valley)

Lynmar Winery (Russian River Valley)

MacMurray Ranch (Russian River Valley)

Marimar Estate, Don Miguel Vineyard (Russian River Valley)

Moshin Vineyards, Estate and Lot 4 (Russian River Valley)

Mueller Winery, Emily's Cuvée (Russian River Valley)

Orogeny Vineyards (Green Valley)

Papapietro Perry Winery (Russian River Valley)

Paul Hobbs Wines (Russian River Valley)

Porter Creek Vineyards (Russian River Valley)

Roessler Cellars, Dutton Ranch (Russian River Valley)

Russian Hill Estate (Russian River Valley)

Rutz Cellars, Dutton Ranch (Russian River Valley)

Siduri Wines, Sapphire Hill Vineyard (Russian River Valley)

### High-End Russian River Valley Pinot Noirs, Mostly $50–$75

Arista Winery, Mononi Vineyard and Toboni Vineyard (Russian River Valley)

Davis Bynum Winery, Allen Vineyard (Russian River Valley)

Dehlinger Winery, Estate and Goldridge Vineyard (Russian River Valley)

DuMOL, Russian River Valley and Aidan, Finn, or Ryan Vineyards (Russian River Valley)

Dutton Estate, Jewell Block and Thomas Road Vineyards (Russian River Valley)

Failla, Keefer Ranch (Russian River Valley)

Freeman Vineyard, Keefer Ranch (Russian River Valley)

Hartford Court, Arrendell Vineyard (Russian River Valley)

Hartford Court, Fog Dance Vineyard (Green Valley)

"J" Vineyards, Nicole's and Robert Thomas Vineyards (Russian River Valley)

Kistler Vineyards, Kistler Vineyard (Russian River Valley); over $100

Lynmar Winery, Quail Hill Vineyard (Russian River Valley)

Merry Edwards, Olivet Lane (Russian River Valley); over $75

Rochioli Vineyards, Estate (Russian River Valley)

Williams Selyem Winery, "Westside Road Neighbors" (Russian River Valley)

Williams Selyem Winery, Allen Vineyard (Russian River Valley); over $75

## Anderson Valley

Anderson Valley is in Mendocino County, about 115 miles north of San Francisco. The Valley is in the western part of the county, just 10 to 15 miles from the Pacific Ocean and southeast of the coastal town of Mendocino. Steep mountains surround the 15-mile-long Valley, and the Navarro River runs through it.

## Six top-value Pinot Noirs

These six Pinot Noirs, all $15 and under, are consistently reliable:

☑ Blackstone Winery (Sonoma Coast)

☑ De Loach Vineyards, "Cote De Loach" (California)

☑ Hangtime Cellars (Edna Valley, San Luis Obispo)

☑ Jekel Vineyards (Monterey County)

☑ Mark West (California)

☑ Red Truck, Cline Cellars (California)

In 1994, only 300 acres of Pinot Noir existed in Anderson Valley; by 2005, that number had quadrupled to 1,200 acres. Many of the top Pinot Noir producers — particularly from Sonoma County but also from Napa Valley — had discovered the ideal growing conditions of Anderson Valley. Some leading Pinot Noir producers that are now using Anderson Valley grapes include Williams Selyem, Littorai, Siduri, Duckhorn's Goldeneye, La Crema, Adrian Fog, Roessler, and Copain.

About 25 Anderson Valley wineries make Pinot Noir, and another 17 wineries outside of the Valley use Anderson Valley grapes for one or more of their Pinot Noirs. Expect to find recommended Anderson Valley Pinot Noirs in two price categories: moderate-plus and high-end.

**Moderate-Plus Anderson Valley Pinot Noirs, $20–$50**

Black Kite Cellars, Kite's Rest (Anderson Valley)
Breggo Cellars (Anderson Valley)
Copain Wines, Cerise Vineyard (Anderson Valley)
Greenwood Ridge Vineyards (Mendocino Ridge)
Handley Cellars (Anderson Valley)
Husch Vineyards (Anderson Valley)
La Crema (Anderson Valley)
Lazy Creek Vineyards (Anderson Valley)

Londer Vineyards (Anderson Valley)
MacPhail (Anderson Valley)
Phillips Hill Estates, Toulouse Vineyard (Anderson Valley)
Phillips Hill Estates, Oppenlander Vineyard (Mendocino)
Raye's Hill Winery, Cerise Vineyard (Anderson Valley)
Roessler Cellars, Savoy Vineyard (Anderson Valley)
Saintsbury, Cerise Vineyard (Anderson Valley)

**Book IV**

**California and Elsewhere in North America**

### High-End Anderson Valley Pinot Noirs, Mostly $50–$75

Adrian Fog Winery, Savoy Vineyard (Anderson Valley)

Breggo Cellars, Savoy and Donnelly Vineyards (Anderson Valley)

Copain Wines, Hacienda Secoya Vineyard (Anderson Valley)

Littorai, Savoy Vineyard and Cerise Vineyard (Anderson Valley)

Londer Vineyards, Paraboll Vineyard (Anderson Valley)

MacPhail, Toulouse Vineyard (Anderson Valley)

Williams Selyem, Ferrington Vineyard (Anderson Valley); over $100

Williams Selyem, Weir Vineyard (Yorkville Highlands, Mendocino County); over $100

# Chapter 5

# Major Wine Regions in the Rest of North America

California's growth has stimulated interest in wine throughout the United States. Today, wineries exist in all 50 states. But wine production is an important industry in only four states: California (the largest wine-producing state, by far; see the earlier chapters in Book IV), Washington, Oregon, and New York. The United States is currently fourth in world wine production — although well behind the two leaders, France and Italy. (Spain is a distant third.)

The wines of the United States are the essence of New World wine-think. Winemakers operate freely, planting whatever grape variety they want, wherever they want to plant it. Likewise, they blend wines from different regions together however they please. (Blending among states is trickier, because of federal rules.)

Of course, the United States isn't the only North American country in the wine business. Canada's wine industry has been growing, and the provinces of Ontario and British Columbia have stepped into the lead in Canadian wine production.

If you want a break from your usual Californian, Italian, or French wines, consider this chapter your introductory guide to North America's *other* top wine producers.

# Ocean-Influenced Oregon

Because Oregon is north of California, most people assume that Oregon's wine regions are cool. And they're right. But the main reason for Oregon's cool climate is that no high mountains separate the vineyards from the Pacific Ocean. The ocean influence brings cool temperatures and rain. Grape-growing and winemaking are really completely different in Oregon and California.

Winemaking is a fairly new industry in Oregon, but it's growing rapidly. From a handful of wineries in the early 1970s, the state had more than 350 wineries in 2008! Most of Oregon's wineries are small, family-owned operations. The exception in terms of size is King Estate, Oregon's largest winery, but even King Estate is relatively small compared to some of the wine behemoths of California.

Red wine makes up 60 percent of Oregon's wine production today; the 40 percent of production that is white wine features mainly Pinot Gris, Chardonnay, and Riesling.

The following sections describe the wines Oregon is known for as well as some prominent wine regions in the Beaver State.

## A tale of two Pinots

Oregon is home to two fabulous Pinots, specifically Pinot Noir and Pinot Gris. The state first gained respect in wine circles for its Pinot Noir, a grape that needs cool climates to perform at its best. The Eyrie Vineyards released Oregon's first Pinot Noir in 1970, but national recognition for the state's Pinots came only after the excellent 1983 and 1985 vintages. Pinot Noir is still Oregon's flagship wine, and a vast majority of the state's wineries make this wine. Oregon's Pinot Noirs, with their characteristic black-fruit aromas and flavors, depth, and complexity, have won accolades as among the very best Pinot Noirs in the United States.

On the white side of the Pinot spectrum, Pinot Gris has emerged as a serious challenger to Chardonnay's domination of the Oregon white wine scene. A natural mutation of its ancestor, Pinot Noir, the Pinot Gris variety has grapes that are normally pale pink–yellowish in color when ripe.

David Lett, founder and winemaker of the Eyrie Vineyards and Oregon's Pinot Noir pioneer, is also the man who made Oregon's first Pinot Gris around 1970, followed by Ponzi Vineyards and Adelsheim Vineyards. Today, more than 75 wineries in Oregon make Pinot Gris.

Two styles of Oregon Pinot Gris exist:

- ✔ A lighter, fruity style (for which the grapes are picked early) is always unoaked and can be consumed as soon as six to eight months after the autumn harvest.

- ✔ A medium-bodied, golden-colored wine from grapes left longer on the vine sometimes has a little oak aging and can age for five or six years (or longer).

In general Oregon Pinot Gris is light- to medium-bodied, with aromas that hint of pears, apples, and sometimes of melon, and surprising depth for an inexpensive wine. It's an excellent food wine, even when it's slightly sweet; it works especially well with seafood and salmon, just the kind of food that it's paired with in Oregon. And the best news is the price. Most of Oregon's Pinot Gris wines sell for under $20.

## Who's who in Willamette Valley

The main home of Pinot Noir and Pinot Gris in Oregon is the Willamette Valley, directly south of the city of Portland in northwestern Oregon. The cool Willamette Valley has established itself in the last 30 or so years as the most important wine region in Oregon; in fact, more than 200 wineries, about two-thirds of the state's wineries, are situated there.

Willamette Valley is a convenient wine destination to visit because the vibrant city of Portland, with all of its fine restaurants, hotels, and shops, is 30 minutes north of this wine region.

Willamette Valley is huge and encompasses several counties. Yamhill County, directly southwest of Portland, has the greatest concentration of wineries, all of which produce Pinot Noir. But quite a few wineries are located in Washington County, west of Portland, and in Polk County, south of Yamhill. Six American Viticultural Areas (AVAs) now exist in the Willamette Valley: Chehalem Mountain, Dundee Hills, Yamhill-Carlton District, Ribbon Ridge, McMinnville Foothills, and Eola Hills.

Here are some of the better producers in the Willamette Valley, primarily for Pinot Noir and Pinot Gris (but sometimes also for Chardonnay or Riesling):

| | |
|---|---|
| Adelsheim Vineyard | Bethel Heights Vineyard |
| Amity Vineyards | Brick House Vineyards |
| Anne Amie | Broadley Vineyards |
| Archery Summit | Cameron Winery |
| Argyle Winery | Chehalem |
| Beaux Frères | Cooper Mountain Vineyards |
| Benton Lane Winery | Cristom Vineyards |

**Book IV**

**California and Elsewhere in North America**

Domaine Drouhin Oregon
Domaine Serene
Duck Pond Cellars
Edgefield Winery
Elk Cove Vineyards
Eola Hills Wine Cellars
Erath Vineyards
Evesham Wood Winery
The Eyrie Vineyards
Firesteed Winery
Hamacher Wines
Hinman Vineyards/Silvan Ridge
Ken Wright Cellars
King Estate Winery
Kramer Vineyards
Lange Winery
Montinore Vineyards
Oak Knoll Winery

Panther Creek Cellars
Patricia Green Cellars
Penner-Ash Wine Cellars
Ponzi Vineyards
Redhawk Vineyard
Rex Hill Vineyards
St. Innocent Winery
Shafer Vineyard
Sokol Blosser Winery
Stangeland Vineyards
Torii Mor Winery
Tualatin Vineyards
Van Duzer Vineyards
Willakenzie Estates
Willamette Valley Vineyards
Witness Tree Vineyard
Yamhill Valley Vineyards

## Two other Oregon wine regions

Two other wine regions of note in Oregon are in the southwestern part of the state: the Umpqua Valley (around the town of Roseburg) and the Rogue River Valley (farther south, next to California's northern border).

Considerably warmer than Willamette, the Umpqua Valley is the site of Oregon's first winery, Hillcrest Vineyard, founded in 1962. The main grape varieties in Umpqua are Pinot Noir, Chardonnay, Riesling, and Cabernet Sauvignon. Major wineries are Henry Estate and Girardet Wine Cellars, known for their Pinot Noir and Chardonnay.

The Rogue River Valley is warmer still; therefore, Cabernet Sauvignon and Merlot often perform better than Pinot Noir there. Chardonnay is the leading white wine, but Pinot Gris is becoming popular. Bridgeview Vineyards, the region's largest winery, is doing an admirable job with Pinot Gris as well as Pinot Noir. Four other vineyards to watch are Ashland Vineyards, Valley View Winery, Sarah Powell Wines, and Foris Vineyards — the latter specializes in Merlot and Cabernet Sauvignon.

# The United States' Second-Largest Wine Producer: Washington State

Washington got off to a late start in the wine business. With the exception of Chateau Ste. Michelle and Columbia Winery, both founded in the 1960s, practically none of the current Washington wineries existed as recently as 1980. In 1981, Washington had 19 wineries; today, more than 500 wineries are in business, making Washington the second-largest producer of premium wines in the United States.

Although Washington and Oregon are neighboring states, their wine regions have vastly different climates due to the location of the vineyards relative to the Cascade Mountains, which cut through both states from north to south.

On Washington's western, or coastal, side, the climate is maritime — cool, plenty of rain, and a lot of vegetation. (In Oregon, almost all the vineyards are located on the coastal side.) East of the mountains, Washington's climate is continental, with cold winters and hot, very dry summers. Most of Washington's vineyards are situated in this area, in the sprawling Columbia and Yakima Valleys. Because it's so far north, Washington also has the advantage of long hours of sunlight, averaging an unusually high 17.4 hours of sunshine during the growing season.

Washington does have a few vineyards west of the Cascades, around Puget Sound, where Riesling and Gewürztraminer grow well. In fact, many of the larger wineries, such as Chateau Ste. Michelle and Columbia Winery, are located in the Puget Sound area, near Seattle (but they obtain almost all of their grapes from the Columbia and Yakima Valleys). Chateau Ste. Michelle and the even larger Columbia Crest (both under the same corporate ownership) are the giants in the state; they account for more than 50 percent of Washington's wines. Two other large Washington wineries are The Hogue Cellars and Washington Hills Cellars.

The next sections highlight the varieties and varietals of Washington, map out its American Viticultural Areas (AVAs) of note, and offer recommendations for Washington producers and wines to try.

## *The grapes that thrive and the wines they make*

Washington winemakers have found that with irrigation, many grapes can flourish in the Washington desert. The Bordeaux varieties — Merlot, Cabernet Sauvignon, Cabernet Franc, Sauvignon Blanc, and Sémillon — are the name of the game. Syrah is coming up fast, and Chenin Blanc and the ever-present Chardonnay are also doing well.

In terms of wine, the Evergreen State first became well-known for the quality of its Merlots. (One winery, Columbia Crest, makes the largest-selling Merlot in the United States in the over-$8 price category.) Lately, Washington's Syrah wines are gaining many accolades. In fact, Washington may be the single best region in the United States for this exciting wine. Cabernet Sauvignon and Cabernet Franc are also excellent varietal wines here.

The types of wine produced in Washington have changed dramatically over the years. In 1993, about two-thirds of Washington's wines were white, one-third red. Reflecting Americans' changing tastes in wine, Washington's wines are now about 60 percent red, 40 percent white.

## Washington's wine regions

Washington has one gigantic AVA, Columbia Valley, which encompasses five other AVAs within its macro-appellation (listed in order of their general importance):

- **Yakima Valley:** This region is the second largest in acreage, behind the huge Columbia Valley itself; more wineries are actually located here than in the rest of Columbia Valley.

- **Walla Walla Valley:** Although only 5 percent of the state's *vinifera* grapes grow here, this fast-growing region in the southeastern corner of Washington is home to some of the state's top wineries, such as Leonetti Cellar, Woodward Canyon, Waterbrook Winery, Canoe Ridge Vineyard, and L'Ecole #41.

- **Red Mountain:** The tiny Red Mountain area is actually within the Yakima Valley AVA, but its red clay soil and high altitude earned it a separate appellation. About nine wineries, including Hedges and Kiona Vineyards, concentrate on red varieties: Cabernet Sauvignon, Merlot, Cabernet Franc, and Syrah. Some great vineyards are also located here.

- **Horse Heaven Hills:** Recognized as a separate AVA in 2005, this area in the southernmost part of the Columbia Valley, just north of the Columbia River, has long been known as an ideal location for Cabernet Sauvignon. Many of Washington's leading wineries, including Chateau Ste. Michelle, use grapes from vineyards located in this AVA.

- **Wahluke Slope:** Created in 2006, the Wahluke Slope AVA is one of the state's warmer appellations, known for its Merlot and Cabernet Sauvignon. It's home to Snoqualmie Vineyards.

Other Washington AVAs of note include tiny Rattlesnake Hills, a subappellation of Yakima Valley, and Columbia Gorge, a beautiful area in southwestern Washington crossing into Oregon, which actually has an equal number of both Oregon and Washington wineries. More than 50 wineries are located in the Greater Puget Sound/Seattle Area AVA, which encompasses the Puget Sound Islands; in this cool, moist climate, Pinot Gris and Pinot Noir are leading varieties, as well as Riesling and Gewürztraminer. About nine wineries, including Arbor Crest, are located in the Spokane Area in eastern Washington.

# Lemberger: A Washington oddity

When was the last time you had a Lemberger? No, not the cheese! Lemberger is a little-known grape variety from Germany that's also grown in Austria, where it's called Blaufränkisch. Don't feel bad if you haven't heard of it, because few people in the United States — outside of Washington — have tasted it. Lemberger is a hardy red grape variety that does well in the Yakima Valley; it makes a fruity, dry, inexpensive wine in the Beaujolais or Dolcetto school. Hoodsport, Covey Run, Kiona Vineyards, and The Hogue Cellars are four good producers of Lemberger wine. The Hogue Cellars calls its version Blue Franc.

# Top Washington wine producers

Following are the recommended wine producers in Washington, along with some of their best wines:

- **Andrew Will Cellars:** Cabernet Sauvignon, Merlot
- **Arbor Crest Wine Cellars:** Sauvignon Blanc, Chardonnay, Riesling
- **Badger Mountain Winery:** Chardonnay, Cabernet Franc
- **Barnard Griffin Winery:** Sémillon, Chardonnay, Fumé Blanc, Merlot
- **Betz Family Winery:** Cabernet Sauvignon, Merlot blend, Syrah
- **Bookwalter Winery:** Cabernet Sauvignon, Merlot
- **Canoe Ridge Vineyard:** Merlot, Cabernet Sauvignon
- **Chateau Ste. Michelle:** Merlot, Cabernet Sauvignon, Chardonnay (especially Cold Creek Vineyard of all three), "Eroica" Riesling (with Dr. Loosen)
- **Chinook Winery:** Sauvignon Blanc, Sémillon, Chardonnay
- **Col Solare:** Meritage (mainly Cabernet Sauvignon; a Chateau Ste. Michelle/Piero Antinori collaboration)
- **Columbia Crest Winery:** Reserve Red (Cabernet-Merlot blend), Sémillon, Syrah, Merlot, Cabernet Sauvignon, Sémillon-Chardonnay
- **Columbia Winery:** Cabernet Sauvignon, Cabernet Franc, Syrah, Merlot (especially Red Willow Vineyard of all four)
- **Covey Run Winery:** Chardonnay, Lemberger
- **DeLille Cellars:** Chaleur Estate (Bordeaux-style blend), Chaleur Estate Blanc (Sauvignon Blanc-Sémillon blend), D2 (second label of Chaleur Estate), Harrison Hill (Cabernet Sauvignon), Syrah
- **Gordon Brothers Cellars:** Chardonnay, Merlot, Cabernet Sauvignon

- **Hedges Cellars:** Red Mountain Reserve (Bordeaux-style blend), Cabernet/Merlot, Fumé/Chardonnay, Three Vineyard Red
- **The Hogue Cellars:** Merlot, Cabernet Sauvignon (Reserve), Blue Franc (Lemberger), Chenin Blanc, Sémillon-Chardonnay, Sémillon
- **Hoodsport Winery:** Lemberger, Sémillon
- **Hyatt Vineyard:** Merlot, Cabernet Sauvignon
- **Januik Winery:** Merlot, Cabernet Sauvignon
- **Kiona Vineyards:** Lemberger, Cabernet Sauvignon, Merlot
- **L'Ecole #41:** Merlot (Seven Hills), Cabernet Sauvignon, Sémillon
- **Leonetti Cellar:** Cabernet Sauvignon (especially Seven Hills Vineyard), Merlot, Sangiovese
- **Long Shadows Winery:** Merlot, Syrah, Riesling
- **Matthews Cellars:** Merlot, Yakima Valley Red (Bordeaux-style blend)
- **McCrea Cellars:** Chardonnay, Syrah
- **Northstar:** Merlot
- **Owen-Sullivan Winery:** Syrah, Cabernet Franc, Merlot
- **Pepper Bridge Winery:** Cabernet Sauvignon, Merlot
- **Preston Wine Cellars:** Cabernet Sauvignon, Merlot (Reserves)
- **Quilceda Creek Vintners:** Cabernet Sauvignon
- **Sagelands Vineyard:** Cabernet Sauvignon, Merlot
- **Seven Hills**\*\*:** Merlot, Cabernet Sauvignon
- **Snoqualmie Vineyards:** Cabernet Sauvignon, Merlot, Syrah
- **Tamarack Cellars:** Merlot, Cabernet Sauvignon, Firehouse Red
- **Tefft Cellars:** Sangiovese, Cabernet Sauvignon
- **Thurston Wolfe Winery:** Syrah
- **Washington Hills Cellars:** Cabernet Sauvignon, Merlot, Chardonnay, Sémillon, Cabernet Franc ("Apex" is this winery's premium label; it also uses the "W. B. Bridgman" label)
- **Waterbrook Winery:** Cabernet Sauvignon, Merlot, Chardonnay, Cabernet Franc, Sauvignon Blanc
- **Woodward Canyon Winery:** Chardonnay, Cabernet Sauvignon, Merlot

\*\**Seven Hills Winery is actually just across the border in Oregon, but the vineyard is in Walla Walla Valley, Washington.*

# New York, America's Unsung Wine Hero

New York City may be the capital of the world in many ways, but its state's wines don't get the recognition they deserve, perhaps because of California's overwhelming presence in the U.S. market. New York ranks as the third-largest wine-producing state in the United States. Brotherhood America's Oldest Winery, Ltd., the oldest continuously operating winery in the United States, opened its doors in New York's Hudson Valley in 1839. And the largest wine company in the world, Constellation, has its headquarters in the Finger Lakes region of western New York.

In the early days (prior to 1960), most of New York's wines were made from native American grape varieties, such as Concord, Catawba, Delaware, and Niagara, as well French-American hybrid grapes such as Seyval Blanc, Baco Noir, and Maréchal Foch.

Common wisdom held that the relatively cold New York winters couldn't support *Vitis vinifera* varieties. But a Russian immigrant, the late, great Dr. Konstantin Frank, proved all the naysayers wrong when he succeeded in growing Riesling (followed by many other *vinifera* varieties) in 1953 in Hammondsport, in the Finger Lakes region. (The first New York wines from *vinifera* grapes were actually made in 1961 at his winery, Dr. Frank's Vinifera Wine Cellars.)

The sections that follow lay out the state's key wine regions and suggest some wineries worth checking out.

## Revealing the key wine regions of the Empire State

New York's most important wine region is the Finger Lakes, where four large lakes temper the otherwise cool climate. This American Viticultural Area (AVA) produces about two-thirds of New York's wines. The other two important regions are the Hudson Valley, along the Hudson River north of New York City, and Long Island, which has three AVAs — North Fork of Long Island (the most important); the Hamptons, on the island's South Fork; and Long Island itself, using grapes from all over Long Island.

In 1973, Alec and Louisa Hargrave got the idea that Long Island's North Fork (about a two-hour drive east of New York City) had the ideal climate and soil for *vinifera* grapes. Today, Long Island has 40 wineries and is still growing. Like Washington state, Long Island seems particularly suited to Merlot, but Chardonnay, Riesling, Cabernet Sauvignon, Cabernet Franc, and Sauvignon Blanc are also grown, plus some Gewürztraminer, Pinot Noir, and numerous other varieties.

Book IV

California and Elsewhere in North America

## Listing the best of New York's wineries

The wine industry in New York State has grown from 19 wineries in 1976 to more than 250 wineries today, most of them small, family-run operations. Following are lists of recommended producers in New York's three major wine regions:

### Finger Lakes Region

Anthony Road Wine Company
Casa Larga Vineyards
Dr. Frank's Vinifera Wine Cellars (and its affiliate, Chateau Frank, for sparkling wines)
Fox Run Vineyards
Glenora Wine Cellars
Hazlitt 1852 Vineyards
Hermann J. Wiemer Vineyard
Heron Hill Vineyards
Hunt Country Vineyards

Knapp Vineyards
Lakewood Vineyards
Lamoreaux Landing Wine Cellars
Lucas Vineyards
McGregor Vineyard
Prejean Winery
Standing Stone Vineyards
Swedish Hill Vineyard
Wagner Vineyards
Widmer's Wine Cellars

### Hudson River Valley Region

Adair Vineyards
Baldwin Vineyards
Benmarl Vineyards
Brotherhood Winery
Cascade Mountain Vineyards

Clinton Vineyards
Magnanini Winery
Millbrook Vineyards
Rivendell Winery

### Long Island Region (North Fork, other than noted)

Bedell Cellars
Castello di Borghes Vineyard
Channing Daughters (Hamptons)
Corey Creek Vineyards
Duck Walk Vineyards (Hamptons)
Jamesport Vineyards
Laurel Lake Vineyards
Lenz Winery
Lieb Family Cellars
Loughlin Vineyards
Macari Vineyards

Martha Clara Vineyards
Old Brookville-Banfi (Nassau County)
Osprey's Dominion
Palmer Vineyards
Paumanok Vineyards
Peconic Bay Vineyards
Pelligrini Vineyards
Pindar Vineyards
Pugliese Vineyards
Raphael
Wolffer Estate (Hamptons)

# Oh, Canada

Ask many wine lovers in the United States about Canadian wines, and you'll probably get a blank stare. Canada's wines are known mainly to Canadians, who consume the bulk of their country's production.

The 1990s brought incredible growth to the Canadian wine industry: The number of wineries grew from 30 to more than 500 today. Wine is made in four of Canada's provinces, but Ontario has bragging rights as the largest producer, with more than 108 wineries. British Columbia ranks second. (Quebec and Nova Scotia round out the quartet.)

To identify and promote wines made entirely from local grapes (some Canadian wineries import wines from other countries to blend with local production), the provinces of Ontario and British Columbia have established an appellation system called *VQA*, Vintners' Quality Alliance. This system regulates the use of provincial names on wine labels, establishes which grape varieties can be used (*vinifera* varieties and certain hybrids), regulates the use of the terms *icewine, late harvest,* and *botrytised,* and requires wines to pass a taste and laboratory test.

The next sections get you up to speed on the grape varieties and wine regions of Canada's top two wine-producing provinces.

## Introducing icewine

Canada is the land of ice and snow. So making icewine should be easy, right? Wrong. It's winemaker against winter to make tiny quantities of this luscious dessert wine that sells for about $50 per half-bottle. Icewine must be made from grapes frozen on the vine. Grapes for icewine can't be harvested until the temperature falls to at least 18 degrees Fahrenheit. Harvesters collect the frozen fruit and maintain it in that condition until it reaches the winery and is pressed to get juice that can be fermented into icewine.

Harvesters work after dark so the sun doesn't get a chance to melt the grapes. When squeezed, the frozen grapes produce a concentrated, sugary syrup, which goes into stainless steel vats (or, if the winemaker wants to put a twist on the flavor, wooden barrels) for fermentation.

Most icewines in Canada are made from thick-skinned white grape varieties such as Riesling, Gewürztraminer, or Vidal. Yet Pinot Blanc, Chenin Blanc, and even red varieties such as Cabernet Franc have been turned into icewine.

Icewine is very sweet and very high in acid. Without the acidity, the wine would be just too sweet to taste, and without the sweetness, the acid would taste as if it could take the paint off a car. But together the balance of sugar and acid makes icewine the nectar of the gods! Icewine is a dessert unto itself, or you can serve it as an accompaniment to a fruit tart or other fruit-based dessert. Also try it with pate de foie gras or creamy cheeses.

**Book IV**

**California and Elsewhere in North America**

## Ontario: Well-positioned for icewine

Ontario's vineyards are cool-climate wine zones, despite the fact that they lie on the same parallel as the warmer European wine regions Chianti Classico and Rioja. Sixty percent of the production in Ontario is white wine, from Chardonnay, Riesling, Gewürztraminer, Pinot Blanc, Auxerrois, and the hybrids Seyval Blanc and Vidal. Red wines come from Pinot Noir, Gamay, Cabernet Sauvignon, Cabernet Franc, Merlot, and the hybrids Maréchal Foch and Baco Noir.

Ontario's VQA rules permit the use of the appellation Ontario and also recognize three *Designated Viticultural Areas* (DVAs), listed in order of importance:

- ✔ **Niagara Peninsula:** Along the south shore of Lake Ontario
- ✔ **Pelee Island:** Eleven miles south of the Canadian mainland, in Lake Erie, Canada's most southerly vineyards
- ✔ **Lake Erie North Shore:** The warmest of Ontario's viticultural areas

Because winter temperatures regularly drop well below freezing, *icewine,* made from grapes naturally frozen on the vine, is a specialty of Ontario. It's gradually earning the Canadian wine industry international attention, particularly for the wines of Inniskillin Winery.

## British Columbia: White wine is tops

The rapidly growing wine industry of British Columbia now boasts more than 100 wineries. Production is mainly white wine — from Chardonnay, Gewürztraminer, Pinot Gris, Pinot Blanc, and Riesling — but red wine production is increasing, mainly from Pinot Noir and Merlot.

The Okanagan Valley in southeastern British Columbia, where the climate is influenced by Lake Okanagan, is the center of wine production; Mission Hill is a leading winery. VQA rules recognize five Designated Viticultural Areas, listed in order of importance:

- ✔ Okanagan Valley
- ✔ Similkameen Valley
- ✔ Fraser Valley
- ✔ Vancouver Island
- ✔ Gulf Islands

# Book V

# Australia and New Zealand: Powerhouses of the Southern Hemisphere

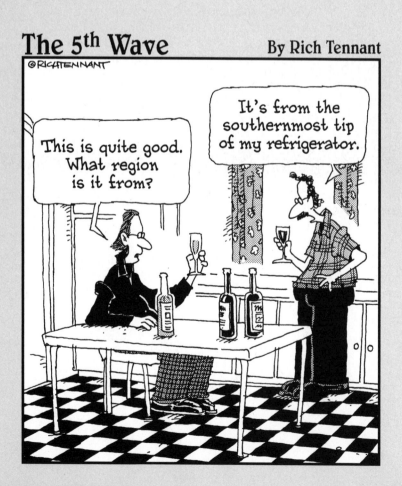

# In This Book . . .

In the 1990s, people around the world were just starting to come to terms with the idea of Australia and New Zealand as serious wine-producing countries. Probably parts of the world are still surprised by the enormous area of vineyards stretching across both countries. That surprise should be fading: Australia is now the sixth biggest wine-producing country in the world.

Being a newer wine power means that wineries in Australia and New Zealand take more risks and embrace new grape varieties. (These countries' diverse terrains and climates also invite experimentation.) From mega-producers to small family wineries, this book leads you through the delicious range of Australian and New Zealand wines.

Here are the contents of Book V at a glance:

# Chapter 1

# Australian and New Zealand Wines: A Success Story

**I**f you'd asked people 10 or 15 years ago what they knew about Australia and New Zealand, you'd likely have gotten the "Three S" response: sun, surf, and sheep. You can probably track this response to the first *Crocodile Dundee* film, which projected the image of Australia as a nation of beer drinkers propping up the bar in outback pubs.

Australia and Australians are, of course, nothing like they're portrayed in the film. And New Zealand is far more than just sheep, hobbits, and spectacular scenery. As for drinking beer . . . well, a great deal of suds is still consumed, but Australians and New Zealanders actually drink a lot more wine than beer. And not only are they great at drinking the stuff, but they're also great at making it. Australia and New Zealand have thriving wine industries that meet the demands of a thirsty local market *and* a booming overseas market. In fact, both Australia and New Zealand export millions of liters of wine annually.

In both countries, the traditional wine regions are expanding to meet the growing demand, and they're being joined by an ever-increasing list of emerging wine regions. More and more Aussies and New Zealanders are becoming winemakers, and vines are being planted in increasingly diverse regions. As a result, wine drinkers all over the world are falling in love with such outstanding wines as Australian Shiraz and Chardonnay, and New Zealand Sauvignon Blanc and Pinot Noir.

This chapter introduces you to the wine styles of Australia and New Zealand, shows you where the wine regions are, and helps you figure out how to digest all the info you see on the countries' wine labels.

# Getting Acclimated in Australia and New Zealand

A quick look at an atlas tells you that Australia and New Zealand take up a fair amount of space on this planet. All that land space means that significant variations in the weather also exist.

Australia's climate ranges from tropical (like in the far north area of Queensland) to temperate (like on the island of Tasmania), so don't expect to find an easy summation of the Australian climate.

Grapes are grown in vineyards inland of Brisbane (in the northern part of Australia) to around Hobart (located on the southern coast of Tasmania); the distance between these two areas is more than 1,100 miles. Taking an east-west perspective, you find grapevines very close to Sydney, on Australia's east coast, and also 2,050 miles away in Perth, on the nation's west coast. Between the two coasts is a lot of desert. Some of Australia's wine regions are coastal, others are inland; some are very hot, some fairly cold; some are at a high altitude, some are on low plains. You get the idea.

New Zealand is no different in its climate variations. The northernmost wine region is Northland, and the southernmost region is Central Otago. The distance between the two is more than 620 miles of diverse landscape, from coastal plains to soaring snow-capped mountains. Don't expect any generalizations here either. In New Zealand, you find vineyards in sheltered maritime locales and on the slopes of mountain ranges.

# Meeting Growing Demand with Diverse Wines

With such diversity in both climate and landscape, it's no surprise that the wines and vines from Australia and New Zealand are also many and varied. The variety in wine production caters to almost all palates and, importantly, most pockets. The choice of what to grow also comes with no strings attached. That is, you can grow whatever grapes you like, wherever you like, with no *appellation* system (a naming system, like the ones in Europe) to prevent you from doing so. The only factor that can stop you in your winemaking tracks is making bad wine.

As of 2008, red grapes reigned supreme in Australia in terms of the quantities grown, making up 53 percent of the total harvest. Of this percentage, Shiraz led the pack with 45 percent of all red grapes grown. Next was Cabernet Sauvignon at 29 percent. Of the white varieties, Chardonnay held the top spot with 51 percent, with Sémillon in second place at 11 percent. Broadly speaking, these four varieties are the best-known Australian varieties, although public demand is also strong for Australian Pinot Noir, Sauvignon Blanc, Merlot, and Riesling, as well as a number of other varieties. In fact, the most fashionable thing happening in the Australian wine industry these days is the enthusiastic reception given to varieties such as Pinot Gris, Sangiovese, and Viognier.

Over in New Zealand, the industry is dominated by white grape varieties, with 72 percent of the grapes grown in 2008 being white. The internationally famous Sauvignon Blanc was the most planted at 48 percent of the total, followed by Chardonnay with 14 percent of the total. Of the red grape varieties grown in New Zealand, the star performer in terms of quantity is Pinot Noir, which makes up 16 percent of the total grapes grown on New Zealand's North and South Islands. New Zealand Merlot is the second most successful red grape.

# Zoning Out: Australia's Wine Regions

To give some clarity as to where all the various grapes are grown throughout Australia, the country's wine industry developed *Geographical Indications* (GIs). This system divides the landmass into wine zones, regions, and subregions. Figure 1-1 shows you Australia's wine zones.

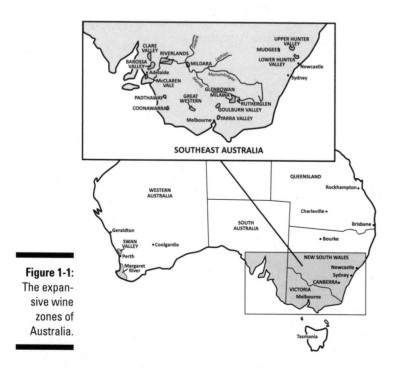

Figure 1-1: The expansive wine zones of Australia.

*Zone* is the most general designation; it's determined by traditional names for the various areas. The breakdowns beyond that get much more specific. *Region* may be classified as an area between two valleys, map coordinates, or roads, for example. Any wine carrying a regional name must have sourced 85 percent of the blend of the fruit from that region.

Don't assume that the grapes in your bottle are from the Barossa Valley just because the winery is located there. Unless the wine's label indicates that the GI is *Barossa Valley,* the grapes could be from anywhere.

Further down Australia's GI index is the *subregion,* which reflects differences in soil type, topography, and climate within a region.

Because the character or quality of wine comes partly from the subregion and also from the winemaker, you may be able to use the subregion as a guide to source similar Australian wines.

The list of regions and subregions in Australia seems to balloon every year, as do the discussions and even occasional court cases as to who's in and who's outside the region. However, the Australian GI determination process has a successful appeal process enshrined therein to protect the fantastic reputation of some regions and the automatic credibility a new vineyard may gain just for being located within a famous region.

For more information on GIs and current information on the GI determination process, visit the Australian Wine and Brandy Corporation's Web site (www.wineaustralia.com), run your mouse over the About Australian Wines link at the top of the page, and click the Wine Regions link.

# Breaking Up New Zealand

When people talk about New Zealand, they often refer to places as being either on the North or the South Island. Although this reference isn't considered to be an official zoning of the country's wine areas, it may act as a starting point for you to picture where a vineyard or winery is located — albeit very approximately.

On a more official basis, New Zealand is broken into ten regions: six in the North Island and four in the South Island.

These ten regions are likely to be broken down into subregions at some point because of the need to classify the distinct areas that exist within each region. For example, within the Otago region (described in Chapter 5 of Book V) are Wanaka and Queenstown, which are separated by a mountain range. Consequently, the vineyards in Wanaka are a good deal cooler than those in Queenstown, and they each produce quite different wines.

# Decoding Australian and New Zealand Wine Labels

What a wine bottle looks like is important not only because it plays a big part in your buying decision but also because it reveals essential information that can help you understand the wine.

Every piece of information on a wine label must be accurate. Like any product, federal and state legislation covers the labeling of wine in Australia and New Zealand. The mandatory items include

✔ **The name and address of the wine company:** This information is legally more important than the winery's name, trademark, or brand name! The address must not be a post office address.

✔ **The country of origin:** The label must state which country the wine comes from. In the unusual yet occasional situation when some wine from another country is blended with an Australian wine, this mix of origin must be stated on the label as a percentage — for example, *75 percent Australian wine plus 25 percent Chilean.*

✔ **The volume of wine:** The volume of wine must be on the front label (flip to Chapter 3 in Book I for help figuring out which label is the front one).

✔ **Any additives or processing aids:** As of 2003, all Australian wine labels must state all products used in the winemaking process. The reason? To warn anyone who has an allergic reaction to any of these products. Consequently, you may find reference to egg products *(egg whites),* beef tissue *(gelatin),* or fish tissue *(isinglass)* on a wine label. These processing aids are sometimes used to clarify the wine, and although it's very unlikely that any of these products remain after the wine has been racked, filtered, and bottled, they must be listed on the label if any trace could possibly remain.

Other additives may include

• **Sulfur dioxide:** Used in both reds and whites, sulfur dioxide, otherwise known as *preservative 220,* is used to prevent oxidation and microbial growth. Yeast also produces it as a byproduct during the fermentation process, so the preservative is, to a degree, a part of every wine — even organic ones.

• **Ascorbic acid:** Some white wines include ascorbic acid, or *preservative 300,* which is used as an aid to preventing oxidation. It isn't used in red wine, however, because it can react with some of the red color pigments and cause a nasty spoilage character.

If the label states that a wine is preservative free, as some organic wine labels do, the wine must have less than 10 milligrams per liter (mg/L) of sulfur dioxide.

✔ **The variety:** If the label says *Cabernet Sauvignon,* then the wine must be between 85 and 100 percent from that variety of grape. Any added variety doesn't have to be declared. If more than one variety is listed on the label, then the one used in the biggest proportion is listed first. So in a Grenache, Shiraz, and Mourvèdre blend, Grenache makes up the largest portion, Shiraz the second, and so on. The actual proportions don't have to be listed, although you may sometimes find this information on the back label.

✔ **A description of the wine:** Listing the variety or varieties of grape in the wine isn't mandatory. However, a description of the wine must be included if the variety isn't listed. So instead of listing the blend — for example, Shiraz, Cabernet, Durif, and Malbec — winemakers can state on the label that their wine is a *dry red wine.*

✔ **The percentage of alcohol and the number of standard drinks per bottle:** Australia has a law that states that the label of any alcoholic beverage must convey the number of standard drinks per bottle (a *standard drink* contains 10 grams of alcohol).

You may sometimes find an over-sticker on a bottle of Australian or New Zealand wine that doesn't quite match the main label. Don't worry; this information isn't an afterthought — wine companies that export their product to other countries use this method to ensure they comply with local labeling requirements. If wine companies were to print a new label to comply with the fine print of every country, they'd be paying the label companies more than their winemakers!

# Chapter 2

# New South Wales: Home to Established Wineries and Upstarts

*I*f New South Wales doesn't sound familiar to you, the Hunter Valley might. This famous Australian wine region, full of established family wine operations (and some newer tourist-focused operations), lies in the northern Australian district of New South Wales. This district also includes Mudgee, an upstart on the wine scene that's shaking its early reputation for inferior grapes and starting to give the Hunter Valley some competition for recognition, mostly with its powerful Shiraz and Cabernet Sauvignon wines.

This chapter takes you on a tour of these two larger regions, as well as some of the smaller spots and the glorious wines that emerge from them.

## Getting to Know the Hunter Valley and Its Wines

The Hunter Valley, about a two-hour drive north from the city of Sydney, is perhaps the best-known grape-growing zone in New South Wales. (It's also the oldest grape-growing region in Australia.) Known simply as "the Hunter," the zone is divided into two regions: the Upper Hunter and the Lower Hunter. The vineyards of the Upper Hunter are centered around the towns of Muswellbrook and Denman; to the southeast, Cessnock and Branxton are the main towns of the Lower Hunter.

Set between the Great Dividing Range and the Pacific Ocean, the Hunter Valley can experience extreme conditions: Hail and excessive rain are just two of the elements to challenge the winemaker. Overall, summers are hot and winters are cool. The region is also pretty dry, receiving only around 30 inches of rain annually.

Compared to some of Australia's other wine zones, the Hunter is largely low land. Consequently, the cooling effect that higher altitudes have on vineyards doesn't come into play much in the Hunter. However, in the Lower Hunter, a break in the Great Dividing Range means that some of the cooler sea breezes from the New South Wales coast flow through to the vineyards. These breezes simultaneously lower the humidity and cool the vines in the afternoon and evening.

The following sections help you get more acquainted with the grapes that thrive in the Hunter and some of the region's top wine producers.

## Taking stock of the Hunter's top grape varieties

The Hunter isn't a great producer of grapes. In fact, many of the Hunter wineries use grapes grown in other Australian wine regions (for example, Riesling grapes come from the Clare Valley and Shiraz grapes come from McLaren Vale). The Hunter Valley, which produces distinctive regional wines, has good luck with the following white and red varieties:

- **Chardonnay:** As one of the main stars of the region, Chardonnay (shar-dohn-nay) makes up about 52 percent of the white grapes grown here. A Hunter Chardonnay is a lovely, rich, nutty-flavored wine. Murray Tyrrell introduced the Chardonnay grape to the region, and today his company makes one of the best Chardonnays in Australia: Tyrrell's Vat 47.

- **Sémillon:** Although less Sémillon (seh-mee-yohn) is grown than Chardonnay (just 30 percent of all white grape varieties), Sémillon has made the Hunter Valley famous for its whites — and the reason stems from inclement weather. The Sémillon grape has a thin, slippery skin, and the bunches are big with the berries packed tightly together. These physical properties mean the grape is particularly susceptible to wet and humid weather — exactly what the Hunter Valley experiences often.

  Because of the danger posed by the bad weather, the Sémillon grapes are picked before they're fully ripe, when the skins aren't soft and vulnerable to disease. The result is a crisp, lemony, pleasant white wine. Initially, this wine can almost be called nondescript, but when left to age in the bottle for 3 to 15 years, Sémillon turns into a magnificent, honeyed, soft, and complex wine.

Book V

Australia
and New
Zealand:
Power-
houses of
the Southern
Hemisphere

- **Verdelho:** The new kid on the block is Verdelho (vehr-*deh*-lyoh), a grape variety that's originally from Portugal. The Verdelho grape (which makes up 12 percent of the Hunter's white grapes) thrives in the region's warm weather. Because it can also cope with bad weather, this grape is increasingly being planted in the Hunter. Some of the best Verdelho wines come from the Broke Fordwich subregion (which you can read about later in this chapter).

- **Shiraz:** Shiraz (shee-rahz), which accounts for 50 to 60 percent of red grapes harvested in the region, put the Hunter Valley winemaking zone on the map, particularly due to the variety's fantastic longevity. Wine buffs still reminisce about the great years of these wines. The style is rustic with earthy characters and big, dense flavors. In the early 1960s and 1970s, Lindemans and Rothbury Estate were particularly famous for this variety, but today you can find some of the best Shiraz at Brokenwood and Tyrrell's.

- **Cabernet Sauvignon:** A red grape variety that makes up 17 percent of the Hunter's red grape total, Cabernet Sauvignon (cab-er-nay saw-vee-nyon) is part of the Hunter's success story. Although the climate is a little too warm to highlight the variety's true flavors, very fine Cabernet Sauvignons come from here. And because Cabernet Sauvignon is a thick-skinned, late-season-ripening variety, it can withstand the Hunter's sometimes difficult harvest conditions.

- **Merlot:** Although Merlot (mer-loh) had been planted in the Hunter over a number of years, only of late has the wine shown its suitability to the zone. A midseason-ripening variety with reasonably tough skin, Merlot can withstand rain and ripen in the month of March, when conditions in the Hunter become a little drier. Merlot is being planted extensively in the Broke Fordwich area; overall it makes up 12 percent of the Hunter's red grape plantings.

## Sampling the best the Lower Hunter offers

The wineries of the Lower Hunter vary enormously in character, ranging from small, family-run businesses to vast cellar-door outlets (*cellar door* is Australian terminology for *tasting room*). Many wineries have restaurants attached, and a large number offer various styles of accommodation.

Some of the best producers of the Lower Hunter include

Brokenwood Wines
Hungerford Hill
Lake's Folly
Lindemans Hunter Valley Winery

McWilliam's Mount Pleasant Winery
The Rothbury Estate
Tower Estate
Tyrell's Wines

# Heading for Broke (Fordwich) wines

The subregion of Broke Fordwich is located to the northwest of the town of Broke. Having the Brokenback Range on the subregion's western edge gives Broke Fordwich a slightly warmer climate than the Hunter Valley as a whole.

As in the Lower Hunter, most rainfall occurs during the growing season, which can result in problems with vine diseases. In addition, the extra fertility of the local soils, which are old and volcanic, means that keeping excess growth under control is vital to prevent higher disease pressures. The types of soil found in the Broke Fordwich subregion produce grapes that have great depth of flavor and color, hence the extensive plantings of Shiraz and Merlot vines.

Overall, Broke Fordwich contributes about one quarter of the wine production in the Hunter Valley. This subregion is home to many of the good Australian labels. Among the wineries producing some outstanding vintages are the following:

Glenguin Wine Company
Hope Estate
Krinklewood Vineyard
Margan Family Winegrowers
Poole's Rock Wines

# Discovering the wines of the Upper Hunter

The Upper Hunter region of the Hunter Valley has the benefit of moderate rainfall and an ever-present thin cloud cover in summer. This cover protects the grapes from the sun and avoids the risk of the grapes becoming overripe, which is vital to capturing flavors in the berries and resulting wines.

Some excellent wines come from the Upper Hunter, as you can see from this list of the top local producers:

- **Arrowfield Wines:** One of the largest wineries in the Hunter Valley, the focus at Arrowfield Wines is on Chardonnay, with Merlot and Verdelho starting to prove their value in the vineyard. The Arrowfield Chardonnay has rich fruit flavors with a hint of melon.

- **Rosemount Estate:** Much of the fame of the Upper Hunter can be attributed to this winery. This large operation has built its Hunter Valley wine fame around Chardonnay and Sémillon. One of Rosemount's most noted wines is the pricey Rosemount Roxburgh Chardonnay, which has won acclaim throughout the world. At the more affordable end of the price spectrum is the Premium Diamond Varietals range, and many people see the Rosemount Estate Chardonnay as the quintessential commercial Australian Chardonnay. Full of tropical fruit with melon characters, this wine is beautifully structured and has a very satisfying finish.

Another Rosemount label is Show Reserve. Some people consider the Rosemount Show Reserve Chardonnay to not be on the same level as the famous Roxburgh Chardonnay, yet it shows the most value for the money. Although not an inexpensive wine, the amount of fruit, alcohol, and oak is comparatively toned down in the Show Reserve Chardonnay so the wine can display a delicate, citrusy Chardonnay character, along with a balanced, midweight texture.

✔ **Yarraman Estate:** Originally Penfolds owned the vineyards, but today Yarraman Estate owns this oldest vineyard in the Upper Hunter with wines dating back to 1958. (The original Rosemount plantings of the 1860s were neglected; today's Rosemount vines were replanted in 1969.) Yarraman Estate Black Cypress Gewürztraminer has the intensity of flavor that can only come from grapes grown on vines more than 40 years old. Like many of the other wineries of the Upper Hunter, Yarraman Estate also produces excellent Shiraz, Chardonnay, and Sémillon wines.

# Exploring the Wine Bounty of Mudgee

After years of being referred to as "Mudgee mud," grapes and wine from the emerging Mudgee region of New South Wales are starting to turn some heads. In fact, many people now hold this region in higher regard than New South Wales's famed Hunter Valley (described earlier in this chapter).

European immigrants initially developed the wine region of Mudgee, like nearly all the grape-growing parts of Australia, as a vineyard area. Descendants of these pioneers and other interested wine growers carried on the tradition. During the 1970s and 1980s, the fruit from Mudgee was blended with grapes from elsewhere, so the region was robbed of public recognition. Gradually though, the area's worth is being noted by winemakers and the wine-drinking public, which isn't surprising because some very fine wines come from this beautiful part of New South Wales.

Overall, Mudgee is a warm region, but like so many of the other inland vineyard areas, the cool nights are a big plus because the wines are allowed to really rest overnight. This rest time prolongs the ripening, allowing the grape time to build up and intensify in flavors and to maintain its natural acidity.

Want to know more about the grape varieties Mudgee favors and the top producers of the region? Check out the sections that follow.

## Noting Mudgee's stylistic reds and shining whites

Mudgee is top heavy with red wine grapes, considering well over half the grapes grown in the region are Shiraz and Cabernet Sauvignon. The best red grape varieties found in Mudgee include

- **Shiraz:** The red grape leader in the area, Shiraz from Mudgee is full-bodied; its flavors, while exhibiting fruitiness, are more on the earthy side of the Shiraz style. Ordinarily, they're long lived in the bottle.

- **Cabernet Sauvignon:** You can expect a Mudgee Cabernet Sauvignon to be fairly full-bodied with plenty of blackberry, as well as a good, firm tannin structure. Like Mudgee's Shiraz, the Cabernet Sauvignon ages well.

- **Merlot:** Merlot may not be as big a player in Mudgee as Shiraz and Cabernet Sauvignon in terms of acres grown and tons processed, but this variety is one to watch in terms of potential. Merlot has the attraction of being a fruit-driven style of wine, which is increasingly appealing to consumers.

Mudgee's claim to fame, in terms of being fashionable, is that the one-time winemaker at Montrose winery, Carlo Corina, was the first to introduce the Italian red varieties to Australia. With the current boom in Sangiovese, Barbera, and Nebbiolo, Mudgee can indeed boast that it's a leader in alternative red wine styles. Although these grapes certainly don't dominate the region, they're nonetheless significant within the wonderful mixture of wines available from Australia.

Of course, red varieties aren't the only grapes grown in the Mudgee region. Two white grape varieties also perform strongly:

- **Chardonnay:** Many people attribute the boom in Chardonnay consumption to the wines that originated from Mudgee in the 1970s. At that time, large tracts of land were planted to this versatile variety, and the local climate suited the grape. The warm days followed by cool nights allow the Chardonnay grown in the Mudgee region to capture intense peach and fig flavors, along with a nicely balanced acidity.

- **Sémillon:** As the lesser-planted white variety, sitting at about 9 percent of the region's grape intake, the Sémillon made in Mudgee is quite different in style from that of the Hunter Valley. In Mudgee, Sémillon achieves a higher degree of ripeness due to the usually fine vintage conditions. So, instead of the wine being lean when young and needing time in the cellar to *fill out* (become a rounder, fuller tasting wine), Mudgee's Sémillons are appealing for immediate drinking.

## Checking out Mudgee's top wineries

Many of Mudgee's top wines are reds known for their dense flavors, as well as for their mineral and earthlike characters. This signature Mudgee style is attributed to the local soils.

Some of the best wines of the Mudgee region come from the following wineries:

Andrew Harris Vineyards
Botobolar Vineyard
Huntington Estate
Logan Wines
Lowe Family Wine Company

Orlando Wyndham Poet's
 Corner Wines
Seldom Seen Vineyards
Simon Gilbert Wines
Thistle Hill Vineyard

Mudgee wines are considered very reasonably priced, perhaps because of their long history of playing second fiddle to the wines of the more famous Hunter Valley. Most Mudgee wines cost less than $20, which certainly makes them a value for the money, especially considering the quality of some of the top red wines in the region.

# Shining the Spotlight on New South Wales's Lesser-Known Wine Regions

New South Wales is home to numerous smaller wine regions that offer a diverse mix of growing conditions, with high humidity in some areas and low humidity in others. (Humidity depends on the flow of air through the regions. For example, the higher-altitude regions are able to get a good breeze throughout the wine canopy, resulting in lower humidity.) Mild temperatures pervade some areas, and reasonably hot temperatures invade others.

Despite these differences, one factor these wine regions have in common is their relative youth. The migrant history so common in Australian grape-growing regions isn't a part of the development of these regions. Instead, Australians of Anglo-Saxon backgrounds, who have a passion for wine and see these areas as worthwhile for growing grapes, pioneered and continue to develop them.

The following sections look at the wines that come from some of the small but interesting wine regions throughout New South Wales.

## Discovering more than oranges in Orange

The Orange region of New South Wales is a mixed agricultural area. Beef cattle, sheep, and orchards dominate the landscape. The development of vineyards is a recent trend that seems likely to continue. The first vines were planted at Bloodwood in 1983, which is pretty recent in Australian terms. Since then, the region has expanded thanks to larger wine companies, such as Rosemount Estate, investing in the area. Although many of the companies that use Orange fruit don't actually run a winery in the area, the numbers of small *cellar doors* (tasting facilities) are increasing. More than 30 wine businesses are run in the region, but because many of them decide to have their wine made at other facilities, only a handful of these local wineries actually make their own wine.

Because of slow, even ripening of grapes in this mild, high-altitude, high-rainfall area, the varieties that do best are those that enjoy showing their fruity flavors. On the white grape front, varieties such as Sauvignon Blanc, Chardonnay, and Riesling benefit from the mild weather, which allows the berries to build up and maintain their flavor profile. As for the red varieties, both Shiraz and Cabernet Sauvignon can do well in Orange during the warmer years, as long as attention is given to the vines. Pinot Noir is the other red grape variety in this region, with plantings increasing gradually. Given that this variety enjoys a cool climate, it has a bright future in the Orange region.

Here's a short list of the top wines of the Orange region:

| | |
|---|---|
| Rosemount Estate Orange Vineyard Merlot | Cumulus Rolling Chardonnay |
| Bloodwork Riesling | Cumulus Climbing Merlot |
| Brangayne of Orange wines | Hungerford Hill Merlot |
| Canobolas-Smith Chardonnay | Hungerford Hill Shiraz |
| | Logan Sauvignon Blanc |

## Feeling the heat in Cowra

More than 35 vineyard operations in Cowra produce around 15,000 tons of fruit a year. By comparison, the Orange region (described in the preceding section) produces around 6,600 tons of fruit a year.

In terms of climate, the Cowra region is considered hot and dry, which means the vineyards need irrigation to be viable. As a result, the local waterways of the Lachlan River and Belbula River, as well as underground bores, are vital to the survival of the region's grapevines. Cool nights temper Cowra's warmth and allow the grapevines to rest, ensuring that the vines don't get overripe and lose their varietal characteristics.

The hot and dry conditions of the Cowra region produce super fruit-flavored grapes from the following white and red varieties:

Book V

Australia and New Zealand: Power-houses of the Southern Hemisphere

- ✔ **Chardonnay:** Chardonnay grapes ripen during the warm late summertime months, producing Chardonnay with intense fruit flavors and high sugar levels. Consequently, the Chardonnay wines from the Cowra region are characteristically full-bodied with plenty of texture and alcohol, typically around 13.5 percent or more.

- ✔ **Shiraz:** The second most favored grape variety in the Cowra region is Shiraz. Here, the fruit flavors are berrylike, with plums and blackberries dominating as opposed to peppery or earthy flavors.

Top wines from small producers in the Cowra region include Hamiltons Bluff Canowindra Grossi Unwooded Chardonnay and Windowrie Family Reserve Chardonnay.

Here's an interesting tidbit: Few actual wineries are located in Cowra. Instead, vineyards are commonly owned by out-of-town wine companies or grape growers that sell their fruit to wineries in other regions. This business approach doesn't mean Cowra's fruit is inferior to that of other regions — quite the opposite in fact. Hunter Valley wineries buy the fruit and either use it to make a specific single label, such as Rothbury Estate Cowra Chardonnay, or to bolster bad years in their own region. (Wines of interest from wineries outside of Cowra that use grapes grown in the region are Hungerford Hill Cowra Chardonnay and Richmond Grove Cowra Vineyard Verdelho.)

# Growing grapes for others in Tumbarumba

Tumbarumba wines aren't made in the Tumbarumba region. Although the fruit is grown here, it's shipped to wineries outside of the region for the *vinification* (winemaking) process. (The two main wineries that benefit from Tumbarumba's grapes are the Charles Sturt Winery in Wagga Wagga and Hungerford Hill in the Hunter Valley.) Regardless, Tumbarumba surely is one of the most beautiful small winegrowing parts of Australia.

Situated at the foothills of the Australian Alps, the Tumbarumba wine region isn't that far from the majestic Mount Kosciusko, Australia's highest mountain. The region has a cool climate (after all, it does sit about 2,250 feet above sea level). But the region isn't vines, vines, and more vines, as far as you can see. Instead, because some parts of the area aren't suited to vines, pockets of vineyards tumble around here and there. Growing grapes in the Tumbarumba region means careful site selection must be a top priority to ensure that the vines are able to maximize sunshine. As a result, you can find vines on the undulating hill, mostly facing north or east to expose them to the sun's rays.

Three specific grape varieties thrive in the cool conditions of the Tumbarumba region, which enable the grapes to ripen so the fruit flavors develop intensity at lower sugar ripeness while simultaneously allowing the grapes to maintain their acidity:

- ✔ **Chardonnay:** Typical Chardonnay is delicate in flavor and weight. Fruits are in the citrus and melon spectrum with some nutty influences from the slow grape ripening.

- ✔ **Pinot Noir:** Table wine and Tumbarumba get along well, too. The cool climate of the region allows the Pinot Noir (pee-noh nwahr) fruit to mature without the occasional superhot day that so often plagues grape growers in other Pinot Noir regions (such as Victoria's Yarra Valley and Mornington Peninsula; flip to Chapter 3 in Book V for details on these wine regions).

  Pinot Noir is sought after from Tumbarumba for sparkling wine, too, because of its delicate flavors and good acidity.

- ✔ **Sauvignon Blanc:** The signature flavor that these grape growers get for their Sauvignon Blanc (saw-vee-nyon blahnk) is gooseberry along with a zesty acidity.

The lack of wineries in the Tumbarumba region means that very few wines actually acknowledge the region on the label. This lack of acknowledgment is due in part to the fact that many of the region's grapes (more than 70 percent, actually) are used to make sparkling wines, which are typically a blend of wines. If you want to find wines that acknowledge the Tumbarumba region on the label, look for Chalkers Crossing Tumbarumba Pinot Noir and Hungerford Hill Tumbarumba series.

Sparkling wines that incorporate the fruit from Tumbarumba are the Charles Sturt Chardonnay Sparkling and the Seppelt Salinger Sparkling.

## *Hightailing it to the Hilltops*

An emerging wine region in the southern portion of the New South Wales zone is Hilltops. Centered around the town of Young, the Hilltops region is about 250 miles west of Sydney. In terms of size, the region is small, with only five wineries in the area. The biggest landowner is McWilliam's with its Barwang property. The fruit, other than what goes to McWilliam's, is mostly sold to the larger winemaking companies (Southcorp Wines and the Hardy Wine Company).

The Hilltops winegrowing region has a cool to mild temperature. Rainfall here is uniform during the growing season. Situated at around 1,440 to 1,980 feet above sea level, this altitude gives the region a touch of coolness that tempers the warm summer days, allowing gradual ripening of the grapes.

The best grape varieties from the Hilltops region, where the red soils tend to give these grapes depth of flavor and a strong berry aroma, are Cabernet Sauvignon and Shiraz.

Wines to note in the region include McWilliam's Barwang Merlot, Chalkers Crossing Hilltops Cabernet Sauvignon, and Chalkers Crossing Hilltops Shiraz.

## Uncorking in Canberra

Most of the wineries in the Canberra District are geographically located in New South Wales. Winters in the Canberra District are bitterly cold, but the weather always warms up come summer. During spring, many of the vineyard sites in this wine region are prone to frost, so the newer planting sites were made to take the need for springtime sun into account. As soon as the cold winter is finished, the rainfall totals begin to diminish, and the vines can't survive the region's hot dry summers without supplementary irrigation coming from surface dams or bore water.

The tempering of these warm days comes from the use of higher-altitude plantings that allow the vines some respite from the warm days and give that all-important nighttime cooling. Being a little elevated means that the potentially damaging cold air drains down to the valleys and away from the vineyards.

The dominant varieties across the Canberra District that make up around 50 percent of the annual crush are

- Cabernet Sauvignon
- Chardonnay
- Shiraz

Other significant plantings are Merlot and Riesling. Additionally, a few outsider varieties manage to do well in these climatic conditions, causing wine lovers to take note as a result; these varieties include Pinot Noir, Riesling, and Viognier.

One of the largest winegrowing ventures in the region is by the Hardy Wine Company (formerly BRL Hardy, before the merger with the U.S.-based Constellation Brands). The company's vineyard development includes planting of 20 hectares of wines and establishing a large winery. So far, the outstanding wines from this venture are Kamberra Chardonnay and Kamberra Meeting Place Pinot Noir/Chardonnay Sparkling Wine.

The main group of wineries of the Canberra District is in the Murrumbateman area. Notable producers are Clonakilla Winery, Dookhuna Estate, Helm's Wines, and Jerk Creek Wines.

# Chapter 3

# Taking In the Diverse Range of Wines from Victoria and Tasmania

From the heat of Rutherglen in the north to the cool maritime region of the Mornington Penninsula, Victoria is quite a diverse state. Not surprisingly, it produces a huge diversity of wine styles. Of course, if you know what you like — particularly if you enjoy a good Pinot Noir or Riesling — and just want to stick with that, you may be more interested in taking a jaunt across Bass Strait to Victoria's neighboring island state, Tasmania. Regardless of your preference, this chapter clues you in to the magic of these two states' wines.

## The Yarra Valley: First in the Region

Victoria's first grape-growing region was the Yarra Valley, located less than an hour's drive east of Melbourne. The men behind these first vineyards were Swiss immigrants, one of whom was Guillaume de Pury, whose family still operates and makes wine at the original Yeringberg property — albeit with modern-day improvements. Today, with significant investment from both Australian and international companies, the Yarra is no longer made up of the odd small, owner-operated winery. Rather, the region is a significant player in both the quantity and quality of the Australian wine scene.

The Yarra Valley region borders the towns of Emerald and Cockatoo to the south; the Plenty River marks the western boundary; and the Yarra River, which begins in the region's east, flows through its center on the way to Melbourne. Most producers are located around the towns of Coldstream,

Healesville, and Yarra Glen, and the historic Lilydale. The Valley is surrounded by the Great Dividing Range to the east, the Plenty Ranges to the west, and the Dandenongs to the south.

The Yarra Valley's cool climate produces a certain style of wine (in fact, it creates some of the best cool-climate wines in all of Australia). The flavors of the grape varieties planted in the Yarra are considered mostly at the delicate or elegant end of the spectrum. Early-ripening grape varieties such as Pinot Noir and Chardonnay are picked around mid-March, along with Sauvignon Blanc. The late-ripening varieties of Cabernet Sauvignon and Petit Verdot are the last to be picked — often not until late April on many sites throughout the Valley.

The timing of the ripening depends on the vineyard site, and the Yarra Valley is quite a diverse area. Properties on the Valley's floor are typically warmer than those perched atop the Valley, which means they can ripen their fruit fully in nearly every season. The higher-altitude vineyards are naturally cooler, so their fruit ripens later in the season.

The following sections break down the best types of Yarra Valley wines to look for and offer recommendations for some top producers and wines from two specific regions of the Valley.

## *Reviewing Yarra's typical wine styles*

The most popular grape varieties planted in the Yarra Valley are Pinot Noir, Chardonnay, Cabernet Sauvignon, Sauvignon Blanc, and, increasingly, Shiraz. Alongside these mainstays, you can also find varieties such as the little-known Roussanne and Marsanne. The attractive and fruity white variety Gewürztraminer is also sprinkled across the Valley, as is the newly fashionable Pinot Gris. All in all, the Yarra is becoming quite a diverse wine region!

Following are some details on the styles of Yarra Valley wines created from the region's diverse range of grape varieties:

- ✔ **Consistent Chardonnay:** Chardonnay (shar-dohn-nay) from cool-climate regions is a seriously good drink (and one of the Yarra's most delicious wines). Unlike many Australian Chardonnays, those from the Yarra typically age very well. As a young wine, they may appear a little subdued, but with time — say three to six years — they turn into complex yet softly sophisticated wines.

- ✔ **Stylish Sauvignon Blanc:** An increasingly popular choice both with the public and among growers, the Yarra's Sauvignon Blanc (saw-vee-nyon blahnk) is better made today than when it was introduced to the area

10 to 15 years ago. Back then it was quite herbaceous, reminiscent of crushed leaves and green grass, whereas today the leafy tag is cone and the variety is much more fruit flavored, with tropical fruits in particular more apparent on your taste buds. This shift in style has mostly been due to the increase in knowledge of how to grow the Sauvignon Blanc grape properly.

✔ **Pleasurable Pinot Noir:** The Yarra's Pinot Noir (pee-noh nwahr) has a definite personality of its own — and interestingly, many of those early producers are still making some of today's best Pinot Noir. None of the wines is a blockbuster in terms of tannin and big fruit, but they all show a gorgeous and feminine character that's always intriguing.

✔ **Classy Cabernet:** The Yarra's Cabernets (cab-er-nay) have always been regarded as some of Australia's finest. Given the flavors and tannin that build up from the long ripening facilitated by the cool climate, you can expect Yarra Cabernets to be of subtle blackberry and cigar box character. The tannin is apparent, but not so gritty that your mouth feels like it has been attacked with sandpaper. Yarra Cabernets are delicious whether a few years old or stored in your wine cellar for eight to ten years. (Head to Chapter 8 in Book I for tips on properly storing your wine.)

✔ **Sassy sparkling:** A relatively new venture in the Yarra is the production of sublime sparkling wines. After the injection of big dollars (okay, millions of them) into the region by Moët & Chandon back in 1986, the Yarra stamped its claim on these wines. Several years later, another Champagne company, Devaux, invested many more French francs. The Yarra had already proved itself in terms of the required sparkling wine grape varieties, namely Pinot Noir and Chardonnay. Some Pinot Meunier was also planted in 1986, establishing a little bit of France in Victoria. Today, the Yarra's sparkling wines are rated among some of the best made in the world (naturally, they're also admired by the French).

## *Listing top picks from Coldstream*

Names of towns are funny things. When the Australian Bureau of Meteorology set up a weather station in Coldstream and started including it in the forecast region, it became apparent how appropriate the town's name is. Coldstream was frequently the coldest place in the Melbourne forecast region — usually by several degrees. Some mornings were just 25 degrees Fahrenheit! As a result, the wineries around this town often experience very cold nighttime conditions.

Here's a list of the top wines in the Coldstream region:

Book V

Australia and New Zealand: Power-houses of the Southern Hemisphere

Coldstream Hills Reserve Pinot Noir

Coldstream Hills Reserve Chardonnay

Coldstream Hills Reserve Cabernet

Domaine Chandon Blanc de Blancs

Chandon Cuvée Riche

Chandon Vintage Brut

Chandon Vintage Brut Rosé

Chandon Z*D Vintage Blanc de Blancs

Dominique Portlet Yarra Valley Cabernet Sauvignon

Dominique Portlet Sauvignon Blanc

Giant Steps Pinot Noir

Giant Steps Chardonnay

Yeringberg Cabernet Merlot

Mount Mary Triolet

Mount Mary Quintet

Oakridge Yarra Valley 864 Cabernet Sauvignon

St Huberts Roussanne

Sticks Pinot Noir

Punt Road Pinot Gris

Punt Road Cabernet Sauvignon

## *Presenting choice wines from Yarra Glen*

Many of the vineyards around Yarra Glen sit pretty low on the Yarra Valley floor, so if any vineyards are going to be frosted or flooded, these are the most likely candidates. However, this location also makes the Yarra Glen vineyards some of the warmer sites in the Yarra Valley, which means you can expect riper, richer-flavored wines from this area.

Some of the best wines from the Yarra Glen region of the Yarra Valley are

De Bortoli Yarra Valley Pinot Noir

De Bortoli Yarra Valley Chardonnay

De Bortoli Yarra Valley Cabernet Sauvignon

De Bortoli Gulf Station Pinot Noir

De Bortoli Gulf Station Sangiovese

De Bortoli Windy Peak Chardonnay

Fergusson Benjamyn Cabernet Sauvignon

TarraWarra Estate Chardonnay

TarraWarra Estate Pinot Noir

Yering Station Pinot Noir

Yering Station Rosé

Yering Station Reserve Pinot Noir

Yering Station Shiraz Viognier

Yering Station Viognier

Yarra Bank Sparkling

## The fun of the Grape Grazing Festival

The Yarra Valley's Grape Grazing Festival is an annual tradition. The idea is to graze your way around the Valley during grape-picking season. Each of the participating wineries teams up with a restaurant — often some of Melbourne's best — and you're able to choose a glass of wine with a suitably matched, entrée-sized plate of food. Then all you need to do is sit under a tree and enjoy! For more info, check out www.grapegrazing.com.au.

# Victoria's Wine-Diverse Heartland: The Central Zone

Australia's Central Victorian wine zone is located roughly to the northeast of the city of Melbourne. It includes the regions of Goulburn Valley (and its subregion, Nagambie Lakes), Bendigo, Heathcote, and Strathbogie Ranges (part of the Central Victorian Mountain District).

Although each Central Victorian region has a unique climate, overall the regions are quite dry, receiving rainfall primarily during winter (June to August) and spring (September to November). As a result, excessive leaf growth isn't a problem, and the risk of disease is lower than in areas that receive high rainfall and/or have too much foliage, which prevents air from circulating easily.

All the regions have well-structured soils that allow free drainage of water down into a clay base, which enables the roots of the grapevines to access the water for use during the dry summer months. Temperature-wise, Central Victoria experiences warm days followed by cool nights. These conditions allow for the all-important slow ripening of the berries for a gradual buildup in the intensity of fruit flavors.

Read on to familiarize yourself with the main types of wine that hail from the Central Victorian wine zone and get up close and personal with the area's different regions.

## Sipping the wines of Central Victoria

Red wine is the star performer in Central Victoria, given the area's mild to warm temperatures. Shiraz is a strong performer, as is Cabernet Sauvignon. In the cooler Strathbogie vineyards, Pinot Noir does well and produces many a fine base for sparkling wines.

Following are the general characteristics of Central Victoria's red wines, plus some recommended reds (organized by region):

- **Shiraz:** Arguably some of Victoria's best Shiraz (shee-rahz) is grown in the central part of the state. The regions that do Shiraz with style include

  - **Goulburn Valley:** Long-living Shiraz is grown in this region of Central Victoria. The fruit is full of rich, ripe plum flavors and is often blended with the sweet Grenache or the savory Mourvèdre grapes. The Mitchelton Crescent blend is definitely one to look for.

- **Bendigo:** You won't be disappointed by the amount of flavor that you get per sip from Bendigo reds, such as the Sutton Grange wines. These wines are typically spicy with a savory background that keeps the fruitiness of the wines in check.

- **Heathcote:** If you're after a blockbuster Shiraz, the Heathcote reds may be what you're looking for. Full of flavor with a backbone of tannin, they often have a high alcohol content. Case in point: The Jasper Hill Shiraz has more than 15 percent alcohol!

✔ **Cabernet Sauvignon:** Often unfairly forgotten thanks to the fame of Central Victoria's Shiraz wines, the local Cabernet Sauvignons (cab-er-nay saw-vee-nyons) are full-bodied and ripe, showing blackberry and cedar flavors with an occasional touch of mint. Although they don't have the reputation of South Australia's Coonawarra Cabernets (which you can read about in Chapter 4 of Book V), the richness is a characteristic that many welcome. A few of the best Central Victorian Cabernet Sauvignons come from the Red Edge winery.

Of course, red wine isn't the only interest of Central Victorian producers. The aromatic white grape varieties such as Sauvignon Blanc, Riesling, and Gewürztraminer all show their strengths in the cooler regions of these areas, and the results are some very stylish wines. By comparison, Chardonnay produced in the area is a little ho-hum, except when the grapes are used for sparkling wine.

White wines to look out for come from these regions of Central Victoria:

✔ **Strathbogie Ranges:** The cool, almost cold nights make this area perfect for capturing and maintaining a fruity, acidic, zingy Riesling (_reese_-ling). The Alexander Park wines, in particular, show these traits.

✔ **Central Victorian Mountain District:** The prize for the most delicious Gewürztraminers (geh-_vairtz_-trah-mee-ners) in the area goes to Delatite Winery. Its Gewürztraminer has a charming, lychee-like fruit and a soft, textured palate.

The wonderful white varieties from Southern France — Marsanne, Roussanne, and Viognier — have moved beyond being fashionably new and are now acclaimed as serious wines. They're particularly at home planted in these warm regions:

✔ **Goulburn Valley:** These varieties have really stamped a name for themselves in this region, and producer Mitchelton has been at the forefront, blending the varieties to make its Airstrip blend. Also look out for the age-worthy Marsanne (mar-sahn) that Tahbilk has been making for years — this inexpensive wine has fantastic cellaring potential.

✔ **Heathcote:** The Viognier (vee-oh-nyay) in this region has seen itself as that added extra. Added to Shiraz at a proportion of something less than 10 percent, Viognier gives the Shiraz a certain fullness and subtlety throughout the mid-palate. Heathcote Winery was one of the pioneers of this style in Australia.

## *Introducing Goulburn Valley and its standout producers*

The main focus for quality wine in the Goulburn Valley region centers on the Nagambie Lakes subregion, located just north of Seymour and about 100 miles north of Melbourne. The wines of this Central Victorian region are known for their rich, intense weight and fruit flavors. When it comes to the weather, the Goulburn River and Nagambie Lakes temper the climates of nearby vineyards by taking the edge off of hot summer days, allowing the grapes to ripen just a little more slowly, thereby ensuring the grapes concentrate their fruit flavor before harvest.

Tahbilk Winery planted the first vines in Goulburn Valley way back in 1860, although most of the planting in this region has been done over the past 30 years. Today, Goulburn Valley is home to 19 wineries, contributing to a vineyard area of 700 hectares — statistics that are growing every year.

Despite being the oldest winery in the area, Tahbilk hasn't stayed still. Its winemaking is up to date, and both the Tahbilk Marsanne and Tahbilk Shiraz are worth buying. In fact, go ahead and buy several — some for the cellar and a couple to drink now because the Marsanne changes from having strong lemon and grapefruit flavors when young to having honey and toasty flavors (along with rich texture) after five or more years in the bottle.

In keeping with a good work ethic, Tahbilk chief executive Alister Purbrick has his own smaller winery, Dalfarras. The Tahbilk value-for-money theme continues here with the spicy and cinnamon-like Dalfarras Shiraz and Dalfarras Sauvignon Blanc, a wine that's reminiscent of lemon zest and fresh herbs. Both wines are particularly good.

Although the Mitchelton winery has always had a high reputation for its Shiraz and Blackwood Park Riesling, the so-called new varieties hailing from France's Rhône Valley have done much for this winery's success. The Airstrip white (consisting of Marsanne, Roussanne, and Viognier) and Crescent red (Shiraz, Mourvèdre, and Grenache) really back up the locals' conviction of the suitability of these grape varieties to this warm, dry climate.

Within the quite large portfolio of wines made at Mitchelton is the Preece line, a reputable, inexpensive choice at a restaurant, cafe, or party.

Although now part of the Dromana Estate consortium, David Traeger Wines is still run as a small affair. The label has paved the way for Verdelho, every year making a wine that seems to burst with sunshine. The David Traeger Shiraz is also very good; it shows the region's famous pepper and spice.

## Tasting the best of Bendigo

Bendigo has four major wine regions: to the southeast around Harcourt; further north around the city of Bendigo; to the northwest around Bridgewater, Inglewood, and Kingower; and to the southwest around Maryborough. Most wineries in the area are small, and nearly all are family owned and operated.

Bendigo's climate is warm, almost hot, in the summertime. The vineyards situated on low-lying country make the most of the heat for ripening their grapes, whereas the vineyards located on the hills use the altitude to develop their style. The granitic soil of the region is tough and not very fertile, so grape yields are low per vine and fruit intensity is high.

Perfumed Shiraz and well-structured Cabernet Sauvignon are just two of the highlights of Bendigo wines. Here are some producers to look for:

Balgownie Estate
Blackjack Vineyards
Chateau Leamon

Passing Clouds
Sutton Grange
Water Wheel Vineyards

## Hunting down quality in Heathcote

The Heathcote region's boundary runs between the Bendigo and Goulburn Valley regions on the northern side of Victoria's Great Dividing Range. Rainfall is low, although what does fall is usually evenly spread across the region. Luckily for the local grape growers, Heathcote's red soil retains water, so during dry spells, the vines' roots can still find water deep down in the soil. (Interesting side note: The top local producers don't opt for irrigation, so their vines produce less fruit and smaller berries — which leads to expensive, more concentrated wines.)

Perhaps the more famous Heathcote wines are those from Wild Duck Creek. This quiet grape grower made news with a wine called Wild Duck Creek Duck Muck, which reached huge price heights after rave reviews from American critics. This wine isn't for lovers of elegant wine styles; it's incredibly intensely flavored and dense in texture, with a huge mouthful of blackberry, chocolate, and licorice.

Other producers to look for include Jasper Hill Vineyard, Heathcote Winery, and Red Edge.

## Producing a variety of varietals in the Central Victorian Mountain District

The Central Victorian Mountain District is quite diverse, spreading east from Seymour across to Mansfield. Around the towns of Seymour and Yea, the temperatures are warm, but they cool down as you move eastward and enter the town of Mansfield, at the foothills of the Great Dividing Range. Here, the winter delivers frosts and the occasional snowfall; in spring, the growing season is slow to get going because the days are still cold. Consequently, ripening occurs much later in autumn, so the grape growers can take advantage of the cold nights.

The Cheviot Bridge Wine Company is a commercial-sized operation in the Central Victorian Mountain District's Yea Valley. It offers three tiers of wine: the Cheviot Bridge Yea Valley range, which is the most expensive; the medium-priced CB range; and the inexpensive Kissing Bridge range. The CB range offers the best value for quality wines, particularly its Shiraz.

As a test of the potential of this area, Murrundindi Vineyard was planted back in 1984. To date, the citrusy and melony Murrundindi Chardonnay proves to be the producer's best wine.

For wines that show loads of full, ripe, fruity flavors, look for Merlot and Shiraz from Plunkett Wines, a winery that's slowly establishing itself as a significant winemaker in the Strathbogie Ranges. Also, look out for Alexander Park Riesling, a fruity bombshell from Dominion Wines.

If you're a fan of white wines, get to know Delatite Vineyard, located near the town of Mansfield. Its aromatic whites, especially the lychee and jasmine Dead Man's Hill Gewürztraminer and the lime and lemon VS Riesling are without a doubt among Australia's finest.

# Traveling to Pyrenees in Victoria's Wild, Wild West

The western part of Victoria makes up quite a large parcel of land. Except for Henty (a tiny winemaking area along the southwestern Victoria coast), no sea is in sight within western Victoria, so the climate is temperate. The region's topography, however, is quite varied. Some vineyards are located on the warm, flat plains; others have opted for higher elevations with cooler microclimates.

The Pyrenees region is about 110 miles from Melbourne, and the area's 16 wineries surround the small townships of Avoca and Moonembel. Most of the vineyards are on flat land at the foot of the Pyrenees Ranges. They tend to experience cool nights that slow down the grapes' ripening after the day's warmth. The soil is gravelly with some clay underneath, which allows rain to drain freely to the clay where the moisture can be retained for use in dry months.

Although this Western Victoria wine region doesn't really resemble the French Pyrenees region (some of the area's early settlers thought it did though, hence the name), plenty of Gallic involvement has occurred here over the years. Taltarni Vineyard was helmed by Frenchman Dominque Portet for many years, and until recently, the Remy Cointreau Group owned Blue Pyrenees Estate, formally known as Château Remy.

Some of the best Shiraz in Australia comes from the Pyrenees region, with Dalwhinnie and Warrenmang Vineyard leading the charge. Both wineries produce excellent standard-release Shiraz, but their special-release wines, such as the Dalwhinnie Eagle Shiraz and the Warrenmang Black Puma Shiraz, are really outstanding. Both wines have a full fruit style but with a backbone of restraint that keeps your interest in the Shiraz for more than one glass.

Dalwhinnie also makes a fine Chardonnay. Over at Warrenmang, the delightful but inexpensive Vinello — a blend of the Italian grape varieties Sangiovese, Barbera, Nebbiolo, and Dolcetto — is a great food wine.

Other top pours of the region come from the following producers:

Blue Pyrenees Estate
Taltarni Vineyards
Mount Avoca Vineyard
Redbank Winery
Summerfield Wines

# Navigating Your Way through Northeast Victoria

Northeast Victoria is centered on the town of Rutherglen, just south of the New South Wales border. The region is steeped in a proud viticultural history. Many of the local wineries date from the 1850s, and generations of winemakers have passed through their gates, passing down their winemaking knowledge from father to son (and the occasional daughter). Northeast Victoria has varied topography and enjoys a range of climates.

Like many wine regions across Australia, the number of hectares of wines planted in the northeast portion of Victoria seems to explode each year. An exciting aspect to this growth is the movement away from the obvious grape choices. Instead of just planting more of the varieties that the rest of Australia grows, the winemakers of Northeast Victoria explore the Italian varieties, increase their experimentation with the Spanish Tempranillo grape on warmer sites, and lean toward such lesser-known French varieties as Gamay on the cooler sites.

Today the five winemaking zones of Northeast Victoria — the Alpine Valley, Beechworth, Glenrowan, King Valley, and Rutherglen — are home to more than 60 wineries, ranging from tiny family affairs to some of Australia's huge wine companies. The sections that follow delve into detail about the grape varieties grown in Northeast Victoria, as well as the region's prominent winemaking zones and the top wines that come from them.

## Celebrating Northeast Victoria's specialties

Winemakers in Northeast Victoria are venturing where most of their Australian fellows haven't dared: nontraditional grape varieties. (Of course, they still make the standard Shiraz and Cabernet Sauvignon too.) The next few sections describe some of the best-known and most popular grape varieties grown in this diverse wine region.

### Fortified wines, Tokay and Muscat

The famous fortified wines known as Tokay and Muscat are made only in Australia. The grape varieties needed to make these wines are Muscadelle for Tokay and Muscat Blanc à Petit Grains (also known in Australia as Brown Muscat) for Muscat.

The grapes that produce these fortified wines need warmth to bring them to their full ripeness, and the warm climate around Rutherglen provides just that. For these types of wines, the grapes need to be super-ripe — and that means staying on the vine a lot longer than usual. Consequently, the weather conditions for the last stage in ripening are vital — little or no rain and lots of warmth.

### Immigrant Italian varieties

The King Valley was originally an area of tobacco plantations established by the predominantly Italian immigrant population. Over time, however, the tobacco planting made way for vineyards, and the tobacco-drying sheds transformed into wineries.

Many second- and third-generation Italian immigrants established wineries in the King Valley region in such towns as Whitfield and Cheshunt. Most of today's King Valley winemakers started off as grape growers though, planting their vineyards and selling their fruit to wine producers. Now, by producing their own wines, they keep a winemaking focus on the region.

Interestingly, by planting the varieties so well-known by their ancestors, the Italian winemakers of King Valley have carved out quite a niche for themselves. The Italian red grapes of Sangiovese, Barbera, and Nebbiolo, and the white grapes of Arneis and Pinot Grigio are putting the region on the winemaking map. And, in true Australian style (which celebrates diversity), the King Valley also produces some fine Chardonnay, Merlot, and Shiraz.

### Traditional red varieties that like their sunshine

Northeast Victoria produces excellent full-bodied red wines, primarily because of its climate. During the ripening season, temperatures get quite high, and the air is usually dry. The grapes can ripen with high levels of sugar that, in turn, produce high levels of alcohol in the finished wine.

During fermentation, yeast uses the sugar in the grapes to produce alcohol, which means the greater the amount of sugar, the higher the level of alcohol.

The sunny disposition of the region helps the following red grape varieties flourish:

- **Durif:** The region's most famous red variety, this little-known French grape is incredibly dense in flavor. However, the tannins are aggressive and quite unpleasant if not handled well during the winemaking process.
- **Shiraz:** Rutherglen Shiraz is quite different in style from that of, say, the cooler Victorian vineyards around the Yarra Valley and the sweet-fruited Shiraz of South Australia (described in Chapter 4 of Book V). Rutherglen Shiraz is earthier in character, displaying the savory style of the grape it's made from.
- **Cabernet Sauvignon:** These reds seem to lose their typical flavors in this warm climate, resulting in an excellent wine that's more like a dry red wine than a typical Cabernet Sauvignon.

## Rutherglen, land of full-bodied reds and fortified wines

The Rutherglen region boasts 19 wineries and is the warmest part of Northeast Victoria. Not surprisingly, some pretty powerful reds, as well as the famous fortified wines, come from this region. Even though the Rutherglen wines being produced these days have become more refined and more sophisticated, they can never be accused of being shy and are still a memorable wine experience.

Here are some of the outstanding wines of the Rutherglen region:

R.L. Buller & Son Shiraz/Grenache/Mourvèdre
R.L. Buller & Son Shiraz/Cabernet
Stanton & Killeen Durif

Chambers Rosewood Vineyards' wine is literally made in a tin shed, in big old barrels that slowly age the world-famous and simply stunning fortified wines. In fact, the wines from here are so good that famed American wine critic Robert Parker has given Chambers's fortified wines the perfect score of 100 — something rarely achieved by any wine in the world.

## King Valley, from the plains to the hills

The great thing about the King Valley is that the surrounding hills allow for a varying climate that gives each vineyard its own personality. For example, some pockets are warmer than others because they're protected from the Alpine winds. Other vineyards flourish in the Alpine breezes that help keep the incidence of disease down by allowing air to circulate through the vine leaf canopy.

Among the standout wineries in the King Valley are the following:

Boggy Creek Vineyards
Brown Brothers
Chrismont Wines

Dal Zotto Estate Wines
John Gehrig Wines
Miranda King Valley Winery

Pizzini Wines initially grew grapes for sale to other wineries, like many of the King Valley's other winemakers. Although these sales are still part of the Pizzini family's income today, so is winemaking. Particularly good red wines from Pizzini are the savory Pizzini Sangiovese and the rose-petal-like Pizzini Nebbiolo. If you enjoy white wine, you have to try the honeyed and floral Pizzini Arneis and the richly flavored Pizzini Verduzzo.

## Alpine Valley, going up and cooling down

The principal towns found in the Alpine Valley are Myrtleford and Bright, southeast of Wangaratta. The Ovens River flows through both towns, and the Kiewa River flows to the north. The smaller Buckland and Buffalo Rivers also water the region.

The higher altitude of the Alpine Valley (most vineyards here are at least 820 feet above sea level) means that the region is distinctly cool. The cold winds that blow straight off the Victorian snowfields also influence the low tempera- tures. Consequently, the ripening of the grapes is slow, which allows them to mature gradually and concentrate their fruity flavors. Generally, the ripening months from late March to May are fairly dry, which means disease isn't a problem at this time.

The most planted grape varieties in the Alpine Valley are Merlot, Cabernet Sauvignon, and Chardonnay, although increasing amounts of Pinot Noir are being planted as well. As of mid-2003, eight wineries had been established in the region.

Two of the Alpine Valley's most impressive wineries are Boynton's Winery and Gapsted Wines.

# Heating Up: The Northwest Region

Northwest Victoria is bordered by New South Wales to the north and South Australia to the west; the city of Mildura sits almost on the New South Wales border. In this region, cast tracts of flat land are planted to vines that rely on water from the nearby Murray River for their survival. It's a dry, almost arid part of the country.

The number of wineries in this region may not be large, but the wineries themselves are large — huge, in fact. If the Lindemans Karadoc winery was the first winery you ever saw, any illusions you may have had that wine-making and grape-growing are romantic activities carried out by happy peasants who regularly prance around on grapes at wine festivals would be shattered. The Lindemans Karadoc complex is reminiscent of an oil refinery. The sheer size of the tanks is mind-boggling, and the factory (as many people call it) is so vast that you practically need a compass and map to find your way around. However, the loss of romance is compensated for by the fact that the wine is made very cost effectively and is the type of wine most commonly consumed by the wine-drinking public.

## Sampling the best from the northwest

Most of Northwest Victoria experiences large variations between day and night temperatures. A day that reaches between 90 and 100 degrees Fahrenheit will cool into a 70-degree Fahrenheit night (which admittedly is still pretty hot). The weather is also dry, especially during the growing season, which means that humidity and, consequently, the risk of fungal disease is low. And while the roots of the vines are getting water through irrigation, the foliage remains dry, thus reducing the need for fungicide sprays — another benefit.

The following list introduces you to Northwest Victoria's top grape varieties:

- ✔ **Chardonnay:** The most favored grape variety in Northwest Victoria is Chardonnay, a versatile grape that can be grown quite cheaply and whose wine can be made cost effectively on a large scale. As a variety, a Chardonnay vine can happily produce a lot of bunches of grapes and still maintain good fruit flavors. Although the grapes may not end up making the world's most complex wine, the end product is good-quality wine. The standout example is the ever-popular Lindemans Bin 65.

- ✔ **Other whites:** The area is also well-known for its multipurpose grapes, Sultana, Colombard, and Muscat Gordo Blanco. These varieties are rarely used to make wines on their own; typically they're used to bulk up the commercial labels sold at rock-bottom prices.

  The wine made from Colombard and Sultana grapes is pretty bland, allowing it to blend with another wine without altering the latter's flavors too much. Muscat Gordo Blanco is very fruity, so it can boost the flavors in a wine that might be lacking.

- ✔ **Shiraz:** Like Chardonnay, Shiraz is a very significant grape variety in the northwest, and it can make pretty decent wine even when lots of grapes are growing per vine. Shiraz grapes love the sunshine, which allows them to ripen into a rich, full-flavored wine.

- ✔ **Other reds:** The other varieties that thrive here are Cabernet Sauvignon and, increasingly, Merlot, Grenache, and Tarrango. Rising crop levels start to affect the true varietal flavor of Cabernet Sauvignon and Merlot, yet they're both still able to make a quality red wine.

## *Looking out over the Murray-Darling region's landscape of vines*

The landscape of the Murray-Darling region (the main winemaking area in Northwest Victoria) is filled with acre after acre of vines, stretching as far as the eye can see. More than 53,000 acres of wine grapes are planted in the Murray-Darling region.

Some of the wineries benefiting from all those grapes include the following:

Deakin Estate

Lindemans Karadoc Winery

Mildara Wines

Robinvale Organic Wines

Trenthan Estate

Zilzie Wines

# Down by the Sea: The Mornington Peninsula

The Mornington Peninsula is a bootlike tract of land (reminiscent of Italy in its shape) that flows south from the city of Melbourne. Surrounded by Port Phillip Bay, Bass Straight, and Western Port Bay, the region's climate is 100-percent maritime.

Like the other cool climates in Australia, the very fact that the weather may be cool during the ripening season limits the grape varieties that do well here. So if a winemaker on the Mornington Peninsula is going to have any chance of producing a really good wine, the grape grower must choose early-ripening varieties. Choice of vineyard site is also paramount to producing top-quality wines in coastal areas.

Starting just past the urban sprawl of the city of Melbourne in a suburb called Mount Aliza, the Mornington region continues southward to include the areas known as Dromana, Main Ridge, Red Hill South, Merricks, and Moorooduc.

Although the Mornington Peninsula isn't Mount Everest, it does have some vineyards on higher altitudes, especially around the Red Hill. This environment makes for lower temperatures, which means slower ripening of the grapes. For this reason, the aspects of the vineyards in this area face north to get plenty of northern sun. (In the Southern Hemisphere, the sun moves from east to west, via the north.) If the vineyard faced south, it'd have no hope of producing fully ripened grapes.

The Mornington Peninsula has earned its reputation as a top wine region based largely on Chardonnay and Pinot Noir wines. Some movement into other varietals, however, has occurred, namely the white wines of Pinot Gris and Viognier and, on the warmer sites, the red wine of Shiraz.

Without doubt, a few grape growers can make a decent Cabernet Sauvignon on the Mornington Peninsula. Many grape growers give the variety a go but most have to graft it onto one of the darlings of the Peninsula: Pinot Noir, Chardonnay, or Pinot Gris.

The following sections take you to some of the Mornington Peninsula's wine regions and provide recommendations of some wines to try.

## Traveling down into Dromana

The Dromana area is one of the warmest on the Mornington Peninsula. Vineyards established here are on flat ground, pretty much at sea level. The

Book V

Australia
and New
Zealand:
Power-
houses of
the Southern
Hemisphere

vines also face the warmer Port Phillip Bay, so the weather is milder. As a result, the grapes ripen earlier than those in vineyards on other parts of the Peninsula.

Turramurra Estate is one of the great wineries in the area. It's owned and operated by David and Paula Leslie. David's other life was as a pathologist, so the scientific aspects of his winemaking are spot on, while still allowing the wines to have plenty of individual character. Wines to try from this producer include the Turramurra Cabernet Sauvignon and the Turramurra Pinot Noir (a firm-structured wine with a balanced amount of fruit and tannin; it shows the warmth possible from this site).

Other wineries of note are Elgee Park, a great Viognier producer, and Dromana Estate, which was one of the first wineries to really make everyone take notice of the Mornington Peninsula and its wines. Check out Elgee Park's smart Pinot Noir and Chardonnay in Dromana's Reserve and normal ranges.

## Rising up on Main Ridge

The Main Ridge area stretches between Arthur's Seat and Red Hill. The area is quite high, with some of the coolest vineyard sites on the Peninsula, but it's also quite beautiful and serene. Among the grapevines you find strawberry farms and cherry orchards, all offering their wares direct to the public — you can even pick your own fruit at some orchards.

The standout wineries of Main Ridge include Main Ridge, which focuses on Pinot Noir and Chardonnay; Ten Minutes by Tractor, a family affair that covers a wide range of wines; and T'Gallant, producer of richly flavored Pinot Gris.

## Centering on Red Hill South and Merricks

As you meander across the Mornington Peninsula and through Red Hill, you come out at the other side of the ridge that separates the Port Phillip Bay–facing vineyards from the Western Port Bay–facing vineyards. The vineyards sitting at the top of the ridge, namely Paringa Estate and Red Hill Estate, are cooler than those on the flat land, such as Stonier Wines.

Here are bottles to watch for from top wineries in the Red Hill South and Merricks regions:

Stonier Chardonnay

Merricks Estate Pinot Noir

Merricks Estate Shiraz

Tuck's Ridge Pinot Noir

Scorpo Shiraz

Scorpo Chardonnay

Box Stallion Arneis

Box Stallion Moscato

Paringa Estate Pinot Noir

## *Meandering around Moorooduc*

Along with the Dromana vineyards, those around Moorooduc are among the warmest of the Mornington Peninsula's vineyards. The combination of warmer climate and poorer soils gives this area the benefit of ripening earlier than Main Ridge and Red Hill. Typically, Moorooduc red wines are more powerful in flavor; they also have higher levels of tannin.

Check out these wineries in the region:

Kooyong
Moorooduc Estate
Stumpy Gully Vineyard
Willow Creek Vineyard
Yabby Lake

# *Macedon: Bubbling Up to Meet You*

The Macedon Ranges wine region is situated less than one hour's drive from Melbourne and has an elevation between 400 and 2,000 feet above sea level. Consequently, the region has a cool climate, and you know you're alive when you visit on a winter's morning!

More than 20 wineries are situated in Macedon. All of them are planted on unique plots of land with varying soil types and altitudes, so each winery makes quite unique wines.

Most of the vineyards in the Macedon Ranges are situated somewhere between 1,000 to 2,000 feet above sea level, which means their climate is cool and bordering on cold, so only certain grape varieties can be grown with success.

The Macedon Ranges are most well-known for their sparkling wines. The local association has agreed to give the sparkling wines of this region the regional appellation of Macedon, as a way to showcase the region. By doing so, the association has identified Macedon sparkling wine as a distinctive product from a specific wine region — just like the Champagne makers of the Champagne region in France did all those years ago.

Macedon sparkling wines are made from the classic Champagne grapes of Pinot Noir and Chardonnay, both of which are cool-climate specialists. Not only do these grapes work well when they're used for sparkling wines, but they also make some pretty good table wines.

Along with Chardonnays and Pinot Noirs, you can also find some Sauvignon Blancs that are made in the intense fruit-flavored style that finishes with a zing of acidity. Hanging Rock "Jim Jim" Sauvignon Blanc is a fantastic example with a tropical, herbal, and acidic style.

A little farther afield is a patch of the Macedon Ranges that's a little warmer. Kyneton produces some very good Shiraz, especially those coming from Knight Granite Hills Wines. Although still at a high elevation, this vineyard makes use of being on the other, warmer side of the mountain range: It has planted its vineyards to face north to optimize the warmth of the sun.

# Tasmania: Wines of a Cool Climate

The grapevine plantings in Tasmania are very small affairs, and many of the island's winemakers are amateurs dabbling in the wine game. But some of Australia's finest wines are made on this island found southeast of the Australian mainland — a fact not overlooked by the big mainland companies that are gradually investing in Tasmania and fueling the growing prominence of its wines.

Being isolated from the mainland and having a relatively small population has enabled Tasmania to maintain its pristine environment: The rivers remain largely unpolluted, and the air is clean. This purity shines through in the state's produce. Tasmania's wine industry has come of age, and the island's wines are now more than ready to take on the best the mainland has to offer.

Officially, Tasmania is just one wine zone. This Geographical Indication (GI) means that no specified regions break up the island. (Refer to Chapter 1 in Book V for the scoop on the GI classification system.) Unofficially, however, Tasmania can be roughly divided into three wine regions:

- ✔ The north coast, including the Tamar Valley of Launceston and the Pipers River area to the northeast of Launceston

- ✔ The east coast, stretching from northeast of Hobart north up to Bincheno

- ✔ The Hobart region, which includes the Coal River Valley, the Derwent Valley, and the Huron Valley

Broadly speaking, most of Tasmania specializes in Pinot Noir and Chardonnay wines. However, the aromatic wines, such as Riesling, Gewürztraminer, and Pinot Gris, do very well in the Tamar Valley.

*Contract winemakers* make much of Tasmania's wine, which means the vineyard owner hands over the grapes to a contract winemaking facility to produce wine according to the grower's specifications.

The following sections take you to Tasmania's unofficial wine regions to help you get to know some of the wines that come from them.

## North coast novelties

Tasmania's unofficial north coast wine region is centered on the city of Launceston, which is located on the Tamar River. Northwest of the city is the Tamar Valley, and to the northeast is Pipers River. The north coast's vineyards made up the lion's share of the total number of vineyards in Tasmania as of 2002.

The premium wineries of Tasmania's north coast include

Bay of Fires
Clover Hill
Jansz Tasmania
Pipers Brook Vineyard
Tamar Ridge

## East coast charmers

The area that follows the coast road from Hobart in the southeast to St Helens on the east coast is loosely considered the east coast wine region. It's among the most beautiful and relatively untouched parts of the world. Top-class wines from this region include those from Apsley Gorge Winery, Freycinet Vineyards, and Spring Vale Vineyards.

## Hobart's finest

In the Hobart region, found in the southern portion of Tasmania, the long autumn makes for intensely flavored and well-structured wines. The key grape varieties in this area are Pinot Noir, Chardonnay, Gewürztraminer, Riesling, and Sauvignon Blanc. Table wines and sparkling wines are the predominant styles.

All the wineries in this region are small affairs, with the largest being Elsewhere Vineyard with 13 hectares. The name came about because the owners felt that the weather report often forecast that it would be fine and sunny elsewhere. The best of the Elsewhere line is the Pinot Noir. Noted other wineries in this region that produce tiny amounts are Tinderbox, Two Bud Spur, and No Regrets.

Book V

Australia
and New
Zealand:
Power-
houses of
the Southern
Hemisphere

# Icewines of the north and south

Originating in Germany in 1794, *icewine* is the result of pressing grapes that have been left on the vine to freeze in winter. Freezing the grapes intensifies their sugar and flavor, and leaving the ice crystals in the wine press further enhances this intensity. Today, Germany, Austria and, increasingly, Canada lead the market in this type of wine.

Down in Tasmania, however, another wine-maker is attempting his own style of icewine. Given that the weather doesn't allow freezing to occur, Andrew Hood freezes his grapes in a cool store after harvest. The result is Iced Riesling, a sweet, dessert-style wine bursting with an array of tropical fruit and citrus lift. Look out for this one under Hood's Wellington label.

Two of Tasmania's best-recognized wineries are in the Derwent Valley. The one closest to Hobart is Moorilla Estate, whose vineyard and winery overlook the Derwent River. As well as the grapes grown on this site, Moorilla Estate also owns the St Mathias vineyard in the northern Tamar Valley region. Moorilla Estate was one of the earliest wineries to be established in Tasmania and remains one with a big reputation, pioneering Gewürztraminer in Tasmania. Try the musk and spice of the Moorilla Estate Gewürztraminer and the lime-dominant Moorilla Estate Riesling. The Moorilla Estate Pinot Noir Reserve, made only in years of exceptional fruit, is well worth tasting for its ripe flavors of plum and truffles.

Another strong-on-quality winery in the Hobart area is Stefano Lubiana Wines. Its Pinot Noir, Chardonnay, Riesling, and Pinot Gris are particularly good. The site of the vineyard is a big factor in the quality of its produce: The vines are planted on a gentle slope that allows for sun exposure, and the Gerwent River acts to keep the summers cooler and the winters warmer.

Other top producers in the Hobart area are as follows:

Craigow Wines
Domaine A
Meadowlark Estate
Wellington Wines

South of Hobart is a group of wineries that make up the Huron Valley wine region. The temperatures here get very cold; in some years, even the stalwart early-ripening varieties struggle. Consequently, vineyard choice is para-mount, with the must-have criteria being a sloping piece of land that receives maximum sunshine and shelter from coastal winds, and soils that can absorb and re-radiate warmth.

## Chapter 4

# The Wine Regions of South and South West Australia

• • • • • • • • • • • • • • • • • • • • • • • • • • • • • • • • • • • • • • • • • • • • • • • • •

### In This Chapter

▶ Appreciating McLaren Vale's Mediterranean climate

▶ Traversing the Valleys: Barossa, Eden, and Clare

▶ Seeing what the Limestone Coast has to offer

▶ Savoring wines from the South West Australia zone

• • • • • • • • • • • • • • • • • • • • • • • • • • • • • • • • • • • • • • • • • • • • • • • • •

Some larger-than-life wine regions exist in South and South West Australia, including the famous Barossa Valley, well known for its brassy reds (and producing some darn fine whites, as well). The sprawling wine zones in this part of Australia are extremely diverse, and some of them span quite a range of geography and technology. Consider this chapter your guide to the prominent and diverse regions in the South and South West zones.

## McLaren Vale: Reaping the Benefits of a Mediterranean Climate

McLaren Vale is located south of Adelaide, the capital of South Australia, on the Fleurieu Peninsula. The region is a wealth of geographical diversity (rivers, ocean proximity, hills) and technological variety. Here you find winemakers using traditional methods alongside those using the most modern facilities. Since 1838, when the first plantings were made in McLaren Vale, the wine region's proximity to Adelaide meant the sprawling residential development from the city toward the tiny township of McLaren Vale was inevitable.

McLaren Vale is only about 7½ miles from the ocean, a proximity that helps create the Vale's Mediterranean climate (warm, dry summers and cool, wet winters). In the Vale, the spring into summer and early autumn weather is typically dry and warm, leading to the need for irrigation on most properties. Those vineyards that don't irrigate tend to have old vines whose roots have searched deep into the ground over the years, looking for water. The yield per vine is tiny, but what berries the vines produce have incredible concentration of flavor and color.

Varying conditions for growing grapes, from soil to climate to exposure due to slope aspect or influence from nearby ocean breezes, means nearly all red and white grape varieties have a chance to flourish in the Vale.

Red grape varieties that thrive in the McLaren Vale wine region include

- **Shiraz:** Without a doubt, Shiraz (shee-rahz) is the king of McLaren Vale. It makes up 60 percent of the red grapes crushed and 45 percent of all grapes grown in the region. The warmth of the climate allows for the buildup of fully ripe, rich, and intensely flavored berries. Tannin development isn't restricted either, so the wines that result are big and bold, filled with sweet fruit and plenty of texture. (Flip to Chapter 5 in Book I for the scoop on tannin.)

- **Cabernet Sauvignon:** This popular grape, pronounced cab-er-nay saw-vee-nyon, is the second most grown red variety in McLaren Vale. These wines are a long way from the Cabernet Sauvignon of Coonawarra — South Australia's renowned Cabernet center. (See the upcoming section "Spending some time in Coonawarra" for a peak at the Coonawarra region.) Cabernet Sauvignon from McLaren Vale is velvety, blackberry-, and mulberry-like, with soft tannin. The wines are an expression of soft fruit and a ripe mid-palate.

- **Grenache:** Big and fruity, Grenache (gren-ahsh) has very sweet-flavored fruit with a touch of spicy clove and nutmeg. Some of the Grenache wines are so ripe that they're almost Port-like in character.

- **Sangiovese, Petit Verdot, Merlot, Tempranillo, Cabernet Franc:** These grape varieties are just some of the "other reds" that are slowly infiltrating the red grapevine plantings across the McLaren Vale. All have great potential to thrive here, especially those that love the warmth, like Italy's Sangiovese (san-joe-vay-say).

White grape varieties that thrive in the McLaren Vale include

- **Chardonnay:** The second most planted grape, taking 16 percent of the total, Chardonnay (shar-dohn-nay) works well in the Vale. As an early-ripening variety, winegrowers easily achieve rich fruitiness in the wines. Typically Chardonnay wines from the McLaren Vale are soft, low-acid wines that are ready for early consumption.

- **Sémillon, Verdelho, Viognier, Marsanne, Roussanne:** These white varieties are all planted, to some degree, in the region. Although Sémillon is the other white of choice for the local grape growers (making up 16 percent of white grapes; 3 percent of all grapes), white grapes make up only 20 percent of the total number of grapes grown in the Vale.

Some of the Vale's white varieties are grown principally to make a crisp, dry white to sell at the wineries' *cellar doors* (tasting rooms). Increasingly, though, the Rhône Valley varieties of Roussanne (roos-sahn), Marsanne (mar-sahn), and Viognier (vee-oh-nyay) are likely to be embraced by the locals, given the region's suitably warm climate as well as the broadening of Australian wine-drinkers' palates.

The following sections provide you with recommendations on good wines to try from some of the McLaren Vale's top producers.

## Coriole wines to cellar and drink now

Wines from Coriole Vineyards are consistently very good. From the top of the range come Coriole Mary Kathleen Cabernet Sauvignon Merlot and Coriole Lloyd Reserve Shiraz.

The reasonably new Coriole Sangiovese and Coriole Nebbiolo wines fly the flag for the Italian varieties here. Their savory characters, rather than big fruity ones, show why these varieties make such food-friendly wines.

## Top-notch Primo vino

Primo Estate is based in the McLaren Vale but has most of its vineyards in the Adelaide Plains. This winery is known for doing things a little differently. Owner Joe Grilli, whose roots are in Italy, makes all of his wines with a touch of class, toning down some of the region's typically super-ripe flavors by monitoring the grapes' ripeness. Grilli bravely makes Colombard — a white grape that doesn't excite many other winemakers because it lacks obvious fruit flavors — and he makes it shine.

### The Bushing Festival

The Bushing Festival, held in October each year in McLaren Vale, is a wine celebration in the Fleurieu region, a picturesque peninsula south of Adelaide. The festival started as a throwback to the medieval times when tavern owners hung ivy outside the tavern to welcome the new wine and *mead* (a low-alcohol mixture of fermented honey and other ingredients). In McLaren Vale they use the local olive branches instead.

The festival coincides with the local wine show, where the region's wines are showcased. After the results of the wine show are finalized, a bushing king or queen is selected. During the celebration, the old monarch is derobed while the newly anointed monarch is crowned — an event that takes on all sorts of hilarity.

Success comes as a first-class drop from Primo Estate when you can find Primo Estate La Biondina Colombard and Primo Estate Joseph Moda Amarone Cabernet.

## Unique names from d'Arenberg

Enjoying the wines from the McLaren Vale means meandering to a winery found on the slightly unusual side of the region: d'Arenberg Wines. Nowhere else in Australia can you find an array of wines with such individual names: Lucky Lizard Chardonnay, Footbolt Old Vine Shiraz, Laughing Magpie Shiraz-Viognier. Highlights from d'Arenberg's range of well-named, good-tasting wines include Olive Grove Chardonnay, Custodian Grenache, and Dead Arm Shiraz.

D'Arenberg Stump Jump Riesling/Sauvignon Blanc/Marsanne and d'Arenberg Stump Jump Grenache/Shiraz are both rich and fruity wines (with the latter red wine possessing soft tannins). They're made to drink on purchase, instead of cellaring for your child's wedding five years in the future. Also, the Rhône varieties can't be missed — look for d'Arenberg Hermit Crab Marsanne Viognier and d'Arenberg Money Spider Roussanne.

## The best from town-based wineries

In the heart of the township of McLaren Vale is Hardys Tintara Winery, which uses fruit from all over the McLaren Vale and beyond. Look for Tintara Reserve Grenache and Tintara Reserve Shiraz.

At the gateway to McLaren Vale, if you're traveling from Adelaide, is Hardys other winery, Hardys Reynella. The vast range of Hardys sparkling wines come from this winery, albeit from grapes that have been grown all over Australia. For example, the fruit for the premium Arras and Sir James lines comes predominantly from the Victorian Hoddles Creek vineyards in Victoria's Yarra Valley and Tasmania (regions covered in Chapter 3 of Book V).

The multiregional labels made at Hardys Reynella are Hardys Eileen Hardy Shiraz and Hardys Eileen Chardonnay, both of which have iconic status among wine drinkers who love the rich side of Australian wines. These wines are made in the fruit-dominant, ripe style with a good lashing of new oak. Some may find this oak dominance a bit too much, but if aged for five to ten years, the wines seem to fit the oak better.

## Well-priced wines from the Vale

Fox Creek Wines makes a range of well-priced, local wines, with Shiraz being the standout so far. The vibrant Fox Creek Verdelho and the Fox Creek Shadow's Run Shiraz/Cabernet (a good everyday wine named after the favored dog that lives on the property) are also worth trying.

Also producing Verdelho is Chapel Hill winery. Chapel Hill was one of the first Vale wineries to produce a Verdelho; because many people discovered the lesser-known white variety through Chapel Hill, the winery continues to have a good following. Sitting up on the hill and overlooking McLaren Vale, Chapel Hill is a modern winery that makes honest (albeit at times quite heavily oaked) wines year after year. Try the Chapel Hill Unwooded Chardonnay, a fresh and white peach wine with medium body — another best from the region — and the Chapel Hill Verdelho, an apple and mixed tropical fruits wine.

On the flats of the Vale is the ever-present, ever-high-quality Wirra Wirra Vineyards. The wine that made Wirra Wirra famous, Wirra Wirra Church Block Red, is a quintessential Australian red blend of Cabernet Sauvignon, Shiraz, and Merlot. It's always top quality at a reasonable price.

If you love ripe, soft reds, find yourself a bottle of Wirra Wirra RSW Shiraz. If you're a Chardonnay fan, you'll enjoy the Wirra Wirra Chardonnay, a full-bodied wine with toasted nut flavors.

## Shiraz to stash from Clarendon

Clarendon Hills is a winery whose Shiraz needs to be hidden away in your cellar and left there for a future celebration. These wines aren't cheap, but they've received very favorable reviews.

The Clarendon Piggott Range Syrah is the wine that some people yearn to have, given its current reputation. The wine is immense in structure with enough tannin and fruit intensity to keep it living for another 15 to 20 years, at least. If you're price conscious, beware: This wine's expensive.

# Big, Bold, and Brassy: The Barossa Valley

Like so many of the Australian and New Zealand wine regions, the Barossa Valley was pioneered by immigrants, many of them from Germany and Poland. Johann Gramp planted his first vines at Jacob's Creek in 1847 (little did he know that these early plantings would be the start of what is now one of the world's biggest-selling red wines, Orlando Jacob's Creek). Many settlers from England were also involved in the early days of the Barossa Valley, which is located in the southeastern end of South Australia. The English brewer Samuel Smith planted a vineyard and called it Yalumba; this winery is still owned by one of his descendants.

As for the Barossa Valley's climate, think hot and dry. Annual rainfall is moderate, with most rain falling during the winter months. Summer heat leads to considerable loss of water due to evaporation. Most of the vineyards are located across the broad flat land that is the Barossa Valley floor. Other vineyards are located in the surrounding low hills at altitudes of up to 1,100 feet above sea level, which makes them a little cooler.

The fertile valleys and gently rolling landscape of the Barossa Valley produce a wide diversity in the region's wine. The Valley is renowned for its reds, but it produces some mean whites, too. Following are some details on the common Barossa Valley wine styles you can expect to find:

- **Shiraz** is the monarch of the Barossa Valley, making up 40 percent of all grapes planted there. The warmth of the region, the lack of rain, and the low cropping levels all contribute to the intensely structured wines. Barossa Valley Shiraz usually has a fairly high alcohol content (14 percent or more). The flavors tend to be a mixture of savory, spice, and licorice. You can easily drink a Barossa Valley Shiraz young, or you can age it in the medium to long term.

- **Cabernet Sauvignon** plays second fiddle to Shiraz in notoriety as well as in the amount of fruit devoted to its making. In a warm climate, Cabernet Sauvignon can lose its trademark elegance. The fruit flavors are certainly ripe; you won't taste any herbaceous tones in a Barossa Valley Cabernet. Instead, you get a high-alcohol wine, blackberry flavor, and some dry, dusty tannins. Much of the Cabernet Sauvignon fruit grown in the Valley goes into making blended wines (so if you love the pure expression of Cabernet Sauvignon, Barossa Valley Cabs may not be for you).

- **Grenache** offers unashamedly fruity, perfumed, and spicy style. Some of the oldest Grenache wines in Australia come from the Barossa Valley, because Grenache has always been part of the Barossa story. Today, Grenache ranks as the third most grown red grape in the Valley, and much of that fruit makes its way into a blended wine.

- **Sémillon** thrives in the heat of the Barossa Valley. The Sémillon (seh-mee-yohn) grapes grown here are fully ripe, and the resulting wines are full-bodied and ready to drink. The climate is also dry, which means there's less threat of fungal disease, something that often afflicts Sémillon in regions that get high rainfall.

When you get down to it, the Barossa Valley is full of history — even some of its ancient vines have interesting stories to tell. Set foot here and you're surrounded by some very interesting wineries producing fascinating vintages. The following sections tell you about the Barossa Valley's most interesting producers and their wines.

## Charles Melton Wines

One of the top wineries in the Barossa Valley is Charles Melton Wines. Everything about this winery smacks of a passion for winemaking. Like so many of the Barossa Valley wines, the wines here are made from both winery-owned vineyards and contract growers. And without a doubt, this is one vineyard that regards its grape suppliers highly — year after year the wines are top class.

Favorite Charles Melton wines include the Charles Melton Nine Popes, which is a blend of Grenache, Shiraz, and Mourvèdre. This wine has a great spiciness, good tannin backbone, and lovely rich fruits. Another wine to try is the Charles Melton Rose of Virginia, a rosé made from Grenache grapes that are fruity without being overly sweet. Last but not least, consider checking out the Charles Melton Shiraz, which definitely has its origins in the Barossa Valley but is balanced in weight without too much oak influence.

## Elderton Wines

A quintessential Barossa Valley winery that makes wines that are unashamedly big in alcohol, oak use, and fruitiness, Elderton Wines has as its flagship wines the Elderton Command Shiraz and the Elderton Ashmead Cabernet Sauvignon. The Command Shiraz is massive in its weight and has loads of new oak flavors, whereas the Cabernet, made from ripe fruit, is in more of a blockbuster style. Be sure to age both wines before drinking them.

## Leo Buring Wines

Leo Buring has long been a name synonymous with extremely high-quality Riesling. Leo Buring's long-time winemaker, John Vickery, built up this reputation, and the current winemakers have kept the quality high.

The top of the range is the Leo Buring Leonay Riesling, a wine that ages incredibly well and develops over time from a lemon-dominated wine to a wine with soft mouthfeel and toasty flavors.

# Orlando-Wyndham

Orlando-Wyndham, a large Australian wine company that also owns Richmond Grove (covered later in this chapter), is headquartered in the Barossa Valley. Part of this winery's portfolio is the world-famous Orlando Jacob's Creek, which is poured into a million wine glasses across the world every day.

The Jacob's Creek label that initially attracted all the attention was the Jacob's Creek Shiraz/Cabernet blend. Although this blend still leads the pack, the entire Jacob's Creek range has gained worldwide success, and a number of well-made, good-value varietals have been developed under the brand name, including Jacob's Creek Riesling, Jacob's Creek Sémillon Sauvignon Blanc, and Jacob's Creek Chardonnay.

Buoyed by the success of the standard Jacob's Creek label, Orlando-Wyndham has added a Reserve label. And, yes, for value — albeit at a higher price — wines bearing the Reserve label are a good drop. Look for the Jacob's Creek Reserve Cabernet Sauvignon.

Another well-priced offering from Orlando-Wyndham is the Orlando Gramp's line of wines. The Gramp's Barossa Grenache is typical of this variety in this region, with loads of cherries, raspberries, and a soft tannin finish. If you're looking for a midpriced sparkling wine, the Orlando Trilogy Brut Non Vintage isn't expensive and has biscuity flavors with a fresh citrus finish.

One of the top wines from this company is the Orlando St. Helga Eden Valley Riesling. Year after year, this Riesling is a zingy, citrusy wine that shows great potential for aging.

# Penfolds Wines

The mammoth headquarters of the large Penfolds Wine company (owned by Southcorp Wines) is on the main street that goes through Nuriootpa, the chief commercial center in the Barossa Valley. A huge range of labels fall under the Penfolds banner, from the lower range but good-quality Penfolds Koonunga Hill Shiraz Cabernet to the famous Penfolds Grange. Much of the Penfolds line of wines is made from a blend of grapes grown in many regions; blending is very much part of the Penfolds winemaking culture. Some of the company's best wines are

- ✔ **Penfolds Grange:** This wine has become one of Australia's best-known wines and is the most sought-after wine on the wine-auction circuit. Buyers are desperate to get a bottle of each vintage so they can have the whole collection. Penfolds Grange is a blend of Shiraz and, depending on the year, some Cabernet Sauvignon. The wine is robust when young, showing loads of blackberry and new wood. Over time, these flavors evolve into nutty, meaty, licorice flavors.

✔ **Penfolds Yattarna Chardonnay:** This wine was dubbed the "white Grange" by many when the 1995 vintage was released. The first few releases of this wine were quite dense in flavor, lacking the right balance of acid and subtlety, and they aged quite quickly. By 1998, the wine had become more restrained in flavors when young, showing hints of citrus, peaches, and new oak, and developing over time into a soft-textured wine reminiscent of toast and honey.

✔ **Penfolds St. Henri Shiraz:** Considered "poor-man's Grange," you could buy at least six bottles of this wine for one bottle of Penfolds Grange. Expect a blackberry and spicy aroma with a generous and soft mouthfeel of licorice and dry tannins. This wine ages well for at least 15 years.

✔ **Penfolds Bin 407 Cabernet Sauvignon:** This wine has had quite a loyal league of followers over the years, because many people look to Penfolds for their Cabernet Sauvignon. Bin 407 is fruit dominant with blackberry and violet aromas, along with a blackcurrant-flavored palate. You can drink it young or age it in your cellar for 9 to 15 years.

✔ **Penfolds Koonunga Hill Shiraz Cabernet:** Always a terrific value, Koonunga Hill is an easy, everyday drinking wine. It's fruity and has soft tannins to balance.

## Peter Lehmann Wines

One of the best-known characters and long-time ambassador for the Barossa Valley is Peter Lehmann. His self-named winery offers a vast array of wine styles, all made to a high quality, from the zesty and citrusy Peter Lehmann Sémillon to the richly weighted Peter Lehmann Chardonnay.

The Peter Lehmann Cabernet Sauvignon, Peter Lehmann Merlot, and Peter Lehmann GSM (a spicy and raspberrylike blend of Grenache, Shiraz, and Mourvèdre) are all top notch and well priced. The flagship Peter Lehmann Stonewell Shiraz shows the Barossa Valley at its best, with an undercurrent of oak and lashings of blackberries and spice.

## Richmond Grove

The Richmond Grove winery falls under the Orlando-Wyndham banner. The Richmond Grove Barossa Shiraz is true to the Barossa style — big and juicy fruited, though these days this Shiraz is less oak dominated.

The jewel in Richmond Groves' crown is the Richmond Grove Watervale Riesling, a refined wine that captures the delicacy of Riesling and lives on in the bottle for years.

## Rockford Wines

One of the Barossa Valley's most renowned wines, the Rockford Basket Press Shiraz, is made by Rockford Wines. This wine is definitely full in body. Instead of being a big fruit bomb of a wine, Rockford Basket Press Shiraz is savory and earthy. Rockford Wines still uses the basket press for this wine, believing that this older pressing method gets the best results.

## St Hallett

One Barossa Valley label you can always turn to for value and reliability is St Hallett. For a long time, St Hallett has honed its winemaking skills on its flagship wine, St Hallett Old Block Shiraz. As is the case throughout the Barossa Valley, the vines are up to 100 years old and are dropped at low levels to add intensity to the fruit flavors.

Also of note is the St Hallett Faith Shiraz, a blend of fruit from the Barossa and Eden Valleys, with the Eden Valley fruit making the wine a little more restrained in weight and power than the Old Block Shiraz. In terms of white wines from the Barossa Valley, St Hallett's Blackwell Sémillon is one of the leaders. Unlike many Sémillons that are made in a fruit-driven style, this wine has been barrel fermented and aged on lees, giving it more nutty tones.

St Hallett's lower-priced everyday drinking wines are the St Hallett's Gamekeeper's Reserve, a red blend of Grenache, Mourvèdre, Shiraz, and Touriga, and the St Hallett's Poacher's Blend, made from Chenin Blanc, Sémillon, and Sauvignon Blanc. Both are well-made, fruit-filled wines that are well worth trying.

## Saltram Wines

Owned by the Beringer Blass Wine Estates, Saltram Wines is making a vast array of wines across all price points. Of note is the Saltram No. 1 Shiraz, the winery's current flagship wine. This is the quintessential "fruit bomb" Barossa Valley Shiraz, layered with loads of American oak. Saltram has plans to release a higher-priced wine as its flagship in the future.

A Saltram label worth looking for is Pepperjack. All Pepperjack wines are fruit filled and soft in tannin. (As an added bonus, they're ready to drink when you buy them!) Look for the Pepperjack Shiraz and Pepperjack Cabernet Sauvignon.

# Seppeltsfield Winery

Book V

Australia
and New
Zealand:
Power-
houses of
the Southern
Hemisphere

Seppeltsfield is well-known for its range of fortified wines. Although Sherry isn't a particularly fashionable style of wine these days, the Seppelt Show Amontillado Sherry DP116 is absolutely one of the best. It's luscious, nutty, and very well priced for the high quality. (*Note:* The "DP116" is simply a winery bin number that has carried through to the naming of the wine.)

Also made by Seppelt is the famous 100-year-old Para Liqueur Port, which is the highest-quality batch of Port that continues the style of the established line. The oak barrel is larger than the average wine barrel. The twist here is that the wine isn't released for 100 years, so the current release is the 1909 vintage.

A less expensive yet still delicious Port is Seppelt Show Tawney Port DP90, which offers the flavors of dried fruits and roasted nuts and has a luscious but not dense texture. (As with the Seppelt Show Amontillado Sherry DP116, the "DP90" indicates the winery bin number.)

# Turkey Flat Vineyards

Turkey Flat Vineyards produces one of the Barossa Valley's famous rosés, the Turkey Flat Rosé. Fruity and with a touch of sweetness, this rosé is a perfect wine for the Australian climate.

Also in the Turkey Flat line of wines is the Turkey Flat Sémillon/Marsanne, a peachy white wine that's an excellent value.

# Wolf Blass Wines

Headquartered in the Barossa Valley and owned by the Beringer Blass Wine Estates, Wolf Blass Wines is known for its house style of wines that are big in fruit and flavor intensity. The winery makes a huge number of quality wines across several price ranges, from the low-priced Wolf Blass Yellow Label Riesling (a fruity, ready-to-drink, summery wine) to the medium-priced Wolf Blass Grey Label Cabernet Sauvignon (a wine with blackberry and mint characteristics) to the very expensive Wolf Blass Black Label Cabernet Sauvignon Shiraz (a Cab-dominant wine that's aged in the bottle for four years before sale).

## Yalumba Winery

Despite being Australia's 12th-largest wine company, the Yalumba Winery is still family owned. Yalumba Winery offers a range of brands, from the Oxford Landing line and Y series at the lower end of the price scale to the regional Yalumba Barossa and Yalumba Eden Valley labels. It also has individual flagship wines such as Heggies, Pewsey Vale, and the Octavius Barossa Shiraz.

Yalumba's skill with making white wine (particularly Riesling) and its passion for the white grape Viognier have combined to make the glorious Yalumba Virgilius Viognier, a luscious wine that's packed with apricots, lychees, and spice flavors.

Added to Yalumba's portfolio is the Yalumba D Sparkling Wine, which is made from fruit largely grown in the cool climates of Tasmania and Victoria (see Chapter 3 in Book V for the scoop on these regions). Both are delicately flavored wines of high quality.

In the regional range, Yalumba produces some noteworthy Barossa reds. The company was one of the first to release a wine that was 100 percent Grenache, before the grape had gained its now-fashionable status. The Yalumba Barossa Bush Vine Grenache is full of ripe Barossa fruit that at times borders on jammy. This full type of wine has a strong following, especially among those who believe that big is good but bigger is better.

# Small, Subdued, and Sassy Eden Valley

The Eden Valley is tiny in comparison with its lower-altitude neighbor, the Barossa Valley (see the previous section) — and not only in area. In 2003, the total amount of grapes crushed in the Eden Valley was almost 10,500 tons; in the Barossa Valley, the amount was close to 55,100 tons. However, size doesn't necessarily matter because a number of very high-profile wineries have chosen to make the Eden Valley their home. In addition, many of the wine companies based in the Barossa Valley source fruit from the Eden Valley.

The Eden Valley is situated to the east of the Barossa Valley, and its eastern boundary is 1,300 feet above sea level in the Barossa Ranges; the highest point in the region is around 2,000 feet above sea level. The altitude naturally means temperatures are a good deal lower than those on the Barossa Valley floor, and rainfall is higher.

If the Barossa Valley is defined by Shiraz, then the Eden Valley is just as strongly identified by its talent for Riesling. (Shiraz, however, isn't overlooked.) Here's a glimpse of the area's premium grapes:

- **Riesling** (*reese*-ling) is the star of the white varieties from the Eden Valley. The cool weather allows for the citrus flavors and the zingy, fresh acid to be captured and retained in the grapes as they ripen. The wine produced from the Riesling grape is tight and citrus dominated, with great aging potential.

- **Chardonnay** also enjoys the cooler climate of the Eden Valley. The lower temperatures mean that the grapes ripen slowly and retain their natural acidity. In comparison to harvest time in the Barossa Valley, harvest time for Chardonnay grapes in the Eden Valley is at least two weeks later, which allows the grapes to ripen in the cooler days.

- Of the red grapes, **Shiraz** is the most-planted variety in the Eden Valley. Most Eden Valley Shiraz is used as part of a blend with Barossa Valley Shiraz. The Eden Valley fruit takes on a more spicy and peppery flavor and is lighter in weight than the full-bodied Barossa Valley Shiraz. Blending grapes from the two regions produces a toned-down wine with less of the Barossa fruit's overt fruitiness and ripeness.

- **Pinot Gris** (pee-noh gree) from the cool Eden Valley produces a soft and elegant wine. The cool climate allows the grapes to maintain their acidity; you won't find an Eden Valley Pinot Gris that's dense in weight. The wine is quite refined, allowing the more minerally flavors to come through rather than loads of pineapple and honey, flavors that are more common in the warmer climates.

- **Merlot** (mer-loh) from the Eden Valley makes wine with savory and quite herbal flavors. The cool climate prevents the Merlot grape from becoming too ripe and turning into a full-bodied wine; instead, the wine is of medium weight.

The following sections detail some Eden Valley wineries and their worth-trying wines.

# Henschke Wines

Now run by the fifth generation of winemakers, the Henschke winery is indeed one of Australia's most highly regarded wine labels. The head of the family is now winemaker Stephen Henschke, assisted by his wife Prue, a leading research viticulturist.

For years, the Henschke line of wines has been built around some core reds, such as the Henschke Mount Edelstone Shiraz and the Cyril Henschke Cabernet Sauvignon. The Shiraz is made from 90-year-old vines and is densely flavored with licorice and blackberries and balanced by a tannin finish. The Cabernet Sauvignon is made from Eden Valley fruit, a fact that shows in the cassis and tobacco flavors so often seen in cool-climate Cabernet Sauvignon.

Henschke's Hill of Grace is the winery's most famous wine with a reputation that rivals Penfolds Grange (described in the earlier "Penfolds Wines" section). This Shiraz is made from old vines (planted in the 1800s, no less!) in the spectacularly beautiful Hill of Grace vineyard. The wine is a mixture of anise, blackberries, and chocolate, balanced by a soft tannin finish.

Henschke also does a wide range of white wines. The Henschke Tilly's Vineyard Dry White is an excellent buy.

## Irvine

James Irvine makes an impressive Eden Valley straight Merlot called Irvine Grand Merlot. This wine was one of the first 100-percent Merlot wines to be made in Australia and is savory rather than fruity, with potential to age well.

## Mountadam Vineyards

David Wynn chose the site for Mountadam Vineyards in order to grow Chardonnay. The High Eden Ridge area, a subregion of the Eden Valley, is perfect for this white variety. Typically, the Mountadam Chardonnay is bottle aged at the winery for a number of years before release, and the wine is well weighted in flavor and alcohol, giving it a rich texture.

Another good Mountadam Vineyards wine to try is the Mountadam Pinot Noir/Chardonnay sparkling wine, which is aged in the bottle for five years before leaving the cellars. This wine has soft bubbles plus complex nutty and savory tones.

## Tin Shed Wines

Recently coming to the attention of wine lovers are the wines from Tin Shed Wines. Yes, the wines were originally made in a tin shed down on the floor of the Barossa Valley, but now the two partners use a naturally insulated 18th-century stone building in the cool Eden Valley, which is more suitable for winemaking. Each partner owns a vineyard, one in the Barossa Valley and one in the Eden Valley, so the wines are often a blend of the two regions. The range from this winery is fairly limited. The wines are made without much intervention and are fermented by using wild yeasts. Worth trying is the Tin Shed 3 Vines MSG, a blend of Mourvèdre, Shiraz, and Grenache that's loaded with spices and licorice, with a touch of tar.

# Classy Clare Valley

Because the Clare Valley wine region is the most northern vineyard area in South Australia, you might think it's also the hottest. Although the days can get quite warm in the summer, the nights are quite the opposite. The combination of the region's elevation and the cool afternoon breezes that blow in during the summer from the Spencer Gulf to the west of the Clare have the effect of producing wines with cool-climate characteristics. This sort of climate allows the fruit to achieve full ripeness and allows the natural acidity to be maintained along with the varietal characters of the fruit.

The Clare Valley is very proud, and rightly so, of the wines it produces. The name *Clare Valley* sits prominently on the labels of wines whose Clare Valley grape totals sit at 85 percent or higher. Here's a rundown of the region's top grapes:

- ✔ **Riesling:** This white variety is the star of the Clare Valley. Although third in terms of the plantings in the region (behind Shiraz and Cabernet Sauvignon), Riesling's recent leap up the fashion stakes has seen it enjoying the limelight. Certain areas in the region have becomes famous for their style of Riesling — the Watervale area makes wines that are approachable when young and are still delicious after 10 to 12 years.

- ✔ **Shiraz:** The most-planted variety across the Clare, Shiraz is mainly found on the lower slopes (which leaves the higher slopes for the Riesling grapes that like it cool). Although the Clare Valley has pockets that are quite hilly and difficult to plant on, large tracts of land exist that allow for reasonably big vineyards. Because of the mild climate, Shiraz from the Clare takes on a more savory, elegant, and refined style in contrast to its big fruity cousins in the Barossa Valley. However, Clare Valley Shiraz still offers plenty of fruit-driven flavors.

- ✔ **Cabernet Sauvignon:** Although the climate of the Clare Valley allows the fruit for Cabernet Sauvignon to ripen satisfactorily each year, the wine doesn't enjoy the kind of reputation that Shiraz has made for itself. However, if you're a fan of Cabernet, you won't be disappointed. A Clare Valley Cabernet is usually good, with briary tones and the blackberry fruit flavors that are so often associated with this red variety.

The Clare Valley is full of small- to medium-sized wineries. The region has an old-world feeling about it, accentuated by the beautiful old buildings that dot the landscape and adorn the towns. The vineyards trail up the hills and over onto the plains and look like they've always been a part of the landscape.

The following sections acquaint you with some of the Clare Valley's top wine producers. Enjoy!

# Annie's Lane

Annie's Lane is a large-production label to some from the Clare Valley, and it's owned by Beringer Blass Wine Estates. Two wine labels are available: the standard Annie's Lane label and the Annie's Lane Copper Trail label. Wines bearing the standard label are commercial, medium-priced wines that, despite varying a little from year to year in quality, are usually good, honest drops.

The Annie's Lane Copper Trail Riesling and Annie's Lane Copper Trail Shiraz are both fine wines. The Riesling shows the citrus and musk flavors so typical to the Clare Valley, whereas the Shiraz resists the temptation to be too dense and ripe and is instead a refined, albeit full-bodied, Clare Valley Shiraz.

# Grosset Wines

A Clare Valley winery producing top-notch Riesling is Grosset Wines. Riesling with the Grosset label was one of the Rieslings that prompted wine lovers to end their love affairs with Chardonnay and Sauvignon Blanc. (The Grosset Polish Hill Riesling is a leader in popularity.) Grosset Wines also makes Grosset Gaia Cabernet Sauvignon, which comes from a small vineyard perched on the side of a hill and is quite blackberry and herbal with a soft finish.

# Knappstein Wines

The Lion Nathan wine and brewing company today owns Knappstein Wines, which is fitting considering the winery is housed partly in an old brewery. At this winery, you find honest, well-made wines that deliver on fruit flavor at a competitive price.

Look for the fruity and herbal Knappstein Sémillon/Sauvignon Blanc, the lychee- and musk-loaded Knappstein Dry Style Gewürztraminer, and the more-expensive nutty and cassis-flavored Knappstein Enterprise Cabernet Sauvignon.

# Leasingham Wines

Leasingham Wines is now owned by the Hardy Wine Company (formerly BRL Hardy) and is another medium-sized label within a large company portfolio. As part of its commitment to showing you just how good aged Riesling from the Clare Valley can be, the Leasingham Classic Clare Riesling isn't released until it has been aged in the bottle for four to five years. When eventually sold, the wine is full of nuttiness and soft acidity.

For an inexpensive and good-quality Riesling, you can buy the Leasingham Bin 7 Riesling and age it yourself. The wine has citrus and mineral tones when young that continue to develop softly with age. The other steals from this winery are the Leasingham Bin 61 Shiraz, a full-flavored, blackberry-fruited wine, and the densely textured cassis and chocolate Leasingham Bin 56 Cabernet Malbec.

The Leasingham Classic Clare Sparkling Shiraz is a fine example of that quirky Australian sparkling red style of wine — big and juicy ripe fruits with some pepper and spice topped off with fizz.

## Taylors Wines

The vineyards of the largest vineyard owner in the region, Taylors Wines, fit the contours of the Clare Valley perfectly. The quality of the wine from Taylors Wines has improved enormously in recent years. The three wines in its premium range are Taylors St Andrews Cabernet Sauvignon, Taylors St Andrews Shiraz, and Taylors St Andrews Riesling, all of which are particularly well made and show the characteristics of the Clare — plenty of flavor but without overripeness or a thick texture.

Taylors Promised Land Cabernet Merlot and Taylors Promised Land Shiraz Cabernet in particular are inexpensive wines from this label that are worth tracking down. These wines are multiregional blends that show a good balance of medium body and flavor.

# Tasting along the Limestone Coast

The Limestone Coast, a Geographical Indications zone (refer to Chapter 1 in Book V for the scoop on the GI classification system), lies roughly halfway between the cities of Melbourne in Victoria and Adelaide in South Australia. Even if you've never heard of the Limestone Coast, you've likely heard of the Coonawarra wine region. Why? Because it's the most well-known of the Limestone Coast's wine regions (although its other regions — Padthaway, Wrattonbully, and Mount Benson — are far from insignificant).

Except for Mount Benson, the climate of the Limestone Coast can be described as Mediterranean with maritime influences. That is, the climate is warm to hot during the day and is cooled off at night by the breezes that come in off the Southern Ocean. Over at Mount Benson, where the vineyards surround the coastal towns of Robe and Kingston, the climate is pure maritime. Winds, though, can often be very strong; coastal winds in spring can rip the young shoots from the vines and disrupt flowering. The result is a low number of berries and reduced numbers of bunches.

During the growing season, temperatures can be high during the day, but they drop considerably after night falls. The wide variation between day- and nighttime temperatures contributes to the success of the grape-growing regions of the Limestone Coast. The grapes are exposed to full sun during the day and have the night to recover, thereby retaining the natural acidity of the grapes.

Rainfall is low along the Limestone Coast, averaging 24 inches a year and falling mainly during the winter. Summer is very dry; sometimes as little as 3 inches of rain falls from January to April. Therefore, irrigation is used to supplement the vines' water supply during the important ripening period. The soil structure allows water to drain away from the vines' roots, which prevents waterlogging.

The next two sections clue you in to the grape varieties that thrive in the Limestone Coast zone and get you up to speed on some Coonawarra wineries that produce pretty tasty wines.

## Picking the best grape varieties

Red grapes dominate the vineyards here, with Cabernet Sauvignon coming in as the most-grown grape. Following are the Limestone Coast's best grape varieties:

- ✔ **Cabernet Sauvignon:** This red grape variety is most often linked with Coonawarra and the Limestone Coast. It thrives in the *terroir* — the soil conditions, climate, and so on — of the area. The cooling influence from the afternoon ocean breezes tempers the warm days, and the grapes ripen quite slowly, gradually building up in intensity of flavor. Because Cabernet Sauvignon is a late-ripening variety, the best years for it are those that have a prolonged autumn, which ensures the grapes ripen fully. In the occasional year when the autumn weather turns cold too soon, the Cabernet Sauvignon from some vineyards may retain a green, herbaceous tone.

- ✔ **Shiraz:** This red variety is having some success in the Mount Benson region, where the French winemaking company M. Chapoutier grows grapes. Although Shiraz from Coonawarra is consistently good, the wine hasn't yet built up the reputation of the Shiraz from McLaren Vale and the Barossa Valley. Shiraz from Coonawarra tends to be a good, solid red wine without the big, ripe characteristics of Shiraz from other South Australia regions.

✔ **Merlot:** The third most-grown red variety in the Limestone Coast zone is Merlot. In the Coonawarra region, Merlot is used mainly for blending, but in the Wrattonbully and Padthaway regions, Merlot is made into a wine in its own right. Straight Merlot is a sweet-fruited wine of medium intensity.

✔ **Sauvignon Blanc, Riesling, and Chardonnay:** Although these white varieties play second fiddle to red grapes on the Limestone Coast, they're grown all across the zone. Riesling tends to do well in Coonawarra, where the cool nighttime temperatures maintain the fresh, fruity style of the grapes.

Riesling wines from Coonawarra differ from the Rieslings produced in the Eden or Clare Valleys; the fruit flavors are bigger and the acids, albeit balanced, are less. These are Rieslings that you can enjoy early in their lives.

## Spending some time in Coonawarra

Coonawarra is really the only wine region of the Limestone Coast zone that caters to the wine tourist. As you drive along the Riddoch Highway, signs start to appear announcing the various cellar doors that are open to visitors. (*Cellar door* is the Australian term for a tasting room within a winery.) Before long, you find yourself surrounded by vineyards.

Many lovers of Coonawarra wines have been disappointed when they arrive at the region. The utterly flat and unromantic Coonawarra landscape is hardly picturesque. However, people quickly forget their disappointment with the landscape as soon as they start sampling what that landscape produces.

Be sure to check out these Coonawarra wineries if you're ever in the area:

| | |
|---|---|
| Balnaves of Coonawarra | Orlando Wines |
| Bowen Estate | Parker Coonawarra Estate |
| Brand's of Coonawarra | Penley Estate Winery |
| Katnook Estate | Punters Corner |
| Lindemans Wines | Rymill Coonawarra |
| Majella Wines | Wynns Coonawarra Estate |
| Mildara Wines | Zema Estate |

# South West Australia: Beaches, Forests, and Sunshine

Margaret River is the main, and perhaps the best-known, region of the South West Australia wine zone. Other regions are Pemberton, Manjimup, Geographe, and Blackwood Valley.

Once attracting only surfers in search of the coast's world-famous waves, Margaret River now hosts upward of 90 wineries, many of which were started in the 1970s by doctors looking for a weekend diversion. Today, Margaret River is very much a wine destination as well as a magnet for surfers keen on catching big waves.

The wine regions within the South West Australia wine zone are inevitably influenced by their proximity to the coast — both in terms of weather and soil fertility. But after you move inland where the giant trees grow, both the fertility of the soil and the higher altitudes change the conditions dramatically.

The following sections help you understand the factors affecting the vines in the various regions of the South West Australia wine zone. They also acquaint you with the grape varieties that thrive in the area and some producers (and wines!) worth checking out.

## Cooling winds and varied soils in Margaret River and Geographe

The climate of the Geographe region is influenced by its proximity to the coast. In the summer months, cooling ocean breezes flow in, and in winter, the closeness of the ocean keeps the temperatures mild. The ocean also influences the climate of Margaret River region. The sea breezes that flow in from the Indian Ocean in the west and the Southern Ocean to the south are responsible for the region's cool-to-warm maritime climate. The regions are located on the southwest coast of Western Australia.

The temperature range in both the Margaret River and Geographe regions is very small — and that's a boon to the grapes grown there. Consistent temperatures mean grapes have a predictable climate in which to ripen.

Rainfall in the Margaret River and Geographe regions is relatively high, and nearly all of the annual 46 inches of rain fall during the winter months. For that reason, you often see cereal crops planted in between the rows of vines.

The cereal crops absorb some of the excess water and prevent the soil — and the roots of the vines — from becoming waterlogged. In spring, the cereal crops are slashed and become mulch for the vines so as to retain moisture through the very dry growing season.

Soils in the Geographe and Margaret River regions vary a little. Right on the coast, the soils are poor and lack nutrients, becoming more fertile inland around the Ferguson River valley. Vineyards are planted in both soil types. Vines planted in the less fertile soils have to struggle a little but ultimately make good, full-flavored wines. Vines planted in the more fertile soils need to be managed well so their *vigor* (leaf and shoot growth) doesn't jeopardize their ability to ripen the grapes.

**Book V**

**Australia and New Zealand: Power-houses of the Southern Hemisphere**

## Vigor in the Blackwood Valley

Being inland and away from the coast, the Blackwood Valley region isn't dominated by a coastal climate. During the ripening season, the days here are warm, but often in the late afternoon, ocean breezes find their way through to the Valley. Summer nights are often quite cool. This temperature balance allows the vines to recover overnight from the day's warmth and helps to slow down ripening (which means the flavors of the grapes become more intense than they would've been had the nights also remained warm).

The soils in the Blackwood Valley are fertile. As a result, careful vineyard management is required to prevent the vines from becoming excessively vigorous.

## Cooling altitudes and rich soils in Pemberton and Manjimup

Pemberton and Manjimup enjoy a similar climate. Being inland and less influenced by breezes from the ocean, these two regions escape the summer heat because of their altitude. Vineyards in the Pemberton area are planted at 330 to 650 feet above sea level; Manjimup is a little higher in elevation than Pemberton, with vineyards established around 820 to 1,000 feet above sea level. Manjimup also gets more sunshine than Pemberton, making it warmer and less humid.

Pemberton and Manjimup have extremely old soils. The *karri loam* of the Pemberton region is a deep-red, fertile soil — almost too fertile, really, because it leads to excessive vigor in the vines. Manjimup's *marri* soil is less fertile and has more sand and gravel than Pemberton's karri loam.

Rainfall in these two regions occurs mainly in winter and spring, although sometimes a storm occurs during ripening season. Depending on the stage of growth the grapes have reached, this rain may or may not be a problem — a lot of the grapes may be spoiled, or the rain may merely provide a gentle drink for the vines.

## The grapes that Margaret River and her neighbors do best

The grapes that have made Margaret River famous are Chardonnay and Cabernet Sauvignon, two varieties that enjoy the slow ripening the region's cool-to-warm maritime climate offers. Here's a rundown of the other grapes that thrive in the South West Australia wine zone:

- **Sémillon and Sauvignon Blanc:** These two varieties feature significantly in the Western Australian white wine portfolio and are frequently blended. Their wines are always incredibly fruity, with loads of tropical flavors and an herbaceous hint. Some of that herbaceousness comes naturally from the Sauvignon Blanc grapes, but it's also seen (unusually) in the Sémillon grapes.

- **Merlot:** This red variety is mainly used to blend with Cabernet Sauvignon. Its fruitiness adds to the savory elegance of the Cabernet and helps fill out the flavors in the mid-palate. Often Cabernet Sauvignon is described as a *doughnut wine,* that is, a wine with a hole in the middle of its flavor profile. When it's blended with Cabernet, Merlot's job is to fill that hole.

- **Shiraz:** The Shiraz produced in the South West zone appeals to lovers of a more refined style of the grape. Shiraz grapes grown in this zone ripen slowly and are picked at a level of ripeness below that of the super-ripe grapes of South Australia. Due to the different climate and soils, the wines tend to be more savory, offering earthy and plum-dominated flavors in medium-bodied wines.

If you're a fan of McLaren Vale and Barossa Valley Shiraz, a Shiraz from the South West zone may not be for you.

## Recommended producers of the South West zone

The Geographe region has relatively few wineries. However, after you swing around to the southern coastline of Geographe Bay, you know you're in serious wine country. The farther south you go, the more vineyards and wineries you see — on both sides of the road no less! The next sections describe some of the good wineries that call the South West zone home.

### Geographe

The Geographe wine region, found inland from Geographe Bay, can lay claim to just a handful of wineries, but these few wineries represent quality.

Check out Capel Vale, which is the area's standout and offers a memorable CV Cabernet Merlot with soft fruit. Look also for Hackersley, which primarily grows fruit for other wineries but is notable for its Sémillon.

### From Cape Naturaliste to Margaret River

The stretch of land from Cape Naturaliste to Margaret River is absolutely laden with wineries. By the time you reach Metricup Road, all you can see is vineyards in a gently rolling and very attractive landscape. Following are some producers to look for:

| | |
|---|---|
| Amberley Estate | Moss Wood |
| Brookland Valley Vineyard | Howard Park Wines |
| Cullen Wines | Pierro Vineyard |
| Evans & Tate | Sandalford Wines |
| Fermoy Estate | Vasse Felix |
| Hay Shed Hill | Wise Vineyards |

### From Margaret River to the Blackwood Valley

The wine region in the southern part of the Margaret River region is top heavy with well-known and super-high-quality wine labels. You can find a handful of them in the following list:

| | |
|---|---|
| Alexandra Bridge Winery | Leeuwin Estate |
| Cape Mentelle | Voyager Estate |
| Devil's Lair | Xanadu Wines |

# Chapter 5

# New Zealand's Islands and Their Wines

Many similarities exist between the wines and wine regions of Australia and New Zealand thanks to the intense competition between the winemakers of both countries. (Then again, having rivalries with your closest neighbor is almost compulsory — Australia and New Zealand's started with the sport of rugby.)

New Zealand boasts a diverse group of vineyards from its northern tip to the bottom of its southern islands. Merlot reigns along the coast of Auckland, and Pinot Noir is the stunning fruit of the Martinborough region (Otago, at the bottom of the South Island, is developing a good reputation for Pinot Noir too). And chances are good that the Sauvignon Blanc you find so memorable got its start on New Zealand's South Island.

This chapter takes you on a tour of New Zealand's wine regions and introduces you to the grape varieties that grow there and the wineries that make some of the nation's best wines.

## Discovering Diversity on New Zealand's North Island

The North Island of New Zealand offers a diverse group of vineyards. The vineyards and wineries off the coast of Auckland on Waiheke Island produce some pretty smart Cabernet wines. And the famous Martinborough

(Wairarapa) region put New Zealand Pinot Noir on the world wine map. Add to these the beautiful wines of Hawke's Bay, one of the few regions in New Zealand that can make top wines from the Merlot grape. The North Island is also home to the third-largest producer of New Zealand wine, the Gisborne region. (Figure 5-1 shows you the island's various wine regions.) The following sections give you more details on the grapes and wines from each of these regions. (Although the Waikato and Bay of Plenty region is larger than the rest, its vineyards constitute a very small percentage of the total planted vines in New Zealand.)

**Figure 5-1:**
The wine regions of New Zealand's North Island.

# Finding good Chardonnay and Merlot in and around Auckland

Auckland, New Zealand's capital city, is situated in the northern part of the nation's North Island. It was once the center of New Zealand's wine industry. These days most of the country's large winemaking firms have wine-processing facilities in the Auckland region, but much of the wine coming out of Auckland-based wineries is actually made from fruit grown as far away as the South Island's Marlborough region (which you can read about later in this chapter).

The Auckland wine region includes five subregions: Matakana/Mahurangi, Kumeu/Huapai, Henderson, Waiheke Island, and South Auckland.

Given Auckland's latitude (just a little bit south of Sydney, in neighboring Australia) and its proximity to the coast, most of the vineyards in the Auckland region have to cope with both high rainfall and high humidity — not unlike Australia's Hunter Valley region (described in Chapter 2 of Book V).

The most-planted grape varieties in the Auckland region are Chardonnay and Merlot, which are almost equal in the number of planted acres, with 23 and 21 percent of the total, respectively. The second most popular red variety in the region (after Merlot) is Cabernet Sauvignon. However, because getting the grapes for Cabernet Sauvignon to fully ripen is so difficult, this variety is gradually being replaced with Merlot and, increasingly, Cabernet Franc.

Here's a closer look at Auckland's top grapes:

- **Chardonnay:** Auckland Chardonnay (shar-dohn-nay) is typically fruit driven, showing aromas of peaches, cashews, and stone fruits. Compared to Chardonnay from other parts of New Zealand, these wines are rich with soft acidity.

- **Pinot Gris:** Some very impressive Pinot Gris (pee-noh gree) wines have been making a name for themselves. Typically, these wines exhibit the nutty and pearlike characteristics of Pinot Gris in a rich, full style.

- **Sauvignon Blanc:** Although the fruit mostly comes from the Gisborne region or from the Marlborough region of New Zealand's South Island, some excellent Sauvignon Blanc (saw-vee-nyon blahnk) comes from Auckland. You may run into an aggressive, herbaceous style of Sauvignon Blanc or a soft, grapefruity style (usually a little more expensive than its intense sibling, but still decidedly affordable).

- **Merlot:** Auckland's best reds are Merlot (mer-loh). Much of the Merlot grown in the Auckland region goes into a blend, almost always as part of a classic Bordeaux blend of Cabernet Sauvignon, Merlot, and Cabernet Franc.

In spite of high rainfall and high humidity, some of the best-performing Auckland wines come from the coastal area in the northern part of the region. A number of wineries have managed to overcome the climatic obstacles of the region and are producing wines of note. Here are bottles to watch for:

Babich Wines Irongate Chardonnay

Babich Wines Irongate Cabernet Merlot

Goldwater Estate Cabernet Sauvignon Merlot

Harrier Rise Uppercase Merlot

Harrier Rise Monza Cabernet

Kumeu River Wines Mate's Vineyard Chardonnay

Kumeu River Chardonnay

*(continued)*

*(continued)*

Matakana Estate Syrah

Matua Valley Shingle Peak Sauvignon Blanc

Matua Valley Shingle Peak Pinot Noir

Nobilo Drylands Marlborough Sauvignon Blanc

Selaks Premium Selection Marlborough Chardonnay

Obsidian Vineyard, The Obsidian

Ransom Clos de Valerie Pinot Gris

Ransom Barrique Fermented Chardonnay

Stonyridge Larose Red Blend

## Proudly producing white wines in Gisborne

Gisborne is the most eastern vineyard region on the North Island (shown in Figure 5-1) and is flanked by the Pacific Ocean. Although no vineyards are located right on the coast, the region does experience cooling sea breezes. Like the Auckland region (see the preceding section), Gisborne is fairly flat, and vineyards are planted at low altitudes.

Today, the Gisborne region produces about 25 percent of the grapes grown throughout New Zealand. Yet despite this impressive quantity, only 16 wine companies are established in Gisborne, and fewer than 10 wineries are operating in the region because the grapes are mostly shipped off to be processed at wineries in other areas. Much of the fruit grown in Gisborne finds its way into reasonably priced commercial labels; for example, New Zealand's largest wine company, Montana, has extensive vineyards here, but the wine itself is made at the company's Auckland or Wake's Bay wineries.

Climate-wise, the most significant characteristics about the Gisborne region are the warmth and high rainfall it experiences. The grape varieties that ripen early, such as Chardonnay, soak up the sun, becoming ripe before being ruined by the heavy rains. On average, the region receives more than 20 inches of rain during the growing season, October to April; often much of this rain falls in the critical months of February, March, and April, when the grapes are most susceptible to damage. Thus, the earlier the grapes ripen, the more likely a successful harvest becomes.

Chardonnay dominates the Gisborne region — almost 60 percent of the region's vines produce this grape. Gisborne is also home to the lesser-known white varieties of Chenin Blanc, Müller Thurgau, and Muscat, which together make up around 16 percent of the grapes planted in Gisborne. You won't necessarily find bottles with labels on them stating that the wine is made from any of these varieties; more often than not, the grapes are used to make inexpensive sparkling wine, blended together and sold under the name of "classic white," or made into a wine that's given a specially devised name. For example, Pouparae Park Winery's blend of Müller Thurgau and Muscat is known as Pouparae Park Solstice Blanc.

Gisborne's red grape varieties, Pinot Noir and Merlot, aren't of a particularly high quality; they make up just about 8 percent of the region's total plantings. Both varieties ripen too late for this region and so are susceptible to the midseason rains.

Here's how Gisborne's dominant grapes shape up:

- The appeal of a Gisborne **Chardonnay** is found in its early ripening, because grape growers can ripen the fruit and then harvest it before the damaging rains arrive. Chardonnay responds well to abundant sunshine and heat, resulting in full-flavored wines that have instant appeal to the consumer. The Chardonnay from the Gisborne area, which is usually ready to drink, is bursting with peaches, honey, and ripe citrus flavors.

- Although **Gewürztraminer** (geh-*vairtz*-trah-mee-ner) makes up only around 3 percent of the vines planted in the Gisborne region, the wines made from this variety are becoming well-known. The grape's delicious spicy and lychee character develops in the warmth of the region's sunshine. The only problem with this variety, though, is that in the wet years, the tight-berried bunches are likely to suffer from *botrytis cinerea,* or noble rot, which ruins the delicate fruit flavors.

Selecting the best is never easy, but four wineries that set the standard for the Gisborne region are Matawhero Wines, Millton Vineyard, Montana, and Thorpe Brothers Wines.

## Delving into Hawke's Bay, east of the ranges

Hawke's Bay is one of the best known wine regions in New Zealand (check out Figure 5-1). In terms of vineyard area planted, the region is the second biggest after Marlborough on the South Island. The main centers in the region are Napier, on the coast, and Hastings, a little inland. Most of the vineyards are located on the flat Heretaunga Plains (near Hastings), with the odd vineyard located closer to the coast.

The climate of the Hawke's Bay region is by no means a hot one, but sunny days are common. The main indicator as to whether a particular season is going to be a good one is the amount of rain (although Hawke's Bay is less prone to disastrous autumn rains than Gisborne, its neighbor to the north). Because they're located on the eastern side of the Ruahine and Kaweka Ranges, the Hawke's Bay vineyards experience less rainfall than other places on the island's east coast.

In the summer months, the sea breezes that arrive in the early afternoon keep the Hawke's Bay vineyards that are closest to the coast several degrees cooler than those vineyards found farther inland. As a result, these vineyards

Book V

Australia and New Zealand: Power-houses of the Southern Hemisphere are less able to ripen late-maturing grape varieties like Cabernet Sauvignon. A little farther inland, around Havelock North, just south of Hastings and on the Heretaunga Plains, the temperature is warmer, enhancing the vineyards' ability to grow Cabernet Sauvignon, Cabernet Franc, and Shiraz.

Like other wine regions in New Zealand, Chardonnay is the most-planted grape variety in Hawke's Bay, making up around 27 percent of all the varieties found there. Hawke's Bay wineries proudly make their wines from locally grown grapes, while also supplying grapes to many of the wineries in Auckland and the Bay of Plenty.

Hawke's Bay is increasingly forging a reputation as the best region in New Zealand to make high-quality Bordeaux-style wines from Cabernet Sauvignon, Merlot, and Cabernet Franc. The sunshine that extends from summer into autumn gives these varieties a chance to fully ripen, with the only possible hitch being rainfall during or before ripening. Site selection is crucial, too, to avoid too much influence from cool afternoon sea breezes.

Following is a rundown of Hawke's Bay's top grapes:

- ✓ **Chardonnay:** New Zealand's best Chardonnay comes from Hawke's Bay. The fruit flavors are at times more restrained compared to the full flavors of wines produced in the Gisborne region.

- ✓ **Sauvignon Blanc:** Although Sauvignon Blanc from Hawke's Bay may suffer in reputation compared to the famous Marlborough Sauvignon Blanc, some fine wines are being made here from this variety.

- ✓ **Cabernet Sauvignon and Merlot:** These are the most successful straight reds in Hawke's Bay; they're actually among the best in the country. When these wines are blended together, along with a touch of Cabernet Franc (cab-er-nay frahn), some outstanding wines result.

The top wineries in the Hawke's Bay region, which produce some memorable Merlots and Chardonnays, among other excellent drops, are as follows:

CJ Pask

Craggy Range Vineyards

Ngatarawa Wines

Stonecroft Wines

Te Mata Estate

Vidal Estate

## *Checking out the rugged Wairarapa Region and its Pinot Noir*

Most people don't associate the name Wairarapa with any wine region in New Zealand. The name most often heard in connection with the wine of this area is Martinborough, the best known of the winegrowing districts in the Wairarapa region (see Figure 5-1) and the focus of this section.

The Wairarapa region is flanked to the west by the rugged Rimutaka and Tararua mountain ranges; to the southeast are the Aorangi Mountains. Below these ranges lies a flat plain where the vineyards are located. Naturally, the surrounding mountain ranges have a great influence on the climate of the Wairarapa region. The presence of the ranges to the west of the vineyards means that rainfall is reduced. As the rain-bearing clouds travel from west to east over the ranges, much of the rain falls on the mountains, leaving the air above the vineyard plains relatively dry.

**Book V**

**Australia and New Zealand: Power-houses of the Southern Hemisphere**

The rain and wind that come up from the south pose the greatest threat to the vineyards (but when the storm fronts aren't too wild, they can actually be beneficial). During *fruit set* (the time in spring when the flowering vines create the berries for the coming season), the wind can have quite an impact. Strong winds blowing through the vineyards can negatively affect the transition from the flower stage to the berry stage. Where fewer berries have formed, each vine naturally reduces the amount of fruit it can produce. On the one hand, the grape growers obtain less fruit; on the other hand, the quality of that fruit is believed to be higher. Vines that yield lower crops are linked to the production of higher-quality, more intensely flavored fruit.

The Wairarapa region is located just 20 to 25 miles away from the coast, and nights in Martinborough are cooled by the evening sea breeze. This nightly drop in temperature is highly desirable for the region's flagship grape variety, Pinot Noir (pee-noh nwahr). The cool night air produces Pinot Noir grapes that make deeply colored, flavorful wines with firm tannin and good aging potential. Pinot Noir accounts for more than 40 percent of the region's vines.

Pinot Noir owes its success in Martinborough to the equable climate, which isn't too hot or too wet. These conditions allow the grapes to struggle a bit and intensify in flavor, and the cool night air permits the vines their all-important overnight rest period. Vines that get the chance to rest overnight in cooler temperatures produce more intensely flavored grapes. In climates where the overnight temperature isn't much less than the daytime temperature, the vines keep working through the night (poor things). As a result, the fruit on the vines ripens quickly without having had any time to intensify in flavor.

Sauvignon Blanc is the second-most-planted variety, a smidgen more popular than Chardonnay at 19 percent versus 16 percent. Coming from vines that typically produce low crops, the region's Sauvignon Blanc wines are intensely flavored and tropical, with great acid zing. Compared to the Sauvignon Blanc produced in the Marlborough region, these wines are riper and a little less herbal.

A number of outstanding wineries from the Wairarapa region, clustered around Martinborough, enjoy a good reputation internationally. Because most are quite small producers, their wines, unfortunately, can be hard to find. Search out wines from Dry River Wines, the Escarpment Vineyard, Martinborough Vineyard, and Palliser Estate.

# *Liquid Distinction from New Zealand's Cool South Island*

If you haven't been there, you might believe that the South Island is the sleepier of New Zealand's two islands. For years, the South Island made its name as the sheep-farming capital of the world — after all, it has more sheep to its name than people — and apart from tourism, its economy rested on the backs of the woolly critters.

However, the economists long ago stopped joking about the backward nature of New Zealand's southern isle. The boom in wine exports from this beautiful part of the world has very much helped the local economy. In 2008, New Zealand winemakers exported more than 75 percent of their wine, up from a mere 9 percent in 1990. Much of this growth has been due to the huge reputation that the wines of Marlborough have carved for themselves, particularly the Marlborough Sauvignon Blancs. Figure 5-2 gives you the lay of the wine-producing regions of the South Island, and the following sections provide an overview of the top three.

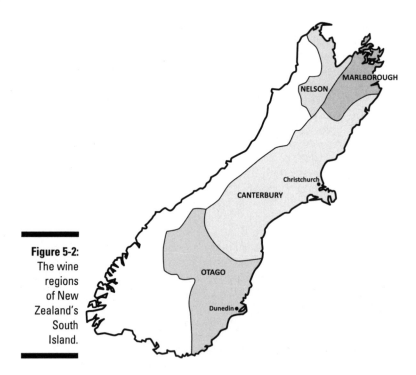

**Figure 5-2:**
The wine regions of New Zealand's South Island.

## *Finding much to admire in Marlborough*

**Book V**

**Australia
and New
Zealand:
Power-
houses of
the Southern
Hemisphere**

Marlborough is arguably the most famous wine region in New Zealand and the most heavily planted. It's also incredibly beautiful. The large flat Wairau Plains stretch for miles and are filled with vineyards as far as the eye can see.

Many of the vineyards take their names from nearby geographical features, such as Cloudy Bay, the bay into which the Wairau River feeds, and Wither Hills, the hilly area surrounding the Wairau Plains. The Wairau Plains lie between the towns of Blenheim and Renwick and are within the Wairau Valley. So you have the Wairau River, Wairau Plains, and Wairau Valley — making the name *Wairau* pretty famous in Marlborough.

The location of the Marlborough region is without a doubt one of the main reasons for its success. The region's topographical advantages include the Marlborough Sounds to the north of Blenheim, which protect the vineyards from the strong northwesterly winds. To the south are the Kaikoura Ranges that stop the cold southerly winds coming up from the Antarctic. And the location of the Richmond Range to the west means that the region has less rainfall than land farther west, because the rain falls on the mountains before the clouds reach the Marlborough region.

The biggest climatic problem the Marlborough region faces is frost. Cool air settles on the wide, flat Wairau Plains very early in the morning. Devastating spring frosts that freeze the young shoots on the vine aren't uncommon. Whenever the danger of frost is likely, grape growers in Marlborough hire local helicopter pilots to hover over the vineyards in an attempt to keep the air moving and bring down the layer of warmer air that's sitting above the vineyards. If a grape grower can't contract a helicopter, he uses other techniques to deter frost, such as running wind machines and building small fires throughout the vineyard.

Many grape varieties grow across Marlborough, but Sauvignon Blanc is the star, totaling more than 50 percent of the varieties planted in the region. The grapes from vineyards on the north bank of the Wairau River produce a Sauvignon Blanc in which tropical fruit is dominant. In contrast, vines growing in the silt and clay of the south bank produce a Sauvignon Blanc that's more herbaceous and grassy. During the day, sunshine allows the fruit to develop its trademark tropical, herbaceous flavors. At night, the drop in temperature means that the vines shut down their activity and the grapes don't continue to ripen. This rest period allows the grapes to maintain their acidity, a key to making top-class Sauvignon Blanc. Leading producers are those who can capture the gorgeous tropical fruit flavors along with a hint of herbal variety.

Of course, Sauvignon Blanc isn't the only grape grown in Marlborough. Other varieties found in the region include

- **Riesling:** The Marlborough climate of mild, warm days and cooler nights contributes to the success of the Riesling (*reese*-ling) grape. Like the other grape varieties grown in Marlborough, Riesling has had to take a back seat to Sauvignon Blanc. Even so, you can find some top-class Rieslings with flavors of lime and lemon.

- **Chardonnay:** The mild days in Marlborough allow Chardonnay grapes to fully develop their fruit flavors, and the cold nights give the grapes the chill they need to maintain their acidity. Marlborough Chardonnays have a weighty mid-palate and a soft acid finish.

- **Pinot Noir:** Of the red varieties, Pinot Noir has forged the biggest reputation, making up 15 percent of the vines planted, whereas the second-most-planted red variety, Merlot, has just 2 percent of plantings. Pinot Noir is an up-and-coming variety in Marlborough. Its vines like the region's varied soil conditions. The stony soils allow the fruit to get some depth in color and body; the water-retaining silt and clay soils allow the fruit to continue ripening throughout the warmer months without becoming stressed by lack of rain, which helps the berries acquire the fruity flavors that fill out the wine's structure.

The reputation of the large wine-producing region of Marlborough is maintained by a large number of notable wineries. Of these, the following deserve special mention:

| | |
|---|---|
| Cloudy Bay | Lawson's Dry Hills |
| Forrest Estate | Montana Brancott Winery |
| Fromm Winery | Nautilus Estate |
| Hunter's Wines | Villa Maria Estate |
| Isabel Estate | Wither Hills |
| Johanneshof Cellars | |

## Cooling off in Canterbury

Although Canterbury is the fifth-largest wine region in New Zealand, in size it's a long way behind its northern neighbor, Marlborough. The Canterbury region can be divided into two distinct subregions: The most planted is the Waipara area, a fairly hilly area north of Christchurch, the main city in the region; the other is the Canterbury Plains.

Both the Waipara area and the Canterbury Plains experience minimal rainfall during the growing season; they're also affected by hot, drying winds that come in from the northwest. Like so many other parts of New Zealand, the surrounding mountain ranges get most of the rainfall, creating a relatively dry climate in the vineyard areas. Because the Waipara region is situated close to the coast, it receives cool night breezes that reduce the nightly temperatures dramatically, giving the grapes the chance to get a good night's sleep. Speaking of the weather, humidity in the Canterbury region is relatively low, which in turn means that the risk of the vines suffering from fungal disease is low — a distinct advantage for grape growers.

Pinot Noir makes up 30 percent of the plantings in the Canterbury region, with Chardonnay making up 24 percent. (Current predictions are that these two varieties, particularly Pinot Noir, will increasingly dominate Canterbury's vineyards.) The other successful grape in this region is Riesling, an aromatic variety that thrives in conditions where it can ripen slowly, thus giving Riesling the chance to retain its zingy acidity.

*TIP*

Naturally, Pinot Noir features prominently in the repertoire of the Canterbury region's outstanding wineries, which include the following:

| | |
|---|---|
| Daniel Schuster Wines | Muddy Water |
| Floating Mountain Winery | Pegasus Bay |
| Giesen Estate | St Helena Wines |
| Kaituna Valley Wines | |

## *Heading south to Otago*

Central Otago — also referred to simply as Otago — is breathtakingly beautiful (you can find it on the map in Figure 5-2). Many of the vineyards lie beneath snow-capped mountains — stunning backdrops for the wine-loving photographer. It's New Zealand's fourth-largest wine region, second only to Marlborough in terms of its reputation within the wine world. When people think of Otago, they think of good-quality wine — and often rather expensive prices.

Several distinct subregions exist within Otago. Queenstown lies at the center of the region; to its north is the Wanaka area with its two vineyards. To the east of Queenstown are the Cromwell Basin and Alexandra subregions; Cromwell is home to more than 60 percent of Otago's vineyards. West from Cromwell on the way to Queenstown is the Gibbston subregion, second only to the Cromwell Basin in terms of hectares planted.

Variations in soil type affect the region's wines. Nearly all the vineyards in the Gibbston area are situated along the Kawarau River and are typically planted on silty, free-draining soils. The wines are less full-bodied than those from the Cromwell Basin, but nevertheless have a fine flavor.

The Otago region is the most southerly winegrowing area in the world, but its climate is far from the cold and wet one you might expect. The region is very dry because it's so far inland, but it's also a land of extremes. Ski resorts sit above vineyards, yet summer temperatures can be some of the highest in the country. When the grapes are ripening in autumn, temperatures are warm to cool by day and cold at night. Conditions can vary even when relatively short distances are involved. For instance, in the Gibbston subregion, the climate is cooler than in the Cromwell Basin. Additionally, the harvesting time of the same grape variety can vary by up to one month.

With such extreme variations in temperature, having the ability to select a good site for a vineyard is critical for a grape grower: The vines need to grow in a warm pocket so they can reach full ripeness. What this climate means, though, is that the ripening period is stretched out, allowing the grapes to accumulate layer upon layer of flavor. The resulting wines possess incredibly intensity.

Pinot Noir reigns supreme in Otago, making up 63 percent of the vines in the region. The Pinot Noirs of the warm Cromwell Basin are amazingly full-bodied with dense, ultra-ripe flavors. The Alexandra and Gibbston subregions produce a Pinot Noir with juicy fruit flavors and a supple texture. The character of Pinot Noirs from the Wanaka area depends greatly on the temperatures of the growing season.

Chardonnay ranks next in importance, with 15 percent of the total vine production in Otago. (The Chardonnays produced in Otago tend to be on the lean and tight side, with citrus flavors and a good acidity.) The other plantings are shared fairly equally among Pinot Gris, Riesling, and Sauvignon Blanc.

As with the Marlborough region, identifying the best wines and wineries of Otago is difficult because so many of them are of a very high standard. However, the following names can lead you to some of the best wines in Otago:

Chard Farm
Felton Road Wines
Gibbston Valley
Rippon Vineyard & Winery
Two Paddocks

# Book VI
# And More Wine Regions!

The 5th Wave                    By Rich Tennant

"The wine is supposed to breathe, Martin, not hyperventilate."

# In This Book . . .

Consider this book your grab bag of other wine regions worth knowing, from countries that rank among the top ten in terms of wine production (think Spain, Argentina, Germany, South Africa, and Chile) to countries such as Portugal, Austria, and Greece that produce exciting wines all their own, albeit in smaller quantities.

In the chapters to come, you cruise through eight nations with truly glorious wines. From South Africa's Pinotage to the Cava of Spain, get ready to take in some recommendations for unique drinkables.

Here are the contents of Book VI at a glance:

# Chapter 1

# Intriguing Wines from Old Spain

*In This Chapter*

▶ Getting to know Spain's top three wine regions

▶ Scoping out several other Spanish wine regions worth knowing

▶ Appreciating the greatness (and value) that is Sherry

Spain is a hot, dry, mountainous country with more vineyard land than any other nation on earth. It ranks third in the world in wine production, after France and Italy.

Spanish wine has awakened from a long period of dormancy and under-achievement. Spain is now one of the wine world's most vibrant arenas. For decades, only Spain's most famous red wine region, Rioja, and the classic fortified wine region, Sherry, had any international presence for fine wines. Now, many other wine regions in Spain are making seriously good wines. In this chapter, you find out more about these regions and the ins and outs of Sherry.

Spain's wine laws, like Italy's, provide for a bilevel Quality Wines Produced in Specified Regions (QWPSR) category: *Denominaciónes de Origen* (DO) and a higher classification, *Denominaciónes de Origen Calificada* (DOC, also known as DOCa), the latter created in 1991. Wines that don't qualify as DO fall into the table wine category *vino de la tierra* (equivalent to the French category *vin de pays*).

## *Rioja Rules the Roost*

Rioja, in north-central Spain (see Figure 1-1), has historically been the country's major red wine region (even if today Ribera del Duero and Priorato are catching up — fast!). Three-quarters of Rioja's wine is red, 15 percent *rosado* (rosé), and 10 percent white.

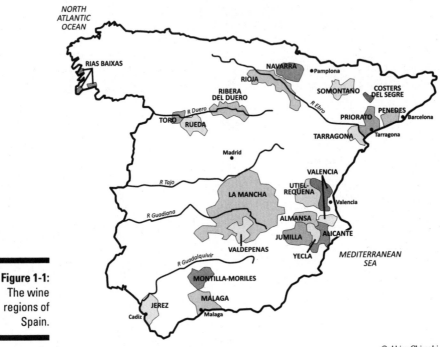

**Figure 1-1:**
The wine
regions of
Spain.

The principal grape in Rioja is Tempranillo (tem-prah-*nee*-yoh), Spain's greatest red variety. But regulations permit another three varieties for reds — Garnacha (Grenache), Graciano (Carignan), and Mazuelo. Red Rioja wine is typically a blend of two or more varieties. Regulations aside, some producers now also use Cabernet Sauvignon in their red Rioja.

The Rioja region has three districts: the cooler, Atlantic-influenced Rioja Alavesa and Rioja Alta areas and the warmer Rioja Baja zone. Most of the best Riojas are made from grapes in the two cooler districts, but some Riojas are blended from the grapes of all three districts.

Traditional production for red Rioja wine involved many years of aging in small barrels of American oak before release, which created pale, gentle, sometimes tired (but lovely) wines that lacked fruitiness. The trend has been to replace some of the oak aging with bottle aging, resulting in wines that taste much fresher. Another trend, among more progressive winemakers, is to use barrels made of French oak along with barrels of American oak — which has traditionally given Rioja its characteristic vanilla aroma.

Regardless of style, red Rioja wines have several faces according to how long they age before being released from the winery. Some wines receive no oak aging at all and are released young. Some wines age (in oak and in the bottle) for two years at the winery and are labeled *crianza;* these wines are still fresh and fruity in style. Other wines age for three years and carry the designation *reserva.* The finest wines age for five years or longer, earning the status of *gran reserva.* These terms appear on the labels (either front or back; see Chapter 3 in Book I for help deciphering which is which) and act as the seal of authenticity for Rioja wines.

Prices start at around $12 for crianza reds and go up to about $45 for some gran reservas. The best recent vintages for red Rioja are 2004, 2001, 1995, and 1994.

The following Rioja producers are particularly consistent in quality for their red wines:

**Book VI**

**And More Wine Regions!**

- ✔ CVNE (Compañía Vinícola del Norte de España), commonly referred to as CUNE
- ✔ Bodegas Muga
- ✔ R. Lopez de Heredia
- ✔ La Rioja Alta
- ✔ Marqués de Murrieta Ygay
- ✔ Marqués de Riscal

Most white Riojas these days are merely fresh, neutral, inoffensive wines, but Marqués de Murrieta and R. Lopez de Heredia still make a traditional white Rioja that's golden-colored, oak-aged, and made from a blend of local white grape varieties, predominantly Viura. Both of these traditional white Riojas are fascinating: flavorful, voluptuous, with attractive traces of oxidation, and capable of aging. These wines aren't everybody's cup of tea, true, but they sure have character! They have so much presence that they can accompany foods normally associated with red wine, as well as traditional Spanish food, such as paella or seafood. The Murrieta white sells for about $16, and the Lopez de Heredia is about $20.

# Ribera del Duero: Drawing New Eyes and Palates to Spain

Ribera del Duero, two hours north of Madrid by car (refer to Figure 1-1), is one of Spain's most dynamic wine regions. Perhaps nowhere else in the world does the Tempranillo grape variety reach such heights, making wines with body, deep color, and finesse. Now famous for its high-quality red wines, this region has helped to ignite world interest in Spanish wines.

For many years, one producer, the legendary Vega Sicilia, dominated the Ribera del Duero area. In fact, Spain's single most famous great wine is Vega Sicilia's Unico (Tempranillo, with 20 percent Cabernet Sauvignon) — an intense, concentrated, tannic red wine with enormous longevity; it ages for ten years in casks and then sometimes ages further in the bottle before it's released. Unico is available mainly in top Spanish restaurants; if you're lucky enough to find it in a retail shop, it can cost about $300 — a bottle, that is. Even Unico's younger, less intense, and more available sibling, the Vega Sicilia Valbuena, retails for about $100.

Vega Sicilia is no longer the only renowned red wine in Ribera del Duero. Alejandro Fernández's Pesquera, entirely Tempranillo, has earned high praise over the past 15 years. Pesquera is a big, rich, oaky, tannic wine with intense fruit character. The reserva sells for about $28, whereas the younger Pesquera is $20. The reserva of Fernández's other winery in the area, Condado de Haza, sells for about $35. Three other fine producers of Ribera del Duero are Bodegas Mauro, Viña Pedrosa, and Bodegas Téofilo Reyes, who all make red wines that rival Pesquera.

# Mountainous Priorato and Its Rich Reds

Back in the 12th century, monks founded a monastery (or *priory*) in the harsh, inaccessible Sierra de Montsant Mountains, about 100 miles southwest of Barcelona in the Catalonia region (refer to Figure 1-1), and planted vines on the steep hillsides. As time passed, the monastery closed, and the vineyards were abandoned because life was simply too difficult in this area (which in time became known as Priorat, or Priorato).

Flash forward to the 20th century, specifically the early 1980s. Enterprising winemakers, among them Alvaro Palacios, rediscovered Priorato and decided that conditions there were ideal for making powerful red wines, especially from old vines planted by locals early in the 20th century.

No Spanish wine region has been in the spotlight lately more than Priorato. And yet Priorato hasn't become a tourist destination, because it's so inaccessible. The region's volcanic soil, composed mainly of slate and *schist* (crystalline rock), is so infertile that not much other than grapes can grow there. The climate is harshly continental: very hot, dry summers and very cold winters. The steep slopes must be terraced; many vineyards can be worked only by hand. And grape yields are very low.

Amazingly rich, powerful red wines — made primarily from Garnacha and Carignan, two of Spain's native varieties — have emerged from this harsh landscape. Many are as rugged as the land, with high tannin and alcohol;

some wines are so high in alcohol that they have an almost Port-like sweetness. Because winemaking in Priorato isn't cost effective (to say the least!) and the quantities of each wine are so small, the wines are necessarily quite expensive; prices begin at about $40.

Priorato reds to look for include Clos Mogador, Clos Erasmus, Alvaro Palacios, Clos Martinet, l'Hermita, Morlanda, Mas d'En Gil, and Pasanau.

# Five Other Spanish Regions to Watch

The action in Spanish wines — especially when value is your concern — definitely doesn't end with Rioja, Ribera del Duero, and Priorato (all of which are described earlier in this chapter). Consider exploring wines from the regions described in the following sections.

**Book VI**

**And More Wine Regions!**

## Penedés

The Penedés wine region is in Catalonia, south of Barcelona (refer to Figure 1-1). It's the home of most Spanish sparkling wines (known as *Cava*); it also produces a large quantity of red and white wines. Cava is made in the traditional method and fermented in the bottle. Most Cavas use local Spanish grapes. As a result, they taste distinctly different (a nice earthy, mushroomy flavor) from California bubblies (see Chapter 3 in Book IV) and from Champagne (see Chapter 6 in Book II). Some of the more expensive blends do contain Chardonnay.

Two gigantic wineries dominate Cava production: Freixenet and Cordorniu. Freixenet's frosted black Cordon Negro bottle has to be one of the most recognizable wine bottles in the world. Other Cava brands to look for are Mont Marçal, Paul Cheneau, Cristalino, Marqués de Monistrol, and Segura Viudas. Juve y Camps, a vintage-dated, upscale Cava, is a worthwhile buy at $16.

Any discussion of Penedés' still wines must begin with Torres, one of the world's great family-owned wineries. Around 1970, Miguel Torres pioneered the making of wines in Spain from French varieties, such as Cabernet Sauvignon and Chardonnay, along with local grapes, such as Tempranillo and Garnacha.

All the Torres wines are clean, well-made, reasonably priced, and widely available. They start in the $10 range for the red Sangre de Toro (Garnacha-Carignan) and Coronas (Tempranillo-Cabernet Sauvignon) and the white Viña Sol. The top-of-the-line Mas La Plana Black Label, a powerful yet elegant Cabernet Sauvignon, costs about $45.

Freixenet, the leading Cava producer, is now also in the still wine business. Its wines include the inexpensive René Barbier–brand varietals and two fascinating wines from Segura Viudas (a Cava brand owned by Freixenet), both $15 to $16. Creu de Lavit is a subtle but complex white that's all Xarel-lo (pronounced sha-*rel*-lo), a native grape used mainly for Cava production. The red Mas d'Aranyo is mainly Tempranillo.

## Rías Baixas

Galicia, in northwest Spain next to the Atlantic Ocean and Portugal (refer to Figure 1-1), wasn't a province known for its wine. But from a small area called Rías Baixas, tucked away in the southern part of Galicia, an exciting, white wine has emerged — Albariño (ahl-ba-*ree*-nyo), made from the Albariño grape variety. Rías Baixas is, in fact, one of the world's hottest white wine regions. (Hot as in "in demand," not climate; Rías Baixas is cool and damp a good part of the year, and green year-round.)

This region now boasts about 200 wineries, compared to only 60 in the 1990s. Modern winemaking, the cool climate, and low-yielding vines have combined to make Rías Baixas's Albariño wines a huge success, especially in the United States, its leading market. Albariño is a lively, (mainly) unoaked white with vivid, floral aromas and flavors reminiscent of apricots, white peaches, pears, and green apples. It's a perfect match with seafood and fish. The Albariño grape makes wines that are fairly high in acidity, which makes them fine apéritif wines.

Albariños to look for include Bodega Morgadío, Lusco, Bodegas Martin Codax, Fillaboa, Pazo de Señorans, Pazo San Mauro, Pazo de Barrantes, and Vionta; all are in the $16 to $23 range.

## Navarra

Once upon a time, the word *Navarra* conjured up images of inexpensive, easy-drinking dry rosé wines (or, to the more adventurous, memories of running the bulls in Pamplona, Navarra's capital city). Today, Navarra, just northeast of Rioja (see Figure 1-1), is known for its red wines, which are similar to, but somewhat less expensive than, the more famous wines of Rioja.

Many Navarra reds rely on Tempranillo, along with Garnacha, but you can also find Cabernet Sauvignon, Merlot, and various blends of all four varieties in the innovative Navarra region. Look for the wines of the following three Navarra producers: Bodegas Julian Chivite, Bodegas Guelbenzu, and Bodegas Magana.

# A brief guide to Spanish wine-label terminology

Expect to see some of the following terms on a Spanish wine label:

- **Blanco:** White.

- **Bodega:** Winery.

- **Cosecha or Vendimia:** The vintage year.

- **Crianza:** For red wines, this means that the wine has aged for two years with at least six months in oak; for white and rosé wines, *crianza* means that the wines aged for a year with at least six months in oak. (Some regions have stricter standards.)

- **Gran reserva:** Wines produced only in exceptional vintages. Red wines must age at least five years, including a minimum of two years in oak; white gran reservas must age at least four years before release, including six months in oak.

- **Joven:** Little or no oak aging.

- **Reserva:** Wines produced in the better vintages. Red reservas must age a minimum of three years, including one year in oak; white reservas must age for two years, including six months in oak.

- **Tinto:** Red.

## Toro

The Toro region in northwest Spain, west of Ribera del Duero (see Figure 1-1), made wines in the Middle Ages that were quite famous in Spain. But it's a hot, arid area with poor soil, so winemaking was practically abandoned there for centuries.

In Spain's current wine boom, Toro has been rediscovered. Winemakers have determined that the climate and soil are ideal for making powerful, tannic red wines — mainly from the Tempranillo grape variety — which rival the wines of Toro's neighbors in Ribera del Duero (one of Spain's most dynamic wine regions, as explained earlier in this chapter).

Toro producers to buy include Bodegas Fariña, Vega Sauco, Estancia Piedra, Bodegas y Viñas Dos Victorias, Gil Luna, and Dehesa La Granja (owned by Pesquera's Alejandro Fernandez).

## Rueda

The Rueda region, west of Ribera del Duero (see Figure 1-1), produces one of Spain's best white wines from the Verdejo grape. The wine is clean and fresh, has good fruit character, and sells for an affordable $9 to $10. The Rioja producer Marquis de Riscal makes one of the leading and most available examples.

# Sherry: A Misunderstood Wine

The late comedian Rodney Dangerfield built a career around the line, "I get no respect!" His wine of choice should've been Sherry, because it shares the same plight. Sherry is a wine of true quality and diversity, but it remains undiscovered by most of the world. The upside of that negligence is that the price of good Sherry is attractively low. The following sections introduce you to all the intricacies of Sherry, an underappreciated, little-known wine.

## Entering the Jerez triangle

Sherry comes from the Andalucía region of sun-baked, southwestern Spain. The wine is named after Jerez de la Frontera, an old town of Moorish and Arab origin where many of the Sherry bodegas are located. (*Bodega* can refer to the actual building in which Sherry is matured or to the Sherry firm itself.)

Actually, the town of Jerez is just one corner of a triangle that makes up the Sherry region. Another corner is Puerto de Santa María, a beautiful, old coast town southwest of Jerez that's home to a number of large bodegas. The third point of the triangle, Sanlúcar de Barrameda (also on the coast but northwest of Jerez), is so blessed with sea breezes that the lightest and driest of Sherries, *manzanilla* (mahn-zah-*nee*-yah), can legally be made only there. Aficionados of Sherry swear they can detect the salty tang of the ocean in manzanilla.

Traveling from Sanlúcar to Jerez, you pass vineyards with dazzling white soil. This soil is *albariza,* the region's famous chalky earth, rich in limestone from fossilized shells. Summers are hot and dry, but balmy sea breezes temper the heat.

The Palomino grape — the main variety used in Sherry — thrives only here in the hot Sherry region on albariza soil. Palomino is a complete failure for table wines because it's so neutral in flavor and low in acid, but it's perfect for Sherry production. Two other grape varieties, Pedro Ximénez (pronounced *pay*-dro he-*main*-ehz) and Moscatel (Muscat), are used for dessert types of Sherry.

## Exploring the duality of Sherry: Fino and oloroso

Sherry consists of two basic types: *fino* (pronounced *fee*-no; light, very dry) and *oloroso* (pronounced oh-loh-*roh*-soh; rich and full, but also dry). Sweet Sherries are made by sweetening either type.

After fermentation, the winemaker decides which Sherries will become finos or olorosos by judging the appearance, aroma, and flavor of the young, unfortified wines. If a wine is to be a fino, the winemaker fortifies it lightly (until its alcohol level reaches about 15.5 percent). She strengthens future olorosos to 18 percent alcohol.

At this point, when the wines are in casks, the special Sherry magic begins: A yeast called *flor* grows spontaneously on the surface of the wines destined to be finos. The flor eventually covers the whole surface, protecting the wine from oxidation. The flor feeds on oxygen in the air and on alcohol and glycerin in the wine. It changes the wine's character, contributing a distinct aroma and flavor and rendering the wine thinner and more delicate in texture.

Flor doesn't grow on olorosos-to-be, because their higher alcohol content prevents it. Without the protection of the flor (and because the casks are never filled to the brim), these wines are exposed to oxygen as they age. This deliberate oxidation protects olorosos against further oxidation — for example, after you open a bottle.

## Aging communally

Both fino and oloroso Sherries age in a special way that's unique to Sherry production: Unlike most other wines, young Sherry isn't left to age on its own. To make room for the young wine, some of the older wine is emptied out of the casks and is added to casks of even older wine. To make room in those casks, some of the wine is transferred to casks of even older wine, and so on. At the end of this chain, four to nine generations away from the young wine, the winemaker takes some of the finished Sherry from the oldest casks and bottles it for sale.

This system of blending wines is called the *solera* system. It takes its name from the word *solera* (floor), the term also used to identify the casks of the oldest wine.

As wines are blended, no more than a third of the wine is emptied from any cask. In theory, then, each solera contains small (and ever-decreasing) amounts of very old wine. As each younger wine mingles with older wine, it takes on characteristics of the older wine; within a few months, the wine of each generation is indistinguishable from what it was before being refreshed with younger wine. Thus, the solera system maintains infinite consistency of quality and style in Sherry.

Because the casks of Sherry age in dry, airy bodegas aboveground (rather than in humid cellars underground, like most other wines), some of the wine's water evaporates, thereby increasing the wine's alcoholic strength. Some olorosos aged for more than ten years can be as much as 24 percent alcohol, compared to their starting point of 18 percent.

## Turning two into a dozen (at least)

Sherry begins to get a bit confusing when you realize that the 2 types of it (fino and oloroso) branch into at least 12 types. New styles occur when the natural course of aging changes the character of a Sherry so that its taste no longer conforms to one of the two categories. Deliberate sweetening of the wine also creates different styles.

Among dry Sherries, the main styles are

- **Fino:** This style of Sherry is pale, straw-colored, light-bodied, dry, and delicate. Fino Sherries are always matured under flor, either in Jerez or Puerto de Santa María. They have 15 to 17 percent alcohol. After they lose their protective flor (by bottling), finos become very vulnerable to oxidation spoilage. You must therefore store them in a cool place, drink them young, and refrigerate them after opening. They're best when chilled.

- **Manzanilla:** Pale, straw-colored, delicate, light, tangy, and very dry fino-style Sherry, manzanilla is made only in Sanlucar de Barrameda. (Although various styles of manzanilla are produced, *manzanilla fina,* the fino style, is by far the most common.) The temperate sea climate causes the flor to grow thicker in this town, and manzanilla is thus the driest and most pungent of all the Sherries. Handle it similarly to a fino Sherry.

- **Manzanilla pasada:** A manzanilla that has been aged in a cask about seven years and has lost its flor is referred to as *manzanilla pasada.* It's more amber in color than a manzanilla fina and fuller-bodied. Close to a dry amontillado (see the next item) in style, manzanilla pasada is still crisp and pungent. Serve it cool.

- **Amontillado:** An aged fino that has lost its flor in the process of cask aging, amontillado (ah-moan-tee-*yah*-doh) is deeper amber in color and richer and nuttier than the previous styles. It's dry but retains some of the pungent tang from its lost flor. True amontillado is fairly rare; most of the best examples are in the $25 to $40 price range. Cheaper Sherries labeled *amontillado* are common, so be suspicious if one costs less than $15 a bottle. Serve amontillado slightly cool and, for best flavor, finish the bottle within a week.

- **Oloroso:** Dark gold to deep brown in color (depending on its age), full-bodied with rich, raisiny aroma and flavor, but dry, oloroso lacks the delicacy and pungency of fino Sherries. Olorosos are usually between 18 and 20 percent alcohol and can keep for a few weeks after you open the bottle because they've already been oxidized in their aging. Serve them at room temperature.

- **Palo cortado:** The rarest of all Sherries, palo cortado (*pah*-loe cor-*tah*-doh) starts out as a fino, with flor, and develops as an amontillado, losing its flor. But then, for some unknown reason, it begins to resemble the richer, more fragrant oloroso style, all the while retaining the elegance of an amontillado. In color and alcohol content, palo cortado is similar to an oloroso, but its aroma is quite like an amontillado. Like amontillado Sherry, beware of cheap imitations. Serve palo cortado at room temperature. It keeps as well as olorosos.

Sweet Sherry is dry Sherry that has been sweetened. The sweetening can come in many forms, such as the juice of Pedro Ximénez grapes that have been dried like raisins. All the following sweet styles of Sherry are best served at room temperature:

- **Medium Sherry:** Amontillados and light olorosos that have been slightly sweetened, medium Sherries are light brown in color.

- **Pale cream:** Made by blending fino and light amontillado Sherries and lightly sweetening the blend, pale cream Sherries have a very pale gold color. This is a fairly new style.

- **Cream Sherry:** Cream and the lighter "milk" Sherries are rich *amorosos* (the term for sweetened olorosos). They vary in quality, depending on the oloroso used, and can improve in the bottle with age. Cream Sherries are a popular style.

- **Brown Sherry:** This Sherry style is a very dark, rich, sweet, dessert wine that usually contains a coarser style of oloroso.

- **East India Sherry:** This one's a type of Brown Sherry that has been deeply sweetened and colored.

- **Pedro Ximénez and Moscatel:** Extremely sweet, dark brown, syrupy dessert wines, Pedro Ximénez and Moscatel Sherries are made from raisined grapes of these two varieties. As varietally labeled Sherries, they're quite rare today. Often lower in alcohol, these Sherry styles are delicious over vanilla ice cream (really!).

Some wines from elsewhere in the world, especially the United States, also call themselves "Sherry." Many of these are inexpensive wines in large bottles. Occasionally you can find a decent one, but usually they're sweet and not very good. Authentic Sherry is made only in the Jerez region of

**Book VI**

**And More Wine Regions!**

Spain and carries the official name, *Jerez-Xérès-Sherry* (the Spanish, French, and English names for the town) on the front or back label (flip to Chapter 3 in Book I for help distinguishing the front label from the back one).

## Storing and serving Sherry

The light, dry Sherries — fino and manzanilla — must be fresh. Buy them from stores with rapid turnover; a fino or manzanilla that has been languishing on the shelf for several months won't give you the authentic experience of these wines.

Although fino or manzanilla can be an excellent apéritif, be careful when ordering a glass in a restaurant or bar. Never accept a glass from an already-open bottle unless the bottle has been refrigerated. Even then, ask how long it has been open — more than two days is too much. After you open a bottle at home, refrigerate it and finish it within a couple days.

Manzanilla and fino Sherry are ideal with almonds, olives, shrimp or prawns, all kinds of seafood, and those wonderful tapas in Spanish bars and restaurants. Amontillado Sherries can accompany tapas before dinner but are also fine at the table with light soups, cheese, ham, or salami (especially the Spanish type, *chorizo*). Dry olorosos and palo cortados are best with nuts, olives, and hard cheeses (such as the excellent Spanish sheep-milk cheese, Manchego). All the sweet Sherries can be served with desserts or enjoyed on their own.

## Recommending specific Sherries

Sherries are among the great values in the wine world: You can buy decent, genuine Sherries for $7 or $8. But if you want to try the best wines, you may have to spend $15 or more. Following are some top Sherries, according to type.

### Fino

All of these fino Sherries cost about $15 to $18:

- González Byass's Tío Pepe
- Pedro Domecq's La Ina
- Emilio Lustau's Jarana
- Valdespino's Inocente

### Manzanilla

Keep your eyes peeled for these two stellar manzanilla Sherries:

- Hidalgo's La Gitana (a great buy at $12, or $9 for a 500-milliliter bottle)
- Hidalgo's Manzanilla Pasada (about $20)

### Amontillado

A great number of cheap imitations exist in this category. For a true amontillado, stick to one of the following brands:

- González Byass's Del Duque (the real thing, at $48; half-bottle, $27)
- Emilio Lustau (any of his amontillados labeled *Almacenista,* $35 to $40)
- Hidalgo's Napoleon (about $18)
- Osborne's Solera A.O.S. ($40)

### Oloroso

If you're dying to try oloroso Sherry, you won't miss out by tasting any of these wines:

- González Byass's Matusalem ($48; half-bottle, $27)
- Emilio Lustau (any of his olorosos labeled *Almacenista,* $35 to $40)
- Osborne's "Very Old" ($38)

### Palo cortado

You find many imitations in this category, too. True palo cortados are quite rare, so stick with the following:

- González Byass's Apostoles ($48; half-bottle, $27)
- Emilio Lustau (any of his palo cortados labeled *Almacenista,* $35 to $40)
- Hidalgo's Jerez Cortado (about $35)

### Cream

For an introduction to cream Sherry that's sure to impress, try

- Sandeman's Armada Cream ($12 to $13)
- Emilio Lustau's Rare Cream Solera Reserva ($25 to $27)

### East India, Pedro Ximénez, Moscatel

You can't go wrong with either of these sweet Sherries:

- ✔ Emilio Lustau (a quality brand for all three Sherries; all about $25)
- ✔ González Byass's Pedro Ximénez "Noe" ($48; half-bottle, $27)

## Presenting Montilla: A Sherry look-alike

Northeast of Spain's Sherry region is the Montilla-Moriles region (commonly referred to as Montilla; see Figure 1-1), where wines very similar to Sherry are made in fino, amontillado, and oloroso styles. The two big differences between Montilla (moan-*tee*-yah) and Sherry are as follows:

- ✔ Pedro Ximénez is the predominant grape variety in Montilla.
- ✔ Montillas usually reach their high alcohol levels naturally (without fortification).

Alvear is the leading brand of Montilla. Reasonably priced (about $14), these wines are widely available as finos or amontillados.

# Chapter 2

# Portugal: Port Wine and Beyond

. . . . . . . . . . . . . . . . . . . . . . . . . . . . . . . . . . . . . . . . . . . . . . . . . . . .

*In This Chapter*

▶ Pouring over Portugal's legendary dessert wine

▶ Tasting some striking whites and reds, including white Vinho Verde

▶ Appreciating how Madeira just gets better with age

. . . . . . . . . . . . . . . . . . . . . . . . . . . . . . . . . . . . . . . . . . . . . . . . . . . .

*P*ortugal is justifiably famous for its great dessert wine, Port. But gradually, wine lovers are discovering the other dimensions of Portuguese wine — its dry wines, especially its reds. Most of these wines come from native Portuguese grape varieties, of which the country has hundreds. Expect Portugal's well-priced wines to play a larger role in world wine markets in the 21st century. For now, use this chapter as your guide to the main wines of Portugal.

Portugal's highest rank for wines is *Denominação de Origen* (DO), which has been awarded to the wines of 32 regions. The table wine category includes eight *vinho regional* (VR) regions, equivalent to France's *vin de pays,* and the simple *vinho de mesa* (table wines).

## Port: The Glory of Portugal

Port is the world's greatest fortified red wine. Without question.

The British invented Port, thanks to one of their many wars with the French, when they were forced to buy Portuguese wine as an alternative to French wine. To ensure that the Portuguese wines were stable enough for shipment by sea, the British had a small amount of brandy added to the finished wine and thereby created early Port. The British established their first Port house, Warre, in the city of Oporto in 1670, and several others followed.

Ironically, the French, who drove the British to Portugal, today drink three times as much Port as the British! But, of course, the French have the highest per capita consumption of wine in the world.

The sections that follow delve into the details of Port, including the various styles available and how to store and serve them.

## Home, home on the Douro

Port takes its name from the city of Oporto, situated where the northerly Douro River empties into the Atlantic Ocean. But its vineyards are far away, in the hot, mountainous Douro Valley. (In 1756, this wine region became one of the first in the world to be officially recognized by its government.) Some of the most dramatically beautiful vineyards anywhere are on the slopes of the upper Douro — still very much a rugged, unspoiled area.

Port wine is typically fermented and fortified in the Douro Valley before traveling downriver to the coast. The large shippers' wine is finished and matured in the Port lodges of Vila Nova de Gaia, a suburb of Oporto, whereas most small producers mature their wine in the Valley. From Oporto, the wine is shipped all over the world.

To stop your wine-nerd friends in their tracks, ask them to name the authorized grape varieties for Port. (That's more than 80, by the way.) In truth, most wine lovers — even Port lovers — can't name more than one variety. These grapes are mostly local and unknown outside of Portugal. For the record, the five most important varieties are Touriga Nacional, Tinta Roriz (Tempranillo), Tinta Barroca, Tinto Cão, and Touriga Franca.

## A Port style for every persuasion

Think Sherry (described in Chapter 1 of Book VI) is complicated? In some ways, Port is even trickier. Although all Port is sweet and most is red, a zillion styles exist. The styles vary according to the quality of the base wine (ranging from ordinary to exceptional), how long the wine is aged in wood before bottling (ranging from 2 to 40-plus years), and whether the wine is from a single year or blended from wines of several years.

Following is a brief description of the main Port styles, from simplest to most complex:

- **White Port:** Made from white grapes, this gold-colored wine can be off-dry or sweet. When served with tonic and ice, white Port can be a bracing warm-weather apéritif.

✔ **Ruby Port:** This young, nonvintage style is aged in wood for about three years before it's released. Fruity, simple, and inexpensive (around $12 for major brands), it's the best-selling type of Port. If labeled *Reserve* or *Special Reserve,* the wine has usually aged about six years and costs a few dollars more.

Ruby Port is a good introduction to the Port world.

✔ **Vintage Character Port:** Despite its name, this wine isn't single-vintage Port — it just tries to taste like one. Vintage Character Port is actually premium ruby blended from higher-quality wines of several vintages and matured in wood for about five years. Full-bodied, rich, and ready-to-drink when released, these wines are a good value at about $17 to $19. But the labels don't always say *Vintage Character;* instead, they often bear proprietary names such as Founder's Reserve (from Sandeman), Bin 27 (Fonseca), Six Grapes (Graham), First Estate (Taylor Fladgate), Warrior (Warre), and Distinction (Croft). As if *Vintage Character* wouldn't have been confusing enough!

**Book VI**

**And More Wine Regions!**

✔ **Tawny Port:** Tawny is the most versatile Port style. The best tawnies are good-quality wines that fade to a pale garnet or brownish red color during long wood aging. Their labels carry an indication of their *average age* (the average age of the wines from which they were blended) — 10, 20, 30, or 40-plus years. Ten-year-old tawnies cost about $30; 20-year-olds sell for $45 to $50; and 30- and over-40-year-old tawnies cost a lot more ($90 to well over $100). The best buys are generally the 10- and 20-year-old tawnies; the older ones aren't always worth the extra bucks. Tawny Ports have more finesse than other styles and are appropriate both as apéritifs and after dinner. Inexpensive tawnies that sell for about the same price as ruby Port are usually weak in flavor and not worth buying.

A serious tawny Port can be enjoyed in warm weather (even with a few ice cubes!) when a Vintage Port would be too heavy and tannic.

✔ **Colheita Port:** Often confused with Vintage Port because it's vintage-dated, colheita is actually a tawny Port from a single vintage. In other words, it has aged (and softened and tawnied) in wood for many years. Unlike an aged tawny, though, it's the wine of a single year. Niepoort is one of the few Port houses that specializes in colheita Port. It can be very good, but older vintages are quite expensive (about $100). Smith Woodhouse and Delaforce offer colheita Ports for $50 or less.

✔ **Late Bottled Vintage (LBV) Port:** This type *is* from a specific vintage, but usually not from a top year. The wine ages four to six years in wood before bottling and is then ready to drink, unlike Vintage Port. Quite full-bodied, but not as hefty as Vintage Port, it sells for $18 to $23.

✔ **Vintage Port:** The pinnacle of Port production, Vintage Port is the wine of a single year blended from several of a house's best vineyards. It's bottled at about two years of age, before the wine has much chance to shed its tough tannins. It therefore requires an enormous amount of bottle aging to accomplish the development that didn't occur in wood. Vintage Port usually isn't *mature* (ready to drink) until about 20 years after the vintage, but it can live 70 or more years in top vintages.

Because it's very rich and very tannic, this wine throws a heavy sediment and *must* be decanted, preferably several hours before drinking (see Chapter 4 in Book I for more on decanting wine).

Most good Vintage Ports sell for $75 to $100 when they're first released (years away from drinkability). Mature Vintage Ports can cost well over $100. Producing a Vintage Port amounts to a *declaration of that vintage* (a phrase you hear in Port circles) on the part of an individual Port house.

✔ **Single Quinta Vintage Port:** These are Vintage Ports from a single estate *(quinta)* that's usually a producer's best property (such as Taylor's Vargellas and Graham's Malvedos). They're made in good years, but not in the best vintages, because then their grapes are needed for the Vintage Port blend. They have the advantage of being readier to drink than declared Vintage Ports — at less than half their price — and of usually being released when they're mature. You should decant and aerate them before serving, however.

Don't let all the complicated styles of Port deter you from picking up a bottle and trying it. If you've never had Port before, you're bound to love it — almost no matter which style you try. Later, you can fine-tune your preference for one style or another.

## Suggestions for storing and serving Port

Treat Vintage Ports like all other fine red wines: Store the bottles on their sides in a cool place. You can store other Ports either on their sides (if they have a cork rather than a plastic-topped cork stopper) or upright. All Ports, except white, ruby, and older Vintage Ports, keep well for a week or so after opening, with aged-stated tawny capable of keeping for a few weeks.

You can now find Vintage Ports and some Vintage Character Ports, such as Fonseca Bin 27, in half-bottles — a brilliant development for Port lovers. Enjoying a bottle after dinner is far easier to justify when it's just a half-bottle. The wine evolves slightly more quickly in half-bottles, and considering the wine's longevity, that may even be a bonus!

Serve Port at cool room temperature, 64 degrees Fahrenheit, although tawny Port can be an invigorating pick-me-up when served chilled during warm weather. The classic complements to Port are walnuts and strong cheeses, such as Stilton, Gorgonzola, Roquefort, Cheddar, and aged Gouda.

## Recommended Port producers

In terms of quality, with the exception of a few clunker producers, Port is one of the most consistent of all wines. The following Port producers are organized into two categories: outstanding and very good. As you might expect, wines in the first group tend to be a bit more expensive. (*Note:* These ratings are based mainly on Vintage Port but can be generally applied to all the various Port styles of the house.)

Book VI

And More Wine Regions!

### Outstanding

| | |
|---|---|
| Taylor-Fladgate | Dow |
| Fonseca | Smith-Woodhouse |
| Graham | Cockburn |
| Quinta do Noval "Nacional" | |

### Very Good

| | |
|---|---|
| Ramos Pinto | Cálem |
| Warre | Churchill |
| Quinta do Noval | Delaforce |
| Niepoort | Gould Campbell |
| Croft | Martinez |
| Sandeman | Osborne |
| Quinta do Infantado | Offley |
| Quinta do Vesuvio | Rozes |
| Ferreira | |

Recent good vintages of Vintage Port to buy include 2000, 1994, 1992, and 1991, with both 2003 and 2007 (to be released beginning in 2009) showing promise for the future.

---

## Another Portuguese classic

One of the great dessert wines made mainly from the white or pink Muscat grape is Setúbal (*shtoo*-bahl). Produced just south of Lisbon, Setúbal is made similarly to Port, with alcohol added to stop fermentation. Like Port, it's a rich, long-lasting wine. The most important producer is J.M. da Fonseca.

# *Portugal's "Green" White: Vinho Verde*

On hot summer evenings, the most appropriate Portuguese wine can be a bottle of bracing, slightly effervescent, white Vinho Verde (*veen*-yo *vaird*). The high acidity of Vinho Verde refreshes your mouth and particularly complements grilled fish or seafood.

The Minho region, Vinho Verde's home, is in the northwest corner of Portugal, directly across the border from the Rías Baixas wine region of Spain. (The region is particularly verdant because of the rain from the Atlantic Ocean — one theory behind the wine's name.)

Two styles of white Vinho Verde exist on the market. The most commonly found brands (Aveleda and Casal Garcia), which sell for $7 or $8, are medium-dry wines of average quality that are best served cold.

The more expensive Vinho Verdes ($15 to $20) are varietal wines made from either the Alvarinho grape (Rías Baixas's Albariño), Loureiro, or Trajadura. These are Portugal's best whites; they're more complex, drier, and more concentrated than basic Vinho Verde. Unfortunately, these finer wines are more difficult to find than the inexpensive ones; look for them in better wine shops or in Portuguese neighborhoods — or on your next trip to Portugal!

The majority of wines from Vinho Verde are red. However, these wines are *highly* acidic; you definitely need to acquire a taste for them.

# *Noteworthy Portuguese Red Wines*

Possibly the best dry red wine in Portugal, Barca Velha, comes from the Douro region, where the grapes for Port grow. Made by the Ferreira Port house, Barca Velha is a full-bodied, intense, concentrated wine that needs years to age — Portugal's version of Vega Sicilia's Unico, but at a considerably lower price ($65 to $70). Like Unico, not much is made, and it's produced only in the best vintages.

Fortunately, the Port house of Ramos Pinto (now owned by Roederer Champagne) makes inexpensive, top-quality, dry red Douro wines that are readily available. Duas Quintas (about $12) has ripe, plummy flavors and a velvety texture; it's surprisingly rich but supple, and it's a great value.

The Douro region boasts other terrific dry red wines, most of them fairly new and based on grapes traditionally used for Port. Brands to look for include Quinta do Vale D. Maria, Quinta do Vallado, Quinta do Crasto, Quinta do Cotto, Quinta de la Rosa, Quinta do Vale Meão, Quinta de Roriz, Quinta da Leda Vale do Bomfim, and Chryseia.

## Recognizing Portuguese wine terms

The following terms may appear on Portuguese wine labels:

✔ **Colheita:** Vintage year

✔ **Garrafeira:** A reserva that has aged at least two years in a cask and one in a bottle if it's red, or six months in a cask and six months in a bottle if it's white

✔ **Quinta:** Estate or vineyard

✔ **Reserva:** A wine of superior quality from one vintage

✔ **Tinto:** Red

Other good red Portuguese wines to try include

✔ **Quinta do Carmo:** The majority owner of this estate in the dynamic Alentejo region in southern Portugal is Château Lafite-Rothschild. A rich, full-bodied wine, Quinta do Carmo sells for $25. Don Martinho, a second-label wine from the estate, is less than half the price of Quinta do Carmo.

✔ **Quinta de Pancas:** One of the few Cabernet Sauvignons in Portugal, Quinta de Pancas comes from the Alenquer region, north of Lisbon; it sells for about $15.

✔ **Quinta de Parrotes:** Made from the local Castelão Frances grape variety, Quinta de Parrotes (from the same estate in Alenquer as the Quinta de Pancas) is a steal at $10.

✔ **Quinta da Bacalhôa:** An estate-bottled Cabernet Sauvignon-Merlot from the esteemed Portuguese winemaker Joào Pires in Azeitao (south of Lisbon), Bacalhôa has the elegance of a Bordeaux and sells for $27.

✔ **The red wines of J.M. da Fonseca Successores:** This firm (which is no relation to the Fonseca Port house) is producing some of the best red wines in Portugal. Look for Quinta da Camarate, Morgado do Reguengo, Tinto Velho Rosado Fernandes, and all da Fonseca's Garrafeiras.

✔ **The wines of Joao Portugal Ramos:** A tireless winemaker who consults for various wineries and also owns three properties, Ramos has a golden touch and yet maintains the typicity of his wines. Some wines sell under his own name; others are Marquês de Borba and Vila Santa.

# Madeira: A Long-Lived Island Wine

The legendary wine called Madeira (pronounced muh-*deer*-uh) comes from the island of the same name, which sits in the Atlantic Ocean nearer to Africa than Europe. Madeira is a subtropical island whose precarious hillside vineyards rise straight up from the ocean. The island is a province of Portugal, but the British have always run its wine trade. (Historically, Madeira could even be considered something of an American wine because the American colonists drank it.)

Although Madeira's fortified wines were quite the rage 200 years ago, the island's vineyards were devastated at the end of the 19th century, first by mildew and then by the phylloxera louse. Most vineyards were replanted with lesser grapes, and Madeira has spent a long time recovering from these setbacks. In the 19th century, more than 70 companies were shipping Madeira all over the world; now only six companies of any size exist: Barbeito, H. M. Borges, Henriques & Henriques, Justino Henriques, the Madeira Wine Company (the largest by far), and Pereira d'Oliveira.

The very best Madeira wines are still those from the old days: vintage-dated wines from 1920 back to 1795. Surprisingly, you can still find a few Madeiras from the 19th century. The prices aren't outrageous, either ($300 to $400 a bottle), considering what other wines that old, such as Bordeaux, cost.

The following sections reveal the true magic of Madeira, from its timeless taste to its long life.

## *Seeing how Madeira's made*

A curiosity of most Madeira production is a baking process called the *estufagem,* which follows fermentation. The fact that Madeira improves with heat was discovered back in the 17th century. When trading ships crossed the equator with casks of Madeira as ballast in their holds, the wine actually improved! Of course, today's practice of baking the wine at home on the island is a bit more practical than sending it around the world in a slow boat.

In the estufagem process, Madeira spends a minimum of three months, often longer, in heated tanks in *estufas* (heating rooms). Any sugars in the wine become caramelized, and the wine becomes thoroughly *maderized* (oxidized through heating) without developing any unpleasant aroma or taste.

A more laborious and considerably more expensive way of heating Madeira is the *canteiro* method, in which barrels are left in warm lofts or exposed to the sun (the weather on the island stays warm year-round) for as long as three years. The same magical metamorphosis takes place in the wines. The *canteiro* method is best for Madeira because the wines retain their high acidity and color and extract much better in the slow, natural three-year process; only the finer Madeiras use this method of aging.

# Enjoying the timeless taste of Madeira

The best Madeira comes in four styles, two fairly dry and two sweet. The sweeter Madeiras generally have their fermentation halted somewhat early by the addition of alcohol. Drier Madeiras have alcohol added after fermentation.

Technically, almost all the best Madeira starts as white wine, but the heating process and years of maturation give it an amber color. It has a tangy aroma and a flavor that's uniquely its own, as well as an impressively long finish on the palate. When Madeira is made from any of the island's five noble grapes (listed in the following section), the grape name indicates the style. When Madeira doesn't carry a grape name — and most younger Madeiras don't — the words *dry, medium-dry, medium-sweet,* and *sweet* indicate the style.

**Book VI**

**And More Wine Regions!**

Vintage Madeira must spend at least 20 years in a cask, but in the old days, the aging was even longer. The aroma of an old Madeira is divine, and you continue tasting the wine long after you've swallowed it. (Spitting is out of the question.) Words truly are inadequate to describe this wine.

If you can afford to buy an old bottle of vintage-dated Madeira (the producer's name is relatively unimportant), you're likely to develop a passion for it. And maybe some day when Madeira production gets back on its feet, every wine lover will be able to experience Vintage Madeira. In the meantime, for a less expensive Madeira experience, look for wines labeled *15 years old, 10 years old,* or *5 years old.* Don't bother with any other type, because it'll be unremarkable.

Never fret about Madeira getting too old. It's indestructible. The enemies of wine — heat and oxygen — have already had their way with Madeira during the winemaking and maturing processes. Nothing you do after opening a bottle of Madeira can make the wine blink.

If a Madeira is dated with the word Solera — for example, Solera 1890 — it is not a Vintage Madeira but a blend of many younger vintages whose original barrel, or solera, dates back to 1890. Solera-dated Madeiras can be very fine and generally aren't as expensive — nor as great — as Vintage Madeiras. But Solera Madeiras are becoming obsolete today. In their place is a new style of Madeira, called Colheita or Harvest. This style is modeled after colheita Port in that colheita Madeira is a single vintage-dated Madeira wine. Colheita Madeira doesn't have to spend a minimum of 20 years aging in a cask, as does Vintage Madeira, but only five — or seven for the driest, Sercial. (For example, the 1994 colheita Madeira debuted in 2000 at only six years of age.) Colheita Madeira is much less expensive than vintage Madeira. Most of the six major Madeira shippers are now selling colheita; sales of vintage-dated Madeira have doubled since the introduction of this style.

## Presenting the varieties that make Madeira

Vintage, colheita, and solera-dated Madeiras are made from a single grape variety and are varietally labeled. The grapes include five noble white grape varieties and one less-noble red variety. (Another noble red variety, Bastardo, is no longer used for commercial production.) Each variety corresponds to a specific style of wine; they're listed here, from driest to sweetest.

- **Sercial:** The Sercial (*ser*-shuhl) grape grows at the highest altitudes. Consequently, these grapes are the least ripe and make the driest Madeira. Sercial Madeira is high in acidity and very tangy. It's an outstanding apéritif wine with almonds, olives, or light cheeses. Unfortunately, true Sercial is quite rare today.

- **Verdelho:** The Verdelho (vehr-*deh*-lyoh) grape makes a medium-dry style, with nutty, peachy flavors and a tang of acidity. It's good as an apéritif or with consommé.

- **Bual (or Boal):** Darker amber in color, Bual (boh-*ahl*) is a rich, medium-sweet Madeira with spicy flavors of almonds and raisins and a long, tangy finish. Bual is best after dinner. Like Sercial, true Bual is rare today.

- **Malmsey:** Made from the Malvasia grape, Malmsey (*mahm*-zee) is dark amber, sweet, and intensely concentrated with a very long finish. Drink it after dinner.

The less-noble red Tinta Negra Mole (*teen*-tuh *nay*-gruh *moh*-leh) variety is the dominant grape for today's Madeira production (used for more than 85 percent of Madeira wines), because it grows more prolifically than the five noble white varieties and without the diseases to which they're prone. Also, it's less site-specific; it can grow anywhere on the island, unlike the noble varieties, which grow in vineyards close to the sea where the urban sprawl of Funchal, Madeira's capital city, encroaches on them. Previously, the less-regarded Tinta Negra Mole wasn't identified as a variety on bottles of Madeira, but now the huge Madeira Wine Company is beginning to varietally label Tinta Negra Mole Madeiras.

Two rare grape varieties, whose names you may see on some very old Madeira bottles, are

- **Terrantez:** Medium-sweet, between Verdelho and Bual in style, this is a powerful, fragrant Madeira with lots of acidity. For some Madeira lovers, Terrantez is the greatest variety of all. Unfortunately, very little Terrantez is available today; Henriques & Henriques still produces it though. If you can get your hands on a bottle, drink it after dinner.

- **Bastardo:** This is the only red grape of the noble varieties. Old Bastardos from the last century are mahogany-colored and rich, but not as rich as the Terrantez.

# Chapter 3

# Finding Little-Known Treasures in Greece

*Y*ou may find it hard to comprehend that a country that practically invented wine, way back in the seventh century BC, could be an emerging wine region today. But that's the way it is. Greece never stopped making wine for all those centuries, but her wine industry took the slow track, inhibited by Turkish rule, political turmoil, and other real-life issues.

The modern era of Greek winemaking didn't begin until the 1960s. Fortunately, it has made some particularly strong strides since then. Today, Greek wines are worth knowing. This chapter helps you do just that by introducing you to Greece's main native grape varieties and its wine regions (as well as their best producers!) and naming regulations. *Opa!*

## Glimpsing the Grapes of Greece

Although Greece is a southern country and famous for its sunshine, its grape-growing climate is actually quite varied, because many vineyards are situated at high altitudes where the weather is cooler. (Most of Greece is mountainous, in fact.) Its wines are mainly (60 percent) white; some of those whites are sweet dessert wines, but most are dry.

One of Greece's greatest wine assets — and handicaps, at the same time — is its abundance of native grape varieties, more than 300 of them if you really want to know. (Only Italy has more indigenous grape varieties.) These native grapes make Greek wines particularly exciting for curious wine lovers to explore, but their unfamiliar names make the wines difficult to sell. Fortunately for the marketers, Greece also produces wines from internationally famous grape varieties such as Chardonnay, Merlot, Syrah, and Cabernet Sauvignon, and those wines can be very good. These days, however, producers seem more committed than ever to their native varieties rather than international grapes.

Of Greece's many indigenous grape varieties, four in particular stand out as the most important — two are white and two are red:

- **Assyrtiko:** Pronounced ah-*seer*-tee-koe, this white variety makes delicate, bone-dry, crisp, very long-lived wines with citrusy and minerally aromas and flavors. Although Assyrtiko grows in various parts of Greece, the best Assyrtiko wines come from the volcanic island of Santorini. Any wine called Santorini is made at least 90 percent from Assyrtiko.

- **Moschofilero:** A very aromatic, pink-skinned variety, Moschofilero (mos-cho-*feel*-eh-roe) makes both dry white and pale-colored dry rosé wines. It grows mainly around Mantinia, in the central, mountainous Peloponnese region. If a wine is named Mantinia, it must be at least 85 percent Moschofilero. Wines made from Moschofilero have high acidity and are fairly low in alcohol, with aromas and flavors of apricots and/or peaches.

  Because they're so easy to drink, Moschofilero wines are a great introduction to Greek wines.

- **Agiorghitiko:** The name of the Agiorghitiko (eye-your-*yee*-tee-koe) grape translates in English to "St. George," and a few winemakers call it that on the labels of wines destined for English-speaking countries. Greece's most-planted and probably most important native red variety, it grows throughout the mainland. Its home turf, where it really excels, is in the Nemea district of the Peloponnese region; any wine named Nemea is made entirely from Agiorghitiko. Wines from this variety are medium to deep in color, have complex aromas and flavors of plums and/or blackcurrants, and often have a resemblance to Cabernet Franc or spicy Merlot wines. Agiorghitiko also blends well with other indigenous or international varieties.

- **Xinomavro:** The most important red variety in the Macedonia region of Northern Greece, Xinomavro (ksee-*no*-mav-roe) produces highly tannic wines with considerable acidity that have been compared to the Nebbiolo wines of Piedmont, Italy (see Chapter 2 in Book III). Wines made from Xinomavro have complex, spicy aromas, often suggesting dried tomatoes, olives, and/or berries. Xinomavro wines are dark in color but lighten with age; they have great longevity. Their home base is the Naoussa district of Macedonia; any wine named Naoussa is made entirely from Xinomavro.

Other important white indigenous varieties in Greece include Roditis (actually a pink-skinned grape), which makes Patras white; and Savatiano, the most widely planted white grape. Retsina, a traditional Greek wine made by adding pine resin to fermenting grape juice (resulting in a flavor not unlike some oaky Chardonnays), is made mainly from Savatiano. Mavrodaphne is an indigenous Greek red variety that's becoming increasingly important, both for dry and sweet red wines.

# Introducing Greece's Wine Regions and the Wines They Yield

Some of the Greek wine regions whose names you're likely to see on wine labels include

- **Macedonia:** The northernmost part of Greece, with mountainous terrain and cool climates. Naoussa wine comes from here.

- **The Peloponnese:** A large, mainly mountainous, peninsula in south-western Greece with varied climate and soil. Noteworthy wines include the soft, red Nemea; the dry whites Patras and Mantinia; and the sweet wines Mavrodaphne de Patras (red) and Muscat de Patras (white).

- **Crete:** The largest Greek island, which makes both white and red wines, many of which are varietally named along with the place-name of Crete.

- **Other Greek islands:** Besides Crete, the four most important islands that make wine are Santorini, Rhodes, Samos, and Cephalonia.

Many Greek wines today are top quality, especially the wines of small, independent wineries. Following are some top Greek wine producers:

- From Macedonia: Alpha Estate, Domaine Gerovassilou, Kir Yianni Estate, and Tsantali-Mount Athos Vineyards

- From the Peloponnese: Antonopoulos Vineyards, Gaia Estate (also has wineries in Santorini), Katogi & Strofilia (with operations also in Macedonia), Mercouri Estate, Papantonis Winery, Domaine Skouras, Domaine Spiropoulos, and Domaine Tselepos

- From the islands: Boutari Estates (six estates throughout Greece, including Crete and Santorini), Gentilini (in Cephalonia), and Domaine Sigalas (Santorini)

# Understanding the Naming Regulations of Greek Wines

Greece is a member of the European Union, and its appellation system for wine therefore conforms to the EU's two-tiered structure. At the top (QWPSR) level, Greece has two categories:

- AOQS, *Appellation d'Origine de Qualité Supérieure* (yes, that's French!), for dry and off-dry wines
- AOC, *Appellation d'Origine Contrôlée,* for dessert and fortified wines

Table wines with a geographic name are called *vins de pays* (regional wines). Many of Greece's better wines actually carry a vins de pays appellation.

Other terms that have formal definitions under Greek wine regulations include *reserve* (QWPSR wines with a minimum of two or three years of aging, for whites and reds respectively), *grande reserve* (one additional year of aging), and *cava* (a table wine — in the EU sense of being at the lower appellation tier — with the same aging requirements as reserve).

# Chapter 4

# A Sampling of Wines from Germany, Austria, and Hungary

Many people think of Germany as a beer-drinking country, and they're not wrong. Yet Germany ranks sixth in the world in wine production, and Germany's per capita wine consumption is about four times higher than that of the United States (although well behind the really big wine drinkers: the French, Italians, and Portuguese).

Neighboring Austria boasts gorgeous vineyard regions, classic beauty, and winning wines. What makes Austrian wines all the more interesting is how they're evolving, as winemakers gradually discover how to best express their land and their grapes through wine.

Tucked into mountains and balmy, Hungary shows off its independence with a renowned dessert wine and a range of whites and reds that offer excellent value.

Consider this chapter your overview of the somewhat familiar and somewhat unusual varieties and varietals of these three lesser-known but worthy wine-producing countries.

## Germany: Europe's Individualist

German wines march to the beat of a different drummer. They come in mainly one color: white. (A whopping 85 percent of Germany's wines are white.) They're fruity in style, low in alcohol, rarely oaked, and often off-dry or sweet. Their labels carry grape names, which is an anomaly in Europe.

Germany is the northernmost major wine-producing country in Europe — which means its climate is cool. Except in warmer pockets of Germany, red grapes don't ripen adequately, which is why most German wines are white. The climate is also erratic from year to year, so vintages really matter for fine German wines. Germany's finest vineyards are situated along rivers, such as the Rhine and the Mosel, and on steep, sunny slopes to temper the extremes of the weather and help the grapes ripen.

The following sections introduce you to Germany's main grape varieties, the ins and outs of Germany's wine laws and styles, and some wine regions (and producers!) you should really get to know.

## Riesling and its cohorts

In Germany's cool climate, the noble Riesling (*reese*-ling) grape finds true happiness. Riesling represents just over 20 percent of Germany's vineyard plantings.

Another major, but less distinguished, German variety is Müller-Thurgau (pronounced *mool*-lair *toor*-gow), a cross between the Riesling and Silvaner (or possibly Chasselas) grapes. Its wines are softer than Riesling's, with less character and little potential for greatness.

After Müller-Thurgau and Riesling, the most-planted grapes in Germany are Silvaner, Kerner, Scheurebe, and Ruländer (Pinot Gris). Among Germany's red grapes, Spätburgunder (Pinot Noir) is the most widely planted, mainly in the warmer parts of the country.

## Germany's wine laws in a nutshell

Germany's wine-classification system isn't based on the French AOC system (described in Chapter 1 of Book II), unlike those of most other European countries. German wines, like most European wines, are in fact named after the places they come from. In the best wines, the name is usually a combination of a village name and a vineyard name, such as Piesporter (town) Goldtröpfchen (vineyard).

Unlike most European wines, however, the grape name is also usually part of the wine name (as in Piesporter Goldtröpfchen *Riesling*). And the finest German wines have yet another element in their name — a *Prädikat,* which is an indication of the ripeness of the grapes at harvest (as in Piesporter Goldtröpfchen Riesling *Spätlese*). Wines with a Prädikat hold the highest rank in the German wine system.

Germany's system of assigning the highest rank to the ripest grapes is completely different from the concept behind most other European systems, which is to bestow the highest status on the best vineyards or districts. Germany's system underscores the country's grape-growing priority: Ripeness — never guaranteed in a cool climate — is the highest goal.

German wine law divides wines with a Prädikat into six levels. From the least ripe to the ripest (that is, from the lowest to the highest), they are

- ✔ Kabinett (*kab*-ee-net)

- ✔ Spätlese (*shpate*-lay-seh)

- ✔ Auslese (*ouse*-lay-seh)

- ✔ Beerenauslese (*beer*-en-*ouse*-lay-seh), abbreviated as BA

- ✔ Eiswein (*ice*-vine)

- ✔ Trockenbeerenauslese (*troh*-ken-*beer*-en*ouse*-lay-seh), abbreviated as TBA

At the three highest Prädikat levels, the amount of sugar in the grapes is so high that the wines are inevitably sweet. Many people, therefore, mistakenly believe that the Prädikat level of a German wine is an indication of the wine's sweetness. In fact, the Prädikat is an indication of the amount of sugar in the *grapes at harvest,* not the amount of sugar in the wine. At lower Prädikat levels, the sugar in the grapes can ferment fully, to dryness, and for those wines there's no direct correlation between Prädikat level and sweetness of the wine.

Less than 10 percent of Germany's wine production falls into the lower, table wine categories: *Landwein* (table wines with geographic indication) or *Deutscher Tafelwein.* Most of the inexpensive German wines that you see in wine shops are QbA wines. (In case you're wondering, QbA stands for *Qualitätswein bestimmter Anbaugebiet.* It indicates quality wine from a specified region.)

The next two sections help you discover more about the range of styles found in Germany's wines.

### Deciphering what it means to be dry, half-dry, or gentle

The common perception of German wines is that they're all sweet. Yet many German wines taste either dry or fairly dry. In fact, you can find German wines at just about any sweetness or dryness level you like.

Most inexpensive German wines, such as Liebfraumilch, are light-bodied, fruity wines with pleasant sweetness — wines that are easy to enjoy without food. The German term for this style of wine is *lieblich,* which translates as "gentle" — a poetic but apt descriptor. The very driest German wines are called *trocken* (dry). Wines that are sweeter than trocken but drier than lieblich are called *halbtrocken* (half-dry). The words *trocken* and *halbtrocken* sometimes appear on the label, but not always.

You can make a good stab at determining how sweet a German wine is by reading the alcohol level on the label. If the alcohol is low — about 9 percent, or less — the wine probably contains grape sugar that didn't ferment into alcohol and is therefore sweet. Higher alcohol levels suggest that the grapes fermented completely, to dryness.

Even if you generally prefer dry white wines, you might find that a bit of sweetness in German wines can be appealing — and helpful in improving the quality of the wine. That's because sweetness undercuts the wines' natural high acidity and gives the wines better balance. In truth, most off-dry German wines don't really taste as sweet as they are, thanks to their acidity.

One way that German winemakers keep some sweetness in their wines is called the *süssreserve* (sweet reserve) method. In this method, a winemaker holds back as much as 25 percent of his grape juice and doesn't allow it to ferment. He then ferments the rest of his juice fully, until it's dry wine. Later, he blends the unfermented grape juice into his dry wine. The grape juice (the süssreserve) contributes a natural, juicy sweetness to the wine.

### Discovering what's noble about rot

Wine connoisseurs all over the world recognize Germany's sweet, dessert-style wines as among the greatest wines on the planet. Most of these legendary wines owe their sweetness to an ugly but magical fungus known as *botrytis cinerea,* commonly called *noble rot.* (Noble rot is the same fungus that gives Sauternes its richness. Find out more about Sauternes in Chapter 2 of Book II.)

Noble rot infects ripe grapes in late autumn if a certain combination of humidity and sun is present. This fungus dehydrates the berries and concentrates their sugar and flavors. The wine from these infected berries is sweet, amazingly rich, and complex beyond description. It can also be expensive, costing $100 a bottle or more.

Wines at the BA and TBA Prädikat levels are usually made entirely from grapes infected with noble rot (called *botrytised* grapes) and are generally richly textured and sweet. Auslese-level wines often come from some partially botrytised grapes, and when they do, they're likely to be sweet, although never to the extent of a BA- or TBA-level wine.

## A secret code of German place-names

If you don't speak German and you don't know German geography intimately, deciphering German wine names is tricky, to say the least. Here's a bit of info that can help: In the German language, the possessive is formed by adding the suffix *-er* to a noun. When you see names like Zeller or Hochheimer — names that end in *-er* — on a wine label, the next word is usually a vineyard area that "belongs" to the commune or district with the *-er* on its name (Zell's Swartze Katz, Hochheim's Kirchenstück). The name of the region itself always appears on labels of QbA and Prädikat wines.

Another way Mother Nature can contribute exotic sweetness to German wines is by freezing the grapes on the vine in early winter. When the frozen grapes are harvested and pressed, most of the water in the berries separates out as ice. The sweet, concentrated juice that's left to ferment makes a luscious sweet Prädikat-level wine called *Eiswein* (literally, "icewine"). Eisweins differ from BAs and TBAs because they lack a certain flavor that derives from *botrytis,* sometimes described as a honeyed character.

Both botrytised wines and Eisweins are referred to as *late-harvest wines,* not only in Germany but also throughout the world, because the special character of these wines comes from conditions that normally occur only when the grapes are left on the vine beyond the usual point of harvest.

## *The wine regions of Deutschland*

Germany has 13 wine regions: 11 in the west and 2 in the eastern part of the country (see Figure 4-1). The most famous of these 13 regions are the Mosel-Saar-Ruwer region, named for the Mosel River and two of its tributaries (along which the region's vineyards lie), and the Rheingau region, along the Rhine River. The Rhine River also lends its name to other German wine regions, including Rheinhessen and Pfalz (formerly called the Rheinpfalz). Rounding out the top five German wine regions is, Nahe, named after the Nahe River. The following sections provide a few more details about these exciting German wine regions and recommend some producers to watch for from each area.

**Figure 4-1:**
The wine
regions of
Germany.

### Mosel-Saar-Ruwer

The Mosel-Saar-Ruwer is a dramatically beautiful region, with its vineyards rising steeply on the slopes of the twisting and turning Mosel River. The wines of the region are among the lightest in Germany (usually containing less than 10 percent alcohol); they're generally delicate, fresh, and charming. Riesling dominates the Mosel-Saar-Ruwer with 57 percent of all plantings. Wines from this region are instantly recognizable because they come in green bottles rather than the brown bottles that other German regions use.

The Mosel boasts dozens of excellent winemakers who produce exciting Riesling wines. Some of the top producers include the following:

Egon Mülle
Dr. Fischer
Friedrich Wilhelm Gymnasium
Karlsmühle
Dr. Loosen
Maximin Grünhauser
Merkelbach

Meulenhof
J.J. Prüm
Reichsgraf Von Kesselstatt
Willi Schaefer
Selbach-Oster
Zilliken

# Sampling Germany's wine festivals

✔ Cochem is a medieval town near the Mosel River that's surrounded by vineyards, making it a popular spot for wine tastings and festivals. Mosel Wine Week celebrates the region's offerings with tasting booths and a street fair in the first week of June. A similar event, Weinfest, takes place the last weekend of August. Contact the Cochem tourist information office to find out more; you can find it at `www.cochem.de`.

✔ Each August, the Stuttgart Wine Festival brings together thousands of wine lovers with regional food and more than 350 Württemberg wines. For dates and times, visit the city's Web site at `www.stuttgart-tourist.de`.

✔ Also in August, Freiburg — an alpine town surrounded by 1,600 acres of vineyards — hosts Weinkost. Get to town earlier for a four-day public wine-tasting festival in late June; this one takes place in the square around the city's magnificent cathedral. Contact the tourist information office through the city's Web site, `www.freiburg.de`.

✔ Rounding out August's offerings is the Traditional Rüdesheim Wine Festival, which takes place in the Rhine village most famous for red wines. Visit `www.rudesheim.de` for details.

**Book VI**

**And More Wine Regions!**

## Rheingau

The Rheingau is among Germany's smaller wine regions. It too has some dramatically steep vineyards bordering a river, but here the river is Germany's greatest wine river, the Rhine. The Riesling grape occupies more than 80 percent of the Rheingau's vineyards, many of which are south-facing slopes that give the Riesling grapes an extra edge of ripeness. Rheingau wine styles tend toward two extremes: trocken wines on the one hand (see the earlier "Deciphering what it means to be dry, half-dry, or gentle" section for more on trocken wines) and sweet late-harvest wines on the other hand. Recommended Rheingau producers include Georg Breuer, Knyphausen, Franz Küntsler, Schloss Schönborn, Leitz, and Robert Weil.

## Rheinhessen

Rheinhessen is Germany's largest wine region, producing huge quantities of simple wines for everyday enjoyment. Liebfraumilch originated here, and it's still one of the most important wines of the region, commercially speaking. The Rheinhessen's highest quality wines come from the Rheinterrasse, a vineyard area along the river. Producers from that area who are particularly good include Gunderloch, Heyl Zu Herrnsheim, and Strub.

## Pfalz

Almost as big as the Rheinhessen, the Pfalz has earned somewhat more respect from wine lovers for its fairly rich and full-bodied white wines and its very good reds — all of which owe their style to the region's relatively warm climate. Müller-Thurgau, Riesling, Silvaner, and Kerner are among the most-planted grape varieties of the Pfalz, but qualitatively Scheurebe and Blauburgunder (Pinot Noir) are important. To experience the best of the Pfalz, look for wines from Dr. Bürklin-Wolf, Rainer Lingenfelder, Müller-Catoir, and Basserman-Jordan.

### Nahe

One other German region of importance for the quality of its wines is Nahe, named for the Nahe River and situated west of Rheinhessen. The Riesling wines here are relatively full and intense. Top producers include Diel, Kruger-Rumpf, Prinz zu Salm-Dahlberg, and Dönnhoff.

# Austria's Exciting Whites (And Reds)

Austria makes less than 1 percent of all the wine in the world — about 28 million cases a year. All of it comes from the eastern part of the country, where the Alps recede into hills, and most of it comes from small wineries. Although some inexpensive Austrian wines do make their way to export markets, the Austrians have embraced a high-quality image, and most of their wines therefore command premium prices.

Although the excellence of Austria's sweet whites has long been recognized, its dry whites and reds have gained recognition only in the past two decades. Reds are in the minority, claiming about 25 percent of the country's production, because many of Austria's wine regions are too cool for growing red grapes. The country's red wines hail mainly from the area of Burgenland, bordering Hungary, one of the warmest parts of Austria. They're medium- to full-bodied, often engagingly spicy, with vivid fruity flavor — and often the international touch of oaky character. Many of them are based on unusual, native grape varieties such as the spicy Blaufrankish (Lemberger), the gentler St. Laurent, or Blauer Zweigelt (a crossing of the other two).

Austria's white wines — apart from the luscious, late-harvest dessert wines made from either botrytised, extremely ripe, or dried grapes — are dry wines ranging from light- to full-bodied that are generally unoaked.

The country's single most important grape variety is the native white Grüner Veltliner (*grew*-ner *velt*-lee-ner). Its wines are full-bodied yet crisp, with rich texture and herbal or sometimes spicy-vegetal flavors (especially green pepper). They're extremely food-friendly and usually high in quality. Some people in the wine trade have nicknamed Grüner Veltliner "GruVe."

Riesling, grown mainly in the region of Lower Austria, in the northeast, is another key grape for quality whites. In fact, some experts believe that Austria's finest wines are its Rieslings (whereas others prefer Grüner Veltliner). Other grape names you may see on bottles of Austrian wine include Müller-Thurgau, which makes dry whites with a great deal of character; Welschriesling, a grape popular in Eastern Europe for inexpensive wines that achieves high quality only in Austria; Pinot Blanc, which can excel here; and Muscat. Sauvignon Blanc is a specialty of the region of Styria, in the south, bordering Slovenia.

In some parts of Austria, for example in the Wachau district, along the Danube River, wines are named in the German system — a town name ending in *-er* followed by a vineyard name and a grape variety. In other parts of Austria, the wine names are generally a grape name (or, increasingly, a proprietary name) followed by the name of the region.

Austria's wine laws draw from the German model (explained in the earlier "Germany's wine laws in a nutshell" section), with QWPSR wine divided into *Qualitätswein* and *Prädikatswein* categories. (One difference is that Kabinett falls into the Qualitätswein category.) But some people believe that an appellation system based on *terroir* rather than ripeness levels would better express the diversity of Austria's vineyard regions. Authorities introduced a new system called *Districtus Austria Controllatus* (DAC) on a limited basis in early 2003.

**Book VI**

**And More Wine Regions!**

# Hungary: A Promising Wine-Producing Nation

Of all the wine-producing countries in Eastern Europe that broke free from Communism in the late 1980s and early 1990s and have resumed wine production under private winery ownership, Hungary seems to have the greatest potential. In addition to a winemaking tradition that dates back to pre-Roman times, Hungary has a wealth of native and international grape varieties and plenty of land suited to vineyards, with a wide range of climates, soils, and altitudes.

Hungarians' wine consumption has increased significantly since the country gained its independence, fueling an improvement in wine quality. International investment in vineyards and wineries has also made a huge contribution.

Hungary produces the equivalent of about 68 million cases of wine a year, most of which is white. Although the country is northerly — its capital, Budapest, sits at the same latitude as Quebec City in Canada — its climate is relatively warm because the country is landlocked and nearly surrounded by mountains. Three large bodies of water affect the microclimate of certain wine regions: Lake Neusiedel, between Hungary and Austria in the northwest; Lake Balaton, Europe's largest lake, in the center of Hungary's western half (which is called Transdanubia); and the Danube River, which runs north to south right through the middle of the country. Hungary has 22 official wine regions, but their names aren't yet particularly important outside of Hungary.

The one Hungarian wine region that does have international fame is Tokaj-Hegyalja, which takes its name from the town of Tokaj and owes its reputation to its world-class dessert wine, Tokaji Azsu (toe-*kye* as-*zoo*). The word *Aszu* refers to botrytised grapes (described earlier in this chapter in the "Discovering what's noble about rot" section). The wine comes from Furmint (*foor*-mint) and Harslevelu (*harsh*-leh-veh-*loo*) grapes, both native white varieties, and sometimes Muscat grapes that have been infected by *botrytis cinerea*. This region also makes dry table wines, such as the varietal Tokaji Furmint.

Tokaji Azsu wines are labeled as three, four, five, or six Puttonyos, according to their sweetness, with six Puttonyos wines being the sweetest. (*Puttonyos* are baskets used to harvest the botrytised grapes, as well as a measure of sweetness.) All Tokaji Azsu wines sell in 500-milliliter bottles, and they range in price from about $35 to $150 per bottle, depending on their sweetness level.

Tokaji Azsu wines vary not only according to their sweetness but also according to their style. Some wines have a fresher, more vibrant fruity character, for example; some have aromas and flavors that suggest dried fruits; some have the smoky character and tannin of new oak barrels; and some have complex, nonfruity notes such as tea leaves or chocolate. This range of styles is due mainly to different winemaking techniques among producers.

Tokaji Azsu has a complicated production method that involves using a certain amount of botrytised grapes (which are compressed into a paste of sorts) as well as healthy, nonmoldy grapes; the more moldy grapes that are used, the sweeter the wine. The production method leaves plenty of room for individual interpretation. Some of the issues that winemakers differ on — besides the normal issues of grape blend — include

- ✔ What the botrytised grapes soak in to create the liquid that then ferments into the final wine: partially fermented wine or simply juice (in either case, from nonmoldy grapes)
- ✔ Whether the wine should mature in new or old oak barrels
- ✔ Whether the wine should be exposed to oxygen during aging (by leaving airspace in the barrels)

Beyond the famous Tokaj-Hegyalja region, Hungary has numerous other wine regions that produce a range of dry and semidry wines, both white and red. Most of these wines are named for their grape variety and are quite inexpensive. Kadarka (*kah*-dahr-kah) is Hungary's best-known native red grape variety.

Hungary is a member of the European Union, and its categories of wine therefore resemble those of EU countries. Wines at the highest level are classified as *Minosegi Bor,* followed by *Tájbor* (country wine) and *Asztali Bor* (table wine).

# Chapter 5

# From South America to South Africa: Rounding Out the Top Wine Nations

The name most often used in wine circles for wines produced outside of Europe is the *New World*. Undoubtedly this phrase, with its ring of colonialism, was coined by a European. Europe, home of all the classic wine regions of the world and producer of more than 60 percent of the world's wine, is the Old World. Everything else is nouveau riche.

Maybe that's fair. Europeans have been making wines for so long that grape-growing and winemaking practices are now codified into detailed regulations. Which hillsides to plant, which grapes should grow where, how dry or sweet a particular wine should be — these decisions were all made long ago, by the grandparents and great-great-grandparents of today's winemakers. But elsewhere, the grape-growing and winemaking game is wide open; every winery owner gets to decide for himself where to grow grapes, what variety to plant, and what style of wine to make. The wines of the New World do have that in common.

Fortunately, New World wines are easy for you to explore without a detailed road map: In the New World, there's little encoded tradition to decipher and relatively little historical backdrop against which the wines need to be appreciated. But having a bit of info on New World wine countries can't hurt, especially if you're just starting to venture into a particular country's offerings. This chapter gets you acquainted with some of the smaller (yet still worthwhile) New World wine-producing nations: Chile, Argentina, and South Africa.

# Chile Discovers Itself

The Spanish first established vineyards in Chile in the mid-16th century, and the country has maintained a thriving wine industry for its home market for several centuries. Nothing new about that. What *is* new about Chile, however, is the growth of her wine industry since the mid-1980s, her rapid development of a strong export market, and her shift toward French grape varieties such as Cabernet Sauvignon, Merlot, and Chardonnay — with an almost-forgotten red Bordeaux variety called Carmenère definitely in the running.

With the Pacific Ocean to the west and the Andes Mountains to the east, Chile is an isolated country. This isolation has its advantages in terms of grape-growing: Phylloxera hasn't yet taken hold in Chile — as it's done in just about every other winemaking country — and *vinifera* vines can therefore grow on their own roots. Chile's other viticultural blessings include a range of mountains along the coast, which blocks the ocean dampness from most vineyards, and the ocean's general tempering influence on a relatively hot climate.

The next sections describe Chile's diverse wine regions and the taste and quality of the country's wines.

## Checking out Chile's wine regions

As in every other country, grape growers and wine producers in Chile originally planted vineyards in the most obvious locations, where grapes would grow prolifically. Trial and error have gradually enabled them to discover the less-obvious locations — many of them cooler and less accessible areas — that offer the opportunity to make truly distinctive wines.

Initially considered the ideal place to plant grapes, Maipo Valley is part of Chile's vast Central Valley, which lies between the coastal range and the Andes. Convenience played a large role: The Maipo Valley surrounds Santiago, Chile's capital and its largest and most important city. Most of Chile's vineyards are still in the Central Valley, but today, vineyards also exist in regions that no one had heard of just ten years ago.

From north to south, here's a summary of Chile's wine regions, both old and new:

 ✔ **Limari Valley:** This is a small region northwest of Santiago, near the Pacific Ocean. Although the climate is hot and dry — it's close to the Atacama Desert and nearer to the equator than any of Chile's other important regions — its unique microclimate, caused by the Valley's proximity to the Pacific, features cooling morning fog and ocean breezes that blow through during the day. Chile's three largest wineries, Concha y Toro, San Pedro, and Santa Rita, all have bought land in Limarí. Promising wines so far are Sauvignon Blanc, Chardonnay, and Syrah. This is one of the country's hot emerging regions.

✔ **Aconcagua Valley:** North of Santiago, Aconcagua Valley is named for the country's highest mountain, the magnificent Mount Aconcagua, and is one of the warmest areas for fine grapes. But Aconcagua also includes many cooler high-altitude sections. Cabernet Sauvignon grows especially well here and, more recently, so does Syrah. Viña Errázuriz is Aconcagua Valley's most important winery.

✔ **Casablanca Valley:** Once considered part of the Aconcagua Valley, the cooler Casablanca Valley, near the Pacific Ocean, now has its own identity. The first-established of the newer Chilean wine regions, it's still one of the best. Some of Chile's finest Chardonnays and Sauvignon Blancs grow in one part of Casablanca; good Merlots and Pinot Noirs come from a more mountainous part. Veramonte is Casablanca's best-known winery, but many other wineries own vineyards in this region.

✔ **San Antonio Valley:** Tiny San Antonio Valley, south of Casablanca Valley and next to the ocean, is arguably Chile's most exciting new wine region. Pinot Noir and Syrah are growing especially well on its cool, steep slopes. Now making one of the world's best Pinot Noirs outside of Burgundy (as well as a fine Syrah), Viña Matetic is the winery to watch in San Antonio Valley.

✔ **Maipo Valley:** Chile's most-established wine region, just south of Santiago, Maipo Valley is home to most of the country's wineries. Concha y Toro, Santa Rita, and Almaviva are a few of Maipo's premium producers. Cabernet Sauvignon is king in this region, and Merlot also does very well.

✔ **Cachapoal Valley:** This red wine region is located near the Andes and is strong in Merlot and Cabernet Sauvignon. Morandé and Altair are two rising star wineries here.

✔ **Colchagua Valley:** Ocean breezes have transformed the formerly quiet Colchagua Valley into one of Chile's most important new red wine regions. Carmenère, Cabernet Sauvignon, Merlot, and Syrah grow especially well here. Colchagua's two leading wineries are Casa Lapostolle and Montes.

✔ **Curicó Valley:** One of Chile's oldest and largest wine regions, both red and white grape varieties grow well in the Curicó Valley because of the Valley's diverse microclimates. The huge San Pedro Winery and Viña Miguel Torres are located in Curicó.

✔ **Maule:** Maule Valley is both Chile's largest wine region in terms of area and the southernmost of its important wine regions. Because it's so huge, it has many diverse microclimates. Red and white varieties grow well here, especially Sauvignon Blanc, Cabernet Sauvignon, and Merlot. Viña Calina is Maule Valley's best-known winery.

# Taking a closer look at Chilean taste and style

Stylistically, Chile's wines generally lack the exuberant fruitiness of Californian and Australian wines (see Book IV and Book V, respectively, for more on these wines). Yet they're not quite as subtle and understated as European wines. Although red wines have always been Chile's strength, today the white wines, especially those from cooler regions, are very good. Chile's Sauvignon Blancs are generally unoaked, whereas most of its Chardonnays are oaked.

Like most New World wines, Chile's wines are generally named for their grape varieties; they carry a regional (or sometimes a district) indication, too. The reasonable prices of the basic wines — mainly from $6 to $10 in the United States — make these wines excellent values. The most important wineries for the export market include, in alphabetical order, Calina, Caliterra, Carmen, Casa Lapostolle, Concha y Toro, Cousiño Macul, Errazuriz, Haras de Pirque, Los Vascos, Montes, Mont Gras, Santa Carolina, Santa Rita, and Undurraga. Viña Matetic, a rising star from the San Antonio Valley, is just beginning to appear on the export markets.

Chile's new challenge is to produce good-quality high-end wines along with its inexpensive varietals. Many of the top producers now make a superpremium red wine in the $45 to $90 price range. These elite Chilean reds are often blends rather than varietal wines, and many are styled along international lines — aged in small French oak barrels and made from very ripe grapes that give rich, fruity flavors and high (14 percent or higher) alcohol levels. What many (but not all) of them lack, however, is a sense of place: They don't taste particularly Chilean. With time, though, Chile will undoubtedly reach its goal and begin producing fine wines that merit their high prices.

Keep an eye out for some of Chile's top superpremium red wines:

- Concha y Toro's Don Melchor Cabernet Sauvignon (about $45)

- Errázuriz's Don Maximiano Founder's Reserve (mainly Cabernet Sauvignon, about $50)

- Albis, a wine from a joint venture between the Chilean Haras de Pirque winery and the Italian Antinori company (Cabernet Sauvignon and Carmenère, about $52)

- Montes Alpha M (a "Bordeaux blend," about $75)

- Almaviva (a sleek and subtle red, mainly Cabernet Sauvignon with Carmenère and Cabernet Franc, about $90)

- Casa Lapostolle's Clos Apalta (a blend of Carmenère, Merlot, and Cabernet Sauvignon, about $80)

✔ Seña, from an estate in Aconcagua that was originally a partnership between the Robert Mondavi and Eduardo Chadwick (of Viña Errázuriz) families and is now owned by the Chadwicks (Cabernet Sauvignon, Merlot, and Carmenère, about $65)

# Argentina, a Major League Player

Argentina produces about four times as much wine as Chile does — that's almost as much as the entire United States. It boasts the largest wine production in South America and the fifth-largest wine production in the world. In recent years, Argentine winemaking has shifted away from large-volume wines suited to the domestic market and toward higher-quality wines that suit wine drinkers outside of Argentina. Not only is Argentina now a major player in the world wine market, but it's also one of the world's most exciting countries for wine production.

Wine grapes have grown in Argentina since the mid-16th century, as they have in Chile (see the earlier sections in this chapter), but Argentina's source of vines was more diverse. For example, many vines were brought over by the vast numbers of Italian and Basque immigrants. As a result, Argentina boasts grape varieties such as Bonarda and Malbec that are insignificant in Chile.

The following sections zero in on Argentina's two main wine regions and suggest numerous Argentine producers, plus a few specific wines, that you should definitely get to know.

## Meeting Mendoza and San Juan — and the grapes they favor

Argentina's wine regions are situated mainly in the western part of the country, where the Andes Mountains divide Argentina from Chile. High altitude tempers the climate, but the vineyards are still very warm by day, cool by night, and desert dry. Rivers flow through the area from the Andes, providing water for irrigation.

The vast majority of Argentina's vineyards are in the state of Mendoza, Argentina's largest wine region, which lies at roughly the same latitude as Santiago, Chile. Within the Mendoza region are various wine districts (the names of which sometimes appear on wine labels) such as Maipú, San Martín, Tupungato, and Luján de Cuyo. Most of Argentina's oldest wineries and their vineyards are clustered close to Mendoza city, but the Uco Valley, south of the city, has attracted many newcomers who are building impressive wineries.

San Juan, just north of Mendoza and considerably hotter, is Argentina's second-largest wine region. La Rioja, Argentina's oldest wine-producing region, is east of San Juan.

San Juan is particularly famous for Torrontés, a variety that's probably indigenous to Galicia, Spain. It produces an inexpensive ($6 to $10), light-bodied, high-acid, aromatic white wine that's one of Argentina's signature whites. It's especially fine with appetizers, seafood, and fish.

Argentina's red wines are generally higher in quality than its whites. The Malbec grape variety — now seldom used in Bordeaux, where it originated — has emerged as Argentina's flagship variety and is gaining popularity at a dizzying pace. Malbec has adapted extremely well to the Mendoza region, and winemakers are busy discovering how it varies in Mendoza's subzones.

Arguments continue as to which variety makes Argentina's greatest red wines, Cabernet Sauvignon or Malbec. But the fact remains that good Cabernet Sauvignon wines come from almost every wine-producing country; only Argentina and Cahors, a small region in southwestern France, have had success with Malbec. The same logic suggests that Bonarda and Barbera, two northern Italian varieties that are widely planted in Argentina (especially Bonarda), have a good future there.

## Naming Argentine producers worth knowing

Thanks in part to its high altitudes and sunny days, Argentina's natural resources for grape-growing are among the strongest in the world. Increasingly, foreign investment continues to bring the capital and the winemaking know-how to make the most of these natural resources. Bodega Norton, for example, a winery that was purchased by an Austrian crystal producer in 1989, now makes some of the country's best wines. Moët & Chandon, another immigrant, is already Argentina's largest sparkling wine producer; it also makes the Terrazas varietal table wines. A Dutchman owns the state-of-the-art Bodegas Salentein winery and its sister winery, Finca El Portillo. You also find several Bordeaux producers, such as Bordeaux's Lurton family, which owns Bodega J & F Lurton.

The homegrown Catena Zapata has emerged as one of Argentina's top wine producers. At $10 a bottle, its Alamos Malbec is one of the greatest wine values around. Catena Cabernet Sauvignon or Malbec (both about $21) and the superpremium Malbec Alta or Cabernet Sauvignon Alta (both about $50) are higher-end wines, among the finest being made in South America today.

Other recommended Argentine producers include Bodega Norton, Bodega J & F Lurton, Bodegas Salentein, Bodega Weinert, Trapiche, Etchart, Finca Sophenia, Achaval Ferrer, Pascual Toso, Michel Torino, Las Terrazas, Navarro Correas, Santa Julia, El Portillo, Dona Paula, and Valentín Bianchi. Some of Argentina's basic wines are priced in the $6 to $10 price range, but a few wineries make costlier wines that start in the $18 to $20 price range and head upwards of $100.

# Embarking on a South African Wine Safari

Vines came to South Africa in the 1650s with the Dutch, the first European settlers; in the same period, French Huguenots (Protestants) escaping religious persecution brought winemaking expertise. At the end of the 18th century, South Africa was producing a luscious fortified wine called Constantia, which became sought after in European royal courts. The country began focusing seriously on table wine production only in the 1980s. Today, South Africa ranks ninth in the world in wine production.

Most of South Africa's table wines come from an area known as the Coastal Region, around the Cape of Good Hope. Traditionally, large firms dominated South Africa's wine industry, and they continue to do so. KWV, formerly a wine growers' cooperative, is one of the country's largest wineries. South Africa's largest winery, the gigantic Distell firm, owns two groups of wineries that had been among the country's largest wine companies: Stellenbosch Farmers' Winery Group and the Bergkelder Group.

If the wines of South Africa are a new adventure for you, the following sections, which detail the country's chief wine regions and the grapes South Africa is known for, will get you more comfortable with the wines from this exciting area.

## South Africa's principal wine regions

South Africa has some vineyard areas with cool microclimates, especially around the southern coast (near the Cape of Good Hope) and in higher altitudes, but the climate in most of its wine regions is warm and dry.

South Africa's Wine of Origin legislation in 1973 created various wine regions, districts, and wards. Almost all the country's vineyards are near its southwestern coast, in Cape Province, within 90 miles of Cape Town, the country's most fascinating and picturesque city.

The five major districts, mainly in the Coastal Region area, are

- ✔ **Constantia:** The oldest wine-producing area in the country (located south of Cape Town)

- ✔ **Stellenbosch:** East of Cape Town; the most important wine district in quantity and quality

- ✔ **Paarl:** North of Stellenbosch; home of the KWV and the famous, beautiful Nederburg Estate; the second-most important wine district

- ✔ **Franschhoek Valley:** A subdistrict of Paarl; many innovative winemakers here

- ✔ **Robertson:** East of Franschhoek, the only major district not in the Coastal Region; a hot, dry area, known mainly for its Chardonnays

The small, cool Hermanus/Walker Bay area, bordering the Indian Ocean, is also showing promise with Pinot Noir and Chardonnay, led by the innovative Hamilton Russell Winery. A new wine district, Elgin, is on the coast between Stellenbosch and Walker Bay. A cool area, Elgin shows promise for its Pinot Noirs and intensely flavored Sauvignon Blancs. The latest area to show promise is Darling Hills, north of Cape Town, led by an up-and-coming winery, Groote Post.

Varietal wines in South Africa must contain at least 75 percent of the named grape variety; exported wines (complying with the stricter European Union regulations) must contain 85 percent of the named variety. About 35 percent of South Africa's wines qualify as Wine of Origin (WO). Wine of Origin regulations are based on the French *Appellation Contrôlée* laws (explained in Chapter 1 of Book II), and they strictly designate vineyards, allowable grape varieties, vintage-dating, and so on.

## *Steen, Pinotage, and company*

The most-planted grape variety in South Africa is Chenin Blanc, often locally called *Steen*. This versatile grape primarily makes medium-dry to semisweet wines, but also dry wines, sparkling wines, late harvest botrytis wines, and rosés.

Cabernet Sauvignon, Merlot, Shiraz, and Pinot Noir have become increasingly important red varieties, and Sauvignon Blanc and Chardonnay are popular white varieties. Cabernet Sauvignon and Sauvignon Blanc do particularly well in South Africa's climate. (Producers here make a very assertive version of Sauvignon Blanc.)

## South Africa: The future

Chenin Blanc and Pinotage represent South Africa's recent past — although both are undergoing a revival today. Cabernet Sauvignon, Merlot, and Chardonnay are making fine wines here now, but Sauvignon Blanc and Shiraz seem to hold the most promise in this country.

Sauvignon Blanc is a no-brainer; some of the world's best Sauvignon Blanc varietal wines are already being made here. The flavorful character of Sauvignon Blanc asserts itself in South Africa, especially in Constantia and in a new cool-climate district, Elim, in Cape Agulhas. Although South African Sauvignon Blancs resemble those from New Zealand, they're easier to drink and not quite as assertive.

Shiraz has become the hot, new variety of the Southern Hemisphere, and indeed throughout the world. What South African winemakers love about Shiraz is its versatility. It can grow well in both cool and warm climates. Right now, Shiraz is the fastest-growing variety being planted in South Africa. In ten years or less, it may be the country's biggest-selling varietal wine.

*TIP*

And then you have Pinotage (pee-noh-*tahj*). Uniquely South African, Pinotage is a grape born as a cross between Pinot Noir and Cinsaut (the same as Cinsault, the Rhône variety) back in 1925. However, Pinotage didn't appear as a wine until 1959. Pinotage wine combines the cherry fruit of Pinot Noir with the earthiness of a Rhône wine. It can be a truly delicious, light- to medium-bodied red wine that makes for easy drinking, or a more powerful red. Although many good Pinotage wines sell for $12 to $16, the best Pinotages cost more. Kanonkop Estate, a specialist in this variety, makes a $30 Pinotage. Simonsig Estate makes a fine Pinotage for around $30.

Although Pinotage is a pleasant wine, and certainly one that's worth trying, South Africa's future more likely is in Cabernet Sauvignon, Merlot, and Shiraz (and blends of these grapes) for its red wines and Sauvignon Blanc and Chardonnay for its whites.

# Index

## • *B* •

## Business/Accounting & Bookkeeping

Bookkeeping For Dummies
978-0-7645-9848-7

eBay Business
All-in-One For Dummies,
2nd Edition
978-0-470-38536-4

Job Interviews
For Dummies,
3rd Edition
978-0-470-17748-8

Resumes For Dummies,
5th Edition
978-0-470-08037-5

Stock Investing
For Dummies,
3rd Edition
978-0-470-40114-9

Successful Time
Management
For Dummies
978-0-470-29034-7

## Computer Hardware

BlackBerry For Dummies,
3rd Edition
978-0-470-45762-7

Computers For Seniors
For Dummies
978-0-470-24055-7

iPhone For Dummies,
2nd Edition
978-0-470-42342-4

Laptops For Dummies,
3rd Edition
978-0-470-27759-1

Macs For Dummies,
10th Edition
978-0-470-27817-8

## Cooking & Entertaining

Cooking Basics
For Dummies,
3rd Edition
978-0-7645-7206-7

Wine For Dummies,
4th Edition
978-0-470-04579-4

## Diet & Nutrition

Dieting For Dummies,
2nd Edition
978-0-7645-4149-0

Nutrition For Dummies,
4th Edition
978-0-471-79868-2

Weight Training
For Dummies,
3rd Edition
978-0-471-76845-6

## Digital Photography

Digital Photography
For Dummies,
6th Edition
978-0-470-25074-7

Photoshop Elements 7
For Dummies
978-0-470-39700-8

## Gardening

Gardening Basics
For Dummies
978-0-470-03749-2

Organic Gardening
For Dummies,
2nd Edition
978-0-470-43067-5

## Green/Sustainable

Green Building
& Remodeling
For Dummies
978-0-4710-17559-0

Green Cleaning
For Dummies
978-0-470-39106-8

Green IT For Dummies
978-0-470-38688-0

## Health

Diabetes For Dummies,
3rd Edition
978-0-470-27086-8

Food Allergies
For Dummies
978-0-470-09584-3

Living Gluten-Free
For Dummies
978-0-471-77383-2

## Hobbies/General

Chess For Dummies,
2nd Edition
978-0-7645-8404-6

Drawing For Dummies
978-0-7645-5476-6

Knitting For Dummies,
2nd Edition
978-0-470-28747-7

Organizing For Dummies
978-0-7645-5300-4

SuDoku For Dummies
978-0-470-01892-7

## Home Improvement

Energy Efficient Homes
For Dummies
978-0-470-37602-7

Home Theater
For Dummies,
3rd Edition
978-0-470-41189-6

Living the Country Lifestyle
All-in-One For Dummies
978-0-470-43061-3

Solar Power Your Home
For Dummies
978-0-470-17569-9

## Internet

Blogging For Dummies,
2nd Edition
978-0-470-23017-6

eBay For Dummies,
6th Edition
978-0-470-49741-8

Facebook For Dummies
978-0-470-26273-3

Google Blogger
For Dummies
978-0-470-40742-4

Web Marketing
For Dummies,
2nd Edition
978-0-470-37181-7

WordPress For Dummies,
2nd Edition
978-0-470-40296-2

## Language & Foreign Language

French For Dummies
978-0-7645-5193-2

Italian Phrases
For Dummies
978-0-7645-7203-6

Spanish For Dummies
978-0-7645-5194-9

Spanish For Dummies,
Audio Set
978-0-470-09585-0

## Macintosh

Mac OS X Snow Leopard
For Dummies
978-0-470-43543-4

## Math & Science

Algebra I For Dummies
978-0-7645-5325-7

Biology For Dummies
978-0-7645-5326-4

Calculus For Dummies
978-0-7645-2498-1

Chemistry For Dummies
978-0-7645-5430-8

## Microsoft Office

Excel 2007 For Dummies
978-0-470-03737-9

Office 2007 All-in-One
Desk Reference
For Dummies
978-0-471-78279-7

## Music

Guitar For Dummies,
2nd Edition
978-0-7645-9904-0

iPod & iTunes
For Dummies,
6th Edition
978-0-470-39062-7

Piano Exercises
For Dummies
978-0-470-38765-8

## Parenting & Education

Parenting For Dummies,
2nd Edition
978-0-7645-5418-6

Type 1 Diabetes
For Dummies
978-0-470-17811-9

## Pets

Cats For Dummies,
2nd Edition
978-0-7645-5275-5

Dog Training For Dummies,
2nd Edition
978-0-7645-8418-3

Puppies For Dummies,
2nd Edition
978-0-470-03717-1

## Religion & Inspiration

The Bible For Dummies
978-0-7645-5296-0

Catholicism For Dummies
978-0-7645-5391-2

Women in the Bible
For Dummies
978-0-7645-8475-6

## Self-Help & Relationship

Anger Management
For Dummies
978-0-470-03715-7

Overcoming Anxiety
For Dummies
978-0-7645-5447-6

## Sports

Baseball For Dummies,
3rd Edition
978-0-7645-7537-2

Basketball For Dummies,
2nd Edition
978-0-7645-5248-9

Golf For Dummies,
3rd Edition
978-0-471-76871-5

## Web Development

Web Design All-in-One
For Dummies
978-0-470-41796-6

## Windows Vista

Windows Vista
For Dummies
978-0-471-75421-3

# How-to?
# How Easy.

Go to www.Dummies.com

From hooking up a modem to cooking up a casserole, knitting a scarf to navigating an iPod, you can trust Dummies.com to show you how to get things done the easy way.

Visit us at Dummies.com